*To the
Junior Classes
in Church History*

*The
Duke University
Divinity
School*

1937–1962

Baker Book House   Grand Rapids, Michigan 49506

A
HISTORY
OF
CHRISTIANITY

Readings
in the History
of the Church

VOLUME 1
The Early
and Medieval
Church

Edited by
RAY C. PETRY

PHOTOLITHOPRINTED BY CUSHING - MALLOY, INC.
ANN ARBOR, MICHIGAN, UNITED STATES OF AMERICA

ACKNOWLEDGMENTS Grateful acknowledgment is made for use of the material designated here by chapters (Roman numerals) and itemized Arabic numbers. The Archabbey Press, IX, 31, 55, 60. G. Bell and Sons Ltd., VI, 20; VII, 1; IX, 1. Benziger Brothers Inc., VI, 45–47; IX, 28, 38, 86. The Bodley Head Ltd., IX, 113–115. The Bruce Publishing Co., VI, 41–44. Burns & Oates Ltd., VI, 45–47; IX, 28, 38. University of California Press, IX, 19–21. Cambridge University Press (New York and London), I, 43–44; III, 28–30; VII, 6; VIII, 30–31; IX, 7, 9, 29. The Catholic University of America Press, IV, 11. Chatto and Windus, IV, 21. The Clarendon Press (Oxford), V, 38–40. Columbia University Press, III, 66; IV, 28–29; V, 25; IX, 2, 3, 25, 30. The Dublin Institute for Advanced Studies, IV, 34–36. Gerald Duckworth and Co., Ltd., IX, 40, 65. Duke Divinity School Bulletin, I, introd. The Early English Text Society, IX, 97. Faber and Faber Ltd., VII, 12–14; IX, 12, 46–47, 68. Fathers of the Church Inc., IX, 41–43. The Folk-Lore Society, London, VIII, 52–55. The Hakluyt Society, IX, 37. Harper & Brothers, VII, 12–15; IX, 12. The Harvard University Press, II, 16; V, 60; IX, 17, 18, 24, 33, 34, 39. Headley Brothers Ltd. (Invicta Press), IX, 96. Heath Cranton Ltd., IX, 98. B. Herder Book Co., VIII, 6–10; IX, 22. Jarrolds Publishers (London) Ltd., VIII, 65. Alfred A. Knopf, Inc., X, 4, 6, 7, 9–11, 23, 30–33, 37–38. W. Kohlhammer, III, 12–13. Longmans, Green & Co. Inc. (New York), IX, 35, 36, 82–83. The Liturgical Press, IV, 30–33. The Macmillan Company, II, 21; X, 39–40. Methuen & Co., Ltd., IX, 102. University of Minnesota Press, IX, 51. The Newman Press, VII, 17; VIII, 56. W. W. Norton and Co., IX, 46, 47, 68. Oxford University Press (London), V, 36; IX, 48–50. Oxford University Press, Inc. (New York), IX, 70. The University of Pennsylvania Press, VIII, 64. Laurence Pollinger Ltd. (London), IX, 68. Princeton University Press, IX, 48–50. Student Christian Movement Press, I, 1–12, 15–35, 45; II, 11; III, 16; IX, 8, 14–15; X, 13, 18–20, 27–28. Charles Scribner's Sons, II, 1–2, 17, 27, 35, 59; III, 1, 11, 21; IV, 19–20; V, 31–32; IX, 45. The Editor, Shrine of Wisdom, IV, 46–48. SPCK, II, 44; III, 4, 5, 10, 23–27; IV, 4, 9; V, 9, 15–17, 20–22. The Union of American Hebrew Congregations, VIII, 51. The Viking Press, Inc., VI, 33; IX, 16, 67; X, 5. Westminster Press, I, 1–12, 15–35; 45; II, 11; III, 16; VIII, 57–58; IX, 8, 14–15; X, 13, 18–20, 27–28. Others not listed here are acknowledged at specific points within the text.

Preface

This volume attempts to relate Christian history in the words of those who have made and interpreted it through the centuries. Many selections, both short and long, have been held indispensable to the balancing of chronological movement and topical development. The possibility, as well as the desirability, of utilizing only complete documents is categorically denied. Short selections stand in danger of splintering. Complete units without judicious selection and use of connective tissue fare no better. They distort the infinite variety of Christian experiences into an oversimplified picture of comforting clarity. Long passages can pervert the truth as readily as short ones. Both are needed in balanced conjunction under critical editorial selectivity.

The editorial introductions throughout this book make no attempt to compress all essential narrative and basic history. Nor do they harbor the unhealthy suggestion of a kind of objectivity that seeks to cancel out the editor's experienced involvement in the story that he tries to set forth. A history that does not capitalize the bold yet modest insights of those learning its significance while participating in its perplexities is no history at all. The introductions, then, are the editor's effort to put the documents in as representative a setting as his own experience and scholarly integrity will permit. Here, as elsewhere, professional technicalities and apparatus are held to a minimum, in keeping with the demands of scholarly interpretation and the needs of the student and general reader.

The compact headings to the source texts serve purposes

as varied as they are specific. They provide the outlines of the Christian story within a progression at once chronological and thematic. As such, they may be consulted readily, together with other data of more specifically detailed reference nature at the ends of chapters. Furthermore, the headings also supply a comprehensive and detailed analysis of all original sources used, as well as a direct ascription of indebtedness for the translations employed. These headings are keyed to the Table of Contents and the acknowledgments of literary materials. Conventional footnotes are obviated in the interest of greater compactness and unity. The translations themselves are the work of many recognized authorities throughout the history of scholarship. These and the editor's own seek generally not so much a literal rendering as an accurate picturing of the texts in the light of the documents as a whole.

Several distinctive features of the volume reflect the editor's considerable experience as researcher and teacher, even though they may at times run counter to generally approved practice. Source texts and illustrations—the latter a seemingly unavoidable though hopelessly slanted term—are designed to exemplify inseparability rather than priority and subordination. Thus, the literary texts are no more basic than the pictures that illustrate them. Texts illustrate the plastic materials even as the plates illustrate texts. Such facts, and not the editor's whimsey, have largely determined the massive character of Chapter IX. Student convenience and textbook prejudice have usually seen to it that reasonably short chapters are given to education, the arts, philosophy—as if each of these were separate parts of modern fragmentation. This segmentation, however, is precisely what the medieval world of Chapter IX would have found unintelligible. At the well-calculated risk of undue bulkiness, Chapter IX leaves together what should not be put asunder—regardless of anyone's convenience, including that of the people who experienced it that way. In Chapter IX, also, chronologies naturally become longer and more complicated, as do introductions and reading lists. It cannot be overstressed that chronologies are not merely dates to be learned, but they are visual evidences and range finders. They document the inextricability of art, literature, architecture, liturgy, and education within the warp and woof of complicated human existence. What has been deliberately avoided in the rapid movement of each introduction can be recouped at will from purposeful study of materials at the end of each chapter. The editor is convinced, moreover, that the time has come to regard music and the arts in Christian history not as distant relatives, but as family members and joint heirs; hence, the inclusion of the extended reference section on music and recordings. None of these can be shunted off from the main junction that Chapter IX represents. The book may be divided into small sections for convenience in reading or study, but it is not our privilege to particularize at the expense of historical unity.

Many people who must remain unnamed have helped write this book; some of these have been wholly unaware of their part in it. Some, who will be named, can hardly be unmindful of their work. The National Council on Religion in Higher Education has offered early sponsorship and continuing encouragement; I am especially grateful for the counsel of its Executive Director, Dr. Richard C. Gilman. The Duke University Research Council has also given assistance. Professor Donn Michael Farris of the Duke Divinity School, who teaches in the many ways an effective librarian can, has made a major contribution to this work. His wife, Joyce Lockhart Farris, an excellent typist and an efficient, imaginative, and sympathetic transcriber of unreadable longhand, has been an indispensable factor in the book's essential formation. The staffs of the Duke University and Divinity School Libraries have been graciousness itself. My wife, Ruth Mertz Petry, knows what a book costs in agony and joy and has paid the full price with me. Words cannot properly recognize the many services of the publisher to book and editor. Special gratitude goes to Mr. Richard W. Hansen for supporting the publication of the work in its fullest integrity; to Mrs. Maurine Lewis for sympathetically and constructively identifying herself with the editor's purposes and for actualizing the highest dedication to editorial ideals; to Mr. Chapman L. Runyon for scrutinizing and correcting the typescript for the printer; to Miss Diana J. Powers for enthusiastic help in the production process; to Mr. James Guiher for eliciting the potential of the illustrations in a happy fusion of art and letters; and, finally, to other associates at Prentice-Hall, some unknown to me by name, but never unappreciated. None of these, together with numerous colleagues, can be held responsible for my errors of judgment and execution. All have earned my lasting gratitude.

RAY C. PETRY

Contents

I

THE FOUNDATION, ORGANIZATION,
AND INSTITUTIONALIZATION OF THE CHRISTIAN CHURCH   1

I. Clement of Rome's Letter to the Church at Corinth
(c. 96/97). II. Ignatius Calls for Unity Consolidated
about the Bishopric (110/117). III. Polycarp's
Letter to the Philippians (c. 110–135). IV. The
"Shepherd" of Hermas: an Apocryphal Apocalypse
(c. 115–140). V. The Didache: Purported Teachings
of the Twelve Apostles (c. 120–150). VI. The Pseudo
Clementine Second Letter: An Early Christian Sermon
(c. 130–150). VII. The Epistle to Diognetus: A
Christian Apologia (c. 130–180). VIII. Second-Century
Christian Worship. IX. Clement of Alexandria (c. 215)
and the Instruction of Christ, the True Pedagogue
(c. 195, 208/11). X. Hippolytus and the Apostolic
Tradition: a Third-Century Order of Worship (c. 217).
XI. Origen the Confessor (c. 185–253/54) on Prayer
(233/34).

II

EARLY RELATIONS OF SPIRITUAL AND TEMPORAL POWERS;
PERSECUTION, TOLERATION, AND COUNCILS   35

I. Reflections of Popular Hostility to Early Christianity.
II. Early Governmental Policy and Sporadic Outbreaks
Against Christians. III. Early Christian Martyrs and
the Christian Witness. IV. Selected Apologists: the
Literary Spokesmen for Christianity in Reply to Typical
Charges Against It. V. Attacks Against Christians
Before the Great Persecutions. VI. The Decian-Valerian
Persecution (c. 249–51, 257/59). VII. Persecutions
under Diocletian, Galerius, and Maximian (c. 302/303–
312). VIII. The Failure of Persecution and the Edicts
of Toleration. IX. Constantine's Favors to Christianity
(313–337); Donatism and the Synod of Arles (314).

III

IV

V

THE PAPACY, THE BARBARIAN KINGDOMS, ISLAM AND THE CAROLINGIAN CHURCH 177

I. Petrine Priority, The Rise of the Bishop of Rome, and His Primacy According to Fathers, Councils, and Popes. II. Assertions of Primacy and Demonstrations of Leadership from the Popes Themselves. III. The Barbarian Infiltration and the New Gothic-Roman-Christian Society. IV. Mohammed (570–632) and the Challenge of Islam to the Pope and to the Franks. V. The Conversion of Germany, the Decline of the Merovingians, and the Rise of the Carolingian Church. VI. Charlemagne (768–814), His Caesaropapism and the Church. VII. Justinian, an Earlier Caesaropapist (527–565); His Patronage of Art and Letters and His Compilation of Laws on the Church and Society Compared with Those of Charles.

VI

THE CHURCH, THE PAPACY, AND THE ECONOMIC-SOCIAL MILIEU; FEUDALISM, INVESTITURE STRUGGLE, CRUSADES, TOWNS, AND TRADE 221

I. Feudal Institutions, Church Lands, and Christian Society. II. Feudal Investiture of Church Offices and Feudal Reform. III. The English Church as a Pawn in the Feudal Game. IV. Pilgrimage and Crusade; Papal Propaganda and Social Susceptibility. V. The Crusades in the Era of Pope Innocent III (1198–1216). VI. Emperor Frederick II (1215–1250) and the Sixth Crusade (1228–1229). VII. St. Louis (IX): The Virtues and Limitations of a Crusading Feudal King (1226–1270). VIII. The Church and Social Tension in the Crusading Period; the Transition from Agrarian Feudalism to Town Economy and Mercantilism.

VII

VIII

IX

to the Pre-University Clerical Schools, Canons Regular, Secular Chapter, and Cathedral Schools; The Liberal Arts and Early Scholasticism. III. The *Studium Generale* and the *Universitas;* Guilds of the Liberal Arts and Scholastic Servants of the Common Life; the Mendicants and the New *Mobilitas*. IV. Gothic Architecture, Scholasticism and the *Summas* of the Common Life; Mental Habit, Order, Measure, Light; Aesthetics and Gothic Symbolism. V. The Cathedral as the Four-Fold Mirror of the World and of the Common Life; Vincent de Beauvais' *Speculum Majus*. VI. The Literacy of the Artists, Builders and Musicians; Order, Measure and Light; Music, the Dance, and Theology; the Liturgy and the Common Life. VII. Illuminated Books: Missals, Breviaries, and Books of Hours; the Literacy of the Clergy and Laity; the Arts and the Common Life. VIII. Books of Contemplative Vision: The "Ages" of Church and World; New Spiritual Monastics; the Divine-Human "Comedy" and the Common Life. IX. Miscellaneous Open Picture Books of Gothic Painting: Frescoes, Murals, Wood, Glass, Stone, Pavement "Graffiti," Bronze, Marble, and Tapestry; the Cities of Assisi, Siena, and Florence. X. The Waning of the Middle Ages; the Dance of Death; the *Ars Moriendi;* Living and Dying in the Common Life.

THE LATE MEDIEVAL PAPACY AND THE CONCILIAR EPOCH; CHRISTIAN REVOLUTION AND REFORM; THE WANING OF THE MIDDLE AGES   497

I. Representative Theories of Christian Unity and Duality in Spiritual and Temporal Powers. II. Early Conciliar Theorists and Political Reformers During the Avignon Papacy. III. The Great Schism (1378–1417/55) and the Dissipation of Christian Unity. IV. Reform Critiques and Early Appeals for a General Council to End the Schism. V. Jean Gerson (1363–1429), Pierre D'Ailly (1350–1420), and the Groundwork for the Council of Pisa (1409). VI. Conciliar Treatises of Reformers Between Pisa and Constance. VII. The Council of Constance and Conciliar Utterances. VIII. The Conciliar Movement and Reform after Constance.

I

The Foundation,

Organization, and Institutionalization

of the Christian Church

Jesus Christ founded the Christian Church.
This assertion cannot easily be contested. How the fact came
to be, however, has frequently been the subject of
debate. This process of founding and organizing has long
fascinated both practicing Christians and
secular historians. Quite basic concerns lie
obscured beneath more obvious traditions and overt acts
of establishment. But Christ was primary in the process,
in a way that transcended the obvious statements attributed to him.

Jesus' basic interest seems to have been the Kingdom of God, and not a new ecclesiastical institution. This eschatological consideration revolved about the last days of one era and the inauguration of a new world. Jesus' concern with the transition from a temporal society to an eternal community took precedence over any social consciousness in the more limited sense. He was not committed to the perpetuation of the human social order as he found it. For him, the Kingdom of God came first. This was the primary community. It already existed, and it was revealed forthwith in his appearance as God's herald. He announced and revealed the "constitution" of this eternal society in the name of God the Father, and it at once became mandatory for all the Son's followers.

Perhaps the most mysterious thing about the Kingdom was that it was at once a secret to the uninitiated and an open fact to those instructed by its special vocation. This was the ministry to divine ends that was already devolving upon those who accepted Christ's call to discipleship. Jesus taught a doctrine of last things (or last days, in the sense of the old order) and new times (in terms of the new age already being ushered in), in which the final community was held to be both immanent and actual. The Kingdom was historically present in the midst of men, though its full realization was future to their present comprehension and experience.

The Church arose as a community—a koinonia, or communio—of penitents. These penitents freely accepted the divine gift of salvation, which they had in no way earned. The very recognition of unworthiness which all Christ's followers confessed in common conferred upon them a new kind of justness or rightness. Those alone were justified who had a full sense of their own unrighteousness. They therefore stood ready to accept redemption out of God's graciousness. Their distinctive society was not esoteric in the sense of its being a privileged clique. They were simply a grateful people no longer blinded by human striving to the magnanimous operation of this divine action.

The community set up by God and revealed by Christ created from the most ordinary people a society that was an outpost of heaven. It was a koinonia, responding to the eternal fellowship. This community became a social reagent in humanity's midst. It was engendered by, and answerable to, the will of the Kingdom. The new ecclesiastical community came to think of itself as the servant of the eternal Kingdom in the temporal world. This royal society swept through and beyond the time-span. It both transcended and transformed earthly history and the interim universe. These would finally be superseded and reborn into a new heaven and a new earth.

Jesus' "Beatitudes" focused the happiness of a new kind of men. Though a part of the old society and under the pull of its ways, they were already living in the new age and subject to its unique constitution. In their "blessedness" they already possessed the joyous orientation of Kingdom sons. Their joy, their righteousness, and their peace were pivoted in God's own kingdom of divine love and perfection. Their standard and their power had already become that community of love whose basic character was God's enabling agape. The triumph of this divine-human society was presently infiltrating the entire universe through God's Holy Spirit.

The nascent church gradually sensed its dual consecration to eternity and time. It recorded, historically, its dedication to final purposes and the earthly genesis that served them. In a world attuned to Greek cycles (i.e., cycles of recurring, self-contained existence), the Church adopted an increasingly linear view of history. That is, the Church on earth, like humanity itself, had a beginning in time as it would have an end to its historical pilgrimage. Those in the Hebraic-Christian tradition moved from historical beginnings to destined religious ends because of such ends. They knew their way by faith only. They journeyed away from their human beginnings without slavish affection for earthly origins. Unlike purely scientific origins that start from whatever has already been, their beginnings were informed with meaning and power by the ends that had preceded them. Christians had fully societal instincts. They knew the meaning of traditio. In living tradition one passed on to another's hands what had been placed in his own. Hands joined hands from age to age in vital transmission of what hands must not merely hold, but hold out, or offer. The City of God was heavenly and future to their earthly hope. Yet, in its supreme corporateness, it begot social beings on earth. Its foundations were in heaven, but its citizens to be were commingled with all of humanity. This citizenry of the eternal city (*civitas*) was not deprived, in the interim, of a living bond with the heavenly *koinonia*. By faith and in love they passed to the Fatherland (*patria*) in the tradition of hand-to-hand community, or *traditio*.

As a resourceful colonist of the heavenly country, the Christian was on pilgrimage within a temporal community of wayfarers. As a Christian traveler—or *viator*—he was sustained throughout the stages of his journey from the knapsack of heaven. He munched angel's food, the celestial sandwich bread. Eucharistically, thankfully, he partook of the *viaticum*, or wayfarer's bread. Set athwart the boundaries joining this temporal neighborhood and the everlasting homeland were deep gorges and rugged peaks; but traffic was maintained. Life in the Christian community was always in contact with that of the Heavenly City. The City of God, the *Civitas Dei*, did indeed beget citizens below. The Church of Christ was the agglutinating bond that knit the temporal society to its parent community. It was a two-in-one society, both divine and human.

On earth, Christians ate the bread of heaven. They sat as a family at the table of the Lord. The divine leadings that drew them together in sorrow and in joy were celestially oriented. They were, even then, dwelling within the Kingdom, though not fully. Its final realization would eventuate in a new heaven and a new earth, a wholly revitalized and unified cosmic community. This community pre-dedicated each member to complete householding with Father, Son, and heavenly hosts. It conditioned each of its members for an economy governing the entire Commonwealth of the divinely renovated universe. This was ultimate ecumenicity, a dwelling in the many rooms (*monai, mansiones*) of the Father's house (*oikos*).

These householders moved about within this newly domesticated universe, undisturbed and calm, with the poised assurance of uncontested heirs. The natural-born citizen of the Father's house was the true guild member of the Christian *universitas*, or *collegium*. He was the initiate into the mystical body of Christ's *agape*. He was graduated for the joyous symmetry of genuine patriotism within the *patria*, the Fatherland. He had the presence of a Prince, for he was a child of the King (*Basileus*). He was conceived and directed from before his earthly genesis for his precise heavenly ending. Thus it was that the children of the Father were at home even when they were abroad. All their traveling was in terms of Home. While on journey, they were no less referable to the norms of their abiding place than when they were in full residence. "This old house" of their present abiding would be taken down. But its design, having been drafted by the Master Architect, would find its transmutation within the Great Hall of the new heaven and the new earth. The earthly city, the *urbs terrena*, would yield to dissolution and reincorporation within the City Eternal, the *Urbs Eterna*. All orbitings of souls in outer space would be reoriented about the City of God.

Such language, however fanciful to the ears of later Christians, came to be common parlance during the early centuries of the Church. The most characteristic progression of Christian thought and action is still discernible within this language.

Early in the Church's record there emerged a common preoccupation with the "cure of souls" (*cura animarum*) and the "school of souls" (*schola animarum*). Earliest Christian life was a genuine *koinonia* or *communio*. It was a *collegium* in the sense of a close-knit, interpenetrating community. It was a mystical *universitas* of head and members. Before *collegium* and *universitas* meant academic institutions they referred to social vitalities and traditions. These were first pre-Christian, then Christian corporations. At the outset, Christian communities of souls implied associations of teaching and learning, as well as societies of divine worship. Long before Christians were academically

3

self-conscious they were cast in seminars with the Great Teacher. "Master" and "Disciple" were sacred terms. Theirs was the urgency of breathless expectation, of genuinely Christian hope. The Christian *collegium* of worship and social response to brothers' needs became also the *koinonia* of instruction, of teaching and learning. This tutelage of Kingdom men on earth, by the Kingdom's servant community in time, registered a desperate need. It was imperative that they know the truth where right doctrine meant eternal beatitude, even as error spelled death to the presence of God and of his people.

Christian manuals of instruction were not marks of luxury, but of survival. Such was the teaching handbook, or *enchiridion*, called Matthew's Gospel. Other examples were the evolving "Church Orders," or books of discipline, such as the *Didache* and the *Apostolic Constitutions*. The catechetical writings and disciplines of the Christian school at Alexandria were also part of this *didascalia*. Preaching and teaching, like pastoral care and indoctrination, were solidly allied, though not identical preoccupations of the Church. Martyrs, confessors, and missionaries were developed only through instruction and catechesis. The Christian community was doomed without tradition or transmission. Augustine contended that Christian associations needed their seals as much as the merchant fraternity. The Christian Credo or Symbol was just such an oral badge or seal. In it the Christians' confession of faith rose up out of memory and reflection. They registered their hearing and doing of the Word as it was preached, taught, and practiced in the community. The increasing spiritual prestige of the teaching authority was only in part an institutionalizing of the Church's pneumatic life. Here was also a regularizing of spiritual respiration, a committing to the everyday, orderly routine of the living faith and Gospel. Profound instruction was essential to the preaching and teaching community of Origen. It was equally indispensable to the leveling of heresy and the validating of truth in the apostolic tradition of Irenaeus. The early Christian church was a witnessing to the Kingdom

through the unity of worship and social ministry, through preaching and teaching. In it, daily work and fiery prophesying were combined; *Kerygma* (the proclamation of the gospel) and diaconate (a deacon's official ministry) were mingled. Martyr suffering and going to school under the Master were part of it, too. For those challenged by the sophisticated world and the eclectic seekers after truth, Christ was the true Gnostic as he was the great Pedagogue.

The vicissitudes of Christian householding on earth were many. To be in the Christian tradition was to respond to the Rule of Faith. It was to minister in the "curacy of souls," to serve in the "school of souls." In Ignatius and in Cyprian, the divine hierarchy was held up as the eliciting pattern of Christian polity and ecclesiastical unity on earth. Likewise, in the early Church, the good pastor was the true teacher. The heavenly hierarchy was the solicitous School of Heaven instructing Christians of earth. Borne within it was the model for the analogue of earthly hierarchy. This applied to temporal government, faith, charity, and the hope of life eternal. The centuries themselves could not wholly denature this pristine Christian simplicity. Nothing could quite obliterate the symbols of the Master. Conveyed by them was the iconography of the Saviour, the image writing of his spiritual presence.

The documents of Chapter I confirm the idealistic bent of this early Christian orientation. They also reflect the rough awakening of those who superficially grasped the import of Jesus' objectives without the full implications of his realistic foresightedness. These later writings, like the canonical literature, show how Christians tried to meet the ultimate demands of their rigorous faith; they also show how they adjusted themselves to daily exigencies among people of quite different views. Following Christ's admonition to be in the world, but not of it, proved a bruising if exhilarating experience.

The first source reading, though actually anonymous, was early ascribed to one Clement, presumably third bishop of Rome. He was writing to the strife-torn Christians at Corinth. The pneumatic emphasis of early Pauline days was then being challenged by

4

worldly bickerings and the practical demands of common-sense Christians. Already, Roman Christian officialdom was beginning to inject into its fraternal exchanges a tone of commiseration subtly charged with patronizing unction. Perhaps certain ministers had been expelled from their offices. Regularity in worship and the ordered church life so cherished at old Rome had been endangered. As a more sophisticated and well-organized Christian society, the ranking priesthood or hierarchy of the Roman community felt called upon to intervene. They pleaded for the larger Christian unity now being threatened by local schism.

No less impassioned in its plea for unity was the correspondence of Ignatius. This depicted the concern for his flock of a second-century bishop on his way to martyrdom. A brief, violent uprising against Christians in his episcopal city of Antioch, in Syria, had broken out. He had been condemned to face wild beasts in the Roman arena. He made an expectant martyr's triumphant tour of certain towns while receiving Christian delegations from others. His coveted crown of martyrdom was about to seal his Christian discipleship with sure victory. The unity he was thus about to serve in his death, as in his life, had been customarily aided on the local, congregational level of church organization by placing a bishop at the head. Supporting him was a council of presbyters, or priests, assisted by deacons. This council featured a planned hierarchy, culminating in the so-called *monepiscopate*. In this hierarchy, or graded priestly rule by earthly officials, the heavenly pattern was to be followed. The bishop, representing God himself, was administrator, liturgical leader, and prophetic teacher. The elders, moreover, represented the apostles. The deacons recalled Christ's ministry of service. Out of this background Ignatius wrote his moving spiritual will and testament.

Polycarp, later to be encountered in the third section of Chapter II, also placed the daily perplexities of Christian life in relation to ultimate crises and the functions of ordered Christian officialdom. The strange, visionary writings of the "Shepherd" reveal the passionate convictions of one having proved worthy under testing. Fresh trials yet loomed for the Church before Christ's return to judge mankind at the end of the world. The Church, arrayed as a matron in white, urged the apocalyptist to admonish his own family and all the churches to do penance. Good Christians would be built into that tower which was the Church. Untrue members would be cast aside.

The *Didache*, traditionally ascribed to the twelve apostles, was in fact a later compilation of pre-Christian and early Christian materials. It preserved the outlines of the Church's gradual but sure transition from spiritual urgency under minimum organization to a more fixed institutional life of increasing complexity. Portions of the work reflect a time when the monepiscopate was not yet fully established and when gifts of prophecy were still reverenced as the mark of leadership. In the main, this manual of church order seems designed to guide rural churches through the growing perplexities of a more systematized corporate life. The layers of older and newer tradition, in their very syncretizing of disparate times and ideals, witness to the institutionalizing process well under way. The Church's eschatological passions are forcefully, if not always realistically, coupled with its daily worship, its economic and social pressures, and its ethical demands. Called to mind are the comparably sobering problems and measures of the contemporary "Pastoral Epistles."

Another work attributed to Clement is actually an early Christian homily, or sermon. The ends and methods of indoctrination are instructively, if not always inspiringly, preserved in it. The need for moral purity and stability in the face of persecution is as marked as the emphasis on the coming Kingdom and the Last Judgment. Primitive enthusiasms had sometimes prompted grave irregularities. These were to be countered with disciplined Christian integrity. All must repent and make ready by means of the true spiritual church for the *parousia*, the imminent return of Christ.

The purported letter to Diognetus seems to have been an authentic Christian expression. It is basically apologetic in the true, positive sense of stating the case for an unaccepted position or group. The distinctive character of Christians in human society is stressed. Christianity is a mystery of transcendent origin. Through it, the fulfillment of the divine purpose is worked out in history. Those not indoctrinated in this salutary mystery cannot discern the divine operation. Christians alone apprehend the secret force generated by God in heaven and revealed by Christ on earth. Here its working goes forward in and through a commonwealth that is on earth, but not of its genius. Yet, the Church is to the world what soul is to the body. Its ultimate purposes bless temporal society.

Early examples of Christian worship are implicit in all these readings. The accounts of Justin and Tertullian, however, are justly famous. Justin was an apologist worthy of the name. He stated the Christian case and made a plea for its toleration. Even more, he pressed the claims of a converter who was, himself, a confessor of the faith and a martyr, or witness, to the true tradition. His *Apology* constitutes a valuable manual of Christian thought and life in the second century. A native of ancient Schechem and a Gentile, he was well acquainted with Jewish life and ideology. Greek by cultural background, he had been influenced by Platonism. He bowed before the Old Testament prophets as propounded by the Christian church. Herein was the true philosophy he had formerly sought elsewhere. A Christian teacher who had once worn the philosopher's cloak and the professor's toga, he described Christian practices in worship as he had participated in them.

Tertullian was born of a pagan centurion father at Carthage. Educated for the law, he was established in his profession before his conversion in 193. By 213 he had left the "great church" to join the company of ascetic Montanist spiritualizers. Their rigorism and pneumatic propensities rebuked the laxity he found all too current in the Christian profession. He lacked Justin's penchant for philosophy. Actually he thought it the parent of gnostic error. Church and academy were, for him, enemies rather than the friends Clement and Origen of Alexandria held them to be. He is sometimes termed the

father of Latin theology, though he was scarcely a speculative theologian. For him Christianity was a divine foolishness not to be reconciled with philosophical systems. Christianity he conceived to be a new law. He entertained a deep sense of sin and the condign need of grace. It was on grace that salvation was based. Tertullian transposed old Latin terms into new Christian meanings. Such words as *sacramentum, substantia, traditio, corona,* and *satisfactio* focused a new divine-human encounter, referring now to these concepts in a new social-eternal context. His *Apologeticum* is outstanding for its critique of pagan and Christian social antithesis. At the heart of this stood his description of the Christian *cultus.*

Clement and his student Origen grew out of Greek culture and maintained an irenic regard for it to the last. Where Tertullian was intransigent and harsh, Clement was flexible and mild. Modest regard for truth from all quarters and reverence for Christ as the epitome of all knowledge and true gnosis were characteristic of him. Probably born at Athens, he later went to Alexandria, the center of Hellenistic intellectualism. There, he became head of the catechetical school. This made converts ready, by instruction and examination in the Christian scriptures and tradition, for responsible places in the Christian community. He knew the Scriptures and Christian literature well. He was conversant with philosophical lore and classical letters, though not always at first hand. The Christian revelation was held relatable to all true knowledge and pre-Christian philosophy. The philosophy of the Greeks, like the law of the Jews, might lead to Christ. Contrary to the inflated and provincial wisdom of esoteric gnostics, the privilege of the true Christian gnostic was the free search for universal truth in Christ. In him was the epitome of all genuine gnosis, both in elevated thought and wise conduct.

Clement's attempted harmonization of Christian faith and current philosophy held real dangers. His eulogies in classroom and via public and private example exalted Christ as the true pedagogue of the world and the only effective instructor of the redeemed. The life of natural man was not to be legalistically indicted and vilified. It was, rather, to be ennobled and enjoyed, with the disciplined Christian liberty properly accorded God's gifts of creation. The *Hymn to Christ* is possibly the early doxology of the Alexandrian school. Evicted from Alexandria by the imminent persecution of Severus, Clement is traditionally accorded a martyr's death.

Origen, whose work is to be represented in greater detail later, combined the scholarly catholicity of his teacher Clement with the exacting consecration, though not the censorious rigorism, of Tertullian. The life of prayer and martyrdom which he incited and elicited was the true teacher's confession. Sought in it was the experience of spiritual perfection exemplified by the ever tutoring, patient, redeeming Christ.

The church order of Hippolytus is a precious deposit from early Christian worship. This good bishop was venerated for learning and eloquence. On one occasion he was supposedly deputized to preach before the erudite, dedicated Origen. Actually elevated at one time as a counter-pope to the Roman bishop, he opposed fearlessly what he regarded as a record of lax ineptitude in the Roman hierarchy. It has been said that in a unique sense he imparted to "the laws and the liturgy of the Eastern Church their permanent form."

I. Clement of Rome's Letter to the Church at Corinth (c. 96/97)

1. The Corinthian Schism, a Blot on Christian Integrity (1:1–2)

This and the succeeding items in this section are in the translation of C. C. Richardson, *et al., Early Christian Fathers* [Library of Christian Classics, Vol. I] (Philadelphia: Westminster Press; London: Student Christian Movement Press, Ltd., 1953), pp. 43, 45–46, 62–64.

Due, dear friends, to the sudden and successive misfortunes and accidents we have encountered, we have, we admit, been rather long in turning our attention to your quarrels. We refer to the abominable and unholy schism, so alien and foreign to those whom God has chosen, which a few impetu-

I-1. Peter and Paul Reunited at Rome. *Mosaic, 12th century, Palatine Chapel, Palermo.*

ous and headstrong fellows have fanned to such a pitch of insanity that your good name, once so famous and dear to us all, has fallen into the gravest ill repute. Has anyone, indeed, stayed with you without attesting the excellence and firmness of your faith? without admiring your sensible and considerate Christian piety? without broadcasting your spirit of unbounded hospitality? without praising your perfect and trustworthy knowledge?

2. Rivalry Responsible for Sufferings of Peter, Paul, and Others (5–6)

But passing from examples in antiquity, let us come to the heroes nearest our own times. Let us take the noble examples of our own generation. By reason of rivalry and envy the greatest and most righteous pillars [of the Church] were persecuted, and battled to the death. Let us set before our eyes the noble apostles: Peter, who by reason of wicked jealousy, not only once or twice but frequently endured suffering and thus, bearing his witness, went to the glorious place which he merited. By reason of rivalry and contention Paul showed how to win the prize for patient endurance. Seven times he was in chains; he was exiled, stoned, became a herald [of the gospel] in East and West, and won the noble renown which his faith merited. To the whole world he taught righteousness, and reaching the limits of the West he bore his witness before rulers. And so, released from this world, he was taken up into the holy place and became the greatest example of patient endurance.

To these men who lived such holy lives there was joined a great multitude of the elect who by reason of rivalry were the victims of many outrages and tortures and who became outstanding examples among us. By reason of rivalry women were persecuted in the roles of Danaïds and Dircae. Victims of dreadful and blasphemous outrages, they ran with sureness the course of faith to the finish, and despite their physical weakness won a notable prize. It was rivalry that estranged wives from their husbands and annulled the saying of our father Adam, "This is now bone of my bone and flesh of my flesh." Rivalry and contention have overthrown great cities and uprooted mighty nations.

3. The Master's Injunctions Concerning the Role of Priests and Laymen in Worship (40)

Now that this is clear to us and we have peered into the depths of the divine knowledge, we are bound to do in an orderly fashion all that the Master has bidden us to do at the proper times he set. He ordered sacrifices and services to be performed; and required this to be done, not in a careless and disorderly way, but at the times and seasons he fixed. Where he wants them performed, and by whom, he himself fixed by his supreme will, so that everything should be done in a holy way and with his approval, and should be acceptable to his will. Those, therefore, who make their offerings at the time set win his approval and blessing. For they follow the Master's orders and do no wrong. The high priest is given his particular duties: the priests are assigned their special place, while on the Levites particular tasks are imposed. The layman is bound by the layman's code.

4. Rules Laid Down for the Ministry and the Order of Worship (41)

"Each of us," brothers, "in his own rank" must win God's approval and have a clear conscience. We must not transgress the rules laid down for our ministry, but must perform it reverently. Not everywhere, brothers, are the different sacrifices—the daily ones, the freewill offerings, and those for sins and trespasses—offered, but only in Jerusalem. And even there sacrifices are not made at any point, but only in front of the sanctuary, at the altar, after the high priest and the ministers mentioned have inspected the offering for blemishes. Those, therefore, who act in any way at variance with his will, suffer the penalty of death. You see, brothers, the more knowledge we are given, the greater risks we run.

5. The Apostolic Preaching, the Scriptures, Bishops, and Deacons (42)

The apostles received the gospel for us from the Lord Jesus Christ; Jesus, the Christ, was sent from God. Thus Christ is from God and the apostles from Christ. In both instances the orderly procedure depends on God's will. And so the apostles, after receiving their orders and being fully convinced by the resurrection of our Lord Jesus Christ and assured by God's word, went out in the confidence of the Holy Spirit to preach the good news that God's Kingdom was about to come. They preached in country and city, and appointed their first converts, after testing them by the Spirit, to be the bishops and deacons of future believers. Nor was this any novelty, for Scripture had mentioned bishops and deacons long before. For this is what Scripture says somewhere: "I will appoint their bishops in righteousness and their deacons in faith."

6. The Function of the Episcopacy and the Present Strife over It (44)

Now our apostles, thanks to our Lord Jesus Christ, knew that there was going to be strife over the title of bishop. It was for this reason and because they had been given an accurate knowledge of the future, that they appointed the officers we have mentioned. Furthermore, they later added a codicil to the effect that, should these die, other approved men should succeed to their ministry. In the light of this, we view it as a breach of justice to remove from their ministry those who were appointed either by them [i.e., the apostles] or later on and with the whole church's consent, by others of the proper standing, and who, long enjoying everybody's approval, have ministered to Christ's flock faultlessly, humbly, quietly, and unassumingly. For we shall be guilty of no slight sin if we eject from the episcopate men who have offered the sacrifices with innocence and holiness. Happy, indeed, are those presbyters who have already passed on, and who ended a life of fruitfulness with their task complete. For they need not fear that anyone will remove them from their secure positions. But you, we observe, have removed a number of people, despite their good conduct, from a ministry they have fulfilled with honor and integrity.

II. Ignatius Calls for Unity Consolidated about the Bishopric (110/117)

7. Unity and Harmony through Regarding the Bishop as the Lord, Himself

The translations in this and the succeeding items are those of Richardson, et al., Early Christian Fathers [LCC, Vol. I], pp. 89, 95, 98–99, 109–110, 114–15—for the Letters to the Ephesians, Magnesians, Trallians, Philadelphians, and Smyrneans. Ep. Eph. 5:2–6:2.

If anyone is not inside the sanctuary, he lacks God's bread. And if the prayer of one or two has great avail, how much more that of the bishop and the total Church. He who fails to join in your worship shows his arrogance by the very fact of becoming a schismatic. It is written, moreover, "God resists the proud." Let us, then, heartily avoid resisting the bishop so that we may be subject to God.

The more anyone sees the bishop modestly silent, the more he should revere him. For everyone the Master of the house sends on his business, we ought to receive as the One who sent him. It is clear, then, that we should regard the bishop as the Lord himself. Indeed, Onesimus spoke very highly of your godly conduct, that you were all living by the truth and harboring no sectarianism. Nay, you heed nobody beyond what he has to say truthfully about Jesus Christ.

8. The Bishop to Preside in God's Place; the Presbyters to Take the Place of the Apostolic Council

Ep. Magn. 6:1.

I believed, then, that I saw your whole congregation in these people I have mentioned, and I loved you all. Hence I urge you to aim to do everything in godly agreement. Let the bishop preside in God's place, and the presbyters take the place of the apostolic council, and let the deacons (my special favorites) be entrusted with the ministry of Jesus Christ who was with the Father from eternity and appeared at the end [of the world].

9. The Bishop to Be Obeyed as Christ; Presbyters as Ministers of Christ's Mysteries; Deacons to Be Respected

Ep. Trall, 1:1–3:2.

Well do I realize what a character you have—above reproach and steady under strain. It is not just affected, but it comes naturally to you, as I gathered from Polybius, your bishop. By God's will and that of Jesus Christ, he came to me in Smyrna, and so heartily congratulated me on being a prisoner for Jesus Christ that in him I saw your whole congregation. I welcomed, then, your godly good will, which reached me by him, and I gave thanks that I found you, as I heard, to be following God.

For when you obey the bishop as if he were Jesus Christ, you are (as I see it) living not in a merely human fashion but in Jesus Christ's way, who for our sakes suffered death that you might believe in his death and so escape dying yourselves. It is essential, therefore, to act in no way without the bishop, just as you are doing. Rather submit even to the presbytery as to the apostles of Jesus Christ. He is our Hope, and if we live in union with him now, we shall gain eternal life. Those too who are deacons of Jesus Christ's "mysteries" must give complete satisfaction to everyone. For they do not serve mere food and drink, but minister to God's Church. They must therefore avoid leaving themselves open to criticism, as they would shun fire.

Correspondingly, everyone must show the deacons respect. They represent Jesus Christ, just as the bishop has the role of the Father, and the presbyters are like God's council and an apostolic band. You cannot have a church without these. I am sure that you agree with me in this.

In your bishop I received the very model of your love, and I have him with me. His very bearing is a great lesson, while his gentleness is most forceful. I imagine even the godless respect him.

10. Ignatius in the Spirit Cries out for Unity about the Hierarchy

Ep. Phil., 7:1-2.

Some there may be who wanted in a human way to mislead me, but the Spirit is not misled, seeing it comes from God. For "it knows whence it comes and whither it goes," and exposes what is secret. When I was with you I cried out, raising my voice— it was God's voice—"Pay heed to the bishop, the presbytery, and the deacons." Some, it is true, suspected that I spoke thus because I had been told in advance that some of you were schismatics. But I swear by Him for whose cause I am a prisoner, that from no human channels did I learn this. It was the Spirit that kept on preaching in these words: "Do nothing apart from the bishop; keep your bodies as if they were God's temple; value unity; flee schism; imitate Jesus Christ as he imitated his Father."

11. Where the Bishop Is, There Is the Catholic Church; also a Valid Eucharist and Baptism

Ep. Smyr., 6–9.

Let no one be misled: heavenly beings, the splendor of angels, and principalities, visible and invisible, if they fail to believe in Christ's blood, they too are doomed. "Let him accept it who can." Let no one's position swell his head, for faith and love are everything—there is nothing preferable to them.

Pay close attention to those who have wrong notions about the grace of Jesus Christ, which has come to us, and note how at variance they are with God's mind. They care nothing about love: they have no concern for widows or orphans, for the oppressed, for those in prison or released, for the hungry or the thirsty. They hold aloof from the Eucharist and from services of prayer, because they refuse to admit that the Eucharist is the flesh of our Saviour Jesus Christ, which suffered for our sins and which, in his goodness, the Father raised [from the dead]. Consequently those who wrangle and dispute God's gift face death. They would have done better to love and so share in the resurrection. The right thing to do, then, is to avoid such people and to talk about them neither in private nor in public. Rather pay attention to the prophets and above all to the gospel. There we get a clear picture of the Passion and see that the resurrection has really happened.

Flee from schism as the source of mischief. You should all follow the bishop as Jesus Christ did the Father. Follow, too, the presbytery as you would the apostles; and respect the deacons as you would God's law. Nobody must do anything that has to do with the Church without the bishop's approval. You should regard that Eucharist as valid which is celebrated either by the bishop or by someone he authorizes. Where the bishop is present, there let the congregation gather, just as where Jesus Christ is, there is the Catholic Church. Without the bishop's supervision, no baptisms or love feasts are permitted. On the other hand, whatever he approves pleases God as well. In that way everything you do will be on the safe side and valid. It is well for us to come to our senses at last, while we still have a chance to repent and turn to God. It is a fine thing to acknowledge God and the bishop. He who pays the bishop honor has been honored by God. But he who acts without the bishop's knowledge is in the devil's service.

III. Polycarp's Letter to the Philippians (c. 110–135)

12. The Commandments of Righteousness; the Role of Wives, Widows, Deacons, Presbyters

Ep. 3–7, Richardson, *et al.*, *Early Christian Fathers* [LCC, Vol. I], pp. 132–37.

I write these things about righteousness, brethren, not at my own instance, but because you first invited me to do so. Certainly, neither I nor anyone like me can follow the wisdom of the blessed and glorious Paul, who, when he was present among you face to face with the generation of his time, taught you accurately and firmly "the word of truth." Also when absent he wrote you letters that will enable you, if you study them carefully, to grow in the faith delivered to you—"which is a mother of us all," accompanied by hope, and led by love to God and Christ and our neighbor. For if anyone is occupied in these, he has fulfilled the commandment of righteousness; for he who possesses love is far from all sin. But "the love of money is the beginning of all evils." Knowing, therefore, that "we brought nothing into the world, and we cannot take anything out," let us arm ourselves "with the weapons of righteousness," and let us first of all teach ourselves to live by the commandment of the Lord.

Then you must teach your wives in the faith delivered to them and in love and purity—to cherish their own husbands in all fidelity, and to love all others equally in all chastity, and to educate their children in the fear of God. And the widows should be discreet in their faith pledged to the Lord, praying unceasingly on behalf of all, refraining from all slander, gossip, false witness, love of money—in fact, from evil of any kind—knowing that they are God's altar, that everything is examined for blemishes, and nothing escapes him whether of thoughts or sentiments, or any of "the secrets of the heart." Knowing, then, that "God is not mocked," we ought to live worthily of his commandment and glory.

Likewise the deacons should be blameless before his righteousness, as servants of God and Christ and not of men; not slanderers, or double-tongued, not lovers of money, temperate in all matters, compassionate, careful, living according to the truth of the Lord, who became "a servant of all"; to whom, if we are pleasing in the present age, we shall also obtain the age to come, inasmuch as he promised to raise us from the dead. And if we bear our citizenship worthy of him, "we shall also reign with him"—provided, of course, that we have faith.

Similarly also the younger ones must be blameless in all things, especially taking thought of purity and bridling themselves from all evil. It is a fine thing to cut oneself off from the lusts that are in the world, for "every passion of the flesh wages war against the Spirit," and "neither fornicators nor the effeminate nor homosexuals will inherit the Kingdom of God," nor those who do perverse things. Wherefore it is necessary to refrain from all these things, and be obedient to the presbyters and deacons as unto God and Christ. And the young women must live with blameless and pure conscience.

Also the presbyters must be compassionate, merciful to all, turning back those who have gone astray, looking after the sick, not neglecting widow or orphan or one that is poor; but "always taking thought for what is honorable in the sight of God and of men," refraining from all anger, partiality, unjust judgment, keeping far from all love of money, not hastily believing evil of anyone, nor being severe in judgment, knowing that we all owe the debt of sin. If, then, we pray the Lord to forgive us, we ourselves ought also to forgive, for we are before the eyes of the Lord and God, and "everyone shall stand before the judgment seat of Christ and each of us shall give an account of himself." So then let us "serve him with fear and all reverence," as he himself has commanded, and also the apostles who preached the gospel to us and the prophets who foretold the coming of the Lord.

11

I-2. The Shepherd Milking. (*Cf. Martyrdom of SS. Perpetua and Felicitas, 4:8–10,* A.D. *202.*) *Fragment of a sarcophagus, Museo delle Terme, Rome.*

Let us be zealous for that which is good, refraining from occasions of scandal and from false brethren, and those who bear in hypocrisy the name of the Lord, who deceive empty-headed people. For "whosoever does not confess that Jesus Christ has come in the flesh is antichrist"; and whosoever does not confess the testimony of the cross "is of the devil"; and whosoever perverts the sayings of the Lord to suit his own lusts and says there is neither resurrection nor judgment—such a one is the first-born of Satan. Let us, therefore, forsake the vanity of the crowd and their false teachings and turn back to the word delivered to us from the beginning, "watching unto prayer" and continuing steadfast in fasting, beseeching fervently the all-seeing God "to lead us not into temptation," even as the Lord said, "The spirit indeed is willing, but the flesh is weak."

IV. The "Shepherd" of Hermas: an Apocryphal Apocalypse (c. 115–140)

13. Sin, Repentance, and the Church

Vis. 2:ii, trans. *ANF,* II, 11.

Fifteen days after, when I had fasted and prayed much to the Lord, the knowledge of the writing was revealed to me. Now the writing was to this effect: "Your seed, O Hermas, has sinned against God, and they have blasphemed against the Lord, and in their great wickedness they have betrayed their parents, and by their treachery did they not reap profit. And even now they have added to their sins lusts and iniquitous pollutions, and thus their iniquities have been filled up. But make known these words to all your children, and to your wife, who is to be your sister. For she does not restrain her tongue, with which she commits iniquity; but, on hearing these words, she will control herself, and will obtain mercy. For after you have made known to them these words which my Lord has commanded me to reveal to you, then shall they be forgiven all the sins which in former times they committed, and forgiveness will be granted to all the saints who have sinned even to the present day, if they repent with all their heart, and drive all doubts from their minds. For the Lord has sworn by His glory, in regard to His elect, that if any one of them sin after a certain day which has been fixed, he shall not be saved. For the repentance of the righteous has limits. Filled up are the days of repentance to all the saints; but to the heathen, repentance will be possible even to the last day. You will tell, therefore, those who preside over the Church, to direct their ways in righteousness, that they may receive in full the promises with great glory.

14. The Church and Her Presbyters

Vis. 2:iv, trans. *ANF,* II, 12.

Now a revelation was given to me, my brethren, while I slept, by a young man of comely appearance, who said to me, "Who do you think that old woman is from whom you received the book?" And I said, "The Sibyl." "You are in a mistake," says he; "it is not the Sibyl." "Who is it then?" say I. And he said, "It is the Church." And I said to him, "Why then is she an old woman?" "Because," said he, "she was created first of all On this account is she old. And for her sake was the world made." After that I saw a vision in my house, and that old woman came and asked me, if I had yet given the book to the presbyters. And I said that I had not. And then she said, "You have done well, for I have some words to add. But when I finish all the words, all the elect will then become acquainted with them through you. You will write therefore two books, and you will send the one to Clemens and the other to Grapte. And Clemens will send his to foreign countries, for permission has been granted to him to do so. And Grapte will admonish the widows and the orphans. But you will read the words in this city, along with the presbyters who preside over the Church.[11]

V. The Didache: Purported Teachings of the Twelve Apostles (c. 120–150)

The translations of sections 6–16 inclusive are those of Richardson, *et al., Early Christian Fathers* [LCC, Vol. I], 174–79.

15. *The Law of Perfection and Foods* (6)

See "that no one leads you astray" from this way of the teaching, since such a one's teaching is godless.

If you can bear the Lord's full yoke, you will be perfect. But if you cannot, then do what you can.

Now about food: undertake what you can. But keep strictly away from what is offered to idols, for that implies worshiping dead gods.

16. *Preparation for Baptism and Its Modes* (7)

Now about baptism: this is how to baptize. Give public instruction on all these points, and then "baptize" in running water, "in the name of the Father and of the Son

and of the Holy Spirit." If you do not have running water, baptize in some other. If you cannot, in cold, then in warm. If you have neither, then pour water on the head three times "in the name of the Father, Son, and Holy Spirit." Before the baptism, moreover, the one who baptizes and the one being baptized must fast, and any others who can. And you must tell the one being baptized to fast for one or two days beforehand.

17. *Fasts and Prayers* (8)

Your fasts must not be identical with those of the hypocrites. They fast on Mondays and Thursdays; but you should fast on Wednesdays and Fridays.

You must not pray like the hypocrites, but "pray as follows" as the Lord bid us in his gospel:

"Our Father in heaven, hallowed be your name; your Kingdom come; your will be done on earth as it is in heaven; give us today our bread for the morrow; and forgive us our debts as we forgive our debtors. And do not lead us into temptation, but save us from the evil one, for yours is the power and the glory forever."

You should pray in this way three times a day.

18. *Eucharist, Church, and Kingdom of God* (9–10)

Now about the Eucharist: This is how to give thanks: First in connection with the cup:

"We thank you, our Father, for the holy vine of David, your child, which you have revealed through Jesus, your child. To you be glory forever."

Then in connection with the piece [broken off the loaf]:

"We thank you, our Father, for the life and knowledge which you have revealed through Jesus, your child. To you be glory forever.

"As this piece [of bread] was scattered over the hills and then was brought together and made one, so let your Church be brought together from the ends of the earth into your Kingdom. For yours is the glory and the power through Jesus Christ forever."

You must not let anyone eat or drink of your Eucharist except those baptized in the Lord's name. For in reference to this the Lord said, "Do not give what is sacred to dogs."

After you have finished your meal, say grace in this way:

"We thank you, holy Father, for your sacred name which you have lodged in our hearts, and for the knowledge and faith and immortality which you have revealed through Jesus, your child. To you be glory forever.

"Almighty Master, 'you have created everything' for the sake of your name, and have given men food and drink to enjoy that they may thank you. But to us you have given spiritual food and drink and eternal life through Jesus, your child.

"Above all, we thank you that you are mighty. To you be glory forever.

"Remember, Lord, your Church, to save it from all evil and to make it perfect by your love. Make it holy, 'and gather' it 'together from the four winds' into your Kingdom which you have made ready for it. For yours is the power and the glory forever."

"Let Grace come and let this world pass away."

"Hosanna to the God of David!"

"If anyone is holy, let him come. If not, let him repent."

"Our Lord, come!"

"Amen."

In the case of prophets, however, you should let them give thanks in their own way.

19. Traveling Evangelists; True and False Prophets (11–13)

Now, you should welcome anyone who comes your way and teaches you all we have been saying. But if the teacher proves himself a renegade and by teaching otherwise contradicts all this, pay no attention to him. But if his teaching furthers the Lord's righteousness and knowledge, welcome him as the Lord.

Now about the apostles and prophets: Act in line with the gospel precept. Welcome every apostle on arriving, as if he were the Lord. But he must not stay beyond one day. In case of necessity, however, the next day too. If he stays three days, he is a false prophet. On departing, an apostle must not accept anything save sufficient food to carry him till his next lodging. If he asks for money, he is a false prophet.

While a prophet is making ecstatic utterances, you must not test or examine him. For "every sin will be forgiven," but this sin "will not be forgiven." However, not everybody making ecstatic utterances is a prophet, but only if he behaves like the Lord. It is by their conduct that the false prophet and the [true] prophet can be distinguished. For instance, if a prophet marks out a table in the Spirit, he must not eat from it. If he does, he is a false prophet. Again, every prophet who teaches the truth but fails to practice what he preaches is a false prophet. But every attested and genuine prophet who acts with a view to symbolizing the mystery of the Church, and does not teach you to do all he does, must not be judged by you. His judgment rests with God. For the ancient prophets too acted in this way. But if someone says in the Spirit, "Give me money, or something else," you must not heed him. However, if he tells you to give for others in need, no one must condemn him.

Everyone "who comes" to you "in the name of the Lord" must be welcomed. Afterward, when you have tested him, you will find out about him, for you have insight into right and wrong. If it is a traveler who arrives, help him all you can. But he must not stay with you more than two days, or, if necessary, three. If he wants to settle with you and is an artisan, he must work for his living. If, however, he has no trade, use your judgment in taking steps for him to live with you as a Christian without being idle. If he refuses to do this, he is trading on Christ. You must be on your guard against such people.

Every genuine prophet who wants to settle with you "has a right to his support." Similarly, a genuine teacher himself, just like a "workman, has a right to his support." Hence take all the first fruits of vintage and harvest, and of cattle and sheep, and give these first fruits to the prophets. For they are your high priests. If, however, you have no prophet, give them to the poor. If you make bread, take the first fruits and give in accordance with the precept. Similarly, when you open a jar of wine or oil, take the first fruits and give them to the prophets. Indeed, of money, clothes, and of all your possessions, take such first fruits as you think right, and give in accordance with the precept.

20. Worship on the Lord's Day (14)

On every Lord's Day—his special day—come together and break bread and give thanks, first confessing your sins so that your sacrifice may be pure. Anyone at variance with his neighbor must not join you, until they are reconciled, lest your sacrifice be defiled. For it was of this sacrifice that the Lord said, "Always and everywhere offer me a pure sacrifice; for I am a great King, says the Lord, and my name is marveled at by the nations."

I-3. Good Shepherd; Story of Jonah; Prayer. *Painted ceiling, 3rd century. Catacomb of SS. Pietro e Marcellino, Rome.*

21. The Unity of Bishop and Deacons (15)

You must, then, elect for yourselves bishops and deacons who are a credit to the Lord, men who are gentle, generous, faithful, and well tried. For their ministry to you is identical with that of the prophets and teachers. You must not, therefore, despise them, for along with the prophets and teachers they enjoy a place of honor among you.

Furthermore, do not reprove each other angrily, but quietly, as you find it in the gospel. Moreover, if anyone has wronged his neighbor, nobody must speak to him, and he must not hear a word from you, until he repents. Say your prayers, give your charity, and do everything just as you find it in the gospel of our Lord.

22. Eschatology: Last Things and the Great Day of Christ's Coming (16)

"Watch" over your life: do not let "your lamps" go out, and do not keep "your loins ungirded"; but "be ready," for "you do not know the hour when our Lord is coming."

Meet together frequently in your search for what is good for your souls, since "a lifetime of faith will be of no advantage" to you unless you prove perfect at the very last. For in the final days multitudes of false prophets and seducers will appear. Sheep will turn into wolves, and love into hatred. For with the increase of iniquity men will hate, persecute, and betray each other. And then the world deceiver will appear in the guise of God's Son. He will work "signs and wonders" and the earth will fall into his hands and he will commit outrages such as have never occurred before. Then mankind will come to the fiery trial "and many will fall away" and perish, "but those who persevere" in their faith "will be saved" by the Curse himself. Then "there will appear the signs" of the Truth: first the sign of stretched-out [hands] in heaven, then the sign of "a trumpet's blast," and thirdly the resurrection of the dead, though not of all the dead, but as it has been said: "The Lord will come and all his saints with him. Then the world will see the Lord coming on the clouds of the sky."

15

VI. The Pseudo Clementine Second Letter: An Early Christian Sermon (c. 130–150)

23. Righteousness and Purity as Preparation for the Kingdom (8–11)

The translations in this and the following items are those of Richardson, *et al., Early Christian Fathers* [LCC, Vol. I], pp. 196–99, 201–2.

So while we are on earth, let us repent. For we are like clay in a workman's hands. If a potter makes a vessel and it gets out of shape or breaks in his hands, he molds it over again; but if he has once thrown it into the flames of the furnace, he can do nothing more with it. Similarly, while we are in this world, let us too repent with our whole heart of the evil we have done in the flesh, so that we may be saved by the Lord while we have a chance to repent. For once we have departed this world we can no longer confess there or repent any more. Thus, brothers, by doing the Father's will and by keeping the flesh pure and by abiding by the Lord's commands, we shall obtain eternal life. For the Lord says in the Gospel: "If you fail to guard what is small, who will give you what is great? For I tell you that he who is faithful in a very little, is faithful also in much." This, then, is what he means: keep the flesh pure and the seal undefiled, so that we may obtain eternal life.

Moreover, let none of you say that this flesh will not be judged or rise again. Consider this: In what state were you saved? In what state did you regain your sight, if it was not while you were in this flesh? Therefore we should guard the flesh as God's temple. For just as you were called in the flesh, you will come in the flesh. If Christ the Lord who saved us was made flesh though he was at first spirit, and called us in this way, in the same way we too in this very flesh will receive our reward. Let us, then, love one another, so that we may all come to God's Kingdom. While we have an opportunity to be healed, let us give ourselves over to God, the physician, and pay him in return. How? By repenting with a sincere heart. For he foreknows everything, and realizes what is in our hearts. Let us then praise him, not with the mouth only, but from the heart, so that he may accept us as sons. For the Lord said, "My brothers are those who do the will of my Father."

So, my brothers, let us do the will of the Father who called us, so that we may have life; and let our preference be the pursuit of virtue. Let us give up vice as the forerunner of our sins, and let us flee impiety, lest evils overtake us. For if we are eager to do good, peace will pursue us. This is the reason men cannot find peace. They give way to human fears, and prefer the pleasures of the present to the promises of the future. For they do not realize what great torment the pleasures of the present bring, and what delight attaches to the promises of the future. If they did these things by themselves, it might be tolerable. But they persist in teaching evil to innocent souls, and do not realize that they and their followers will have their sentence doubled.

Let us therefore serve God with a pure heart and we shall be upright. But if, by not believing in God's promises, we do not serve him, we shall be wretched. For the word of the prophet says, "Wretched are the double-minded, those who doubt in their soul and say, 'We have heard these things long ago, even in our fathers' times, and day after day we have waited and have seen none of them.' You fools! Compare yourselves to a tree. Take a vine: first it sheds its leaves, then comes a bud, and after this a sour grape, then a ripe bunch. So my people too has had turmoils and troubles; but after that it will receive good things." So, my brothers, we must not be double-minded. Rather must we patiently hold out in hope so that we may also gain our reward. For "he can be trusted who promised" to pay each one the wages due for his work. If, then, we have done what is right in God's eyes, we shall enter his Kingdom and receive the promises "which ear has not heard or eye seen, or which man's heart has not entertained."

I-4. Episodes in Christ's Passion. *To the right of central panel: the arrest of Jesus and judgment by Pilate; to the left of center panel: Jesus crowned with thorns, and the ascent to Calvary; central motif: allegory of triumphant Resurrection. Christian sarcophagus, Museo Laterano, Rome.*

24. The True, Spiritual Church, the Body of Christ (14)

So, my brothers, by doing the will of God our Father we shall belong to the first Church, the spiritual one, which was created before the sun and the moon. But if we fail to do the Lord's will, that passage of Scripture will apply to us which says, "My house has become a robber's den." So, then, we must choose to belong to the Church of life in order to be saved. I do not suppose that you are ignorant that the living "Church is the body of Christ." For Scripture says, "God made man male and female." The male is Christ; the female is the Church. The Bible, moreover, and the Apostles say that the Church is not limited to the present, but existed from the beginning. For it was spiritual, as was our Jesus, and was made manifest in the last days to save us. Indeed, the Church which is spiritual was made manifest in the flesh of Christ, and so indicates to us that if any of us guard it in the flesh and do not corrupt it, he will get it in return by the Holy Spirit. For this flesh is the antitype of the spirit. Consequently, no one who has corrupted the antitype will share in the reality. This, then, is what it means, brothers: Guard the flesh so that you may share in the spirit. Now, if we say that the Church is the flesh and the Christ is the spirit, then he who does violence to the flesh, does violence to the Church. Such a person, then, will not share in the spirit, which is Christ. This flesh is able to share in so great a life and immortality, because the Holy Spirit cleaves to it. Nor can one express or tell "what things the Lord has prepared" for his chosen ones.

25. Repentance and Charity Befitting the Coming Judgment (16)

So, brothers, since we have been given no small opportunity to repent, let us take the occasion to turn to God who has called us, while we still have One to accept us. For if we renounce these pleasures and master our souls by avoiding their evil lusts, we shall share in Jesus' mercy. Understand that "the day" of judgment is already "on its way like a furnace ablaze," and "the powers of heaven will dissolve" and the whole earth will be like lead melting in fire. Then men's secret and overt actions will be made clear. Charity, then, like repentance from sin, is a good thing. But fasting is better than prayer, and charity than both. "Love covers a multitude of sins," and prayer, arising from a good conscience, "rescues from death." Blessed is everyone who abounds in these things, for charity lightens sin.

26. *Training in the Present Life for the Eventual Laurels of the Future (19–20)*

So my brothers and sisters, after God's truth I am reading you an exhortation to heed what was there written, so that you may save yourselves and your reader. For compensation I beg you to repent with all your heart, granting yourselves salvation and life. By doing this we will set a goal for all the young who want to be active in the cause of religion and of God's goodness. We should not, moreover, be so stupid as to be displeased and vexed when anyone admonishes us and converts us from wickedness to righteousness. There are times when we do wrong unconsciously because of the double-mindedness and unbelief in our hearts, and "our understanding is darkened" by empty desires. Let us, then, do what is right so that we may finally be saved. Blessed are they who observe these injunctions; though they suffer briefly in this world, they will gather the immortal fruit of the resurrection. A religious man must not be downcast if he is miserable in the present. A time of blessedness awaits him. He will live again in heaven with his forefathers, and will rejoice in an eternity that knows no sorrow.

But you must not be troubled in mind by the fact that we see the wicked in affluence while God's slaves are in straitened circumstances. Brothers and sisters, we must have faith. We are engaged in the contest of the living God and are being trained by the present life in order to win laurels in the life to come. None of the upright has obtained his reward quickly, but he waits for it. For were God to give the righteous their reward at once, our training would straightway be in commerce and not in piety, since we would give an appearance of uprightness, when pursuing, not religion, but gain. That is why the divine judgment punishes a spirit which is not upright, and loads it with chains.

"To the only invisible God," the Father of truth, who dispatched to us the Saviour and prince of immortality, through whom he also disclosed to us the truth and the heavenly life—to him be glory forever and ever. Amen.

VII. The Epistle to Diognetus: A Christian Apologia (c. 130–180)

27. *The Strange Story of a Mysterious "New" Race (1–2)*

The translations, by sections, are those of Richardson, *et al.*, *Early Christian Fathers* [LCC, Vol. I], pp. 213–19.

To His Excellency, Diognetus:

I understand, sir, that you are really interested in learning about the religion of the Christians, and that you are making an accurate and careful investigation of the subject. You want to know, for instance, what God they believe in and how they worship him, while at the same time they disregard the world and look down on death, and how it is that they do not treat the divinities of the Greeks as gods at all, although on the other hand they do not follow the superstition of the Jews. You would also like to know the source of the loving affection that they have for each other. You wonder, too, why this new race or way of life has appeared on earth now and not earlier. I certainly welcome this keen interest on your part, and I ask God, who gives us the power to speak and the power to listen, to let me speak in such a way that you may derive the greatest possible benefit from listening, and to enable you to listen to such good effect that I may never have a reason for regretting what I have said. Now, then, clear out all the thoughts that take up your attention, and pack away all the old ways of looking at things that keep deceiving you. You must become like a new man from the beginning, since, as you yourself admit, you are going to listen to a really new message.

THE STUPIDITY OF IDOLATRY

Look at the things that you proclaim and think of as gods. See with your outward eyes and with your mind what material they are made of and what form they happen to have. Is not one a stone, like the stones we walk on, and another bronze, no better than the utensils that have been forged for our use? Here is a wooden one, already rotting away, and one made of silver, that needs a watchman to protect it from being stolen.

Yet another one is made of iron, eaten by rust, and another of pottery, no more attractive than something provided for the most ignoble purpose. Were not all these things made out of perishable material? Were they not forged by iron and fire? Surely the stonemason made one of them, and the blacksmith another, the silversmith a third, and the potter a fourth! These things have been molded into their present shapes by the arts of these craftsmen. Before they were shaped, they could just as easily have been given a different form—and would this not be possible even now? Could not vessels like them be made out of the same material, if the same craftsmen happened to be available? Moreover, could not these things that you worship now be made by men into vessels like any others? They are all dumb, after all, and blind. They are without life or feeling or power of movement, all rotting away and decaying. These are the things you call gods, the things you serve. You Gentiles adore these things, and in the end you become like them. That is why you hate the Christians, because they do not believe that these objects are gods. But is it not you yourselves who, when in your own thoughts you suppose that you are praising the gods, are in reality despising them? Surely it is mockery and insult to worship your stone and earthenware gods without bothering to guard them, while you lock up your gods of silver and gold at night, and set guards over them during the day, to keep them from being stolen.

Moreover, if they are not lacking in sensation, you punish them by the very honors you try to pay them, while, if they are senseless, you show them up by the mere act of worshiping them with blood and sacrificial fat. Just picture one of yourselves enduring this kind of thing, or allowing it to be done to him! There is not one man who would willingly tolerate this sort of punishment, because he has feeling and intelligence, but the stone tolerates it, because it has no feeling. Do you not then really disprove its power of feeling? I could say a good deal more about the fact that Christians are not the slaves of gods like these, but if anyone cannot see the force of these arguments, I

think that nothing is to be gained by arguing the matter further.

28. *The Mystery of Christianity Not to Be Learned from Men (4:6)*

All this being so, I think that you have learned enough to see that Christians are right in holding themselves aloof from the aimlessness and trickery of Greeks and Jews alike, and from the officiousness and noisy conceit of the Jews. But as far as the mystery of the Christians' own religion is concerned, you cannot expect to learn that from man.

29. *Christians in the World but Not of It; Social Obligations on Earth, Citizenship in Heaven (5)*

For Christians cannot be distinguished from the rest of the human race by country or language or customs. They do not live in cities of their own; they do not use a peculiar form of speech; they do not follow an eccentric manner of life. This doctrine of theirs has not been discovered by the ingenuity or deep thought of inquisitive men, nor do they put forward a merely human teaching, as some people do. Yet, although they live in Greek and barbarian cities alike, as each man's lot has been cast, and follow the customs of the country in clothing and food and other matters of daily living, at the same time they give proof of the remarkable and admittedly extraordinary constitution of their own commonwealth. They live in their own countries, but only as aliens. They have a share in everything as citizens, and endure everything as foreigners. Every foreign land is their fatherland, and yet for them every fatherland is a foreign land. They marry, like everyone else, and they beget children, but they do not cast out their offspring. They share their board with each other, but not their marriage bed. It is true that they are "in the flesh," but they do not live "according to the flesh." They busy themselves on earth, but their citizenship is in heaven. They obey the established laws, but in their own lives they go far beyond what the laws require. They love all men, and by all men are persecuted. They are unknown, and still they are condemned; they are put to death, and yet they are brought to life. They are poor, and yet they make many rich; they are completely destitute, and yet they enjoy complete abundance. They are dishonored, and in their very dishonor are glorified; they are defamed, and are vindicated. They are reviled, and yet they bless; when they are affronted, they still pay due respect. When they do good, they are punished as evildoers; undergoing punishment, they rejoice because they are brought to life. They are treated by the Jews as foreigners and enemies, and are hunted down by the Greeks; and all the time those who hate them find it impossible to justify their enmity.

30. What the Soul Is to the Body, That Christians Are to the World (6)

To put it simply: What the soul is in the body, that Christians are in the world. The soul is dispersed through all the members of the body, and Christians are scattered through all the cities of the world. The soul dwells in the body, but does not belong to the body, and Christians dwell in the world, but do not belong to the world. The soul, which is invisible, is kept under guard in the visible body; in the same way, Christians are recognized when they are in the world, but their religion remains unseen. The flesh hates the soul and treats it as an enemy, even though it has suffered no wrong, because it is prevented from enjoying its pleasures; so too the world hates Christians, even though it suffers no wrong at their hands, because they range themselves against its pleasures. The soul loves the flesh that hates it, and its members; in the same way, Christians love those who hate them. The soul is shut up in the body, and yet itself holds the body together; while Christians are restrained in the world as in a prison, and yet themselves hold the world together. The soul, which is immortal, is housed in a mortal dwelling; while Christians are settled among corruptible things, to wait for the incorruptibility that will be theirs in heaven. The soul, when faring badly as to food and drink, grows better; so too Christians, when punished, day by day, increase more and more. It is to no less a post than this that God has ordered them, and they must not try to evade it.

31. The King's Son Sent to Men: the Christian Revelation (7)

As I have indicated, it is not an earthly discovery that was committed to them; it is not a mortal thought that they think of as worth guarding with such care, nor have they been entrusted with the stewardship of merely human mysteries. On the contrary, it was really the Ruler of all, the Creator of all, the invisible God himself, who from heaven established the truth and the holy, incomprehensible word among men, and fixed it firmly in their hearts. Nor, as one might suppose, did he do this by sending to men some subordinate—an angel, or principality, or one of those who administer earthly affairs, or perhaps one of those to whom the government of things in heaven is entrusted. Rather, he sent the Designer and Maker of the universe himself, by whom he created the heavens and confined the sea within its own bounds—him whose hidden purposes all the elements of the world faithfully carry out, him from whom the sun has received the measure of the daily rounds that it must keep, him whom the moon obeys when he commands her to shine by night, and whom the stars obey as they follow the course of the moon. He sent him by whom all things have been set in order and distinguished and placed in subjection—the heavens and the things that are in the heavens, the earth and the things in the earth, the sea and the things in the sea, fire, air, the unfathomed pit, the things in the heights and in the depths and in the realm between; God sent him to men.

Now, did he send him, as a human mind might assume, to rule by tyranny, fear, and terror? Far from it! He sent him out of kindness and gentleness, like a king sending his son who is himself a king. He sent him as God; he sent him as man to men. He willed to save man by persuasion, not by compulsion, for compulsion is not God's way of working. In sending him, God called men, but did not pursue them; he sent him in love, not in judgment. Yet he will indeed send him someday as our Judge, and who shall stand when he appears? . . .

Do you not see how they are thrown to wild animals to make them deny the Lord, and how. they are not vanquished? Do you not see that the more of them are punished, the more do others increase? These things do not seem to come from a human power; they are a mighty act of God, they are proofs of his presence.

VIII. Second-Century Christian Worship

A. ACCORDING TO JUSTIN'S APOLOGY I (c. 150/155)

32. Men Reborn for the Kingdom through Baptismal Washing, or Illumination (61)

Trans. of Chaps. 61, 65–67, Richardson, et al., *Early Christian Fathers* [LCC, Vol. I], pp. 282–83, 286–88.

How we dedicated ourselves to God when we were made new through Christ I will explain, since it might seem to be unfair if I left this out from my exposition. Those who are persuaded and believe that the things we teach and say are true, and promise that they can live accordingly, are instructed to pray and beseech God with fasting for the remission of their past sins, while we pray and fast along with them. Then they are brought by us where there is water, and are reborn by the same manner of rebirth by which we ourselves were reborn; for they are then washed in the water in the name of God the Father and Master of all, and of our Saviour Jesus Christ, and of the Holy Spirit. For Christ said, "Unless you are born again you will not enter into the Kingdom of heaven." Now it is clear to all that those who have once come into being cannot enter the wombs of those who bore them. But as I quoted before, it was said through the prophet Isaiah how those who have sinned and repent shall escape from their sins. He said this: "Wash yourselves, be clean, take away wickednesses from your souls, learn to do good, give judgment for the orphan and defend the cause of the widow, and come and let us reason together, says the Lord. And though your sins be as scarlet, I will make them as white as wool, and though they be as crimson, I will make them white as snow. If you will not listen to me, the sword will devour you; for the mouth of the Lord has spoken these things." And we learned from the apostles this reason for this [rite]. At our first birth we were born of necessity without our knowledge, from moist seed, by the intercourse of our parents with each other, and grew up in bad habits and wicked behavior. So that we should not remain children of necessity and ignorance, but [become sons] of free choice and knowledge, and obtain remission of the sins we have already committed, there is named at the water, over him who has chosen to be born again and has repented of his sinful acts, the name of God the Father and Master of all. Those who lead to the washing the one who is to be washed call on [God by] this term only. For no one may give a proper name to the ineffable God, and if anyone should dare to say that there is one, he is hopelessly insane. This washing is called illumination, since those who learn these things are illumined within. The illuminand is also washed in the name of Jesus Christ, who was crucified under Pontius Pilate, and in the name of the Holy Spirit, who through the prophets foretold everything about Jesus.

33. Post-Baptismal Assembly; Eucharistic Prayers; Distribution of Bread, Wine, and Water (65)

We, however, after thus washing the one who has been convinced and signified his assent, lead him to those who are called brethren, where they are assembled. They then earnestly offer common prayers for themselves and the one who has been illuminated and all others everywhere, that we may be made worthy, having learned the truth, to be found in deed good citizens and keepers of what is commanded, so that we may be saved with eternal salvation. On finishing the prayers we greet each other with a kiss. Then bread and a cup of water and mixed wine are brought to the president of the brethren and he, taking them, sends up praise and glory to the Father of the universe through the name of the Son and of the Holy Spirit, and offers thanksgiving at some length that we have been deemed worthy to receive these things from him. When he has finished the prayers and the thanksgiving, the whole congregation present assents, saying, "Amen." "Amen" in the Hebrew language means, "So be it." When the president has given thanks and the whole congregation has assented, those whom we call deacons give to each of those present a portion of the consecrated bread and wine and water, and they take it to the absent.

34. Participation of the Eucharistic Food; Communion of the Flesh and Blood of the Incarnate Jesus (66)

This food we call Eucharist, of which no one is allowed to partake except one who believes that the things we teach are true, and has received the washing for forgiveness of sins and for rebirth, and who lives as Christ handed down to us. For we do not receive these things as common bread or common drink; but as Jesus Christ our Saviour being incarnate by God's word took flesh and blood for our salvation, so also we have been taught that the food consecrated by the word of prayer which comes from him, from which our flesh and blood are nourished by transformation, is the flesh and blood of the incarnate Jesus. For the apostles in the memoirs composed by them, which are called Gospels, thus handed down what was commanded them: that Jesus, taking bread and having given thanks, said, "Do this for my memorial, this is my body"; and likewise taking the cup and giving thanks he said, "This is my blood"; and gave it to them alone. This also the wicked demons in imitation handed down as something to be done in the mysteries of Mithra; for bread and a cup of water are brought out in their secret rites of initiation, with certain invocations which you either know or can learn.

35. Eucharistic Communion and Social Cohesiveness at the Sunday Assembly (67)

After these [services] we constantly remind each other of these things. Those who have more come to the aid of those who lack, and we are constantly together. Over all that we receive we bless the Maker of all things through his Son Jesus Christ and through the Holy Spirit. And on the day called Sunday there is a meeting in one place of those who live in cities or the country, and the memoirs of the apostles or the writings of the prophets are read as long as time permits. When the reader has finished, the president in a discourse urges and invites [us] to the imitation of these noble things. Then we all stand up together and offer prayers. And, as said before, when we have finished the prayer, bread is brought, and wine and water, and the president similarly sends up prayers and thanksgivings to the best of his ability, and the congregation assents, saying the Amen; the distribution, and reception of the consecrated [elements] by each one, takes place and they are sent to the absent by the deacons. Those who prosper, and who so wish, contribute, each one as much as he chooses to. What is collected is deposited with the president, and he takes care of orphans and widows, and those who are in want on account of sickness or any other cause, and those who are in bonds, and the strangers who are sojourners among [us], and, briefly, he is the protector of all those in need. We all hold this common gathering on Sunday, since it is the first day, on which God transforming darkness and matter made the universe, and Jesus Christ our Saviour rose from the dead on the same day. For they crucified him on the day before Saturday, and on the day after Saturday, he appeared to his apostles and disciples and taught them these things which I have passed on to you also for your serious consideration.

B. FROM THE ACCOUNT IN TERTULLIAN'S APOLOGY (c. 197)

36. The Assembly in Worship of the Christian Society; Prayers for Church and World; Sacred Readings, Exhortations, Discipline; Piety's "Community Chest" Fund

Apologeticum, 39, trans. ANF, III, p. 46. See Tertullian's, De Corona, 3, in Chap. III, No. 19 of this source book.

I shall at once go on, then, to exhibit the peculiarities of the Christian society, that, as I have refuted the evil charged against it, I may point out its positive good. We are a body knit together as such by a common religious profession, by unity of discipline, and by the bond of a common hope. We meet together as an assembly and congregation, that, offering up prayer to God as with united force, we may wrestle with Him in our supplications. This violence God delights in. We pray, too, for the emperors, for their ministers and for all in authority, for the welfare of the world, for the prevalence of peace, for the delay of the final consummation. We assemble to read our sacred writings, if any peculiarity of the times makes either forewarning or reminiscence needful. However it be in that respect, with the sacred words we nourish our faith, we animate our hope, we make our confidence more stedfast; and no less by inculcations of God's precepts we confirm good habits. In the same place also exhortations are made, rebukes and sacred censures are administered. For with a great gravity is the work of judging carried on among us, as befits those who feel assured that they are in the sight of God; and you have the most notable example of judgment to come when any one has sinned so grievously as to require his severance from us in prayer, in the congregation and in all sacred intercourse. The tried men of our elders preside over us, obtaining that honour not by purchase, but by established character. There is no buying and selling of any sort in the things of God. Though we have our treasurechest, it is not made up of purchase-money, as of a religion that has its price. On the monthly day, if he likes, each puts in a small donation; but only if it be his pleasure, and only if he be able: for there is no compulsion; all is voluntary. These gifts are, as it were, piety's deposit fund. For they are not taken thence and spent on feasts, and drinking-bouts, and eating-houses, but to support and bury poor people, to supply the wants of boys and girls destitute of means and parents, and of old persons confined now to the house; such, too, as have suffered shipwreck; and if there happen to be any in the mines, or banished to the islands, or shut up in the prisons, for nothing but their fidelity to the cause of God's Church, they become the nurslings of their confession. But it is mainly the deeds of a love so noble that lead many to put a brand upon us. *See*, they say, *how they love one another*, for themselves are animated by mutual hatred; how they are ready even to die for one another, for they themselves will sooner put to death.

IX. Clement of Alexandria (c. 215) and the Instruction of Christ, the True Pedagogue (c. 195, 208/11)

37. *The Character of the True Gnostic*

Strom. 4:22, trans. *ANF*, II, p. 434.

The man of understanding and perspicacity is, then, a Gnostic. . . . But only the doing of good out of love, and for the sake of its own excellence, is to be the Gnostic's choice. Now, in the person of God it is said to the Lord, "Ask of Me, and I will give the heathen for Thine inheritance;" teaching Him to ask a truly regal request—that is, the salvation of men without price, that we may inherit and possess the Lord. For, on the contrary, to desire knowledge about God for any practical purpose, that this may be done, or that may not be done, is not proper to the Gnostic; but the knowledge itself suffices as the reason for contemplation. For I will dare aver that it is not because he wishes to be saved that he, who devotes himself to knowledge for the sake of the divine science itself, chooses knowledge. For the exertion of the intellect by exercise is prolonged to a perpetual exertion. And the perpetual exertion of the intellect is the essence of an intelligent being, which results from an uninterrupted process of admixture, and remains eternal contemplation, a living substance. Could we, then, suppose any one proposing to the Gnostic whether he would choose the knowledge of God or everlasting salvation; and if these, which are entirely identical, were separable, he would without the least hesitation choose the knowledge of God, deeming that property of faith, which from love ascends to knowledge, desirable, for its own sake. This, then, is the perfect man's first form of doing good, when it is done not for any advantage in what pertains to him, but because he judges it right to do good; and the energy being vigorously exerted in all things, in the very act becomes good; not, good in some things, and not good in others; but consisting in the habit of doing good, neither for glory, nor, as the philosophers say, for reputation, nor from reward either from men or God; but so as to pass life after the image and likeness of the Lord.

38. *Christ the Instructor, Tutor of the Soul*

Paed. 1:1, trans. *ANF*, II, p. 209.

When, then, the heavenly guide, the Word, was inviting men to salvation, the appellation of *hortatory* was properly applied to Him: his same word was called rousing (the whole from a part). For the whole of piety is hortatory, engendering in the kindred faculty of reason a yearning after true life now and to come. But now, being at once curative and preceptive, following in His own steps, He makes what had been prescribed the subject of persuasion, promising the cure of the passions within us. Let us

then designate this Word appropriately by the one name *Tutor* (or *Paedagogue*, or *Instructor*). . . .

There is a wide difference between health and knowledge; for the latter is produced by learning, the former by healing. One, who is ill, will not therefore learn any branch of instruction till he is quite well. For neither to learners nor to the sick is each injunction invariably expressed similarly; but to the former in such a way as to lead to knowledge, and to the latter to health. As, then, for those of us who are diseased in body a physician is required, so also those who are diseased in soul require a paedagogue to cure our maladies; and then a teacher, to train and guide the soul to all requisite knowledge when it is made able to admit the revelation of the Word. Eagerly desiring, then, to perfect us by a gradation conducive to salvation, suited for efficacious discipline, a beautiful arrangement is observed by the all-benignant Word, who first exhorts, then trains, and finally teaches.

I-5. Sermon on the Mount. Miracles of Healing Woman, Paralytic, and Man Born Blind. *From a sarcophagus, c. 300, Museo delle Terme, Rome.*

I-6. Christ Enthroned. *Marble sarcophagus of Julius Bassus, c. 359, Vatican Grottoes, Rome.*

39. *Prayer to the Paedagogue*

Paed. 3:12, trans. *ANF*, II, p. 295.

Be gracious, O Instructor, to us Thy children, Father, Charioteer of Israel, Son and Father, both in One, O Lord. Grant to us who obey Thy precepts, that we may perfect the likeness of the image, and with all our power know Him who is the good God and not a harsh judge. And do Thou Thyself cause that all of us who have our conversation in Thy peace, who have been translated into Thy commonwealth, having sailed tranquilly over the billows of sin, may be wafted in calm by Thy Holy Spirit, by the ineffable wisdom, by night and day to the perfect day; and giving thanks may praise, and praising thank the Alone Father and Son, Son and Father, the Son, Instructor and Teacher, with the Holy Spirit, all in One, in whom is all, for whom all is One, for whom is eternity, whose members we all are, whose glory the aeons are; for the All-good, All-lovely, All-wise, All-just One. To whom be glory both now and for ever. Amen.

40. *Hymn to Christ the Saviour in Praise of His Instruction*

Paed. 3:12, trans. *ANF*, II, pp. 295–96.

A HYMN TO CHRIST THE SAVIOUR

Composed by St. Clement

I

Bridle of colts untamed,
  Over our wills presiding;
Wing of unwandering birds,
  Our flight securely guiding.
Rudder of youth unbending,
  Firm against adverse shock;
Shepherd, with wisdom tending
  Lambs of the royal flock:
Thy simple children bring
In one, that they may sing
In solemn lays
Their hymns of praise
With guileless lips to Christ their King.

II

King of saints, almighty Word
Of the Father highest Lord;
Wisdom's head and chief;

Assuagement of all grief;
Lord of all time and space,
Jesus, Saviour of our race;
Shepherd, who dost us keep;
Husbandman, who tillest,
Bit to restrain us, Rudder
To guide us as Thou willest;
Of the all-holy flock celestial wing;
Fisher of men, whom Thou to life dost bring;
From evil sea of sin,
And from the billowy strife,
Gathering pure fishes in,
Caught with sweet bait of life:
Lead us, Shepherd of the sheep,
Reason-gifted, holy One;
King of youths, whom Thou dost keep,
So that they pollution shun:
Steps of Christ, celestial Way;
Word eternal, Age unending;
Life that never can decay;
Fount of mercy, virtue-sending;
Life august of those who raise
Unto God their hymn of praise,
                              Jesus Christ!

III

Nourished by the milk of heaven,
To our tender palates given;
Milk of wisdom from the breast
Of that bride of grace exprest;
By a dewy spirit filled
From fair Reason's breast distilled;
Let us sucklings join to raise
With pure lips our hymns of praise
As our grateful offering,
Clean and pure, to Christ our King.
Let us, with hearts undefiled,
Celebrate the mighty Child.
We, Christ-born, the choir of peace;
We, the people of His love,
Let us sing, nor ever cease,
To the God of peace above.

41. Baptism, Grace, and Illumination

Paed. 1:6, trans. *ANF*, II, p. 215.

But He is perfected by the washing—of baptism—alone, and is sanctified by the descent of the Spirit? Such is the case. The same also takes place in our case, whose exemplar Christ became. Being baptized, we are illuminated; illuminated, we become sons; being made sons, we are made perfect; being made perfect, we are made immortal. "I," says He, "have said that ye are gods, and all sons of the Highest." This work is variously called grace, and illumination, and perfection, and washing: washing, by which we cleanse away our sins; grace, by which the penalties accruing to transgressions are remitted; and illumination, by which that holy light of salvation is beheld, that is, by which we see God clearly.

42. The Church, the Virgin Mother, and the Eucharistic Milk

Paed. 5:6, trans. *ANF*, II, p. 220.

O mystic marvel! The universal Father is one, and one the universal Word; and the Holy Spirit is one and the same everywhere, and one is the only virgin mother. I love to call her the Church. This mother, when alone, had not milk, because alone she was not a woman. But she is once virgin and mother—pure as a virgin, loving as a mother. And calling her children to her, she nurses them with holy milk, viz., with the Word for childhood. Therefore she had not milk; for the milk was this child fair and comely, the body of Christ, which nourishes by the Word the young brood, which the Lord Himself brought forth in throes of the flesh, which the Lord Himself swathed in His precious blood. O amazing birth! O holy swaddling bands! The Word is all to the child, both father and mother, and tutor and nurse. "Eat ye my flesh," He says, "and drink my blood." Such is the suitable food which the Lord ministers, and He offers His flesh and pours forth His blood, and nothing is wanting for the children's growth. O amazing mystery! We are enjoined to cast off the old and carnal corruption, as also the old nutriment, receiving in exchange another new regimen, that of Christ, receiving Him if we can, to hide Him within; and that, enshrining the Saviour in our souls, we may correct the affections of our flesh.

But you are not inclined to understand it thus, but perchance more generally. Hear it also in the following way. The flesh figuratively represents to us the Holy Spirit; for the flesh was created by Him. The blood points out to us the Word, for as rich blood

26

the Word has been infused into life; and the union of both is the Lord, the food of the babes—the Lord who is Spirit and Word. The food—that is, the Lord Jesus—that is, the Word of God, the Spirit made flesh, the heavenly flesh sanctified. The nutriment is the milk of the Father, by which alone we infants are nourished. The Word Himself, then, the beloved One, and our nourisher, hath shed His own blood for us, to save humanity; and by Him, we, believing on God, flee to the Word, "the care-soothing breast" of the Father. And He alone, as is befitting, supplies us children with the milk of love, and those only are truly blessed who suck this breast. Wherefore also Peter says: "Laying therefore aside all malice, and all guile, and hypocrisy, and envy, and evil speaking, as new-born babes, desire the milk of the word, that ye may grow by it to salvation; if ye have tasted that the Lord is Christ."

X. Hippolytus and the Apostolic Tradition: a Third-Century Order of Worship (c. 217)

43. Tradition our Teacher; the Ordination of Bishops, Presbyters, and Deacons

1:1–15. The translation of this and the following item is that of B. S. Easton, *The Apostolic Tradition of Hippolytus* (Cambridge: Cambridge University Press, 1934), pp. 33–41.

1. We have duly completed what needed to be said about "Gifts," describing those gifts which God by His own counsel has bestowed on men, in offering to Himself His image which had gone astray. But now, moved by His love to all His saints, we pass on to our most important theme, "The Tradition," our teacher. And we address the churches, so that they who have been well trained, may, by our instruction, hold fast that tradition which has continued up to now and, knowing it well, may be strengthened. This is needful, because of that lapse or error which recently occurred through ignorance, and because of ignorant men. And [the] Holy Spirit will supply perfect grace to those who believe aright, that they may know how all things should be transmitted and kept by them who rule the church.

PART I

2. Let the bishop be ordained after he has been chosen by all the people. When he has been named and shall please all, let him, with the presbytery and such bishops as may be present, assemble with the people on a Sunday. While all give their consent, the bishops shall lay their hands upon him, and the presbytery shall stand by in silence. All indeed shall keep silent, praying in their heart for the descent of the Spirit. Then one of the bishops who are present shall at the request of all, lay his hand on him who is ordained bishop, and shall pray as follows, saying:

3. God and Father of our Lord Jesus Christ, Father of mercies and God of all comfort, who dwellest on high yet hast respect to the lowly, who knowest all things before they come to pass. Thou hast appointed the borders of thy church by the word of thy grace, predestinating from the beginning the righteous race of Abraham. And making them princes and priests, and leaving not thy sanctuary without a ministry, thou hast from the beginning of the world been well pleased to be glorified among those whom thou hast chosen. Pour forth now that power, which is thine, of thy royal Spirit, which thou gavest to thy beloved Servant Jesus Christ, which he bestowed on his holy apostles, who established the church in every place, the church which thou hast sanctified unto unceasing glory and praise of thy name. Thou who knowest the hearts of all, grant to this thy servant, whom thou hast chosen to be bishop, [to feed thy holy flock] and to serve as thy high priest without blame, ministering night and day, to propitiate thy countenance without ceasing and to offer thee the gifts of thy holy church. And by the Spirit of high-priesthood to have authority to remit sins according to thy commandment, to assign the lots according to thy precept, to loose every bond according to the authority which thou gavest to thy apostles, and to please thee in meekness and purity of heart, offering to thee an odour of sweet savour. Through thy Servant Jesus Christ our Lord, through whom be to thee glory, might, honour, with

[the] Holy Spirit in [the] holy church, both now and always and world without end. Amen.

4. And when he is made bishop, all shall offer him the kiss of peace, for he has been made worthy. To him then the deacons shall bring the offering, and he, laying his hand upon it, with all the presbytery, shall say as the thanksgiving:

The Lord be with you.

And all shall say

And with thy spirit.
Lift up your hearts.
We lift them up unto the Lord.
Let us give thanks to the Lord.
It is meet and right.

And then he shall proceed immediately:

We give thee thanks, O God, through thy beloved Servant Jesus Christ, whom at the end of time thou didst send to us a Saviour and Redeemer and the Messenger of thy counsel. Who is thy Word, inseparable from thee; through whom thou didst make all things and in whom thou art well pleased. Whom thou didst send from heaven into the womb of the Virgin, and who, dwelling within her, was made flesh, and was manifested as thy Son, being born of [the] Holy Spirit and the Virgin. Who, fulfilling thy will, and winning for himself a holy people, spread out his hands when he came to suffer, that by his death he might set free them who believed on thee. Who, when he was betrayed to his willing death, that he might bring to nought death, and break the bonds of the devil, and tread hell under foot, and give light to the righteous, and set up a boundary post, and manifest his resurrection, taking bread and giving thanks to thee said: Take, eat: this is my body, which is broken for you. And likewise also the cup, saying: This is my blood, which is shed for you. As often as ye perform this, perform my memorial.

Having in memory, therefore, his death and resurrection, we offer to thee the bread and the cup, yielding thee thanks, because thou hast counted us worthy to stand before thee and to minister to thee.

And we pray thee that thou wouldest send thy Holy Spirit upon the offerings of thy holy church; that thou, gathering them into one, wouldest grant to all thy saints who partake to be filled with [the] Holy Spirit, that their faith may be confirmed in truth, that we may praise and glorify thee. Through thy Servant Jesus Christ, through whom be to thee glory and honour, with [the] Holy Spirit in the holy church, both now and always and world without end. Amen.

5. If anyone offers oil, he shall give thanks as at the offering of the bread and wine, though not with the same words but in the same general manner, saying:

That sanctifying this oil, O God, wherewith thou didst anoint kings, priests and prophets, thou wouldest grant health to them who use it and partake of it, so that it may bestow comfort on all who taste it and health on all who use it.

6. Likewise, if anyone offers cheese and olives, let him say thus:

Sanctify this milk that has been united into one mass, and unite us to thy love. Let thy loving kindness ever rest upon this fruit of the olive, which is a type of thy bounty, which thou didst cause to flow from the tree unto life for them who hope on thee.

But at every blessing shall be said:

Glory be to thee, with [the] Holy Spirit in the holy church, both now and always and world without end. [Amen.]

8. But when a presbyter is ordained, the bishop shall lay his hand upon his head, while the presbyters touch him, and he shall say according to those things that were said above, as we have prescribed above concerning the bishop, praying and saying:

God and Father of our Lord Jesus Christ, look upon this thy servant, and grant to him the Spirit of grace and counsel of a presbyter, that he may sustain and govern thy people with a pure heart; as thou didst look upon thy chosen people and didst command Moses that he should choose presbyters, whom thou didst fill with thy Spirit, which thou gavest to thy servant. And now, O Lord, grant that there may be unfailingly preserved amongst us the Spirit of thy grace, and make us worthy that, believing, we may minister to thee in simplicity of heart, praising thee. Through thy Servant Jesus Christ, through whom be to thee glory and honour, with [the] Holy Spirit in the holy church, both now and always and world without end. Amen.

9. But the deacon, when he is ordained, is chosen according to those things that were said above, the bishop alone in like manner laying his hands upon him, as we have prescribed. When the deacon is ordained, this is the reason why the bishop alone shall lay his hands upon him: he is not ordained to the priesthood but to serve the bishop and to carry out the bishop's commands. He does not take part in the council of the clergy; he is to attend to his own duties and to make known to the bishop such things as are needful. He does not receive that Spirit that is possessed by the presbytery, in which the presbyters share; he receives only what is confided in him under the bishop's authority.

For this cause the bishop alone shall make a deacon. But on a presbyter, however, the presbyters shall lay their hands because of the common and like Spirit of the clergy. Yet the presbyter has only the power to receive; but he has no power to give. For this reason a presbyter does not ordain the clergy; but at the ordination of a presbyter he seals while the bishop ordains.

Over a deacon, then, he shall say as follows:

O God, who hast created all things and hast ordered them by thy Word, the Father of our Lord Jesus Christ, whom thou didst send to minister thy will and to manifest to us thy desire; grant [the] Holy Spirit of grace and care and diligence to this thy servant, whom thou hast chosen to serve the church and to offer in thy holy sanctuary the gifts that are offered to thee by thine appointed high priests, so that serving without blame and with a pure heart he may be counted worthy of this exalted office, by thy goodwill, praising thee continually. Through thy Servant Jesus Christ, through whom be to thee glory and honour, with [the] Holy Spirit, in the holy church, both now and always and world without end. Amen.

10. On a confessor, if he has been in bonds for the name of the Lord, hands shall not be laid for the diaconate or the presbyterate, for he has the honour of the presbyterate by his confession. But if he is to be ordained bishop, hands shall be laid upon him.

But if he is a confessor who was not brought before the authorities nor was punished with bonds nor was shut up in prison, but was insulted (?) casually or privately for the name of the Lord, even though he confessed, hands are to be laid upon him for every office of which he is worthy.

The bishop shall give thanks [in all ordinations] as we have prescribed. It is not, to be sure, necessary for anyone to recite the exact words that we have prescribed, by learning to say them by heart in his thanksgiving to God; but let each one pray according to his ability. If, indeed, he is able to pray competently with an elevated prayer, it is well. But even if he is only moderately able to pray and give praise, no one may forbid him; only let him pray sound in the faith.

11. When a widow is appointed, she shall not be ordained but she shall be appointed by the name. If her husband has been long dead, she may be appointed [without delay]. But if her husband has died recently, she shall not be trusted; even if she is aged she must be tested by time, for often the passions grow old in those who yield to them.

The widow shall be appointed by the word alone, and [so] she shall be associated with the other widows; hands shall not be laid upon her because she does not offer the oblation nor has she a sacred ministry. Ordination is for the clergy on account of their ministry, but the widow is appointed for prayer, and prayer is the duty of all.

12. The reader is appointed by the bishop's giving him the book, for he is not ordained.

13. Hands shall not be laid upon a virgin, for it is her purpose alone that makes her a virgin.

14. Hands shall not be laid upon a subdeacon, but his name shall be mentioned that he may serve the deacon.

15. If anyone says, "I have received the

gift of healing," hands shall not be laid upon him: the deed shall make manifest if he speaks the truth.

44. The Examination and Instruction of New Converts; the Catechumenate and Baptism

Ibid., 2:16–20, trans. Easton, op. cit., pp. 41–45.

PART II

16. New converts to the faith, who are to be admitted as hearers of the word, shall first be brought to the teachers before the people assemble. And they shall be examined as to their reason for embracing the faith, and they who bring them shall testify that they are competent to hear the word. Inquiry shall then be made as to the nature of their life; whether a man has a wife or is a slave. If he is the slave of a believer and he has his master's permission, then let him be received; but if his master does not give him a good character, let him be rejected. If his master is a heathen, let the slave be taught to please his master, that the word be not blasphemed. If a man has a wife or a woman a husband, let the man be instructed to content himself with his wife and the woman to content herself with her husband. But if a man is unmarried, let him be instructed to abstain from impurity, either by lawfully marrying a wife or else by remaining as he is. But if any man is possessed with demons, he shall not be admitted as a hearer until he is cleansed.

Inquiry shall likewise be made about the professions and trades of those who are brought to be admitted to the faith. If a man is a pander, he must desist or be rejected. If a man is a sculptor or painter, he must be charged not to make idols; if he does not desist he must be rejected. If a man is an actor or pantomimist, he must desist or be rejected. A teacher of young children had best desist, but if he has no other occupation, he may be permitted to continue. A charioteer, likewise, who races or frequents races, must desist or be rejected. A gladiator or a trainer of gladiators, or a huntsman [in the wild-beast shows], or anyone connected with these shows, or a public official in charge of gladiatorial exhibitions must desist or be rejected. A heathen priest or anyone who tends idols must desist or be rejected. A soldier of the civil authority must be taught not to kill men and to refuse to do so if he is commanded, and to refuse to take an oath; if he is unwilling to comply, he must be rejected. A military commander or civic magistrate that wears the purple must resign or be rejected. If a catechumen or a believer seeks to become a soldier, they must be rejected, for they have despised God. A harlot or licentious man or one who has castrated himself, or any other who does things not to be named, must be rejected, for they are defiled. A magician must not [even] be brought for examination. An enchanter, an astrologer, a diviner, a soothsayer, a user of magic verses, a juggler, a mountebank, an amulet-maker must desist or be rejected. A concubine, who is a slave and has reared her children and has been faithful to her master alone, may become a hearer; but if she has failed in these matters she must be rejected. If a man has a concubine, he must desist and marry legally; if he is unwilling, he must be rejected.

If, now, we have omitted anything (any trade?), the facts [as they occur] will instruct your mind; for we all have the Spirit of God.

17. Let catechumens spend three years as hearers of the word. But if a man is zealous and perseveres well in the work, it is not the time but his character that is decisive.

18. When the teacher finishes his instruction, the catechumens shall pray by themselves, apart from the believers. And [all] women, whether believers or catechumens, shall stand for their prayers by themselves in a separate part of the church.

And when [the catechumens] finish their prayers, they must not give the kiss of peace, for their kiss is not yet pure. Only believers shall salute one another, but men with men and women with women; a man shall not salute a woman.

And let all the women have their heads covered with an opaque cloth, not with a veil of thin linen, for this is not a true covering.

19. At the close of their prayer, when their instructor lays his hand upon the catechumens, he shall pray and dismiss them; whoever gives the instruction is to do this, whether a cleric or a layman.

If a catechumen should be arrested for the name of the Lord, let him not hesitate about bearing his testimony; for if it should happen that they treat him shamefully and kill him, he will be justified, for he has been baptized in his own blood.

20. They who are to be set apart for baptism shall be chosen after their lives have been examined: whether they have lived soberly, whether they have honoured the widows, whether they have visited the sick, whether they have been active in well-doing. When their sponsors have testified that they have done these things, then let them hear the Gospel. Then from the time that they are separated from the other catechumens, hands shall be laid upon them daily in exorcism and, as the day of their baptism draws near, the bishop himself shall exorcise each one of them that he may be personally assured of their purity. Then, if there is any of them who is not good or pure, he shall be put aside as not having heard the word in faith; for it is never possible for the alien to be concealed.

Then those who are set apart for baptism shall be instructed to bathe and free themselves from impurity and wash themselves on Thursday. If a woman is menstruous, she shall be set aside and baptized on some other day.

They who are to be baptized shall fast on Friday, and on Saturday the bishop shall assemble them and command them to kneel in prayer. And, laying his hand upon them, he shall exorcise all evil spirits to flee away and never to return; when he has done this he shall breathe in their faces, seal their foreheads, ears and noses, and then raise them up. They shall spend all that night in vigil, listening to reading and instruction.

They who are to be baptized shall bring with them no other vessels than the one each will bring for the eucharist; for it is fitting that he who is counted worthy of baptism should bring his offering at that time.

XI. Origen the Confessor (c. 185–253/54) on Prayer (233/34)

45. The Subjects of Prayer

Chap. 33, trans. J. E. L. Oulton and H. Chadwick, *Alexandrian Christianity* [LCC, Vol. II] (Philadelphia: Westminster Press; London: Student Christian Movement Press, Ltd., 1954), pp. 327–29.

XXXIII, 1. Before bringing this treatise to an end, I think I ought to say something about the subjects of prayer. It seems to me that four subjects, which I have found here and there throughout the Scriptures, may be outlined, and that every one should form his prayer accordingly. The subjects are these. At the beginning and preamble of the prayer, so far as possible, God is to be glorified, through Christ glorified together with him, in the Holy Spirit hymned together with him. And next in order after this each one must offer general thanksgiving including blessings bestowed on many besides himself, together with those he has personally obtained from God. After thanksgiving, it seems to me that he ought to accuse himself bitterly before God of his own sins, and then ask God, first for healing that he may be delivered from the habit that causes him to sin, and secondly for forgiveness of the past. After confession, it seems to me that in the fourth place he should add his request for great and heavenly things, his own and general, and also for his family and his dearest. And finally he should bring his prayer to a close glorifying God through Christ in the Holy Spirit.

2. These subjects of prayer, as we said before, we found in one place or another of the Scriptures. The subject concerned with giving glory to God is thus expressed in the one hundred and third Psalm: "O Lord, my God, how greatly art thou magnified! Thou art clothed with praise and majesty; who coverest thyself with light as with a garment; who stretchest out the heavens like a curtain, who layeth the beams of his chambers in the waters; who maketh the clouds a place for his feet, who walketh upon the wings of the winds; who maketh winds his

I-7. Attitude of Prayer. *Velatio (lunetti), 3rd century, Catacomb of Priscilla, Rome.*

messengers, his ministers a flame of fire: who layeth the foundations of the earth to remain stedfast; it shall not be removed for ever and ever. The deep is his covering as a vesture: the waters shall stand upon the mountains. At thy rebuke they shall flee: at the voice of thy thunder they shall be afraid." And the greater part of this Psalm contains a glorification of the Father. And each one can collect many other passages for himself, and he will thus see how widely the subject of glorification is dispersed.

3. As for thanksgiving, this example may be cited from the second [book] of the Kingdoms. After the promises made to David through Nathan, David was astonished at the gifts of God, and is reported to have given thanks for them in these words: "Who am I, O Lord my Lord, and what is my house, that thou lovedst me thus far? And I was made little in thy sight, my Lord, and thou hast spoken concerning the house of thy servant for a long time to come; but this is the law of man, O Lord my Lord. And what

can David say more unto thee? And now thou knowest thy servant, O Lord. For thy servant's sake thou hast done it, and according to thine heart hast thou wrought all this thy greatness to make it known unto thy servant, that he may magnify thee, O Lord my Lord."

4. An example of confession: "From all my transgressions deliver me"; and elsewhere: "My wounds stink and are corrupt, because of my foolishness. I am pained and bowed down to the uttermost: I go mourning all the day long."

5. Of requests, in the twenty-seventh Psalm: "Draw me not away with sinners, and with workers of iniquity destroy me not"; and like words.

6. And having begun by glorifying God it is fitting to conclude and bring the prayer to an end by glorifying him, hymning and glorifying the Father of the universe through Jesus Christ in the Holy Spirit, "to whom be the glory for ever."

Duchesne, L., *Early History of the Christian Church.* 3 vols. New York: Longmans, Green & Co., Inc., 1908–1924.

Elliott-Binns, L. E., *The Beginnings of Western Christendom.* London: Lutterworth Press, 1948.

Flew, R. N., *Jesus and His Church.* Nashville, Tennessee: Abingdon Press, 1938.

Goodspeed, E. J., *A History of Early Christian Literature.* Chicago: University of Chicago Press, 1942.

Kidd, B. J., *A History of the Church to A. D. 461.* 3 vols. New York: Oxford University Press, Inc., 1922.

Lietzmann, H., *The Beginnings of the Christian Church,* trans. B. L. Woolf. New York: Charles Scribner's Sons, 1937.

Petry, R. C., *Christian Eschatology and Social Thought.* Nashville, Tennessee: Abingdon Press, 1956.

Quasten, J., *Patrology,* Vols. I–III. Westminster, Maryland: Newman Press, 1951, 1953, 1960.

Richardson, C. C., *et al., Early Christian Fathers,* Library of Christian Classics, Vol. I. Philadelphia: Westminster Press, and London: Student Christian Movement Press, Ltd., 1953.

Streeter, B. H., *The Primitive Church.* New York: The Macmillan Co., 1929.

CHRONOLOGY

30 B.C.–14 A.D.	*The Augustan Age*
c. 30/33	*Crucifixion of Jesus*
43/44	*Herod Agrippa I executes St. James*
c. 50–63	*Missionary travels, letters, and career of St. Paul*
64	*Burning of Rome; Nero persecutes the Christians; death of St. Paul?*
c. 69–110	*The Gospels*
70	*Jerusalem taken; Temple burnt by Titus*
79–81	*Titus*
81–96	*Domitian*
93–94	*Josephus' Antiquities*
96–98	*Nerva*
96/97	*Epistle of Clement of Rome to the Corinthians*
98–117	*Trajan, Tacitus (Journals, Annals, Histories)*
c. 110/117	*Epistles of Ignatius of Antioch*
c. 110–135	*Polycarp to the Philippians*
112	*Correspondence of Pliny with Trajan*
c. 115–140	*"Shepherd" of Hermas*
c. 117–138	*Hadrian*
c. 120–150	*Didache*
c. 130	*Epistle of Barnabus*
130–150	*Pseudo-Clement*
130–180	*Epistle to Diognetus*
132–135	*Jewish Revolt under Bar Kokba*
138–161	*Antoninus Pius*
c. 150/155	*Justin's Apology*
c. 150	*Melito of Sardis' Homily on the Passion*
161–180	*Marcus Aurelius*
c. 185–253/54	*Origen*
c. 197	*Tertullian's Apology*
c. 215	*Clement of Alexandria*
c. 217	*Hippolytus' Apostolic Tradition*
c. 233/34	*Origen on Prayer*

Equestrian Statue of Marcus
Aurelius, 161–180 A.D. *Bronze.*
Piazza de Campidoglio, Rome.

II

Early Relations of

Spiritual and Temporal Powers;

Persecution, Toleration,

and Councils

The earliest hostility to Christians came
from the Jews, who had been blamed by many of them for Christ's
death. They resented the Christian deification of
Jesus the man. These renegades were guilty of exorcism in his
name. Furthermore, they expropriated sacred
Jewish writings for their own nefarious ends.
Indeed they claimed them for their own by original intent.
The Jews were not infrequently charged with having
diverted these writings to their intermediate purposes.

The first strong Roman opposition to Christianity did not stem from governmental policy. Popular suspicion and fear prompted it. The society of the time was most religious. Every possible placation of all conceivable divine powers was sought for the blessing of society. The Christians appeared bent on compromising the general welfare at the expense of their own eccentric customs. Their disparagement of all gods except their own threatened the popular cults and the well-being of the masses. From the Graeco-Roman perspective, Christians were atheists. They ruled out what at that time seemed to most men the chief sources of divine benevolence. As compensation, they offered the dubious blessing of their own jealous, provincial deity. The terms of his favor were set by Christian exclusivism. Theirs was a kill-joy aversion to all that normal people held dear.

These Christians were charged by other Jews with meddling in demonic operations. Tales were rife in Roman society that Christianity's founder had himself visited Egypt when a boy. Everyone knew the Egyptian reputation for the black arts. The Christians themselves admitted a spiritual lineage running back to a certain prophet, Moses. He was no mean practitioner with staff and wand, having flaunted his Hebrew sorcery to the great embarrassment of delta magicians. It was to this area that the Christ had fled. Subsequently, the crude symbolism of his own shepherd's crook revived associations with the necromancer's wand.

On every hand Christians endangered normal commerce with society's manifold deities, recklessly inviting divine reprisals on human society. They tampered at will with the usual operations of business and trade. Wherever they got a foothold, the traffic in idols and images fell off and bank deposits showed a decline. Christian views on marriage bonds, sex rights and family ethics seeped into the old order with dire effects for previous norms. Husbands having left pliant enough wives in the morning might return at night to marriage partners with strangely modified responses. Neighbors hinted that Christian missionaries who called during the day might have had something to do with this. Strange new values applied by the Christians to women, children, slaves, and even the dregs of society played havoc with existing mores. Above all, the Christians were feared as a class apart, a peculiar sort of beings, less than human, haters of the human race. Most of their more normal neighbors thought these Christians' own morals shady at best.

Official Rome was at first indifferent to Christians as such. They were generally thought of as just another sect of the Jews— when they were considered at all. Jews might protest this, but then Jews protested everything. No Jew was satisfied, even with what another Jew did. In fact, all religious groups were tolerated by the Romans on principle as potential invokers of the divine graces upon state and society. But none was excused from the privileged duty of supporting the imperial cult. The Jews actually received special favors. This was partly because of the usual turmoil among the Jews caused by any incursions on their fancied rights as keepers of ancient laws and sacred writings. It was also in part because of the often demonstrated ability of the Jews to turn any rigorism on the part of their overlords to their own propaganda advantage.

The limits of Roman tolerance accorded other cults were also wide. Religious bodies, however, could not set themselves up to serve self-conscious ends divergent from those of state and society as a whole. They dared not snap the very elastic bonds defining public decency. Here, again, Christians managed, apparently without effort, to break all the rules at once. "Exclusivism" was their middle name. They held no one to be decent but themselves. They were a self-constituted, esoteric society judgmentally separate from all others. On occasion, they castigated with heaven's special curse all customary perspectives and all practicing mores not their own. The dictates of their heavenly king, their *Basileus*, was what counted; not the will of the emperor or the timidities of earthlings bowing obsequiously before false gods. For a considerable time, however, the Roman government was unaware of, or affected a studied indifference to, all of this.

The Roman populace, out of growing fear, forced the Christian divergence from social and governmental practice upon the state's attention. It is erroneous, however, to look for anything like a general policy of state persecution until the mid-third century. Admittedly, there was some vicious as well as much nondescript opposition throughout fairly wide areas well before this time. Varying degrees of local cultic agitation and provincial governmental nervousness were back of this. Such collisions, however, were almost invariably precipitated by a jittery populace, and were limited, with few exceptions, to the regional exercises of official policy. Cities and, after a time, provinces might be embroiled. The emperor's rule was not for a long time—except in atypical instances like that of Nero.

Early Christian chroniclers were quite understandably inclined to exaggerate the severity as well as the extensiveness of this persecution. Later Christian historians read back into such occurrences a pervasiveness and an imperial persecution policy that did not exist in the earliest centuries. It is not too strange that the "worst" emperors were equated with the "sternest" persecutors. Actually, those rulers who best embodied the admirable Roman qualities of earlier days might in their very embodiment most conscientiously prosecute this unpleasant task. Reducing the Christian "state within a state" to the fuller loyalties called for by the commonwealth would constitute a vice or a virtue as viewed from different perspectives. Intermingled in the first 200 years were the paranoic reactions of a Nero, the slightly less marked abnormalities of a Domitian, the noble intent of a Trajan to preserve the Roman equilibrium, and the dedicated severities of a Marcus Aurelius. Nevertheless, a well-defined Roman policy was long in coming. When it did arrive, it was accompanied by considerable vacillation. Official actions reflected the vagaries of mounting social pressure at least as much as the cumulative wisdom of honest statesmanship.

Christian apologists tried increasingly to counteract the patently ludicrous indictments of popular opposition. More and more they pointed out the unfairness, as they saw it, of the state's punishing Christians just because they were Christians, that is, merely

because of their "name." Since Trajan, especially, the imperial tendency had been not to hunt Christians down, but to apprehend them only as they were pointed out and/or confessed to the "name." But even Tertullian himself could not sustain this as a complete illogicality for Romans—especially as Christians themselves made so much of loyalty to, and confession of, Christ's name. It was Tertullian, by the way, who somehow managed to regard Marcus Aurelius as friendly to Christians, in spite of flagrant evidences to the contrary. The source-readings emanating from Lyons and Vienne in Gaul show the serious, if intermittent, measures taken by "good" Roman emperors against the Christian "menace."

Not until the time of Decius, however, may the historian speak of a concerted imperial persecution. By that time, a host of Christian martyrs had paid the price of confessing and witnessing to Christ's name. Peter and Paul had suffered under Nero, Ignatius under Trajan, the blessed Polycarp under Antoninus Pius, and Justin and his companions in the time of Marcus Aurelius. These were merely a few of the more famous figures. With Decius, however, a different trend was discernible.

The year 249—the thousandth anniversary of Rome's legendary founding—touched off a painful review by historians, social critics, government officials, and the people themselves of Roman greatness that was no more. Surely the palliating of Christian dissidence in their very midst was in no small measure responsible for the decline of the old Roman integrity. Roman tolerance and indifference had paid off in decadence. Motivating factors included sentimental nostalgia and hurt pride. Literary men did not fail to observe the conjunction of Christianity's rising star with Rome's waning fortunes. Rome had been great under the old gods. Her sun was setting in the false radiance of an upstart luminary.

Quite likely, as Allard suggests, the ancient Roman religion was confused by Decius with the Divinity of the Roman state. To separate from the one was to revolt against the other. He was scarcely one to remark the fine distinction between civil and religious order, between patriotism and belief. He could not see how anyone could serve Rome by serving any God other than the gods of Rome.

The course Decius settled upon was not that of fanatical annihilation of dissent. It was one far more dangerous to Christianity. This coldly calculated persecution emanated from what Allard calls an implacable theorician. Lactantius agrees. Decius was not out to kill Christians. This would compound the difficulty by robbing the state of its rightful potential in supplicants before the divine favor. He would, instead, subvert Christian prayers from their own ends to Roman needs. He would make apostates, not martyrs. Every means was to be used—even occasional violence—as required. The chief measures applied to subversion were, however, those of brainwashing and psychological warfare. The more subtle the threat required to shake Christian stubbornness and the less damage to the person of the apostate, the clearer the victory of Decius. The less required to prompt Christian rationalization of conscience the better the imperial purpose would be served. The diabolical ease with which a Christian could suborn himself and his Christ—while still sincerely believing that he was being loyal to his faith —was frightening.

This was, as Lactantius opined, the worst persecution of all. Overt sacrificing to the gods was desirable, but not mandatory. If a Christian would voluntarily submit to his name being entered behind his back on an official list, that sufficed. He need not "know" anything about it or be "responsible" for it. The dodges by which one could be enticed to self-deception with face-saving devices were innumerable. Some Christians were outright *traditores,* or traitors. They "lapsed" from their Christian profession with overt capitulation. They were the sacrificers (*sacrificati*). Others, the *libellatici,* bought their way or otherwise got on—or were, without overt objection, smuggled on—the official lists (*libelli*) of sacrificers. Within these larger classes of apostates or *lapsi* were subdivisions of self-deception. All such persons, however subtle or physically painful the pressure of their temptation, constituted the

non-confessors. Their number, unlike that of "confessors dying as martyrs," was all too large. Still, the purposes of Decius were not achieved. In the main Christians stood firm, as confessors and martyrs, however painfully in evidence their lapsed brethren might be. Even the more rigorous measures of the Valerian persecution were not enough. Bishops and priests were required to worship the gods on penalty of death. Lay members were forbidden on like penalty to frequent cemeteries or hold assemblies for worship. A second set of edicts put even more cruel pressure on the hierarchy. Christians of noble birth were to lose their property. Graduated scales of severity affected every level of Christian life. Some stood to revert to slavery. Roman bishops and deacons confessed their Christ and won crowns of martyrdom. In Africa, bishop Cyprian won his reward after having once been argued into retirement for the good of the Church.

The Decian-Valerian persecution was severe, intermittent, and, in the main, short. Sporadic outbreaks characterized the later period, to the time of Diocletian. Then, the last great test was launched. There was little subtlety in his old-soldier's attack. He had made sweeping administrative reforms. These involved the partition of the empire and the large-scale induction of barbarians into the army. Included were revisions of finance, together with a fateful debasement of the currency—in fact, an economic and social reorganization that struck at the root of old Roman customs. Personally simple in his tastes, he affected oriental pageantry for the boosting of imperial prestige. Diocletian had Christian friends. Some of these tried to excuse his ruthless anti-Christian measures by attributing them to the over-influence of his governmental associates and subordinates. This explanation may have had some basis in fact, although probably very little. He was honestly intent upon undoing the damage to Roman unity that he felt Christian growth had caused. His own measures were even more calculated to accelerate the Roman decline. Once started, however, his assault against Christianity rapidly attained furious momentum. In a series of edicts the way was prepared for churches to be destroyed, scriptures burnt, Christian hierarchs degraded, and humble Christians enslaved. Of course his main, pile-driving offensive was against official Christianity. Christians were compelled to sacrifice. Their lives as well as their prayers were to be conserved if possible. Both were to be surrendered if they did not yield.

The Christians suffered horribly. Yet they did not break. Diocletian admitted himself beaten and retired into obscurity. Persecution in the West fell off rapidly after 305. Galerius, in particular, increased the tempo of savagery in the East until 311. Then he granted tolerance to the Christians that he could not easily withhold. Constantine and Licinius followed with their edicts in 313. Constantine was soon to outdistance his competitor in imperial ambition and to look with increasing favor upon Christianity. His motives in embracing the new faith have been variously estimated. Some have seen in them the boldest opportunism. The legendary account of his conquering by the "Sign of the Cross" has been piously regarded and cynically ridiculed. Perhaps a genuine measure of religious conviction can no more be withheld from him than from countless others. Their nobler motives have, like his, been generously mixed with compromising concerns. The effect of his increasing kindnesses to Christianity has been endlessly debated. Whatever the complexity of his allied purposes, Constantine's chief end was to unify the empire. The Christians who had resisted all Roman attacks could surely be counted upon to form the core of the new Roman unity. Eusebius saw in him the God-willed saviour of Christianity and its protector in history. Christianity found that its victory under the "new Cyrus" entailed fresh problems and mounting embarrassments, as well as rich opportunities heretofore unknown.

The exact relation of Christ to Caesar had puzzled the earliest disciples. The proper balance of due loyalty to earthly kings and prior regard for divine claims had precipitated unending agonies of spirit. Rendering to God the things belonging to God, and to Caesar the prerogatives rightly his, was no easy service. It was to prove as difficult under Christian rulers as it had been under hostile ones.

Constantine proposed by his favors to make Christianity's rising star—which Rome could not bring down—the symbol of Rome's hoped-for renaissance. The danger of being thus cast in a role of responsible privilege was a real one for the Church. But the "fall" of Christianity was not necessarily implicit in this crucial opportunity. When, however, the Christian emperor began to recast the role of doctrinal statement to accord with optimum political unity, a warning signal was called for. The early Christian Fathers attending the councils called at the imperial initiative did not apparently resent Constantine's concern over Christian disunity. Church historians indicate that they were grateful, if anything. The Church's stakes involved at Arles, Nicaea, and subsequent councils were certainly no less than the emperor's. The source-texts from these councils and from men like Athanasius serve several purposes, at least. They document the growth in complexity of Christian dogma. The manner in which Christian doctrine is tied up with state prerogatives is most instructive. In all of this the precarious balance of Christian spiritual loyalties and temporal, social obligations is illuminated. Here again Athanasius deserves on all counts to be surveyed for the vigor of his orthodox Christian premises, as for the heroism with which he countered the undue manifestations of temporal power. Under Julian, the Church learned, if only briefly and partially, what a difference an emperor of non-Christian sympathies could make in its plans. The strain of keeping God's rights and those of the emperor unconfused under Theodosius the Great proved acute, even for such a stalwart as Ambrose. Neither bishop nor emperor had his way entirely while learning to walk the tightrope of spiritual and temporal balancing. The discipline accepted by Theodosius at the hands of the Christian hierarch, Ambrose, did the secular ruler credit. So did the courage of Milan's bishop redound to the Church's spiritual prestige. Under Justinian the line of spiritual-temporal cooperation and independence was drawn tauter still. Much of the vain emperor's theological dilettantism reflects what his administrative fiat and legislative arbitrariness also demonstrate. He could be a dictator to the Church on grounds of both spiritual and temporal precedence. He could and did dare to tell the Church what, and what not, to do. Yet he could, on occasion, put all of this down to his being a humble, responsible servant of the Christian cause. This riddle the Church could not solve then, nor has it since. There must have been those in 392 who viewed with alarm the denial to non-Christian consciences of the freedom Christians had died for earlier. How grateful could they afford to be for imperial piety such as this? Justinian did not ask and he did not care. Pagans and heretics had nothing coming to them but deprivation and death. As a Christian emperor he was prepared to give them both, regardless of the means he had to employ.

I. Reflections of Popular Hostility to Early Christianity

1. Celsus' True Word as Recapitulated in Origen

Con. Cels. 1:1, 4, 9, 38; 2:55, 63; 3:59. Translations for this and the following item are acknowledged as follows: Selections from *A Source Book for Ancient Church History*, pp. 56–58, 62–64, by Joseph Cullen Ayer are reprinted with the permission of Charles Scribner's Sons © 1913 Charles Scribner's Sons; renewal © 1941 Joseph Cullen Ayer, Jr.

I, 1. (MSG, 11:651.) Wishing to throw discredit upon Christianity, the first point Celsus brings forward is that the Christians have entered secretly into associations with each other which are forbidden by the laws; saying that "of associations some are public, others again secret; and the former are permitted by the laws; the latter are prohibited by the laws."

I, 4. (MSG, 11:661.) Let us notice, also, how he thinks to cast discredit upon our system of morals as neither venerable nor a new branch of instruction, inasmuch as it is common to other philosophers.

I, 9. (MSG, 11:672.) He says that "Cer-tain of them do not wish either to give or to receive reasons for those things to which they hold; saying, 'Do not examine, only believe and your faith will save you!' "; and he alleges that such also say: "The wisdom of this life is bad, but foolishness is a good thing."

I, 38. (MSG, 11:733.) He admits somehow the miracles which Jesus wrought and by means of which He induced the multitude to follow Him as the Christ. He wishes to throw discredit on them, as having been done not by divine power, but by the help of magic, for he says: "That he [Jesus], having been brought up secretly and having served for hire in Egypt, and then coming to the knowledge of certain miraculous powers, returned from thence, and by means of those powers proclaimed himself a god."

II, 55. (MSG, 11:884.) "Come, now, let us grant to you that these things [the prediction made by Christ of His resurrection] were said. Yet how many others are there who have used such wonders to deceive their simple hearers, and who made gain of their deception? Such was the case, they say, with Zalmoxis in Scythia, the slave of Pythagoras; and with Pythagoras himself in Italy. . . . But the point to be considered is, whether any one who was really dead ever rose with a veritable body. Or do you imagine the statements of others not only are myths, but appear as such, but you have discovered a becoming and credible termination of your drama, the voice from the cross when he breathed his last, the earthquake and the darkness? that while living he was of no help to himself, but when dead he rose again, and showed the marks of his punishment and his hands as they had been. Who saw this? A frantic woman, as you state, and, if any other, perhaps one of those who were engaged in the same delusion, who, owing to a peculiar state of mind, had either dreamed so, or with a wandering fancy had imagined things in accordance with his own wishes, which has happened in the case of very many; or, which is most probable, there was some one who desired to impress the others with this portent, and by such a falsehood to furnish an occasion to other jugglers."

II, 63. (MSG, 11:896.) "If Jesus desired to show that his power was really divine, he ought to have appeared to those who had ill-treated him, and to him who had condemned him, and to all men universally."

III, 59. (MSG, 11:997.) "That I bring no heavier charge than what truth requires, let any one judge from the following. Those who invite to participation in other mysteries make proclamation as follows: 'Every one who has clean hands and a prudent tongue'; others again thus: 'He who is pure from every pollution, and whose soul is conscious of no evil, and who has lived well and justly.' Such is the proclamation made by those who promise purification from sins. But let us hear whom the Christians invite. 'Whoever,' they say, 'is a sinner, whoever is devoid of understanding, whoever is a child,' and, to speak generally, 'whoever is unfortunate, him will the kingdom of God receive.' Do you not call him a sinner, then, who is unjust and a thief and a housebreaker and a poisoner, a committer of sacrilege and a robber of the dead? Whom else would a man invite if he were issuing a proclamation for an assembly of robbers?"

2. Christians Charged with Immorality and Cultic Excesses by the Heathen Populace

Minucius Felix, *Octavius*, 8:9–10, trans., as acknowledged.

Ch. 9. And now, as wickeder things are advancing more successfully and abandoned manners are creeping on day by day, those foul shrines of an impious assembly are increasing throughout the whole world. Assuredly this confederacy should be rooted out and execrated. They know one another by secret marks and signs. They love one another almost before they know one another. Everywhere, also, there is mingled among them a certain religion of lust; and promiscuously they call one another brother and sister, so that even a not unusual debauchery might, by the employment of those sacred names, become incestuous. It is thus that their vain and insane superstition glories in crimes. Nor, concerning these matters,

would intelligent report speak of things unless there was the highest degree of truth, and varied crimes of the worst character called, from a sense of decency, for an apology. I hear that they adore the head of an ass, that basest of creatures, consecrated by I know not what silly persuasion—a worthy and appropriate religion for such morals. Some say that they worship the genitalia of their pontiff and priest, and adore the nature, as it were, of their parent. I know not whether these things be false; certainly suspicion has place in the case of secret and nocturnal rites; and he who explains their ceremonies by reference to a man punished by extreme suffering for wickedness, and to the deadly wood of the cross, bestows fitting altars upon reprobate and wicked men, that they may worship what they deserve. Now the story of their initiation of young novices is as detestable as it is well known. An infant covered with meal, so as to deceive the unwary, is placed before him who is to be defiled with their rites; this infant is slain with dark and secret wounds by the young novice, who has been induced to strike harmless blows, as it were, on the surface of the meal. Thirstily—O horror!—they lick up its blood; eagerly they divide its limbs. By this victim they are confederated, with the consciousness of this wickedness they are pledged to a mutual silence. These sacred rites are more foul than any sort of sacrilege. And of their banqueting it is well known what is said everywhere; even the speech of our Cirtensian testifies to it. On a solemn day they assemble at a banquet with all their children, their sisters and mothers, people of every sex and age. There, after much feasting, when the sense of fellowship has waxed warm and the fervor of incestuous lust has grown hot with drunkenness, a dog that has been tied to a chandelier is provoked to rush and spring about by throwing a piece of offal beyond the length of the line by which he is bound; and thus the light, as if conscious, is overturned and extinguished in shameless darkness, while unions of abominable lust involve them by the uncertainty of chance. Although if all are not in fact, yet all are in their conscience, equally incestuous; since whatever might happen by the act of the individuals is sought for by the will of all.

Ch. 10. I purposely pass over many things, for there are too many, all of which, or the greater part of them, the obscurity of their vile religion declares to be true. For why do they endeavor with such pains to conceal and cloak whatever they worship, since honorable things always rejoice in publicity, but crimes are kept secret? Why have they no altars, no temples, no acknowledged images? Why do they never speak openly, never congregate freely, unless it be for the reason that what they adore and conceal is either worthy of punishment or is something to be ashamed of? Moreover, whence or who is he, or where is the one God, solitary and desolate, whom no free people, no kingdoms, and not even Roman superstition have known? The sole, miserable nationality of the Jews worshipped one God, and one peculiar to itself; but they worshipped him openly, with temples, with altars, with victims, and with ceremonies; and he has so little force or power that he is enslaved together with his own special nation to the Roman deities. But the Christians, moreover, what wonders, what monstrosities, do they feign, that he who is their God, whom they can neither show nor see, inquires diligently into the conduct of all, the acts of all, and even into their words and secret thoughts. They would have him running about everywhere, and everywhere present, troublesome, even shamelessly inquisitive, since he is present at everything that is done, and wanders about in all places. When he is occupied with the whole, he cannot give attention to particulars; or when occupied with particulars, he is not enough for the whole. Is it because they threaten the whole earth, the world itself and all its stars, with a conflagration, that they are meditating its destruction? As if either the natural and eternal order constituted by the divine laws would be disturbed, or, when the league of the elements has been broken up and the heavenly structure dissolved, that fabric in which it is contained and bound together would be overthrown!

II. Early Governmental Policy and Sporadic Outbreaks Against Christians

3. The So-called "Persecution" under Nero

Tacitus, *Annales*, 15:44, trans. *PTR*, IV, 1 (ii), p. 4.

Therefore to check this rumor, those, who were called Christians by the mob and hated for their moral enormities, were substituted in his place as culprits by Nero and afflicted with the most exquisite punishments. Christ, from whom the name was given, was put to death during the reign of Tiberius, by the procurator Pontius Pilate. Although checked for the time, this pernicious superstition broke out again not only in Judea, where the evil originated, but throughout the City, in which the atrocities and shame from all parts of the world center and flourish. Therefore those who confessed were first seized, then on their information a great multitude were convicted, not so much of the crime of incendiarism, as of hatred of the human race. The victims who perished also suffered insults, for some were covered with the skins of wild beasts and torn to pieces by dogs, while others were fixed to crosses and burnt to light the night when daylight had failed. Nero had offered his gardens for the spectacle and was giving a circus show, mingling with the people in the dress of a driver, or speeding about in a chariot. Although they were criminals who deserved the most severe punishment, yet a feeling of pity arose, since they were put to death not for the public good but to satisfy the rage of an individual.

4. "Persecution" by Domitian (95)

Cassius Dio, *Hist. Rom.*, 67:14, trans. *PTR*, IV, 1 (iii), p. 7.

At this time [95 A.D.] the road leading from Sinuessa to Puteoli was paved with stones. And in the same year Domitian put to death, besides many others, his cousin Flavius Clemens, who was then consul, and the wife of Flavius, Flavia Domitilla, who was his own relative. The crime charged against both was sacrilege. On the same charge many others who had adopted Jewish customs were condemned. Some were put to death, others had their property confiscated. Domitilla was exiled alone on Pandataria.

5. Pliny, Governor of Bithynia, Queries the Emperor Trajan (98–117) Concerning the Imperial Policy Toward Christians (112)

Ep. 10:96, trans. *PTR*, IV, 1 (iv), pp. 8–9.

It is my custom, my Lord, to refer to you all things concerning which I am in doubt. For who can better guide my indecision or enlighten my ignorance?

I have never taken part in the trials of Christians: hence I do not know for what crime nor to what extent it is customary to punish or investigate. I have been in no little doubt as to whether any discrimination is made for age, or whether the treatment of the weakest does not differ from that of the stronger; whether pardon is granted in case of repentance, or whether he who has ever been a Christian gains nothing by having ceased to be one; whether the *name* itself without the proof of crimes, or the crimes, inseparably connected with the *name*, are punished. Meanwhile, I have followed this procedure in the case of those who have been brought before me as Christians. I asked them whether they were Christians a second and a third time and with threats of punishment; I questioned those who confessed; I ordered those who were obstinate to be executed. For I did not doubt that, whatever it was that they confessed, their stubbornness and inflexible obstinacy ought certainly to be punished. There were others of similar madness, who because they were Roman citizens, I have noted for sending to the City. Soon, the crime spreading, as is usual when attention is called to it, more cases arose. An anonymous accusation containing many names was presented. Those who denied that they were or had been

Christians, ought, I thought, to be dismissed since they repeated after me a prayer to the gods and made supplication with incense and wine to your image, which I had ordered to be brought for the purpose together with the statues of the gods, and since besides they cursed Christ, not one of which things they say, those who are really Christians can be compelled to do. Others, accused by the informer, said that they were Christians and afterwards denied it; in fact they had been but had ceased to be, some many years ago, some even twenty years before. All both worshipped your image and the statues of the gods, and cursed Christ. They continued to maintain that this was the amount of their fault or error, that on a fixed day they were accustomed to come together before daylight and to sing by turns a hymn to Christ as a god, and that they bound themselves by oath, not for some crime but that they would not commit robbery, theft, or adultery, that they would not betray a trust nor deny a deposit when called upon. After this it was their custom to disperse and to come together again to partake of food, of an ordinary and harmless kind, however; even this they had ceased to do after the publication of my edict in which according to your command I had forbidden associations. Hence I believed it the more necessary to examine two female slaves, who were called deaconesses, in order to find out what was true, and to do it by torture. I found nothing but a vicious, extravagant superstition. Consequently I have postponed the examination and make haste to consult you. For it seemed to me that the subject would justify consultation, especially on account of the number of those in peril. For many of all ages, of every rank, and even of both sexes are and will be called into danger. The infection of this superstition has not only spread to the cities but even to the villages and country districts. It seems possible to stay it and bring about a reform. It is plain enough that the temples, which had been almost deserted, have begun to be frequented again, that the sacred rites, which had been neglected for a long time, have begun to be restored, and that fodder for victims, for which till now there was scarcely a purchaser, is sold. From which one may readily judge what a number of men can be reclaimed if repentance is permitted.

6. Trajan's Reply

Ep. 10:97, trans. *PTR,* IV, 1 (iv), pp. 9–10.

You have followed the correct procedure, my Secundus, in conducting the cases of those who were accused before you as Christians, for no general rule can be laid down as a set form. They ought not to be sought out; if they are brought before you and convicted they ought to be punished; provided that he who denies that he is a Christian, and proves this by making supplication to our gods, however much he may have been under suspicion in the past, shall secure pardon on repentance. In the case of no crime should attention be paid to anonymous charges, for they afford a bad precedent and are not worthy of our age.

II-1. Trajan's Column. *Marble, 106–113* A.D. *Rome.*

III. Early Christian Martyrs and the Christian Witness

7. The Sufferings of Polycarp (c. 155/156)

Martyr. S. Polycarpi, Introd. and 1, 9, 10, 11, trans. ANF, I, pp. 39, 41.

The Church of God which sojourns at Smyrna, to the Church of God sojourning in Philomelium, and to all the congregations of the Holy and Catholic Church in every place: Mercy, peace, and love from God the Father, and our Lord Jesus Christ, be multiplied.

CHAP. I.—SUBJECT OF WHICH WE WRITE

We have written to you, brethren, as to what relates to the martyrs, and especially to the blessed Polycarp, who put an end to the persecution, having, as it were, set a seal upon it by his martyrdom. For almost all the events that happened previously [to this one], took place that the Lord might show us from above a martyrdom becoming the Gospel.

Now, as Polycarp was entering into the stadium, there came to him a voice from heaven, saying, "Be strong, and show thyself a man, O Polycarp!" No one saw who it was that spoke to him; but those of our brethren who were present heard the voice. And as he was brought forward, the tumult became great when they heard that Polycarp was taken. And when he came near, the proconsul asked him whether he was Polycarp. On his confessing that he was, [the proconsul] sought to persuade him to deny [Christ], saying, "Have respect to thy old age," and other similar things, according to their custom, [such as], "Swear by the fortune of Caesar; repent, and say, Away with the Atheists." But Polycarp, gazing with a stern countenance on all the multitude of the wicked heathen then in the stadium, and waving his hand towards them, while with groans he looked up to heaven, said, "Away with the Atheists." Then, the proconsul urging him, and saying, "Swear, and I will set thee at liberty, reproach Christ;" Polycarp declared, "Eighty and six years have I served Him, and He never did me any injury: how then can I blaspheme my King and my Saviour?"

And when the proconsul yet again pressed him, and said, "Swear by the fortune of Caesar," he answered, "Since thou art vainly urgent that, as thou sayest, I should swear by the fortune of Caesar, and pretendest not to know who and what I am, hear me declare with boldness, I am a Christian. And if you wish to learn what the doctrines of Christianity are, appoint me a day, and thou shalt hear them." The proconsul replied, "Persuade the people." But Polycarp said, "To thee I have thought it right to offer an account [of my faith]; for we are taught to give all due honour (which entails no injury upon ourselves) to the powers and authorities which are ordained of God. But as for *these*, I do not deem them worthy of receiving any account from me.

The proconsul then said to him, "I have wild beasts at hand; to these will I cast thee, except thou repent." But he answered, "Call them then, for we are not accustomed to repent of what is good in order to adopt that which is evil; and it is well for me to be changed from what is evil to what is righteous." But again the proconsul said to him, "I will cause thee to be consumed by fire, seeing thou despisest the wild beasts, if thou wilt not repent." But Polycarp said, "Thou threatenest me with fire which burneth for an hour, and after a little is extinguished, but art ignorant of the fire of the coming judgment and of eternal punishment, reserved for the ungodly. But why tarriest thou? Bring forth what thou wilt."

8. The Witness of Justin (165)

Acta S. Justinii et sociorum, 1, 2, 45, trans. ANF, I, 305–6.

In the time of the lawless partisans of idolatry, wicked decrees were passed against the godly Christians in town and country, to force them to offer libations to vain idols; and accordingly the holy men, having been apprehended, were brought before the prefect of Rome, Rusticus by name. And when they had been brought before his judgment-seat, Rusticus the prefect said to Justin, "Obey the gods at once, and submit to the kings." Justin said, "To obey the command-

ments of our Saviour Jesus Christ is worthy neither of blame nor of condemnation." Rusticus the prefect said, "What kind of doctrines do you profess?" Justin said, "I have endeavoured to learn all doctrines; but I have acquiesced at last in the true doctrines, those namely of the Christians, even though they do not please those who hold false opinions." Rusticus the prefect said, "Are those the doctrines that please you, you utterly wretched man?" Justin said, "Yes, since I adhere to them with right dogma." Rusticus the prefect said, "What is the dogma?" Justin said, "That according to which we worship the God of the Christians, whom we reckon to be one from the beginning, the maker and fashioner of the whole creation, visible and invisible; and the Lord Jesus Christ, the Son of God, who had also been preached before hand by the prophets as about to be present with the race of men, the herald of salvation and teacher of good disciples. And I, being a man, think that what I can say is insignificant in comparison with His boundless divinity, acknowledging a certain prophetic power, since it was prophesied concerning Him of whom now I say that He is the Son of God. For I know that of old the prophets foretold His appearance among men."

Rusticus the prefect said, "Where do you assemble?" Justin said, "Where each one chooses and can: for do you fancy that we all meet in the very same place? Not so; because the God of the Christians is not circumscribed by place; but being invisible, fills heaven and earth, and everywhere is worshipped and glorified by the faithful." Rusticus the prefect said, "Tell me where you assemble, or into what place do you collect your followers?" Justin said, "I live above one Martinus, at the Timiotinian Bath; and during the whole time (and I am now living in Rome for the second time) I am unaware of any other meeting than his. And if any one wished to come to me, I communicated to him the doctrines of truth." Rusticus said, "Are you not, then, a Christian?" Justin said, "Yes, I am a Christian."

The prefect says to Justin, "Hearken, you who are called learned, and think that you know true doctrines; if you are scourged and beheaded, do you believe you will ascend into heaven?" Justin said, "I hope that, if I endure these things, I shall have His gifts. For I know that, to all who have thus lived, there abides the divine favour until the completion of the whole world." Rusticus the prefect said, "Do you suppose, then, that you will ascend into heaven to receive some recompense?" Justin said, "I do not suppose it, but I know and am fully persuaded of it." Rusticus the prefect said, "Let us, then, now come to the matter in hand, and which presses. Having come together, offer sacrifice with one accord to the gods." Justin said, "No right-thinking person falls away from piety to impiety." Rusticus the prefect said, "Unless ye obey, ye shall be mercilessly punished." Justin said, "Through prayer we can be saved on account of our Lord Jesus Christ, even when we have been punished, because this shall become to us salvation and confidence at the more fearful and universal judgment-seat of our Lord and Saviour." Thus also said the other martyrs: "Do what you will, for we are Christians, and do not sacrifice to idols."

Rusticus the prefect pronounced sentence, saying, "Let those who have refused to sacrifice to the gods and to yield to the command of the emperor be scourged, and led away to suffer the punishment of decapitation, according to the laws." The holy martyrs having glorified God, and having gone forth to the accustomed place, were beheaded, and perfected their testimony in the confession of the Saviour. And some of the faithful having secretly removed their bodies, laid them in a suitable place, the grace of our Lord Jesus Christ having wrought along with them, to whom be glory for ever and ever. Amen.

9. Martyrdoms at Lyons and Vienne (c. 177/78) Under the "Good" Emperor Marcus Aurelius (161–180)

Eusebius, *Hist. Ecc.*, 6:1, 3, trans. *PTR*, IV, 1 (v), pp. 11–13.

"The servants of Christ, living at Vienne and Lyons in Gaul, to the brethren throughout Asia and Phrygia who have the same faith and hope of redemption that we have, peace, grace and glory from God the Father and Christ Jesus our Lord."

Then after some other preliminary remarks they begin their account in the following words: "The magnitude of the tribulation here, the great fury of the heathen against the saints, and how much the blessed martyrs endured, we cannot fully recount, nor indeed is it possible to express these in writing. For with all his might the adversary broke loose upon us, showing even now how unrestrained his future coming would be. He tried every means of training and exercising his followers against the servants of God, so that not only were excluded from houses, baths and markets, but also forbidden, every one of us, to appear in any place whatsoever.

But the grace of God fought against the adversary, rescued the weak, and arrayed firm pillars, able through patience to withstand every attack of the Evil One. They engaged in conflict with him, suffering every kind of shame and injury, and, counting their great trials as small, they hastened to Christ, showing that 'the sufferings of this present time are not worthy to be compared with the glory which shall be revealed to us ward.'

First, indeed, they endured nobly the sufferings heaped upon them by the general populace: clamors, blows, being dragged along, robberies, stonings, imprisonments, and all that an enraged mob loves to inflict on opponents and enemies. Then they were taken to the forum by the chiliarch and the ordained authorities of the city and were examined in the presence of the whole multitude. Having confessed, they were imprisoned until the arrival of the governor. When they were afterwards brought before him and he treated us with all manner of cruelty, Vettius Epagathus, one of the brethren, filled with love for God and his neighbor, interfered. His daily life was so consistent that, although young, he had a reputation like the elder Zacharias, for he 'walked in all the commandments and ordinances of the Lord blameless' and was untiring in every good office for his neighbor, filled with zeal for God and fervent in spirit. Such a man could not endure the unrighteous judgment against us, but was filled with indignation and demanded that he should be permitted to testify in behalf of the brethren, that there was no atheism nor impiety in us. Those about the tribunal cried out against him, and with reason, for he was a man of mark; and the governor denied his just request, but asked only this one question, if he also was a Christian; and on his confessing this most distinctly, placed him also in the number of the martyrs. He was called the advocate of the Christians, but he had the Advocate [παράκλητον] in himself, the Spirit more fully than Zacharias. This he manifested by the fulness of his love, counting himself happy to lay down his own life in the defence of the brethren. For he was and is a true disciple of Christ, 'following the Lamb whithersoever he goeth.'

After that the others were divided and the proto-martyrs were known and held in readiness. They with all eagerness finished the confession of martyrdom. But some appeared unprepared and untrained and still weak, unable to endure the strain of a great contest. Of these about ten became apostates, who caused us great pain and excessive sorrow, and weakened the zeal of the others who had not yet been seized, and who, although suffering all kinds of evil, were constantly with the martyrs and did not abandon them. Then indeed all were in great fear on account of the uncertainty of the confession, not fearing the sufferings to be endured, but looking to the end and fearing lest some one should apostatize. Yet those who were worthy were seized each day, filling up their number, so that all the zealous and those through whom especially our affairs had been managed were gathered together from the two churches. And some of our servants who were heathens were seized because the governor had ordered that we should all be examined in public.

These, by the wiles of Satan, fearing the tortures which they saw the saints suffering and urged by the soldiers to do this, accused us falsely of Thyestean banquets and Oedipodean incests and of deeds which it is not lawful for us to speak or think of, and which we do not believe men ever committed. When these accusations were reported all raged like wild beasts against us, so that even those who had previously restrained themselves on account of kinship, then became exceedingly enraged and gnashed

their teeth against us. And the saying of our Lord was fulfilled that 'the time will come when whosoever killeth you will think that he doth God's service.' Then finally the holy martyrs endured suffering beyond all description and Satan strove earnestly that some blasphemies might be uttered by them also.

But the whole rage of the people, governor and soldiers was aroused exceedingly against Sanctus, deacon from Vienne, and against Maturus, a recent convert but a noble combatant, and against Attalus, a native of Pergamus, who had always been a pillar and a foundation in that place, and against Blandina through whom Christ showed that what appears mean, deformed and contemptible to men is of great glory with God through love for Him, shown in power and not boasting in appearance. For while we all, together with her mistress on earth, who was herself also one of the combatants among the martyrs, feared lest in the strife she should be unable to make her confession on account of her bodily weakness, Blandina was filled with such power that she was delivered and raised above those who took turns in torturing her in every manner from dawn till evening; and they confessed that they were defeated and had nothing more which they could do to her. They marvelled at her endurance, for her whole body was mangled and broken; and they testified that one form of torture was sufficient to destroy life, to say nothing of so many and so great tortures. But the blessed one, like a noble athlete, renewed her strength in the confession; and her comfort, refreshment and relief from suffering was in saying, 'I am a Christian' and 'Nothing vile is done by us.'

IV. Selected Apologists: The Literary Spokesmen for Christianity in Reply to Typical Charges Against It

10. Aristides

Apologia (c. 140), 15–16, trans. *ANF*, X, pp. 276–78.

XV. But the Christians, O King, while they went about and made search, have found the truth; and as we learned from

47

their writings, they have come nearer to truth and genuine knowledge than the rest of the nations. For they know and trust in God, the Creator of heaven and of earth, in whom and from whom are all things, to whom there is no other god as companion, from whom they received commandments which they engraved upon their minds and observe in hope and expectation of the world which is to come. Wherefore they do not commit adultery nor fornication, nor bear false witness, nor embezzle what is held in pledge, nor covet what is not theirs. They honour father and mother, and show kindness to those near to them; and whenever they are judges, they judge uprightly. They do not worship idols [made] in the image of man; and whatsoever they would not that others should do unto them, they do not to others; and of the food which is consecrated to idols they do not eat, for they are pure. And their oppressors they appease [lit: comfort] and make them their friends; they do good to their enemies; . . . And when they see a stranger, they take him in to their homes and rejoice over him as a very brother; for they do not call them brethren after the flesh, but brethren after the spirit and in God. And whenever one of their poor passes from the world, each one of them according to his ability gives heed to him and carefully sees to his burial. And if they hear that one of their number is imprisoned or afflicted on account of the name of their Messiah, all of them anxiously minister to his necessity, and if it is possible to redeem him they set him free. And if there is among them any that is poor and needy, and if they have no spare food, they fast two or three days in order to supply to the needy their lack of food. They observe the precepts of their Messiah with much care, living justly and soberly as the Lord their God commanded them. Every morning and every hour they give thanks and praise to God for His loving-kindnesses toward them; and for their food and their drink they offer thanksgiving to Him. And if any righteous man among them passes from the world, they rejoice and offer thanks to God; and they escort his body as if he were setting out from one place to another near.

XVI . . . And as for their words and

their precepts, O King, and their glorying in their worship, and the hope of earning according to the work of each one of them their recompense which they look for in another world,—you may learn about these from their writings. It is enough for us to have shortly informed your Majesty concerning the conduct and the truth of the Christians. For great indeed, and wonderful is their doctrine to him who will search into it and reflect upon it. And verily, this is a new people, and there is something divine [lit: a divine admixture] in the midst of them.

11. Justin

Apologia, I (c. 150/55), 9, 11, 13, trans., C. C. Richardson, *et al.*, *Early Christian Fathers* [LCC, Vol. I] (Philadelphia: Westminster Press; London: Student Christian Movement Press, Ltd.), pp. 246–47, 249.

Certainly we do not honor with many sacrifices and floral garlands the objects that men have fashioned, set up in temples, and called gods. We know that they are lifeless and dead and do not represent the form of God—for we do not think of God as having the kind of form which some claim that they imitate to be honored—but rather exhibit the names and shapes of the evil demons who have manifested themselves [to men]. You know well enough without our mentioning it how the craftsmen prepare their material, scraping and cutting and molding and beating. And often they make what they call gods out of vessels used for vile purposes, changing and transforming by art merely their appearance. We consider it not only irrational but an insult to God, whose glory and form are ineffable, to give his name to corruptible things which themselves need care. You are well aware that craftsmen in these [things] are impure and—not to go into details—given to all kinds of vice; they even corrupt their own slave girls who work along with them. What an absurdity, that dissolute men should be spoken of as fashioning or remaking gods for public veneration, and that you should appoint such people as guardians of the temples where they are set up—not considering that it is unlawful to think or speak of men as guardians of gods. . . .

When you hear that we look for a kingdom, you rashly suppose that we mean something merely human. But we speak of a Kingdom with God, as is clear from our confessing Christ when you bring us to trial, though we know that death is the penalty for this confession. For if we looked for a human kingdom we would deny it in order to save our lives, and would try to remain in hiding in order to obtain the things we look for. But since we do not place our hopes on the present [order], we are not troubled by being put to death, since we will have to die somehow in any case. . . .

What sound-minded man will not admit that we are not godless, since we worship the Fashioner of the universe, declaring him, as we have been taught, to have no need of blood and libations and incense, but praising him by the word of prayer and thanksgiving for all that he has given us? We have learned that the only honor worthy of him is, not to consume by fire the things he has made for our nourishment, but to devote them to our use and those in need, in thankfulness to him sending up solemn prayers and hymns for our creation and all the means of health, for the variety of creatures and the changes of the seasons, and sending up our petitions that we may live again in incorruption through our faith in him. It is Jesus Christ who has taught us these things, having been born for this purpose and crucified under Pontius Pilate, who was procurator in Judea in the time of Tiberius Caesar. We will show that we honor him in accordance with reason, having learned that he is the Son of the true God himself, and holding him to be in the second place and the prophetic Spirit in the third rank. It is for this that they charge us with madness, saying that we give the second place after the unchanging and ever-existing God and begetter of all things to a crucified man, not knowing the mystery involved in this, to which we ask you to give your attention as we expound it.

12. Athenagoras

Legatio pro Christianis (c. 177), 3, trans. *ANF*, II, p. 130.

Three things are alleged against us: atheism, Thyestean feasts, Oedipodean intercourse. But if these charges are true,

spare no class: proceed at once against our crimes; destroy us root and branch, with our wives and children, if any Christian is found to live like the brutes. And yet even the brutes do not touch the flesh of their own kind; and they pair by a law of nature, and only at the regular season, not from simple wantonness; they also recognize those from whom they receive benefits. If any one, therefore, is more savage than the brutes, what punishment that he can endure shall be deemed adequate to such offences? But, if these things are only idle tales and empty slanders, originating in the fact that virtue is opposed by its very nature to vice, and that contraries war against one another by a divine law (and you are yourselves witnesses that no such iniquities are committed by us, for you forbid informations to be laid against us), it remains for you to make inquiry concerning our life, our opinions, our loyalty and obedience to you and your house and government, and thus at length to grant to us the same rights (we ask nothing more) as to those who persecute us. For we shall then conquer them, unhesitatingly surrendering, as we now do, our very lives for the truth's sake.

V. Attacks Against Christians Before the Great Persecutions

13. *Under Septimius Severus* (202)

Tert., *Ad Scapulam*, 4, and Eusebius, *Hist. Ecc.*, 6:1, trans. *PTR*, IV, 1 (vi), pp. 20–21.

Under threat of severe punishment he forbade men to become Jews. Moreover, he decreed the same in the case of Christians. . . .

Even Severus himself, father of Antoninus, was mindful of the Christians. For the Christian Proculus, who was called Torpacion, procurator of Euhodias, and who had once wrought a cure for him with ointment, Severus sought out and kept in the palace until the time of his death. Antoninus, who was nourished on Christian milk, was very well acquainted with this man. The most noble women and men, whom Severus knew belonged to this sect, he not only did not harm, but he even set forth the truth by his own testimony and openly restored them to us from the raging populace. . . .

When Severus set in motion a persecution against the churches, brilliant testimonies were given everywhere by the athletes of religion. Especially did these abound in Alexandria, whither athletes of God were sent in accordance with their worth, from Egypt and all Thebais, as if to a very great contest, and where they obtained their crowns from God through their most patient endurance of various tortures and kinds of death. Among these was Leonides, who was called the father of Origen, and who was beheaded, leaving his son still a young boy. . . .

14. *Under Maximinus Thrax*

Eusebius, *Hist. Ecc.*, 6:28, trans. *PTR*, IV, 1 (vi), p. 21.

Maximinus Caesar succeeded to Alexander, Emperor of the Romans, who had ruled thirteen years. On account of his hatred for the household of Alexander, which contained many believers, he began a persecution, but commanded that the rulers of the churches alone should be put to death, on the ground that they were the authors of the teaching of the Gospels. Then Origen composed his work "On Martyrdom," and dedicated the book to Ambrose and Protoctetus, who was presbyter of the parish in Caesarea, because both had incurred unusual peril in this persecution. The report is that in this peril these men were prominent in confession. Maximinus did not survive more than three years. Origen has marked this as the time of the persecution in the twenty-second book of his Commentaries on John and in different letters.

VI. The Decian-Valerian Persecution (c. 249–51, 257/59)

15. *Lactantius on Decius*

De Mort. Persecut. 4, trans. *PTR*, IV, 1 (vi), pp. 21–22.

For after many years the accursed beast, Decius, arose who harrassed the Church,— for who but an evil man can persecute righteousness?—And as if he had been raised to that high position for this purpose, he began at once to rage against God so that he immediately fell. For having proceeded against the Carpi, who had then occupied Dacia and Moesia, he was immediately surrounded by the barbarians and destroyed with a great part of his army. Nor could he be honored by burial, but, stripped and naked, he lay exposed as food to wild beasts and birds, as was becoming to an enemy of God.

16. *Libelli from the Decian Persecution*

Trans. J. R. Knipfing, *Harvard Theological Review* (Cambridge, Mass.: Harvard University Press, 1923), XVI, pp. 346–47, 363–64. Reprinted by permission of the publishers.

[A complete, though hypothetical, text of such a libellus, the composite result of a combination of the data of our forty-one texts, would read somewhat as follows:]

1st Hand. To the Commission of . . . chosen to superintend the (sacred offerings and) sacrifices. From . . . son (*or* daughter) of . . . (and of . . .) (together with his brother and their wives) (and his children), who comes from the village of . . . (in the division of . . .), and is domiciled in the village of . . . (*or* in the . . . quarter of the city) (*or* dwelling beyond the town gates), (aged . . . years with a scar on the right eyebrow) (and member of the household of . . . , who functioned as exegete in the famous city of Alexandria, not to mention the offices he now holds) (*or* priestess of the god Petesouchos the great, the mighty, the immortal, and priestess of the gods in the . . . quarter). I (*or* we) have always and (all [my] life) without interruption sacrificed and poured libations and manifested piety toward the gods (in accordance with the divine decree), and now (again) in your presence in accordance with the edict's decree, I (*or* we) have made sacrifice and poured a libation (*or* poured a libation and sacrificed) and partaken of the sacred victims (in company with my wife and children) (acting through me). (Wherefore I present this petition and) I (*or* we) request you to certify this (for me, *or* for us) below. Farewell. I (*or* we) have presented this petition (aged . . . and injured) (*or* aged . . .) (and I . . . wrote in his behalf, for he is illiterate) (*or 2d hand,* I . . . presented this petition, I . . . signed for him since he is illiterate).

2d Hand. I . . . (prytanis) (and I . . .) saw you sacrificing (together with your son, *or* sons).

3d Hand. I . . . have signed.

1st Hand. The year one of the emperor Caesar Gaius Messius Quintus Trajanus Decius Pius Felix Augustus, June 12 (*or any date thereafter up to July 14*). . . .

1st Hand. To the commission of the village of Alexandru Nesus, chosen to superintend the sacrifices. From Aurelius Diogenes, son of Satabous, of the village of Alexandru Nesus, aged 72 years, with a scar on the right eyebrow. I have always and without interruption sacrificed to the gods, and now in your presence in accordance with the edict's decree I have made sacrifice, and poured a libation, and partaken of the sacred victims. I request you to certify this below. Farewell. I, Aurelius Diogenes, have presented this petition.

2d Hand. I, Aurelius Syrus, saw you and your son sacrificing.

3d Hand. . . . onos. . . .

1st Hand. The year one of the Emperor Caesar Gaius Messius Quintus Trajanus Decius Pius Felix Augustus, Epeiph 2 (June 26, 250). . . .

1st Hand. To the commission of the village of Philadelphia, chosen to superintend the sacrifices. From Aurelius Syrus and Aurelius Pasbeius, his brother, and of Demetria and Sarapias, our wives, dwelling beyond the town gates. We have always and without interruption sacrificed to the gods, and now in your presence in accordance with the edict's decree we have poured a libation, and partaken of the sacred victims. We request you to certify this for us below. Farewell.

2d Hand. We, Aurelius Syrus and Aurelius Pasbeius, presented this petition. I, Isidore, wrote in their behalf, for they are illiterate.

17. Origen (c. 185–253/54) a Confessor Calls for the Christian Witness

Exhortatio ad Martyrium, 30, 50. Selections from *A Source Book for Ancient Church History,* p. 213, by Joseph Cullen Ayer are re-

printed with the permission of Charles Scribner's Sons © 1913 Charles Scribner's Sons; renewal © 1941, Joseph Cullen Ayer, Jr.

Ch. 30. We must remember that we have sinned and that it is impossible to obtain forgiveness of sins without baptism, and that according to the evangelical laws it is impossible to be baptized a second time with water and the Spirit for the forgiveness of sins, and therefore the baptism of martyrdom is given us. For thus it has been called, as may be clearly gathered from the passage: "Can ye drink of the cup that I drink of, and be baptized with the baptism that I am baptized with?" [Mark 10:38]. And in another place it is said: "But I have a baptism to be baptized with; and how am I straightened until it be accomplished!" [Luke 12:50]. For be sure that just as the expiation of the cross was for the whole world, it (the baptism of martyrdom) is for the cure of many who are thereby cleansed. For as according to the law of Moses those placed near the altar are seen to minister forgiveness of sins to others through the blood of bulls and goats, so the souls of those who have suffered on account of the testimony of Jesus are not in vain near that altar in heaven [cf. Rev. 6:9ff.], but minister forgiveness of sins to those who pray. And at the same time we know that just as the high priest, Jesus Christ, offered himself as a sacrifice, so the priests, of whom He is the high priest, offer themselves as sacrifices, and on account of this sacrifice they are at the altar as in their proper place.

Ch. 50. Just as we have been redeemed with the precious blood of Christ, who received the name that is above every name, so by the precious blood of the martyrs will others be redeemed.

18. Cyprian (c. 200–258), the Bishop Becomes a Martyr (c. 258)

Acta Proconsularia, Cypriani, trans. PTR, IV, 1 (vi), pp. 24–26.

And thus on the next day, the eighteenth before the Kalends of October, early in the morning, a great crowd came to Sexti according to the order of Galerius Maximus, the proconsul. And accordingly Galerius Maximus, the proconsul, ordered Cyprian to be brought before him that day, while he was sitting in the Sauciolian court. And when he had been brought, Galerius Maximus, the proconsul, said to Bishop Cyprian: "You are Thascius Cyprian?" Bishop Cyprian replied: "I am." Galerius Maximus, the proconsul, said: "The most sacred Emperors have commanded you to sacrifice." Bishop Cyprian said: "I will not." Galerius Maximus said: "Reflect on it." Bishop Cyprian replied: "Do what you are ordered to do. In such a just case there is no need of reflection."

Galerius Maximus, having spoken with the council, pronounced the sentence weakly and reluctantly in the following words: "For a long time you have lived in sacrilege, you have gathered about you many associates in your impious conspiracy, you have put yourself in hostility to the Roman gods and to the sacred rites, nor could the pious and most sacred princes, Valerian and Gallienus, Emperors, and Valerian, the most noble Caesar, bring you back to the practice of their worship. And therefore, since you are found to be the author of the vilest crimes, and the standard bearer, you shall be a warning to those whom you have gathered about you in your crime; by your blood, discipline shall be established." And having said this he read out the decree from his tablet: "We command that Thascius Cyprian be executed by the sword." Bishop Cyprian said: "Thank God."

After this sentence the crowd of brethren kept saying: "And we will be beheaded with him." On account of this a commotion arose among the brethren and a great crowd followed him. And thus Cyprian was brought in to the country near Sexti; here he laid aside his red cloak, kneeled on the ground, and prostrated himself before the Lord in prayer. And when he had laid aside his priestly robe and given it to the deacons, he stood in his linen under-garments, and waited for the executioner. Moreover, when the executioner had come, he ordered his followers to give this executioner twenty-five pieces of gold. Indeed, linen cloths and handkerchiefs were being sent before him by the brethren. After this the blessed Cyprian covered his eyes with his hand. When he could not bind

the handkerchiefs to himself, Julian, the presbyter, and Julian, the subdeacon, bound them. Thus the blessed Cyprian died, and his body was placed near at hand on account of the curiosity of the heathen. Hence, being borne away in the night with tapers and torches, it was brought with prayers and great triumph to the courts of the procurator Macrobius Candidianus, which are on the Via Mappaliensis, near the fish ponds. Moreover, after a few days, Galerius Maximus, the proconsul, died.

The blessed martyr Cyprian suffered on the eighteenth before the Kalends of October under the Emperors Valerian and Gallienus, Jesus Christ, the true God, reigning, to whom be honor and glory for ever and ever. Amen.

VII. Persecutions under Diocletian, Galerius, and Maximian (c. 302/303–312)

19. Lactantius on the Persecution

De Mort. Persec., 7, 11–14, trans. *ANF*, VII, pp. 303, 305–6.

While Diocletian, that author of ill, and deviser of misery, was ruining all things, he could not withhold his insults, not even against God. This man, by avarice partly, and partly by timid counsels, overturned the Roman empire. For he made choice of three persons to share the government with him; and thus, the empire having been quartered, armies were multiplied, and each of the four princes strove to maintain a much more considerable military force than any sole emperor had done in times past. There began to be fewer men who paid taxes than there were who received wages; so that the means of the husbandmen being exhausted by enormous impositions, the farms were abandoned, cultivated grounds became woodland, and universal dismay prevailed. Besides, the provinces were divided into minute portions, and many presidents and a multitude of inferior officers lay heavy on each territory, and almost on each city. There were also many stewards of different degrees, and deputies of presidents. Very few civil causes came before them: but there were condemnations daily, and forfeitures frequently inflicted; taxes on numberless commodities, and those not only often repeated, but perpetual, and, in exacting them, intolerable wrongs.

.　　.　　.　　.　　.

The mother of Galerius, a woman exceedingly superstitious, was a votary of the gods of the mountains. Being of such a character, she made sacrifices almost every day, and she feasted her servants on the meat offered to idols: but the Christians of her family would not partake of those entertainments; and while she feasted with the Gentiles, they continued in fasting and prayer. On this account she conceived ill-will against the Christians, and by woman-like complaints instigated her son, no less superstitious than herself, to destroy them. So, during the whole winter, Diocletian and Galerius held councils together, at which no one else assisted; and it was the universal opinion that their conferences respected the most momentous affairs of the empire. The old man long opposed the fury of Galerius, and showed how pernicious it would be to raise disturbances throughout the world and to shed so much blood; that the Christians were wont with eagerness to meet death; and that it would be enough for him to exclude persons of that religion from the court and the army. Yet he could not restrain the madness of that obstinate man. He resolved, therefore, to take the opinion of his friends. Now this was a circumstance in the bad disposition of Diocletian, that whenever he determined to do good, he did it without advice, that the praise might be all his own; but whenever he determined to do ill, which he was sensible would be blamed, he called in many advisers, that his own fault might be imputed to other men: and therefore a few civil magistrates, and a few military commanders, were admitted to give their counsel; and the question was put to them according to priority of rank. Some, through personal ill-will towards the Christians, were of opinion that they ought to be cut off, as enemies of the gods and adversaries of the established religious ceremonies. Others thought differently, but, having understood the will of Galerius, they, either from dread of displeasing or from a desire of gratifying him, concurred in the opinion given against the Christians. Yet not even then could the emperor be prevailed upon to yield his assent. He determined above all to consult his gods; and to that end he despatched a soothsayer to inquire of Apollo at Miletus, whose answer was such as might be expected from an enemy of the divine religion. So Diocletian was drawn over from his purpose. But although he could struggle no longer against his friends, and against Caesar and Apollo, yet still he attempted to observe such moderation as to command the business to be carried through without bloodshed; whereas Galerius would have had all persons burnt alive who refused to sacrifice.

.　　.　　.　　.　　.

A fit and auspicious day was sought out for the accomplishment of this undertaking; and the festival of the god Terminus, celebrated on the seventh of the kalends of March, was chosen, in preference to all others, to terminate, as it were, the Christian religion.

That day, the harbinger of death, arose,
First cause of ill, and long enduring woes;

of woes which befell not only the Christians, but the whole earth. When that day dawned, in the eighth consulship of Diocletian and seventh of Maximian, suddenly, while it was yet hardly light, the prefect, together with chief commanders, tribunes, and officers of the treasury, came to the church in Nicomedia, and the gates having been forced open, they searched everywhere for an image of the Divinity. The books of the Holy Scriptures were found, and they were committed to the flames; the utensils and furniture of the church were abandoned to pillage; all was rapine, confusion, tumult. That church, situated on rising ground, was within view of the palace; and Diocletian and Galerius stood, as if on a watchtower, disputing long whether it ought to be set on fire. The sentiment of Diocletian prevailed, who dreaded lest, so great a fire being once kindled, some part of the city might be burnt; for there were many and large buildings that surrounded the church. Then the Pretorian Guards came in battle array, with axes and other iron instruments, and having been let loose everywhere, they in a few hours levelled that very lofty edifice with the ground.

. . . . .

Next day an edict was published, depriving the Christians of all honours and dignities; ordaining also that, without any distinction of rank or degree, they should be subjected to tortures, and that every suit at law should be received against them; while, on the other hand, they were debarred from being plaintiffs in questions of wrong, adultery, or theft; and, finally, that they should neither be capable of freedom, nor have right of suffrage. A certain person tore down this edict, and cut it in pieces, improperly indeed, but with high spirit, saying in scorn, "These are the triumphs of Goths and Sarmatians." Having been instantly seized and brought to judgment, he was not only tortured, but burnt alive, in the forms of law; and having displayed admirable patience under sufferings, he was consumed to ashes.

. . . . .

But Galerius, not satisfied with the tenor of the edict, sought in another way to gain on the emperor. That he might urge him to excess of cruelty in persecution, he employed private emissaries to set the palace on fire; and some part of it having been burnt, the blame was laid on the Christians as public enemies; and the very appellation of *Christian* grew odious on account of that fire. It was said that the Christians, in concert with the eunuchs, had plotted to destroy the princes; and that both of the princes had well-nigh been burnt alive in their own palace. Diocletian, shrewd and intelligent as he always chose to appear, suspected nothing of the contrivance, but, inflamed with anger, immediately commanded that all his own domestics should be tortured to force a confession of the plot.

20. *The Edicts of Diocletian Against the Christians*

Eusebius, *Hist. Ecc.,* 8:2, 6; Eusebius, *De Mart. Palest.,* 3, 4, 9, trans. *PTR,* IV, 1 (vii), pp. 26–28.

(Hist. Ecc. viii 2.) This was the nineteenth year of the reign of Diocletian, in Dystrus (which the Romans call March), when the feast of the Saviour's passion was near at hand, and royal edicts were published everywhere, commanding that the churches should be razed to the ground, the Scriptures destroyed by fire, those who held positions of honor degraded, and the household servants, if they persisted in the Christian profession, be deprived of their liberty.

And such was the first decree against us. But issuing other decrees not long after, the Emperor commanded that all the rulers of the churches in every place should be first put in prison and afterwards compelled by every device to offer sacrifice.

(Hist. Ecc. viii 6.) Then as the first decrees were followed by others commanding that those in prison should be set free, if they would offer sacrifice, but that those who refused should be tormented with countless tortures; who could again at that time count the multitude of martyrs throughout each province, and especially throughout Africa and among the race of the Moors, in Thebais and throughout Egypt, from which having already gone into other cities and provinces, they became illustrious in their martyrdoms!

(De Mart. Pal. ch. 3.) During the second year the war against us increased greatly. Urbanus was then governor of the province and imperial edicts were first issued to him, in which it was commanded that all the people throughout the city should sacrifice and pour out libations to the idols. . . .

(De Mart. Pal. ch. 4.) . . . For in the second attack upon us by Maximinus, in the third year of the persecution against us, edicts of the tyrant were issued for the first time, that all the people should offer sacrifice and that the rulers of the city should see to this diligently and zealously. Heralds went through the whole city of Caesarea, by the orders of the governor, summoning men, women and children to the temples of the

II-2. Procession of Martyrs. *Included are Stephen, Popes Clement and Sextus II, Cyprian, and antipope Hippolytus on nave wall of the Basilica, S. Apollinare Nuovo, c. 520 A.D., Ravenna.*

idols, and in addition the chiliarchs were calling upon each one by name from a roll. (De Mart. Pal. ch. 9.) . . . All at once decrees of Maximinus again got abroad against us everywhere throughout the province. The governors, and in addition the military prefects, incited by edicts, letters and public ordinances the magistrates, together with the generals and the city clerks in all the cities, to fulfill the imperial edicts which commanded that the altars of the idols should be rebuilt with all zeal; and that all the men, together with the women and children, even infants at the breast, should offer sacrifice and pour out libations; and these urged them anxiously, carefully to make the people taste of the sacrifices; and that the viands in the market should be polluted by the libations of the sacrifices; and that watches should be stationed before the baths, so as to defile those who washed in these with the all-abominable sacrifices. . . .

21. Christian Clergy Forced to Surrender Their Scriptures and Books

Gesta apud Zenophilium. Reprinted from *Constantine and the Conversion of Europe* by A. H. M. Jones, 1948, pp. 51–54. Used with permission of The Macmillan Company, New York, and The English Universities Press, Ltd., London.

"In the eighth and seventh consulships of Diocletian and Maximian, 19th May, from the records of Munatius Felix, high priests of the province for life, mayor of the colony of Cirta. Arrived at the house where the Christians used to meet, the Mayor said to Paul the bishop: 'Bring out the writings of the law and anything else you have here, according to the order, so that you may obey the command.'"

The Bishop: "The readers have the scriptures, but we will give what we have here."

The Mayor: "Point out the readers or send for them."

The Bishop: "You all know them."

The Mayor: "We do not know them."

The Bishop: "The municipal office knows them, that is, the clerks Edusius and Junius."

The Mayor: "Leaving over the matter of the readers, whom the office will point out, produce what you have."

Then follows an inventory of the church plate and other property, including large stores of male and female clothes and shoes, produced in the presence of the clergy, who include three priests, two deacons, and four subdeacons, all named, and a number of "diggers."

The Mayor: "Bring out what you have."

55

Silvanus and Carosus (two of the subdeacons): "We have thrown out everything that was here."

The Mayor: "Your answer is entered on the record."

After some empty cupboards had been found in the library, Silvanus then produced a silver box and a silver lamp, which he said he had found behind a barrel.

Victor (the mayor's clerk): "You would have been a dead man if you hadn't found them."

The Mayor: "Look more carefully, in case there is anything left here."

Silvanus: "There is nothing left. We have thrown everything out."

And when the dining-room was opened, there were found there four bins and six barrels.

The Mayor: "Bring out the scriptures that you have so that we can obey the orders and command of the emperors."

Catullinus (another subdeacon) produced one very large volume.

The Mayor: "Why have you given one volume only? Produce the scriptures that you have."

Marcuclius and Catullinus (two subdeacons): "We haven't any more, because we are subdeacons; the readers have the books."

The Mayor: "Show me the readers."

Marcuclius and Catullinus: "We don't know where they live."

The Mayor: "If you don't know where they live, tell me their names."

Marcuclius and Catullinus: "We are not traitors: here we are, order us to be killed."

The Mayor: "Put them under arrest."

They apparently weakened so far as to reveal one reader, for the Mayor now moved on to the house of Eugenius, who produced four books.

The Mayor now turned on the other two subdeacons, Silvanus and Carosus:

The Mayor: "Show me the other readers."

Silvanus and Carosus: "The bishop has already said that Edusius and Junius the clerks know them all: they will show you the way to their houses."

Edusius and Junius: "We will show them, sir."

The Mayor went on to visit the six remaining readers. Four produced their books without demur. One declared he had none, and the Mayor was content with entering his statement on the record. The last was out, but his wife produced his books; the Mayor had the house searched by the public slave to make sure that none had been overlooked. This task over, he addressed the subdeacons: "If there has been any omission, the responsibility is yours."

VIII. The Failure of Persecution and the Edicts of Toleration

22. *The Edict of Galerius (311)*

Lact., *De Mort. Persec.*, 34, 35, trans. *PTR*, IV, 1 (vii), pp. 28–29.

(ch. 34.) Among other arrangements which we are always accustomed to make for the prosperity and welfare of the republic, we had desired formerly to bring all things into harmony with the ancient laws and public order of the Romans, and to provide that even the Christians who had left the religion of their fathers should come back to reason; since, indeed, the Christians themselves, for some reason, had followed such a caprice and had fallen into such a folly that they would not obey the institutes of antiquity, which perchance their own ancestors had first established; but at their own will and pleasure, they would thus make laws unto themselves which they should observe and would collect various peoples in divers places in congregations. Finally, when our law had been promulgated to the effect that they should conform to the institutes of antiquity, many were subdued by the fear of danger, many even suffered death. And yet since most of them persevered in their determination, and we saw that they neither paid the reverence and awe due to the gods nor worshipped the God of the Christians, in view of our most mild clemency and the constant habit by which we are accustomed to grant indulgence to all, we thought that we ought to grant our most prompt indulgence also to these, so that they may again be Christians and may hold their conventicles, provided they do nothing contrary to good order. But we shall tell the magistrates in another letter what they ought to do.

Wherefore, for this our indulgence, they ought to pray to their God for our safety, for that of the republic, and for their own, that the republic may continue uninjured on every side, and that they may be able to live securely in their homes.

(ch. 35.) This edict is published at Nicomedia on the day before the Kalends of May, in our eighth consulship and the second of Maximinus.

23. *The Edict of Constantine and Licinius* (*Milan, 313*)

Lact., *De Mort. Persec.*, 48, trans. PTR, IV, 1 (vii), pp. 29–30.

When I, Constantine Augustus, as well as I, Licinius Augustus, had fortunately met near Mediolanum (Milan), and were considering everything that pertained to the public welfare and security, we thought that, among other things which we saw would be for the good of many, those regulations pertaining to the reverence of the Divinity ought certainly to be made first, so that we might grant to the Christians and to all others full authority to observe that religion which each preferred; whence any Divinity whatsoever in the seat of the heavens may be propitious and kindly disposed to us and all who are placed under our rule. And thus by this wholesome counsel and most upright provision we thought to arrange that no one whatsoever should be denied the opportunity to give his heart to the observance of the Christian religion, or of that religion which he should think best for himself, so that the supreme Deity, to whose worship we freely yield our hearts, may show in all things His usual favor and benevolence. Therefore, your Worship should know that it has pleased us to remove all conditions whatsoever, which were in the rescripts formerly given to you officially, concerning the Christians, and now any one of these who wishes to observe the Christian religion may do so freely and openly, without any disturbance or molestation. We thought it fit to commend these things most fully to your care that you may know that we have given to those Christians free and unrestricted opportunity of religious worship. When you see that this has been granted to them by us, your Worship will know that we have also conceded to other religions the right of open and free observance of their worship for the sake of the peace of our times, that each one may have the free opportunity to worship as he pleases; this regulation is made that we may not seem to detract aught from any dignity or any religion. Moreover, in the case of the Christians especially, we esteemed it best to order that if it happens that anyone heretofore has bought from our treasury or from anyone whatsoever, those places where they were previously accustomed to assemble, concerning which a certain decree had been made and a letter sent to you officially, the same shall be restored to the Christians without payment or any claim of recompense and without any kind of fraud or deception. Those, moreover, who have obtained the same by gift, are likewise to return them at once to the Christians. Besides, both those who have purchased and those who have secured them by gift, are to appeal to the vicar if they seek any recompense from our bounty, that they may be cared for through our clemency. All this property ought to be delivered at once to the community of the Christians through your intercession, and without delay. And since these Christians are known to have possessed not only those places in which they were accustomed to assemble, but also other property, namely the churches, belonging to them as a corporation and not as individuals, all these things which we have included under the above law, you will order to be restored, without any hesitation or controversy at all, to these Christians, that is to say to the corporations and their conventicles:—providing, of course, that the above arrangements be followed so that those who return the same without payment, as we have said, may hope for an indemnity from our bounty. In all these circumstances you ought to tender your most efficacious intervention to the community of the Christians, that our command may be carried into effect as quickly as possible, whereby, moreover, through our clemency, public order may be secured. Let this be done so that, as we have said above,

Divine favor towards us, which, under the most important circumstances we have already experienced, may, for all time, preserve and prosper our successes together with the good of the state. Moreover, in order that the statement of this decree of our good will may come to the notice of all, this rescript, published by your decree, shall be announced everywhere and brought to the knowledge of all, so that the decree of this, our benevolence, cannot be concealed.

IX. Constantine's Favors to Christianity (313–337); Donatism and the Synod of Arles (314)

24. Grant of Financial Support to African Churches (c. 313)

Ep. ad Caecilianum, Euseb. *Hist. Ecc.*, 10:6, trans. *NPNF*, 2nd ser., I, 382–83.

Constantine Augustus to Caecilianus, bishop of Carthage. Since it is our pleasure that something should be granted in all the provinces of Africa and Numidia and Mauritania to certain ministers of the legitimate and most holy catholic religion, to defray their expenses, I have written to Ursus, the illustrious finance minister of Africa, and have directed him to make provision to pay to thy firmness three thousand folles. Do thou therefore, when thou hast received the above sum of money, command that it be distributed among all those mentioned above, according to the brief sent to thee by Hosius. But if thou shouldst find that anything is wanting for the fulfillment of this purpose of mine in regard to all of them, thou shalt demand without hesitation from Heracleides, our treasurer, whatever thou findest to be necessary. For I commanded him when he was present that if thy firmness should ask him for any money, he should see to it that it be paid without delay. And since I have learned that some men of unsettled mind wish to turn the people from the most holy and catholic Church by a certain method of shameful corruption, do thou know that I gave command to Anulinus, the proconsul, and also to Patricius, vicar of the prefects, when they were present, that they should give proper attention not only to other matters but also above all to this, and that they

should not overlook such a thing when it happened. Wherefore if thou shouldst see any such men continuing in this madness, do thou without delay go to the above-mentioned judges and report the matter to them; that they may correct them as I commanded them when they were present. The divinity of the great God preserve thee for many years.

25. Clergy to Be Exempt from Political Duties (313)

Ep. ad Anulinum, Euseb., *Hist. Ecc.*, 10:7, trans. *NPNF*, 2nd ser., I, p. 383.

"Greeting to thee, our most esteemed Anulinus. Since it appears from many circumstances that when that religion is despised, in which is preserved the chief reverence for the most holy celestial Power, great dangers are brought upon public affairs; but that when legally adopted and observed it affords the most signal prosperity to the Roman name and remarkable felicity to all the affairs of men, through the divine beneficence,—it has seemed good to me, most esteemed Anulinus, that those men who give their services with due sanctity and with constant observance of this law, to the worship of the divine religion, should receive recompense for their labors. Wherefore it is my will that those within the province entrusted to thee, in the catholic Church, over which Caecilianus presides, who give their services to this holy religion, and who are commonly called clergymen, be entirely exempted from all public duties, that they may not by any error or sacrilegious negligence be drawn away from the service due to the Deity, but may devote themselves without any hindrance to their own law. For it seems that when they show greatest reverence to the Deity, the greatest benefits accrue to the state. Farewell, our most esteemed and beloved Anulinus."

26. The Emperor Convokes the Synod of Arles (314)

Euseb., *Hist. Ecc.*, 10:v, 21–24, trans. *NPNF*, 2nd ser., pp. 381–82.

"Constantine Augustus to Chrestus, bishop of Syracuse. When some began wickedly and perversely to disagree among themselves in regard to the holy worship and celestial power and Catholic doctrine, wishing to put an end to such disputes among them, I formerly gave command that certain bishops should be sent from Gaul, and that the opposing parties who were contending persistently and incessantly with each other, should be summoned from Africa; that in their presence, and in the presence of the bishop of Rome, the matter which appeared to be causing the disturbance might be examined and decided with all care. But since, as it happens, some, forgetful both of their own salvation and of the reverence due to the most holy religion, do not even yet bring hostilities to an end, and are unwilling to conform to the judgment already passed, and assert that those who expressed their opinions and decisions were few, or that they had been too hasty and precipitate in giving judgment, before all the things which ought to have been accurately investigated had been examined,—on account of all this it has happened that those very ones who ought to hold brotherly and harmonious relations toward each other, are shamefully, or rather abominably, divided among themselves, and give occasion for ridicule to those men whose souls are aliens to this most holy religion. Wherefore it has seemed necessary to me to provide that this dissension, which ought to have ceased after the judgment had been already given by their own voluntary agreement, should now, if possible, be brought to an end by the presence of many. Since, therefore, we have commanded a number of bishops from a great many different places to assemble in the city of Arles, before the kalends of August, we have thought proper to write to thee also that thou shouldst secure from the most illustrious Latronianus, corrector of Sicily, a public vehicle, and that thou shouldst take with thee two others of the second rank, whom thou thyself shalt choose, together with three servants who may serve you on the way, and betake thyself to the above-mentioned place before the appointed day; that by thy firmness, and by the wise unanimity and harmony of the others present, this dispute, which has disgracefully continued until the present time, in consequence of certain shameful strifes, after all has been heard which those have to

say who are now at variance with one another, and whom we have likewise commanded to be present, may be settled in accordance with the proper faith, and that brotherly harmony, though it be but gradually, may be restored. May the Almighty God preserve thee in health for many years."

27. Synodical Decrees of Arles Concerning Easter, Rebaptism and the "Lapsed"

Synod. Ep. to Sylvester, Bishop of Rome (Bruns II, 107). Selections from *A Source Book for Ancient Church History*, pp. 291–92, by Joseph Cullen Ayer, are reprinted with the permission of Charles Scribner's Sons © 1913 Charles Scribner's Sons; renewal © 1941 Joseph Cullen Ayer, Jr.

Marinus and the assembly of bishops, who have come together in the town of Arles, to the most holy lord and brother Sylvester. What we have decreed with general consent we signify to your charity that all may know what ought to be observed in the future.

1. In the first place, concerning the observation of the Lord's Easter, we have determined that it be observed on one day and at one time throughout the world by us, and that you send letters according to custom to all.

8. Concerning the Africans, because they make use of their own law, to the effect that they rebaptize, we have determined that if any one should come from heresy to the Church they should ask him the creed; and if they should perceive that he had been baptized in the name of the Father and of the Son and of the Holy Ghost, hands only should be laid upon him that he might receive the Holy Ghost. That if when asked he should not reply this Trinity, let him be baptized.

9. Concerning those who bring letters of the confessors, it pleased us that these letters having been taken away, they should receive other letters of communion.

13. Concerning those who are said to have given up the Holy Scriptures or the vessels of the Lord or the name of their brethren, it has pleased us whoever of them shall have been convicted by public documents and not by mere words, should be removed from the clerical order; though if the same have been found to have ordained

any, and those whom they have ordained are worthy, it shall not render their ordination invalid. And because there are many who are seen to oppose the law of the Church and think that they ought to be admitted to bring accusation by hired witnesses, they are by no means to be admitted, except, as we have said above, they can prove their accusations by public documents.

X. The Arian Controversy and the Council of Nicaea (325)

28. The Outbreak of the Dispute

Socrates, *Hist. Ecc.*, 1:5, trans. *NPNF*, 2nd ser., II, p. 3.

He, [Alexander] in the fearless exercise of his functions for the instruction and government of the Church, attempted one day in the presence of the presbytery and the rest of his clergy, to explain, with perhaps too philosophical minuteness, that great theological mystery—*the Unity of the Holy Trinity*. A certain one of the presbyters under his jurisdiction, whose name was Arius, possessed of no inconsiderable logical acumen, imagining that the bishop was subtly teaching the same view of this subject as Sabellius the Libyan from love of controversy took the opposite opinion to that of the Libyan, and as he thought vigorously responded to what was said by the bishop. 'If,' said he, 'the Father begat the Son, he that was begotten had a beginning of existence: and from this it is evident, that there was a time when the Son was not. It therefore necessarily follows, that he had his subsistence [essence] from nothing.'

29. The Heresy of Arius

Sozomen, *Hist. Ecc.*, 1:15, trans. *NPNF*, 2nd ser., II, p. 251.

Although, as we have shown, religion was in a flourishing condition at this period, yet the churches were disturbed by sore contentions; for under the pretext of piety and of seeking the more perfect discovery of God, certain questions were agitated, which had not, till then, been examined. Arius was the originator of these disputations. He was a presbyter of the church at Alexandria in Egypt, and was at first a zealous thinker about doctrine, and upheld the innovations of Melitius. Eventually, however, he abandoned this latter opinion, and was ordained deacon by Peter, bishop of Alexandria, who afterwards cast him out of the church, because when Peter anathematized the zealots of Melitius and rejected their baptism, Arius assailed him for these acts and could not be restrained in quietness. After the martyrdom of Peter, Arius asked forgiveness of Achillas, and was restored to his office as deacon, and afterwards elevated to the presbytery. Afterwards Alexander, also, held him in high repute, since he was a most expert logician; for it was said that he was not lacking in such knowledge. He fell into absurd discourses, so that he had the audacity to preach in the church what no one before him had ever suggested; namely, that the Son of God was made out of that which had no prior existence, that there was a period of time in which he existed not; that, as possessing free will, he was capable of vice and virtue, and that he was created and made: to these, many other similar assertions were added as he went forward into the arguments and the details of inquiry. Those who heard these doctrines advanced, blamed Alexander for not opposing the innovations at variance with doctrine. But this bishop deemed it more advisable to leave each party to the free discussion of doubtful topics, so that by persuasion rather than by force, they might cease from contention; hence he sat down as a judge with some of his clergy, and led both sides into a discussion. But it happened on this occasion, as is generally the case in a strife of words, that each party claimed the victory. Arius defended his assertions, but the others contended that the Son is consubstantial and co-eternal with the Father. The council was convened a second time, and the same points contested, but they came to no agreement amongst themselves. During the debate, Alexander seemed to incline first to one party and then to the other; finally, however, he declared himself in favor of those who affirmed that the Son was consubstantial and co-eternal with the Father, and he commanded Arius to receive this doctrine, and to reject his former opinions.

30. Bishop Alexander of Alexandria and His Clergy Officially Anathematize Arius (c. 319)

Socrates, *Hist. Ecc.*, 1:6, trans. *NPNF*, 2nd ser., II, p. 4.

The dogmas they have invented and assert, contrary to the Scriptures, are these: That God was not always the Father, but that there was a period when he was not the Father; that the Word of God was not from eternity, but was made out of nothing; for that the ever-existing God ('the I AM'—the eternal One) made him who did not previously exist, out of nothing; wherefore there was a time when he did not exist, inasmuch as the Son is a creature and a work. That he is neither like the Father as it regards his essence, nor is by nature either the Father's true Word, or true Wisdom, but indeed one of his works and creatures, being erroneously called Word and Wisdom, since he was himself made by God's own Word and the Wisdom which is in God, whereby God both made all things and him also. Wherefore he is as to his nature mutable and susceptible of change, as all other rational creatures are: hence the Word is alien to and other than the essence of God; and the Father is inexplicable by the Son, and invisible to him, for neither does the Word perfectly and accurately know the Father, neither can he distinctly see him. The Son knows not the nature of his own essence: for he was made on our account, in order that God might create us by him, as by an instrument; nor would he ever have existed, unless God had wished to create us.

Some one accordingly asked them whether the Word of God could be changed, as the devil has been? and they feared not to say, 'Yes, he could; for being begotten, he is susceptible of change.' We then, with the bishops of Egypt and Libya, being assembled together to the number of nearly a hundred, have anathematized Arius for his shameless avowal of these heresies, together with all such as have countenanced them.

31. Arius Curries Favor with Bishop Eusebius of Nicomedia (c. 320)

Theodoret, *Hist. Ecc.*, 1:4, trans. *NPNF*, 2nd ser., III, p. 41.

"To his very dear lord, the man of God, the faithful and orthodox Eusebius, Arius, unjustly persecuted by Alexander the Pope, on account of that all-conquering truth of which you also are a champion, sendeth greeting in the Lord.

"Ammonius, my father, being about to depart for Nicomedia, I considered myself bound to salute you by him, and withal to inform that natural affection which you bear towards the brethren for the sake of God and His Christ, that the bishop greatly wastes and persecutes us, and leaves no stone unturned against us. He has driven us out of the city as atheists, because we do not concur in what he publicly preaches, namely, God always, the Son always; as the Father so the Son; the Son co-exists unbegotten with God; He is everlasting; neither by thought nor by any interval does God precede the Son; always God, always Son; he is begotten of the unbegotten; the Son is of God Himself. Eusebius, your brother bishop of Caesarea, Theodotus, Paulinus, Athanasius, Gregorius, Aetius, and all the bishops of the East, have been condemned because they say that God had an existence prior to that of His Son; except Philogonius, Hellanicus, and Macarius, who are unlearned men, and who have embraced heretical opinions. Some of them say that the Son is an eructation, others that He is a production, others that He is also unbegotten. These are impieties to which we cannot listen, even though the heretics threaten us with a thousand deaths. But we say and believe, and have taught, and do teach, that the Son is not unbegotten, nor in any way part of the unbegotten; and that He does not derive His subsistence from any matter; but that by His own will and counsel He has subsisted before time, and before ages, as perfect God, only begotten and unchangeable, and that before He was begotten, or created, or purposed, or established, He was not. For He was not unbegotten. We are persecuted, because we say that the Son has a beginning, but that God is without beginning. This is the cause of our persecution, and likewise, because we say that He is of the non-existent. And this we say, because He is neither part of God, nor of any essential being. For this are we persecuted; the rest you know. I bid thee farewell in the Lord, remembering our afflictions, my fellow-Lucianist, and true Eusebius."

32. The Letter of Arius to Bishop Alexander (c. 320)

Athanasius, *Ep. de Synodis Armini et Seleuciae habitis* (359), 16, trans. *NPNF*, 2nd ser., IV, p. 458.

And what they wrote by letter to the blessed Alexander, the Bishop, runs as follows:—

To Our Blessed Pope and Bishop, Alexander, the Presbyters and Deacons send health in the Lord.

Our faith from our forefathers, which also we have learned from thee, Blessed Pope, is this:—We acknowledge One God, alone Ingenerate, alone Everlasting, alone Unbegun, alone True, alone having Immortality, alone Wise, alone Good, alone Sovereign; Judge, Governor, and Providence of all, unalterable and unchangeable, just and good, God of Law and Prophets and New Testament; who begat an Only-begotten Son before eternal times, through whom He has made both the ages and the universe; and begat Him, not in semblance, but in truth; and that He made Him subsist at His own will, unalterable and unchangeable; perfect creature of God, but not as one of things begotten; nor as Valentinus pronounced that the offspring of the Father was an issue; nor as Manichaeus taught that the offspring was a portion of the Father, one in essence; or as Sabellius, dividing the Monad, speaks of a Son-and-Father; nor as Hieracas, of one torch from another, or as a lamp divided into two; nor that He who was before, was afterwards generated or new-created into a Son, as thou too thyself, Blessed Pope, in the midst of the Church and in session hast often condemned; but, as we say, at the will of God, created before times and before ages, and gaining life and being from the Father, who gave subsistence to His glories together with Him. For the Father did not, in giving to Him the inheritance of all things, deprive Himself of what He has ingenerately in Himself; for He is the Fountain of all things. Thus there are Three Subsistences. And God, being the cause of all things, is Unbegun and altogether Sole, but the Son being begotten apart from time by the Father, and being created and founded before ages, was not before His generation, but being begotten apart from time before all things, alone was made to subsist by the Father. For He is not eternal or co-eternal or co-unoriginate with the Father, nor has He His being together with the Father, as some speak of relations, introducing two ingenerate beginnings, but God is before all things as being Monad and Beginning of all. Wherefore also He is before the Son; as we have learned also from thy preaching in the midst of the Church. So far then as from God He has being, and glories, and life, and all things are delivered unto Him, in such sense is God His origin. For He is above Him, as being His God and before Him. But if the terms 'from Him,' and 'from the womb,' and 'I came forth from the Father, and I am come' (Rom. xi. 36; Ps. cx. 3; John xvi. 28), be understood by some to mean as if a part of Him, one in essence or as an issue, then the Father is according to them compounded and divisible and alterable and material, and, as far as their belief goes, has the circumstances of a body, Who is the Incorporeal God.

33. Fragmentary Quotations from Arius' Thalia

Athanasius, *Ep. ad syn. Arm. et Sel.*, 15, trans. *NPNF*, 2nd ser., IV, pp. 457–58.

God Himself then, in His own nature, is ineffable by all men. Equal or like Himself He alone has none, or one in glory. And Ingenerate we call Him, because of Him who is generate by nature. We praise Him as without beginning because of Him who has a beginning. And adore Him as everlasting, because of Him who in time has come to be. The Unbegun made the Son a beginning of things originated; and advanced Him as a Son to Himself by adoption. He has nothing proper to God in proper subsistence. For He is not equal, no, nor one in essence with Him. Wise is God, for He is the teacher of

Wisdom. There is full proof that God is invisible to all beings; both to things which are through the Son, and to the Son He is invisible. I will say it expressly, how by the Son is seen the Invisible; by that power by which God sees, and in His own measure, the Son endures to see the Father, as is lawful. Thus there is a Triad, not in equal glories. Not intermingling with each other are their subsistences. One more glorious than the other in their glories unto immensity. Foreign from the Son in essence is the Father, for He is without beginning. Understand that the Monad was; but the Dyad was not, before it was in existence. It follows at once that, though the Son was not, the Father was God. Hence the Son, not being (for He existed at the will of the Father), is God Only-begotten, and He is alien from either. Wisdom existed as Wisdom by the will of the Wise God. Hence He is conceived in numberless conceptions: Spirit, Power, Wisdom, God's glory, Truth, Image, and Word. Understand that He is conceived to be Radiance and Light. One equal to the Son, the Superior is able to beget; but one more excellent, or superior, or greater, He is not able. At God's will the Son is what and whatsoever He is. And when and since He was, from that time He has subsisted from God. He, being a strong God, praises in His degree the Superior. To speak in brief, God is ineffable to His Son. For He is to Himself what He is, that is, unspeakable. So that nothing which is called comprehensible does the Son know to speak about; for it is impossible for Him to investigate the Father, who is by Himself. For the Son does not know His own essence, For, being Son, He really existed, at the will of the Father. What argument then allows, that He who is from the Father should know His own parent by comprehension? For it is plain that for that which hath a beginning to conceive how the Unbegun is, or to grasp the idea, is not possible.

34. Constantine's Call for a Council at Nicaea (325)

Euseb., *Vita Const.*, 3:6, trans. *NPNF*, 2nd ser., I, p. 521.

Then as if to bring a divine array against this enemy, he convoked a general council, and invited the speedy attendance of bishops from all quarters, in letters expressive of the honorable estimation in which he held them. Nor was this merely the issuing of a bare command, but the emperor's good will contributed much to its being carried into effect: for he allowed some the use of the public means of conveyance, while he afforded to others an ample supply of horses for their transport. The place, too, selected for the synod, the city Nicaea in Bithynia (named from "*Victory*"), was appropriate to the occasion. As soon then as the imperial injunction was generally made known, all with the utmost willingness hastened thither, as though they would outstrip one another in a race; for they were impelled by the anticipation of a happy result to the conference, by the hope of enjoying present peace, and the desire of beholding something new and strange in the person of so admirable an emperor.

35. The Creed of the Council of Nicaea (325)

Socrates, *Hist. Ecc.*, 1:8. Selections from *A Source Book for Ancient Church History*, pp. 305–6, by Joseph Cullen Ayer are reprinted with the permission of Charles Scribner's Sons © 1913 Charles Scribner's Sons; renewal © 1941 Joseph Cullen Ayer, Jr.

We believe in one God, Father Almighty, maker of all things visible and invisible; and in one Lord Jesus Christ, the Son of God, begotten of His Father, only begotten, that is of the *ousia* of the Father, God of God, Light of Light, true God of true God; begotten, not made, of one substance with the Father, by whom all things were made, both things in heaven and things in earth, who for us men and for our salvation, came down from heaven and was made [became] flesh and was made [became] man, suffered and rose again on the third day, ascended into the heavens and comes to judge living and dead.

But those who say there was when He was not, and before being begotten He was not, and He was made out of things that were not or those who say that the Son of God was from a different substance [hypostasis] or being [*ousia*] or a creature, or capable of change or alteration, these the Catholic Church anathematizes.

36. *The Emperor Reviews the Work of the Council of Nicaea and Calls for Unity*

Socrates, *Hist. Ecc.*, 1:9, trans. *NPNF*, 2nd ser., II, pp. 13–14.

But in order that this might be done, by divine admonition I assembled at the city of Nicaea most of the bishops; with whom I myself also, who am but one of you, and who rejoice exceedingly in being your fellow-servant, undertook the investigation of the truth. Accordingly, all points which seemed in consequence of ambiguity to furnish any pretext for dissension, have been discussed and accurately examined. And may the Divine Majesty pardon the fearful enormity of the blasphemies which some were shamelessly uttering concerning the mighty Saviour, our life and hope; declaring and confessing that they believe things contrary to the divinely inspired Scriptures. While more than three hundred bishops remarkable for their moderation and intellectual keenness, were unanimous in their confirmation of one and the same faith, which according to the truth and legitimate construction of the law of God can only be *the* faith; Arius alone beguiled by the subtlety of the devil, was discovered to be the sole disseminator of this mischief, first among you, and afterwards with unhallowed purposes among others also. Let us therefore embrace that doctrine which the Almighty has presented to us: let us return to our beloved brethren from whom an irreverent servant of the devil has separated us: let us go with all speed to the common body and our own natural members. For this is becoming your penetration, faith and sanctity; that since the error has been proved to be due to him who is an enemy to the truth, ye should return to the divine favor. For that which has commended itself to the judgment of three hundred bishops cannot be other than the doctrine of God; seeing that the Holy Spirit dwelling in the minds of so many dignified persons has effectually enlightened them respecting the Divine will. Wherefore let no one vacillate or linger, but let all with alacrity return to the undoubted path of duty; that when I shall arrive among you, which will be as soon as possible, I may with you return due thanks to God, the inspector of all things, for

having revealed the pure faith, and restored to you that love for which ye have prayed.

XI. Athanasius Combats the Arians, *Contra Arianos*

37. *Co-eternity of Father and Son; the Father's Eternity Implies the Eternity of That Radiance Which Is His Word*

(1:25), trans. *NPNF*, 2nd ser., IV, p. 321.

. . . —whereas God is, He was eternally; since then the Father is ever, His Radiance ever is, which is His Word. And again, God who is, hath from Himself His Word who also is; and neither hath the Word been added, whereas He was not before, nor was the Father once without Reason. For this assault upon the Son makes the blasphemy recoil upon the Father; as if He desired for Himself a Wisdom, and Word, and Son from without; for whichever of these titles you use, you denote the offspring from the Father, as has been said. So that this their objection does not hold; and naturally; for denying the Logos they in consequence ask questions which are illogical. As then if a person saw the sun, and then inquired concerning its radiance, and said, 'Did that which is make that which was, or that which was not,' he would be held not to reason sensibly, but to be utterly mazed, because he fancied what is from the Light to be external to it, and was raising questions, when and where and whether it were made; in like manner, thus to speculate concerning the Son and the Father and thus to inquire, is far greater madness, for it is to conceive of the Word of the Father as external to Him, and to idly call the natural offspring a work, with the avowal, 'He was not before His generation.'

38. *The Father Is in the Son as the Sun Is in Its Radiance* (3:3)

Trans. *NPNF*, 2nd ser., IV, p. 395.

For the Son is in the Father, as it is allowed us to know, because the whole Being of the Son is proper to the Father's essence, as radiance from light, and stream from fountain; so that whoso sees the Son, sees what is proper to the Father, and knows that the Son's Being, because from the Father, is therefore in the Father. For the Father is in the Son, since the Son is what is from the Father and proper to Him, as in the radiance the sun, and in the word the thought, and in the stream the fountain: for whoso thus contemplates the Son, contemplates what is proper to the Father's Essence, and knows that the Father is in the Son.

39. Father and Son Are Two; but the Nature Is One (Sun and Radiance Are Two; but the Light from the Sun Is One)

(3:4), trans. *NPNF,* 2nd ser., IV, p. 395.

For they are one, not as one thing divided into two parts, and these nothing but one, nor as one thing twice named, so that the Same becomes at one time Father, at another His own Son, for this Sabellius holding was judged an heretic. But They are two, because the Father is Father and is not also Son, and the Son is Son and not also Father; but the nature is one; (for the offspring is not unlike its parent, for it is his image), and all that is the Father's, is the Son's. Wherefore neither is the Son another God, for He was not procured from without, else were there many, if a godhead be procured foreign from the Father's; for if the Son be other, as an Offspring, still He is the Same as God; and He and the Father are one in propriety and peculiarity of nature, and in the identity of the one Godhead, as has been said. For the radiance also is light, not second to the sun, nor a different light, nor from participation of it, but a whole and proper offspring of it. And such an offspring is necessarily one light; and no one would say that they are two lights, but sun and radiance two, yet one the light from the sun enlightening in its radiance all things. So also the Godhead of the Son is the Father's; whence also it is indivisible; and thus there is one God and none other but He. And so, since they are one, and the Godhead itself one, the same things are said of the Son, which are said of the Father, except His being said to be Father:—for instance, that He is God, 'And the Word was God;' Almighty, 'Thus

saith He which was and is and is to come, the Almighty;' Lord, 'One Lord Jesus Christ;' that He is Light, 'I am the Light;' . . .

40. Whoever Worships the Son, Worships the Father in the Son

(3:6), trans. *NPNF,* 2nd ser., IV, pp. 396–97.

Wherefore also is He implied together with the Father. For, a son not being, one cannot say father; whereas when we call God a Maker, we do not of necessity intimate the things which have come to be; for a maker is before his works. But when we call God Father, at once with the Father we signify the Son's existence. Therefore also he who believes in the Son, believes also in the Father: for he believes in what is proper to the Father's Essence; and thus the faith is one in one God. And he who worships and honours the Son, in the Son worships and honours the Father; for one is the Godhead; and therefore one the honour and one the worship which is paid to the Father in and through the Son. And he who thus worships, worships one God; . . .

41. The Arians Strive to Separate the Son from the Father, the Brightness from the Light

Ad episcopos Aegypti (c. 356/61), 13, trans. *LF,* XIII, pp. 141–42.

. . . Infidelity is coming in through these men, or rather a Judaism beside the Scriptures, which has close upon it Gentile superstition; so that he who holds these opinions can no longer be called a Christian, for they are all contrary to the Scriptures.

John, for instance, saith, "In the beginning was the Word;" but these men say, "He was not before he was begotten." And again he has written, "And we are in Him that is true, even in His Son Jesus Christ; this is the true God, and eternal life;" but these men, as if in contradiction to this, allege that Christ is not the true God, but that He is only called God, as are other creatures, in regard of His participation in the Divine nature. And the Apostle blames the Gentiles, because they worship creatures, saying, "They served the creature more than" God "the Creator." But if these men say that the Lord is a creature,

II-3. Orthodox Christians Fleeing from the Arians, *Sermons of Gregory Nazianzen*, c. 880.

and worship Him as a creature, how do they differ from the Gentiles? If they hold this opinion, is not this passage also against them; and does not the blessed Paul write as blaming them? The Lord also says, "I and my Father are one"; and "He that hath seen Me hath seen the Father"; and the Apostle, who was sent by Him to preach, writes, "Who being the brightness of His glory, and the express Image of His Person." But these men dare to separate them, and to say that he is alien from the substance and eternity of the Father; and impiously to represent Him as changeable, not perceiving that, by speaking thus, they make Him to be not one with the Father, but one with created things. Who does not see that the brightness cannot be separated from the light, but that it is by nature proper to it and coexistent with it, and is not produced after it?

XII. Athanasius on Incarnation, Redemption, and Deification (c. 318)

42. *Christ Was Incarnated so that the Law Involving Man's Ruin Might Be Undone*

De Incar., 8, trans. *NPNF*, 2nd ser., IV, p. 40.

For this purpose, then, the incorporeal and incorruptible and immaterial Word of God comes to our realm, howbeit he was not far from us before. For no part of Creation is left void of Him: He has filled all things everywhere, remaining present with His own Father. But He comes in conde-

scension to shew loving-kindness upon us, and to visit us. . . . He took pity on our race, and had mercy on our infirmity, and condescended to our corruption, and, unable to bear that death should have the mastery —lest the creature should perish, and His Father's handiwork in men be spent for nought—He takes unto Himself a body, and that of no different sort from ours. . . . And thus taking from our bodies one of like nature, because all were under penalty of the corruption of death He gave it over to death in the stead of all, and offered it to the Father—doing this, moreover, of His loving-kindness, to the end that, firstly, all being held to have died in Him, the law involving the ruin of men might be undone (inasmuch as its power was fully spent in the Lord's body, and had no longer holding-ground against men, his peers), and that, secondly, whereas men had turned toward corruption, He might turn them again toward incorruption, and quicken them from death by the appropriation of His body and by the grace of the Resurrection, banishing death from them like straw from the fire.

43. *So that Man's Redemption and Deification Might Be Sure*

Cont. Arian., 2:70, trans. *NPNF*, 2nd ser., IV, p. 386.

For therefore did He assume the body originate and human, that having renewed it as its Framer, He might deify it in Himself, and thus might introduce us all into the kingdom of heaven after His likeness. For man had not been deified if joined to a creature, or unless the Son were very God; nor had man been brought into the Father's presence, unless He had been His natural and true Word who had put on the body. And as we had not been delivered from sin and the curse, unless it had been by nature human flesh, which the Word put on (for we should have had nothing common with what was foreign), so also the man had not been deified, unless the Word who became flesh had been by nature from the Father and true and proper to Him. For therefore the union was of this kind, that He might unite what is man by nature to Him who is in the nature of the Godhead, and his salvation and deification might be sure.

XIII. Typical Decisions and Canons of Early Christian Councils

A. ARLES (314)

44. Canon 14 (13): On Donatist Ordination

Trans. O. R. Vassall-Phillips, *St. Optatus*, App. IV. See IX, 27 on Easter, etc., in this chapter.

14(13) Concerning those who are said to have surrendered the Holy Scriptures or communion vessels, or the names of their brethren, we decree that whoever of them has been proved from public documents to have done these things shall be removed from the clergy. For if the same persons are found to have carried out ordinations, and a question has arisen about those whom they have ordained, such ordination should not be prejudicial to them. And seeing that there are many who seem to oppose the church, and through bribed witnesses think that they should be allowed to bring accusations, their plea is absolutely disallowed, unless, as we said above, they produce evidence from written documents.

B. ANCYRA (314–319)

45. Canon 3: On Readmission of Those Having "Lapsed" under Persecution

Trans. *NPNF*, 2nd ser., XIV, p. 64.

Those who have fled and been apprehended, or have been betrayed by their servants; or those who have been otherwise despoiled of their goods, or have endured tortures, or have been imprisoned and abused, declaring themselves to be Christians; or who have been forced to receive something which their persecutors violently thrust into their hands, or meat [offered to idols], continually professing that they were Christians; and who, by their whole apparel, and demeanour, and humility of life, always give evidence of grief at what has happened; these persons, inasmuch as they are free from sin, are not to be repelled from the communion; and if, through an extreme strictness or ignorance of some things, they have been repelled, let them forthwith be re-admitted. This shall hold good alike of clergy and laity. It has also been considered whether laymen who have fallen under the same compulsion may be admitted to orders, and we have decreed that, since they have in no respect been guilty, they may be ordained; provided their past course of life be found to have been upright.

C. NICAEA (325)

46. Canon 6: All Sees to Retain Ancient Rights

Trans. *PTR*, IV, 2 (i), p. 6.

Let the ancient customs prevail which obtain in Egypt and Libya and Pentapolis, and which give the bishop of Alexandria jurisdiction over all these provinces, since there is a similar custom in the case of the bishop of Rome. And likewise also at Antioch, and in the other provinces, their prerogatives are to be preserved to the churches. Now it is perfectly plain that if any one has become a bishop without the consent of the metropolitan, the great Synod has decreed that such a one ought not to be a bishop. If, however, two or three, through their own contentiousness, antagonize the common vote of all the bishops, the same being reasonable and in accordance with church law, the vote of the majority must prevail.

47. Canon 10: Against Ordaining Those Having Lapsed

Trans. *PTR*, IV, 2 (i), p. 7.

If any from the number of the lapsed have been promoted to office, either in ignorance, or with the ordainers' full knowledge, this shall not prejudice the church's rule; for when the fact is discovered, they must be deposed.

48. Canon 13: Communion to Be Given the Dying

Trans. *PTR*, IV, 2 (i), p. 8.

With regard to those [penitents] who are departing this life, the old and regular law is still to be observed: viz. that if any one is at the point of death, he should not be deprived of the last and most necessary provision for the journey [ἐφοδίος—viaticum]. But if, after one's life has been despaired of, and he has partaken of the communion, he is again restored to the number of the living, he shall be in the class of those who join in the prayers only.

And, in general, if any one whatsoever is departing, and begs to partake of the eucharist, the bishop, after due examination of his fitness, shall give it to him.

49. Canon 17: Against Clerics Taking Usury

Trans. *PTR*, IV, 2 (i), p. 9.

Inasmuch as many enrolled among the clergy, in covetous pursuit of sordid gain, have forgotten the divine Scripture which says: "He put not his money out at interest" [Ps. 14:5 LXX]; and when they make loans, demand 1 per cent. a month; the holy and great Synod has deemed it just to decree that if, after the publication of this ordinance, any one is found taking interest by explicit contract, or seeking to accomplish the same result in another way, or exacting half as much again when the debt falls due, or, in fine, resorting to any other contrivance whatsoever for the sake of base gain, he shall be deposed from the clerical office, and his name erased from the list.

D. CONSTANTINOPLE (381)

50. Canon 3: The Bishop of Constantinople Next in Rank to the Bishop of Rome

Trans. *PTR*, IV, 2 (i), p. 13.

Next to the bishop of Rome, the bishop of Constantinople shall have priority of rank, because Constantinople is New Rome.

E. CHALCEDON (451)

51. Definition of the Faith of Chalcedon

Trans. *NPNF*, 2nd ser., XIV, 264–65.

Following the holy Fathers we teach with one voice that the Son [of God] and our Lord Jesus Christ is to be confessed as one and the same [Person], that he is perfect in Godhead and perfect in manhood, very God and very man, of a reasonable soul and [human] body consisting, consubstantial with the Father as touching his Godhead, and consubstantial with us as touching his manhood; made in all things like unto us, sin only excepted; begotten of his Father before the worlds according to his Godhead; but in these last days for us men and for our salvation born [into the world] of the Virgin Mary, the Mother of God according to his manhood. This one and the same Jesus Christ, the only-begotten Son [of God] must be confessed to be in two natures, unconfusedly, immutably, indivisibly, inseparably [united], and that without the distinction of natures being taken away by such union, but rather the peculiar property of each nature being preserved and being united in one Person and subsistence, not separated or divided into two persons, but one and the same Son and only-begotten, God the Word, our Lord Jesus Christ, as the Prophets of old time have spoken concerning him, and as the Lord Jesus Christ hath taught us, and as the Creed of the Fathers hath delivered to us.

These things, therefore, having been expressed by us with the greatest accuracy and attention, the holy Ecumenical Synod defines that no one shall be suffered to bring forward a different faith [ἑτέραν πίστιν], nor to write, nor to put together, nor to excogitate, nor to teach it to others. But such as dare either to put together another faith, or to bring forward or to teach or to deliver a different Creed [ἕτερον σύμβολον] to such as wish to be converted to the knowledge of the truth from the Gentiles, or Jews or any heresy whatever, if they be Bishops or clerics let them be deposed, the Bishops from the Episcopate, and the clerics from the clergy; but if they be monks or laics: let them be anathematized.

52. Canon 3: Clerics Not to Undertake Secular Business

Trans. *PTR*, IV, 2 (iv), pp. 22–23.

It has come to the holy Synod that certain men who are registered among the clergy have become, through their love of base gain, farmers of other men's estates, and managers of secular affairs, thus becoming remiss in the service of God; that they also insinuate themselves into the houses of worldly persons, and in covetousness accept the management of their property. Wherefore the holy and great Synod has decreed that in the future no bishop, or cleric, or monk shall either farm estates, or administer property, or busy himself with secular administrations, except when he is legally compelled to assume the guardianship of minors, or is entrusted by the bishop with the care of ecclesiastical business, or of orphans, or widows not otherwise provided for, and in general of persons who most need help from the church, through fear of the Lord. Now if any one in the future attempts to transgress these decrees, he shall incur the ecclesiastical penalties.

53. Canon 10: Against Pluralists

Trans. *PTR*, IV, 2 (iv), p. 25.

A cleric is not permitted to be registered in two cities at once, that is in the church in which he was originally ordained, and in that to which, through love of vain glory, he has fled because it is larger; and those who do this must be restored to their own church in which they were first ordained and must there alone minister. If, however, a man has already been transferred from one church to another, he shall have nothing more to do with the affairs of the former church, or with the martyries, or almshouses, or hospices under its jurisdiction. The holy Synod has therefore decreed, that those who are so bold as to do anything thus forbidden, after the publication of the ordinance of this great and ecumenical Synod, shall be deposed from their rank.

XIV. The Relation of Spiritual and Temporal Powers after Constantine

A. UNDER JULIAN THE APOSTATE (361–363)

54. Julian Reopens Pagan Temples

Sozomen, *Hist. Ecc.*, 5:3, trans. *NPNF*, 2nd ser., II, p. 328.

When Julian found himself sole possessor of the empire, he commanded that all the pagan temples should be reopened throughout the East; that those which had been neglected should be repaired; that those which had fallen into ruins should be rebuilt, and that the altars should be restored. He assigned considerable money for this purpose; he restored the customs of antiquity and the ancestral ceremonies in the cities, and the practice of offering sacrifice.

He himself offered libations openly and publicly sacrificed; bestowed honors on those who were zealous in the performance of these ceremonies; restored the initiators and the priests, the hierophants and the servants of the images, to their old privileges; and confirmed the legislation of former emperors in their behalf; he conceded exemption from duties and from other burdens as was their previous right; he restored the provisions, which had been abolished, to the temple guardians, and commanded them to be pure from meats, and to abstain from whatever according to pagan saying was befitting him who had announced his purpose of leading a pure life.

55. Under the Guise of Tolerating Christianity He Seeks Its Ruin

Sozomen, *Hist. Ecc.*, 5:5, trans. *NPNF*, 2nd ser., II, pp. 329–30.

It was from these motives that Julian recalled from exile all Christians who, during the reign of Constantius, had been banished on account of their religious sentiments, and restored to them their property that had been confiscated by law. He charged the people not to commit any act of injustice against the Christians, not to insult them, and not to constrain them to offer sacrifice unwillingly. . . . He deprived the clergy, however, of the immunities, honors, and provisions which Constantine had conferred; repealed the laws which had been enacted in their favor, and reinforced their statute liabilities. He even compelled the virgins and widows, who, on account of their poverty, were reckoned among the clergy, to refund the provision which had been assigned them from public sources. . . .

Nothing, however, could diminish the enmity of the ruler against religion. In the intensity of his hatred against the faith, he seized every opportunity to ruin the Church. He deprived it of its property, votives, and sacred vessels, and condemned those who had demolished temples during the reign of Constantine and Constantius, to rebuild them, or to defray the expenses of their re-erection. On this ground, since they were unable to pay the sums and also on account of the inquisition for sacred money, many of the priests, clergy, and the other Christians were cruelly tortured and cast into prison.

It may be concluded from what has been said, that if Julian shed less blood than preceding persecutors of the Church, and that if he devised fewer punishments for the torture of the body, yet that he was severer in other respects; for he appears as inflicting evil upon it in every way, except that he recalled the priests who had been condemned to banishment by the Emperor Constantius; . . .

B. UNDER THEODOSIUS I (379–395) IN RELATION TO AMBROSE (340–397), BISHOP OF MILAN

56. Tension During Holy Week at Milan (385)

Ambrose, Ep. 20:19, 22–28, trans. LF, XLV, p. 128ff.

[19] At length came the command, "Deliver up the Basilica"; I reply, "It is not lawful for us to deliver it up, nor for your Majesty to receive it. By no law can you violate the house of a private man, and do you think that the house of God may be taken away? It is asserted that all things are lawful to the Emperor, that all things are his. But do not burden your conscience with the thought that you have any right as Emperor over sacred things. Exalt not yourself, but if you would reign the longer, be subject to God. It is written, *God's to God and Caesar's to Caesar*. The palace is the Emperor's, the Churches are the Bishop's. To you is committed jurisdiction over public, not over sacred buildings." Again the Emperor is said to have issued his command, "I also ought to have one Basilica"; I answered "*It is not lawful for thee to have her*. What hast thou to do with an adulteress who is not bound with Christ in lawful wedlock?"

[22] Thus I spoke, wondering that the Emperor's mind could be softened by the zeal of the soldiers, by the entreaties of the Counts, by the prayers of the people. Meanwhile I am informed that a Secretary was come with the mandate. I retired a little, and he notified to me the mandate. "What has been your design," says he, "in acting against the Emperor's orders?" I replied, "What has been ordered I know not, nor am I aware what is alleged to have been wrongly done." He says, "Why have you sent presbyters to the Basilica? If you are a tyrant I would fain know it, that I may know how to arm myself against you." I replied by saying that I had done nothing which assumed too much for the Church, but when I heard it was filled with soldiers, I only uttered deeper groans, and though many exhorted me to proceed thither, I replied, "I cannot give up the Basilica, yet I must not fight." That afterwards, when I was told that the Imperial hangings were removed, and that the people required me to go thither, I had directed the presbyters to do so, but that I was unwilling to go myself, saying, "I trust in Christ that the Emperor himself will espouse our cause."

[23] If this seems like domineering, I grant indeed that I have arms, but only in the name of Christ; I have the power of offering up my body. Why, I asked, did he delay to strike if he considered my power unlawful? By ancient right Priests have conferred sovereignty, never assumed it, and it is a common saying that Emperors have coveted the Priesthood more often than Priests sovereignty. Christ fled that He might not be made a king. We have a power of our

own. The power of a Priest is his weakness; *When I am weak,* it is said, *then am I strong.* But let him against whom God has raised up no adversary beware lest he raise up a tyrant for himself. Maximus did not say that I domineered over Valentinian, though he complains that my embassage prevented his passing over into Italy. I added, that priests were never usurpers, but that they had often suffered from usurpers.

[24] The whole of that day was passed in this affliction; meanwhile the boys tore in derision the Imperial hangings. I could not return home, because the Church was surrounded by a guard of soldiers. We recited the Psalms with our brethren in the little Basilica belonging to the Church.

[25] On the following day, the book of Jonah was read in due course, after which, I began this discourse; We have read a book, my brethren, wherein it is foretold that sinners shall return again to repentance. They are accepted on this footing, that their present state is considered an earnest of the future. I added that this just man was even willing to incur blame, rather than behold or denounce destruction on the city; and, since that prophecy was mournful, that he was also grieved because the gourd had withered; that God had said to the prophet, *Art thou greatly angry for the gourd?* and Jonah had answered, *I am greatly angry.* Then the Lord said if the withering of the gourd was a grief to him, how much more ought he to care for the salvation of so many souls; and therefore that He had suspended the destruction which had been prepared for the whole city.

[26] Immediate tidings are brought to me that the Emperor had commanded the soldiers to retire from the Church; and that the fine which had been imposed on the merchants on their condemnation should be restored. What joy then prevailed among the whole people, what applause, what congratulations! Now it was the day whereon the Lord delivered Himself up for us, the day whereon there is a relaxation of penance in the Church. The soldiers eagerly brought the tidings, running in to the altars, and giving the kiss, the emblem of peace. Then I perceived that God had smitten *the worm* *which came when the morning rose,* that the whole city might be preserved.

[27] These are the past events, and would that they were terminated, but the excited words of the Emperor show that heavier trials are awaiting us. I am called a tyrant, and even more than tyrant. For when the Counts besought the Emperor to go to the Church, and said that they did so at the request of the soldiers, he replied, "You would deliver me up to chains, if Ambrose bade you." I leave you to judge what awaits us after these words; all shuddered at hearing them, but there are those about him who exasperate him.

[28] Lastly Calligonus the Grand Chamberlain ventured to address himself specially to me. "Do you, while I live, despise Valentinian? I will have your head." I replied, "May God grant you to fulfil your threat: I shall suffer as becomes a Bishop, you will act as befits an eunuch." May God indeed turn them aside from the Church; may all their weapons be directed against me, may they satiate their thirst in my blood!

57. *The Affair at Callinicum* (388)

Ambrose, Ep. 41:26–28, trans. *LF,* XLV.

Seeing therefore, O Emperor (for I will now not only discourse of you but address myself to you) how severe the Lord's censures are wont to be, you must take care, in proportion as you become more illustrious, to submit so much the more humbly to your Maker. For it is written: When the Lord thy God shall have brought thee into a foreign land, and thou shalt eat the fruits of others, say not, "By my own strength and righteousness I obtained these things," but, "The Lord God gave them to me, Christ in His mercy conferred them on me," and therefore by loving His body, that is, the Church, pour water on His feet and kiss His feet; thus shalt thou not only absolve those who have been taken in sin, but in giving to them peace you will bring them into concord and restore to them rest. Pour ointment on His feet, that the whole house wherein Christ sits at meat may be filled with the odour of thy ointment, and let all who sit at meat with Him rejoice in thy fragrance; that is to say,

71

pay such regard even to the lowest, that in their absolution the Angels may rejoice, as they do over one sinner that repenteth, the Apostles may be glad, the Prophets may exult. For *the eye cannot say unto the hand, I have no need of thee, nor the head to the feet, I have no need of you.* Since therefore each member is necessary, do thou protect the whole body of the Lord Jesus, that He also of His divine mercy may protect thy kingdom.

On my coming down he says to me, "You have been preaching at me to-day." I replied that in my discourse I had his benefit in view. He then said, "It is true, I did make too harsh a decree concerning the reparation of the synagogue by the Bishop, but this has been rectified. As for the monks, they commit many crimes." Then Timasius, one of the Generals-in-chief, began to be very vehement against the monks. I replied to him, "With the Emperor I deal as is fitting, because I know that he fears God, but with you, who speak so rudely, I shall deal differently."

After standing for some time, I said to the Emperor, "Enable me to offer for you with a safe conscience, set my mind at rest." The Emperor sat still, and nodded, but did not promise in plain words; then, seeing that I still remained standing, he said that he would amend the order. I said at once that he must quash the whole enquiry, for fear the Count should make it an opportunity for inflicting wrong on the Christians. He promised that it should be done. I said to him, "I act on your promise," and repeated the words again. "Do so," said he. Then I went to the altar; but I would not have gone, if he had not given me his distinct promise. And indeed so great was the grace attending the oblation, that I myself was sensible that this favour he had granted was very acceptable to our God, and that the divine Presence had not been withheld. Then all was done as I wished.

58. The Massacre at Thessalonika (390)

Ambrose, Ep. 51:4, 12, 13, trans. *LF*, XLV, pp. 325, 328.

Suffer me, gracious Emperor. You have a zeal for the faith, I own it, you have the fear of God, I confess it; but you have a vehemence of temper, which if soothed may readily be changed into compassion, but if inflamed becomes so violent that you can scarcely restrain it. If no one will allay it, let no one at least inflame it. To yourself I would willingly trust, for you are wont to exercise self-control, and by your love of mercy to conquer this violence of your nature.

I advise, I entreat, I exhort, I admonish; for I am grieved that you who were an example of singular piety, who stood so high for clemency, who would not suffer even single offenders to be put in jeopardy, should not mourn over the death of so many innocent persons. Successful as you have been in battle, and great in other respects, yet mercy was ever the crown of your actions. The devil has envied you your chief excellence: overcome him, while you still have the means. Add not sin to sin by acting in a manner which has injured so many.

For my part, debtor as I am to your clemency in all other things; grateful as I must ever be for this clemency, which I have found superior to that of many Emperors and equalled only by one, though I have no ground for charging you with contumacy, I have still reason for apprehension: if you purpose being present, I dare not offer the Sacrifice. That which may not be done when the blood of one innocent person has been shed, may it be done where many have been slain? I trow not.

59. The Emperor Prohibits Pagan Worship as a Crime (392)

Codex Theodosianus, 16:10, 12. Selections from *A Source Book for Ancient Church History*, pp. 346–48, by Joseph Cullen Ayer are reprinted with the permission of Charles Scribner's Sons © 1913 Charles Scribner's Sons; renewal © 1941 Joseph Cullen Ayer, Jr.

Hereafter no one of whatever race of dignity, whether placed in office or discharged therefrom with honor, powerful by birth or humble in condition and fortune, shall in any place or in any city sacrifice an innocent victim to a senseless image, venerate with fire the household deity by a more private offering, as it were the genius of the house, or the Penates, and burn lights, place incense, or hang up garlands. If any one undertakes by way of sacrifice to slay a victim or to consult the smoking entrails, let him, as guilty of lese-majesty, receive the appropriate sentence, having been accused by a lawful indictment, even though he shall not have sought anything against the safety of the princes or concerning their welfare. It constitutes a crime of this nature to wish to repeal the laws, to spy into unlawful things, to reveal secrets, or to attempt things forbidden, to seek the end of another's welfare, or to promise the hope of another's ruin. If any one by placing incense venerates either images made by mortal labor, or those which are enduring, or if any one in ridiculous fashion forthwith venerates what he has represented, either by a tree encircled with garlands or an altar of cut turfs, though the advantage of such service is small, the injury to religion is complete, let him as guilty of sacrilege be punished by the loss of that house or possession in which he worshipped according to the heathen superstition. For all places which shall smoke with incense, if they shall be proved to belong to those who burn the incense, shall be confiscated. But if in temples or public sanctuaries or buildings and fields belonging to another, any one should venture this sort of sacrifice, if it shall appear that the acts were performed without the knowledge of the owner, let him be compelled to pay a fine of twenty-five pounds of gold, and let the same penalty apply to those who connive at this crime as well as those who sacrifice. We will, also, that this command be observed by judges, defensors, and curials of each and every city, to the effect that those things noted by them be reported to the court, and by them the acts charged may be punished. But if they believe anything is to be overlooked by favor or allowed to pass through negligence, they will lie under a judicial warning. And when they have been warned, if by any negligence they fail to punish they will be fined thirty pounds of gold, and the members of their court are to be subjected to a like punishment.

C. JUSTINIAN (527–565) CONSOLIDATES EARLIER LEGISLATION CONCERNING SPIRITUAL AND TEMPORAL POWERS

60. Constantine on Church Properties and Privileges (321)

The Code, Bk. I, Tit. II, No. 1, trans. S. P. Scott, *The Civil Law* (Cincinnati: The Central Trust Co., 1932), XII, 15. Grateful acknowledgment of permission to reprint Items 60–65 is made to the Central Trust Company (Executor of the Estate of Samuel P. Scott, deceased), The Estate of Elizabeth W. Scott, deceased, and the Jefferson Medical College of Philadelphia, the copyright owners of *The Civil Law*.

1. THE EMPEROR CONSTANTINE TO THE PEOPLE

Let everyone, at the time of his death, have the liberty to leave any portion of his property that he chooses to a most holy and venerable Catholic congregation, and let his dispositions not be set aside; for there is nothing to which men are more entitled than to have free power to exert their last will, as afterwards they cannot do so, and let them be unrestrained, for the right exercised then does not return.

Given at Rome, on the fifth of the *Nones* of July during the Consulate of Crispus and Constantine-Caesar, each Consul for the second time, 321.

61. Honorius and Theodosius on the Relics of the Martyrs (386)

Ibid., I, ii, 3, trans. Scott, *CL*, XII, p. 16.

3. THE EMPERORS HONORIUS AND THEODOSIUS

Let no one sell or purchase the relics of martyrs.

Given at Constantinople, on the fourth of the *Kalends* of March, during the Consulate of the Prince Honorius, and Evodius, 386.

62. The Same Concerning Churches and Church Property (423)

Ibid., I, ii, 7, trans. Scott, *CL*, XII, 17.

7. THE SAME TO ASCLEPIODOTUS, PRAETORIAN PREFECT

We freely place the care of the Divine Houses and Venerable Churches in the same honorable class with that of highways and bridges, because these are not included among base employments.

Given at Constantinople, on the fifteenth of the *Kalends* of March, during the Consulate of Asclepiodotus and Marinian, 423.

63. *Justinian on Donations for Pious Purposes* (528)

Ibid., I, ii, 16, trans. Scott, *CL*, XII, p. 26.

16. THE EMPEROR JUSTINIAN TO MENNA, PRAETORIAN PREFECT

The principle set forth in the ancient laws, although obscurely stated, that donations made for pious purposes were valid, even though they had not been inserted into written instruments, We plainly and clearly direct shall stand; just as in other cases, where ancient rights remain intact if they have reference to gifts of this description. When, however, anyone makes a donation of property up to the value of fifty *solidi*, either to a holy church, to a house for the entertainment of strangers, an infirmary, an orphan asylum, an establishment where indigent persons are sheltered, an old men's home, a foundling hospital to the poor themselves or to some city; such donations shall be valid, if the necessary legal formalities have been complied with.

If, however, the donation should be for a larger sum than that above mentioned (except, of course, where one is made by the Emperor), it will be void unless it is set forth in a proper instrument, for no one shall have the right for any reason, and under the pretext of piety, to change the rules established by the ancients concerning such donations, with the exception of those which We have expressly mentioned.

Given 528.

64. *Justinian on the Privileged State of Church Holdings*

Ibid., I, ii, 18, trans. Scott, *CL*, XII, p. 27.

18. THE SAME, TO DEMOSTHENES, PRAETORIAN PREFECT

We order that property that comes into the hands of churches, hospitals, monasteries, orphan asylums, old men's homes, foundling hospitals, insane asylums, or any other

II-4. Emperor Justinian, Imperial Architect Julianus Argentarius, the Consecrating Archbishop, Maximian, Soldiers, and Others. *Mosaic, c. 547 A.D., San Vitale, Ravenna.*

establishments of this kind, whether it is derived from the liberality of the people, or from donations *inter vivos* or *mortis causa*, or from a last will, or has been acquired by any other lucrative title, shall be free and immune from interference; for although the law enacted on this subject exerts all its force with reference to other persons, still, in consideration of piety, its vigor should be relaxed so far as the Church or any other institutions which have been set apart for pious uses are concerned. For why should we not make a distinction between Divine and human things? And why should not the privileges to which it is entitled be reserved in favor of Heaven?

(1) This law shall not only be observed in cases which may arise hereafter, but also in those which are at present pending, and which have not yet been determined, either by a judicial decision or by amicable compromise.

Published at the seventh milliary of this renowned City, in the new Consistory of the Palace of Justinian.

65. *Priesthood and Empire According to Justinian*

The Novels, Tit. VI, *Sixth New Constitution, First Collection,* Preface, trans. Scott, CL, XVI, p. 30.

The priesthood and the Empire are the two greatest gifts which God, in His infinite clemency, has bestowed upon mortals; the former has reference to Divine matters, the latter presides over and directs human affairs, and both, proceeding from the same principle, adorn the life of mankind; hence nothing should be such a source of care to the emperors as the honor of the priests who constantly pray to God for their salvation. For if the priesthood is everywhere free from blame, and the Empire full of confidence in God is administered equitably and judiciously, general good will result, and whatever is beneficial will be bestowed upon the human race. Therefore We have the greatest solicitude for the observance of the divine rules and the preservation of the honor of the priesthood, which, if they are maintained, will result in the greatest ad-

II-5. Empress Theodora with Ladies and Dignitaries of Her Court. *Mosaic, 6th century, San Vitale, Ravenna.*

vantages that can be conferred upon us by God, as well as in the confirmation of those which We already enjoy, and whatever We have not yet obtained We shall hereafter acquire. For all things terminate happily where the beginning is proper and agreeable to God. We think that this will take place if the sacred rules of the Church which the just, praiseworthy, and adorable Apostles, the inspectors and ministers of the Word of God, and the Holy Fathers have explained and preserved for Us, are obeyed.

SUGGESTED READINGS

Cadoux, C. J., *The Early Church and the World*. London: T. & T. Clark, 1925.

Canfield, L. H., *The Early Persecutions of the Christians*. New York: Columbia University Press, 1913.

Case, S. J., *The Social Triumph of the Ancient Church*. New York: Harper & Brothers, 1933.

Diehl, C., *History of the Byzantine Empire*. Princeton, N. J.: Princeton University Press, 1925.

———, *Byzantium: Greatness and Decline*, trans. N. Walford, introduction and bibliography by P. Charanis. New Brunswick, N. J.: Rutgers University Press, 1957.

Dill, S., *Roman Society in the Last Century of the Western Empire*, rev. ed. New York: The Macmillan Co., 1960.

Hardy, E. G., *Christianity and the Roman Government*, 3rd ed. London: G. Allen & Unwin, 1925.

Harnack, A., *Mission and Expansion of Christianity in the First Three Centuries*, 2nd ed., 3 vols., trans. J. Moffatt. London: Williams & Norgate, Ltd., 1908.

Hefele, C. J., *A History of the Christian Councils*, 4 vols. (to 680). London: T. & T. Clark, 1872–1895.

Jones, A. H., *Constantine and the Conversion of Europe*. London: English Universities Press, 1948.

Lietzmann, H., *The Founding of the Church Universal*, trans. B. L. Woolf. New York: Charles Scribner's Sons, 1938.

———, *From Constantine to Julian*, trans. B. L. Woolf. New York: Charles Scribner's Sons, 1950.

McIlwain, C. H., *The Growth of Political Thought in the West*. New York: The Macmillan Co., 1933.

Mackinnon, J., *From Christ to Constantine*. New York: Longmans, Green & Co., Inc., 1936.

McNeill, J. T., *et al.*, *Environmental Factors in Christian History*. Chicago: University of Chicago Press, 1939. Especially, articles by Colwell, Oborn, Laing, and Willoughby.

Phillips, C. S., *The New Commandment*. London: SPCK, 1930.

Riddle, D. W., *The Martyrs: A Study in Social Control*. Chicago: University of Chicago Press, 1931.

Vasiliev, A. A., *History of the Byzantine Empire*, 2 vols., 2nd ed. Madison: University of Wisconsin Press, 1952.

Workman, H. B., *Persecution in the Early Church*. London: Epworth Press, 1923.

A Christian Family Group.
Portrait of Galla Placidia and her children, 4th century, Museo Civico Christiano, Brescia.

III

The Catholic Church

and Christian Tradition; Early Heretics,

Fathers, Theologians, and Historians

The early Church came to self-consciousness
amid a bewildering chorus of affirmations and counter-assertions.
Its catholicity or universalizing character was
partly shaped by self-authenticating ideas that it fully approved.
Avowals of ecclesiastical integrity were
likewise elicited by interpretations of the Church
that it could not support. The Church was catholic by
virtue of its comprising the whole body of the faithful.
No simple reiteration of primitive beliefs could suffice indefinitely
for all its members. Reinterpretation of early
teachings was needed to stabilize new circumstances.
The application of original ideals to both
anticipated and unforeseen developments had constantly to be made.

Tradition was necessary, in the sense of a vital delivering up and carrying forward from one age to the next of teachings and ideals destined for later times and peoples. A living credo, or confession of belief, must be able to hark back receptively to voices out of the past and look forward expectantly to invitations from God's future. The Rule of Faith was a true reincarnation of the pristine Christian commission and an unstereotyped reissuance of it for each succeeding age. Genuine catholicity required that total potentialities as well as formally registered statements of the faith be committed to ensuing generations of believers for living reinvestment. Tradition did not mean a dead-hand grip on an idea or ideal once espoused. The vital transferral or transmission of concepts and practices was the very genius of tradition. Present believers received from predecessors the heritage of pulsing life that was to be handed on to their successors. The faith delivered once and for all to the saints was not to be handed over once only, but constantly, in perpetuity. Nor was it to be given to all at once, but at once—forthwith and forever—until it reached all. The process demanded transmission by each to all, and by all to each.

Catholic or universal life put a premium on common heritage and a community of experience. Tradition was the cumulative acquisition and dispensation of the total inheritance for comprehensively shared existence. Consensus was less important as arbitrary foreclosure on dissent than as the transcending of sheer, cantankerous, individualistic whim. Herein, to be sure, lay a grave danger. Some things might seem precious enough to most people to warrant burying them like a single talent in a well-folded napkin. The sensitized, prophetic conscience of the individual bent on new, courageous investment might even be voted down by the masses, obsessed with caution.

Quite early, the word heresy tended to connote divergence from positions commonly held. Actually, heresy was not indictable on the grounds of individual difference of opinion. What was reprehensible in it was the selfish preoccupation with personal views and actions. These were often nurtured in

cherished immunity from the discerning judgment and possible rejection of the entire community. One who dissented from majority conclusions might not be a heretic at all. He could well be a misguided idealist, a professional negator, or even an indispensable prophet. Dangerous or unacceptable belief did not, in itself, constitute heresy. Stubborn persistence in having one's way, regardless of everyone and everything, was an almost infallible clue to it.

In the very nature of human affairs, people—including Christians—were not always discriminating in their evaluation of motives and ideals. The source-readings on typical heresies are supplied for different reasons. They serve as much for the discernment of creative norms and ephemeral enthusiasms in Christian community life as to facilitate learning who, and what, heretics were. It was no easy thing for the Church to foster growth in genuine catholicity and tested Christian tradition, while according free reign to newly discovered truth and the prophetic spirit. The ecclesiastical institution did not always escape rigidifying influences and the stereotyping of earlier visions in the name of authoritative revelation. This need not be surprising. Frequently, the collective judgment by early Christians of what they held to be wholesome community standards and dissipating aberrations strikes the later observer as being singularly justified, or at least understandably tenable. This is the astonishing fact.

The chief heresies stigmatized by the official church were seldom the attacks of outsiders alone. Had they been, the concentration of counter-propaganda would have been much simpler than it actually was. Frequently, these shocking or insinuating divergences in doctrine came from inside the Christian community, itself. Departures might be introduced via shrewd manipulation or with naive convictions. Their proponents might champion them as original Christian teachings latterly neglected or distorted. Or perhaps they might insist on merely bringing out hitherto unrealized potentialities in the implicitness of the gospel. In any case such views and their propounders appeared, not so much to be enemies attacking, as friends challenging, the Church. Their fellow members were, after all, simply being proffered a further explication of the ever-resourceful gospel.

The necessity of disentangling original beliefs and transmissable, growing doctrines from an alarming accumulation of specious perversions was painful. The task often baffled the Christian community and its hierarchy. Short of relinquishing its heritage, the Church could not fail, however, to accept the wager of battle. In the process, it examined and rediscovered afresh, for itself and for its critics, much of what it had been, was then, and might hope to be. This was an essential part of the Church's coming of age. To say that the heresies brought the Church to self-awareness and integrity would probably be an exaggeration. Looking honestly and critically at the heretical interpretation of what church life had presumably been, and should properly be, served a good purpose. The Church was goaded into an ever more positive reinterpretation of its true character and historic mission.

Certainly there were Christian thinkers of undoubtedly able loyalties who had entertained profound questions and sketched out positive systems before. The major heresies no doubt prompted vigorous counter-offensives. These threats alerted Christian Fathers, theologians, and historians increasingly to their task of penitential reinquiry and critical reinterpretation. Reiteration of choice phrases—even though they were the Master's own—would not be enough to empower Christian ideals for an evangelizing confrontation of the world. Ultimately, though not without protest from many quarters, the whole current of philosophical and theological speculation that antedated and environed Christianity would have to be considered in relation to the gospel. The gospel would have to be restated and reissued out of a context correlated with this entire world view. The category of "Christian apologist" could not be limited to those who merely refuted non-Christian charges of immorality and lèse-majesté while re-echoing scriptural passages. The total mind, body, and spirit of humanity was now in contention and under the claim of Christ. Included

were not only the humble acquiescences of the naive but also the fullest cogitations of the fastidious intellect.

Christianity, of course, would not be forced off its own ground of *kerygma, didascalia,* and *agape* service into being just another philosophy or set of theosophical speculations. None of these would be ignored, however. All would be commandeered, countermanded, and exploited as the total Christian mission required. Those who helped bring all this about were rightly to be called the "Patristics," the veritable "Fathers" of the Church. Only in relation to such perspectives as theirs, as well as within the ken of historical theologians and under the scrutiny of Church historians, could the Church's founders and functions be rightly appraised. There were discriminating stations to be filled by Christian social critics—even by those not wholly balanced in their historical purview. The Church could not truly exist, unless it maintained a practiced awareness of its shortcomings and a perennially reconsecrated vocation of reform. Historians must record and weigh the Church's pilgrimage over against its human beginning and its ultimate ends. Men of letters were indispensable in the Church's reinterpretation of itself, to itself—and to all the world.

"Gnosis" was held by the gnostic to be true teaching or dogma. As such, it was revealed doctrine referable to universal reality. The gnosticism of so-called heretics and that of Christian Alexandrians like Clement and Origen had at least one basic element in common. Both groups took seriously the Christian necessity of assessing and exemplifying the true wisdom of total revelation. The Church was vulnerable to a late date because of a false assumption. Naive commitment to Christ and oral tradition was supplemented, it is true, by canonical and other writings. These, however, were thought adequate for validating Christian doctrine without recourse to philosophy. Gnosticism, inside and outside the Church, deemed it dishonest to do less than speculate about total human destiny in relation to the whole universe. Christianity, to be what it claimed, must surely correlate its ends and intermediate purposes. These must be referable to all that see-ers and doers throughout history had yearned for. This was germane to what apostles had testified to and died for.

The Alexandrians rightly divined that for Christianity to accept sub-Christian views of wisdom and esoteric philosophizings would be to lose the gospel. They were also convinced that to disparage all gnosticism, or the spiritual discernments of wisdom as such, would also entail a rejection of evangelical truth. What Clement and Origen really desired was to redefine Gnosis in its most Christian sense. They would do this while honoring the valid instincts recapturable from it for Christian catholicity. The cultic syncretisms and docetic affectations attached to non-Christian wisdom would thus be replaced with Christian realism.

In the classic gnostic systems of the Graeco-Roman world there was not one gnosticism but many. Generally recurrent emphases included certain tenets in highly individualized detail. Dualism in some form was usually present. This was no mere differentiation of mental and bodily functions. Customarily implied was a more or less rigid separation of flesh and spirit at the very heart of the cosmos. The universe was parcelled out as the creation of two coeval forces. One of these was good, the other evil. The spiritual world was the creation of the good God. The physical universe bore the stamp of its evil, creating deity. Pristine spirit, though created good, fell away into evil, to the degree that it became imprisoned in matter and flesh. Man, himself, in his spirit, inherited the patrimony of light and good. Through his fleshly existence, imparted to him by the evil creator, or a fumbling world-maker, he became mired in evil and darkness. His redemption must be secured from flesh for a return to spirit, from darkness back to light. This was effected by divine election with little or no volition on the part of the redeemed. He enjoyed an arbitrary selectness, an esoteric enrollment among the divinely favored. There was here no unmerited graciousness extended to all, out of divine generosity. Rather was this a cult of those judged worthy on the basis of superior gnosis and the "know-how" of the elite. Liberation was by a series of gradations and intermediaries, themselves uniquely guarded

from, yet in imminent danger of, contamination by the material world. What was implied was the very opposite of the Christian gospel. Gnosticism was no fellowship bound together by open avowal of unworthiness, and the laying hold upon free grace. Instead, gnostic coteries congratulated themselves upon being culled out for special favor, in terms of their speculative sensibilities. The accent was placed upon wisdom, revealed to a select few. Christ, Paul insisted, had held out the revealed secret of free salvation. The heart of universal mystery had been broken open by the Saviour for all men. In the gnostic systems, however, cliques of favored speculatives stressed their spiritual understanding to the exclusion of lesser insights and inferior, fleshly humanity.

For the gnostic, Revelation was central but Christ was not. He was only one, though admittedly an important, intermediary among subtly graduated forces deputized by the world of spirit. Together, they labored for sophistical liberation of the chosen from evil and darkness to good and light. In the world, pneumatic and material elements were intermingled. Stratifications of psychic, hylic, and pneumatic beings jostled each other in splendid syncretistic confusion. So the Valentinians were reported to have differentiated animal, material, and spiritual men. Only the latter were destined to final release. Between the good God and the material universe, which was no creation of his, countless middle-workers and heavenly Aeons were employed. Christ was sometimes declared to be one of these. His earthly manifestation was the historical Jesus. In the intricate cosmologies of different gnostic systems, Jesus' earthly body might be conceived as possessing varying degrees of genuine humanity. From this temporary diversion his spirit must be brought back to realistic Christhood in the Celestial Aeon. Or, again, his body might be invested with all the vagaries of docetic imagery as being fleshly in appearance but not such in actuality. The physical universe itself was considered by many to be the creation of the Demiurge, the in-between worker or artificer.

Was there before, or has there been since, such a hopeless confusion of competing gods, wandering Aeons in the crowded Pleroma, and half-noble, half-ignoble World-Framers? Against all this, Irenaeus pitted the saving clarity of Gospel redemption centralized in Christ. Many gnostic systems were at once aristocratic and esoteric, fatalistic and presumptuous, ascetic and antinomian. The flesh might well be disciplined to the point of denaturing the inherent dignity of the spirit, or disparaged by the obloquy of shameful excesses befitting the realm of matter. Jesus the Christ would here bring no voluntary incarnation of the Godhead into the physical world of man's own flesh. What had the God of righteousness, protected in haughty aloofness from all materiality, to do, at first hand, with earthlings? How could a Christ redeem flesh, who was himself a pallid go-between, his spirit veiled in bodily apparition? Irenaeus, for one, would have none of this fanciful debasement of God's universal creation and his redemptive catholicity. In the Christ who took on man's flesh, God's creative will touched his world and his children, hand to hand.

Out of opposition to dualistic propaganda and docetic slurs on Christian salvation, the Church was jolted into painful self-examination. What was its true nature and its distinctive role in a universe that could harbor such bizarre lucubrations? No longer could the hierarchy reiterate the simple assertions of the unlettered. The issue must be joined with cosmologists, however blasé or naive, at all points involving the essence, character, and operation of the divine creativity. The soteriological intent of the Divinity and the agencies set up by it in the Church for saving humanity must be systematically conceived and publicly clarified. The Church's teaching witness as well as the vicarious martyrdom of shed blood and monastic renunciation must be placed at the disposal of the entire Christian community. The Christian tradition was scrutinized and reactivated. The cultus, which was the living invocation of the divine graces and the offering of human praises to God, was reinvigorated and safeguarded. More and more recourse was had to those officials held responsible for mediating divine blessing and for preparing the doctrines received from the past for transmission to the future. Increasingly, the Church looked to the bishops in crucial areas. These were symbolic of teaching authority. At the same time, they were the divinely empowered protectors and propagators of worship. Pneumatic spontaneity and apostolic priority receded quickly before the authoritarian character of the teaching administrator. The trend was toward Christian universality as opposed to local independence. Captious self-interpretation and personal claims to unique witness in the spirit were subjected to hierarchical examination and collective judgment. The bishop and his graded associates, together with their specially commissioned teachers, were the interpreters of scriptural testimony and cumulative tradition. Out of the old apostolic consensus came The Rule of Faith, the appeal to universal authority, and the beginnings of catholic theology. Manuals of instruction multiplied. The systematic formulations of doctrinal synthesizers were joined to earlier Christian catechizing for the reinterpretation of the gospel.

Each of the heretical challenges evoked new apologies of authoritative faith and reliable teaching. Fathers like Irenaeus, Hippolytus, and Tertullian countered various assaults of dualistic and docetic character. Irenaeus, especially, sought their repudiation in an appeal to tradition. This he found exemplified in the authoritative unity of the Roman hierarchy. Hippolytus, no less than Irenaeus, stressed the ludicrous inadequacies of complicated gnostic cosmology and theogony when contrasted with the vicarious centrality of the all-saving Christ. Tertullian scornfully attacked Marcion. Though perhaps less given than some gnostics to speculative frenzy, this wily heretic clearly opposed the God of the Old Testament to that of the New, the Creator of Genesis to the Father of Christ. God and his Son were both denatured in the process, and the workings of the Holy Spirit were deformed. Yet, with the rigoristic demands of the Montanists, Tertullian showed definite sympathy. He even supported the pneumatic claims of certain prophetesses of theirs—at least by implication. He was to draw the ire of other Christian leaders in the "Great Church" for his own heterodoxy.

Gravely threatening tenets of dualism had long since been imported from ancient

83

Zoroastrianism. These had been syncretistically mingled with non-Christian gnosticism and quasi-Christian doctrines. The grotesques born of such unions are strongly visible in Manichaean documents. No one can read them fairly, however, without sympathy for the honest searchings of soul there reflected. Nor can he be unimpressed by the febrile philosophizings there manifested. The subordination of Christ and the Church to the more precious cogitations of a non-Christian character cannot well be ignored. The fateful extension of such views was coupled with the importation of other resourceful syncretisms of the ancient world for the invasion of medieval civilization. The quandaries thus occasioned will come into later focus.

Out of sheer self-preservation, the Church sought heightened intellectual appeal with poignant urgency. A body of admissible interpretation was needed that could do more than refute unsound insinuations. The process of the Church's clarifying its positive intent may have been accelerated by growing dissension. Actually, the propagandizing of Christian propositions soon outstripped mere collision with unorthodox points of view. The predominant involvement became that of locating the Church's own center of being, and of reinterpreting this to herself and to the world at large. These were the positive preoccupations of the Church Fathers.

Here, many talented and devoted leaders served multiple callings. Irenaeus' contribution was not limited to a virulent disparagement of heretics. He lodged in the Church's growing self-consciousness an awareness of her need for unitive authority and a resourceful tradition of Christian teaching. Tertullian was not usually charitable in his excoriation of latitudinarian tendencies in fellow Christians. He pressed hard on the heels of those he deemed heretical. Apparently, he entertained no doubt of his own orthodoxy. He could find validity in the militant ecstasies of the primitive church and her recurrent prophets. At the same time he insisted on a reverent sense of the Church's corporate dedication and expanding mission. The Rule of Faith and scriptural authority came to life in him. So did the un-compromising tenor of his rigorist ethics. The new vocabulary and literary usage demanded by a vitalizing Christian society were intensified by him.

Clement of Alexandria had never become so intrigued with gnostic cozenings as to forget the genuine heritage of the true gnostic, Christ. He and his even more perceptive student, Origen, left behind an immortal legacy of Christian instruction. Origen's intellectual powers were joined to a consistent daily piety. He witnessed to the life of spiritual perfection, no less in his scholarly writings than in his example of prayer and martyrdom. Technically a confessor only because he did not die under torture, he was no less a martyr in both flesh and spirit.

Origen wrote, taught, and edited prodigiously. His reflections on the universe were centered in his praise of the educator-God. The manner in which the divine tutor leads the human learner from grade to grade was one of his cherished ligatures between the life of scholarship and that of devotion. The "school" of souls and the "cure" of souls were inseparable for him. His critical honesty in the study of Holy Scriptures was inspiring, if not always free from dangerous implications. Scripture should not—and in fact could not—be taken in a completely literal sense. The responsibility of the Church to breed critical, yet consecrated, interpreters of faith and devotion was as great as its ethical obligation to serve the Kingdom. Throughout, there was need of living the life both renounced and perfected under the gospel. This witness must be prosecuted daily in the midst of jealously demanding and conflicting loyalties. His own veracity in answering the captious cynicism of the Hellenistic temper is observable in his work *Against Celsus*. His support for a genuinely Christian, if not always currently acceptable, eschatology is fascinatingly broached in this writing. The subject is suggestively, though not exhaustively or satisfactorily, developed in his great book *On the Principal Doctrines* (or theological foundation stones of Christianity). Needless to say, his views did not always meet with the approval of later Fathers. His insights were often considerably more procreative than those of more cautious thinkers.

The Greek Fathers recall the Church's early stake in the Greek language and in the traditions of the ancient and more contiguous East. In spite of the growing influence of the Latin tongue, the speech of Hellas would, nonetheless, continue to hold fascination for precise and communicative minds. Language eccentricities, fixities, and flexibilities would never cease to account in sizeable measure for the controversial encounters of Greek and Latin doctrine.

Basil, with all his versatile interests, stands forth as a representative of the Greek concern over the prescientific world in relation to the more scriptural *Weltanschauung*. His addiction to the monastic life, like his consecration to his episcopal task, was clearly marked. These vocations focalized the concentrations of his socially sensitized, Christian conscience. His explications of the social gospel have been essentially preserved in the currently exaggerated panegyrics of Gregory Nazianzen.

Chrysostom's eminence as a preacher should not blind us to other expressions of his ethical perceptiveness. Nor should one ignore his significance as a courageous witness to spiritual prerogatives, however hard pressed he might be by temporal authorities. His liturgical influence is preserved in the readings of Chapter IV.

Jerome was noteworthy for his extravagant endorsements of the monastic life. He was not less distinguished as a biographer of early Christian leaders in the style of the Romans. His was one of the earliest passions for Jewish-Christian geography and topography. His Biblical scholarship and textual researches were to become classics of Western literature. No mean liturgical stimulation was traceable to him.

Cyprian, like another African, Tertullian, whom he regarded as his "master," demonstrated in his early career the civic concern of the professional *rhetor*, or teacher of rhetoric. The practical bearing of the gospel on the Church's life is found both in his laudation of ecclesiastical unity and in his personal dedication as diocesan leader and martyr. Even under the strain of imperial persecution, his life was one prolonged search for Christian unification. He counseled and practiced fairness for the "lapsed."

He also administered the Church's disciplinary measures with firmness. Christian catholicity was, for him, the practicing universality of the Church's unifying example to society. The episcopal dignity was a shared character and function. Perhaps no testimony bearing on the crucial Roman episcopacy has been more controverted than his.

With Augustine, Western Christianity found a philosopher of history and a theologian of rare power. He was a profound yet facile commentator upon almost every aspect of human introspection and action. This man was to become for later centuries the recognized catholicizer of the Western Church, the universalizing re-creator of the ecclesiastical conscience in operation. Into his catholic spirit there debouched a confluence of intellectual and social currents, Christian and non-Christian. These included presentiments both Platonic and Ciceronian, Manichaean and Ambrosian, Biblical and aesthetic. From him flowed the fast coursing streams of the private, though no less universal *Confessions* and the Christian social energies of the *City of God*. Homilies, musicological treatises, psychological studies, Biblical commentaries, tracts on human polity, and volumes of sacramental theology were shaped by his unwearying pen. Charlemagne and the medieval scholastics, the Jansenists and their Jesuit critics, the classical Protestant Reformers, and the twentieth-century neo-orthodox theologians—all found in him their inspiration to new revivals of the ancient Christian tradition.

I. Early Heretics and the Challenge to Christian Catholicity

A. BASILIDES' GNOSTIC SYSTEM (C. 130)

1. The Ultimate Dualism of Light and Darkness

Acta Archelai, 55. Selections from *A Source Book for Ancient Church History*, pp. 83–84, by Joseph Cullen Ayer are reprinted with the permission of Charles Scribner's Sons © 1913 Charles Scribner's Sons; renewal © 1941 Joseph Cullen Ayer, Jr.

Among the Persians there was also a certain preacher, one Basilides, of more ancient date, not long after the time of our Apostles. Since he was of a shrewd disposition himself, and observed that at that time all other subjects were preoccupied, he determined to affirm that dualism which was maintained also by Scythianus. And so, since he had nothing to advance which he might call his own, he brought the sayings of others before his adversaries. And all his books contain some matters difficult and extremely harsh. The thirteenth book of his Tractates, however, is still extant, which begins thus:

"In writing the thirteenth book of our Tractates, the word of salvation furnished us with the necessary and fruitful word. It illustrates under the figure of a rich [principle] and a poor [principle], a nature without root and without place and only supervenes upon things. This is the only topic which the book contains." Does it not, then, contain a strange word, as also certain persons think? Will ye not all be offended with the book itself, of which this is the beginning? But Basilides, returning to the subject, some five hundred lines intervening, more or less, says: "Give up this vain and curious variation, and let us rather find out what inquiries the Barbarians [*i.e.*, the Persians] have instituted concerning good and evil, and to what opinions they have come on all these subjects. For certain among them have said that there are for all things two beginnings [or principles], to which they have referred good and evil, holding these principles are without beginning and ingenerate; that is to say, that in the origins of things there were light and darkness, which existed of themselves, and which were not declared to exist. When these subsisted by themselves, they each led its own proper mode of life as it willed to lead, and such as was competent to it. For in the case of all things, what is proper to it is in amity with it, and nothing seems evil to itself. But after they came to the knowledge of each other, and after the darkness contemplated the light, then, as if fired with a passion for something superior, the darkness rushed to have intercourse with the light."

2. The Docetic Principles of the System

Irenaeus, *Adv. Haer.*, 1:24, trans. *ANF*, I, p. 349.

Basilides again, that he may appear to have discovered something more sublime and plausible, gives an immense development to his doctrines. He sets forth that Nous was first born of the unborn father, that from him, again, was born Logos, from Logos Phronesis, from Phronesis Sophia and Dynamis, and from Dynamis and Sophia the powers, and principalities, and angels, whom he also calls the *first;* and that by them the first heaven was made. Then other powers, being formed by emanation from these, created another heaven similar to the first; and in like manner, when others, again, had been formed by emanation from them, corresponding exactly to those above them, these, too, framed another third heaven; and then from this third, in downward order, there was a fourth succession of descendants; and so on, after the same fashion, they declare that more and more principalities and angels were formed, and three hundred and sixty-five heavens. Wherefore the year contains the same number of days in conformity with the number of the heavens.

Those angels who occupy the lowest heaven, that, namely, which is visible to us, formed all the things which are in the world, and made allotments among themselves of the earth and of those nations which are upon it. The chief of them is he who is thought to be the God of the Jews; and inasmuch as he desired to render the other nations subject to his own people, that is, the Jews, all the other princes resisted and opposed him. Wherefore all other nations were at enmity with his nation. But the father without birth and without name, perceiving that they would be destroyed, sent his own first-begotten Nous (he it is who is called Christ) to bestow deliverance on them that believe in him, from the power of those who made the world. He appeared, then, on earth as a man, to the nations of these powers, and wrought miracles. Wherefore he did not himself suffer death, but Simon, a certain man of Cyrene, being compelled, bore the cross in his stead; so that this latter being transfigured by him, that he might be thought to be Jesus, was crucified, through ignorance and error, while Jesus himself received the form of Simon, and standing by, laughed at them. For since he was an incorporeal power, and the Nous (mind) of the unborn father, he transfigured himself as he pleased, and thus ascended to him who had sent him, deriding them, inasmuch as he could not be laid hold of, and was invisible to all. Those, then, who know these things have been freed from the principalities who formed the world; so that it is not incumbent on us to confess him who was crucified, but him who came in the form of a man, and was thought to be crucified, and was called Jesus, and was sent by the father, that by this dispensation he might destroy the works of the makers of the world. If any one, therefore, he declares, confesses the crucified, that man is still a slave, and under the power of those who formed our bodies; but he who denies him has been freed from these beings, and is acquainted with the dispensation of the unborn father.

3. Cosmology, Creation, and Restitution

Hippolytus, *Ref. Om. Haer.*, 7:15, trans. *ANF*, V, p. 108.

When, therefore, he says, the entire Sonship shall have come, and shall be above the conterminous spirit, then the creature will become the object of mercy. For (the creature) groans until now, and is tormented, and waits for the manifestation of the sons of God, in order that all who are men of the Sonship may ascend from thence. When this takes place, God, he says, will bring upon the whole world enormous ignorance, that all things may continue according to nature, and that nothing may inordinately desire anything of the things that are contrary to nature. But (far from it); for all the souls of this quarter of creation, as many as possess the nature of remaining immortal in this (region) only, continue (in it), aware of nothing superior or better (than their present state). And there will not prevail any rumour or knowledge in regions below, concerning beings whose dwelling is placed above, lest subjacent souls should be wrung

with torture from longing after impossibilities. . . . All things, therefore, that abide in (this) quarter are incorruptible, but corruptible if they are disposed to wander and cross over from the things that are according to nature. In this way the Archon of the Hebdomad will know nothing of superjacent entities. For enormous ignorance will lay hold on this one likewise, in order that sorrow, and grief, and groaning may depart from him; for he will not desire aught of impossible things, nor will he be visited with anguish. In like manner, however, the same ignorance will lay hold also on the Great Archon of the Ogdoad, and similarly on all the creatures that are subject unto him, in order that in no respect anything may desire aught of those things that are contrary to nature, and may not (thus) be overwhelmed with sorrow. And so there will be the restitution of all things which, in conformity with nature, have from the beginning a foundation in the seed of the universe, but will be restored at (their own) proper periods.

B. VALENTINUS' GNOSTICISM (C. 135–165/ 70)

4. The Heart Purified by the Good, Alone

Clem. Alex., *Strom.*, 2:xx, 114, trans. R. M. Grant, *Second-Century Christianity* (London: SPCK, 1946), p. 25.

2. "There is one Good, whose presence is manifested by the Son. By him alone can the heart become pure, by the expulsion of every evil spirit from the heart; for the many spirits dwelling in it do not allow it to be pure, but each of them performs his own deeds, insulting it often with unseemly lusts. And the heart seems to me to be treated somewhat like an inn, for that has holes and ruts in it, and is often filled with dung by men who live filthily in it and take no care of the place since it belongs to others. So it happens with the heart as long as there is no thought taken for it; it remains unclean and the abode of many demons. But when the Father, who alone is good, visits it, it is sanctified and gleams with light. And he who possesses such a heart is so blessed that 'he shall see God' [Matt. v. 8]."

5. *Theosophical Premises of a Valentinian Tractate*

Epiphanius, *Haer.*, 31:5f., trans. R. M. Grant, *op. cit.*, pp. 27–29.

"Never-ceasing Nous to the never-ceasing ones, greeting.

"I am going to discuss with you nameless and unspeakable and superheavenly mysteries, which are subject neither to principalities nor to powers nor to subjects nor to anything which can be understood by the intelligence, but can be revealed only by the Thought of the Changeless. For when in the beginning the Father himself held all things in himself, which rested in him without consciousness—in him whom they call the never ageing, eternally young, male-female Aeon, who everywhere surrounds all things and yet is not surrounded by them—then Thought contained in him (that power whom some call Thought, others Grace—and to be sure quite rightly, for she has graciously relinquished treasures of Greatness to those who stem from Greatness—and others correctly call her Silence, because Greatness completed all things through thought without words)—then, as I was saying, immortal thought desired to break the eternal bonds, and aroused the tendency of Greatness toward marriage, from longing to lie with her. And when she had had intercourse with Greatness, she brought forth the Father of Truth to light, one whom the perfected rightly named Man because he was the type of the unbegotten-before-all-being yet to come. After this, Silence incited the physical union of Light with Man (their coming together existed by her will alone) and brought forth Truth. Truth is rightly so called by the perfected because in truth she was like her mother Silence, who desired lights to be divided equally into male and female, so that through the lights themselves the unity actually in them might be manifest in those of them who were [merely] lights visible to the senses. After this there was aroused in Truth the lustful tendency of her mother, and she attracted the attention of her father to herself, and they lived together, and in immortal intercourse and in never-ageing fusion they brought forth the

pneumatic male-female tetrad, the type of the pre-existent tetrad which is composed of Depth, Silence, Father, and Truth. This [former] tetrad descended from Father and Truth is composed of Man, Church, Logos, and Life. Then, by the will of all-surrounding Depth, Man and Church were united, mindful of the Father's words, and brought forth the Dodecad of the productive male-female beings. The male beings are Helper, Paternal, Maternal, Eternal, Wilful (who is Light) and Ecclesiastical; the female are Faith, Hope, Love, Intelligence, Blessedness, Wisdom. After these come Logos and Life. They remodelled the gift of unity and had fellowship with each other (their fellowship is volition), and brought forth a decad of productive male-female beings. The male beings are Deep, Ageless, Self-Existent, Only-Begotten, Immovable (these took their names for the glory of the All-Surrounding). The female are Intercourse, Union, Blending, Unity, Pleasure (and these took their names for the glory of Silence). When then according to the will of the Father of Truth the Thirty was perfected, who is the Number that mortal men on earth count, without knowing anything about her, and with whom they turn round and begin to count again (when they have reached her and cannot count beyond [*i.e.*, days of the month])—she is composed of Depth, Silence, Father, Truth, Man, Church, Logos, Life, Helper, Paternal, Maternal, Eternal, Wilful, Ecclesiastical, Faith, Hope, Love, Intelligence, Blessedness, Wisdom, Deep, Ageless, Self-Existent, Only-Begotten, Immovable, Intercourse, Union, Blending, Unity, Pleasure—then the All-Surrounding resolved, in unsurpassable understanding, to call forth another Ogdoad opposite the authentic pre-existent one, though remaining within the number of Thirty, and he placed the male numbers opposite to the male beings—the One, the Three, the Five, the Seven; and the female opposite the female —the Two, the Four, the Six, the Eight. This then is the Ogdoad which was called forth from the pre-existent Ogdoad, that is, that composed of Depth, Father, Man, Logos, and Silence, Truth, Church, Life; and it was united with the lights. So arose the separated Thirty. The pre-existent Ogdoad, however, remained composed and at rest."

C. MARCION'S GNOSTIC PROPENSITIES (c. 140/144)

6. Separation of Law and Gospel; a Diversity of Gods

Tert., *Adv. Marc.*, 1:19, trans. *ANF*, III, p. 285.

Marcion's special and principal work is the separation of the law and the gospel; and his disciples will not deny that in this point they have their very best pretext for initiating and confirming themselves in his heresy. These are Marcion's *Antitheses,* or contradictory propositions, which aim at committing the gospel to a variance with the law, in order that from the diversity of the two documents which contain them, they may contend for a diversity of gods also.

7. Marcion's Good, Weak God

Ibid., 1:27, trans. *ANF*, III, pp. 292–93.

Listen, ye sinners; and ye who have not yet come to this, hear, that you may attain to such a pass! A better god has been discovered, who never takes offence, is never angry, never inflicts punishment, who has prepared no fire in hell, no gnashing of teeth in the outer darkness! He is purely and simply good. He indeed forbids all delinquency, but only in word. He is in you, if you are willing to pay him homage, for the sake of appearances, that you may seem to honour God; for your fear he does not want. And so satisfied are the Marcionites with such pretences, that they have no fear of their god at all. They say it is only a bad man who will be feared, a good man will be loved. Foolish man, do you say that he whom you call Lord ought not to be feared, whilst the very title you give him indicates a power which must itself be feared? . . . Come, then, if you do not fear God as being good, why do you not boil over into every kind of lust, and so realize that which is, I believe, the main enjoyment of life to all who fear not God? Why do you not frequent the customary pleasures of the maddening circus, the bloodthirsty arena, and the lascivious thea-

tre? Why in persecutions also do you not, when the censer is presented, at once redeem your life by the denial of your faith? God forbid, you say with redoubled emphasis. So you do fear sin, and by your fear prove that He is an object of fear Who forbids the sin.

8. Docetism Denatures Christ's Incarnation

Ibid., 3:8, trans. *ANF*, III, p. 327.

Now, the more firmly the antichrist Marcion had seized this assumption, the more prepared was he, of course, to reject the bodily substance of Christ, since he had introduced his very god to our notice as neither the author nor the restorer of the flesh; and for this very reason, to be sure, as pre-eminently good, and most remote from the deceits and fallacies of the Creator. His Christ, therefore, in order to avoid all such deceits and fallacies, and the imputation, if possible, of belonging to the Creator, was not what he appeared to be, and feigned himself to be what he was not—incarnate without being flesh, human without being man, and likewise a divine Christ without being God! But why should he not have propagated also the phantom of God? Can I believe him on the subject of the internal nature, who was all wrong touching the external substance? How will it be possible to believe him true on a mystery, when he has been found so false on a plain fact?

D. MONTANISM (c. 155/170) AND THE REVIVAL OF PNEUMATISM AND RIGORISM

9. Montanist Prophetesses, Priscilla and Maximilla

Hipp., *Ref. Om. Haer.*, 8:12, trans. *ANF*, V, pp. 123–24.

But there are others who themselves are even more heretical in nature (than the foregoing), and are Phrygians by birth. These have been rendered victims of error from being previously captivated by (two) wretched women, called a certain Priscilla and Maximilla, whom they supposed (to be) prophetesses. And they assert that into these the Paraclete Spirit had departed; and antecedently to them, they in like manner consider Montanus as a prophet. And being in possession of an infinite number of their books, (the Phrygians) are overrun with delusion; and they do not judge whatever statements are made by them, according to (the criterion of) reason; nor do they give heed unto those who are competent to decide; but they are heedlessly swept onwards by the reliance which they place on these (impostors). And they allege that they have learned something more through these, than from law, and prophets, and the Gospels. But they magnify these wretched women above the Apostles and every gift of Grace, so that some of them presume to assert that there is in them a something superior to Christ. These acknowledge God to be the Father of the universe, and Creator of all things, similarly with the Church, and (receive) as many things as the Gospel testifies concerning Christ. They introduce, however, the novelties of fasts, and feasts, and meals of parched food, and repasts of radishes, alleging that they have been instructed by women. And some of these assent to the heresy of the Noetians, and affirm that the Father himself is the Son, and that this (one) came under generation, and suffering, and death.

10. Some Montanist Oracles from Representative Sources

Trans. R. M. Grant, *op. cit.*, pp. 95–96.

1. Montanus: "I am the Lord God Omnipotent dwelling in man." (Epiphanius, *Haer.* xlviii. 11.)

2. Montanus: "I am neither an angel nor an envoy, but I the Lord God, the Father, have come." (*Ibid.*)

3. Montanus: "I am the Father and the Son and the Paraclete." (Didymus, *De trinitate* iii. 41. 1.)

4. Montanus: "Why do you say 'the superman who is saved'? Because the righteous man will shine a hundred times brighter than the sun, and even the little ones among you who are saved, a hundred times brighter than the moon." (Epiphanius, *Haer.* xlviii. 10.)

5. Montanus: "Behold, man is as a lyre,

and I hover over him as a plectrum; man sleeps but I watch; behold, the Lord is removing the hearts of men and giving them (new) hearts." (*Ibid.*, xlviii. 4.)

6. Montanus: "You are exposed to public reproach? It is for your good. He who is not reproached by men is reproached by God. Do not be disconcerted; your righteousness has brought you into the midst (of all). Why are you disconcerted, since you are gaining praise? Your power arises when you are seen by men." (Tertullian, *De fuga* 9.)

7. Montanus: "Do not hope to die in bed nor in abortion nor in languishing fevers, but in martyrdom, that he who suffered for you may be glorified." (*Ibid.*)

8. Montanus: "For God brought forth the Word as a root brings forth a tree, and a spring a river, and the sun a ray." (Tertullian, *Adv. Prax.* 8.)

9. Montanus: "The Church is able to remit sins; but I will not do so, lest others also sin." (Tertullian, *De pudic.* 21.)

10. Maximilla: "After me there will be no more prophecy, but the End." (Epiphanius, *Haer.* xlviii. 11.)

11. Maximilla: "I am driven as a wolf from the sheep. I am not a wolf; I am word, spirit, and power." (Eusebius, *H. E.* v. 16. 17.)

12. Maximilla: "Do not listen to me, but listen to Christ." (Epiphanius, *Haer.* xlviii. 12.)

13. Maximilla: "The Lord sent me as a partisan of this task, a revealer of this covenant, an interpreter of this promise, forced, whether I will or not, to learn the knowledge of God." (*Ibid.* xlviii. 13.)

14. Prisca: "For continence brings harmony, and they see visions, and, bowing their heads, they also hear distinct voices, saving and mysterious." (Tertullian, *De exh. cast.* 10.)

15. Prisca: "They are flesh, yet they hate the flesh." (Tertullian, *De res. carn.* 11.)

16. Prisca: "Appearing as a woman clothed in a shining robe, Christ came to me [in sleep]; he put wisdom into me and revealed to me that this place is sacred and that here Jerusalem will come down from heaven." (Epiphanius, *Haer.* xlix. 1.)

E. MANICHAEAN LIGHT AND DARKNESS
(c. 250)

11. Traditional Writings on the Life of Mani

An Nadim, Fihrist. Selections from *A Source Book for Ancient Church History*, pp. 252–54, by Joseph Cullen Ayer are reprinted with the permission of Charles Scribner's Sons. © 1913 Charles Scribner's Sons; renewal © 1941 Joseph Cullen Ayer, Jr.

Mohammed ibn Isak says: Mani was the son of Fatak, of the family of the Chaskanier. Ecbatana is said to have been the original home of his father, from which he emigrated to the province of Babylon. He took up his residence in Al Madain, in a portion of the city known as Ctesiphon. In that place was an idol's temple, and Fatak was accustomed to go into it, as did also the other people of the place. It happened one day that a voice sounded forth from the sacred interior of the temple, saying to him: "Fatak, eat no flesh, drink no wine and refrain from carnal intercourse." This was repeated to him several times on three days. When Fatak perceived this, he joined a society of people in the neighborhood of Dastumaisan which were known under the name of Al-Mogtasilah, *i.e.*, those who wash themselves, baptists, and of whom remnants are to be found in these parts and in the marshy districts at the present time. These belonged to that mode of life which Fatak had been commanded to follow. His wife was at that time pregnant with Mani, and when she had given him birth she had, as they say, glorious visions regarding him, and even when she was awake she saw him taken by some one unseen, who bore him aloft into the air, and then brought him down again; sometimes he remained even a day or two before he came down again. Thereupon his father sent for him and had him brought to the place where he was, and so he was brought up with him in his religion. Mani, in spite of his youthful age, spake words of wisdom. After he had completed his twelfth year there came to him, according to his statement, a revelation from the King of the Paradise of Light, who is God the Exalted, as he said. The angel which brought him the revelation was called Eltawan; this name means "the

Companion." He spoke to Mani, and said: "Separate thyself from this sort of faith, for thou belongest not among its adherents, and it is obligatory upon you to practise continence and to forsake the fleshly desires, yet on account of thy youth the time has not come for thee to take up thy public work." But when he was twenty-four years old, Eltawan appeared to him and said: "Hail, Mani, from me and from the Lord who has sent me to thee and has chosen thee to be his prophet. He commands thee now to proclaim thy truth and on my announcement to proclaim the truth which is from him and to throw thyself into this calling with all thy zeal."

The Manichaeans say: He first openly entered upon his work on the day when Sapor, the son of Ardaschir, entered upon his reign, and placed the crown upon his head; and this was Sunday, the first day of Nisan (March 20, 241), when the sun stood in the sign Aries. He was accompanied by two men, who had already attached themselves to his religion; one was called Simeon, the other Zakwa; besides these, his father accompanied him, to see how his affairs would turn out.

Mani said he was the Paraclete, whom Jesus, of blessed memory, had previously announced. Mani took the elements of his doctrine from the religion of the Magi and Christianity. . . . Before he met Sapor Mani had spent about forty years in foreign lands. Afterward he converted Peroz, the brother of Sapor, and Peroz procured him an audience with his brother Sapor. The Manichaeans relate: He thereupon entered where he was and on his shoulders were shining, as it were, two candles. When Sapor perceived him, he was filled with reverence for him, and he appeared great in his eyes; although he previously had determined to seize him and put him to death. After he had met him, therefore, the fear of him filled him, he rejoiced over him and asked him why he had come and promised to become his disciple. Mani requested of him a number of things, among them that his followers might be unmolested in the capital and in the other territories of the Persian Empire, and that they might extend themselves whither they wished in the provinces. Sapor granted him all he asked.

Mani had already preached in India, China, and among the inhabitants of Turkestan, and in every land he left behind him disciples.

12. Doctrines of Light and Darkness

Psalms of the Bema, 223, ed. and trans. by C. R. C. Allberry, *et al.*, *A Manichaean Psalm-Book*, Pt. II [Manichaean Manuscripts in the Chester Beatty Collection, Vol. II] (Stuttgart: W. Kohlhammer, 1938), pp. 9–11.

Let us worship the Spirit of the Paraclete.

Let us bless our Lord Jesus who has sent to us the Spirit of Truth. He came and separated us from the Error (πλάνη) of the world (κόσμος), he brought us a mirror, we looked, we saw the Universe in it.

When the Holy Spirit came he revealed to us the way of Truth and taught us that there are two Natures (φύσις), that of Light and that of Darkness, separate one from the other from the beginning.

The Kingdom of Light, on the one hand (μέν), consisted in five Greatnesses, and they are the Father and his twelve Aeons and the Aeons of the Aeons, the Living Air (ἀήρ), the Land of Light; the great Spirit breathing in them, nourishing them with his Light.

But the Kingdom of Darkness consists of five storehouses (ταμιεῖον), which are Smoke (καπνός) and Fire and Wind and Water and Darkness; their Counsel creeping in them, moving them and inciting (?) them to make war (πόλεμος) with one another.

Now (οὖν) as they were making war (πόλεμος) with one another they dared (τολμᾶν) to make an attempt upon the Land of Light, thinking that they would be able to conquer it. But they know not that which they have thought to do they will bring down upon their own heads.

But (δέ) there was a multitude of angels in the Land of the Light, having the power to go forth to subdue the enemy of the Father, whom it pleased that by his Word that he would send, he should subdue the rebels who desired to exalt themselves above that which was more exalted than they.

Like unto a shepherd that shall see a lion coming to destroy his sheep-fold: for he uses guile and takes a lamb and sets it as a snare that he may catch him by it (i.e. the lamb); for by a single lamb he saves his sheep-fold. After these things he heals the lamb that has been wounded by the lion:

This too is the way of the Father, who sent his strong son; and *he* produced from himself his Maiden equipped with five powers, that she might fight against the five abysses of the Dark.

When the Watcher (?) stood in the boundaries of light, he shewed to them his Maiden who is his soul; they bestirred themselves in their abyss, desiring to exalt themselves over her, they opened their mouth desiring to swallow her.

He held her power (ἀρχή) fast, he spread her over them, like nets over fishes, he made her rain down upon them like purified clouds of water, she thrust herself within them like piercing lightning. She crept in their inward parts, she bound them all, they not knowing it.

When the First Man had finished (?) his war (πόλεμος), the Father sent his second son.

He came and helped his brother out of the abyss; he established this whole world (κόσμος) out of the mixture that took place of the Light and the Darkness.

He spread out all the powers of the abyss to ten heavens and eight earths, he shut them up into this world (κόσμος) once, he made it a prison too for all the powers of Darkness, it is also a place of purification for the Soul that was swallowed (?) in them.

The sun and moon he founded, he set them on high, to purify the Soul. Daily they take up the refined part to the height, but (δέ) the dregs however they erase . . . mixed (?), they convey [it above and below.

This whole world (κόσμος) stands firm for (πρός) a season, there being a great building which is being built outside

92

this world ($\kappa\acute{o}\sigma\mu os$). So soon as that builder shall finish, the whole world ($\kappa\acute{o}\sigma\mu os$) will be dissolved and set on fire that the fire may smelt it away.

All life, the relic of Light wheresoever it be, he will gather to himself and of it depict ($Z\omega\gamma\rho\alpha\phi\epsilon\hat{\imath}\nu$) an image ($\dot{\alpha}\nu\delta\rho\iota\acute{a}s$). And the counsel of death too, all the Darkness, he will gather together and make a likeness ($Z\omega\gamma\rho\alpha\phi\epsilon\hat{\imath}\nu$) of its very self, it and the] Ruler ($\ddot{a}\rho\chi\omega\nu$).

In a moment the living Spirit will come . . . he will succour the Light. But the counsel of death and the Darkness he will shut up in the dwelling ($\tau\alpha\mu\epsilon\hat{\imath}o\nu$) that was established for it, that it might be bound in it for ever.

There is no other means to bind the Enemy save this means; for he will not be received to the Light because he is a stranger to it; nor again can he be left in his land of Darkness, that he may not wage a war ($\pi\acute{o}\lambda\epsilon\mu os$) greater than the first.

A new Aeon will be built in the place of the world ($\kappa\acute{o}\sigma\mu os$) that shall dissolve, that in it the powers of the Light may reign, because they have performed and fulfilled the will of the Father entire, they have subdued the hated one, they have . . . over him for ever.

This is the Knowledge of Mani, let us worship him and bless him. Blessed is he every man that shall trust [in him, for he it is shall live with all the Righteous ($\delta\acute{\iota}\kappa\alpha\iota os$).

Glory and victory to our Lord Mani, the Spirit of Truth, that cometh from the Father, who has revealed to us the Beginning, the Middle and the End. Victory to the soul of the blessed ($\mu\alpha\kappa\alpha\rho\acute{\iota}\alpha$) Mary, Theona, Pshaijmnoute.

13. Fragments on Christ, the Church, and Mary

Psalmoi Sarakoton, trans. Allberry, MPB, pp. 158–60. Observe the connection of these materials with those of the medieval period in Chapter VIII.

Taste and know that the Lord is sweet.

Christ is the word of Truth: he that hears it shall live.

I tasted a sweet taste, I found nothing sweeter than the word of Truth.

Taste.

I tasted a sweet taste, I found nothing sweeter than the name of God.

Taste.

I] tasted a sweet taste, I found nothing sweeter than Christ.

Where is there a kind mother like my mother, Love ($\dot{\alpha}\gamma\acute{a}\pi\eta$)?

Where is there a kind father like my father, Christ?

What honey is so sweet as this name, Church?

Wisdom ($\sigma o\phi\acute{\iota}\alpha$) invites ($\kappa\alpha\lambda\epsilon\hat{\imath}\nu$) you, that you may eat with your Spirit.

Lo, the new wine has been broached: lo, the cups have been brought in.

Drink what you shall drink, gladness surrounding you.

Eat that you may eat, being glad in your [Spirit.

. . . are they that preach, they that hear are . . .

The Bride] is the Church, the Bridegroom is . . .

Taste.

The Bride] is the soul, the Bridegroom is Jesus.

[l. 4 illegible]

. . . the sons of the Light . . .

This is the] true joy [that will] endure with us.

. . . which does not change or pass.

. . . they rejoice, but ($\dot{\alpha}\lambda\lambda\acute{a}$) . . .

Taste.

. . . but ($\dot{\alpha}\lambda\lambda\acute{a}$) . . .   Taste.

. . . outside, they rejoicing . . .   Taste.

[l. 14 fragmentary]

He that] humbleth himself shall be received, he that [exalteth himself] shall be humbled (?).

He that] dies lives, he that labours has his rest. . . . the labour is the rest, after . . . there is joy again.

Let us] rejoice in this joy from everlasting to everlasting.

Glory] and honour to Jesus, the King of the holy ones, and] his holy Elect, and the soul of the blessed ($\mu\alpha\kappa\alpha\rho\acute{\iota}\alpha$) Mary.

Put in me a holy heart, my God: let an upright Spirit be new within me.

The holy heart is Christ: if he rises in us, we also shall rise in him.

Christ has risen, the dead shall rise with him. If we believe in him, we shall pass beyond death and come to life.

The] sons of faith,—they shall see faith: lo, . . . come, let us put oil in our lamps (λαμπάς).

Let us gather] in and become warm milk; this creature (?) . . . hope (ἐλπίς) which has come from on high.

The creature] of the Darkness is this body (σῶμα) which we wear (φορεῖν): the] soul which is in it is the First [Man.

The] First Man who was victorious in the Land of the Darkness, he also today will be victorious in the body (σῶμα) of [death.

The Living Spirit that gave help to the First [Man, he also today is the Paraclete-Spirit.

One is the Mind (νοῦς) that is to come, that reveals, gathering (?) in, choosing his holy Church.

Purify [me, my God], purify me within, without: purify (?) the [body (? σῶμα), the] soul and the Spirit.

Let . . . be a holy body (σῶμα) for me; the knowledge . . . Spirit and Mind (νοῦς) for me.

Purify me, [my God,] . . . me in (?) these three . . . , my mouth, . . . , and the purity of my virginity (παρθενία).

Jesus has risen: he has risen in three days, the Cross (σταυρός) of Light that rises in three powers.

The sun and the moon and the Perfect Man, —these three powers are the Church of the Great World (κόσμος).

Jesus, the Maiden, and the Mind (νοῦς) which is in their midst,—[these three powers are the Church of the Little World (κόσμος).

The Kingdom of the heavens,—behold, it is within us, behold, it is outside us; if we believe in it we shall live in it for ever.

Glory, victory to every man [that] has heard these things and believed in them and fulfilled them in joy. Victory to the soul of the blessed (μακαρία) Mary.

94

II. The Early Christian Fathers, and Their Confrontation of the Heresies with the Rule of Faith and Tradition

A. IRENAEUS (C. 140–202) AND THE CHRISTIAN TRADITION

14. The Faith of the Church versus the Gnostic Demiurge, Aeons, Pleroma

Adv. Haer., 1:10, trans. Richardson, *et al.*, *Early Christian Fathers* [LCC, Vol. I], pp. 360–62.

Now the Church, although scattered over the whole civilized world to the end of the earth, received from the apostles and their disciples its faith in one God, the Father Almighty, who made the heaven, and the earth, and the seas, and all that is in them, and in one Christ Jesus, the Son of God, who was made flesh for our salvation, and in the Holy Spirit, who through the prophets proclaimed the dispensations of God—the comings, the birth of a virgin, the suffering, the resurrection from the dead, and the bodily reception into the heavens of the beloved, Christ Jesus our Lord, and his coming from the heavens in the glory of the Father to restore all things, and to raise up all flesh, that is, the whole human race, so that every knee may bow, of things in heaven and on earth and under the earth, to Christ Jesus our Lord and God and Saviour and King, according to the pleasure of the invisible Father, and every tongue may confess him, and that he may execute righteous judgment on all. The spiritual powers of wickedness, and the angels who transgressed and fell into apostasy, and the godless and wicked and lawless and blasphemers among men he will send into the eternal fire. But to the righteous and holy, and those who have kept his commandments and have remained in his love, some from the beginning [of life] and some since their repentance, he will by his grace give life incorrupt, and will clothe them with eternal glory.

Having received this preaching and this faith, as I have said, the Church, although scattered in the whole world, carefully preserves it, as if living in one house. She believes these things [everywhere] alike, as if she had but one heart and one soul, and preaches them harmoniously, teaches them, and hands them down, as if she had but one mouth. For the languages of the world are different, but the meaning of the [Christian] tradition is one and the same. Neither do the churches that have been established in Germany believe otherwise, or hand down any other tradition, nor those among the Iberians, nor those among the Celts, nor in Egypt, nor in Libya, nor those established in the middle parts of the world. But as God's creature, the sun, is one and the same in the whole world, so also the preaching of the truth shines everywhere, and illumines all men who wish to come to the knowledge of the truth. Neither will one of those who preside in the churches who is very powerful in speech say anything different from these things, for no one is above [his] teacher, nor will one who is weak in speech diminish the tradition. For since the faith is one and the same, he who can say much about it does not add to it, nor does he who can say little diminish it.

This matter of having more or less understanding does not mean that men change the basic idea, and imagine another God above the Demiurge and Maker and Nourisher of this universe, as if he were not enough for us, or another Christ or another Only-begotten. But it consists in working out the things that have been said in parables, and building them into the foundation of the faith: in expounding the activity and dispensation of God for the sake of mankind; in showing clearly how God was long-suffering over the apostasy of the angels who transgressed, and over the disobedience of men; in declaring why one and the same God made some things subject to time, others eternal, some heavenly, and some earthly; in understanding why God, being invisible, appeared to the prophets, not in one form, but differently to different ones; in showing why there were a number of covenants with mankind, and in teaching what is the character of each of the covenants; in searching out why God shut up all in disobedience that he might have mercy on all; in giving thanks that the Word of

God was made flesh, and suffered; in declaring why the coming of the Son of God [was] in the last times, that is, the Beginning was made manifest at the end; in unfolding what is found in the prophets about the end and the things to come; in not being silent that God has made the despaired-of Gentiles fellow heirs and of the same body and partners with the saints; and in stating how this mortal and fleshly [body] will put on immortality, and this corruptible incorruption; and in proclaiming how he says, "What was not a people, is a people, and what was not beloved, is beloved," and, "Many more are the children of the desolate than of her who has a husband." With reference to these things and others like them the apostle exclaimed, "O depth of the riches and wisdom and knowledge of God; how unsearchable are his judgments and his ways past finding out!" But [this greater skill] does not consist in imagining beyond the Creator and Demiurge the Mother of these things and of him, the Desire of a wandering Aeon, and coming to such a point of blasphemy, nor in falsely conceiving of the Pleroma above her, now with thirty, now with an innumerable crowd of Aeons, as these teachers who are indeed void of divine understanding say. But as I said before, the real Church has one and the same faith everywhere in the world.

15. The Heretics Attacked for Their Rejection of Scripture and Tradition

Adv. Haer., 3:2, trans. ANF, I, p. 415.

1. When, however, they are confuted from the Scriptures, they turn round and accuse these same Scriptures, as if they were not correct, nor of authority, and [assert] that they are ambiguous, and that the truth cannot be extracted from them by those who are ignorant of tradition. For [they allege] that the truth was not delivered by means of written documents, but *vivâ voce:* wherefore also Paul declared, "But we speak wisdom among those that are perfect, but not the wisdom of this world." And this wisdom each one of them alleges to be the fiction of his own inventing, forsooth; so that, according to their idea, the truth prop-

erly resides at one time in Valentinus, at another in Marcion, at another in Cerinthus, then afterwards in Basilides, or has even been indifferently in any other opponent, who could speak nothing pertaining to salvation. For every one of these men, being altogether of a perverse disposition, depraving the system of truth, is not ashamed to preach himself.

2. But, again, when we refer them to that tradition which originates from the apostles, [and] which is preserved by means of the successions of presbyters in the Churches, they object to tradition, saying that they themselves are wiser not merely than the presbyters, but even than the apostles, because they have discovered the unadulterated truth. For [they maintain] that the apostles intermingled the things of the law with the words of the Saviour; and that not the apostles alone, but even the Lord Himself, spoke as at one time from the Demiurge, at another from the intermediate place, and yet again from the Pleroma, but that they themselves, indubitably, unsulliedly, and purely, have knowledge of the hidden mystery: this is, indeed, to blaspheme their Creator after a most impudent manner! It comes to this, therefore, that these men do now consent neither to Scripture nor to tradition.

3. Such are the adversaries with whom we have to deal, my very dear friend, endeavouring like slippery serpents to escape at all points. Wherefore they must be opposed at all points, if perchance, by cutting off their retreat, we may succeed in turning them back to the truth. For, though it is not an easy thing for a soul under the influence of error to repent, yet, on the other hand, it is not altogether impossible to escape from error when the truth is brought alongside it.

16. Irenaeus' Doctrine of Recapitulation

Adv. Haer., 5:19–21, trans. Richardson, *et al.*, *Early Christian Fathers* [LCC, Vol. I], pp. 389–90.

So the Lord now manifestly came to his own, and, born by his own created order which he himself bears, he by his obedience on the tree renewed [and reversed] what was done by disobedience in [connection with] a tree; and [the power of] that seduction by which the virgin Eve, already betrothed to a man, had been wickedly seduced was broken when the angel in truth brought good tidings to the Virgin Mary, who already [by her betrothal] belonged to a man. For as Eve was seduced by the word of an angel to flee from God, having rebelled against his Word, so Mary by the word of an angel received the glad tidings that she would bear God by obeying his Word. The former was seduced to disobey God [and so fell], but the latter was persuaded to obey God, so that the Virgin Mary might become the advocate of the virgin Eve. As the human race was subjected to death through [the act of] a virgin, so was it saved by a virgin, and thus the disobedience of one virgin was precisely balanced by the obedience of another. Then indeed the sin of the first-formed man was amended by the chastisement of the First-begotten, the wisdom of the serpent was conquered by the simplicity of the dove, and the chains were broken by which we were in bondage to death.

Therefore he renews these things in himself, uniting man to the Spirit; and placing the Spirit in man, he himself is made the head of the Spirit, and gives the Spirit to be the head of man, for by him we see and hear and speak.

He therefore completely renewed all things, both taking up the battle against our enemy, and crushing him who at the beginning had led us captive in Adam, trampling on his head, as you find in Genesis that God said to the serpent, "And I will put enmity between you and the woman, and between your seed and her seed; he will be on the watch for your head, and you will be on the watch for his heel." From then on it was proclaimed that he who was to be born of a virgin, after the likeness of Adam, would be on the watch for the serpent's head—this is the seed of which the apostle says in the Letter to the Galatians, "The law of works was established until the seed should come to whom the promise was made." He shows this still more clearly in the same Epistle when he says, "But when the fullness of time was come, God sent his Son, made of a woman." The enemy would not have been justly conquered unless it had been a man

[made] of woman who conquered him. For it was by a woman that he had power over man from the beginning, setting himself up in opposition to man. Because of this the Lord also declares himself to be the Son of Man, so renewing in himself that primal man from whom the formation [of man] by woman began, that as our race went down to death by a man who was conquered we might ascend again to life by a man who overcame; and as death won the palm of victory over us by a man, so we might by a man receive the palm of victory over death.

B. TERTULLIAN (C. 160–C. 220), THE CATH- OLIC INTRANSIGENT AND LATER DEFEC- TOR TO MONTANISM

17. His Summary of the Creed or Rule of Faith

De Praes. Haer., 13, trans. ANF, III, p. 249.

Now with regard to this rule of faith— that we may from this point acknowledge what it is which we defend—it is, you must know, that which prescribes the belief that there is one only God, and that He is none other than the Creator of the world, who produced all things out of nothing through His own Word, first of all sent forth; that this Word is called His Son, *and*, under the name of God, was seen "in diverse man- ners" by the patriarchs, heard at all times in the prophets, at last brought down by the Spirit and Power of the Father into the Virgin Mary, was made flesh in her womb, and, being born of her, went forth as Jesus Christ; thenceforth He preached the new law and the new promise of the kingdom of heaven, worked miracles; having been cruci- fied, He rose again the third day; (then) having ascended into the heavens, He sat at the right hand of the Father; sent instead of Himself the Power of the Holy Ghost to lead such as believe; will come with glory to take the saints to the enjoyment of ever- lasting life and of the heavenly promises, and to condemn the wicked to everlasting fire, after the resurrection of both these classes shall have happened, together with the restoration of their flesh. This rule, as it will be proved, was taught by Christ, and raises amongst ourselves no other questions than those which heresies introduce, and which make men heretics.

18. Denial of the Heretics' Right to the Scriptures

Ibid., 37, trans. ANF, III, p. 261.

Thus, not being Christians, they have acquired no right to the Christian Scrip- tures; and it may be very fairly said to them, "Who are you? When and whence did you come? As you are none of mine, what have you to do with that which is mine? Indeed, Marcion, by what right do you hew my wood? By whose permission, Valentinus, are you diverting the streams of my fountain? By what power, Apelles, are you removing my landmarks? This is my property. Why are you, the rest, sowing and feeding here at your own pleasure? This (I say) is my property. I have long possessed it; I pos- sessed it before you. I hold sure title-deeds from the original owners themselves, to whom the estate belonged. I am the heir of the apostles. Just as they carefully prepared their will and testament, and committed it to a trust, and adjured (the trustees to be faithful to their charge), even so do I hold it. As for you, they have, it is certain, always held you as disinherited, and rejected you as strangers—as enemies."

19. The Christian Tradition on Baptism and Eucharist

De Corona, 3, trans. ANF, III, pp. 94–95. See Tertullian's Apologeticum, 39, in Chap. I, Item 36 of this source book.

Let us inquire, therefore, whether tradi- tion, unless it be written, should not be ad- mitted. Certainly we shall say that it ought not be be admitted, if no cases of other practices which, without any written instru- ment, we maintain on the ground of tradi- tion alone, and the countenance thereafter of custom, affords us any precedent. To deal with this matter briefly, I shall begin with baptism. When we are going to enter the water, but a little before, in the presence of the congregation and under the hand of the president, we solemnly profess that we dis- own the devil, and his pomp, and his angels. Hereupon we are thrice immersed, making a somewhat ampler pledge than the Lord has appointed in the Gospel. Then, when we are taken up (as new-born children), we taste first of all a mixture of milk and honey, and from that day we refrain from the daily bath for a whole week. We take also, in congregations before daybreak, and from the hand of none but the presidents, the sacrament of the Eucharist, which the Lord both commanded to be eaten at meal-times, and enjoined to be taken by all alike. As often as the anniversary comes round, we make offerings for the dead as birthday honours. We count fasting or kneeling in worship on the Lord's day to be unlawful. We rejoice in the same privilege also from Easter to Whitsunday. We feel pained should any wine or bread, even though our own, be cast upon the ground. At every forward step and movement, at every going in and out, when we put on our clothes and shoes, when we bathe, when we sit at table, when we light the lamps, on couch, on seat, in all the ordinary actions of daily life, we trace upon the forehead the sign.

20. His Account of an Ecstatic Vision by a Montanist Woman

De Anima, 9, trans. ANF, III, p. 188.

We have now amongst us a sister whose lot it has been to be favoured with sundry gifts of revelation, which she experiences in the Spirit by ecstatic vision amidst the sacred rites of the Lord's day in the church: she converses with angels, and sometimes even with the Lord; she both sees and hears mysterious communications; some men's hearts she understands, and to them who are in need she distributes remedies. Whether it be in the reading of Scriptures, or in the chanting of psalms, or in the preaching of sermons, or in the offering up of prayers, in all these religious services matter and opportunity are afforded to her of seeing visions. It may possibly have happened to us, whilst this sister of ours was rapt in the Spirit, that we had discoursed in some ineffable way about the soul. After the people are dismissed at the conclusion of the sacred services, she is in the regular habit of reporting to us whatever things she may have seen in vision (for all her communications are examined with the most

scrupulous care, in order that their truth may be probed). "Amongst other things," says she, "there has been shown to me a soul in bodily shape, and a spirit has been in the habit of appearing to me; not, however, a void and empty illusion, but such as would offer itself to be even grasped by the hand, soft and transparent and of an etherial colour, and in form resembling that of a human being in every respect." This was her vision, and for her witness there was God; and the apostle most assuredly foretold that there were to be "spiritual gifts" in the church.

21. Some of His Observations on Marriage

Ad Uxorem, 1:3; 2:8. Selections from *A Source Book for Ancient Church History*, p. 168, by Joseph Cullen Ayer are reprinted with the permission of Charles Scribner's Sons © 1913 Charles Scribner's Sons; renewal © 1941 Joseph Cullen Ayer, Jr. See Item 34 of this chapter in this source book.

I, 3. There is no place at all where we read that marriages are prohibited; of course as a "good thing." What, however, is better than this "good," we learn from the Apostle in that he permits marriage, indeed, but prefers abstinence; the former on account of the insidiousness of temptations, the latter on account of the straits of the times (I Cor. 7:26). Now by examining the reason for each statement it is easily seen that the permission to marry is conceded us as a necessity; but whatever necessity grants, she herself deprecates. In fact, inasmuch as it is written, "It is better to marry than to burn" (I Cor. 7:9), what sort of "good" is this which is only commended by comparison with "evil," so that the reason why "marrying" is better is merely that "burning" is worse? Nay; but how much better is it neither to marry nor to burn?

II, 8. Whence are we to find adequate words to tell fully of the happiness of that marriage which the Church cements and the oblation confirms, and the benediction seals; which the angels announce, and the Father holds for ratified? For even on earth children do not rightly and lawfully wed without their father's consent. What kind of yoke is that of two believers of one hope, one discipline, and the same service? The two are brethren, the two are fellow-servants; no difference of spirit or flesh; nay, truly, two in one flesh; where there is one flesh the spirit is one.

C. ORIGEN OF ALEXANDRIA (C. 185–C. 253/54), THE CHRISTIAN TEACHER

22. His Early Life and Teaching

Eusebius, *Hist. Ecc.*, 6:iii, 1, 3, 8–10, 13, trans. *NPNF*, 2nd ser., I, pp. 251–52.

But while he was lecturing in the school, as he tells us himself, and there was no one at Alexandria to give instruction in the faith, as all were driven away by the threat of persecution, some of the heathen came to him to hear the word of God. . . .

He was in his eighteenth year when he took charge of the catechetical school. He was prominent also at this time, during the persecution under Aquila, the governor of Alexandria, when his name became celebrated among the leaders in the faith, through the kindness and goodwill which he manifested toward all the holy martyrs, whether known to him or strangers. . . .

But when he saw yet more coming to him for instruction, and the catechetical school had been entrusted to him alone by Demetrius, who presided over the church, he considered the teaching of grammatical science inconsistent with training in divine subjects, and forthwith he gave up his grammatical school as unprofitable and a hindrance to sacred learning. Then, with becoming consideration, that he might not need aid from others, he disposed of whatever valuable books of ancient literature he possessed, being satisfied with receiving from the purchaser four oboli a day. For many years he lived philosophically in this manner, putting away all the incentives of youthful desires. Through the entire day he endured no small amount of discipline; and for the greater part of the night he gave himself to the study of the Divine Scriptures. He restrained himself as much as possible by a most philosophic life; sometimes by the discipline of fasting, again by limited time for sleep. And in his zeal he never lay upon a bed, but upon the ground. Most of all, he thought that the words of the Saviour in the Gospel should be observed, in which

he exhorts not to have two coats nor to use shoes, nor to occupy oneself with cares for the future. . . . so that prominent men even of the unbelieving heathen and men that followed learning and philosophy were led to his instruction. Some of them having received from him into the depth of their souls faith in the Divine Word, became prominent in the persecution then prevailing; and some of them were seized and suffered martyrdom.

23. His Doctrine on Cycles of Existence

De Prin., 2:viii, 3, trans. G. W. Butterworth, *Origen on First Principles* (London: SPCK, 1936), p. 126. Items 23–26 reprinted with the permission of the publisher, SPCK.

Those rational beings who sinned and on that account fell from the state in which they were, in proportion to their particular sins were enveloped in bodies as a punishment; and when they are purified they rise again to the state in which they formerly were, completely putting away their evil and their bodies. Then again a second or a third or many more times they are enveloped in different bodies for punishment. For it is probable that different worlds have existed and will exist, some in the past and some in the future . . . .

24. Speculations Concerning the School of Souls (Schola Animarum) and Universal Salvation

De Prin., 1:6, trans. Butterworth, *OFP*, pp. 56–57.

GREEK	LATIN
But I think that, from among those that have been made subject to the worse kind of rulers and authorities and world-powers, in each world or in certain worlds, there are some who, by reason of their good deeds and their desire to be transferred from these powers, will speedily attain manhood	But whether among those orders that live under the chieftainship of the devil and conform to his wickedness there are some who will one day in the ages to come succeed in turning to goodness

by reason of the power of free-will which is in them, or whether it be true that long-continued and deep-rooted wickedness turns at last from a habit into a kind of nature, you, reader, must judge; whether, that is, this portion of the creation shall be utterly and entirely out of harmony even with that final unity and concord, both in the ages that are 'seen' and 'temporal' and in those that are 'not seen' and eternal. But in the meantime, alike in these ages that are 'seen' and 'temporal' and in those that are 'not seen' and 'eternal,' all those beings are arranged in a definite order proportionate to the degree and excellence of their merits. And so it happens that some in the first, others in the second, and others even in the last times, through their endurance of greater and more severe punishments of long duration, extending, if I may say so, over many ages, are by these very stern methods of correction renewed and restored, first by the instruction of angels and afterwards by that of powers yet higher in rank, so that they advance through each grade to a higher one, until at length they reach the things that are 'invisible' and 'eternal,' having traversed in turn, by some form of instruction, every single office of the heavenly powers. It appears to follow from this, in my opinion, that every rational nature can, in the process of passing from one order to another, travel through each order to all the rest, and from all to each, while undergoing the various movements of progress or the reverse in accordance with its own actions and endeavours and with the use of its power of free will.

25. The Threefold Interpretation of the Scriptures

De Prin., 4:ii, 4, trans. Butterworth, *OFP,* pp. 275–76.

4.   The right way, therefore, as it appears to us, of approaching the scriptures and gathering their meaning, is the following, which is extracted from the writings themselves. We find some such rule as this laid down by Solomon in the Proverbs concerning the divine doctrines written therein: 'Do thou pourtray them threefold in counsel and knowledge, that thou mayest answer words of truth to those who question thee.' One must therefore pourtray the meaning

of the sacred writings in a threefold way upon one's own soul, so that the simple man may be edified by what we may call the flesh of the scripture, this name being given to the obvious interpretation; while the man who has made some progress may be edified by its soul, as it were; and the man who is perfect and like those mentioned by the apostle: 'We speak wisdom among the perfect; yet a wisdom not of this world, nor of the rulers of this world, which are coming to nought; but we speak God's wisdom in a mystery, even the wisdom that hath been hidden, which God foreordained before the worlds unto our glory"—this man may be edified by the spiritual law, which has 'a shadow of the good things to come.' For just as man consists of body, soul and spirit, so in the same way does the scripture, which has been prepared by God to be given for man's salvation.

26. Limits to the Literal Interpretation of Scripture

De Prin., 4:iii, 1, trans. Butterworth, *OFP,* pp. 288–90.

1.   Now what man of intelligence will believe that the first and the second and the third day, and the evening and the morning existed without the sun and moon and stars? And that the first day, if we may so call it, was even without a heaven? And who is so silly as to believe that God, after the manner of a farmer, 'planted a paradise eastward in Eden,' and set in it a visible and palpable 'tree of life,' of such a sort that anyone who tasted its fruit with his bodily teeth would gain life; and again that one could partake of 'good and evil' by masticating the fruit taken from the tree of that name? And when God is said to 'walk in the paradise in the cool of the day' and Adam to hide himself behind a tree, I do not think anyone will doubt that these are figurative expressions which indicate certain mysteries through a semblance of history and not through actual events.

Further, when Cain 'goes out from the face of God' it seems clear to thoughtful men that this statement impels the reader to inquire what the 'face of God' is and how anyone can 'go out' from it. And what more need I say, when those who are not altogether blind can collect thousands of such instances, recorded as actual events, but which did not happen literally?

Even the gospels are full of passages of this kind, as when the devil takes Jesus up into a 'high mountain' in order to show him from thence 'the kingdoms of the whole world and the glory of them.' For what man who does not read such passages carelessly would fail to condemn those who believe that with the eye of the flesh, which requires a great height to enable us to perceive what is below and at our feet, the kingdoms of the Persians, Scythians, Indians and Parthians were seen, and the manner in which their rulers are glorified by men? And the careful reader will detect thousands of other passages like this in the gospels, which will convince him that events which did not take place at all are woven into the records of what literally did happen.

27. The Church Warned Against "Stale" Teaching

In Levit. Hom. v. 8 (Lat.), trans. R. B. Tollinton, *Selections from the Commentaries and Homilies of Origen* (London: SPCK, 1929), pp. 177, 178–79.

The Law forbade the Israelites to eat yesterday's meat. So too should stale teaching be avoided in the Church. (In Levit.

Hom. v. 8; Lomm. ix. 258–60; B. vi. 348–50. From the Latin.)

Hearken to this, all ye priests of the Lord; give ye careful attention to what is said. This flesh, which is allotted to the priests from the sacrifices, is the word of God, which they teach in the church. Thus they are warned in this passage, by forms which have mystic meaning, not to bring out yesterday's fare, when they set about to address the people; not to set forth stale doctrines according to the letter, but by God's grace ever to bring forth new truth, ever to discover the spiritual lessons. If you produce to-day in the church what you learned yesterday from the Jews, this is just eating yesterday's flesh in the sacrifice. If you remember, the Lawgiver also uses the

same language in regard to the offering of firstfruits; they must, he says, be fresh and new. Everywhere, you see, what belongs to the praise of God—for this is what the sacrifice of praise means—must be new and fresh, so that there be no risk of your lips speaking but your mind being fruitless, while you produce old teaching in the church.

28. The Nature of Christian Citizenship

Contra Celsum, 8:73, trans. H. Chadwick, *Origen: Contra Celsum* (Cambridge: Cambridge University Press, 1953), p. 509.

73. Then Celsus next exhorts us to *help the emperor with all our power, and cooperate with him in what is right, and fight for him, and be fellow-soldiers if he presses for this, and fellow-generals with him.* We may reply to this that at appropriate times we render to the emperors divine help, if I may so say, by taking up even the whole armour of God. And this we do in obedience to the apostolic utterance which says: 'I exhort you, therefore, first to make prayers, supplications, intercessions, and thanksgivings for all men, for emperors, and all that are in authority.' Indeed, the more pious a man is, the more effective he is in helping the emperors—more so than the soldiers who go out into the lines and kill all the enemy troops that they can.

We would also say this to those who are alien to our faith and ask us to fight for the community and to kill men: that it is also your opinion that the priests of certain images and wardens of the temples of the gods, as you think them to be, should keep their right hand undefiled for the sake of the sacrifices, that they may offer the customary sacrifices to those who you say are gods with hands unstained by blood and pure from murders. And in fact when war comes you do not enlist the priests. If, then, this is reasonable, how much more reasonable is it that, while others fight, Christians also should be fighting as priests and worshippers of God, keeping their right hands pure and by their prayers to God striving for those who fight in a righteous cause and for the emperor who reigns righteously, in order that everything which is opposed and hostile to those who act rightly may be destroyed? Moreover, we who by our prayers destroy all daemons which stir up wars, violate oaths, and disturb the peace, are of more help to the emperors than those who seem to be doing the fighting. We who offer prayers with righteousness, together with ascetic practices and exercises which teach us to despise pleasures and not to be led by them, are cooperating in the tasks of the community. Even more do we fight on behalf of the emperor. And though we do not become fellow-soldiers with him, even if he presses for this, yet we are fighting for him and composing a special army of piety through our intercessions to God.

29. An Apologia for Christian Views of the Present and the Future Life

Con. Cels., 4:10, trans. Chadwick, *OCC*, p. 190.

10. After this again Celsus as usual produces no argument or proof at all, and as though we babbled about God impiously and impurely says: *It is quite clear that they babble about God impiously and impurely.* And he thinks that we do this *to arouse the amazement of the uneducated people,* and that we *do not speak the truth about the punishments* which are necessary *for those who have sinned.* For this reason he compares us to *those in the Bacchic mysteries who introduce phantoms and terrors.* Now concerning the Bacchic mysteries it is for the Greeks to say whether there is a convincing interpretation of them, or if there is nothing of the kind; and Celsus and his associates may listen to them. But we defend our teaching by saying that we are concerned with the improvement of the human race, whether we use threats of punishments which, we have been persuaded, are necessary for the whole world, and probably also not unbeneficial to those who will suffer them, or whether we use promises of what is in store for those who have lived good lives, which include promises of the blessed life after death in the kingdom of God for those worthy to be under His rule.

30. A Further Defense of Christian Eschatology

Con. Cels., 5:14, 15, trans. Chadwick, *OCC*, pp. 274–76. See Item 34 of this chapter of the source book.

14. This is what he says! *It is foolish of them also to suppose that, when God applies the fire (like a cook!), all the rest of mankind will be thoroughly roasted and that they alone will survive, not merely those who are alive at the time but those also long dead who will rise up from the earth possessing the same bodies as before. . . .*

15. See now, to start with, how he pours ridicule upon the idea of the conflagration of the world, which is a doctrine maintained also by some Greeks whose philosophy cannot be despised, and wants to make out that when we teach the doctrine of the world-conflagration we are making God like a cook. He has not realized that according to the opinion of some Greeks (probably borrowing from the very ancient nation of the Hebrews) the fire that is brought on the world is purifying, and it is probable that it is applied to each individual who needs judgment by fire together with healing. The fire burns but does not consume utterly those who have no matter which needs to be destroyed by it, while it burns and does utterly consume those who have built 'wood, hay, or stubble' on the building (as it is allegorically called) by their actions, words, and thoughts. The divine scriptures say that the Lord 'like the fire of a smelting-furnace and like a cleaner's herb' will visit each individual who is in need, because they have been adulterated by the evil flood of matter, as it were, which results from sin; and I say that they need fire which, so to speak, refines those adulterated by copper, tin, and lead. Anyone who is interested may learn these things from the prophet Ezekiel.

That we do not say *God applies fire like a cook,* but that God is a benefactor of those who are in need of pain and fire, the prophet Isaiah will also bear witness, where he is recorded to have said to a sinful nation: 'Because thou hast a coal-fire sit on it; it shall be a help to thee.' The Logos, accommodating himself to what is appropriate to the masses who will read the Bible, wisely utters threatening words with a hidden meaning to frighten people who cannot in any other way turn from the flood of iniquities. Even so, however, the observant person will find an indication of the end for which the threats and pains are inflicted on those who suffer. At the present moment it is enough to quote from Isaiah, 'For my name's sake will I show mine anger, and I will bring my honours upon thee, so that I will not destroy thee.' But we have been compelled to hint at truths which are not suitable for the simple-minded believers who need elementary words which come down to their own level, in order that we may not seem to allow Celsus' attack to pass without refutation when he says *When God applies the fire like a cook.*

D. CYPRIAN (c. 200–258) THE MARTYR, PROTAGONIST OF CATHOLIC UNITY

31. An Apostrophe to the Church's Unity

De Catholicae Ecclesiae Unitate (c. 251), 4–6, trans. ANF, V, pp. 422–23.

If any one consider and examine these things, there is no need for lengthened discussion and arguments. There is easy proof for faith in a short summary of the truth. The Lord speaks to Peter, saying, "I say unto thee, that thou art Peter; and upon this rock I will build my Church, and the gates of hell shall not prevail against it. And I will give unto thee the keys of the kingdom of heaven; and whatsoever thou shalt bind on earth shall be bound also in heaven, and whatsoever thou shalt loose on earth shall be loosed in heaven." And again to the same He says, after His resurrection, "Feed my sheep." And although to all the apostles, after His resurrection, He gives an equal power, and says, "As the Father hath sent me, even so send I you: Receive ye the Holy Ghost: Whose soever sins ye remit, they shall be remitted unto him; and whose soever sins ye retain, they shall be retained;" yet, that He might set forth unity, He arranged by His authority the origin of that unity, as beginning from one. Assuredly the rest of the apostles were also the same as

was Peter, endowed with a like partnership both of honour and power; but the beginning proceeds from unity. Which one Church, also, the Holy Spirit in the Song of Songs designated in the person of our Lord, and says, "My dove, my spotless one, is but one. She is the only one of her mother, elect of her that bare her." Does he who does not hold this unity of the Church think that he holds the faith? Does he who strives against and resists the Church trust that he is in the Church, when moreover the blessed Apostle Paul teaches the same thing, and sets forth the sacrament of unity, saying, "There is one body and one spirit, one hope of your calling, one Lord, one faith, one baptism, one God?"

And this unity we ought firmly to hold and assert, especially those of us that are bishops who preside in the Church, that we may also prove the episcopate itself to be one and undivided. Let no one deceive the brotherhood by a falsehood: let no one corrupt the truth of the faith by perfidious prevarication. The episcopate is one, each part of which is held by each one for the whole. The Church also is one, which is spread abroad far and wide into a multitude by an increase of fruitfulness. As there are many rays of the sun, but one light; and many branches of a tree, but one strength based in its tenacious root; and since from one spring flow many streams, although the multiplicity seems diffused in the liberality of an overflowing abundance, yet the unity is still preserved in the source. Separate a ray of the sun from its body of light, its unity does not allow a division of light; break a branch from a tree,—when broken, it will not be able to bud; cut off the stream from its fountain, and that which is cut off dries up. Thus also the Church, shone over with the light of the Lord, sheds forth her rays over the whole world, yet it is one light which is everywhere diffused, nor is the unity of the body separated. Her fruitful abundance spreads her branches over the whole world. She broadly expands her rivers, liberally flowing, yet her head is one, her source one; and she is one mother, plentiful in the results of fruitfulness: from her womb we are born, by her milk we are nourished, by her spirit we are animated.

The spouse of Christ cannot be adulterous; she is uncorrupted and pure. She knows one home; she guards with chaste modesty the sanctity of one couch. She keeps us for God. She appoints the sons whom she has born for the kingdom. Whoever is separated from the Church and is joined to an adulteress, is separated from the promises of the Church; nor can he who forsakes the Church of Christ attain to the rewards of Christ. He is a stranger; he is profane; he is an enemy. He can no longer have God for his Father, who has not the Church for his mother.

E. BASIL (C. 330–379) CATHOLIC BISHOP, PREACHER, AND SOCIAL SERVANT

32. *Sermon on the Creation According to the Scriptures and Human Science*

Hom. Hex., 1:2, 4, trans. *NPNF*, 2nd ser., VIII, pp. 53–54.

"In the beginning God created the heaven and the earth." I stop struck with admiration at this thought. What shall I first say? Where shall I begin my story? Shall I show forth the vanity of the Gentiles? Shall I exalt the truth of our faith? The philosophers of Greece have made much ado to explain nature, and not one of their systems has remained firm and unshaken, each being overturned by its successor. It is vain to refute them; they are sufficient in themselves to destroy one another. Those who were too ignorant to rise to a knowledge of a God, could not allow that an intelligent cause presided at the birth of the Universe; a primary error that involved them in sad consequences. Some had recourse to material principles and attributed the origin of the Universe to the elements of the world. Others imagined that atoms, and indivisible bodies, molecules and ducts, form, by their union, the nature of the visible world. Atoms reuniting or separating, produce births and deaths and the most durable bodies only owe their consistency to the strength of their mutual adhesion: a true spider's web woven by these writers who give to heaven, to earth, and to sea so weak an origin and so

little consistency! It is because they knew not how to say "In the beginning God created the heaven and the earth." Deceived by their inherent atheism it appeared to them that nothing governed or ruled the universe, and that was all given up to chance. To guard us against this error the writer on the creation, from the very first words, enlightens our understanding with the name of God; "In the beginning God created." What a glorious order! He first establishes a beginning, so that it might not be supposed that the world never had a beginning. Then he adds "Created" to show that that which was made was a very small part of the power of the Creator. In the same way that the potter, after having made with equal pains a great number of vessels, has not exhausted either his art or his talent; thus the Maker of the Universe, whose creative power, far from being bounded by one world, could extend to the infinite, needed only the impulse of His will to bring the immensities of the visible world into being. If then the world has a beginning, and if it has been created, enquire who gave it this beginning, and who was the Creator: or rather, in the fear that human reasonings may make you wander from the truth, Moses has anticipated enquiry by engraving in our hearts, as a seal and a safeguard, the awful name of God: "In the beginning God created"—It is He, beneficent Nature, Goodness without measure, a worthy object of love for all beings endowed with reason, the beauty the most to be desired, the origin of all that exists, the source of life, intellectual light, impenetrable wisdom, it is He who "in the beginning created heaven and earth."

One day, doubtless, their terrible condemnation will be the greater for all this worldly wisdom, since, seeing so clearly into vain sciences, they have wilfully shut their eyes to the knowledge of the truth. These men who measure the distances of the stars and describe them, both those of the North, always shining brilliantly in our view, and those of the southern pole visible to the inhabitants of the South, but unknown to us; who divide the Northern zone and the circle of the Zodiac into an infinity of parts, who

III-1. Left: Latin Fathers Gregory, Augustine, and Silvester. Right: Greek Fathers Basil, Chrysostom, Gregory Nazianzen. *Mosaics, c. 1148, choir of the Cathedral of Cefalù, Sicily.*

observe with exactitude the course of the stars, their fixed places, their declensions, their return and the time that each takes to make its revolution; these men, I say, have discovered all except one thing: the fact that God is the Creator of the universe, and the just Judge who rewards all the actions of life according to their merit. They have not known how to raise themselves to the idea of the consummation of all things, the consequence of the doctrine of judgment, and to see that the world must change if souls pass from this life to a new life. In reality, as the nature of the present life presents an affinity to this world, so in the future life our souls will enjoy a lot conformable to their new condition. But they are so far from applying these truths, that they do but laugh when we announce to them the end of all things and the regeneration of the age. Since the beginning naturally precedes that which is derived from it,

the writer, of necessity, when speaking to us of things which had their origin in time, puts at the head of his narrative these words —"In the beginning God created."

33. *His Social Contributions, Especially, the New City, or Hospital at Constantinople, Evaluated in the Panegyric of Gregory Nazianzen*

Orat., 63, trans. *NPNF*, 2nd ser., VII, p. 416.

What more? A noble thing is philanthropy, and the support of the poor, and the assistance of human weakness. Go forth a little way from the city, and behold the new city, the storehouse of piety, the common treasury of the wealthy, in which the superfluities of their wealth, aye, and even their necessaries, are stored, in consequence of his exhortations, freed from the power of the moth, no longer gladdening the eyes of the thief, and escaping both the emulation of envy, and the corruption of time: where disease is regarded in a religious light, and disaster is thought a blessing, and sympathy is put to the test. . . . My subject is the most wonderful of all, the short road to salvation, the easiest ascent to heaven. There is no longer before our eyes that terrible and piteous spectacle of men who are living corpses, the greater part of whose limbs have mortified, driven away from their cities and homes and public places and fountains, aye, and from their own dearest ones, recognizable by their names rather than by their features: they are no longer brought before us at our gatherings and meetings, in our common intercourse and union, no longer the objects of hatred, instead of pity on account of their disease; composers of piteous songs, if any of them have their voice still left to them. Why should I try to express in tragic style all our experiences, when no language can be adequate to their hard lot? He however it was, who took the lead in pressing upon those who were men, that they ought not to despise their fellowmen, nor to dishonour Christ, the one Head of all, by their inhuman treatment of them; but to use the misfortunes of others as an opportunity of firmly establishing their own lot, and to lend to God that mercy of which they stand in need at His hands. . . . Basil's care was for the sick, and the relief of their wounds, and the imitation of Christ, by cleansing leprosy, not by a word, but in deed.

F. JEROME (C. 340–420), CHRISTIAN SCHOLAR, TRANSLATOR, AND INTERPRETER

34. *He Writes on Origen and Tertullian*

De Inlustr. viri, 53 and 54, trans. NPNF, 2nd ser., III, pp. 373–74.

Who is there, who does not also know that he [Origen] was so assiduous in the study of Holy Scriptures, that contrary to the spirit of his time, and of his people, he learned the Hebrew language, and taking the Septuagint translation, he gathered the other translations also in a single work, namely, that of Aquila, of Ponticus the

Proselyte, and Theodotian the Ebonite, and Symmachus an adherent of the same sect who wrote commentaries also on the gospel according to Matthew, from which he tried to establish his doctrine. And besides these, a fifth, sixth, and seventh translation, which we also have from his library, he sought out with great diligence, and compared with other editions. And since I have given a list of his works, in the volumes of letters which I have written to Paula, in a letter which I wrote against the works of Varro, I pass this by now, not failing however, to make mention of his immortal genius, how that he understood dialectics, as well as geometry, arithmetic, music, grammar, and rhetoric, and taught all the schools of philosophers, in such wise that he had also diligent students in secular literature, and lectured to them daily, and the crowds which flocked to him were marvellous. These, he received in the hope that through the instrumentality of this secular literature, he might establish them in the faith of Christ.

Tertullian the presbyter, now regarded as chief of the Latin writers after Victor and Apollonius, was from the city of Carthage in the province of Africa, and was the son of a proconsul or Centurion, a man of keen and vigorous character, he flourished chiefly in the reign of the emperor Severus and Antoninus Caracalla and wrote many volumes which we pass by because they are well known to most. I myself have seen a certain Paul an old man of Concordia, a town of Italy, who, while he himself was a very young man had been secretary to the blessed Cyprian who was already advanced in age. He said that he himself had seen how Cyprian was accustomed never to pass a day without reading Tertullian, and that he frequently said to him, "Give me the master," meaning by this, Tertullian. He was presbyter of the church until middle life, afterwards driven by the envy and abuse of the clergy of the Roman church, he lapsed to the doctrine of Montanus, and mentions the new prophecy in many of his books.

He composed, moreover, directly against the church, volumes: *On modesty, On persecution, On fasts, On monogamy*, six books

III-2. St. Jerome in His Study. *Jacopo di Paolo da Bologna, Italian, active 1384–1426.*

On ecstasy, and a seventh which he wrote *Against Apollonius.* He is said to have lived to a decrepit old age, and to have composed many small works, which are not extant.

35. His Diffidence at Revising the Old Latin, and Supplying the New Vulgate, Version of the Gospels

Ep. ad Damasum, Praef. (383), trans. *NPNF,* 2nd ser., VI, pp. 487–88.

You urge me to revise the old Latin version, and, as it were, to sit in judgment on the copies of the Scriptures which are now scattered throughout the whole world; and, inasmuch as they differ from one another, you would have me decide which of them agree with the Greek original. The labour is one of love, but at the same time both perilous and presumptuous; for in judging others I must be content to be judged by all; and how can I dare to change the language of the world in its hoary old age, and carry it back to the early days of its infancy? Is there a man, learned or un-learned, who will not, when he takes the volume into his hands, and perceives that what he reads does not suit his settled tastes, break out immediately into violent lan-guage, and call me a forger and a profane person for having the audacity to add any-thing to the ancient books, or to make any changes or corrections therein? Now there are two consoling reflections which enable me to bear the odium—in the first place, the command is given by you who are the su-preme bishop; and secondly, even on the showing of those who revile us, readings at variance with the early copies cannot be right. For if we are to pin our faith to the Latin texts, it is for our opponents to tell us *which;* for there are almost as many forms of texts as there are copies. If, on the other hand, we are to glean the truth from a comparison of *many,* why not go back to the original Greek and correct the mistakes introduced by inaccurate translators, and the blundering alterations of confident but ignorant critics, and, further, all that has been inserted or changed by copyists more asleep than awake? I am not discussing the Old Testament, which was turned into Greek by the Seventy elders, and has reached us by a descent of three steps. I do not ask what Aquila and Symmachus think, or why Theodotion takes a middle course between the ancients and the moderns. I am willing to let that be the true translation which had apostolic approval. I am now speaking of the New Testament. This was undoubtedly composed in Greek, with the exception of the work of Matthew the Apostle, who was the first to commit to writing the Gospel of Christ, and who pub-lished his work in Judaea in Hebrew char-acters. We must confess that as we have it in our language it is marked by discrep-ancies, and now that the stream is dis-tributed into different channels we must go back to the fountainhead. I pass over those manuscripts which are associated with the names of Lucian and Hesychius, and the authority of which is perversely maintained by a handful of disputatious persons. It is obvious that these writers could not amend anything in the Old Testament after the labours of the Seventy; and it was useless to correct the New, for versions of Scripture which already exist in the languages of many nations show that their additions are false. I therefore promise in this short Preface the four Gospels only, which are to be taken in the following order, Matthew, Mark, Luke, John, as they have been revised by a comparison of the Greek manuscripts. Only early ones have been used. But to avoid any great divergences from the Latin which we are accustomed to read, I have used my pen with some restraint, and while I have corrected only such passages as seemed to convey a different meaning, I have allowed the rest to remain as they are.

G. JOHN OF ANTIOCH (CHRYSOSTOM, C. 344/45–C. 407), THE "GOLDEN MOUTHED" PREACHER AND SOCIAL SENSITIZER

36. He Preaches on Christian Ethics Befitting Kingdom Citizens

Ad pop. Antioch., de Statuis (387), Hom. 16: 17, trans. *NPNF*, 1st ser., IX, pp. 451–52.

This homily was delivered on the occasion of the prefect entering the church, for the purpose of pacifying the minds of the people, in consequence of a rumour of an intended sack having been announced to him, when all were meditating flight. It treats also on the subject of avoiding oaths, and on the words of the Apostle, "Paul, a prisoner of Jesus Christ." Philem. 1:1 (Homily XVI Concerning the Statues)

17. And now, it is time that you should be teachers and guides of others; that friends should undertake to instruct and lead on their neighbours; servants their fellow-servants; and youths those of their own age. What if any one had promised thee a single piece of gold for every man who was reformed, wouldest thou not then have used every exertion, and been all day long sitting by them, persuading and exhorting? Yet now God promises thee not one piece of gold, nor ten, or twenty, or a hundred, or a thousand; no, nor the whole earth, for thy labours, but He gives thee that which is greater than all the world, the kingdom of heaven; and not only this, but also another thing besides it. And what kind of thing is that? *He who taketh forth the precious from the vile,* saith He, *shall be as my mouth* (Jer. 15:19). What can be equal to this in point of honour or security? What kind of excuse or pardon can be left to those, who after so great a promise neglect their neighbour's safety? Now if you see a blind man falling into a pit, you stretch forth a hand, and think it a disgraceful thing to overlook one who is about to perish. But daily beholding all thy brethren precipitated into the wicked custom of oaths, dost thou not dare even to utter a word? Thou hast spoken once, perhaps, and he hath not heard. Speak therefore twice, and thrice, and as often as it may be, till thou hast persuaded him. Every day God is addressing us, and we do not hear; and yet He does not leave off speaking. Do thou, therefore, imitate this tender care towards thy neighbour. For this reason it is that we are placed with one another; that we inhabit cities, and that we meet together in churches, in order that we may bear one another's burdens, that we may correct one another's sins. And in the same manner as persons inhabiting the same shop, carry on a separate traffic, yet put all afterwards into the common fund, so also let us act. Whatever advantages each man is able to confer upon his neighbour, let him not grudge, nor shrink from doing it, but let there be some such kind of spiritual commerce, and reciprocity; in order that having deposited every thing in the common store, and obtained great riches, and procured a large treasure, we may be all together partakers of the kingdom of heaven; through the grace and lovingkindness of our Lord Jesus Christ, by Whom and with Whom, to the Father, and the Holy Ghost,

be glory, both now and ever, and world without end. Amen.

37. *His Sermon on Christian Example to the Greeks*

Ibid., Hom. 43:7, trans. *NPNF*, 1st ser., X, pp. 277–78.

"Then certain of the scribes and pharisees answered him, saying, Master, we would see a sign from Thee. But He answered and said, an evil and adulterous generation seeketh after a sign, and there shall no sign be given to it, but the sign of the Prophet Jonas." (Homily XLIII. On Matt. 12:38, 39)

Let us show forth then a new kind of life. Let us make earth, heaven; let us hereby show the Greeks, of how great blessings they are deprived. For when they behold in us good conversation, they will look upon the very face of the kingdom of Heaven. Yea, when they see us gentle, pure from wrath, from evil desire, from envy, from covetousness, rightly fulfilling all our other duties, they will say, "If the Christians are become angels here, what will they be after their departure hence? if where they are strangers they shine so bright, how great will they become when they shall have won their native land!" Thus they too will be reformed, and the word of godliness "will have free course," not less than in the apostles' times. For if they, being twelve, converted entire cities and countries; were we all to become teachers by our careful conduct, imagine how high our cause will be exalted. For not even a dead man raised so powerfully attracts the Greek, as a person practising self-denial. At that indeed he will be amazed, but by this he will be profited. That is done, and is past away; but this abides, and is constant culture to his soul.

H. AUGUSTINE (354–430), THE CATHOLICIZER OF CHRISTIAN DOCTRINE

38. *The Catholicity of the Church*

Serm. 283:3. The translations of items 38–41, 43–44, 47–48, abbreviated as Prz., AS by number and page, are reprinted with the kind permission of the publishers. From *An Augustine Synthesis* by Erich Przywara, published by Sheed & Ward, Inc., New York (1939); also Sheed & Ward, Ltd., London. This item Prz. AS No. 377, pp. 223–24.

The Church is spread throughout the whole world: all nations have the Church. Let no one deceive you; it is the true, it is the Catholic Church. Christ we have not seen, but we have her; let us believe as regards Him. The Apostles on the contrary saw Him, they believed as regards her. . . . They saw Christ, they believed in the Church which they did not see; and we who see the Church, let us believe in Christ, whom we do not yet see.

39. *The Holy Spirit as Soul of the Church*

Serm., 267:iv, 4, trans. Prz., AS, No. 440, p. 255.

If you wish to have the Holy Spirit, mark this well, my brethren. Our spirit by which man is a living being is called the soul, . . . so you see what the soul does in the body. It gives life to all the members; it sees through the eyes, it hears through the ears, it smells through the nostrils, it talks through the tongue, it works through the hands, it walks through the feet; it is present at one and the same time to all the members so that they may live; to each it gives life, to each it assigns its duty. The eye does not hear, nor the ear see, nor the tongue see, nor does the ear or eye talk; but yet it lives, the ear lives, the tongue lives; their duties are diverse, life they share in common. So is the Church of God: in some saints she works miracles, in other saints she preaches the truth, in others she protects virginity, in yet others she preserves conjugal chastity, in some she does one thing, in others another; all do that which is severally proper to them, but all share life in an equal degree. Now what the soul is to the body of man, that the Holy Spirit is in the body of Christ, which is the Church. The Holy Spirit does that in the whole Church, which the soul does in all the members of a single body. . . . If therefore you wish to live by the Holy Spirit, hold fast to charity, love truth, long for unity, so that you may attain to eternity.

40. Behold the Mediator

Serm., 47:xii, 21, trans. Prz., *AS*, No. 296, p. 185.

'The prince in the midst of them' (Ezech. xxxiv, 24). And therefore Mediator of God and Man; since He is God with the Father, man with men: not a man-mediator without a divine nature, nor a God-Mediator without a human nature. Behold the mediator! Divinity without humanity is not a mediator; humanity without divinity is not a Mediator; but between divinity alone and humanity alone there is as mediator the human divinity and the divine humanity of Christ.

41. Lost Man, God-Man, and Grace

Serm. (*de Script., N.T.*), 174:ii, 2, trans. Prz., *AS*, No. 305, pp. 188–89.

Man was lost by free-will; the God-Man came by liberating grace. Dost thou ask what power for evil free-will hath? Call to mind man sinning. Dost thou ask what power to aid He who is God and Man hath? Mark in Him the liberating grace. In no way could it be so shewn what is the power of man's will, if unaided by God, in avoiding evil; it could not be better shewn than in the case of the first man. . . . Verily, in no way doth the benevolence of God's grace and the bounty of His omnipotence so plainly appear as in the Man who is the 'mediator of God and men, the Man Christ Jesus' (I Tim. II 5).

42. Christ as Mediator, Priest, and Sacrifice

De Civ. Dei, 10:6, trans. *NPNF*, 1st ser., II, p. 184.

. . . it follows that the whole redeemed city, that is to say, the congregation or community of the saints, is offered to God as our sacrifice through the great High Priest, who offered Himself to God in His passion for us, that we might be members of this glorious head, according to the form of a servant. For it was this form He offered, in this He was offered, because it is according to it He is Mediator, in this He is our Priest, in this the Sacrifice.

43. The Sacrament of the Body and Blood of Christ

In Joan. Evang., 26:15, 17, trans. Prz., *AS*, No. 400, p. 233.

He would have, then, this meat and drink to be understood as being the fellowship of His body and members, which is the holy Church, in His predestinated and called and justified and glorified saints and His faithful. Of these the first is already effected, namely predestination; the second and third, that is vocation and justification, have taken place, are taking place, and will take place; but the fourth, namely the glorifying, is now in hope, while in the reality it is of the future. The Sacrament of this thing, that is of the unity of the body and blood of Christ, is prepared on the Lord's Table in some places every day, in some places at certain intervals of days, and from the Lord's Table it is taken by some to life, by some to destruction. But the thing itself, of which it is the Sacrament, is for every man to life, for none to destruction, whosoever shall have been partaker thereof. . . . For whilst by meat and drink men seek to attain to this, neither to hunger nor to thirst, there is nothing that truly affords this save only this meat and drink which maketh them by whom it is taken immortal and incorruptible, namely the very fellowship of the saints, where shall be peace and unity full and perfect. For to this end, as men of God before us have also understood, did Our Lord Jesus Christ betoken His body and blood in things which from being many are reduced to some one thing. For out of many grains several are made into one thing and out of many grapes several flow together into one thing.

44. Bread, Wine, Divine Mystery, and Unity

Serm. 272, Prz., *AS*, No. 403, p. 235.

If then you wish to understand the body of Christ, hear what the Apostle says to believers: 'Now you are the body of Christ and members' (1 Cor. xii, 27). If therefore you are the body of Christ and members, your divine mystery is set on the table of the Lord; you receive your mystery. To that which you are, you answer Amen, and by so answering give your assent. For thou hearest, the Body of Christ, that thy Amen may be true. Why then in bread? . . . Let us again and again hear what the Apostle himself says, when speaking of this Sacrament: 'We, being many, are one bread, one body' (*id.* x, 17). Understand and rejoice: unity, truth, piety, charity. One bread, who is this one bread? Being many, one body. Remember that bread is not made of one grain but of many. When you were exorcized, it was as if you were ground in the mill; when you were baptized, it was as if you were moistened with water; when you received the fire of the Holy Spirit, it was as if you were baked. Be what you see and receive what you are. This the Apostle has said about the bread. And what we should understand about the Chalice, though not actually expressed, he sufficiently shows. For just as, in order that the visible shape of bread may exist, many grains are moistened together into one mass, as in the case of the believers, of whom Holy Scripture says, 'they had but one soul and one heart unto God' (Acts iv, 32), so it is with the wine. Brethren, remember from what the wine is made. Many grapes hang on the vine, but the juice of the grapes is mingled into a unity. Thus also has Christ the Lord designated us. He willed that we should belong to Him, and consecrated the mystery of our peace and of our unity on His table.

45. Law, Grace, and Free Will

De correp. et gratia, 2, trans. *NPNF,* 1st ser., V, p. 472.

Now the Lord Himself not only shows us what evil we should shun, and what good we should do, which is all that the letter of the law is able to effect; but He moreover helps us that we may shun evil and do good, which none can do without the Spirit of grace; and if this be wanting, the law comes in merely to make us guilty and to slay us. It is on this account that the apostle says, "The letter killeth, but the Spirit giveth life." He, then, who lawfully uses the law learns therein evil and good, and, not trusting in his own strength, flees to grace, by the help of which he may shun evil and do good. But who is there who flees to grace except when "the steps of a man are ordered by the Lord, and He shall determine his way"? And thus also to desire the help of grace is the beginning of grace; of which, says he, "And I said, Now I have begun; this is the change of the right hand of the Most High." It is to be confessed, therefore, that we have free choice to do both evil and good; but in doing evil every one is free from righteousness and a servant of sin, while in doing good no one can be free, unless he have been made free by Him who said, "If the Son shall make you free, then you shall be free indeed." Neither is it thus, that when any one has been made free from the dominion of sin, he no longer needs the help of his Deliverer; but rather thus, that hearing from Him, "Without me ye can do nothing," he himself also says to Him, "Be thou my helper! Forsake me not."

46. The Nature and Number of the Predestinated

De correp. et gratia, 23, 39, trans. *NPNF,* 1st ser., V, pp. 481, 487–88.

Whosoever, therefore, in God's most providential ordering, are foreknown, predestinated, called, justified, glorified,—I say not, even although not yet born again, but even although not yet born at all, are already children of God, and absolutely cannot perish. . . . From Him, therefore, is given also perseverance in good even to the end; for it is not given save to those who shall not perish, since they who do not persevere shall perish. . . .

I speak thus of those who are predestinated to the kingdom of God, whose number is so certain that one can neither be added to them nor taken from them; not of those who, when He had announced and spoken, were multiplied beyond number.

For they may be said to be called but not chosen, because they are not called according to the purpose.

47. Two Kingdoms, Celestial and Terrestrial

In Ps. 51:4, trans., Prz., AS, No. 464, p. 271.

There is to-day, in this age, a terrestrial kingdom where dwells also the celestial kingdom. Each kingdom—the terrestrial kingdom and the celestial, the kingdom to be rooted up and that to be planted for eternity—has its various citizens. Only in this world the citizens of each kingdom are mingled; the body of the terrestrial kingdom and the body of the celestial kingdom are commingled. The celestial kingdom groans amid the citizens of the terrestrial kingdom, and sometimes (for this too must not be hushed) the terrestrial kingdom doth in some manner exact service from the citizens of the kingdom of heaven and the kingdom of heaven doth exact service from the citizens of the terrestrial kingdom.

48. Two Cities, Two Loves, Selfish and Social

De Gen. ad Litt., 11:xv, 20, trans. Prz., AS, No. 456, p. 266.

There are two kinds of love; of these the one is holy, the other impure; the one is social, the other selfish; the one consults the common good for the sake of the supernal fellowship, the other reducing the affairs of the commonality to their own power for the sake of arrogant domination; the one subject to God, the other endeavouring to equal Him; the one tranquil, the other turbulent; the one working for peace, the other seditious; the one preferring truth to the praise of those who are in error, the other greedy for praise however got; the one friendly, the other envious; the one wishing for the neighbour what it would wish for itself, the other wishing to subject the very neighbour to itself; the one guiding the neighbour in the interest of the neighbour's good, the other in that of its own. . . . These two kinds of love distinguish the two cities established in the human race, . . . in the so to speak commingling of which the ages are passed.

49. The Origins and Destinies of the Two Cities

De Civ. Dei, 14:28, 15:1, trans. *NPNF,* 1st ser., II, pp. 282–83, 284–85.

Accordingly, two cities have been formed by two loves: the earthly by the love of self, even to the contempt of God; the heavenly by the love of God, even to the contempt of self. The former, in a word, glories in itself, the latter in the Lord. For the one seeks glory from men; but the greatest glory of the other is God, the witness of conscience. The one lifts up its head in its own glory; the other says to its God, "Thou art my glory, and the lifter up of mine head." In the one, the princes and the nations it subdues are ruled by the love of ruling; in the other, the princes and the subjects serve one another in love, the latter obeying, while the former take thought for all. The one delights in its own strength, represented in the persons of its rulers; the other says to its God, "I will love Thee, O Lord, my strength." And therefore the wise men of the one city, living according to man, have sought for profit to their own bodies or souls, or both, and those who have known God "glorified Him not as God, neither were thankful, but became vain in their imaginations, and their foolish heart was darkened; professing themselves to be wise,"—that is, glorying in their own wisdom, and being possessed by pride,—"they became fools, and changed the glory of the uncorruptible God into an image made like to corruptible man, and to birds, and four-footed beasts, and creeping things." For they were either leaders or followers of the people in adoring images, "and worshipped and served the creature more than the Creator, who is blessed for ever." But in the other city there is no human wisdom, but only godliness, which offers due worship to the true God, and looks for its reward in the society of the saints, of holy angels as well as holy men, "that God may be all in all.". . . Yet I trust we have already done justice to these great and difficult questions regarding the beginning of the world, or of the soul, or of the human race itself. This race we have distributed into two parts, the one consisting of those who live according to man, the other of those who live according to God. And these we also mystically call the two cities, or the two communities of men, of which the one is presdestined to reign eternally with God, and the other to suffer eternal punishment with the devil. . . . When these two cities began to run their course by a series of deaths and births, the citizen of this world was the first-born, and after him the stranger in this world, the citizen of the city of God, predestinated by grace, elected by grace, by grace a stranger below,—and by grace a citizen above. By grace,—for so far as regards himself he is sprung from the same mass, all of which is condemned in its origin: but God, like a potter (for this comparison is introduced by the apostle judiciously, and not without thought), of the same lump made one vessel to honor, another to dishonor.

50. The City of God Begets Citizens Below

De Civ. Dei, 15:1, trans. *NPNF*, 1st ser., II, p. 285.

For the city of the saints is above, although here below it begets citizens, in whom it sojourns till the time of its reign arrives, when it shall gather together all in the day of the resurrection; and then shall the promised kingdom be given to them, in which they shall reign with their Prince, the King of the ages, time without end.

51. Co-Citizenship with the Angels in the City of God

De Civ. Dei, 10:25, trans. *NPNF*, 1st ser., II, p. 196.

This is the most glorious city of God; this is the city which knows and worships one God: she is celebrated by the holy angels, who invite us to their society, and desire us to become fellow-citizens with them in this city; for they do not wish us to worship them as our gods, but to join them in worshipping their God and ours; nor to sacrifice to them, but, together with them, to become a sacrifice to God.

52. The Character of the Citizenry in the City of God

De Civ. Dei, 15:3, trans. *NPNF*, 1st ser., II, p. 286.

Fitly, therefore, does Isaac, the child of promise, typify the children of grace, the citizens of the free city, who dwell together in everlasting peace, in which self-love and self-will have no place, but a ministering love that rejoices in the common joy of all, of many hearts makes one, that is to say, secures a perfect concord.

53. The Life in the City of God, a Social Life

De Civ. Dei, 19:5, trans. *NPNF*, 1st ser., II pp. 403–4.

We give a much more unlimited approval to their idea that the life of the wise man must be social. For how could the city of God (concerning which we are already writing no less than the nineteenth book of this work) either take a beginning or be developed, or attain its proper destiny, if the life of the saints were not a social life?

54. The Customs of War Tempered by Christian Influence

De Civ. Dei, 1:7, trans. *NPNF*, 1st ser., II, p. 5.

All the spoiling, then, which Rome was exposed to in the recent calamity—all the slaughter, plundering, burning, and misery —was the result of the custom of war. But what was novel, was that savage barbarians showed themselves in so gentle a guise, that the largest churches were chosen and set apart for the purpose of being filled with the people to whom quarter was given, and that in them none were slain, from them none forcibly dragged; that into them many were led by their relenting enemies to be set at liberty, and that from them none were led into slavery by merciless foes. Whoever does not see that this is to be attributed to the name of Christ, and to the Christian temper, is blind; whoever sees this, and gives no praise, is ungrateful; whoever hinders any one from praising it, is mad. Far be it from any prudent man to impute this

III-3. St. Augustine Reading *The City of God. The angel lends divine inspiration. The eagle signifies the profound thought of the saint. The auditory includes people of high rank animatedly discussing the work. King Clovis represents royalty. The City of God appears in the distance.*

clemency to the barbarians. Their fierce and bloody minds were awed, and bridled, and marvellously tempered by Him who so long before said by His prophet, "I will visit their transgression with the rod, and their iniquities with stripes; nevertheless my loving-kindness will I not utterly take from them."

55. *The Misery of War, Even Just War*

> De Civ. Dei, 19:7, trans. NPNF, 1st ser., II, p. 405.

But the imperial city has endeavored to impose on subject nations not only her yoke, but her language, as a bond of peace, so that interpreters, far from being scarce, are numberless. This is true; but how many great wars, how much slaughter and bloodshed, have provided this unity! And though these are past, the end of these miseries has not yet come. For though there have never been wanting, nor are yet wanting, hostile nations beyond the empire, against whom wars have been and are waged, yet, supposing there were no such nations, the very extent of the empire itself has produced wars of a more obnoxious description —social and civil wars—and with these the whole race has been agitated, either by the actual conflict or the fear of a renewed outbreak. If I attempted to give an adequate

III-4. St. Augustine and the City of God, *c.* 1475.

description of these manifold disasters, these stern and lasting necessities, though I am quite unequal to the task, what limit could I set? But, say they, the wise man will wage just wars. As if he would not all the rather lament the necessity of just wars, if he remembers that he is a man; for if they were not just he would not wage them, and would therefore be delivered from all wars. For it is the wrong-doing of the opposing party which compels the wise man to wage just wars; and this wrong-doing, even though it gave rise to no war, would still be matter of grief to man because it is man's wrong-doing. Let every one, then, who thinks with pain on all these great evils, so horrible, so

ruthless, acknowledge that this is misery. And if any one either endures or thinks of them without mental pain, this is a more miserable plight still, for he thinks himself happy because he has lost human feeling.

56. *The Character of Peace and Order*

De Civ. Dei, 19:13, trans. *NPNF,* 1st ser., II, p. 409.

The peace of the body then consists in the duly proportioned arrangement of its parts. The peace of the irrational soul is the harmonious repose of the appetites, and that of the rational soul the harmony of knowledge and action. The peace of body and soul is the well-ordered and harmonious life and health of the living creature. Peace between man and God is the well-ordered obedience of faith to eternal law. Peace between man and man is well-ordered concord. Domestic peace is the well-ordered concord between those of the family who rule and those who obey. Civil peace is a similar concord among the citizens. The peace of the celestial city is the perfectly ordered and harmonious enjoyment of God, and of one another in God. The peace of all things is the tranquillity of order.

57. Peace, and the Social Life of the Heavenly City

De Civ. Dei, 19:17, trans. *NPNF,* 1st ser., II, p. 413.

When we shall have reached that peace, this mortal life shall give place to one that is eternal, and our body shall be no more this animal body which by its corruption weighs down the soul, but a spiritual body feeling no want, and in all its members subjected to the will. In its pilgrim state the heavenly city possesses this peace by faith; and by this faith it lives righteously when it refers to the attainment of that peace every good action towards God and man; for the life of the city is a social life.

I. VINCENT OF LERINS (†C. 450), CRITIC OF ST. AUGUSTINE AND PROTAGONIST OF THE FAITH

58. The Rule for Distinguishing the Truth of the Catholic Faith and Scriptures from Heretical Assumptions

Commonitorium (c. 434), 2:5–6, trans. *NPNF,* 2nd ser., XI, p. 132.

But here some one perhaps will ask, Since the canon of Scripture is complete, and sufficient of itself for everything, and more than sufficient, what need is there to join with it the authority of the Church's interpretation? For this reason,—because, owing to the depth of Holy Scripture, all do not accept it in one and the same sense, but one understands its words in one way, another in another; so that it seems to be capable of as many interpretations as there

are interpreters. For Novatian expounds it one way, Sabellius another, Donatus another, Arius, Eunomius, Macedonius, another, Photinus, Apollinaris, Priscillian, another, Iovinian, Pelagius, Celestius, another, lastly, Nestorius another. Therefore, it is very necessary, on account of so great intricacies of such various error, that the rule for the right understanding of the prophets and apostles should be framed in accordance with the standard of Ecclesiastical and Catholic interpretation.

Moreover, in the Catholic Church itself, all possible care must be taken, that we hold that faith which has been believed everywhere, always, by all. For that is truly and in the strictest sense "Catholic," which, as the name itself and the reason of the thing declare, comprehends all universally. This rule we shall observe if we follow universality, antiquity, consent. We shall follow universality if we confess that one faith to be true, which the whole Church throughout the world confesses; antiquity, if we in no wise depart from those interpretations which it is manifest were notoriously held by our holy ancestors and fathers; consent, in like manner, if in antiquity itself we adhere to the consentient definitions and determinations of all, or at the least of almost all priests and doctors.

59. What to Do in Case of Dissent

Comm., 3:7–8, trans. *NPNF,* 2nd ser., XI, pp. 132–33.

What then will a Catholic Christian do, if a small portion of the Church have cut itself off from the communion of the universal faith? What, surely, but prefer the soundness of the whole body to the unsoundness of a pestilent and corrupt member? What, if some novel contagion seek to infect not merely an insignificant portion of the Church, but the whole? Then it will be his care to cleave to antiquity, which at this day cannot possibly be seduced by any fraud of novelty.

But what, if in antiquity itself there be found error on the part of two or three men, or at any rate of a city or even of a province? Then it will be his care by all means, to prefer the decrees, if such there be, of an ancient General Council to the rashness and ignorance of a few. But what, if some error should spring up on which no such decree is found to bear? Then he must collate and consult and interrogate the opinions of the ancients, of those, namely, who, though living in divers times and places, yet continuing in the communion and faith of the one Catholic Church, stand forth acknowledged and approved authorities: and whatsoever he shall ascertain to have been held, written, taught, not by one or two of these only, but by all, equally, with one consent, openly, frequently, persistently, that he must understand that he himself also is to believe without any doubt or hesitation.

60. Communion with the Universal Church; This the Only Protection Against the Evils Resulting from the Novel Doctrines of the Donatists

Comm., 4:9, trans. *NPNF,* 2nd ser., XI, p. 133.

But that we may make what we say more intelligible, we must illustrate it by individual examples, and enlarge upon it somewhat more fully, lest by aiming at too great brevity important matters be hurried over and lost sight of.

In the time of Donatus, from whom his followers were called Donatists, when great numbers in Africa were rushing headlong into their own mad error, and unmindful of their name, their religion, their profession, were preferring the sacrilegious temerity of one man before the Church of Christ, then they alone throughout Africa were safe within the sacred precincts of the Catholic faith, who, detesting the profane schism, continued in communion with the universal Church, leaving to posterity an illustrious example, how, and how well in future the soundness of the whole body should be preferred before the madness of one, or at most of a few.

61. Children of the Faith to Defend It to the Death

Comm., 33:86, trans. *NPNF,* 2nd ser., XI, p. 156.

Whoever then gainsays these Apostolic and Catholic determinations, first of all necessarily insults the memory of holy Celestine, who decreed that novelty should cease to assail antiquity; and in the next place sets at naught the decision of holy Sixtus, whose sentence was, "Let no license be allowed to novelty, since it is not fit that any addition be made to antiquity;" moreover, he contemns the determination of blessed Cyril, who extolled with high praise the zeal of the venerable Capreolus, in that he would fain have the ancient doctrines of the faith confirmed, and novel inventions condemned; yet more, he tramples upon the Council of Ephesus, that is, on the decisions of the holy bishops of almost the whole East, who decreed, under divine guidance, that nothing ought to be believed by posterity save what the sacred antiquity of the holy Fathers, consentient in Christ, had held, who with one voice, and with loud acclaim, testified that these were the words of all, this was the wish of all, this was the sentence of all, that as almost all heretics before Nestorius, despising antiquity and upholding novelty, had been condemned, so Nestorius, the author of novelty and the assailant of antiquity, should be condemned also. Whose consentient determination, inspired by the gift of sacred and celestial grace, whoever disapproves must needs hold the profaneness of Nestorius to have been condemned unjustly; finally, he despises as vile and worthless the whole Church of Christ, and its doctors, apostles, and prophets, and especially the blessed Apostle Paul: he despises the Church, in that she hath never failed in loyalty to the duty of cherishing and preserving the faith once for all delivered to her; he despises St. Paul, who wrote, "O Timothy, guard the deposit intrusted to thee, shunning profane novelties of words;" and again, "If any man preach unto you other than ye have received, let him be accursed." But if neither apostolical injunctions nor ecclesiastical decrees may be violated, by which, in accordance with the sacred consent of universality and antiquity, all heretics always, and, last of all, Pelagius, Coelestius, and Nestorius have been rightly and deservedly condemned, then assuredly it is incumbent on all Catholics who are anxious to approve themselves genuine sons

of Mother Church, to adhere henceforward
to the holy faith of the holy Fathers, to be
wedded to it, to die in it; but as to the
profane novelties of profane men—to detest
them, abhor them, oppose them, give them
no quarter.

III. Church Historians, Social Critics, and Christian Literati

A. EUSEBIUS OF CAESAREA (C. 263/65–
340), CHURCH HISTORIAN AND ADULATOR
OF THE EMPEROR

62. *Constantine Elevated to the Empire by God*

Vita Const., 1:24, trans. NPNF, 2nd ser., I,
p. 489.

Thus then the God of all, the Supreme
Governor of the whole universe, by his own
will appointed Constantine, the descendant
of so renowned a parent, to be prince and
sovereign: so that, while others have been
raised to this distinction by the election of
their fellow-men, he is the only one to whose
elevation no mortal may boast of having
contributed.

63. *Constantine, Pilot of the Ship of Empire*

Orat. Const., 2:1–5, trans. NPNF, 2nd ser., I,
p. 583.

This only begotten Word of God reigns,
from ages which had no beginning, to infinite and endless ages, the partner of his
Father's kingdom. And [our emperor] ever
beloved by him, who derives the source of
imperial authority from above, and is strong
in the power of his sacred title, has controlled the empire of the world for a long
period of years. Again, that Preserver of the
universe orders these heavens and earth,
and the celestial kingdom, consistently with
his Father's will. Even so our emperor whom
he loves, by bringing those whom he rules
on earth to the only begotten Word and
Saviour renders them fit subjects of his kingdom. And as he who is the common Saviour
of mankind, by his invisible and Divine
power as the good shepherd, drives far away
from his flock, like savage beasts, those apos-

tate spirits which once flew through the
airy tracts above this earth, and fastened
on the souls of men; so this his friend,
graced by his heavenly favor with victory
over all his foes, subdues and chastens the
open adversaries of the truth in accordance
with the usages of war. He who is the pre-
existent Word, the Preserver of all things,
imparts to his disciples the seeds of true
wisdom and salvation, and at once enlightens and gives them understanding in the
knowledge of his Father's kingdom. Our
emperor, his friend, acting as interpreter to
the Word of God, aims at recalling the
whole human race to the knowledge of God;
proclaiming clearly in the ears of all, and
declaring with powerful voice the laws of
truth and godliness to all who dwell on the
earth. Once more, the universal Saviour
opens the heavenly gates of his Father's
kingdom to those whose course is thither-
ward from this world. Our emperor, emulous
of his Divine example, having purged his
earthly dominion from every stain of impious
error, invites each holy and pious worshiper
within his imperial mansions, earnestly desiring to save with all its crew that mighty
vessel of which he is the appointed pilot.

B. SALVIAN (C. 400–C. 480/85), BISHOP
AND EXAGGERATED SOCIAL CRITIC

64. *Roman-Christian Social Life Compared Unfavorably with That of the Barbarians*

De Gub. Dei, 5:4, trans. J. H. Robinson, *Readings in European History* (New York: Ginn &
Co., 1904), I, pp. 28–30.

In what respects can our customs be
preferred to those of the Goths and Vandals, or even compared with them? And
first, to speak of affection and mutual charity
(which, our Lord teaches, is the chief virtue,
saying, "By this shall all men know that ye
are my disciples, if ye have love one to
another"), almost all barbarians, at least
those who are of one race and kin, love
each other, while the Romans persecute
each other. For what citizen does not envy
his fellow-citizen? What citizen shows to
his neighbor full charity?

[The Romans oppress each other with
exactions] nay, not each other: it would be

quite tolerable, if each suffered what he inflicted. It is worse than that; for the many are oppressed by the few, who regard public exactions as their own peculiar right, who carry on private traffic under the guise of collecting the taxes. And this is done not only by nobles, but by men of lowest rank; not by judges only, but by judges' subordinates. For where is the city—even the town or village—which has not as many tyrants as it has curials? . . . What place is there, therefore, as I have said, where the substance of widows and orphans, nay even of the saints, is not devoured by the chief citizens? . . . None but the great is secure from the devastations of these plundering brigands, except those who are themselves robbers.

[Nay, the state has fallen upon such evil days that a man cannot be safe unless he is wicked] Even those in a position to protest against the iniquity which they see about them dare not speak lest they make matters worse than before. So the poor are despoiled, the widows sigh, the orphans are oppressed, until many of them, born of families not obscure, and liberally educated, flee to our enemies that they may no longer suffer the oppression of public persecution. They doubtless seek Roman humanity among the barbarians, because they cannot bear barbarian inhumanity among the Romans. . . .

. . . All the barbarians, as we have already said, are pagans or heretics. The Saxon race is cruel, the Franks are faithless, the Gepidae are inhuman, the Huns are unchaste,—in short, there is vice in the life of all the barbarian peoples. But are their offenses as serious as ours? Is the unchastity of the Hun so criminal as ours? Is the faithlessness of the Frank so blameworthy as ours? Is the intemperance of the Alemanni so base as the intemperance of the Christians? Does the greed of the Alani so merit condemnation as the greed of the Christians? If the Hun or the Gepid cheat, what is there to wonder at, since he does not know that cheating is a crime? If a Frank perjures himself, does he do anything strange, he who regards perjury as a way of speaking, not as a crime?

65. *Christians Charged with Preferring Theaters to Churches*

De Gub. Dei, 6:vii, 35–36, trans. R. T., London, 1700, pp. 171–73.

I cannot forbear, therefore, to return to what I have said often before. What is there like this among the barbarians? Where are there any Cirque-Games among them? Where are their theatres? Where is the abomination of all kinds of impurities, that is, the destruction of our hopes and salvation? And although they, as pagans, did make use of all these, yet their error would be much less culpable in the sight of God; because, although there would be uncleanness in the seeing of them, yet would there be no breach of a sacred obligation.

But as to us, what can we answer for ourselves? We hold the Creed—and yet destroy it; we confess the gift of salvation, and at the same time deny it. And where is our Christianity this while, who have received the sacrament of salvation to no other purpose but that we might transgress afterward with greater sin and wickedness? We prefer plays before the churches of God. We despise the altars, and honour the theatres. We love them all. We respect them all. 'Tis only God Almighty who seems little to us in comparison of them all.

C. CASSIODORUS SENATOR (C. 480/85–573), STATESMAN AND CHRISTIAN MAN OF LETTERS

66. *Some Christian Historians and Their Works Evaluated*

Institutiones, 1:17, trans. L. W. Jones, *An Introduction to Divine and Human Readings by Cassiodorus Senator,* "The Records of Civilization—Sources and Studies," XL, ed. A. P. Evans (New York: Columbia University Press, 1946), pp. 115–19.

1. In addition to the various writers of treatises Christian studies also possess narrators of history, who, calm in their ecclesiastical gravity, recount the shifting movements of events and the unstable history of kingdoms with eloquent but very cautious splendor. Because they narrate ecclesiastical matters and describe changes which occur at various times, they must al-

ways of necessity instruct the minds of readers in heavenly affairs, since they strive to assign nothing to chance, nothing to the weak power of gods, as pagans have done, but to assign all things truly to the will of the Creator. Such is Josephus, almost a second Livy, who is very diffuse in his *Jewish Antiquities,* a prolix work which, in a letter to Lucinus Betticus, Father Jerome says he himself could not translate because of its great size. We, however, have had it laboriously translated into Latin in twenty-two books by our friends, since it is exceedingly subtle and extensive. Josephus has also written with remarkable grace seven other books entitled *The Jewish Captivity,* the translation of which is ascribed by some to Jerome, by others to Ambrose, and by still others to Rufinus; and since the translation is ascribed to men of this sort, its extraordinary merits are explicitly shown. The next work to be read is the history written by Eusebius in Greek in ten books, but translated and completed in eleven books by Rufinus, who has added subsequent events. Among the Greek writers Socrates, Sozomenus, and Theodoretus have written on events subsequent to Eusebius' history; with God's help we have had the work of these men translated and placed in a single codex in twelve books by the very fluent Epiphanius, lest eloquent Greece boast that it has something essential which it judges you do not possess. Orosius, who compares Christian times with pagan, is also at hand, if you desire to read him. Marcellinus too has traversed his journey's path in laudable fashion, completing four books on the nature of events and the location of places with most decorous propriety; I have likewise left his work for you.

2. Eusebius has written chronicles, which are the mere shadows of history and very brief reminders of the times, in Greek; and Jerome has translated this work into Latin and extended it to his own time in excellent manner. Eusebius has been followed in turn by the aforesaid Marcellinus the Illyrian, who is said to have acted first as secretary of the patrician Justinian, but who later, with the Lord's help, upon the improvement of his employer's civil status, faithfully guided his work from the time of the emperor Theodosius to the beginning of the triumphant rule of the emperor Justinian, in order that he who had first been grateful in the service of his employer might later appear to be most devoted during his imperial rule. St. Prosper has also written chronicles which extend from Adam to the time of Genseric and the plundering of the City. Perhaps you will find other later writers, inasmuch as there is no dearth of chroniclers despite the continual succession of one age after another. But when, O diligent reader, you are filled with these works and your mind gleams with divine light, read St. Jerome's book *On Famous Men,* a work whose brief discussion has honored the various Fathers and their works; then read a second book, by Gennadius of Marseilles, who has very faithfully treated and carefully examined the writers on divine law. I have left you these two books joined in a single volume, lest delay in learning the matter be caused by the need of using various codices.

3. The authors of many venerable texts follow. These most learned authors either compose books with divine inspiration, or comfort each other with the easy elegance of letters, or describe the people in a very charming sermon, or strive in an exceedingly lively contest with heretics in such a way that certain ones of their number enter controversies with unusual zeal and contend in the midst of judges with glorious disputation. Thus, with the Lord's help the faithful are strengthened by the destruction of the faithless. You will, then, be able to choose for yourself amid this most holy and most eloquent multitude of Fathers the one with whom you converse most pleasantly. It is, moreover, difficult to state how frequently they effectually reveal the Sacred Scriptures at most suitable points, so that, as you read along, you unexpectedly become acquainted with that which you realize you have carelessly neglected. These most learned authors are extraordinary witnesses because of their various merits, and the ecclesiastical sky shines with them as if with glittering stars.

XVIII. ON ST. HILARY

1. Among their number St. Hilary, bishop of Poitiers, a profoundly subtle and cautious disputant, walks majestically and, reverently bringing the deep mysteries of the Sacred Scriptures before us, with God's help causes the things which were previously veiled in dark parables to be seen clearly.

XIX. ON ST. CYPRIAN

1. It is impossible to explain completely how useful, among other writers, the very blessed Cyprian is (except in the matter of repetition of baptism, which the practice and theory of the Church have rejected); a remarkably skillful declaimer and a wonderful teacher, he is like the ointment that runs down to make all things pleasant. How many doubters he has saved from apostasy! How many apostates he has restored to spiritual health with his very powerful preaching! How many martyrs he has led all the way to martyrdom! And, lest he fail to attain the ideal described in his preaching, he too, with the Lord's aid, was adorned with the crown of martyrdom. Among the other famous monuments of his erudition which he has left us is a little book written with rhetorical charm to explain the Lord's Prayer, which is ever set as an invincible shield against the deceitful vices.

XX. ON ST. AMBROSE

1. St. Ambrose, too, utterer of eloquent speech, impassioned, but dignified, very agreeable in his calm persuasion, a man whose teaching was like his own life, since the divine grace indicated its approval of him by no small miracles. . . .

SUGGESTED READINGS

Altaner, B., *Patrology*, trans. H. C. Graef. New York: Herder & Herder, Inc., 1960.

Battenhouse, R. W., ed., *A Companion to the Study of St. Augustine*. New York: Oxford University Press, Inc., 1955.

Bethune-Baker, J. F., *Introduction to the Early History of Christian Doctrine*, 5th ed. Cambridge: Cambridge University Press, 1933.

Bigg, Charles, *The Christian Platonists of Alexandria*, 2nd ed. New York: Oxford University Press, Inc., 1913.

Blackman, E. C., *Marcion and His Influence*. London: SPCK, 1948.

Case, S. J., *Makers of Christianity*. New York: Holt, Rinehart, and Winston, Inc., 1934.

Chadwick, O., and J. E. L. Oulton, *Alexandrian Christianity*, Library of Christian Classics, Vol. II. Philadelphia: Westminster Press, 1954.

Cochrane, C. N., *Christianity and Classical Culture*. New York: Oxford University Press, Inc., 1940.

Greenslade, S. L., *Early Latin Theology*, Library of Christian Classics, Vol. V. Philadelphia: Westminster Press, 1956.

Kelly, J. W. D., *Early Christian Creeds*. New York: Longmans, Green & Co., Inc., 1950.

————, *Early Christian Doctrines*. New York: Harper & Brothers, 1959.

Lietzmann, H., *The Founding of the Church Universal*. New York: Charles Scribner's Sons, 1938.

McGiffert, A. C., *A History of Christian Thought*, Vol. I. New York: Charles Scribner's Sons, 1932.

van der Meer, F. and C. Morhmann, *Atlas of the Early Christian World*, trans. and ed. by M. F. Hedlund and H. H. Rowley. New York: Thomas Nelson & Sons, 1958.

Quasten, J., *Patrology*, 3 vols. Westminster, Maryland: The Newman Press, 1951–1960.

Runciman, S., *The Medieval Manichee: A Study of the Christian Dualist Heresy*. Cambridge: Cambridge University Press, 1947.

Seeberg, R., *Text-Book of the History of Doctrines*, 2 vols., trans. C. E. Hay. Philadelphia: United Lutheran Publication House, 1905.

CHRONOLOGY

Illustration, page 124: **Representation of an Ancient Benedictine.**

IV

Christian Worship and Contemplation; the Rise of Renunciatory Asceticism and Monasticism

The Church began as a community of worshipers. The word *ecclesia* denoted those called into assembly to pay divine honors. This connotation preceded any suggestion of a constitutionally approved body administering a human organization. Organization at first was virtually nonexistent. The Church in its earliest self-analysis and in its avowed teachings described itself as a *koinonia*, or fellowship, set up on earth from a pre-existent, heavenly world. Its temporal pilgrimage would lead back to its original homeland. Primary loyalty during its sojourn was to the community of heaven, with services to fellow human beings en route. Such organization as was found indispensable naturally elicited a leadership for service. This followed the pattern of the eternal companionship revealed by the Church's founder.

Inevitably, the Church became conscious of itself and of its stake in the human order. It succumbed to the growing demands of social complexity and organizational functions. Officials slowly became consolidated in form and procedure. They continued, however, to project their service in terms of far-off ends. Their activities focused a growing body of interim preoccupations, as well.

Nevertheless, the Church proceeded through the centuries to restate its primary obligation as a worshiping society. Paramount was the voluntary proffering of confession, praise, thanks, and petitions. These were presented to the Eternal *Basileus*, the Great King, the God and Father of Jesus Christ, and of his brethren in the world. Such community in worship did not prevent an ever-widening separation between the people and their clergy. The hierarchy, or rule of priests, soon came to be accepted by the laity as a reflection on earth of the ordered gradations of heavenly administration. Bishops, priests, deacons, and a body of minor officials gradually replaced the more spontaneously evoked prophets, evangelists, and teachers of earlier days.

Basic in this development was the rise of the episcopal office. Almost everything associated with the more pneumatically disparate activities of the old community now came to be grouped under the systematic exercise of the bishop's power. Primitive charismatic gifts and the administrative responsibilities of a more sophisticated pastorate were allocated to him. The teaching authority of one increasingly appealed to as the final arbiter of doctrine and cultic integrity was also granted him. He was looked upon as the successor of the apostles, the vicar of Christ, the representative of God Himself. He was the guarantor of the apostolic tradition, the intermediary between God and man, and the mystagogic indoctrinator for those being initiated into heavenly secrets. Above all, the bishop was the chief hierarch, the great high priest, the offerer on the altar of the eucharistic Body and Blood of Christ. Overseer of things both spiritual and temporal, he was preceptor and judge of the community. He was also the bearer and transmitter of that binding and loosing which activated on earth the mandates of the celestial ordering.

Comparison of the present sources with those in Chapter I reveals a heightened level of worldly wisdom and theological expression. A measure of uneasiness and strain may be detected in the balancing of worship and everyday routines. No compromising of eternal loyalties under temporal pressures is, however, admitted. The increasing difficulty of maintaining proper equilibrium between the love of God and the love of man may be conceded. Yet the worship of Christians and the way in which they regulate their devotional existence still takes precedence over every other activity.

A premium was thus placed upon discipline and regularity in the early church. This applied to the eminent leader borne down with practical decisions. It also governed the specialist courting divine visitations in contemplative retreats. The claims of the habitual, disciplined response were also placed upon the lowliest worshiper in the most secular activities of the workaday world.

The accommodation, however grudging, of the worshiping Christian to his demanding environment was already beginning to be reflected in the *Didache*, in the primitive homilists, and in the more tutored Alexandrians, for example, studied at the outset. The tortuous strains of the world visited upon fourth-century worshipers are clearly evident in the later selections. Still, the avowed foci are much the same. Practical realities, to be sure, are always more excruciatingly balanced against the exactions of non-Christian society.

The leaders of the cult from 300–500 A.D. were able thinkers and active participants in the world scene. They knew the necessity of systematic instruction and habitual worship if the distinctive Christian testimony were to be maintained. Bishop Cyril of Jerusalem realized that spontaneity was a good thing, but that it could not suffice against the bludgeoning routines of everyday life. A deep layer of regular suggestion and habitual response woven into daily experience seemed to him the only safe counter against the insidiousness of subordinate, competing concerns. The Christian community was born and nurtured in *catechesis*. These exercises did not provide set answers for stilted queries. They did stress the quick-witted fitting of understanding to procreative questioning and answering as these were exemplified in the sentencious interplay of Jesus' conversation with his disciples. Worship was not to be guaranteed at the price of hard questions avoided. Nor was it to overlook the painful exigencies of life in conflict with a demanding society. Cyril held Christian experience to be as real and as earnest—if not as spiced with subtle humor—as it had been for the Master. Faith and practice for both were not two things but one profession. Christian action was not forthcoming where there was no established reserve of Christian doctrine and reflection. These placed the distinctive worth of the individual judgment and decision within the supporting motivations of the spiritually disciplining group. Cyril's catechetical lectures were not exactly syllogisms from a professor's notebook. They were a manual of hard-bitten instructions for survival in a seductive world. The Christian credo he held to be the basis of a Christian's participation in reality. It had to be inculcated until it became a habit, not parroted like set questions for an examination.

Similarly, the early Christian preoccupation with eucharistic food was more than a figure of speech. Talk about the nutriment of the sacraments referred to the edification of soul by nourishment on spiritual reality. This true being could be sustained only by the genuine food of Christians—the Lord's Body and Blood.

The extended passages drawn from fourth- and fifth-century liturgy are chosen for their representative qualities. They depict the deepening, versatile expansion of the tradition of worship. These resources document the means taken to habituate both ordinary and unusual personalities to the daily life of devotion. The assumption throughout is that one does not truly learn without professing. Confessing the faith is not possible without the learning that comes from reading, reflecting, repeating, questioning, answering, reconsidering, testing, and applying. The Christian needed the Creed as the wayfarer required food. These thanksgiving morsels of the eucharistic banquet were the hungry soul's "journey bread." The *viaticum* was the sandwich of the *viator*, or pilgrim. His survival called for spiritual and bodily sustenance as well as the "know-how" of heart and mind. Indoctrination for neophytes was practiced to be sure. Societies bent on continuation in hostile or ingratiating surroundings pool their shrewdest experience for replenishing and propagating their group resources.

The Body and Blood of Christ were not eaten in any crass sense. They were the spiritual nourishment of those being recruited and matured into an eternal corporation. Early Church orders permit an intimate glimpse into the objectives and procedures of faithful worshipers. They show how Christians shared their sense of purpose, where they succumbed to hypocrisy, and to what extent they balanced innovation and conservation.

These orders of Christian worship reveal the gathering of a core of tradition that was to be transmitted through the generations. They indicate the inseparability of symbolic expression and realistic faith. The close connection between places of worship and the times and rituals of public prayer are established. The shifting emphases as well as the cumulative habits of worship are put into living connection. Rites, special observances, scripture readings, architectural objectives, aesthetic principles, and the gradations of instruction conducing to group solidarity are all observable. Some of these liturgical collections depict the Eastern, some the Western, usages of the Christian cult. The Egyptian Sacramentary, or prayer book, of Bishop Sarapion is a priceless treasure from a scholar and saint whose name suggests Egyptian mythology but whose friendships were with Athanasius and Anthony. The *Apostolic Constitutions*, called by Easton "the most ambitious of all the Church Orders," collated an entire treasury of earlier legal and liturgical sources to provide a practical manual of church life. The *Didache, Didascalia*, Christian prayers with Jewish models, and a version of Hippolytus' *Apostolic Tradition* are among those freshly edited. They are reset from older Judaeo-Christian experience into the late, fourth-century vitality of an ongoing tradition. These pages are a vivid, if closely edited, documentary on the seasons and liturgical regularity of that day and past eras.

Similarly, the eucharistic treatises of Ambrose, the liturgy of St. Martin, the Psalters of Jerome's Vulgate and the Augustinian quandary over hymnody described in the *Confessions* mine rich deposits of Western liturgy. There was a far-ranging diversity within the Greek tradition. It is suggested by a comparison of the emphases in the Liturgy of St. Chrysostom with that of the Pseudo-Dionysius. The musical innovations developed in the West, most significantly at Milan, provide a commentary on the emergence of St. Augustine from Christian tutelage under St. Ambrose. More dramatically still they provide an example of Christian indoctrination and maturation under a leadership and community participation that was both conserving of old values and brilliantly innovating as needs dictated. Within this liturgical experiment at Milan a rich tradition was being developed. It included scripture reading, preaching, teaching, catechizing, praying, and singing—all with a maximum of community expression. The living history of the Church cannot be assessed apart from such documents.

Ambrose's hymn, "On Cock Crow," may seem naive to the twentieth-century layman and student. One may smile at Augustine's qualms over the possibly deleterious effects of musical joys. Who may safely deride these, however, without a twinge of fellow-feeling? Who, especially, in an age that provides lush harmony and heroically planned discord in such a welter of confusion as ours? Again, Dionysius may not be discussed as a merely irritating antiquarian without doing violence to his great historical influence throughout the Middle Ages. His is an intricate, but nonetheless cogent, analysis of how the sacred gradations of the heavenly world become the pattern for priestly ministrations by the earthly church. In the paraphrases and commentaries of John Scotus Eriugena, especially, this Dionysian recapitulation of the heavenly in relation to the earthly hierarchy became a major inspiration of medieval scholars and churchmen.

There is no intention in this chapter of setting worship over against monasticism. Nor is there a desire either to equate these with mystical experience or to sever them from it. Each of these had historically distinctive connotations. Together they focused the life of prayer and Christian devotion. The renunciants here referred to were far from being negativists or repudiators of a full human existence. Renunciation in its proper gospel context was no minus quantity, no merely negative concept or action. For the worshiper—whether in a parish church, a monastic community, or in mystic solitariness—to renounce was not to seek the obliteration of his true selfhood or to disparage his true humanity. It was, positively, to remove himself from the position of eminence that belongs to God. It was to surrender his selfish preoccupations that mutilated human commerce with the divine. In so doing one placed himself in reverential subordination to the divine will for the divinely ordered end of unobstructed communion with God. Such was the avowed purpose of Christian worship. It was the unifying propensity and the major end of monastic association. For this, one placed himself under discipline (*ascesis*) for the proper structuring of every human thought and action in a hierarchy of positive evaluations and actions. This was the offering of the self without prudential reservations to the divine will, and for divine-human companionship. Such might be forthcoming, out of the bewildering complexities of the usual existence in the world. Again it might grow out of the "common life," that is, the distinctively community vocation of the monastic household. Here and elsewhere one might yearn for, and, if it were God's will, be granted an intimate communion with Divinity. This constituted the contemplative life and the mystic vision, the *visio Dei*.

In Eastern Christianity, ascetic prescriptions sometimes went to individualized extremes. On occasion these approximated a metaphysical dualism of flesh and spirit that recalled gnostic aberrations. The eremitic or hermit life had its special and often legitimate appeal to men like St. Anthony. Pachomius and Basil, however, showed a clear sympathy for the rigors of personal discipline balanced and stabilized within the corporate life of a worshiping community. This was the cenobitic existence, literally that of the common life (*koinos bios*). To this Benedict gave his practicing approval. In so doing he paid tribute to his own experienced regard for eremitic instincts as tutored and sublimated by the more disciplined, communal living. He levied upon the desert Fathers and Western experience as well, with a special affection for the spiritual leadership of Cassian and Basil. Selections drawn from these shrewd Christian practitioners may help explain why.

Benedict placed special emphasis upon the Rule (*Regula*) to be subscribed to by every individual within the disciplining liberation of the monastic community. Here the primary obligations and opportunities were those of the *Opus Dei*, the habitual participation in the Liturgy (*leitourgia*) or divine service, with recurring cycles of prayer, reading, meditation, and manual labor. These regularized activities of mind, body, and spirit were coordinated by an abbot to whom all owed explicit obedience and implicit deference as to God himself. Here the worship of God was central. This was no bureau for the dissemination of humanitarian social service. Specifically, it was a Christian family regulated by its hours of devotion. To worship God was primary. To serve men became as valid a by-product as the second commandment derived from the first. The monastery became, with Benedict, the prime example of the well-regulated family of vocational renunciants. The old Roman genius had stressed unifying principles set to simple practicing virtues. These were at once methodical and moderate. Benedict gave new application under Christian monitoring to these Roman instincts for organizational stability and productive routines.

For Cassian, Basil, and Benedict, as for Gregory the Great and Columban, an orderly life was one that was voluntarily subordinated to God. In the monastic community a well-disciplined society was primarily a community habituated to divine worship. The derivative benefits to the world at large from Columban's monastic missions and from Gregory's also was a dividend from the larger investment. Through the earlier Christian centuries this was understood fairly well, though it has long since tended toward increasing distortions. The chief role of the monk was to set up a research institute for specialized service. Its distinctive specialism was prayer to God. When no instrumental considerations obtruded themselves, this community of spiritual researchers benefited all mankind by intercessory prayers and vicarious efforts arising from it. They did not have to prove the validity for the world of their "monastic withdrawal." Their validation was in their dedicated community of service to God—first, last, and always. Outer ministries simply footnoted that dedication.

The perusal of Rules such as Benedict's and Columban's will show how different, yet how alike, are the conditionings of the monastic habit. The little and even picayune considerations of daily institutional rigor help to make understandable the more dramatic dedications of Benedictine and Irish missions.

In a sense, the early centuries had a point in seeking within monasticism a substitute for the old martyr testimony. This witness, normally "one without blood," was one where blood told. Only the graduated renunciant, one habituated to spiritual routines under inspiring dedications, might be depended upon to preserve the true hierarchy of human values. He, alone, who was bred in the sublimation of lesser desires for the service of uncalculating devotion, might be expected to "witness" for others, also, in the service of God.

There was a real danger in earlier Christian tendencies to think of humanity as divided into workers, fighters, and prayers; just as there was certainly peril in classifying them later as top-priority scientists, day-laborers, and professional men. Officially at least, the Church did not declare monks to be truer worshipers than ordinary mortals, any more than it called virginity good and marriage bad. These were thought of as specialized functions and vocations that were intended to safeguard the necessary integrity of all Christians. Inevitably, the popular mind did deduce, without serious official rebuke, that special rewards followed the higher life of vocational renunciation.

Regularity in worship has produced distinctive Christian fruitage throughout Christian history. This has by no means been limited to monastics. A goodly proportion of spiritual leaders has, quite understandably, emanated from these outstanding centers of devotional regularity. It is certainly no accident that many, though by no means all, practicing contemplatives have come from the regulated devotions of monastic life. Still, one did not have to be a monk to be a mystic; nor would being a monk guarantee contemplative attainments. Contemplation was a gift of God, not an earned reward. Significantly enough, however, monastic habitude was held to be an excellent training for mystic receptivity to the divinely initiated graces.

Some early Eastern fathers stressed the theoretical purity of the contemplative summit (*theoria*) in conjunction with moral purity and the renounced life of the virtues (*apatheia*). In pure, perpetual prayer as the monastic life knew it, *theoria* and *apatheia* were united. Action and contemplation were joined in true Christian practice. Outside the monastery and beyond any particular contemplative retreat, the genuine Christian might be given the divine vocation. God might choose whom he would to walk alone with him in silent communion and to praise him in the company of the righteous.

Unfortunately, good words with clearly delimited usage have a way of slipping out of historical focus. Recent generations have some quite oversimplified connotations in street and classroom for Christian terms that deserve a better fate. Thus "theory," "practice," "monastic retreat," "normal" activities, social "apathy," "mystical visionaries," "humanitarian concern," and a host of other built-in value judgments are rife. Too often these are united to current usages as if others from Stoic, early Christian, and medieval

times had never been. "Mysticism," especially, needs rescuing from its contemporary morass of meanings. "Contemplation" fares scarcely better. The sources at the end of this chapter seek to familiarize the reader with terminologies in living historical contexts. Sometimes this is the only feasible corrective for unduly pre-empted meanings.

In résumé, however, the honest inquirer into Christian history must be prepared to know the inflections given specific words and concepts, not only by his own era but by others who used them with equally good right. This chapter requires that words like worship, liturgy, Opus Dei, sacrament, hierarchy, contemplation, mysticism, Regula, asceticism, and evangelical poverty be put in historical perspective. Latin and Greek words are not injected artificially, but neither are they withdrawn because their current English use is patronizingly reserved for our own special ends. In the process, it may be well to remember that the drab work of the world as well as the exciting liberation of new lands to conversion, civilization, and commercial exploitation were not always, or even mainly, the contributions of the worldly-wise. Predominantly, the most realistic confrontation of crucial events with solid principles in the Middle Ages was the work of graduates "regulated" by the cenobium. They had been conditioned by habit to improvise feasible action in a skeptical or even hostile world. How much their "contemplation" resulted in "action," and why their "action" so often led back to "contemplation," the sources themselves must help to clarify.

I. Worship and the Sacraments from c. 300–500

A. CYRIL OF JERUSALEM (C. 315–386)

1. On Learning and Professing the Faith

Catecheses (c. 398), 5:12, trans. *NPNF*, 2nd ser., VII, p. 32.

But in learning the Faith and in professing it, acquire and keep that only, which is now delivered to thee by the Church, and

IV-1. Interior of Old St. Peter's, Rome, early 4th Century. *Portion of a Renaissance fresco in S. Martino ai Monti, Rome.*

which has been built up strongly out of all the Scriptures. For since all cannot read the Scriptures, some being hindered as to the knowledge of them by want of learning, and others by a want of leisure, in order that the soul may not perish from ignorance, we comprise the whole doctrine of the Faith in a few lines. This summary I wish you both to commit to memory when I recite it, and to rehearse it with all diligence among yourselves, not writing it out on paper, but engraving it by the memory upon your heart, taking care while you rehearse it that no Catechumen chance to overhear the things which have been delivered to you. I wish you also to keep this as a provision through the whole course of your life, and beside this to receive no other, neither if we ourselves should change and contradict our present teaching, nor if an adverse angel, *transformed into an angel of light*, should wish to lead you astray. *For though we or an angel from heaven preach to you any other gospel than that ye have received, let him be to you* anathema. So for the present listen while I simply say the Creed, and commit it to memory; but at the proper season expect the confirmation out of Holy Scripture of each part of the contents.

2. On the Eucharistic Food

Myst. Cat. 4:1–9, trans. R. W. Church, *LF* (1838).

I COR. 11:23

I have received of the Lord that which also I delivered unto you, That the Lord Jesus, the same night in which He was betrayed, took bread, &c.

1. This teaching of the Blessed Paul is alone sufficient to give you a full assurance concerning those Divine Mysteries, which when ye are vouchsafed, ye are of *the same body* and blood with Christ. For he has just distinctly said, *That our Lord Jesus Christ the same night in which He was betrayed, took bread, and when He had given thanks*

131

He brake it, and said, Take, eat, this is My Body: and having taken the cup and given thanks, He said, Take, drink, this is My Blood. Since then He Himself has declared and said of the Bread, *This is My Body,* who shall dare to doubt any longer? And since He has affirmed and said, *This is My Blood,* who shall ever hesitate, saying, that it is not His blood?

2. He once turned water into wine, in Cana of Galilee, at His own will, and is it incredible that He should have turned wine into blood? That wonderful work He miraculously wrought, when called to an earthly marriage; and shall He not much rather be acknowledged to have bestowed the fruition of His Body and Blood on the children of the bridechamber?

3. Therefore with fullest assurance let us partake as of the Body and Blood of Christ: for in the figure of Bread is given to thee His Body, and in the figure of Wine His Blood; that thou by partaking of the Body and Blood of Christ, mightest be made of the same body and the same blood with Him. For thus we come to bear Christ in us, because His Body and Blood are diffused through our members; thus it is that, according to the blessed Peter, *we become partakers of the divine nature.*

4. Christ on a certain occasion discoursing with the Jews said, *Except ye eat My flesh and drink My blood, ye have no life in you.* They not receiving His saying spiritually were offended, and went backward, supposing that He was inviting them to eat flesh.

5. Even under the Old Testament there was shew-bread; but this as it belonged to the Old Testament, came to an end; but in the New Testament there is the Bread of heaven, and the Cup of salvation, sanctifying soul and body; for as the Bread has respect to our body, so is the Word appropriate to our soul.

6. Contemplate therefore the Bread and Wine not as bare elements, for they are, according to the Lord's declaration, the Body and Blood of Christ; for though sense suggests this to thee, let faith stablish thee. Judge not the matter from taste, but from faith be fully assured without misgiving,

that thou hast been vouchsafed the Body and Blood of Christ.

7. The blessed David also shall advise thee the meaning of this, saying, *Thou hast prepared a table before me in the presence of mine enemies.* What he says, is to this effect. Before Thy coming, evil spirits prepared a table for men, foul and polluted and full of all devilish influence; but since Thy coming, O Lord, *Thou hast prepared a table before me.* When the man says to God, *Thou hast prepared before me a table,* what other does he mean but that mystical and spiritual Table, which God hath prepared *over against,* that is, contrary and in opposition to the evil spirits? And very truly; for that had fellowship with devils, but this, with God. *Thou has anointed my head with oil.* With oil He anointed thine head upon thy forehead, by the seal which thou hast of God; that thou mayest be made *the impression of the seal, Holiness of God.* And *my cup runneth over.* Thou seest that cup here spoken of, which Jesus took in His hands, and gave thanks, and said, *This is My blood, which is shed for many for the remission of sins.*

8. Therefore Solomon also, pointing at this grace, says in Ecclesiastes, *Come hither, eat thy bread with joy,* (that is, the spiritual bread; *Come hither,* calling with words of salvation and blessing,) *and drink thy wine with a merry heart;* (that is, the spiritual wine;) *and let thy head lack no ointment,* (thou seest he alludes even to the mystic Chrism;) *and let thy garments be always white, for God now accepteth thy works;* for before thou camest to Baptism, thy works were *vanity of vanities.* But now, having put off thy old garments, and put on those which are spiritually white, thou must be continually robed in white; we mean not this, that thou must always wear white raiment; but with truly white and glistering and spiritual attire, thou must be clothed withal, that thou mayest say with the blessed Esaias, *My soul shall be joyful in my God; for He hath clothed me with the garments of salvation, He hath covered me with the robe of gladness.*

9. These things having learnt, and being fully persuaded that what seems bread is

IV-2. Interior, Church of St. Ambrose, Milan, 8th and 9th Century.

not bread, though bread by taste, but the Body of Christ; and that what seems wine is not wine, though the taste will have it so, but the Blood of Christ; and that of this David sung of old, saying, *And bread which strengtheneth man's heart, and oil to make his face to shine,* 'strengthen thine heart,' partaking thereof as spiritual, and 'make the face of thy soul to shine.' And so having it unveiled by a pure conscience, mayest thou *behold as in a glass the glory of the Lord,* and proceed from *glory to glory,* in Christ Jesus our Lord:—To whom be honour, and might, and glory, for ever and ever. Amen.

B. AMBROSE OF MILAN (c. 339/40–397)

3. Concerning the Sacrament of Christ's Body and Blood

De Sacram., 4, v, 21–23; 4, vi, 26–27, trans. and ed. T. Thompson and J. H. Srawley, *St. Ambrose On the Sacraments and On the Mysteries* (London: SPCK, 1950), pp. 90–91, 92–93.

21. Wilt thou know that it is consecrated by heavenly words? Hear what the words are. The priest speaks. "Make for us," he says, "this oblation approved, ratified, reasonable, acceptable, seeing that it is the figure of the body and blood of our Lord Jesus Christ, who the day before he suffered

took bread in his holy hands, and *looked up to heaven* to thee, holy Father, almighty, everlasting God, and *giving thanks, he blessed, brake, and* having broken, delivered it *to* his *apostles* and *to his disciples, saying, Take, and eat* ye all of this; for *this is my body, which shall be broken for many.*

22. "*Likewise* also *after supper,* the day before he suffered he *took the cup, looked up to heaven* to thee, holy Father, almighty, everlasting God, and *giving thanks,* blessed it and delivered it to his apostles and to his disciples, *saying, Take, and drink ye all of this; for this is my blood.*" Observe all those expressions. Those words are the Evangelists' up to *Take,* whether the body or the blood. After that they are the words of Christ: *Take, and drink ye all of this; for this is my blood.* And observe them in detail.

23. *Who the day before he suffered,* he says, *in his holy hands took bread.* Before it is consecrated, it is bread, but when the words of Christ have been added, it is the body of Christ. Therefore hear him saying: *Take and eat ye all of it; for this is my body.* And before the words of Christ it is a cup full of wine and water. When the words of Christ have operated, then and there it is made to be the blood of Christ which redeemed the people. Therefore, see in how

133

many ways the word of Christ is mighty to change all things. There the Lord Jesus himself testifies to us that we receive his body and blood. Ought we to doubt of his trustworthiness and testimony? . . .

26. But that thou mayest know that this is a sacrament, it was prefigured beforehand. Then learn how great is the sacrament. See what he says: *As often as ye do this, so often will ye make a memorial of me until I come again.*

27. And the priest says: "Therefore having in remembrance his most glorious passion and resurrection from the dead and ascension into heaven, we offer to thee this spotless offering, reasonable offering, unbloody offering, this holy bread and cup of eternal life: and we ask and pray that thou wouldst receive this oblation on thy altar on high by the hands of thy angels, as thou didst vouchsafe to receive the presents of thy righteous servant Abel, and the sacrifice of our patriarch Abraham, and that which the high priest Melchizedek offered to thee."

C. BISHOP SARAPION OF THMUIS (†c. 362)

4. Eucharistic Anaphora

Sacramentary (c. 350–356), I, 1–4, trans. J. Wordsworth, *Bishop Sarapion's Prayer Book* (London: SPCK, 1923), pp. 60–66.

1. *Offertory Prayer of Bishop Sarapion.*

[A. PREFACE]

It is meet and right to praise, to hymn, to glorify thee the uncreated Father of the only-begotten Jesus Christ. We praise thee, O uncreated God, who art unsearchable, ineffable, incomprehensible by any created substance. We praise thee who are known of thy Son (St. Matt. xi. 27; St. John x. 14, 15), the only-begotten, who through him art spoken of and interpreted and made known to created nature. We praise thee who knowest the Son and revealest to the Saints the glories that are about him: who art known of thy begotten Word, and art brought to the sight and interpreted to the understanding

IV-3. Interior, St. Paul Outside the Walls, 4th Century, Rome. *Etching by G. B. Piranesi, 1749.*

of the Saints. We praise thee, O unseen Father, provider of immortality. Thou art the fount of life, the fount of light, the fount of all grace and all truth, O lover of men, O lover of the poor, who reconcilest thyself to all, and drawest all to thyself through the advent (ἐπιδημία) of thy beloved Son. We beseech thee make us living men. Give us a spirit of light, that "we may know thee the true [God] and him whom thou didst send, (even) Jesus Christ" (St. John xvii. 3). Give us holy Spirit, that we may be able to tell forth and to enuntiate thy unspeakable mysteries. May the Lord Jesus speak in us and holy Spirit, and hymn thee through us.

For thou art "far above all rule and authority and power and dominion, and every name that is named, not only in this world but also in that which is to come" (Eph. i. 21). Beside thee stand thousand thousands and myriad myriads of angels (Dan. vii. 10; Heb. xii. 22), archangels, thrones, dominions, principalities, powers (*lit.* rules, authorities): by thee stand the two most honourable six-winged seraphim, with two wings covering the face, and with two the feet, and with two flying and crying holy (ἀγιάζοντα, *cp.* Isa. vi. 2, 3), with whom receive also our cry of "holy" (ἀγιασμόν) as we say: Holy, holy, holy, Lord of Sabaoth, full is the heaven and the earth of thy glory.

[B. OBLATION AND RECITAL OF THE INSTITUTION]

Full is the heaven, full also is the earth of thy excellent glory. Lord of Hosts (*lit.* powers), fill also this sacrifice with thy power and thy participation (μεταλήψεως): for to thee have we offered this living sacrifice (Rom. xii. 1), this bloodless oblation (*cp.* Eph. v. 2). To thee we have offered this bread the likeness (ὁμοίωμα) of the body of the only-begotten. This bread is the likeness of the holy body, because the Lord Jesus Christ in the night in which he was betrayed took bread and broke and gave to his disciples saying, "Take ye and eat, this is my body which is being broken for you for remission of sins" (cp. *Lit. of St. Mark, etc.*). Wherefore we also making the likeness of the death have offered the bread, and beseech thee through this sacrifice, be reconciled to all of us and be merciful, O God of truth: and as this bread had been scattered on the top of the mountains and gathered together came to be one, so also gather thy holy Church out of every nation and every country and every city and village and house and make one living catholic church. We have offered also the cup, the likeness of the blood, because the Lord Jesus Christ, taking a cup after supper (Luc. xxii. 20; I Cor. xi. 25), said to his own disciples, "Take ye, drink, this is the new covenant, which (ὅ) is my blood, which is being shed for you for remission of sins (ἁμαρτημάτων)." Wherefore we have also offered the cup, presenting a likeness of the blood.

[C. INVOCATION OF THE LOGOS]

O God of truth, let thy holy Word come upon this bread (ἐπιδημησάτω...ἐπὶ τ.ἀ.τ.) that the bread may become body of the Word, and upon this cup that the cup may become blood of the Truth; and make all who communicate to receive a medicine of life for the healing of every sickness and for the strengthening of all advancement and virtue, not for condemnation, O God of truth, and not for censure and reproach. For we have invoked thee, the uncreated, through the only-begotten in holy Spirit.

[D. INTERCESSION FOR THE LIVING]

Let this people receive mercy, let it be counted worthy of advancement, let angels be sent forth as companions to the people for bringing to naught of the evil one and for establishment of the Church.

[E. INTERCESSION FOR THE DEPARTED]

We intercede also on behalf of all who have been laid to rest, whose memorial we are making.

After the recitation (ὑποβολήν) *of the names:* Sanctify these souls: for thou knowest all. Sanctify all (souls) laid to rest in the Lord. And number them with all thy holy powers and give to them a place and a mansion in thy kingdom.

[F. PRAYER FOR THOSE WHO HAVE OFFERED]

Receive also the thanksgiving (eucharist) of the people, and bless those who have offered the offerings (τὰ πρόσφορα) and the thanksgivings, and grant health and soundness and cheerfulness and all advancement of soul and body to this whole people through the only-begotten Jesus Christ in holy Spirit; as it was and is and shall be to generations of generations and to all the ages of the ages. Amen.

[G. THE LORD'S PRAYER?]
[THE MANUAL ACTS AND COMMUNION]

2. *After the [Lord's?] prayer (comes) the fraction, and in the fraction a prayer.*

Count us worthy of this communion also, O God of truth, and make our bodies to contain purity (χωρῆσαι ἁγνείαν) and our souls prudence and knowledge. And make us wise, O God of compassions, by the participation of the body and the blood, because through thy only-begotten to thee (is) the glory and the strength in holy Spirit, now and to all the ages of the ages. Amen.

[THE INCLINATION]

3. *After giving the fraction (i.e. the broken bread) to the clerics, imposition of hands (i.e. Benediction) of the people.*

I stretch out the hand upon this people and pray that the hand of the truth may be stretched out and blessing given to this people on account of thy loving kindness (φιλανθρωπίαν), O God of compassions, and the mysteries that are present. May a hand of piety and power and sound discipline (σωφρονισμοῦ) and cleanness and all holiness bless this people, and continually preserve it to advancement and improvement through thy only-begotten Jesus Christ in holy Spirit both now and to all (the) ages of the ages. Amen.

[POST COMMUNION PRAYER]

4. *After the distribution of (i.e. to) the people (is this) prayer.*

We thank thee, Master, that thou hast called those who have erred, and hast taken to thy self those who have sinned, and hast set aside the threat that was against us, giving indulgence by thy loving kindness, and wiping it away by repentance, and casting it off by the knowledge that regards thyself (τῇ πρὸς σὲ γνώσει ἀποβαλών). We give thanks to thee, that thou hast given us communion of (the) body and blood. Bless us, bless this people, make us to have a part with the body and the blood through thy only-begotten Son, through whom to thee (is) the glory and the strength in holy Spirit both now and ever and to all the ages of the ages. Amen.

D. ST. MARTIN OF TOURS (316–400) AND HIS LITURGY (C. 370–378)

5. *His Catechumenate and Baptism*

Vincent of Lerins, *Vita Martini*, 3, trans. *NPNF*, 2nd ser., XI, p. 5. See sources in Chap. IX.

Accordingly, at a certain period, when he had nothing except his arms and his simple military dress, in the middle of winter, a winter which had shown itself more severe than ordinary, so that the extreme cold was proving fatal to many, he happened to meet at the gate of the city of Amiens a poor man destitute of clothing. He was entreating those that passed by to have compassion upon him, but all passed the wretched man without notice, when Martin, that man full of God, recognized that a being to whom others showed no pity, was, in that respect, left to him. Yet, what should he do? He had nothing except the cloak in which he was clad, for he had already parted with the rest of his garments for similar purposes. Taking, therefore, his sword with which he was girt, he divided his cloak into two equal parts, and gave one part to the poor man, while he again clothed himself with the remainder. Upon this, some of the by-standers laughed, because he was now an unsightly object, and stood out as but partly dressed. Many, however, who were of sounder understanding, groaned deeply because they themselves had done nothing similar. They especially felt this, because, being possessed of more than Martin, they could have clothed the poor man without reducing themselves to nakedness. In the following night, when Martin had resigned himself to sleep, he had a vision of Christ arrayed in that part of his cloak with which he had clothed the poor man. He contemplated the Lord with the greatest attention, and was told to own as his the robe which he had given. Ere long, he heard Jesus saying with a clear voice to the multitude of angels standing round—"Mar-

IV-4. Interior, S. Maria Maggiore, 432–440 A.D. *Ceiling c. 1500.*

tin, who is still but a catechumen, clothed me with this robe." The Lord, truly mindful of his own words (who had said when on earth—"Inasmuch as ye have done these things to one of the least of these, ye have done them unto me"), declared that he himself had been clothed in that poor man; and to confirm the testimony he bore to so good a deed, he condescended to show him himself in that very dress which the poor man had received. After this vision the sainted man was not puffed up with human glory, but, acknowledging the goodness of God in what had been done, and being now of the age of twenty years, he hastened to receive baptism. He did not, however, all at once, retire from military service, yielding to the entreaties of his tribune, whom he admitted to be his familiar tent-companion. For the tribune promised that, after the period of his office had expired, he too would retire from the world. Martin, kept back by the expectation of this event, continued, although but in name, to act the part of a soldier, for nearly two years after he had received baptism.

E. **CONSTITUTIONS OF THE HOLY APOSTLES** (c. 375/400)

6. *The Church, the Clergy, and the Assembly for Worship*

Constit. Apost., 2, vii, 57, trans. ANF, VII, pp. 421–22.

But be thou, O bishop, holy, unblameable, no striker, not soon angry, not cruel; but a builder up, a converter, apt to teach, forbearing of evil, of a gentle mind, meek, long-suffering, ready to exhort, ready to comfort, as a man of God.

When thou callest an assembly of the Church as one that is the commander of a great ship, appoint the assemblies to be made with all possible skill, charging the deacons as mariners to prepare places for the brethren as for passengers, with all due care and decency. And first, let the building be long, with its head to the east, with its vestries on both sides at the east end, and so it will be like a ship. In the middle let the bishop's throne be placed, and on each side of him let the presbytery sit down; and let

IV-5. Sanctuary of San Vitale, 6th Century Ravenna.

the deacons stand near at hand, in close and small girt garments, for they are like the mariners and managers of the ship: with regard to these, let the laity sit on the other side, with all quietness and good order. And let the women sit by themselves, they also keeping silence. In the middle, let the reader stand upon some high place: let him read the books of Moses, of Joshua the son of Nun, of the Judges, and of the Kings and of the Chronicles, and those written after the return from the captivity; and besides these, the books of Job and of Solomon, and of the sixteen prophets. But when there have been two lessons severally read, let some other person sing the hymns of David, and let the people join at the conclusions of the verses. Afterwards let our Acts be read, and the Epistles of Paul our fellow-worker, which he sent to the churches under the conduct of the Holy Spirit; and afterwards let a deacon or a presbyter read the Gospels, both those which I Matthew and John have delivered

to you, and those which the fellow-workers of Paul received and left to you, Luke and Mark. And while the Gospel is read, let all the presbyters and deacons, and all the people, stand up in great silence; for it is written: "Be silent, and hear, O Israel." And again: "But do thou stand there, and hear." In the next place, let the presbyters one by one, not all together, exhort the people, and the bishop in the last place, as being the commander. Let the porters stand at the entries of the men, and observe them. Let the deaconesses also stand at those of the women, like shipmen. For the same description and pattern was both in the tabernacle of the testimony and in the temple of God. But if any one be found sitting out of his place, let him be rebuked by the deacon, as a manager of the foreship, and be removed into the place proper for him; for the Church is not only like a ship, but also like a sheepfold. For as the shepherds place all the brute creatures distinctly, I mean goats and sheep, according to their kind and age, and still every one runs together, like to his like; so is it to be in the Church. Let the young persons sit by themselves, if there be a place for them; if not, let them stand upright. But let those that are already stricken in years sit in order. For the children which stand, let their fathers and mothers take them to them. Let the younger women also sit by themselves, if there be a place for them; but if there be not, let them stand behind the women. Let those women which are married, and have children, be placed by themselves; but let the virgins, and the widows, and the elder women, stand or sit before all the rest; and let the deacon be the disposer of the places, that every one of those that comes in may go to his proper place, and may not sit at the entrance. In like manner, let the deacon oversee the people, that nobody may whisper, nor slumber, nor laugh, nor nod; for all ought in the church to stand wisely, and soberly, and attentively, having their attention fixed upon the word of the Lord. After this, let all rise up with one consent, and looking towards the east, after the catechumens and penitents are gone out, pray to God eastward, who ascended up to the heaven of heavens to the east; remembering also the ancient situation of paradise in the east, from whence the first man, when he had yielded to the persuasion of the serpent, and disobeyed the command of God, was expelled. As to the deacons, after the prayer is over, let some of them attend upon the oblation of the Eucharist, ministering to the Lord's body with fear. Let others of them watch the multitude, and keep them silent. But let that deacon who is at the high priest's hand say to the people, Let no one have any quarrel against another; let no one come in hypocrisy. Then let the men give the men, and the women give the women, the Lord's kiss. But let no one do it with deceit, as Judas betrayed the Lord with a kiss. After this let the deacon pray for the whole Church, for the whole world, and the several parts of it, and the fruits of it; for the priests and the rulers, for the high priest and the king, and the peace of the universe. After this let the high priest pray for peace upon the people, and bless them, as Moses commanded the priests to bless the people, in these words: "The Lord bless thee, and keep thee: the Lord make His face to shine upon thee, and give thee peace." Let the bishop pray for the people, and say: "Save Thy people, O Lord, and bless Thine inheritance, which Thou hast obtained with the precious blood of Thy Christ, and hast called a royal priesthood, and an holy nation." After this let the sacrifice follow, the people standing, and praying silently; and when the oblation has been made, let every rank by itself partake of the Lord's body and precious blood in order, and approach with reverence and holy fear, as to the body of their king. Let the women approach with their heads covered, as is becoming the order of women; but let the door be watched, lest any unbeliever, or one not yet initiated, come in.

F. JEROME (C. 340/47–420) AND THE VULGATE

7. The Roman Psalter (c. 383) and the Gallican (c. 387–388)

Praef. in Lib. Ps., trans. NPNF, 2nd ser., VI, p. 494.

Long ago, when I was living at Rome, I revised the Psalter, and corrected it in a great measure, though but cursorily, in accordance with the Septuagint version. You now find it, Paula and Eustochium, again corrupted through the fault of copyists, and realise the fact that ancient error is more powerful than modern correction; and you therefore urge me, as it were, to cross-plough the land which has already been broken up, and, by means of the transverse furrows, to root out the thorns which are beginning to spring again; it is only right, you say, that rank and noxious growths should be cut down as often as they appear. And so I issue my customary admonition by way of preface both to you, for whom it happens that I am undertaking the labour, and to those persons who desire to have copies such as I describe. Pray see that what I have carefully revised be transcribed with similar painstaking care. Every reader can observe for himself where there is placed either a horizontal line or mark issuing from the centre, that is, either an obelus (†) or an asterisk (⁂). And wherever he sees the former, he is to understand that between this mark and the two stops (:) which I have introduced, the Septuagint translation contains superfluous matter. But where he sees the asterisk (⁂), an addition to the Hebrew books is indicated, which also goes as far as the two stops.

G. GREGORY OF NYSSA († 394)

8. The Purpose and Method of Catechetical Instruction

Orat. Cat. (c. 390), Praef., trans. NPNF, 2nd ser., V, pp. 473–74.

The presiding ministers of the "mystery of godliness" have need of a system in their instructions, in order that the Church may be replenished by the accession of such as should be saved, through the teaching of the word of Faith being brought home to the hearing of unbelievers. Not that the same method of instruction will be suitable in the case of all who approach the word. The catechism must be adapted to the diversities of their religious worship; with an eye, indeed, to the one aim and end of the system, but not using the same method of preparation in each individual case. The Judaizer has been preoccupied with one set of notions, one conversant with Hellenism, with others; while the Anomoean, and the Manichee, with the followers of Marcion, Valentinus, and Basilides, and the rest on the list of those who have wandered into heresy, each of them being prepossessed with their peculiar notions, necessitate a special controversy with their several opinions. The method of recovery must be adapted to the form of the disease. You will not by the same means cure the polytheism of the Greek, and the unbelief of the Jew as to the Only-begotten God: nor as regards those who have wandered into heresy will you, by the same arguments in each case, upset their misleading romances as to the tenets of the Faith. No one could set Sabellius right by the same instruction as would benefit the Anomoean. The controversy with the Manichee is profitless against the Jew. It is necessary, therefore, as I have said, to regard the opinions which the persons have taken up, and to frame your argument in accordance with the error into which each has fallen, by advancing in each discussion certain principles and reasonable propositions, that thus, through what is agreed upon on both sides, the truth may conclusively be brought to light. When, then, a discussion is held with one of those who favour Greek ideas, it would be well to make the ascertaining of this the commencement of the reasoning, *i.e.* whether he presupposes the existence of a God, or concurs with the atheistic view. Should he say there is no God, then, from the consideration of the skilful and wise economy of the Universe he will be brought to acknowledge that there is a certain over-mastering power manifested through these channels. If, on the other hand, he should have no doubt as to the existence of Deity, but should be inclined to entertain the presumption of a plurality of Gods, then we will adopt against him some such train of reasoning as this: "does he think Deity is perfect or defective?" and if, as is likely, he bears testimony to the perfection in the Divine nature, then we will demand of him to grant a perfection throughout in everything that is observable in that divinity, in order that Deity may not be regarded as a mixture of opposites, defect and perfection.

140

H. SUNDAY OFFICES: PILGRIMAGE OF ETHERIA (C. 390)

9. Lord's Day Vigil and Eucharist

S. *Silviae Peregrinatio*, 24:8, trans. and ed. by M. L. McClure and C. L. Feltoe, *The Pilgrimage of Etheria* (London: SPCK, 1920), pp. 49–51.

But on the seventh day, that is on the Lord's Day, the whole multitude assembles before cockcrow, in as great numbers as the place can hold, as at Easter, in the basilica which is near the Anastasis, but outside the doors, where lights are hanging for the purpose. And for fear that they should not be there at cockcrow they come beforehand and sit down there. Hymns as well as antiphons are said, and prayers are made between the several hymns and antiphons, for at the vigils there are always both priests and deacons ready there for the assembling of the multitude, the custom being that the holy places are not opened before cockcrow. Now as soon as the first cock has crowed, the bishop arrives and enters the cave at the Anastasis; all the doors are opened and the whole multitude enters the Anastasis, where countless lights are already burning. And when the people have entered, one of the priests says a psalm to which all respond, and afterwards prayer is made; then one of the deacons says a psalm and prayer is again made, a third psalm is said by one of the clergy, prayer is made for a third time and there is a commemoration of all. After these three psalms and three prayers are ended, lo! censers are brought into the cave of the Anastasis so that the whole basilica of the Anastasis is filled with odours. And then the bishop, standing within the rails, takes the book of the Gospel, and proceeding to the door, himself reads the (narrative of the) Resurrection of the Lord. And when the reading is begun, there is so great a moaning and groaning among all, with so many tears, that the hardest of hearts might be moved to tears for that the Lord had borne such things for us. After the reading of the Gospel the bishop goes out, and is accompanied to the Cross by all the people with hymns, there again a psalm is said and prayer is made, after which he blesses the faithful and the dismissal takes place, and as he comes out all approach to his hand. And forthwith the bishop betakes himself to his house, and from that hour all the monks return to the Anastasis, where psalms and antiphons, with prayer after each psalm or antiphon, are said until daylight; the priests and deacons also keep watch in turn daily at the Anastasis with the people, but of the lay people, whether men or women, those who are so minded, remain in the place until daybreak, and those who are not, return to their houses and betake themselves to sleep.

2. MORNING SERVICES

Now at daybreak because it is the Lord's Day every one proceeds to the greater church, built by Constantine, which is situated in Golgotha behind the Cross, where all things are done which are customary everywhere on the Lord's Day. But the custom here is that of all the priests who take their seats, as many as are willing, preach, and after them all the bishop preaches, and these sermons are always on the Lord's Day, in order that the people may always be instructed in the Scriptures and in the love of God. The delivery of these sermons greatly delays the dismissal from the church, so that the dismissal does [not] take place before the fourth or perhaps the fifth hour.

I. THE (DIVINE) LITURGY OF ST. CHRYSOSTOM (C. 344/45–407)

10. The Great Entrance and the Communion

Trans. J. M. Neale & R. F. Littledale, *The Liturgies of SS. Mark, James, Clement, Chrysostom, and The Church of Malabar* (London: J. T. Hayes, 1859), pp. 107–8, 120–23.

And the Priest raising the Air [veil over paten and chalice], *puts it on the left shoulder of the Deacon, saying,*

Lift up your hands in the sanctuary, and bless the Lord.

Then, taking the holy disk [paten], *he puts it with all care and reverence on the Deacon's head, the Deacon also holding the censer with one of his fingers. And the Priest himself taking the holy chalice in his hands, they go through the north part, preceded by tapers, and make*

IV-6. The "Great Entrance" and the Eastern Liturgy.

The Great Entrance, *both praying for all, and saying,* The Lord God remember us all in His kingdom, always, now and ever, and to ages of ages.

And the Deacon, going within the holy doors, stands on the right hand; and when the Priest is about to enter in, he saith to him,

The Lord God remember thy Priesthood in His kingdom.

Priest. The Lord God remember thy Diaconate in His kingdom, always, now and ever, and to ages of ages.

And the Priest sets down the chalice on the holy Table, and taking the holy disk from the head of the Deacon, he places it there also, . . .

The Deacon then girds his Orarion [stole] *crosswise, and goes into the holy Bema* [Chancel], *and standing on the right hand,* (*the Priest grasping the holy Bread,*) *saith,*

Sir, break the holy Bread.

And the Priest, dividing It into four parts with care and reverence, places It on the holy disk in the form of a Cross in this fashion:

saying, The Lamb of God is broken and distributed; He That is broken and not divided in sunder; ever eaten and never consumed, but sanctifying the communicants.

And the Deacon, pointing with his Orarion to the holy Cup, saith,

Sir, fill the holy Cup.

And the Priest taking the upper portion, (that is, the ΙΣ,) *makes with It a Cross above the holy Cup, saying,* The fulness of the cup, of faith, of the Holy Ghost: *and thus puts It into the holy Cup.*

Deacon. Amen.

And taking the warm water, he saith to the Priest,

Sir, bless the warm water.

And the Priest blesseth, saying,

Blessed is the fervour of Thy Saints, always, now and ever, and to ages of ages. Amen.

And the Deacon pours forth a sufficiency into the holy Cup, in the form of a Cross, saying,

The fervour of faith, full of the Holy Ghost. Amen. (*Thrice.*)

Then, setting down the warm water, he stands a little way off. And the Priest, taking a particle of the holy Bread, saith,

The blessed and most holy Body of our Lord and God and Saviour Jesus Christ, is communicated to me, N., Priest, for the remission of my sins, and for everlasting life.

I believe, Lord, and confess.

Of Thy Mystic Supper to-day.

Let not, O Lord, the communion of Thy holy mysteries be to my judgment or condemnation, but to the healing of my soul and body.

And thus he partakes of that which is in his hands with fear and all caution. Then he saith,

Deacon, approach.

And the Deacon approaches, and reverently makes an obeisance, asking forgiveness. And the Priest, taking the holy Bread, gives it to the Deacon; and the Deacon, kissing the hand that gives it, saith,

Sir, make me partaker of the precious and holy Body of our Lord and God and Saviour Jesus Christ.

Priest. N. the holy Deacon is made partaker of the precious and holy and spotless Body of our Lord and God and Saviour Jesus Christ, for the remission of his sins, and for eternal life.

And the Deacon going behind the holy Table, boweth his head and prayeth, and so doth the Priest.

Then the Priest standing up, takes the holy Chalice with its covering in both hands, and drinks three times, saying, I, N., Priest, partake of the pure and holy Blood of our Lord and God and Saviour Jesus Christ, for the remission of my sins, and for eternal life.

And then he wipes the holy Cup and his own lips with the covering he has in his hands, and saith,

Behold, this hath touched my lips, and shall take away my transgressions, and purge my sins.

Then he calls the Deacon, saying, Deacon approach. *The Deacon comes, and adores once, saying,*

Behold, I approach the Immortal King.

I believe, Lord, and confess.

Priest. N. the Deacon and servant of God is made partaker of the precious and holy Blood of our Lord and God and Saviour Jesus Christ, for the remission of sins, and for eternal life.

And when the Deacon hath communicated, the Priest saith,

Behold, this hath touched thy lips.

Then the Deacon, taking the holy disk, and holding it over the holy Chalice, wipes it thoroughly with the holy sponge; and with care and reverence covers it with the veil. In like manner he covers the disk with the asterisk, [or star: a framework securing the veil over the paten] *and that with its veil.*

The Priest saith the prayer of Thanksgiving.

We yield Thee thanks, O Lord and Lover of men, Benefactor of our souls, that Thou hast this day thought us worthy of Thy heavenly and immortal mysteries. Rightly divide our path, confirm us all in Thy fear, guard our life, make safe our goings: through the prayers and supplications of the

IV-7. Exaltation of the Cross, Transfiguration Theme, Moses and Elias, Martyr-Bishop S. Apollinare, and the Heavenly Pastures. *Mosaic, 6th century, Sanctuary of S. Apollinare in Classe, Ravenna.*

glorious Mother of God and Ever-Virgin Mary, and all Thy Saints.

And thus they open the doors of the holy Bema; and the Deacon, having made one adoration, takes the Chalice with reverence, and goes to the door, and raising the holy Chalice, shews it to the people, saying, Approach with the fear of God, faith and love.

They who are to communicate draw near with all reverence, and hold their arms crossed on their breast; and the Priest, as he distributes the mysteries to each, saith,

N. the servant of God is made partaker of the pure and holy Body and Blood of our Lord and God and Saviour Jesus Christ, for the remission of his sins, and life everlasting.

Then the Priest blesseth the people, saying aloud,

O God, save Thy people, and bless Thine heritage.

J. DIONYSIUS THE PSEUDO-AREOPAGITE AND THE EARTHLY HIERARCHIES, DEIFICATION, EUCHARISTIC SACRAMENT (C. 500)

11. The Ecclesiastical Hierarchy: Initiation, Deification, Participation in the One, Salvation

De ecclesiastica hierarchis, 1:1–5, trans. T. L. Campbell, Dionysius the Pseudo-Areopagite: The Ecclesiastical Hierarchy Translated and Annotated (Washington, D. C.: Catholic University of America Press, 1955), pp. 1–5.

1. We must show, most pious of sons, that our hierarchy is inspired by God and that it implies a divine and deifying sci-

ence, activity, and perfection. We shall show this from our most sacred and supramundane Scriptures, for the benefit of those who have been initiated by the consecration of sacred initiation in hierarchical mysteries and traditions. However, take care not to reveal indiscretely these most sacred things. Be prudent and respect the hidden things of God by using spiritual and obscure notions. Keep these things undefiled, inaccessible to the uninitiated, reverently communicating sacred things only to holy persons in a holy illumination.

Theology has taught us worshippers that Jesus Himself is the transcendentally divine and supra-essential mind, the source and essence of all hierarchy, holiness, and divine operation, the divinely sovereign power who illumines the blessed beings superior to us in a manner at once more spiritual and clear, assimilating them to His own light as far as possible. As for us, because of our love of the beautiful which attracts us to Him, and by which we are raised up to Him, He folds together our multiple differences and perfects us into a unified divine life, habit, and activity, and grants us the sacred power of the divine priesthood. By our approach to the sacred function of the priesthood, we come nearer to the beings above us through imitating as much as we can the constancy and unchangeableness of their steadfastness in holy things, and by looking upon the constancy of the supremely divine and blessed Jesus. Reverently contemplating whatever we are permitted to see, enlightened by the knowledge of visions, we shall be able to be consecrated and to consecrate others in this mystical knowledge. We shall become images of light and co-workers with God, perfected and making others perfect.

2. What, then, is the hierarchy of the angels and archangels, supramundane principalities and powers, virtues and dominations, divine thrones, or beings of the same rank as thrones which the word of God describes as being perpetually near God, always about Him and with Him, those beings in Hebrew called cherubim and seraphim? These things you are likely to find in our treatise on the orders and sacred divisions of their ranks and hierarchies. You will note

that we have praised that hierarchy according to the theology of the most holy Scriptures, not worthily to be sure, but to the best of our ability. Nevertheless, we must recall here that both that hierarchy and every other hierarchy we are now praising has but the one same power throughout the whole of its hierarchical functions, and that the chief of each sacred order himself receives an initiation in divine things according to his nature, aptitude, and rank. He is himself deified, and makes his subjects, according to the merits of each, participants in the holy deification he has received from God Himself. Inferiors follow their superiors, who urge them to advance, and some go forward and lead others on as far as possible. Through this divine hierarchical harmony, each order can participate as much as possible in Him who is truly beautiful, wise, and good.

The beings and orders above us, of whom I have already made pious mention, are incorporeal, and their hierarchy is spiritual and supramundane. We observe that our own human hierarchy, conformably to our nature, abounds in a manifold variety of sensible symbols which raise us hierarchically, in proportion to our capacity, to the oneness of deification, to God and divine virtue. Since they are spirits, they know according to laws proper to them, but we are raised up to divine contemplations through sensible images as much as we can be. To speak truly, there is one to whom all the godlike aspire, but they do not partake of Him who is one and the same in the same manner, but as the divine ordinance assigns to each according to his merits.

These things have been treated more systematically in the treatise, *On Things Spiritual and Sensible.* Right now I will only attempt to describe the principle and essence of our own hierarchy as best I can, calling upon Jesus, the principle and perfection of every hierarchy.

3. According to our august tradition, every hierarchy gives full account of every sacred reality falling under it, and a most general summary of the rites that pertain to this or that particular hierarchy. Our hierarchy is called, and is, that function embracing all the sacred rites proper to it, and in

accordance with which the divine bishop, once he is consecrated, can participate in all the sacred rites which pertain to him, because he takes his name from "hierarchy." He who speaks of hierarchy speaks at the same time of the orderly arrangement of all sacred things taken together. Likewise, he who says "hierarch" means a man divinely inspired and godlike, one learned in all sacred knowledge, and in whom the whole hierarchy is plainly perfected and recognized.

The source of this hierarchy is the Trinity, the fountain of life, the essence of goodness, the one cause of things that are. From its goodness comes both the being and the well-being of things that exist. This beatitude that divinely transcends all things is the truly existing triune Unity who willed, in a manner incomprehensible to us but most clear to itself, the salvation of rational creatures, both ourselves and the beings above us. This salvation is possible in no other way than by the deification of the saved. This deification is a certain assimilation and unification with God in so far as possible. The common end of every hierarchy is the continued love of God and divine things, a love divinely sanctified into oneness with Him. However, for this there must be an absolute and unswerving flight from whatever is contrary, a knowledge of beings as they are in themselves, a vision and understanding of sacred truth, a divine participation in the One itself as much as possible, and an enjoyment of open vision that nourishes spiritually and deifies every man who is raised up to it.

4. Let us say, then, that the divine Beatitude, the being divine by nature, the principle of deification, whose divine goodness deifies those who are deified, has granted to all rational and spiritual beings the gift of the hierarchy for their salvation. This gift has been given in a manner more spiritual and immaterial to the supramundane and those enjoying a blessed repose, for it is not from without that God moves them to divine things, but spiritually, by illuminating them from within by means of a pure and immaterial light regarding His most divine will. This gift offered to them simply and compactly is given to us through a variety and multiplicity of divisible symbols out of the God-given Scriptures, in so far as it is fitting. The very essence of our hierarchy is the divinely transmitted Scriptures. We deem most venerable these oracles which our divinely inspired initiators have given us in sacred writings and theological books, and further, such as our leaders have revealed to us from these same holy men by a more immaterial initiation that is very similar to the heavenly hierarchy since it is from mind to mind. It is corporeal because it comes through the medium of speech, and yet quite immaterial because it is unwritten. The divinely inspired bishops did not transmit these teachings in undisguised formulas for the common usage of sacred ceremony, but in sacred symbols, because not everyone is holy, nor, as Scripture says, does knowledge belong to all.

5. Necessarily, therefore, after they themselves had been filled with the sacred gift by the supra-essential Deity, they were sent forth by His supremely divine goodness to proclaim this gift to posterity. Ardently desiring its elevation and deification with their own, like gods, the first leaders of our hierarchy transmitted to us the supracelestial in sensible figures in accordance with the sacred ordinances. They transmitted the unified in variety and multiplicity, the divine in the human, the immaterial in the material, the super-essential on our own level, making use of both written and oral instructions. They did this not merely on account of the unholy, for whom it is sacrilegious even to approach the symbols, but, as I said, because our hierarchy is something symbolic, proportioned to our nature that needs material things for our more divine elevation from them to the spiritual. However, to the divine initiators in sacred things, the reasons behind the symbols have been revealed, and they are not to be explained to those still being initiated. It is known that those who make laws concerning what is sacred and divinely handed-down arranged the hierarchy in well-fixed and distinct ranks of orders, and in proportional, sacred distributions of what is proper for each according to its deserts.

Therefore, I have confided this divine gift

to you along with other hierarchical matters, trusting in your sacred promises (for it is well to recall them), that you will not commit to everyone all the holy doctrines of the sublime episcopal order, but only to the godlike teachers of sacred things of the same rank as yourself, whom, according to the hierarchical precept, you will persuade to promise to treat pure things purely, to communicate the works of God only to godly men, things that perfect to those becoming perfect, and most holy things to the holy.

12. Union with Super-essential Deity Surpassing the Intelligible; Each Creature Illumined by Divine Graciousness in Accordance with the Principle of Analogia

De Divinis Nominibus 1:1–2. Freely rendered by the editor from Dom Chevallier *et al.*, *Dionysiaca* (Paris, 1937), I and M. de Gandillac, *Oeuvres Complètes du Pseudo-Denys L'Aréopagite* (Paris: Aubier, 1943), pp. 66–69.

Our rule in accordance with the sacred texts is to enumerate no truth of the divine word in terms of human wisdom, but rather by a revelation of that power which invested the Holy Writers. This enables us to adhere, in a Union without word and without knowledge, to realities both unspeakable and unknowable. . . . No word or thought may be entertained with regard to the hidden Super-Essential Godhead beyond that divinely revealed to us by Holy Writ. Only a super-essential knowledge befits the Unknowing of this same Super-essentiality which transcends reason, thought, and being. We may lift our eyes to lofty things only as we strive to ascend with the aid of those effulgent Rays emanating from the Divine Scriptures. . . . Created intelligences receive a manifestation of Divine secrets that is according to the measure of those powers within each. The Divine Goodness out of its saving concern for humanity reveals itself with an immeasurable graciousness tempered to the clearly measurable limits of human comprehension. . . .

. . . The Scriptures themselves teach us that no being may take in the meaning of this Super-Essence that transcends all Essences, this Good defying the description of all words, this Mind that eludes every mind, this Word beyond Experience, Insight, Name and Category, this Cause of all being that does not itself exist, this Super-Essence that is beyond all Being and all Revelation save its own self-manifestation. Though in its intimate nature perfectly inaccessible to every being, the Good in Itself does not remain wholly incommunicable. Out of Its Divine isolation it sends forth illumination from its Super-Essential Ray. Each creature, according to the measure of its individual powers receives the loving self-revelation of this Divine Goodness. It draws holy souls toward itself for such contemplation of, communion with, and resemblance of Itself as may be in harmony with the Divine plan and each human condition.

13. The Ecclesiastical Hierarchy: Holy Liturgies; Sacrament of Assembly (Synaxis); Sacrament of Union (Koinonia); Communion in the Mysteries; Rites and Symbols

Ecc. Hier., 3, iii, 12. Trans. by the editor from B. Geyer & J. Zellinger, *Florilegium Patristicum* . . . Fasc. VII: *Monumenta eucharistica et liturgica*. . . . Pars VI, ed. J. Quasten (Bonnae: Sumpt. Petri Hanstein, 1937), pp. 311–12, compared with Gandillac, *Oeuvres*, pp. 277–79.

But how indeed could we realize this divine imitation except by the continuous renewal in memory of the most holy working of the divine favor mediated through hierarchical proclamation and priestly ministries? This, then, we do, as the Scriptures say, in commemoration of the Master and of the divine graces (Luke 22:19). That is why the godly hierarch, standing erect before the Holy Altar, extols the divine working that is herein recalled and that Jesus divinely brought to pass. Doing so, he consummated in our behalf the workings of divine providence for the salvation of our race by the good pleasure of the Most Holy Father and in the Holy Spirit, according to the testimony of the Oracle, or Holy Sayings.

Having thus chanted his veneration of the awesome mysteries, and having perceived them by that *theoria* or contemplative insight with which he spiritually regarded

IV-8. The Symbolic Sacrifices. *Abel offering the lamb; Melchizidek, the bread; and Abraham, his son Isaac. Mosaic, 6th century, St. Apollinare in Classe, Ravenna.*

them, the godly hierarch proceeds, then, to their symbolic consecration, as handed down by Divinity, Himself. He prays, therefore, that he may be worthy of bringing about the divine working in imitation of God, of consecrating the divine mysteries, and of distributing them devotedly out of resemblance with Christ. He makes supplication, likewise, for all those about to participate in the divine mysteries that they may communicate worthily in holy things. Then he celebrates and consecrates the most divine mysteries, bringing to the view of every one the mysteries that he will shortly achieve under the species symbolically present. The bread has, heretofore, remained covered and undivided. He now uncovers it and breaks it up into a number of pieces. He likewise shares among all the assistants the single chalice, thus symbolically multiplying and distributing the One. With this, the holiest act of the entire liturgy is consummated.

For the Unique, the Uncompounded, the Hidden of Jesus, the Thearchic (or Super-Essential, God-Principled) Word has taken on our humanity in both composition and appearance. He has generously admitted us to His unifying communion, thereby joining what is lowest in us to His most divine eminence. This remains true only so long as

we adhere to it like members articulated in a common body. . . . If we wish to share in his communion, we must contemplate the most divine life of God incarnate and emulate his holy sinlessness, thus tending toward the perfect purity of a lasting deification.

II. Examples of Music in the Worship of the Early Church

A. ST. AMBROSE (C. 340–397)

14. He Comments on His Hymns (386)

Sermo c. Auxentium, 34, trans. LF, XLV, p. 156.

Moreover they assert that the people have been beguiled by the strains of my hymns. I deny not this either. It is a lofty strain, than which nothing is more powerful. For what can be more powerful than the confession of the Trinity, which is daily celebrated by the mouth of the whole people? All zealously desire to make profession of their faith, they know how to confess in verse the Father and the Son and the Holy Spirit. Thus all are become teachers who were scarcely able to be disciples.

15. One of His Hymns: At Cock-Crowing

Hymnus ad Galli Cantum, Stanzas 1–8, trans. E. Caswell, *Hymns and Poems*, 1849.

AT COCK-CROWING

1   Dread framer of the earth and sky!
      Who dost the circling seasons give!
    And all the cheerful change supply
      Of alternating morn and eve!

2   Loud crows the herald of the dawn,
      Awake amid the gloom of night,
    And guides the lonely traveller on,
      With call prophetic of the light.

3   Forthwith at this, the darkness chill
      Retreats before the star of morn;
    And from their busy schemes of ill,
      The vagrant crews of night return.

4   Fresh hope, at this, the sailor cheers;
      The waves their stormy strife allay;
    The Church's Rock, at this, in tears,
      Hastens to wash his guilt away.

5   Arise ye, then, with one accord!
      Nor longer wrapt in slumber lie;
    The cock rebukes all who their Lord
      By sloth neglect, by sin deny.

6   At his clear cry joy springs afresh;
      Health courses through the sick man's veins;

The dagger glides into its sheath;
    The fallen soul her faith regains.

7   Jesu! look on us when we fall;
      One momentary glance of thine
    Can from her guilt the soul recall
      To tears of penitence divine.

8   Awake us from false sleep profound,
      And through our senses pour thy light;
    Be thy blest name the first we sound
      At early morn, the last at night.

B. ST. AUGUSTINE (354–430)

16. On Ambrose and the Singing at Milan

Confess., 10:33; 9:6, 7, trans. *NPNF*, 1st ser., I, pp. 156, 134.

(10:33) The delights of the ear had more powerfully inveigled and conquered me, but Thou didst unbind and liberate me. Now, in those airs which Thy words breathe soul into, when sung with a sweet and trained voice, do I somewhat repose; yet not so as to cling to them, but so as to free myself when I wish. But with the words which are their life do they, that they may gain admission into me, strive after a place of some honour in my heart; and I can hardly assign them a fitting one. Sometimes I appear to myself to give them more respect than is fitting, as I perceive that our minds are more

IV-9. Christ and St. Peter Before the Cock Crows. *Sarcophagus, Museo Laterano, Rome.*

devoutly and earnestly elevated into a flame of piety by the holy words themselves when they are thus sung, than when they are not; and that all affections of our spirit, by their own diversity, have their appropriate measures in the voice and singing, wherewith by I know not what secret relationship they are stimulated. But the gratification of my flesh, to which the mind ought never to be given over to be enervated, often beguiles me, while the sense does not so attend on reason as to follow her patiently; but having gained admission merely for her sake, it strives even to run on before her, and be her leader. Thus in these things do I sin unknowing, but afterwards do I know it.

Sometimes, again, avoiding very earnestly this same deception, I err out of too great preciseness; and sometimes so much as to desire that every air of the pleasant songs to which David's Psalter is often used, be banished both from my ears and those of the Church itself; and that way seemed unto me safer which I remembered to have been often related to me of Athanasius, Bishop of Alexandria, who obliged the reader of the psalm to give utterance to it with so slight an inflection of voice, that it was more like speaking than singing. Notwithstanding, when I call to mind the tears I shed at the songs of Thy Church, at the outset of my recovered faith, and how even now I am moved not by the singing but by what is sung, when they are sung with a clear and skilfully modulated voice, I then acknowledge the great utility of this custom. Thus vacillate I between dangerous pleasure and tried soundness; being inclined rather (though I pronounce no irrevocable opinion upon the subject) to approve of the use of singing in the church, that so by the delights of the ear the weaker minds may be stimulated to a devotional frame. Yet when it happens to me to be more moved by the singing than by what is sung, I confess myself to have sinned criminally, and then I would rather not have heard the singing.

(9:6) Nor was I satiated in those days with the wondrous sweetness of considering the depth of Thy counsels concerning the salvation of the human race. How greatly did I weep in Thy hymns and canticles, deeply moved by the voices of Thy sweet-speaking Church! The voices flowed into mine ears, and the truth was poured forth into my heart, whence the agitation of my piety overflowed, and my tears ran over, and blessed was I therein.

(9:7) Not long had the Church of Milan begun to employ this kind of consolation and exhortation, the brethren singing together with great earnestness of voice and heart. For it was about a year, or not much more, since Justina, the mother of the boy-Emperor Valentinian, persecuted Thy servant Ambrose in the interest of her heresy, to which she had been seduced by the Arians. The pious people kept guard in the church, prepared to die with their bishop, Thy servant. There my mother, Thy handmaid, bearing a chief part of those cares and watchings, lived in prayer. We, still unmelted by the heat of Thy Spirit, were yet moved by the astonished and disturbed city. At this time it was instituted that, after the manner of the Eastern Church, hymns and psalms should be sung, lest the people should pine away in the tediousness of sorrow; which custom, retained from then till now, is imitated by many, yea, by almost all of Thy congregations throughout the rest of the world.

III. Renunciation, Asceticism, and the Beginnings of Monasticism in the East

A. ST. ANTHONY (C. 251–356) AND EREMITIC BEGINNINGS

17. *Athanasius (295–373) on St. Anthony*

Vita. S. Ant., 3, trans. *NPNF*, 2nd ser., IV, p. 196.

And again as he went into the church, hearing the Lord say in the Gospel, 'be not anxious for the morrow,' he could stay no longer, but went out and gave those things also to the poor. Having committed his sister to known and faithful virgins, and put her into a convent to be brought up, he henceforth devoted himself outside his house to disci-

IV-10. The Temptation of St. Anthony. *Martin Schongauer, engraving, c. 1480–1490.*

pline, taking heed to himself and training himself with patience. For there were not yet so many monasteries in Egypt, and no monk at all knew of the distant desert; but all who wished to give heed to themselves practised the discipline in solitude near their own village. Now there was then in the next village an old man who had lived the life of a hermit from his youth up. Antony, after he had seen this man, imitated him in piety. And at first he began to abide in places outside the village; then if he heard of a good man anywhere, like the prudent bee, he went forth and sought him, nor turned back to his own place until he had seen him; and he returned, having got from the good man as it were supplies for his journey in the way of virtue. So dwelling there at first, he confirmed his purpose not to return to the abode of his fathers nor to the remembrance of his kinsfolk; but to keep all his desire and energy for perfecting his discipline. He worked, however, with his hands, having heard, 'he who is idle let him not eat,' and part he spent on bread and

part he gave to the needy. And he was constant in prayer, knowing that a man ought to pray in secret unceasingly. For he had given such heed to what was read that none of the things that were written fell from him to the ground, but he remembered all, and afterwards his memory served him for books.

B. PACHOMIUS (C. 286/92–346) AND CENOBITIC OUTLINES

18. Sozomen (c. 450) on Pachomius' Call to Community Life

Hist. Ecc., 3:14, trans. NPNF, 2nd ser., II, p. 292.

It is said that Pachomius at first practiced philosophy alone in a cave, but that a holy angel appeared to him, and commanded him to call together some young monks, and live with them, for he had succeeded well in pursuing philosophy by himself, and to train them by the laws which were about to be delivered to him, and now he was to possess and benefit many as a leader of communities.

19. Palladius (c. 363–c. 424) on Pachomius

Historia Lausiaca (c. 419/20), 38. Selections from *A Source Book for Ancient Church History*, pp. 402–6, by Joseph Cullen Ayer are reprinted with the permission of Charles Scribner's Sons © 1913 Charles Scribner's Sons; renewal © 1941 Joseph Cullen Ayer, Jr. This passage, pp. 402–5.

There is a place in the Thebaid called Tabenna, in which lived a certain monk Pachomius, one of those men who have attained the highest form of life, so that he was granted predictions of the future and angelic visions. He was a great lover of the poor, and had great love to men. When, therefore, he was sitting in a cave an angel of the Lord came in and appeared to him and said: Pachomius you have done well those things which pertain to your own affairs; therefore sit no longer idle in this cave. Up, therefore, go forth and gather all the younger monks and dwell with them and give them laws according to the form which I give thee. And he gave him a brass tablet on which the following things were written:

1. Give to each to eat and drink according to his strength; and give labors according to the powers of those eating, and forbid neither fasting nor eating. Thus appoint difficult labors to the stronger and those who eat, but the lighter and easy tasks to those who discipline themselves more and are weaker.

2. Make separate cells in the same place; and let three remain in a cell. But let the food of all be prepared in one house.

3. They may not sleep lying down, but having made seats built inclining backward let them place their bedding on them and sleep seated.

4. But by night let them wear linen tunics, being girded about. Let each of them have a shaggy goatskin, made white. Without this let them neither eat nor sleep. When they go in unto the communion of the mysteries of Christ every Sabbath and Lord's Day, let them loose their girdles and put off the goatskin, and enter with only their cuculla. . . . But he made the cuculla for them without any fleece, as for boys; and he commanded to place upon them certain branding marks of a purple cross.

5. He commanded that there be twenty-four groups of the brethren, according to the number of the twenty-four letters. And he prescribed that to each group should be given as a name a letter of the Greek alphabet, from Alpha and Beta, one after another, to Omega, in order that when the archimandrite asked for any one in so great a company, that one may be asked who is the second in each, how group Alpha is, or how the group Beta; again let him salute the group Rho; the name of the letters following its own proper sign. And upon the simpler and more guileless place the name Iota; and upon those who are more ill-tempered and less righteous the letter Xi. And thus in harmony with the principles and the life and manners of them arrange the names of the letters, only the spiritual understanding the meaning.

6. There was written on the tablet that if there come a stranger of another monastery, having a different form of life, he shall not eat nor drink with them, nor go in with them into the monastery, unless he shall be found in the way outside of the monastery.

7. But do not receive for three years into the contest of proficients him who has entered once for all to remain with them; but when he has performed the more difficult tasks, then let him after a period of three years enter the stadium.

8. When they eat let them veil their faces, that one brother may not see another brother eating. They are not to speak while they eat; nor outside of their dish or off the table shall they turn their eyes toward anything else.

9. And he made it a rule that during the whole day they should offer twelve prayers; and at the time of lighting the lamps, twelve; and in the course of the night, twelve; and at the ninth hour, three; but when it seemed good for the whole company to eat, he directed that each group should first sing a psalm at each prayer.

But when the great Pachomius replied to the angel that the prayers were few, the angel said to him: I have appointed these that the little ones may advance and fulfil the law and not be distressed; but the perfect do not need to have laws given to them. For being by themselves in their cells, they have dedicated their entire life to contemplation on God. But to these, as many as do not have an intelligent mind, I will give a law that as saucy servants out of fear for the Master they may fulfil the whole order of life and direct it properly. When the angel had given these directions and fulfilled his ministry he departed from the great Pachomius. There are monasteries observing this rule, composed of seven thousand men, but the first and great monastery, wherein the blessed Pachomius dwelt, and which gave birth to the other places of asceticism, has one thousand three hundred men.

C. BASIL (330–379) AND HIS PREFERENCE FOR CENOBITIC LIFE (RULE, C. 370)

20. *Edification Through Community Life and Responsibility*

Regula fusius tractata, Q. 7., trans. Ayer, *A Source Book*, pp. 405–6, as acknowledged in Item 19, above.

Questio VII. Since your words have given us full assurance that the life [*i.e.*, the cenobitic life] is dangerous with those who despise the commandments of the Lord, we wish accordingly to learn whether it is necessary that he who withdraws should remain alone or live with brothers of like mind who have placed before themselves the same goal of piety.

Responsio 1. I think that the life of several in the same place is much more profitable. First, because for bodily wants no one of us is sufficient for himself, but we need each other in providing what is necessary. For just as the foot has one ability, but is wanting another, and without the help of the other members it would find neither its own power strong nor sufficient of itself to continue, nor any supply for what it lacks, so it is in the case of the solitary life: what is of use to us and what is wanting we cannot provide for ourselves, for God who created the world has so ordered all things that we are dependent upon each other, as it is written that we may join ourselves to one another [cf. Wis. 13:20]. But in addition to this, reverence to the love of Christ does not permit each one to have regard only to his own affairs, for love, he says, seeks not her own [I Cor. 13:5]. The solitary life has only one goal, the service of its own interests. That clearly is opposed to the law of love, which the Apostle fulfilled, when he did not in his eyes seek his own advantage but the advantage of many, that they might be saved [cf. I Cor. 10:33]. Further, no one in solitude recognizes his own defects, since he has no one to correct him and in gentleness and mercy direct him on his way. For even if correction is from an enemy, it may often in the case of those who are well disposed rouse the desire for healing; but the healing of sin by him who sincerely loves is wisely accomplished. . . . Also the commands may be better fulfilled by a larger community, but not by one alone; for while this thing is being done another will be neglected; for example, by attendance upon the sick the reception of strangers is neglected; and in the bestowal and distribution of the necessities of life (especially when in these services much time is consumed) the care of the work is neglected, so that by this the greatest commandment and the one most helpful to

salvation is neglected; neither the hungry are fed nor the naked clothed. Who would therefore value higher the idle, useless life than the fruitful which fulfils the commandments of God?

3. . . . Also in the preservation of the gifts bestowed by God the cenobitic life is preferable. . . . For him who falls into sin, the recovery of the right path is so much easier, for he is ashamed at the blame expressed by so many in common, so that it happens to him as it is written: It is enough that the same therefore be punished by many [II Cor. 2:6]. . . . There are still other dangers which we say accompany the solitary life, the first and greatest is that of self-satisfaction. For he who has no one to test his work easily believes that he has completely fulfilled the commandments. . . .

4. For how shall he manifest his humility, when he has no one to whom he can show himself the inferior? How shall he manifest compassion cut off from the society of many? How will he exercise himself in patience, if no one opposes his wishes?

IV. Monasticism as Spiritual Martyrdom

A. PACHOMIUS

21. *On the Monk as Another Kind of Martyr*

Syriac Text of Anan-Isho, trans. E. Budge, *The Paradise or Garden of the Holy Fathers* (London: Chatto & Windus, 1907), I, p. 301.

And there was also (there) among those who were very famous a certain brother who cultivated the ascetic life by himself, and when he heard of the divine rule of our holy Father Pachomius he entreated him to receive him in the monastery; and when Rabba had received him, and he had passed a little (time) with the brethren, he desired greatly to bear witness (i.e., to become a martyr), although the world was in a state of peace, and the Church was flourishing and was, by the grace of God, at peace, and the blessed Constantine, who had put on Christ, was at that time reigning. And this brother was continually entreating the blessed man Pachomius, and saying, "Pray for me, O Father, that I may become a martyr"; but Rabba admonished him that he should not permit this thought to enter his mind again, and said unto him, "Brother, endure the strife of the monks mightily and blamelessly, and make straight thy life in the way which will please Christ, and thou shalt have companionship with the martyrs in heaven."

B. MARTIN OF TOURS

22. As Martyr by Intent, His Glory that of Martyrdom

Sulpicius Severus (†c. 420), Ep. 2 ad Aurel., trans. NPNF, 2nd ser., XI, p. 20.

For although the character of our times could not ensure him the honor of martyrdom, yet he will not remain destitute of the glory of a martyr, because both by vow and virtues he was alike able and willing to be a martyr. But if he had been permitted, in the times of Nero and of Decius, to take part in the struggle which then went on, I take to witness the God of heaven and earth that he would freely have submitted to the rack of torture, and readily surrendered himself to the flames: yea, worthy of being compared to the illustrious Hebrew youths, amid the circling flames, and though in the very midst of the furnace, he would have sung a hymn of the Lord.

C. JEROME

23. Paula's Bloodless Martyrdom of the Devout Mind

Ep. 108:32 (31), trans, NPNF, 2nd ser., VI, p. 211.

Be not fearful, Eustochium: you are endowed with a splendid heritage. The Lord is your portion; and, to increase your joy, your mother has now after a long martyrdom won her crown. It is not only the shedding of blood that is accounted a confession: the spotless service of a devout mind is itself a daily martyrdom. Both alike are crowned; with roses and violets in the one case, with lilies in the other. Thus in the Song of Songs it is written: "my beloved is white and ruddy;" for, whether the victory be won in peace or in war, God gives the same guerdon to those who win it. Like Abraham your

mother heard the words: "get thee out of thy country, and from thy kindred, unto a land that I will shew thee;" and not only that but the Lord's command given through Jeremiah: "flee out of the midst of Babylon, and deliver every man his soul." To the day of her death she never returned to Chaldaea, or regretted the fleshpots of Egypt or its strong-smelling meats. Accompanied by her virgin bands she became a fellow-citizen of the Saviour; and now that she has ascended from her little Bethlehem to the heavenly realms she can say to the true Naomi: "thy people shall be my people and thy God my God."

V. John Cassian (c. 360–c. 435) and the Desert Fathers of the East in Relation to the Cenobitic West

24. On Ennui and the Spirit of Accidia

De Institutis coenobiorum et de octo principalium vitiorum remediis (c. 419–426), 10:1–5, trans. NPNF, 2nd ser., XI, pp. 266–68.

CHAPTER I

Our sixth combat is with what the Greeks call ἀκηδία, which we may term weariness or distress of heart. This is akin to dejection, and is especially trying to solitaries, and a dangerous and frequent foe to dwellers in the desert; and especially disturbing to a monk about the sixth hour, like some fever which seizes him at stated times, bringing the burning heat of its attacks on the sick man at usual and regular hours. Lastly, there are some of the elders who declare that this is the "midday demon" spoken of in the ninetieth Psalm.

CHAPTER II

. . . . .

And when this has taken possession of some unhappy soul, it produces dislike of the place, disgust with the cell, and disdain and contempt of the brethren who dwell with him or at a little distance, as if they were careless or unspiritual. It also makes the man lazy and sluggish about all manner of work which has to be done within the enclosure of his dormitory. It does not suffer him to stay in his cell, or to take any pains about reading, and he often groans because

IV-11. Lives of the Fathers. Vitae Patrum, manuscript, 14th century, Naples.

are stopping there, but also that even food for the body cannot be procured without great difficulty. Lastly he fancies that he will never be well while he stays in that place, unless he leaves his cell (in which he is sure to die if he stops in it any longer) and takes himself off from thence as quickly as possible. Then the fifth or sixth hour brings him such bodily weariness and longing for food that he seems to himself worn out and wearied as if with a long journey, or some very heavy work, or as if he had put off taking food during a fast of two or three days. Then besides this he looks about anxiously this way and that, and sighs that none of the brethren come to see him, and often goes in and out of his cell, and frequently gazes up at the sun, as if it was too slow in setting, and so a kind of unreasonable confusion of mind takes possession of him like some foul darkness, and makes him idle and useless for every spiritual work, so that he imagines that no cure for so terrible an attack can be found in anything except visiting some one of the brethren, or in the solace of sleep alone. Then the disease suggests that he ought to show courteous and friendly hospitalities to the brethren, and pay visits to the sick, whether near at hand or far off. He talks too about some dutiful and religious offices; that those kinsfolk ought to be inquired after, and that he ought to go and see them oftener; that it would be a real work of piety to go more frequently to visit that religious woman, devoted to the service of God, who is deprived of all support of kindred; and that it would be a most excellent thing to get what is needful for her who is neglected and despised by her own kinsfolk; and that he ought piously to devote his time to these things instead of staying uselessly and with no profit in his cell.

CHAPTER III

. . . . .

And so the wretched soul, embarrassed by such contrivances of the enemy, is disturbed, until, worn out by the spirit of accidie, as by some strong battering ram, it either learns to sink into slumber, or, driven out from the confinement of its cell, accustoms itself to seek for consolation under

he can do no good while he stays there, and complains and sighs because he can bear no spiritual fruit so long as he is joined to that society; and he complains that he is cut off from spiritual gain, and is of no use in the place, as if he were one who, though he could govern others and be useful to a great number of people, yet was edifying none, nor profiting any one by his teaching and doctrine. He cries up distant monasteries and those which are a long way off, and describes such places as more profitable and better suited for salvation; and besides this he paints the intercourse with the brethren there as sweet and full of spiritual life. On the other hand, he says that everything about him is rough, and not only that there is nothing edifying among the brethren who

154

these attacks in visiting some brother, only to be afterwards weakened the more by this remedy which it seeks for the present. For more frequently and more severely will the enemy attack one who, when the battle is joined, will as he well knows immediately turn his back, and whom he sees to look for safety neither in victory nor in fighting but in flight: until little by little he is drawn away from his cell, and begins to forget the object of his profession, which is nothing but meditation and contemplation of that divine purity which excels all things, and which can only be gained by silence and continually remaining in the cell, and by meditation, and so the soldier of Christ becomes a runaway from His service, and a deserter, and "entangles himself in secular business," without at all pleasing Him to whom he engaged himself.

CHAPTER IV

.　.　.　.　.

All the inconveniences of this disease are admirably expressed by David in a single verse, where he says, "My soul slept from weariness," that is, from accidie. Quite rightly does he say, not that his body, but that his soul slept. For in truth the soul which is wounded by the shaft of this passion does sleep, as regards all contemplation of the virtues and insight of the spiritual senses.

CHAPTER V

.　.　.　.　.

And so the true Christian athlete who desires to strive lawfully in the lists of perfection, should hasten to expel this disease also from the recesses of his soul; and should strive against this most evil spirit of accidie in both directions, so that he may neither fall stricken through by the shaft of slumber, nor be driven out from the monastic cloister, even though under some pious excuse or pretext, and depart as a runaway.

25. *Faith, Divine Grace, the Virtues, and the Way of Perfection*

De Instit., 12:15; trans. *NPNF*, 2nd ser., XI, p. 284.

And so, if we wish in very deed and truth to attain to the crown of virtues, we ought to listen to those teachers and guides who, not dreaming with pompous declamations, but learning by act and experience, are able to teach us as well, and direct us likewise, and show us the road by which we may arrive at it by a most sure pathway; and who also testify that they have themselves reached it by faith rather than by any merits of their efforts. And further, the purity of heart that they have acquired has taught them this above all; viz., to recognize more and more that they are burdened with sin (for their compunction for their faults increases day by day in proportion as their purity of soul advances), and to sigh continually from the bottom of their heart because they see that they cannot possibly avoid the spots and blemishes of those faults which are ingrained in them through the countless triflings of the thoughts. And therefore they declared that they looked for the reward of the future life, not from the merits of their works, but from the mercy of the Lord, taking no credit to themselves for their great circumspection of heart in comparison with others, since they ascribed this not to their own exertions, but to divine grace; and without flattering themselves on account of the carelessness of those who are cold, and worse than they themselves are, they rather aimed at a lasting humility by fixing their gaze on those whom they knew to be really free from sin and already in the enjoyment of eternal bliss in the kingdom of heaven, and so by this consideration they avoided the downfall of pride, and at the same time always saw both what they were aiming at and what they had to grieve over: as they knew that they could not attain that purity of heart for which they yearned while weighed down by the burden of the flesh.

26. *The Nature and Practice of Pure Prayer*

I Conference of Abbot Isaac, *Collationes Patrum* (c. 420–429), 3, trans. *NPNF*, 2nd ser., XII, p. 388.

And therefore in order that prayer may be offered up with that earnestness and purity with which it ought to be, we must by all means observe these rules. First all anxiety about carnal things must be entirely got rid of; next we must leave no room for not merely the care but even the recollection of any business affairs, and in like manner also must lay aside all backbitings, vain and incessant chattering, and buffoonery; anger above all, and disturbing moroseness must be entirely destroyed, and the deadly taint of carnal lust and covetousness be torn up by the roots. And so when these and such like faults which are also visible to the eyes of men, are entirely removed and cut off, and when such a purification and cleansing, as we spoke of, has first taken place, which is brought about by pure simplicity and innocence, then first there must be laid the secure foundations of a deep humility, which may be able to support a tower that shall reach the sky; and next the spiritual structure of the virtues must be built up upon them, and the soul kept free from all conversation and from roving thoughts that thus it may by little and little begin to rise to the contemplation of God and to spiritual insight. For whatever our mind has been thinking of before the hour of prayer, is sure to occur to us while we are praying through the activity of the memory. Wherefore what we want to find ourselves like while we are praying, that we ought to prepare ourselves to be before the time for prayer. For the mind in prayer is formed by its previous condition, and when we are applying ourselves to prayer the images of the same actions and words and thoughts will dance before our eyes, and make us either angry, as in our previous condition, or gloomy, or recall our former lust and business, or make us shake with foolish laughter (which I am ashamed to speak of) at some silly joke, or smile at some action, or fly back to our previous conversation. And therefore if we do not want anything to haunt us while we are praying, we should be careful before our prayer, to exclude it from the shrine of our heart, that we may thus fulfill the Apostle's injunction: "Pray without ceasing;" and: "In every place lifting up holy hands without wrath or disputing." For otherwise we shall not be able to carry out that charge unless our mind, purified from all stains of sin, and given over to virtue as to its natural good, feed on the continual contemplation of Almighty God.

VI. The Rise and Development of Western Cenobitism: the Tradition of Spiritual Regularity and *Stabilitas Loci*

A. BENEDICT OF NURSIA (c. 480/84–543/47/55)

27. *The Benedictine Rule* (c. 543/47)

Regula Monachorum (ed. E. Woelfflin), trans. *ThM*, No. 251, pp. 434–59.

Ch. 1. *The kinds of monks.*—There are four kinds of monks. The first kind is that of the cenobites [that is, those living in common], those who live in a monastery according to a rule, and under the government of an abbot. The second is that of the anchorites, or hermits, who have learned how to conduct the war against the devil by their long service in the monastery and their association with many brothers, and so, being well trained, have separated themselves from the troop, in order to wage single combat, being able with the aid of God to carry on the fight alone against the sins of the flesh. The third kind (and a most abominable kind it is) is that of the sarabites, who have not been tested and proved by obedience to the rule and by the teaching of experience, as gold is tried in the furnace, and so are soft and pliable like a base metal; who in assuming the tonsure are false to God, because they still serve the world in their lives. They do not congregate in the Master's fold, but dwell apart without a shepherd, by twos and threes, or even alone. Their law is their own desires, since they call that holy which they like, and that unlawful which they do not like. The fourth kind is composed of those who are called *gyrovagi* (wanderers), who spend their whole lives wandering about through different regions and living three or four days at a time in the cells of different monks. They are always wandering about and never remain long in one place, and they are governed by their own appetites and desires. They are in every way worse even than the sarabites. But it is better to pass over in silence than to mention their manner of life. Let us, therefore, leaving these aside, proceed, with the aid of God, to the consideration of the cenobites, the highest type of monks.

Ch. 8. *Divine worship at night* [vigils].—During the winter; that is, from the first of November to Easter, the monks should rise at the eighth hour of the night; a reasonable arrangement, since by that time the monks will have rested a little more than half the night and will have digested their food. Those brothers who failed in the psalms or the readings shall spend the rest of the time after vigils (before the beginning of matins) in pious meditation. From Easter to the first of November matins shall begin immediately after daybreak, allowing the brothers a little time for attending to the necessities of nature.

Ch. 9. *The psalms to be said at night.*—During the winter time, the order of service shall be as follows: first shall be recited the verse ["Make haste, O God, to deliver me; make haste to help me, O God," Ps. 70:1]; then this verse three times: "O Lord, open thou my lips and my mouth shall show forth thy praise" [Ps. 51:15]; then the third psalm and the Gloria, the 94th Psalm responsively or in unison, a hymn, and six psalms responsively. After this the abbot shall give the benediction with the aforesaid verse, and the brothers shall sit down. Three lessons from the gospels with three responses shall then be read from the lectern by the brothers in turn. The first two responses shall be sung without the Gloria, but in the third response which follows the last reading the cantor shall sing the Gloria, the monks rising from their seats at the beginning of it to show honor and reverence to the holy Trinity. Passages are to be read from the Old and New Testaments in the vigils, and also the expositions of these passages left by the accepted orthodox Catholic fathers. After the three readings and the responses, six psalms with the Halleluia shall follow, then a reading from the epistles recited from memory, and the usual verses, the vigils concluding with the supplication of the litany, "Kyrie eleison."

Ch. 16. *The order of divine worship during the day.*—The prophet says: "Seven times a day do I praise thee" [Ps. 119:164];

Saint Benoit Patriarche
des Moines D'Occident

IV-12. Representation of St. Benedict, Patriarch of Western Monks.

and we observe this sacred number in the seven services of the day; that is, matins, prime, terce, sext, nones, vespers, and completorium; for the hours of the daytime are plainly intended here, since the same prophet provides for the nocturnal vigils, when he says in another place: "At midnight I will rise to give thanks unto thee" [Ps. 119:62]. We should therefore praise the Creator for his righteous judgments at the aforesaid times: matins, prime, terce, sext, nones, vespers, and completorium; and at night we should rise to give thanks unto Him.

Ch. 20. *The reverence to be shown in prayer.*—When we have any request to make of powerful persons, we proffer it humbly and reverently; with how much greater humility and devotion, then, should we offer our supplications unto God, the

Lord of all. We should realize, too, that we are not heard for our much speaking, but for the purity and the contrition of our hearts. So when we pray, our prayer should be simple and brief, unless we are moved to speak by the inspiration of the spirit. The prayer offered before the congregation also should be brief, and all the brothers should rise at the signal of the superior.

Ch. 22. *How the monks should sleep.*— The monks shall sleep separately in individual beds, and the abbot shall assign them their beds according to their conduct. If possible all the monks shall sleep in the same dormitory, but if their number is too large to admit of this, they are to be divided into tens or twenties and placed under the control of some of the older monks. A candle shall be kept burning in the dormitory all night until daybreak. The monks shall go to bed clothed and girt with girdles and cords, but shall not have their knives at their sides, lest in their dreams they injure one of the sleepers. They should be always in readiness, rising immediately upon the signal and hastening to the service, but appearing there gravely and modestly. The beds of the younger brothers should not be placed together, but should be scattered among those of the older monks. When the brothers arise they should gently exhort one another to hasten to the service, so that the sleepy ones may have no excuse for coming late.

Ch. 30. *The manner of correction for the young.*—The forms of punishment should be adapted to every age and to every order of intelligence. So if children or youths, or those who are unable to appreciate the meaning of excommunication, are found guilty, they should be given heavy fasts and sharp blows for their correction.

Ch. 33. *Monks should not have personal property.*—The sin of owning private property should be entirely eradicated from the monastery. No one shall presume to give or receive anything except by the order of the abbot; no one shall possess anything of his own, books, paper, pens, or anything else; for monks are not to own even their own bodies and wills to be used at their own desire, but are to look to the father [abbot] of the monastery for everything. So they

shall have nothing that has not been given or allowed to them by the abbot; all things are to be had in common according to the command of the Scriptures, and no one shall consider anything as his own property. If anyone has been found guilty of this most grievous sin, he shall be admonished for the first and second offence, and then if he does not mend his ways he shall be punished.

Ch. 38. *The weekly reader.*—There should always be reading during the common meal, but it shall not be left to chance, so that anyone may take up the book and read. On Sunday one of the brothers shall be appointed to read during the following week. He shall enter on his office after the mass and communion, and shall ask for the prayers of all, that God may keep him from the spirit of pride; then he shall say this verse three times, all the brethren uniting with him: "O Lord, open thou my lips, and my mouth shall show forth thy praise;" then after receiving the benediction he enters upon his office. At the common meal, the strictest silence shall be kept, that no whispering or speaking may be heard except the voice of the reader. The brethren shall mutually wait upon one another by passing the articles of food and drink, so that no one shall have to ask for anything; but if this is necessary, it shall be done by a sign rather than by words, if possible. In order to avoid too much talking no one shall interrupt the reader with a question about the reading or in any other way, unless perchance the prior may wish to say something in the way of explanation. The brother who is appointed to read shall be given the bread and wine before he begins, on account of the holy communion which he has received, and lest so long a fast should be injurious; he shall have his regular meal later with the cooks and other weekly servants. The brothers shall not be chosen to read or chant by order of rotation, but according to their ability to edify their hearers.

Ch. 48. *The daily labor of the monks.*— Idleness is the great enemy of the soul, therefore the monks should always be occupied, either in manual labor or in holy reading. The hours for these occupations should be arranged according to the seasons, as follows: From Easter to the first of October, the monks shall go to work at the first hour and labor until the fourth hour, and the time from the fourth to the sixth hour shall be spent in reading. After dinner, which comes at the sixth hour, they shall lie down and rest in silence; but anyone who wishes may read, if he does it so as not to disturb anyone else. Nones shall be observed a little earlier, about the middle of the eighth hour, and the monks shall go back to work, laboring until vespers. But if the conditions of the locality or the needs of the monastery, such as may occur at harvest time, should make it necessary to labor longer hours, they shall not feel themselves ill-used, for true monks should live by the labor of their own hands, as did the apostles and the holy fathers. But the weakness of human nature must be taken into account in making these arrangements. From the first of October to the beginning of Lent, the monks shall have until the full second hour for reading, at which hour the service of terce shall be held. After terce, they shall work at their respective tasks until the ninth hour. When the ninth hour sounds they shall cease from labor and be ready for the service at the second bell. After dinner they shall spend the time in reading the lessons and the psalms. During Lent the time from daybreak to the third hour shall be devoted to reading, and then they shall work at their appointed tasks until the tenth hour. At the beginning of Lent each of the monks shall be given a book from the library of the monastery which he shall read entirely through. One or two of the older monks shall be appointed to go about through the monastery during the hours set apart for reading, to see that none of the monks are idling away the time, instead of reading, and so not only wasting their own time but perhaps disturbing others as well. Anyone found doing this shall be rebuked for the first or second offence, and after that he shall be severely punished, that he may serve as a warning and an example to others. Moreover, the brothers are not to meet together at unseasonable hours. Sunday is to be spent by all the brothers in holy reading, except by such as have regular duties assigned to them for that day. And if any

brother is negligent or lazy, refusing or being unable profitably to read or meditate at the time assigned for that, let him be made to work, so that he shall at any rate not be idle. The abbot shall have consideration for the weak and the sick, giving them tasks suited to their strength, so that they may neither be idle nor yet be distressed by too heavy labor.

Ch. 58. *The way in which new members are to be received.*—Entrance into the monastery should not be made too easy, for the apostle says: "Try the spirits, whether they are of God" [1 John 4:1]. So when anyone applies at the monastery, asking to be accepted as a monk, he should first be proved by every test. He shall be made to wait outside four or five days, continually knocking at the door and begging to be admitted; and then he shall be taken in as a guest and allowed to stay in the guest chamber a few days. If he satisfies these preliminary tests, he shall then be made to serve a novitiate of at least one year, during which he shall be placed under the charge of one of the older and wiser brothers, who shall examine him and prove, by every possible means, his sincerity, his zeal, his obedience, and his ability to endure shame. And he shall be told in the plainest manner all the hardships and difficulties of the life which he has chosen. If he promises never to leave the monastery [*stabilitas loci*] the rule shall be read to him after the first two months of his novitiate, and again at the end of six more months, and finally, four months later, at the end of his year. Each time he shall be told that this is the guide which he must follow as a monk, the reader saying to him at the end of the reading: "This is the law under which you have expressed a desire to live; if you are able to obey it, enter; if not, depart in peace." Thus he shall have been given every chance for mature deliberation and every opportunity to refuse the yoke of service. But if he still persists in asserting his eagerness to enter and his willingness to obey the rule and the commands of his superiors, he shall then be received into the congregation, with the understanding that from that day forth he shall never be permitted to draw back from the service or to leave the monastery. The ceremony of receiving a new brother into the monastery shall be as follows: first he shall give a solemn pledge, in the name of God and his holy saints, of constancy, conversion of life, and obedience (*stabilitas loci, conversio morum, obedientia*); this promise shall be in writing drawn up by his own hand (or, if he cannot write, it may be drawn up by another at his request, and signed with his own mark), and shall be placed by him upon the altar in the presence of the abbot, in the name of the saints whose relics are in the monastery. Then he shall say: "Receive me, O Lord, according to thy word, and I shall live; let me not be cast down from mine expectation" [Ps. 119:116]; which shall be repeated by the whole congregation three times, ending with the "Gloria Patri." Then he shall prostrate himself at the feet of all the brothers in turn, begging them to pray for him, and therewith he becomes a member of the congregation. If he has any property he shall either sell it all and give to the poor before he enters the monastery, or else he shall turn it over to the monastery in due form, reserving nothing at all for himself; for from that day forth he owns nothing, not even his own body and will. Then he shall take off his own garments there in the oratory and put on the garments provided by the monastery. And those garments which he put off shall be stored away in the vestiary, so that if he should ever yield to the promptings of the devil and leave the monastery, he shall be made to put off the garments of a monk, and to put on his own worldly clothes, in which he shall be cast forth. But the written promise which the abbot took from the altar where he placed it shall not be given back to him, but shall be preserved in the monastery.

Ch. 73. *This rule does not contain all the measures necessary for righteousness.*—The purpose of this rule is to furnish a guide to the monastic life. Those who observe it will have at least entered on the way of salvation and will attain at least some degree of holiness. But he who aims at the perfect life must study and observe the teachings of all the holy fathers, who have pointed out in their writings the way of perfection. For

every page and every word of the Bible, both the New and the Old Testament, is a perfect rule for this earthly life; and every work of the holy catholic fathers teaches us how we may direct our steps to God. The Collations, the Institutes, the Lives of the Saints, and the rule of our father, St. Basil, all serve as valuable instructions for monks who desire to live rightly and to obey the will of God. Their examples and their teachings should make us ashamed of our sloth, our evil lives, and our negligence. Thou who art striving to reach the heavenly land, first perfect thyself with the aid of Christ in this little rule, which is but the beginning of holiness, and then thou mayst under the favor of God advance to higher grades of virtue and knowledge through the teaching of these greater works. AMEN.

B. CASSIODORUS (c. 480/85–573)

28. *His Monastic Foundation at Vivarium* (*c. 555*)

Instit., 1, xxix, 1–2, trans. L. W. Jones, *An Introduction to Divine and Human Readings* by Cassiodorus Senator (New York: Columbia University Press, 1946), pp. 131–32.

1. The site of the monastery of Vivarium invites you to prepare many things for strangers and those in need, since you have well-irrigated gardens and, close beside them, the waters of the River Pellena, which abounds in fish—a river which should not be considered dangerous because of the greatness of its waves or contemptible because of their smallness. It flows into your grounds, skillfully directed wherever it is considered necessary, adequate for your gardens and your mills alike. It is indeed present when it is wanted, and when it has satisfied your wishes it goes far away; thus, being dedicated to a definite service, neither is it dangerously rough nor can it be lacking when it is sought. Seas too are so near you that they are accessible for various kinds of fishing, and, when it pleases you, a fish once caught may be shut up in the fish ponds. For there, with the help of the Lord, we have made pleasant ponds, where a multitude of fish may drift beneath the faithful monastery; the situation so much resembles

the caves in mountains that the fish in no way realizes that it is a captive, and it is free to acquire food and to hide itself in the solitary caverns. We have also ordered baths to be built of a sort suitable for sick bodies in a place where fitly flows limpid water, which is most pleasant for drinking and for bathing. Consequently, in all justice your monastery is sought by other people rather than other places by you. But these matters, as you see, are delights in present affairs, not a future hope of the faithful. The former are transitory; the latter will abide without end. But, situated in the monastery as we are, let us be conveyed rather to the desires which make us reign with Christ.

2. Carefully read and willingly hear the priest Cassian, who has written about the instruction of faithful monks; he states in the very beginning of his holy argument that eight cardinal sins are to be avoided. He penetrates so competently into the harmful disturbances of minds that he makes men practically see their excesses in physical form and avoid them, though through confused and dull perception they had no previous knowledge of them. In the matter of free will, however, he has been rightly blamed by the blessed Prosper, and we therefore admonish you that you ought to exercise caution in reading a man who oversteps the mark in topics of this sort. Victor Mattaritanus, bishop of Africa, has with the Lord's help corrected what Cassian has said and added what was lacking with such skill as to be justly awarded the palm in these matters; and we believe that we ought promptly to make this same Cassian, among others, conform to orthodox beliefs about the beginnings of monasticism in Africa. He violently arraigns other kinds of monks. But, dearest brothers, with God's aid choose those parts which Victor Mattaritanus has soundly praised.

29. On Monastic Reading of the Scriptures

Ibid., 1, xxxii, 3, trans. Jones, *DHR*, p. 137.

3. You have therefore been given a city of your own, O pious citizens, and if with the help of the Lord you spend your time concordantly and spiritually, you already enjoy a prefiguration of the heavenly home. Do not delight in slothfulness, which you know is hateful to the Lord. The authentic documents of the Sacred Scriptures together with their interpreters attend you, and they are truly the flowery fields, the sweet fruits of the heavenly paradise, with which faithful souls are imbued to their salvation and by which your tongues are instructed in a diction not destined to die but to bear fruit. Therefore enter ardently upon the mysteries of the Lord, in order that you may be able to point out the way to those who follow, since it is a great shame to have books to read and to be unable to teach their meaning through ignorance.

C. POPE GREGORY I (590–604) AND THE PANEGYRIC ON BENEDICT

30. Benedict's Life and Miraculous Deeds

Dialogi de vita et miraculis patrum Italicorum, Lib. 2: Praef., trans. O. J. Zimmerman and B. R. Avery, *Life and Miracles of St. Benedict* (Collegeville, Minn.: St. Johns Abbey Press, 1949), pp. 1–2.

Some years ago there lived a man who was revered for the holiness of his life. Blessed Benedict was his name, and he was blessed also with God's grace. During his boyhood he showed mature understanding, and a strength of character far beyond his years kept his heart detached from every pleasure. Even while still living in the world, free to enjoy all it had to offer, he saw how empty it was and turned from it without regret.

He was born in Norcia of distinguished parents, who sent him to Rome for a liberal education. When he found many of the students there abandoning themselves to vice, he decided to withdraw from the world he had been preparing to enter; for he was afraid that if he acquired any of its learning he would be drawn down with them to his eternal ruin. In his desire to please God alone, he turned his back on further studies, gave up home and inheritance and resolved to embrace the religious life. He took this step, fully aware of his ignorance; yet he was truly wise, uneducated though he may have been.

31. His Conquest over Temptations of the Flesh

Dial., 2:2, trans. Zimmerman, *LMB*, pp. 7–8.

(2) One day while the saint was alone, the tempter came in the form of a little blackbird, which began to flutter in front of his face. It kept so close that he could easily have caught it in his hand. Instead he made the sign of the Cross and the bird flew away. The moment it left, he was seized with an unusually violent temptation. The evil spirit recalled to his mind a woman he had once seen, and before he realized it his emotions were carrying him away. Almost overcome in the struggle, he was on the point of abandoning the lonely wilderness, when suddenly with the help of God's grace he came to himself.

Just then he noticed a thick patch of nettles and briers next to him. Throwing his garment aside, he flung himself naked into the sharp thorns and stinging nettles. There he rolled and tossed until his whole body was in pain and covered with blood. Yet once he had conquered pleasure through suffering, his torn and bleeding skin served to drain off the poison of temptation from his body. Before long the pain that was burning his whole body had put out the fires of evil in his heart. It was by exchanging these two fires that he gained the victory over sin. So complete was his triumph that from then on, as he later told his disciples,

IV-13. Pope Gregory I, under the Inspiration of the Holy Spirit, Dictates His *Dialogues* to the Deacon, Peter.

IV-14. Miracle of the Poisoned Loaf. *From Gregory's* Dialogues on the Life of St. Benedict.

he never experienced another temptation of this kind.

32. The Miracle of the Poisoned Loaf

Dial., 2:8, trans. Zimmerman, *LMB,* pp. 22–23.

The progress of the saint's work, however, could not be stopped. His reputation for holiness kept on growing and with it the number of vocations to a more perfect state of life. This only infuriated Florentius all the more. He still longed to enjoy the praise the saint was receiving, yet he was unwilling to lead a praiseworthy life himself. At length his soul became so blind with jealousy that he decided to poison a loaf of bread and send it to the servant of God as a sign of Christian fellowship. Though aware at once of the deadly poison it contained, Benedict thanked him for the gift.

At mealtime a raven used to come out of the nearby woods to receive food from the saint's hands. On this occasion he set the poisoned loaf in front of it and said, 'In the name of our Lord Jesus Christ, take this bread and carry it to a place where no one will be able to find it.' The raven started to caw and circled around the loaf of bread with open beak and flapping wings as if to indicate that it was willing to obey but found it impossible to do so. Several times the saint repeated the command. 'Take the bread,' he said, 'and do not be afraid! Take it away from here and leave it where no one can find it.' After hesitating for a long while the raven finally took the loaf in its beak and flew away. About three hours later, when it had disposed of the bread, it returned and received its usual meal from the hands of the man of God.

33. Benedict's Life as Abbot and as Author of the Rule

Dial., 2:36, trans. Zimmerman, *LMB,* p. 74.

(36) I should like to tell you much more about this saintly abbot, but I am purposely passing over some of his miraculous deeds in my eagerness to take up those of others. There is one more point, however, I

163

want to call to your attention. With all the renown he gained by his numerous miracles, the holy man was no less outstanding for the wisdom of his teaching. He wrote a Rule for Monks that is remarkable for its discretion and its clarity of language. Anyone who wishes to know more about his life and character can discover in his Rule exactly what he was like as an abbot, for his life could not have differed from his teaching.

D. COLUMBAN (C. 543–615) AND HIS RULE

34. Of Poverty and of Overcoming Greed

Monks' Rule (*Regula Monachorum*), 4, trans. G. S. M. Walker, *Sancti Columbani Opera* [Scriptores Latini Hiberniae, II] (Dublin: The Dublin Institute for Advanced Studies, 1957), p. 127.

By monks, to whom for Christ's sake the world is crucified and they to the world, greed must be avoided, when indeed it is reprehensible for them not only to have superfluities, but even to want them. In their case not property but will is required; and they, leaving all things and daily following the Lord Christ with the cross of fear, have treasures in heaven. Therefore, while they will have much in heaven, on earth they should be satisfied with the small possessions of utter need, knowing that greed is a leprosy for monks who copy the sons of the prophets, and for the disciple of Christ it is revolt and ruin, for the uncertain followers of the apostles also it is death. Thus then nakedness and disdain of riches are the first perfection of monks, but the second is the purging of vices, the third the most perfect and perpetual love of God and unceasing affection for things divine, which follows on the forgetfulness of earthly things. Since this is so, we have need of few things, according to the word of the Lord, or even of one. For few things are true necessities without which life cannot be led, or even one thing, like food according to the letter. But we require purity of feeling by the grace of God, that we may understand spiritually

IV-15. Representation of a Nun of St. Columban.

what are those few gifts of love which are offered to Martha by the Lord.

35. Perfection Through Community Discipline

Reg. Mon., 10, trans. Walker, *SCO*, pp. 141, 143.

Let the monk live in a community under the discipline of one father and in company with many, so that from one he may learn lowliness, from another patience. For one may teach him silence and another meekness. Let him not do as he wishes, let him eat what he is bidden, keep as much as he has received, complete the tale of his work, be subject to whom he does not like. Let him come weary to his bed and sleep walking, and let him be forced to rise while his sleep is not yet finished. Let him keep silence when he has suffered wrong, let him fear the superior of his community as a lord, love him as a father, believe that whatever he commands is healthful for himself, and let him not pass judgement on the opinion of an elder, to whose duty it belongs to obey and fulfil what he is bidden, as Moses says, Hear, O Israel, and the rest.

36. Monastic Offenses and Punishments

Communal Rule (*Regula Coenobialis*), 4, trans. Walker, *SCO*, pp. 149, 151.

IV. Him who through a cough has not chanted well at the beginning of a psalm, it is ordained to correct with six blows. Likewise him who has bitten the cup of salvation with his teeth, with six blows. Him who has not followed the order for the sacrifice [for celebrating], with six blows. [A priest when celebrating who has not trimmed his nails, and a deacon, whose beard has not been shaved, him who receives the sacrifice, approaches the chalice, straight from farmwork, with six blows.] And him who is smiling at the synaxis, that is, at the office of prayers, with six blows; if his laughter has broken out aloud, with an imposition, unless it has happened pardonably. [A priest, when celebrating, and a deacon, who are holding the sacrifice, should beware lest they wander with roving eyes; and if they neglect this, they must be corrected with six blows. He who has forgotten his chrismal when hurrying out to some work, with five times five blows; if he has dropped it on the ground in a field, and found it at once, with five times ten blows; if he has hung it on a tree, with thrice ten, if it remains there overnight, with an imposition]. He who with unclean hands receives the blessed bread, with twelve blows. He who forgets to make the oblation right until they go to Mass, with a hundred blows.

He who tells idle tales to another, if he censures himself at once, with a mere pardon; but if he has not censured himself [but has declined the way in which he ought to excuse them] with an imposition of silence or fifty blows. He who brings forward an excuse honestly, when examination is made of something, and does not at once say in begging pardon, It is my fault, I am sorry, with fifty blows. He who honestly sets counsel against counsel, with fifty blows. He who has struck the altar, with fifty blows.

E. POPE GREGORY, THE BENEDICTINE RULE, AND THE MISSION TO THE ANGLES, ACCORDING TO THE VENERABLE BEDE (673–735)

37. Gregory Dispatches Augustine (Prior of St. Andrew) to the English Nation

Hist. Ecc., 1:23, trans. J. E. Giles, *Bede's Ecclesiastical History of England* (London: J. Bohn, 1847), pp. 34–35.

In the year of our Lord 582, Maurice, the fifty-fourth from Augustus, ascended the throne, and reigned twenty-one years. In the tenth year of his reign, Gregory, a man renowned for learning and behaviour, was promoted to the apostolical see of Rome, and presided over it thirteen years, six months and ten days. He, being moved by Divine inspiration, in the fourteenth year of the same emperor, and about the one hundred and fiftieth after the coming of the English into Britain, sent the servant of God, Augustine, and with him several other monks, who feared the Lord, to preach the word of God to the English nation. They having, in obedience to the pope's commands, undertaken that work, were, on their journey, seized with a sudden fear, and began to think of returning home, rather than proceed to a barbarous, fierce, and unbelieving nation, to whose very language they were strangers; and this they unanimously agreed was the safest course. In short, they sent back Augustine, who had been appointed to be consecrated bishop in case they were received by the English, that he might, by humble entreaty, obtain of the holy Gregory, that they should not be compelled to undertake so dangerous, toilsome, and uncertain a journey. The pope, in reply, sent them a hortatory epistle, persuading them to proceed in the work of the Divine word, and rely on the assistance of the Almighty. The purport of which letter was as follows:—

"Gregory, the servant of the servants of God, to the servants of our Lord. Forasmuch as it had been better not to begin a good work, than to think of desisting from that which has been begun, it behoves you, my beloved sons, to fulfil the good work, which, by the help of our Lord,

you have undertaken. Let not, therefore, the toil of the journey, nor the tongues of evil speaking men, deter you; but with all possible earnestness and zeal perform that which, by God's direction, you have undertaken; being assured, that much labour is followed by an eternal reward. When Augustine, your chief, returns, whom we also constitute your abbat, humbly obey him in all things; knowing, that whatsoever you shall do by his direction, will, in all respects, be available to your souls. Almighty God protect you with his grace, and grant that I may, in the heavenly country, see the fruits of your labour. Inasmuch as, though I cannot labour with you, I shall partake in the joy of the reward, because I am willing to labour. God keep you in safety, my most beloved sons. Dated the 23rd of July, in the fourteenth year of the reign of our pious and most august lord, Mauritius Tiberius, the thirteenth year after the consulship of our said lord. The fourteenth indiction."

38. Augustine Evangelizes King Ethelbert of Kent (c. 596/97)

Hist. Ecc., 1:25, Giles, BEHE, pp. 36–38.

Augustine, thus strengthened by the confirmation of the blessed Father Gregory, returned to the work of the word of God, with the servants of Christ, and arrived in Britain. The powerful Ethelbert was at that time king of Kent; he had extended his dominions as far as the great river Humber, by which the Southern Saxons are divided from the Northern. On the east of Kent is the large Isle of Thanet containing according to the English way of reckoning, 600 families, divided from the other land by the river Wantsum, which is about three furlongs over, and fordable only in two places, for both ends of it run into the sea. In this island landed the servant of our Lord, Augustine, and his companions, being, as is reported, nearly forty men. They had, by order of the blessed Pope Gregory, taken interpreters of the nation of the Franks, and sending to Ethelbert, signified that they were come from Rome, and brought a joyful message, which most undoubtedly assured to all that took advantage of it everlasting joys in heaven, and a kingdom that would never end, with the living and true God. The king having heard this, ordered them

to stay in that island where they had landed, and that they should be furnished with all necessaries, till he should consider what to do with them. For he had before heard of the Christian religion, having a Christian wife of the royal family of the Franks, called Bertha; whom he had received from her parents, upon condition that she should be permitted to practise her religion with the Bishop Luidhard, who was sent with her to preserve her faith. Some days after, the king came into the island, and sitting in the open air, ordered Augustine and his companions to be brought into his presence. For he had taken precautions that they should not come to him in any house, lest, according to an ancient superstition, if they practised any magical arts, they might impose upon him, and so get the better of him. But they came furnished with Divine, not with magic virtue, bearing a silver cross for their banner, and the image of our Lord and Saviour painted on a board; and singing the litany, they offered up their prayers to the Lord for the eternal salvation both of themselves and of those to whom they were come. When he had sat down, pursuant to the king's commands, and preached to him and his attendants there present, the word of life, the king answered thus:—"Your words and promises are very fair, but as they are new to us, and of uncertain import, I cannot approve of them so far as to forsake that which I have so long followed with the whole English nation. But because you are come from far into my kingdom, and, as I conceive, are desirous to impart to us those things which you believe to be true, and most beneficial, we will not molest you, but give you favourable entertainment, and take care to supply you with your necessary sustenance; nor do we forbid you to preach and gain as many as you can to your religion." Accordingly he permitted them to reside in the city of Canterbury, which was the metropolis of all his dominions, and, pursuant to his promise, besides allowing them sustenance, did not refuse them liberty to preach. It is reported that, as they drew near to the city, after their manner, with the holy cross, and the image of our sovereign Lord and King, Jesus Christ, they, in concert, sung this litany: "We beseech thee, O Lord, in all thy mercy, that thy anger and wrath be turned away from this city, and from thy holy house, because we have sinned. Hallelujah."

39. Augustine Establishes His Episcopal See (c. 602)

Hist. Ecc., 1:26, trans. Giles, *BEHE*, pp. 39–40.

As soon as they entered the dwelling-place assigned them, they began to imitate the course of life practised in the primitive church; applying themselves to frequent prayer, watching and fasting; preaching the word of life to as many as they could; despising all worldly things, as not belonging to them; receiving only their necessary food from those they taught; living themselves in all respects conformably to what they prescribed to others, and being always disposed to suffer any adversity, and even to die for that truth which they preached. In short, several believed and were baptized, admiring the simplicity of their innocent life, and the sweetness of their heavenly doctrine. There was on the east side of the city, a church dedicated to the honour of St. Martin, built whilst the Romans were still in the island, wherein the queen, who, as has been said before, was a Christian, used to pray. In this they first began to meet, to sing, to pray, to say mass, to preach, and to baptize, till the king, being converted to the faith, allowed them to preach openly, and build or repair churches in all places.

When he, among the rest, induced by the unspotted life of these holy men, and their delightful promises, which, by many miracles, they proved to be most certain, believed and was baptized, greater numbers began daily to flock together to hear the word, and, forsaking their heathen rites, to associate themselves, by believing, to the unity of the church of Christ. Their conversion the king so far encouraged, as that he compelled none to embrace Christianity, but only showed more affection to the believers, as to his fellow citizens in the heavenly kingdom. For he had learned from his instructors and leaders to salvation, that the service of Christ ought to be voluntary, not by compulsion. Nor was it long before he gave his teachers a settled residence in his metropolis of Canterbury, with such possessions of different kinds as were necessary for their subsistence.

VII. Monastic Regulae and the Lives of Contemplation and Action in the Mystical Tradition

A. AUGUSTINE, NEO-PLATONISM, AND CONTEMPLATION

40. Experience, with His Mother, of the "Vision" at Ostia

Confess., 9, x, 23–25, trans. *NPNF*, 1st ser., I, pp. 137–38.

As the day now approached on which she was to depart this life (which day Thou knewest, we did not), it fell out—Thou, as I believe, by Thy secret ways arranging it—that she and I stood alone, leaning in a certain window, from which the garden of the house we occupied at Ostia could be seen; at which place, removed from the crowd, we were resting ourselves for the voyage, after the fatigues of a long journey. We then were conversing alone very pleasantly; and, "forgetting those things which are behind, and reaching forth unto those things which are before," we were seeking between ourselves in the presence of the Truth, which Thou art, of what nature the eternal life of the saints would be, which eye hath not seen, nor ear heard, neither hath entered into the heart of man. But yet we opened wide the mouth of our heart, after those supernal streams of Thy fountain, "the fountain of life," which is "with Thee;" that being sprinkled with it according to our capacity, we might in some measure weigh so high a mystery.

And when our conversation had arrived at that point, that the very highest pleasure of the carnal senses, and that in the very brightest material light, seemed by reason of the sweetness of that life not only not worthy of comparison, but not even of mention, we, lifting ourselves with a more ardent affection towards "the Self-same," did gradually pass through all corporeal things, and even the heaven itself, whence sun, and moon, and stars shine upon the earth; yea, we soared higher yet by inward musing, and discoursing, and admiring Thy works; and we came to our own minds, and went beyond them, that we might advance as high as that region of unfailing plenty, where Thou feedest Israel for ever with the food of truth, and where life is that Wisdom by whom all these things are made. . . .

We were saying, then, If to any man the tumult of the flesh were silenced,—silenced the phantasies of earth, waters, and air,—silenced, too, the poles; yea, the very soul be silenced to herself, and go beyond herself by not thinking of herself,—silenced fancies and imaginary revelations, every tongue, and every sign, and whatsoever exists by passing away, since, if any could hearken, all these say, "We created not ourselves, but were created by Him who abideth for ever:" If, having uttered this, they now should be silenced, having only quickened our ears to Him who created them, and He alone speak not by them, but by Himself, that we may hear His word, not by fleshly tongue, nor angelic voice, nor sound of thunder, nor the obscurity of a similitude, but might hear Him—Him whom in these we love—without these, like as we two now strained ourselves, and with rapid thought touched on that Eternal Wisdom which remaineth over all. If this could be sustained, and other visions of a far different kind be withdrawn, and this one ravish, and absorb, and envelope its beholder amid these inward joys, so that his life might be eternally like that one moment of knowledge which we now sighed after, were not this "Enter thou into the joy of Thy Lord"? And when shall that be? When we shall all rise again; but all shall not be changed.

41. Contemplation and Action Allegorized in Rachel and Leah

Contra Faustum Manichaeum, 22:52, trans. *NPNF,* 1st ser., IV, pp. 291–92.

Supposing that the two free wives point to the New Testament, by which we are called to liberty, what is the meaning of there being two? Perhaps because in Scripture, as the attentive reader will find, we are said to have two lives in the body of Christ,—one temporal, in which we suffer pain, and one eternal, in which we shall behold the blessedness of God. We see the one in the Lord's passion, and the other in His resurrection. The names of the women point to this meaning: It is said that Leah means Suffering, and Rachel the First Principle made visible, or the Word which makes the First Principle visible. The action, then, of our mortal human life, in which we live by faith, doing many painful tasks without knowing what benefit may result from them to those in whom we are interested, is Leah, Jacob's first wife. And thus she is said to have had weak eyes. For the purposes of mortals are timid, and our plans uncertain. Again, the hope of the eternal contemplation of God, accompanied with a sure and delightful perception of truth, is Rachel. And on this account she is described as fair and well-formed. This is the beloved of every pious student, and for this he serves the grace of God, by which our sins, though like scarlet, are made white as snow. For Laban means making white; and we read that Jacob served Laban for Rachel. No man turns to serve righteousness, in subjection to the grace of forgiveness, but that he may live in peace in the Word which makes visible the First Principle, or God; that is, he serves for Rachel, not for Leah. For what a man loves in the works of righteousness is not the toil of doing and suffering. No one desires this life for its own sake; as Jacob desired not Leah, who yet was brought to him, and became his wife, and the mother of children. Though she could not be loved of herself, the Lord made her be borne with as a step to Rachel; and then she came to be approved of on account of her children. Thus every useful servant of God, brought into His grace by which his sins are made white, has in his mind, and heart, and affection, when he thus turns to God, nothing but the knowledge of wisdom. This we often expect to attain as a reward for practising the seven precepts of the law which concern the love of our neighbor, that we injure no one: namely, Honor thy father and mother; Thou shalt not commit adultery; Thou shalt not kill; Thou shalt not steal; Thou shalt not bear false witness; Thou shalt not desire thy neighbor's wife; Thou shalt not covet thy neighbor's property. When a man has obeyed these to the best of his ability, and, instead of the bright joys of truth which he desired and hoped for, finds in the darkness of the manifold trials of this world that he is bound to painful endurance, or has embraced Leah instead of Rachel, if there is perseverance in his love, he bears with the one in order to attain the other; and as if it were said to him, Serve seven other years for Rachel, he hears seven new commands,—to be poor in spirit, to be meek, to be a mourner, to hunger and thirst after righteousness, to be merciful, pure, and a peacemaker. A man would desire, if it were possible, to obtain at once the joys of lovely and perfect wisdom, without the endurance of toil in action and suffering; but this is impossible in mortal life. This seems to be meant, when it is said to Jacob: "It is not the custom in our country to marry the younger before the elder." The elder may very well mean the first in order of time. So, in the discipline of man, the toil of doing the work of righteousness precedes the delight of understanding the truth.

B. GREGORY AND THE "MIXED LIFE" OF CONTEMPLATION AND ACTION

42. *Christ as the Example of United Contemplation and Action*

Moralia in Job, 6:56, trans. *LF*, Vol. I, Pt. 2, pp. 355–56.

And whosoever opens his mind in holy works, has over and above to extend it to the secret pursuits of inward contemplation. For he is no perfect preacher, who either, from devotion to contemplation, neglects works that ought to be done, or, from urgency in business, puts aside the duties of contemplation. . . . It is hence that the Redeemer of mankind in the day time exhibits His miracles in cities, and spends the night in devotion to prayer upon the mountain, namely, that He may teach all perfect preachers, that they should neither entirely leave the active life, from love of the speculative, nor wholly slight the joys of contemplation from excess in working, but in quiet imbibe by contemplation, what in employment they may pour back to their neighbours by word of mouth. For by contemplation they rise into the love of God, but by preaching they return back to the service of their neighbour. . . . In the sight of the internal Judge our charity may

IV-16. Rachel (Contemplation) and Leah (Action) on Either Side of Moses. *Michelangelo, Tomba da Giulio II, parte inferior, S. Pietro in Vincoli, Rome.*

be coloured with the love both of God and of our neighbour, that the converted soul may neither so delight in repose for the sake of the love of God, as to put aside the care and service of our neighbour, nor busying itself for the love of our neighbour, be so wedded thereto, that entirely forsaking quiet, it extinguish in itself the fire of love of the Most High. Whosoever then has already offered himself as a sacrifice to God, if he desires perfection, must needs take care that he not only stretch himself out to breadth of practice, but likewise up to the heights of contemplation.

43. Reverberation, Light, and Recoil

Mor., 5:57, 58, trans. *LF*, I, 2, pp. 286–87.

But when the mind is suspended in contemplation, when, exceeding the narrow limits of the flesh, with all the power of her ken, she strains to find something of the freedom of interior security, she cannot for long rest standing above herself, because though the spirit carries her on high, yet the flesh sinks her down below by the yet remaining weight of her corruption. . . . For not even in the sweetness of inward contemplation does the mind remain fixed for long, in that being made to recoil by the very immensity of the light it is called back to itself. And when it tastes that inward sweetness, it is on fire with love, it longs to mount above itself, yet it falls back in broken state to the darkness of its frailty.

44. Contemplation, Light, and the Darkness of Natural Infirmity

Mor., 4:45, trans. *LF*, I, 1, p. 212.

. . . and when we lift up the eye of the mind to that beam of light above, we grow dark with the mere dimness of our natural infirmity. And indeed many in this feeble condition of the flesh have been made strong by so great a force of virtue, that they could shine like stars in the world. Many in the darkness of this present life, while they shew forth in themselves examples above our reach, shine upon us from on high after the manner of stars; but with whatsoever brilliancy of practice they shine, with whatever fire of compunction they enkindle their hearts, it is plain that while they still bear the load of this corruptible flesh, they are unable to behold the light of eternity such as it is.

45. Contemplation, and Light Beheld as in a Mist or Fog

Mor., 31:101, trans. *LF*, III, 2, p. 500.

Because, therefore, holy men raise themselves up to lofty contemplation, and yet cannot behold God as He is, it is well said of this eagle; *Her eyes behold afar off.* As if He were saying; They resolutely direct the keenness of their intention, but they cannot, as yet, behold Him nigh, the greatness of Whose brightness they are not at all able to penetrate. For the mist of our corruption darkens us from the incorruptible light, and when the light can both be seen in a measure, and yet cannot be seen as it is, it shews how distant it is. But if the mind were not to see it in any way, it would not see that it was far off. But if it were already to behold it perfectly, it would not in truth see it through a mist [fog].

VIII. Dionysius the Pseudo-Areopagite: Celestial Hierarchies and Mystical Theology

46. Hierarchies, Illumination, Deification, Symbols, Analogia

De coelesti hierarchia, trans. by the editors of the Shrine of Wisdom, *The Mystical Theology and the Celestial Hierarchies of Dionysius the Areopagite* (Fintry, Brook, Godalming, Surrey, England: The Shrine of Wisdom, 1949), pp. 29–30.

TO MY FELLOW-PRESBYTER TIMOTHY.
DIONYSIUS THE PRESBYTER

That every Divine Illumination, whilst going forth with love in various ways to the objects of its forethought, remains one. Nor is this all: it also unifies the things illuminated.

'Every good gift and every perfect gift is from above and cometh down from the Father of Lights.'

Moreover, every Divine procession of radiance from the Father, whilst constantly and bounteously flowing unto us, fills us anew, as though with a unifying power, by recalling us to things above, and leads us again to the unity of the Shepherding Father and to the Divine ONE. For from Him and into Him are all things, as saith the holy Word.

Calling, then, upon Jesus, the Light of the Father, the Real, the True, 'Which lighteth every man that cometh into the world, by Whom we have access to the Father,' the Origin of Light, let us raise our thought, according to our power, to the illuminations of the most sacred doctrines handed down by the Fathers, and also, as far as we may, let us contemplate the Hierarchies of the Celestial Intelligences revealed to us by them in symbols for our upliftment: and admitting through the spiritual and unwavering eyes of the mind the original and super-original gift of Light of the Father Who is the Source of Divinity, which shows to us images of the all-blessed Hierarchies of the Angels in figurative symbols, let us through them again strive upwards towards Its Primal Ray. For this Light can never be deprived of Its own intrinsic unity, and although in goodness, as is fitting, It becomes a manyness and proceeds into manifestation for the upliftment and unification of those creatures which are governed by Its Providence, yet It abides eternally within Itself in changeless sameness, firmly established in Its own unity, and elevates to Itself, according to their capacity, those who turn towards It, as is meet, uniting them in accordance with Its own unity. For by that first Divine Ray we can be enlightened only in so far as It is hidden by all-various holy veils for our upliftment, and fittingly tempered to our natures by the Providence of the Father.

Wherefore that first institution of the sacred rites, judging it worthy of a supermundane copy of the Celestial Hierarchies, gave us our most holy hierarchy, and described that spiritual Hierarchy in material terms and in various compositions of forms so that we might be led, each according to his capacity, from the most holy imagery to

formless, unific, elevative principles and assimilations. For the mind can by no means be directed to the spiritual presentation and contemplation of the Celestial Hierarchies unless it use the material guidance suited to it, accounting those beauties which are seen to be images of the hidden beauty, the sweet incense a symbol of spiritual dispensations, and the earthly lights a figure of the immaterial enlightenment. Similarly the details of the sacred teaching correspond to the feast of contemplation in the soul, while the ranks of order on earth reflect the Divine Concord and the disposition of the Heavenly Orders. The receiving of the most holy Eucharist symbolizes our participation of Jesus; and everything else delivered in a supermundane manner to Celestial Natures is given to us in symbols.

To further, then, the attainment of our due measure of deification, the loving Source of all mysteries, in showing to us the Celestial Hierarchies, and consecrating our hierarchy as fellow-ministers, according to our capacity, in the likeness of their Divine ministry, depicted those supercelestial Intelligences in material images in the inspired writings of the sacred Word so that we might be guided through the sensible to the intelligible, and from sacred symbols to the Primal Source of the Celestial Hierarchies.

47. Renunciation; the Darkness of Unknowing; and the Radiance of the Divine Darkness

De Mystica theologia, 1, trans. Shrine of Wisdom, *MTCH*, pp. 9, 11.

WHAT IS THE DIVINE DARKNESS?

Supernal Triad, Deity above all essence, knowledge, and goodness; Guide of Christians to Divine Wisdom; direct our path to the ultimate summit of Thy mystical Lord, most incomprehensible, most luminous, and most exalted, where the pure, absolute, and immutable mysteries of theology are veiled in the dazzling obscurity of the secret Silence, outshining all brilliance with the intensity of their Darkness, and surcharging our blinded intellects with the utterly im-

171

palpable and invisible fairness of glories surpassing all beauty.

Let this be my prayer; but do thou, dear Timothy, in the diligent exercise of mystical contemplation, leave behind the senses and the operations of the intellect, and all things sensible and intellectual, and all things in the world of being and non-being, that thou mayest arise, by unknowing (Comment 1) towards the union, as far as is attainable, with Him Who transcends all being and all knowledge. For by the unceasing and absolute renunciation of thyself and of all things, thou mayest be borne on high, through pure and entire self-abnegation, into the superessential Radiance of the Divine Darkness (Comment 2).

It was not without reason that the blessed Moses was commanded first to undergo purification himself and then to separate himself from those who had not undergone it; and after the entire purification heard many-voiced trumpets and saw many lights streaming forth with pure and manifold rays; and that he was thereafter separated from the multitude, with the elect priests, and pressed forward to the summit of the divine ascent (Comment 5). Nevertheless, he did not attain to the Presence of God Himself; he saw not Him (for He cannot be looked upon), but the Place where He dwells. And this I take to signify that the divinest and highest things seen by the eyes or contemplated by the mind are but the symbolical expressions of those that are immediately beneath Him Who is above all. Through these, His incomprehensible Presence is manifested upon those heights of His Holy Places; that then It breaks forth, even from that which is seen and that which sees, and plunges the mystic into the Darkness of Unknowing, whence all perfection of understanding is excluded, and he is enwrapped in that which is altogether intangible and noumenal, being wholly absorbed in Him Who is beyond all, and in none else (whether himself or another); and through the inactivity of all his reasoning powers is united by his highest faculty to Him Who is wholly unknowable; thus by knowing nothing he knows That Which is beyond his knowledge (Comment 6).

48. Affirmative and Negative Theology

Myst. theol., 3, trans. Shrine of Wisdom, *MTCH*, pp. 15–17.

WHAT ARE THE AFFIRMATIONS AND THE NEGATIONS CONCERNING GOD?

In the *Theological Outlines* (Comment 9) we have set forth the principal affirmative expressions concerning God, and have shown in what sense God's Holy Nature is One, and in what sense Three; what is within It which is called Paternity, and what Filiation, and what is signified by the name Spirit; how from the uncreated and indivisible Good, the blessed and perfect Rays of Its Goodness proceed, and yet abide immutably one both within Their Origin and within Themselves and each other, coeternal with the act by which They spring from It (Comment 10); how the superessential Jesus enters an essential state in which the truths of human nature meet; and other matters made known by the Oracles are expounded in the same place.

Again, in the treatise on *Divine Names*, we have considered the meaning, as concerning God, of the titles of Good, of Being, of Life, of Wisdom, of Power, and of such other names as are applied to Him; further, in *Symbolical Theology*, we have considered what are the metaphorical titles drawn from the world of sense and applied to the nature of God; what is meant by the material and intellectual images we form of Him, or the functions and instruments of activity attributed to Him; what are the places where He dwells and the raiment in which He is adorned; what is meant by God's anger, grief, and indignation, or the divine inebriation; what is meant by God's oaths and threats, by His slumber and waking; and all sacred and symbolical representations (Comment 11). And it will be observed how far more copious and diffused are the last terms than the first, for the theological doctrine and the exposition of the *Divine Names* are necessarily more brief than the *Symbolical Theology*.

For the higher we soar in contemplation the more limited become our expressions of that which is purely intelligible; even as now, when plunging into the Darkness which is above the intellect, we pass not merely into brevity of speech, but even into absolute silence, of thoughts as well as of words. Thus, in the former discourse, our contemplations descended from the highest to the lowest, embracing an ever-widening number of conceptions, which increased at each stage of the descent; but in the present discourse we mount upwards from below to that which is the highest, and, according to the degree of transcendence, so our speech is restrained, until, the entire ascent being accomplished, we become wholly voiceless, inasmuch as we are absorbed in Him Who is totally ineffable (Comment 12). 'But why,' you will ask, 'does the affirmative method begin from the highest attributions, and the negative method with the lowest abstractions?' The reason is because, when affirming the subsistence of That Which transcends all affirmation, we necessarily start from the attributes most closely related to It and upon which the remaining affirmations depend; but when pursuing the negative method to reach That Which is beyond all abstraction, we must begin by applying our negations to things which are most remote from It (Comment 13).

For is it not more true to affirm that God is Life and Goodness than that He is air or stone; and must we not deny to Him more emphatically the attributes of inebriation and wrath than the applications of human speech and thought?

SUGGESTED READINGS

Butler, E. C., *Western Mysticism*, 2nd ed. New York: E. P. Dutton & Co., Inc., 1926.

Chadwick, O., *Western Asceticism*, Library of Christian Classics, Vol. XII. Philadelphia: Westminster Press, 1958.

Clarke, W. K. L., *St. Basil the Great*. Cambridge: Cambridge University Press, 1913.

Davies, J. G., *The Origin and Development of Early Christian Architecture*. New York: Philosophical Library, Inc., 1952.

Dix, G., *The Shape of the Liturgy*. London: The Dacre Press, 1945.

Duchesne, L., *Christian Worship, Its Origin and Evolution*, trans. M. L. McClure. London: SPCK, 1931.

Kirk, K. E., ed., *The Apostolic Ministry*. New York: Morehouse-Barlow Co., Inc., 1946.

Lietzmann, H., *The Founding of the Church Universal*. New York: Charles Scribner's Sons, 1938.

Mackean, W. H., *Christian Monasticism in Egypt to the Close of the Fourth Century*. London: SPCK, 1920.

Manson, T. W., *The Church's Ministry*. Naperville, Illinois: Allec R. Allenson, Inc., 1956.

McNeill, J. T., *A History of the Cure of Souls*. New York: Harper & Brothers, 1951.

Pourrat, P., *Christian Spirituality . . .*, Vol. I, trans. W. H. Mitchell and S. P. Jacques. London: Burns and Oates, Ltd., 1922.

Raby, F. J. E., *A History of Christian-Latin Poetry. . . .* New York: Oxford University Press, Inc., 1927.

Rolt, C. E., *Dionysius the Areopagite on the Divine Names and the Mystical Theology*. London: SPCK, 1920.

Srawley, J. H., *The Early History of the Liturgy*, 2nd ed. Cambridge: Cambridge University Press, 1947.

Waddell, H., *The Desert Fathers*. New York: Holt, Rinehart & Winston, Inc., 1936.

Workman, H. B., *The Evolution of the Monastic Ideal. . . .* London: The Epworth Press, Publishers, 1913.

CHRONOLOGY

The Conversion of an Arian by St. Remy. *Master of St. Gilles, Franco-Flemish, c. 1500.*

V

The Papacy,

the Barbarian Kingdoms,

Islam, and the Carolingian Church

In the course of five hundred years the
bishops of Rome ascended from a position of relative obscurity
to claim episcopal pre-eminence throughout the Christian
world. The basis of their contention rested, in historical
retrospect, upon the "Petrine Theory."
According to this assertion, grounded in
Matthew 16:19, Peter as prince of the apostles had received
from Christ himself supreme power over the entire
Church. The keys to the Kingdom of Heaven were uniquely committed
to him. This commission entailed the binding
in heaven of what Peter chose to bind on earth and the
loosing in heaven of what he chose to loose
on earth. His primacy was thus held to have been established with

177

attendant superiority over the other apostles. This precedence in rank Peter in turn transmitted to his successors, the bishops of Rome. As such, they were to be granted the same primacy over the Church and other bishops that Peter had exercised over his fellow apostles.

By the fifth century, the theories of Petrine eminence and apostolic succession had been coordinated in a steadily rising crescendo of insistence upon papal priority. With the passages reproduced in this chapter from Leo I, the claims to papal headship over all other bishops reached a high peak. Conceivably, they represented neither the uncontested concessions from earliest times of all leading ecclesiasts nor even the primitive conception of the earliest Roman bishops themselves. Presumably, these contentions read back into early documents the implications for Roman primacy ascribable to these documents from the vantage point of cumulative pontifical influence.

According to Leo's assertions, Christ had committed the duty of promulgating his truth to all the apostles. But St. Peter had been constituted their head. Separated from him, one might have no share in the divine blessing. Constantinople, for example, had developed its own kind of royal glory, but this could not compete with Rome's apostolicity. Rome had been founded by Peter, the rock, on which foundation in Christ she rested secure. Out of the whole world, Peter had been uniquely chosen by Christ. Subsequently, he presided over the apostles and assembled church Fathers. In the midst of many priests and shepherds ruling God's people, Peter governed supremely with the full authority and all-inclusiveness that Christ had originally exercised. The stability of divine graciousness thus specifically conferred upon Peter was by him then conveyed to the other apostles. Leo seconded his legates' designation of himself as the head of the universal Church. He was endowed with the dignity of St. Peter who was the foundation of the Church, the rock of the faith, and the porter of heaven. From his seat at Rome, Leo exercised the care and headship of all the churches, with direct responsibility

to Christ who had conferred this princedom on Peter. Leo, speaking humbly out of a sense of his own unworthiness, nevertheless invited others to see in him the successor to St. Peter. His was thus the episcopal dignity and precedence inherited immediately from the prince of all the apostles.

The rise of the Roman bishops to claim this primacy on earth and to fulfill these heavenly functions was not a simple process. They were certainly not accorded any such priority either quickly or spontaneously. Their own claims to this eminence were slow in coming to full self-consciousness, let alone to self-expression. No widespread unanimity marked the views of early Christian leaders toward them and their special status. Centuries went by before the tradition of their distinct calling achieved sufficient background in demonstrated leadership for them to rationalize their purportedly original commission into its fullest pretensions. Meanwhile, the testimonies of the Christian Fathers traced the existential pattern of varying circumstances, giving rise to the shifting interpretations of the ages.

A variety of factors served to place the Roman bishop in the foreground for those who scrutinized the gathering tradition of the Church's unity and ultimate destiny. Rome with all her vicissitudes had long been the mistress of the world. An almost indefinable prestige clung, even after her decline, to any administrator of reasonable distinction within her walls. Moreover, early tradition—such as that of Clement's letter to the Corinthians—associated the leadership and martyrdom of both Peter and Paul with this one-time capital of civilization. Then, too, the shift of imperial administration to Constantinople in the East left the bishop of Rome the one major continuing force in the eternal city. Through the centuries, Roman bishops exemplified much of the old Roman genius for adapting the principles of law and order to the surmounting of fluid circumstance. Notably, one penchant of Roman bishops was clearly marked. They had a propensity for avoiding social and theological eccentricities in the interest of spiritual unity.

For example, the mediating efforts credited to Leo I at the council of Chalcedon were entered by later ecclesiastical officials and proponents of the papacy as having been a strong assist to papal prestige in subsequent tradition. Clearly outrunning any verifiable influence upon Attila was Leo's mounting prestige, traditionally ascribed to that episode. More important still for the accretion in papal influence was the role of bishops like Gregory I as they met the onslaught of the Lombards and other barbarians upon Roman-Christian society. This growing reputation was also attributable in no small part to the initiative displayed by the popes in their missions to Britain and Germany. This was significant for the simultaneous recouping of Roman leadership and Christian unity within a society newly formed from older social ingredients. With power and popular deference on the rise for services rendered under public pressures such as these, the Petrine claims of Rome gained at least a respectful hearing throughout Western society. Here was a credible theoretical basis for positions already taken and leadership already exercised. One can with difficulty envisage Roman episcopal headship as being derivable alone from doctrinal claims, however vigorous and apposite. The Roman bishops, however, gave cumulative support by their own aggressive actions to these historic papal contentions.

Actually, as buttresses to the latent claims of the earliest centuries, the later Roman bishops could point to their being head of the only apostolic church in the West. They could stand forth as sole bearers of Roman administrative élan. Their public image grew as the sober guardians of orthodoxy and spiritual conservation in the midst of babbling philosophies and disunifying theologies. They directed attention to themselves as the authorized leaders of that congregation to which Peter had committed his power in all its solidarity. To them Paul had surrendered his missionary vocation with its universalizing proclamation.

The historical variations and the traditional convergence of the Fathers, both Western and Eastern, apropos the Roman episcopal leadership receive large attention in the readings of this chapter. No attempt is made to give them a unity they never exhibited. However dangerous it may be to offer such a scant collection from so vast a field, diversified suggestion is infinitely preferable to generalized, safe conclusions from any single quarter. The directions which further reading may explore are fairly evident.

The logic of following the documents on the rising papacy with those of the barbarian peoples should be apparent. Roman unity had been threatened alike by the exclusivism of Christianity and the pressure of rude Gothic tribesmen. Yet both forces were to help create a new Roman unity out of their common affection for, as well as their distinct aversions to, the old Roman ideal. Roman historians and social critics had observed the fateful Christian capacity for unifying their own exclusivist claims at the expense of Roman tolerance and solidarity. The more sophisticated Roman analysts realized that the Germanic peoples were not seeking to destroy Rome. They were merely trying to huddle in suffocating proximity to her orderly security and pacific bounty. The old *Pax Romana* receded before the Christian triumph over imperial persecution. It succumbed to centuries of Gothic infiltration. This came about more through the crossing of elastic frontiers of barter and trade and the influx of barbarians into the imperial armies than it did by intermittent military skirmishes. Ironically enough the "New Roman Peace" would arise from a collaboration of Roman Christians and Christian barbarians in the erection of a new Roman-Christian society. Strictly speaking, it would not be Roman, or barbarian, or Christian. Its component laws, institutional ideals, religious assumptions, and social flexibility were to reflect the merging of all these cultural forces.

The sources provided here suffice to indicate the odd blend of forces that came to be so misleadingly called "The Barbarian Invasions." These factors were compounded quite naturally of population explosion, tribal frenzy in the face of invading Asiatic hordes, and rapacious Germanic ambitions excited by an indeterminate Roman policy.

Here, actually, was an interpenetration of customs, survival pressures, and latent idealisms that touched every aspect of Germanic as well as Roman and Christian life. This investment of vital new energies profoundly agitated the old Roman society. The high potentiality of a Christian ethos that had often threatened to become effete was gradually joined to the generally untutored, but by no means wholly savage, impulses of the galvanic German peoples.

With all their uncritical description of the Gothic surge into the Roman orbit, Procopius, Jordanes, and others like them exhibit the stuff from which historical significance is deducible. They portray a melee of Teutonic passion and Eastern imperial calculation. These intersected a Roman decadence that was challenged by a renewed sense of Christian destiny. The rash vigor of the Goths was capitalized by Christian missionaries with pacific, if highly Arian, convictions. The muddled viciousness of the Eastern-Western entente—from which Theodoric arose to found an Ostrogothic state—set the stage for new rivalries and alliances. These embroiled Rome and Constantinople in further duplicities of policy toward the Germans. New battles and compromised purposes marked the course of relations between orthodox Christians and Arian Ostrogoths. Some of these, like the self-cultivated Theodoric, were genuine if heterodox admirers of the old Roman culture. They were, at the same time, midwives to a new Christian society.

Theodoric had in his youth been a hostage at Constantinople. When, out of weltering intrigue and barbarian violence, he rose to kingship over Italy, he did not presume to imperial ambitions. His policies were often devious but his admiration for the glories of old Rome was real. The orthodox faithful never forgave his abominable Arianism. Despite his arbitrary cruelties, he ruled Christian Italy with a fairness that seemed justice itself by contrast with later exactions from Justinian's orthodox exarchs. With the aid of men like Cassiodorus and Boethius he effected a cultural renaissance of large proportions centered at Ravenna. Increasingly, Italian Christians turned to

the bishop of Rome as their natural protector against Eastern imperial exploitation as well as Arian-Gothic statecraft. The popes looked wistfully to an alliance with newly evangelized Frankish orthodoxy. Unlike his Ostrogothic brother-in-law Theodoric, Clovis the Frank, upon his dramatic conversion in 496, had accepted orthodox Christianity. Following the urgings of his wife, and after a battlefield vision strongly reminiscent of Constantine's own, Clovis had accepted Christianity. He had previously fallen under the influence of miracles traceable to the orthodox St. Martin of Tours. Now he underwent baptism by Bishop Remy of Rheims. The picture drawn of him by his admirer Gregory of Tours depicts a character as strong as it was willful and cruel: one who was, for Gregory, the anointed of God even as he was the virile progenitor of the all-too-soon decadent Merovingian line. The Roman hierarchy watched with approval the Frankish rise to pre-eminence among their Arian neighbors. They were safely outside the range of Justinian's reconquest. The Franks, however much a travesty upon Roman ideals, grew steadily in their assumption of orthodox Christian ambitions. In due time it was to be their star which would rise in conjunction with that of the papacy. Together they would beat off Islamic threats and help lay the foundation of a New Christian-Roman unity.

In the meantime, the bishops of Rome had, with the aid of Benedictine monasticism, been "regularizing" their relations with Britain and Germany. In the last chapter, apropos of monastic missions, the work of Gregory in evangelizing Kent was noted. The present chapter accents his part in the rise of papal primacy. Gregory was of patrician Roman stock. He was for a time a monastic contemplative. He served for a while as prefect of Rome, the city's highest secular officer. In his unsuccessful mission to Constantinople to secure aid against the Lombards, Gregory developed an animus for Greek—the language and all it entailed. He never lost his predilection for contemplative retreat and himself endowed a monastery. This was St. Andrew, over which he was at one time abbot. Its rule was Benedictine. From it, Augustine was sent on the mission to Kent, by way of Frankish Gaul.

Gregory came to the papacy at a most inopportune hour—at least from the perspective of individual ambition. The Lombards were at the gates of Rome. Famine and plague seized the entire city. Economic resources were throttled. Virtually forced into the pontificate, he had resisted manfully but in vain. He wrote as if the end of all things had come. He acted as if the whole divine program depended upon him. The plague was stayed. Gregory tried armed intervention against the Lombards and later negotiated a truce with them to free the beleaguered city. Social service to the entire populace with sagacious administration of things both small and great fell to his harried lot. This was a man ruling out of the cumulative wisdom of his versatile past. He demonstrated an astute balancing of the most diverse factors potential for the future. He wrote books of homily and hagiographical narrative. His volumes of Bible commentary vied with a stream of letters on rural economy and ecclesiastical diplomacy. He earned the gratitude of succeeding centuries with the homely wisdom of his *Pastoral Rule*. In this he addressed bishops in particular, but all who had ever had a flock as well. Long afterward, King Alfred translated this and other works of Gregory for those governing Christian souls in Britain. In such a man the might of the papacy stood more erect than any claims to Petrine singularity could ever have predicted.

At the outset of the eighth century the tide of papal fortunes, the promise of Benedictine missions, the vigor of rising Islam, and the Reorienting of Frankish ambitions were all moving toward a dramatic climax. Popes like Gregory II (712/15–731), Gregory III (731–741), Zacharias (741–752), and Stephens I (752) and II (752–757) played key roles. For long years Winfred, later called Boniface, carried the combined influences of Benedictinism and the Roman hierarchy even more deeply into the heart of the German apostolate. Next to his dependence on papal Rome and the Benedictine Rule was his cherished alliance with the Austrasian and Neustrian mayors of the palace. These were fast moving to ascendancy over the "do-nothing" kings, as the effete later Merovingians were called. By 687 Pepin of Heristal had established himself in virtual dominance over the whole Frankish realm. Pepin died in 714 without legitimate heirs. His functions as "mayor of the palace" devolved upon his illegitimate son, Charles Martel (714/15–741). While reconsolidating his claims over Aquitaine he ran head-on into the rising tide of the Moors at the battle of Poitiers (732). The pieces of a vast jigsaw puzzle were now ready for arrangement: papacy, monasticism, German missionaries, Frankish mayors, and Islam.

The rise of Islam had marked the transition from the shrewd visions of a crude prophet and social legislator, Mohammed (632), to the corporate rebirth of the Arabic world. The new movement stemmed from the simultaneous fusion and rejection of Judaism and Christianity, alike. It exhilarated the warlike propensities and economic necessities of countless Bedouin and other Arab peoples. Even more, it ennobled conquest and death as the fitting response to Islam. This was obedience to the fateful will of Allah. Entire submission to one true God involved fasting, frequent prayers, regular almsgiving, abstention from alcohol, and other moderately ascetic disciplines. Moslem contempt blazed out against Jewish perversions and the recreant Christian compromising, with Trinitarianism, of true Semitic monotheism. Islam surmounted what it deemed to be Jewish and Christian rebellion against the divine unity, with its own Credo of divinely revealed destiny. Periodically, from the days of the early Franks through the agonies of medieval crusading, the hierarchies of the papal West and the sultanates of the East engaged each other to the death.

One hundred years after the Hegira (622), Pope Gregory II sent a letter recommending Boniface to Charles Martel (722). This prelate had been instructed by the papacy in apostolic doctrine and the traditions of the Holy See. He was on a mission from God Himself, and the Holy Father—an apostolate to the Gentiles dwelling on the eastern side of the Rhine. Gregory appealed to Charles's "religious spirit" to support this Boniface, a bishop by papal appointment (722). At the time, Charles's response was scarcely more than lukewarm. Within ten years (732) Boniface would set up a ring of German bishoprics. He would be installed as archbishop by Gregory III. Charles would have new reason to look respectfully toward Rome. Gregory III would, out of his pressing vexations with the Lombards, look ever more hopefully to the rising power of the Carolingian Franks. Sealing the common concern of pope and mayor was Boniface, whose work in the next twenty years would bear rich fruit in an alliance of pregnant possibilities (751). Upon his death in 741, Charles's sons—Carloman and Pepin—carried forward private enterprises coupled with national ambitions. These saw an increasing deference to Boniface's influence and the Church's ideals. Much of it was, perhaps, subconscious and indirect. One may assess variously the constituent elements of state initiative, national ecclesiastical assemblies, and the influence of Boniface's broadening missionary episcopacy. In no case, however, ought the significance of 751/752 to be underrated. Boniface's work was woven deeply into it. Temporal and spiritual powers found mutual reenforcement and common outgrowths in this necessary alliance. The promises and donations of Pepin and the role of Pope Stephen in guaranteeing the emergence of the Carolingian mayors into full Christian kingship were a downpayment on a new unity. The papacy had its protector against the Lombards. The Christian Franks had coronation at papal hands.

Pepin died in 768. His sons Charles and Carloman ruled jointly until 771. Upon Carloman's death Charles forced his claims over minor heirs into uncontested hegemony. The court biographer Einhard paints a highly congratulatory but not wholly distorted picture of this Charlemagne, the great Charles. He emerges from this and similar sources as a worthy successor to Charles Martel, his grandfather. He was egotistical, lusty, shrewd, and loyal to his lights. He was a fighter born, a hard rider, hunter, and ruthless enemy. His personal morals he held to be his sole concern. He forced discussions with learned men on the nature of the virtues and their relation to Christian ethics and the Kingdom of God. The morals of churchmen and of the Christian populace he regarded as his rightful, royal preoccupation. He was ignorant, perhaps, of the more subtle bouquet of Christian idealism and ethical vicariousness. He was bent, nevertheless, on discerning the solid contributions as well as the cherished vagaries of scholars and theologians. He put their theories to the proof in his own imperially enforced laws, the capitularies.

Early in his reign and until a late date, he ruthlessly fought the Saxons. He finally gave them the choice of conversion or of extinction. If he brought the Church to them, they also brought much of paganism into the Church. Charles organized his whole government around carefully prepared yet somewhat improvised field trips by his imperial messengers, the *missi dominici*. They were the investigators, interpreters, and guarantors of royal justice. They were also the people's indoctrinators in the imperial will and the kingly plan of education.

Religious instruction became an imperial passion with Charlemagne. The pope was informed quite early of his spiritual functions in relation to the military, missionizing responsibilities of the emperor. Charles saw no contradiction of the papal prerogative and no repudiation of his own secular limitations in thus playing the Christian benevolent despot. He made the entire realm a training ground for Christian ecclesiasts —under strictly imperial aegis, of course. He schooled them, even as he controlled them, in the administration of episcopal, parish, and monastic duties. He was a caesaropapist in all the basic meanings of that term. He conceived his secular calling under God as a defining and delimiting of the spiritual vocations of churchmen, the pope included.

Charlemagne scrutinized the activities of ecclesiasts in all their liturgical and administrative aspects. He punished and rewarded laymen and churchmen in terms of landholding, land-dispensing, and a set of near-feudal contracts. He doled out lands and offices in tantalizing balance to bishops and abbots, to ecclesiastical and secular princes. In the so-called palace school at Aachen his was the most voracious inquiry of all into the bearing upon Christian life of the Bible and the Fathers. He avidly sought the implications of Augustine's *City of God* for all Christian sovereigns—and for himself, particularly. He thought of himself as the apotheosis of Augustine's "good king." Likewise, he tried to ferret out the tradition of the liberal arts, the secrets of Roman and Canon Law, the esoterics of symbol and icon, and the potentialities for reform in architecture, liturgy, and manuscript calligraphy. A tyro in contrast with a dilettante theologian like Justinian, he had a rare capacity for rescuing practicable suggestions from academic hair-splitting.

In the process of keeping churchmen, like all others, under careful surveillance and undisguised dominance, Charles disciplined them in the experimental school of social influence and temporal policy. In his very parceling out of the imperial fisc, as in his shrewd playing off of one noble against another, he girded the Church and the papacy itself for the day of weakened empire and augmented feudal powers. Under apprenticeship to Charles the Great as from few others, the hierarchy learned how ecclesiastical society might play at imperial games; how it might realign the power pressures of landholding and legislative fiat into a new economic-social unity.

In retrospect, the arts, laws and Christian manipulation of another caesaropapist, Justinian, seem full of éclat and polish. Against their background of brilliant codification and theological sophistication, Charles's vigor often appears crudely amusing. Yet these very contrasts put in relief all the more the zestful idealism that was implicit in his heady, hardy propagandizing for a Christian commonwealth.

I. Petrine Priority, The Rise of the Bishop of Rome, and His Primacy According to Fathers, Councils, and Popes

A. CLEMENT OF ROME

1. Peter and Paul Placed in the Roman Context. (See Ep. Cor., 5, already reproduced in Chap. I, No. 2.)

B. IRENAEUS RECAPITULATES THE CHURCH'S TRADITION AND THE EPISCOPAL LISTS

2. The Priority of the Roman Church Founded by Peter and Paul

Adv. Haer., 3, iii, 2, trans. ANF, I, pp. 415–16.

2. Since, however, it would be very tedious, in such a volume as this, to reckon up the successions of all the Churches, we do put to confusion all those who, in whatever manner, whether by an evil self-pleasing, by vainglory, or by blindness and perverse opinion, assemble in unauthorized meetings; [we do this, I say,] by indicating that tradition derived from the apostles, of the very great, the very ancient, and universally known Church founded and organized at Rome by the two most glorious apostles, Peter and Paul; as also [by pointing out] the faith preached to men, which comes down to our time by means of the successions of the bishops. For it is a matter of necessity that every Church should agree with this Church, on account of its preeminent authority, that is, the faithful everywhere, inasmuch as the apostolical tradition has been preserved continuously by those [faithful men] who exist everywhere.

3. The Catalogue of Early Popes, the Ecclesiastical Tradition, and Episcopal Succession

Adv. Haer., 3, iii, 3, trans. ANF, I, p. 416.

3. The blessed apostles, then, having founded and built up the Church, com-

mitted into the hands of Linus the office of the episcopate. Of this Linus, Paul makes mention in the Epistles to Timothy. To him succeeded Anacletus; and after him, in the third place from the apostles, Clement was allotted the bishopric. This man, as he had seen the blessed apostles, and had been conversant with them, might be said to have the preaching of the apostles still echoing [in his ears], and their traditions before his eyes. Nor was he alone [in this], for there were many still remaining who had received instructions from the apostles. In the time of this Clement, no small dissension having occurred among the brethren at Corinth, the Church in Rome despatched a most powerful letter to the Corinthians, exhorting them to peace, renewing their faith, and declaring the tradition which it had lately received from the apostles, proclaiming the one God, omnipotent, the Maker of heaven and earth, the Creator of man, who brought on the deluge, and called Abraham, who led the people from the land of Egypt, spake with Moses, set forth the law, sent the prophets, and who has prepared fire for the devil and his angels. From this document, whosoever chooses to do so, may learn that He, the Father of our Lord Jesus Christ, was preached by the Churches, and may also understand the apostolical tradition of the Church, since this Epistle is of older date than these men who are now propagating falsehood, and who conjure into existence another god beyond the Creator and the Maker of all existing things. To this Clement there succeeded Evaristus. Alexander followed Evaristus; then, sixth from the apostles, Sixtus was appointed; after him, Telephorus, who was gloriously martyred; then Hyginus; after him, Pius; then after him, Anicetus. Soter having succeeded Anicetus, Eleutherius does now, in the twelfth place from the apostles, hold the inheritance of the episcopate. In this order, and by this succession, the ecclesiastical tradition from the apostles, and the preaching of the truth, have come down to us. And this is most abundant proof that there is one and the same vivifying faith, which has been preserved in the Church from the apostles until now, and handed down in truth.

C. TERTULLIAN'S STATEMENT ON ROMAN EMINENCE FROM HIS "CATHOLIC" PERIOD; AN ENIGMATIC UTTERANCE FROM HIS "MONTANIST" PHASE

4. How Happy the Church of Rome!

De Praes. Haer. (c. 200), 36, trans. ANF, III, p. 260.

How happy is its church, on which apostles poured forth all their doctrine along with their blood! where Peter endures a passion like his Lord's! where Paul wins his crown in a death like John's! where the Apostle John was first plunged, unhurt, into boiling oil, and thence remitted to his island-exile! See what she has learned, what taught, what fellowship has had with even (our) churches in Africa!

5. An Anonymous Bishop—Probably the Roman Pontiff—Rebuked for Usurping Peter's Personal Prerogatives

De Pudicitia (c. 220), 1, 21, trans. ANF, IV, p. 99.

If, because the Lord has said to Peter, "Upon this rock will I build My Church," "to thee have I given the keys of the heavenly kingdom;" or, "Whatsoever thou shalt have bound or loosed in earth, shall be bound or loosed in the heavens," you therefore presume that the power of binding and loosing has derived to you, that is, to every Church akin to Peter, what sort of man are you, subverting and wholly changing the manifest intention of the Lord, conferring (as that intention did) this (gift) personally upon Peter? "On thee," He says, "will I build My Church"; and, "I will give to thee the keys," not to the Church; and, "Whatsoever thou shalt have loosed or bound," not what they shall have loosed or bound.

D. ORIGEN ON THE MEANING OF THE PETRINE "ROCK"

6. The Promise to Peter Meant for All Disciples Like Him

Comm. in Matt., 12:11, trans. ANF, IX, p. 456.

But if you suppose that upon that one Peter only the whole church is built by God,

what would you say about John the son of
thunder or each one of the Apostles? Shall
we otherwise dare to say, that against Peter
in particular the gates of Hades shall not
prevail, but that they shall prevail against
the other Apostles and the perfect? Does
not the saying previously made, "The gates
of Hades shall not prevail against it," hold
in regard to all and in the case of each of
them? And also the saying, "Upon this rock
I will build My church"? Are the keys of
the kingdom of heaven given by the Lord
to Peter only, and will no other of the
blessed receive them? But if this promise,
"I will give unto thee the keys of the kingdom of heaven," be common to the others,
how shall not all the things previously
spoken of, and the things which are subjoined as having been addressed to Peter,
be common to them? For in this place these
words seem to be addressed as to Peter
only, "Whatsoever thou shalt bind on earth
shall be bound in heaven," etc.; but in the
Gospel of John the Saviour having given
the Holy Spirit unto the disciples by breathing upon them said, "Receive ye the Holy
Spirit," etc. Many then will say to the Saviour, "Thou art the Christ, the Son of the
living God;" but all who say this will say
it to Him, as not at all having learned it
by the revelation of flesh and blood but
by the Father in heaven Himself taking
away the veil that lay upon their heart,
in order that after this "with unveiled face
reflecting as a mirror the glory of the Lord"
they may speak through the Spirit of God
saying concerning Him, "Lord Jesus," and
to Him, "Thou art the Christ, the Son of
the living God." And if any one says this
to Him, not by flesh and blood revealing it
unto Him but through the Father in heaven,
he will obtain the things that were spoken
according to the letter of the Gospel to that
Peter, but, as the spirit of the Gospel
teaches, to every one who becomes such as
that Peter was. For all bear the surname of
"rock" who are the imitators of Christ, that
is, of the spiritual rock which followed those
who are being saved, that they may drink
from it the spiritual draught. But these bear
the surname of the rock just as Christ does.
But also as members of Christ deriving their

surname from Him they are called Christians, and from the rock, Peters.

7. The Episcopacy, Peter, and Ecclesiastical Unity

De Catholicae Ecclesiae Unitate (c. 251), 4–6
[Texts already reproduced in Chap. III, No.
31].

8. Appeals to Rome Not to Compromise the Prerogatives of Other Bishops

Ep. 59 (54):14 (252), trans. Robinson, Readings in European History, II, p. 66.

They dare to appeal to the throne of
Peter, and to the chief church whence
priestly unity takes its source. . . . But
we have all agreed—as is both fair and just
—that every case should be heard there
where the crime has been committed; and
a portion of the flock has been assigned to
each individual pastor, which he is to rule
and govern, having to give an account of
his deeds to the Lord. It certainly behooves
those over whom we are placed not to run
about, nor to break up the harmonious
agreement of the bishops with their crafty
and deceitful rashness, but there to plead
their cause, where they may be able to have
both accusers and witnesses to their crime.

9. The Pope as Leader and Rallying Point of the Western Church

To Silvester (314), trans. O. R. Vassall-Phillips,
St. Optatus (London: SPCK, 1917), p. 389.

To the most beloved Pope Silvester:
Marinus . . . [33 names], eternal life in
the Lord.
Being united by the common tie of
charity, and by that unity which is the bond
of our mother, the Catholic Church, we have
been brought to the city of Arles by the
wish of the most pious emperor, and we
salute you with due reverence, most glorious Pope. Here we have suffered from

troublesome men, dangerous to our law and tradition—men of undisciplined mind, whom both the authority of our God, which is with us, and our tradition and the rule of truth reject, because they have neither reason in their argument, nor any moderation in their accusations, nor was their manner of proof to the point. Therefore *by the judgement of God and of Mother Church*, who knows and approves her own, *they have been either condemned or rejected.* Would, most beloved brother, that you had thought it well to be present at this great spectacle! We believe surely that in that case a more severe sentence would have been passed against them; and our assembly would have rejoiced with a greater joy, had you passed judgement together with us; but since you were by no means able to leave *that region where the apostles daily sit,* and their blood without ceasing bears witness to the glory of God, . . . it did not seem to us, most well-beloved brother, that we ought to deal exclusively with those matters on account of which we had been summoned, but we judged that we also should take counsel on our own affairs; because, as the countries from which we have come are different, so events of various kinds will happen which we think that we ought to watch and regulate. Accordingly, we thought well, in the presence of the Holy Ghost and his angels, that concerning the various matters which occurred to each of us, we should make some decrees to provide for the present state of peace. We also agreed to write first to you who hold the greater dioceses that by you especially they should be brought to the knowledge of all. What it is that we have determined on, we have appended to this poor letter of ours.

In the first place we were bound to discuss a matter that concerned the usefulness of our life. Now since One died and rose again for many, the same season should be observed with a religious mind by all at the same time, lest divisions or dissensions arise in so great a service of devotion. We judge therefore that the Easter of the Lord should be observed throughout the world upon the same day.

G. JEROME ON EPISCOPAL EQUALITY

10. *Wherever There Are Bishops, There Dignity and Priesthood Are One* (356)

Ep. 146:1, trans. *NPNF*, 2nd ser., VI, p. 289.

It is not the case that there is one church at Rome and another in all the world beside. Gaul and Britain, Africa and Persia, India and the East worship one Christ and observe one rule of truth. If you ask for authority, the world outweighs its capital. Wherever there is a bishop, whether it be at Rome or at Engubium, whether it be at Constantinople or at Rhegium, whether it be at Alexandria or at Zoan, his dignity is one and his priesthood is one. Neither the command of wealth nor the lowliness of poverty makes him more a bishop or less a bishop. All alike are successors of the apostles.

H. THE COUNCIL OF SARDICA (342)

11. *The Bishopric of Rome as Court of Appeal*

Canon 3 (Lat.), trans. *NPNF*, 2nd ser., XIV, p. 417.

Bishop Hosius said: . . . But if judgment have gone against a bishop in any cause, and he think that he has a good case, in order that the question may be reopened, let us, if it be your pleasure, honour the memory of St. Peter the Apostle, and let those who tried the case write to Julius, the bishop of Rome, and if he shall judge that the case should be retried, let that be done, and let him appoint judges; but if he shall find that the case is of such a sort that the former decision need not be disturbed, what he has decreed shall be confirmed.

Is this the pleasure of all? The synod answered, It is our pleasure.

I. CYRIL OF JERUSALEM (C. 348/50) ON THE PRIMACY OF PETER

12. *Peter, Chiefest of Apostles*

Catecheses, 2:19, trans. *NPNF*, 2nd ser., VII, p. 13.

Let no man therefore despair of his own salvation. Peter, the chiefest and foremost of the Apostles, denied the Lord thrice before a little maid: but he repented himself, and wept bitterly. Now weeping shews the repentance of the heart: and therefore he not only received forgiveness for his denial, but also held his Apostolic dignity unforfeited.

13. Peter and Paul

Cat., 6:15, trans. *NPNF*, 2nd ser., VII, p. 38.

As the delusion was extending, Peter and Paul, a noble pair, chief rulers of the Church, arrived and set the error right; . . .

14. Peter, Foremost of the Apostles and Chief Herald of the Church

Cat., 11:3, trans. *NPNF*, 2nd ser., VII, p. 64.

And when they all became silent (for the matter was too high for man to learn), Peter, the foremost of the Apostles and chief herald of the Church, neither aided by cunning invention, nor persuaded by human reasoning, but enlightened in his mind from the Father, says to Him, *Thou art the Christ,* not only so, but *the Son of the living God.*

J. OPTATUS OF MILEVE AND THE PERIOD OF POPE DAMASUS (385)

15. Peter's Unique Episcopal Chair

De Schismate Donatistorum, 2:2, trans. Vassall-Phillips, O, p. 64.

2. So we have proved that the Catholic Church is the Church which is diffused throughout the world. We must now mention its ornaments. . . . For one who knows, to err is sin; those who do not know may sometimes be pardoned. You cannot deny that you know that *upon Peter first in the city of Rome was conferred the episcopal chair, on which sat Peter, the head of all the apostles,* whence he was called Cephas, *that in this one chair unity should be preserved by all, lest the other apostles might uphold each for himself separate chairs, so that he who should set up a second chair, against the unique chair, would already be a schismatic and a sinner.*

16. Peter Preferred for the Sake of Unity

De Schism. Don., 7:3, trans. Vassall-Phillips, O, p. 283.

3. . . . You have not wished to bring forward the examples to be found in the gospel, as for instance what has been written concerning the person of the most blessed Peter, where we may read a description of the way in which unity is to be obtained or procured. Without doubt it is evil to do anything against a prohibition, but it is worse not to have unity when you can. We see that this unity was preferred to punishment by Christ himself, who chose that all his disciples should be in unity, rather than punish a sin against himself. For, as he did not wish to be denied, he declared that whosoever should deny him before men would he deny before his Father. And though this has been thus written, nevertheless *for the good of unity blessed Peter,* for whom it would have been enough if after his denial he had obtained pardon only, *deserved to be placed before all the apostles, and alone received the keys of the kingdom of heaven, to be communicated to the rest.* So from this example it is given us to understand that for the sake of unity sins should be buried, since the most blessed apostle Paul says that charity can cover a multitude of sins.

K. AMBROSE ON THE PETRINE PRE-EMINENCE (c. 397)

17. Peter Tempted, Forgiven, and Set Over the Church

Enarratio in Psalmum, 43:40, trans. E. Giles, *Documents Illustrating Papal Authority* (London: SPCK, 1952), p. 145.

40. . . . Peter is sifted, as he is driven on to deny Christ. He falls into temptation, speaking like a man full of chaff. . . . In the end he wept and washed away his chaff, and by those temptations, he was worthy that Christ should intervene for him. . . . At length, after being tempted by the devil, Peter is set over the Church. And so the Lord indicated beforehand that which happened later, namely that he chose him as shepherd of his flock; for he said to him,

"When thou art converted, strengthen thy brethren." And so the holy apostle Peter is converted to good fruit, and sifted like wheat, that he with the saints of the Lord might be one bread which should be our food.

II. Assertions of Primacy and Demonstrations of Leadership from the Popes Themselves

A. JULIUS I (337–352)

18. The Eusebians at Antioch Rebuked for Bypassing Rome (340)

> Athanasius, *Apologia Contra Arianos*, 2:35, trans. *NPNF*, 2nd ser., IV, p. 118.

And why was nothing said to us concerning the Church of the Alexandrians in particular? Are you ignorant that the custom has been for word to be written first to us, and then for a just decision to be passed from this place? If then any such suspicion rested upon the Bishop there, notice thereof ought to have been sent to the Church of this place; whereas, after neglecting to inform us, and proceeding on their own authority as they pleased, now they desire to obtain our concurrence in their decisions, though we never condemned him. Not so have the constitutions of Paul, not so have the traditions of the Fathers directed; this is another form of procedure, a novel practice. I beseech you, readily bear with me: what I write is for the common good. For what we have received from the blessed Apostle Peter, that I signify to you; and I should not have written this, as deeming that these things were manifest unto all men, had not these proceedings so disturbed us.

B. DAMASUS (366–384)

19. Opinions of Rome to be Sought First

> Theodoret, *Hist. Ecc.*, 2:17, trans. *NPNF*, 2nd ser., III, p. 83.

"The bishops assembled at Rome in sacred synod, Damasus and Valerianus and the rest, to their beloved brethren the bishops of Illyria, send greeting in God. . . .

"When first the wickedness of the heretics began to flourish, and when, as now, the blasphemy of the Arians was crawling to the front, our fathers, three hundred and eighteen bishops, the holiest prelates in the Roman Empire, deliberated at Nicaea. The wall which they set up against the weapons of the devil, and the antidote wherewith they repelled his deadly poisons, was their confession that the Father and the Son are of one substance, one godhead, one virtue, one power, one likeness, and that the Holy Ghost is of the same essence and substance. Whoever did not thus think was judged separate from our communion. Their deliberation was worthy of all respect, and their definition sound. But certain men have intended by other later discussions to corrupt and befoul it. Yet, at the very outset, error was so far set right by the bishops on whom the attempt was made at Ariminum to compel them to manipulate or innovate on the faith, that they confessed themselves seduced by opposite arguments, or owned that they had not perceived any contradiction to the opinion of the Fathers delivered at Nicaea. No prejudice could arise from the number of bishops gathered at Ariminum, since it is well known that neither the bishop of the Romans, whose opinion ought before all others to have been waited for, nor Vincentius, whose stainless episcopate had lasted so many years, nor the rest, gave in their adhesion to such doctrines."

C. SIRICIUS (384–399)

20. The Bishop of Rome, Heir of Peter's Government (385)

> *Ep.* 1:1, trans. E. Giles, *Documents Illustrating Papal Authority* (London: SPCK, 1952), p. 142.

1. . . . In view of our office, we are not free to dissemble or to keep silent, for our zeal for the Christian religion ought to be greater than anyone's. We bear the burdens of all who are heavy laden, or rather *the blessed apostle Peter bears them in us, who in all things, as we trust, protects and defends those who are heirs of his government.*

D. INNOCENT I (401–417)

21. Claims Authority Throughout the West (416)

> *Ep.* 25:2, trans. Giles, *DIPA* (London: SPCK, 1952), p. 194.

2. Who does not know or observe that it [the church order] was delivered by

Peter the chief of the apostles to the Roman church, and is kept until now, and ought to be retained by all, and that nothing ought to be imposed or introduced which has no authority, or seems to derive its precedents elsewhere?—especially since it is clear that in all Italy, the Gauls, Spain, Africa, Sicily and the adjacent islands, no one formed these churches except those whom the venerable apostle Peter or his successors made priests. Or let them discover that any other apostle be found to have been or to have taught in these provinces. If not, they ought to follow that which the Roman church keeps, from which they undoubtedly received them first; but while they are keen on foreign statements, they seem to neglect the head of their institution.

E. ZOSIMUS (417–418)

22. The Indisputable Authority of the Roman See (418)

Ep. 12:1–2, trans. E. Giles, *DIPA* (London: SPCK, 1952), pp. 212–13.

1. Although the tradition of the fathers has assigned such great authority to the apostolic see that *no one would dare to dispute its judgement*, and has kept this always by canons and rules and church order, and in the current of its laws pays the reverence which it owes to the name of Peter, from whom it descends; for canonical antiquity, by the consent of all, has willed such power to this apostle, so that the promise of Christ our God, that he should loose the bound and bind the loosed, is equally given to those who have obtained, with his assent, the inheritance of his see; for he has a care for all churches, especially for this where he sat, nor does he permit any of its privileges or decisions to be shaken by any blast, since he established it on the firm and immovable foundation of his own name, which no one shall rashly attack, but at his peril. Peter then is the head of so great authority, and has confirmed the devotion of all the fathers who followed him, so that the Roman church is established by all laws and discipline, whether human or divine. His place we rule, and we inherit the power of his name; you

know this, dearest brothers, and as priests you ought to know it. *Such then being our authority, that no one can revise our sentence,* we have done nothing which we have not of our own accord brought to your notice in our letter, giving this much to our brotherhood, that by consulting together, not because we did not know what ought to be done, or might do something which might displease you as contrary to the good of the Church, but we desired to treat together with you of a man who, as you wrote, was accused before you, and who came to our see asserting his innocence, not refusing judgement from the former appeal; of his own accord calling for his accusers, and condemning the crimes of which he was falsely accused by rumour. We thought, in fact we know, that his entire petition was explained in the earlier letter which we sent you, and we believed that we had sufficiently replied to those you wrote in answer.

2. But we have unfolded the whole roll of your letter which was sent by Subdeacon Marcellinus. You have understood the entire text of our letter as if we had believed Celestius in everything, and had given our assent, so to speak, to every syllable without discussing his words. Matters which need a long treatment are never rashly postponed, nor without great deliberation must anything be decided on which a final judgement has to be given. So let your brotherhood know that we have changed nothing since we wrote to you, or you wrote to us; but we have left all as it was before, when we informed your holiness of the matter in our letter, in order that the supplication you sent to us might be granted. Farewell.

F. LEO THE GREAT (440–461)

23. The Petrine Theory Stated

Trans. *ThM*, No. 35, pp. 85–86.

Col. 628. Our Lord Jesus Christ, the Saviour of the world, caused his truth to be promulgated through the apostles. And while this duty was placed on all the apostles, the Lord made St. Peter the head of them all, that from him as from their head his gifts should flow out into all the body. So that if anyone separates himself from St. Peter he should know that he has no share in the divine blessing.

Col. 656. If any dissensions in regard to church matters and the clergy should arise among you, we wish you to settle them and report to us all the terms of the settlement, so that we may confirm all your just and reasonable decisions.

Col. 995. Constantinople has its own glory and by the mercy of God has become the seat of the empire. But secular matters are based on one thing, ecclesiastical matters on another. For nothing will stand which is not built on the rock [Peter] which the Lord laid in the foundation [Matt. 16:18]. . . . Your city is royal, but you cannot make it apostolic [as Rome is, because its church was founded by St. Peter].

Col. 1031. You will learn with what reverence the bishop of Rome treats the rules and canons of the church if you read my letters by which I resisted the ambition of the patriarch of Constantinople, and you will see also that I am the guardian of the catholic faith and of the decrees of the church fathers.

Col. 991. On this account the holy and most blessed pope, Leo, the head of the universal church, with the consent of the holy synod, endowed with the dignity of St. Peter, who is the foundation of the church, the rock of the faith, and the door-keeper of heaven, through us, his vicars, deprived him of his rank as bishop, etc.

Col. 615. And because we have the care of all the churches, and the Lord, who made Peter the prince of the apostles, holds us responsible for it, etc.

Col. 881. Believing that it is reasonable and just that as the holy Roman church, through St. Peter, the prince of the apostles, is the head of all the churches of the whole world, etc.

Col. 147. This festival should be so celebrated that in my humble person he [Peter] should be seen and honored who has the care over all the shepherds and the sheep committed to him, and whose dignity is not lacking in me, his heir, although I am unworthy.

24. Roman Authority Derived from Petrine Primacy (418)

Sermo 4:2–4, trans. T. W. Allies, *The See of Peter* (London, 1850).

2. . . . It is by far more profitable, and more worthy, to raise the mind's eye to the contemplation of the glory of the most blessed apostle Peter, and to celebrate this day chiefly in honour of him who was watered with so copious streams from the very fountain of all graces that, while *nothing has passed to others without his participation,* yet he received many special privileges of his own. . . . And yet, out of the whole world, one, Peter, is chosen, who presides both at the call of the Gentiles, and over all the apostles and collected fathers of the Church; so that though there be, among God's people, many priests and many shepherds, yet Peter especially rules all whom Christ also rules originally. Beloved, it is a great and wonderful sharing of his own power which the divine honour bestowed on this man, and if he wished that other rulers should be in common with him, *yet did he never give except through him what he denied not to others.* And then the Lord asks all the apostles what men think of him; and they answer in common so long as they set forth the doubtfulness of human ignorance. . . . "And upon this rock I will build my Church, and the gates of hell shall not prevail against it." On this strength, he says, I will build an eternal temple, and the loftiness of my Church, reaching to heaven, shall rise upon the firmness of this faith.

3. . . . "I will give to thee the keys . . . loosed in heaven." The right of this power did indeed pass on to the other apostles, and the order of this decree passed on to all the chiefs of the Church; but not in vain was that which was imparted to all *entrusted to one.* Therefore this is commended to Peter separately, because all the rulers of the Church are invested with the figure of Peter. The privilege therefore of Peter remains, wherever judgement is passed from his equity. Nor is there too much severity or indulgence, where nothing is bound, nothing loosed, except what blessed Peter either looses or binds. Again as his passion pressed

on, which was to shake the firmness of the disciples, the Lord says, "Simon, behold Satan has desired to have you that he may sift you as wheat, but I have prayed for thee that thy faith fail not, and when thou art converted, confirm thy brethren, that ye enter not into temptation." The danger from the temptation of fear was common to all apostles, and they equally needed the help of divine protection, since the devil desired to harass and shatter all; and yet special care is taken of Peter by the Lord, and he asks specially for the faith of Peter, as if the state of the others would be more certain if the mind of the chief were not overcome. So then in Peter the strength of all is fortified, and the help of divine grace is so ordered that the stability which through Christ is given to Peter, *through Peter is conveyed to the apostles.*

4. Since then, beloved, we see such a protection divinely granted to us, reasonably and justly do we rejoice in the merits and dignity of our leader, rendering thanks to the eternal King, our Redeemer, the Lord Jesus Christ, for having given so great a power to him whom he made chief of the whole Church, that if anything, even in our time, by us be rightly done and rightly ordered, it is to be ascribed to his working, to his guidance, unto whom it was said, "And thou, when thou art converted, confirm thy brethren"; and to whom the Lord after his resurrection, in answer to the triple profession of eternal love, thrice said, with mystical intent, "Feed my sheep." And this, beyond a doubt, the pious shepherd does even now, and fulfils the charge of his Lord, confirming us with his exhortations, and not ceasing to pray for us, that we may be overcome by no temptation. But if, as we must believe, he extends this care of his piety to all God's people everywhere, how much more will he condescend to grant his help unto us his children, among whom, on the sacred couch of his blessed repose, he rests in the same flesh in which he ruled! To him, therefore, let us ascribe this anniversary day of us his servant, and this festival, by whose patronage we have been thought worthy to share his seat itself, the grace of our Lord Jesus Christ helping us in all things, who

liveth and reigneth with God the Father and the Holy Ghost for ever and ever. Amen.

25. Leo, Chalcedon (451) and the "Tome" (Letter to Flavian, Ep. 28)

Liber Pontificalis, 47, trans. L. R. Loomis, *The Book of the Popes (Liber Pontificalis),* I, to the Pontificate of Gregory I, "Records of Civilization: Sources and Studies, I," ed. J. T. Shotwell (New York: Columbia University Press, 1916), p. 98.

He, by his own authority, issued precepts and he sent to Marcian Augustus, the orthodox, catholic prince, and an assemblage was called and the bishops were gathered together with the prince and the holy council of the bishops was held at Chalcedon in the confession chapel of the holy Euphemia; and 256 priests were met together, beside 408 bishops who sent their autographs, and they were assembled together with the Tome, that contained the declaration of faith of the apostolic, Roman church and the autograph of the holy bishop Leo. Then in the presence of the catholic prince Marcian Augustus the assembled council of bishops, in number 1200, in company with Marcian Augustus set forth the catholic faith, two natures in one Christ, God and man.

26. Passages from Leo's Tome

Epistola (28) *Dogmatica ad Flavianum,* 3–4, trans. NPNF, 2nd ser., XII, p. 40.

Without detriment therefore to the properties of either nature and substance which then came together in one person, majesty took on humility, strength weakness, eternity mortality: and for the paying off of the debt belonging to our condition inviolable nature was united with passible nature, so that, as suited the needs of our case, one and the same Mediator between God and men, the Man Christ Jesus, could both die with the one and not die with the other. Thus in the whole and perfect nature of true man was true God born, complete in what was His own, complete in what was ours. And by "ours" we mean what the Creator formed in us from the beginning and what He undertook to repair. For what the

Deceiver brought in and man deceived committed, had no trace in the Saviour. Nor, because He partook of man's weaknesses, did He therefore share our faults. He took the form of a slave without stain of sin, increasing the human and not diminishing the divine: because that emptying of Himself whereby the Invisible made Himself visible and, Creator and Lord of all things though He be, wished to be a mortal, was the bending down of pity, not the failing of power. Accordingly He who while remaining in the form of God made man, was also made man in the form of a slave. For both natures retain their own proper character without loss: and as the form of God did not do away with the form of a slave, so the form of a slave did not impair the form of God. The Lord assumed His mother's nature without her faultiness: nor in the Lord Jesus Christ, born of the Virgin's womb, does the wonderfulness of His birth make His nature unlike ours. For He who is true God is also true man: and in this union there is no lie, since the humility of manhood and the loftiness of the Godhead both meet there.

G. GELASIUS (492–496)

27. The Priestly Power Predominant over the Royal

Ad Anastasium Imperatorem, 2, trans. Robinson, *REH*, I, pp. 72–73.

. . . There are two powers, august Emperor, by which this world is chiefly ruled, namely, the sacred authority of the priests and the royal power. Of these, that of the priests is the more weighty, since they have to render an account for even the kings of men in the divine judgment. You are also aware, dear son, that while you are permitted honorably to rule over human kind, yet in things divine you bow your head humbly before the leaders of the clergy and await from their hands the means of your salvation. In the reception and proper disposition of the heavenly mysteries you recognize that you should be subordinate rather than superior to the religious order, and that in these matters you depend on their judgment rather than wish to force them to follow your will.

If the ministers of religion, recognizing the supremacy granted you from heaven in matters affecting the public order, obey your laws, lest otherwise they might obstruct the course of secular affairs by irrelevant considerations, with what readiness should you not yield them obedience to whom is assigned the dispensing of the sacred mysteries of religion. Accordingly, just as there is no slight danger in the case of the priests if they refrain from speaking when the service of the divinity requires, so there is no little risk for those who disdain—which God forbid—when they should obey. And if it is fitting that the hearts of the faithful should submit to all priests in general who properly administer divine affairs, how much the more is obedience due to the bishop of that see which the Most High ordained to be above all others, and which is consequently dutifully honored by the devotion of the whole Church.

H. GREGORY THE GREAT (590–604)

28. Gregory's Career Summarized from the Book of the Popes

Liber Pont., 66, trans. by the editor from *Gestorum Pontificum Romanorum* I, ed. Th. Mommsen, *Monumenta Germaniae Historica*, I (Berlin: Weidmann, 1898), pp. 161–62.

Gregory who belonged to the Roman nation had Gordian for his father. He ruled thirteen years, six months, and ten days. He wrote forty homilies on the Gospels, others on James and Ezekiel. He likewise composed the *Pastoral Rule*, *The Dialogues* and other works too numerous to mention. This was the time when Romanus, patrician and exarch, came to Rome. And when he returned to Ravenna, he recaptured certain cities formerly occupied by the Lombards. . . . At the same period, the blessed Gregory sent the servants of God, Mellitus, Augustine, and John on a mission accompanied by several other god-fearing monks. He dispatched them on a preaching mission to the peoples of the Angles in order that they might be converted to the Lord Jesus Christ. He added to the recitation of the canon the prayer, *Diesque nostros in tua pace disponere,* and several others.

He made a ciborium of pure silver with four columns for the apostle Peter. . . . He decided that masses should be celebrated over the body of St. Peter. He did the same thing for the church of the apostle St. Paul. . . . He died and was buried in the basilica of St. Peter the apostle, in front of the sacristy the twelfth day of March. . . . The pontifical see was vacant five months and eighteen days.

29. *The Forbidding Outset of Gregory's Pontificate*

Mor. (Ep. I), trans. *LF*, I, i, pp. 1–5.

To the Most Devout and Holy Brother, my fellow Bishop Leander, Gregory, the servant of God's servants.

1. When I knew you long since at Constantinople, my most blessed brother, at the time that I was kept there by the affairs of the Apostolical See, and that you had been brought thither by an embassage, with which you were charged, on counts touching the faith of the Wisigoths, I then detailed in your ears all that displeased me in myself, since for late and long I declined the grace of conversion, and after that I had been inspired with an heavenly affection I thought it better to be still shrouded in the secular habit. For though I had now disclosed to me what I should seek of the love of things eternal, yet long-established custom had so cast its chains upon me, that I could not change my outward habit: and while my purpose still compelled me to engage in the service of this world as it were in semblance only, many influences began to spring up against me from caring for this same world, so that the tie which kept me to it was now no longer in semblance only, but what is more serious, in my own mind. At length being anxious to avoid all these inconveniences, I sought the haven of the monastery, and having left all that is of the world, as at that time I vainly believed, I came out naked from the shipwreck of human life. For as the vessel that is negligently moored, is very often (when the storm waxes violent) tossed by the water out of its shelter on the safest shore, so under the cloak of the Ecclesiastical office, I found myself plunged on a sudden in a sea of secular matters, and because I had not held fast the tranquillity of the monastery when in possession, I learnt by losing it, how closely it should have been held. For whereas the virtue of obedience was set against my own inclination to make me take the charge of ministering at the holy Altar, I was led to undertake that upon the grounds of the Church requiring it, which, if it might be done with impunity, I should get quit of by a second time withdrawing myself; and subsequently notwithstanding my unwillingness and reluctance, at the very time when the ministry of the Altar was a heavy weight, the further burden of the Pastoral charge was fastened on me, which I now find so much the more difficulty in bearing, as I feel myself to be unequal to it, and as I cannot take breath in any comfortable assurance in myself. For because, now that the end of the world is at hand, the times are disturbed by reason of the multiplied evils thereof, and we ourselves, who are supposed to be devoted to the inner mysteries, are thus become involved in outward cares; just as it happened then also when I was brought to the ministry of the Altar, this was brought about for me without my knowledge, viz. that I should receive the mighty charge of the Holy Order, to the end that I might be quartered under less restraint in an earthly palace, whither indeed I was followed by many of my brethren from the monastery, who were attached to me by a kindred affection. Which happened, I perceive, by Divine dispensation, in order that by their example, as by an anchored cable, I might ever be kept fast to the tranquil shore of prayer, whenever I should be tossed by the ceaseless waves of secular affairs. For to their society I fled as to the bosom of the safest port from the rolling swell, and from the waves of earthly occupation; and though that office which withdrew me from the monastery had with the point of its employments stabbed me to death as to my former tranquillity of life, yet in their society, by means of the appeals of diligent reading, I was animated with the yearnings of daily renewed compunction. It

was then that it seemed good to those same brethren, you too adding your influence, as you yourself remember, to oblige me by the importunity of their requests to set forth the book of blessed Job; and as far as the Truth should inspire me with powers, to lay open to them those mysteries of such depth; and they made this too an additional burden which their petition laid upon me, that I would not only unravel the words of the history in allegorical senses, but that I would go on to give to the allegorical senses the turn of a moral exercise, with the addition of somewhat yet harder, that I would crown the several meanings with testimonies, and that the testimonies, which I brought forward, should they chance to appear involved, should be disentangled by the aid of additional explanation.

30. Gregory, the Pastoral Rule, and the Cure of Souls

Liber Regulae Pastoralis, 1:1; 2:1; 3, Prolog., trans. *NPNF*, 2nd ser., XII, pp. 1–2, 9, 24.

No one presumes to teach an art till he has first, with intent meditation, learnt it. What rashness is it, then, for the unskilful to assume pastoral authority, since the government of souls is the art of arts! For who can be ignorant that the sores of the thoughts of men are more occult than the sores of the bowels? And yet how often do men who have no knowledge whatever of spiritual precepts fearlessly profess themselves physicians of the heart, though those who are ignorant of the effect of drugs blush to appear as physicians of the flesh! But because, through the ordering of God, all the highest in rank of this present age are inclined to reverence religion, there are some who, through the outward show of rule within the holy Church, affect the glory of distinction. They desire to appear as teachers, they covet superiority to others, and, as the Truth attests, they seek the first salutations in the market-place, the first rooms at feasts, the first seats in assemblies (Matth. xxiii. 6, 7), being all the less able to administer worthily the office they have undertaken of pastoral care, as they have reached the magisterial position of humility out of elation only. For,

indeed, in a magisterial position language itself is confounded when one thing is learnt and another taught. . . .

The conduct of a prelate ought so far to transcend the conduct of the people as the life of a shepherd is wont to exalt him above the flock. For one whose estimation is such that the people are called his flock is bound anxiously to consider what great necessity is laid upon him to maintain rectitude. It is necessary, then, that in thought he should be pure, in action chief; discreet in keeping silence, profitable in speech; a near neighbour to every one in sympathy, exalted above all in contemplation; a familiar friend of good livers through humility, unbending against the vices of evil-doers through zeal for righteousness; not relaxing in his care for what is inward from being occupied in outward things, nor neglecting to provide for outward things in his solicitude for what is inward. . . .

Since, then, we have shewn what manner of man the pastor ought to be, let us now set forth after what manner he should teach. For, as long before us Gregory Nazianzen of reverend memory has taught, one and the same exhortation does not suit all, inasmuch as neither are all bound together by similarity of character. For the things that profit some often hurt others; seeing that also for the most part herbs which nourish some animals are fatal to others; and the gentle hissing that quiets horses incites whelps; and the medicine which abates one disease aggravates another; and the bread which invigorates the life of the strong kills little children. Therefore according to the quality of the hearers ought the discourse of teachers to be fashioned, so as to suit all and each for their several needs, and yet never deviate from the art of common edification. For what are the intent minds of hearers but, so to speak, a kind of tight tensions of strings in a harp, which the skilful player, that he may produce a tune not at variance with itself, strikes variously? And for this reason the strings render back a consonant modulation, that they are struck indeed with one quill, but not with one kind of stroke. Whence every teacher also, that he may edify all in the one virtue of charity, ought to

V-1. Battle of Romans and Barbarians. *From the Ludovisi Sarcophagus, 3rd century* A.D., *Museo delle Terme, Rome.*

touch the hearts of his hearers out of one doctrine, but not with one and the same exhortation.

III. The Barbarian Infiltration and the New Gothic-Roman-Christian Society

A. ACCOUNTS OF THE GOTHS, THEIR EVANGELIZATION, AND THEIR WARS

31. Ulfilas' Arian Creed

Selections from *A Source Book for Ancient Church History*, p. 426, by Joseph Cullen Ayer are reprinted with the permission of Charles Scribner's Sons. © 1913, Charles Scribner's Sons; renewal © 1941, Joseph Cullen Ayer, Jr.

I, Ulfilas, bishop and confessor, have always thus believed, and in this sole and true faith I make my testament before my Lord: I believe that there is one God the Father, alone unbegotten and invisible; and in His only begotten Son, our Lord and God, the fashioner and maker of all creation, not having any one like him—therefore there is one God of all, who, in our opinion, is God—and there is one Holy Spirit, the illuminating and sanctifying power—as Christ said to his apostles for correction, "Behold I send the promise of my Father to you, but remain ye in the city of Jerusalem until ye be indued with power from on high"; and again, "And ye shall receive power coming upon you from the Holy Spirit"—neither God nor Lord, but a minister of Christ in all things; not ruler, but a subject, and obedient in all things to the Son, and the Son himself subject and obedient in all things to his Father . . . through Christ . . . with the Holy Spirit. . . .

32. Ulfilas' Mission to the Goths

Socrates, *Hist. Ecc.,* 4:23, *ibid.,* pp. 426–27.

The barbarians dwelling beyond the Danube, who are called Goths, having been engaged in a civil war among themselves,

195

were divided into two parties; of one of these Fritigernus was the leader, of the other Athanaric. When Athanaric had obtained an evident advantage over his rival, Fritigernus had recourse to the Romans and implored their assistance against his adversary. When these things were reported to the Emperor Valens [364–378], he ordered the troops garrisoned in Thrace to assist those barbarians against the barbarians fighting against them. They won a complete victory over Athanaric beyond the Danube, totally routing the enemy. This was the reason why many of the barbarians became Christians; for Fritigernus, to show his gratitude to the Emperor for the kindness shown him, embraced the religion of the Emperor, and urged those under him to do the same. Therefore it is that even to this present time so many of the Goths are infected with the religion of Arianism, because the emperors at that time gave themselves to that faith. Ulfilas, the bishop of the Goths at that time, invented the Gothic letters and, translating the Holy Scriptures into their own language, undertook to instruct these barbarians in the divine oracles. But when Ulfilas taught the Christian religion not only to the subjects of Fritigernus but to the subjects of Athanaric also, Athanaric, regarding this as a violation of the privileges of the religion of his ancestors, subjected many of the Christians to severe punishments, so that many of the Arian Goths of that time became martyrs. Arius, indeed, failing to refute the opinion of Sabellius the Libyan, fell from the true faith and asserted that the Son of God was a new God; but the barbarians, embracing Christianity with greater simplicity, despised this present life for the faith of Christ.

33. *Procopius' Account of the Gothic and Vandal Wars*

Corpus Script. Hist. Byz., trans. *ThM*, No. 2, pp. 11 and 12.

I, 2. During the reign of Honorius [395–423] in the west the barbarians began to overrun the empire. . . . The invaders were mainly of the Gothic race, the greatest and most important tribes being the East Goths, the Vandals, the West Goths, and the Gepidae. . . . These tribes have different names, but in all other respects they resemble one another very closely; they all have light complexions, yellow hair, large bodies, and handsome faces; they obey the same laws and have the same religion, the Arian; and they all speak the same language, Gothic. I am of the opinion, therefore, that they were originally one people and have separated into tribes under different leaders. They formerly dwelt beyond the Danube; then the Gepidae occupied the land about Sirmium on both sides of that river, where they still dwell.

The first to move were the West Goths. This tribe entered into an alliance with the Romans, but later, since such an alliance could not be permanent, they revolted under Alaric. Starting from Thrace, they made a raid through all of Europe, attacking both emperors.

[Alaric sacks Rome.] Soon after, Alaric died, and the West Goths, under Athaulf, passed on into Gaul.

3. Under the pressure of famine, the Vandals, who formerly dwelt on the shores of the Maeotic Gulf [Sea of Azof], moved on toward the Rhine, attacking the Franks. With them went the Alani. . . . [Crossing the Rhine into Gaul] they proceeded down into Spain, the most western province of the Roman empire, and settled there under their king, Godegisel, Honorius having made an agreement with him by which the Vandals were to be allowed to settle in Spain on condition that they should not plunder the land.

At that time the greatest Roman generals were Boniface and Aëtius, who were political rivals. . . . Boniface sent secretly to Spain and made an agreement with Gunderich and Geiserich, the sons and successors of Godegisel, whereby they were to bring the Vandals into Africa, and the three were to divide the rule of Africa among themselves, mutually supporting one another in case of attacks from outside. Accordingly the Vandals crossed the strait at Gades and entered Africa, while the West Goths moved forward from Gaul into Spain after them. [Gunderich dies, leaving Geiserich sole ruler of the Vandals; Geiserich quarrels with Boniface and drives him out of Africa, ruling the whole territory with his Vandals.]

5. Geiserich now got together a large fleet and attacked Italy, capturing Rome and the palace of the emperor. The usurper Maximus was slain by the populace and his body torn to pieces. Geiserich took back to Carthage Eudoxia, the empress, and her two daughters, Eudocia and Placidia, carrying off also an immense booty in gold and silver. The imperial palace was plundered of all its treasures, as was also the temple of Jupiter Capitolinus, including a large part of the roof, which was made of bronze, heavily plated with gold. . . .

34. Jordanes on the Conversion of the Goths and Alaric's Sack of Rome (410)

De Origine actusque Getarum (c. 551), 25–31, trans. Robinson, *REH*, I, pp. 39–44.

The following account is by Jordanes, himself a Goth, but unlike most of his people, not an Arian, but an orthodox Christian. He wrote about 551, nearly a century and a half after the events which he here narrates:

The West Goths [terrified by the victories of the Huns over the East Goths] requested Emperor Valens to grant them a portion of Thrace or Moesia south of the Danube in which to settle. They promised to obey his laws and commands and, in order still further to gain his confidence, they engaged to become Christians if only the emperor would send to them teachers who knew their language. When Valens heard this he readily agreed to a plan which he might himself have proposed. He received the Goths into Moesia and erected them, so to speak, into a sort of rampart to protect his empire against the other tribes.

Now, since Valens was infected with the heresy of the Arians and had closed all the churches which belonged to our party [i.e. the orthodox], he sent the Goths preachers of his own infection. These missionaries poured out for the newcomers, who were inexperienced and ignorant, the poison of their own false faith. So the West Goths were made Arians rather than Christians by Emperor Valens. Moreover, in their enthu-

siasm they converted their kinsmen, the East Goths and the Gepidae, and taught them to respect this heresy. They invited all nations of their own tongue everywhere to adopt the creed of this sect.

We have seen how, according to Ammianus Marcellinus, the forces of the emperor maltreated the poor Goths and drove them to revolt.

When news of this reached the emperor Valens at Antioch, he hastened with an army into Thrace. Here it came to a miserable battle in which the Goths conquered. The emperor fled to a peasant's hut not far from Adrianople. The Goths, according to the custom of the raging enemy, set fire to the buildings, having no idea that there was an emperor hidden in the little hut, and so he was consumed in his kingly pomp. This was in accordance with God's judgment that he should be burned with fire by them, since when they asked for the true faith he misled them with false teaching and changed for them the fire of love into the fire of hell.

After the great and glorious victory, the West Goths set themselves to cultivate Thrace and the Dacian river valley as if it were their native soil of which they had just gained possession.

[There they remained, hostile to the Empire, and a perpetual menace. Finally Theodosius the Great, the brave and stern, the wise and liberal, ended the war between the Goths and the Romans by a treaty. By his presents and his friendly bearing, he won the friendship of Athanaric, king of the West Goths, and invited him to go to Constantinople.]

When the West Goth entered the royal city he was astounded. "Now I see what I have often heard without believing—the glory of this great city." Looking here and there, he admired the site of the city, and the number of ships, and the magnificent walls. He saw people of many nations, like a stream flowing from different sources into one fountain. He marveled at the martial array of the soldiers and exclaimed, "Doubtless the emperor is a god of this earth, and whoever has raised his hand against him is guilty of his own blood."

A few months later, Athanaric, upon whom the emperor heaped his favors, departed from this world, and the emperor, because of his affection for Athanaric, honored him almost more in death than he had done in life, gave him worthy burial, and was himself present beside the bier at the funeral.

After the death of Athanaric, all his army remained in the service of the emperor Theodosius, submitted to the Roman power, and formed, as it were, one body with its soldiers. They resembled the allies whom Constantine had had, who were called *Foederati*.

After Theodosius, who cherished both peace and the Gothic people, had departed this life, his sons [Honorius and Arcadius], through their lives of indulgence, began to bring ruin down upon their empires and withdrew from their allies, the Goths, the accustomed gifts. The Goths soon grew disgusted with the emperors, and since they were fearful lest their bravery in war should decline by too long a period of peace, they made Alaric their king. . . . So, since the said Alaric was chosen king, he took counsel with his fellows and declared to them that it was preferable to conquer a kingdom through one's own force rather than to live in peace under the yoke of strangers.

He thereupon took his army and advanced, during the consulate of Stilicho and Aurelianus, through Pannonia and Sirmium into Italy. This country was so completely deprived of forces that Alaric approached without opposition to the bridge over the Candiano, three miles from the imperial city of Ravenna. . . .

The Goths sent messengers to the emperor Honorius, who was at Ravenna, requesting that they might be permitted to settle quietly in Italy. Should they be allowed to do this, they would live as one people with the Romans; otherwise they would try which people could expel the other, the victor to remain in control. But the emperor Honorius, fearing both suggestions, took counsel with his senate how they might rid Italy of the Goths. He at last concluded to assign the distant provinces of Gaul and Spain to the West Goths. He had, indeed, already nearly lost these districts, for they

had been devastated by an incursion of Genseric, king of the Vandals. If Alaric and his people could succeed in conquering the region, they might have it as their home.

[The Goths agreed to this, but on their way thither were treacherously attacked by Stilicho, the emperor's father-in-law (402). The Goths, however, held their own in the battle which followed. They turned back, full of wrath, towards Italy, and wasted the northern part of the peninsula during the following years; then moved south into Tuscany.]

Finally they entered the city of Rome and sacked it at Alaric's command. They did not, however, set fire to the city, as is the custom of the wild peoples, and would not permit that any of the holy places should be desecrated. They then proceeded into Campania and Lucania, which they likewise plundered, and came then to Britii. . . .

Alaric, the king of the West Goths, also brought hither the treasures of all Italy which he had won by plunder, and determined to cross from here over to Sicily and thence to Africa, which would offer him a final abode. But a number of his ships were swallowed up by that fearful sea, and many were injured; for man is unable to carry out his wishes when they are opposed to God's will.

While Alaric, discouraged by this misfortune, was considering what he should do, he was struck down by an early death and departed this world. His followers mourned the loss of him they had so dearly loved. They diverted the river Busento from its ordinary bed near the town of Consentia— this river, it may be added, brings salubrious water from the foot of the mountains to the town—and had a grave dug by captives in the middle of the channel. Here they buried Alaric, together with many precious objects. Then they permitted the water to return once more to its old bed. Moreover, in order that the place might never be found, they killed all those who had helped dig the grave.

The Goths transferred the rule to Atavulf, a relative of Alaric's, and a man of fine figure and lofty spirit, who, although he was not distinguished for his size, was remarkable for his figure and face. When Atavulf had assumed the rule he turned back again to Rome, and what had been left there from the first sack was now swept clean away, as a field might be devastated by grasshoppers. He robbed not only individuals of their wealth in Italy, but he also took that of the state, and Emperor Honorius was able in no way to restrain him. He even led away prisoner from Rome Placidia, the sister of Honorius, and daughter of Emperor Theodosius by his second wife.

[Later he married Placidia and strengthened the Gothic cause by this royal alliance. He then moved on to Gaul, where he engaged in a struggle with the other barbarians.]

B. THE CAREER OF THE ARIAN KING, THEODORIC THE OSTROGOTH (471–526)

35. *Procopius on the Ostrogoths, Theodoric and the Church*

Corpus Script. Hist. Byz., trans. ThM, No. 3, pp. 12–14.

I, 1. While Zeno [474–491] was emperor in Byzantium, the west was ruled by Augustus, whom the Romans called Augustulus, because of his youth. The actual government was in the hands of his father Orestes, a most able man. Some time before this, as a result of the reverses which they had suffered at the hands of Attila and Alaric, the Romans had taken the Sciri, Alani, and other German tribes into the empire as allies. The renown of Roman arms had long since vanished, and the barbarians were coming into Italy in ever-increasing numbers, where they were actual masters under the false name of allies (*federati*). They continually seized more and more power, until finally they demanded a third of all the lands of Italy. When Orestes refused to grant this they slew him. Then one of the imperial officers, Odovaker, also a barbarian, promised to secure this for them if they would recognize him as ruler. In spite of the power which he thus acquired, Odovaker did not attack the emperor [Romulus Augustulus], but only forced him to retire to private life. He then gave the barbarians the third of the lands which they had demanded, thus binding them more closely to him, and ruled over Italy unopposed for ten years.

About this time the East Goths, who had been allowed to settle in Thrace, rose against the emperor under their king, Theodorich. He had been brought up at Byzantium, where he had been given the rank of a patrician, and had even held the title of consul. The emperor Zeno, a master in diplomacy, persuaded Theodorich to invade Italy and attack Odovaker, with the chance of winning the whole west for himself and the East Goths. . . . Theodorich seized on this opportunity eagerly, and the whole tribe set out for Italy, taking along with them in wagons their women and children and all their movables. . . . Odovaker hastened with an army to oppose this invasion, but was defeated in several battles, and finally shut up in Ravenna. . . . After the siege had lasted for about three years both parties were willing to come to terms, the Goths being weary of the long siege and the soldiers of Odovaker being on the verge of starvation. So, through the efforts of the bishop of Ravenna, a treaty was made according to which Theodorich and Odovaker were to rule the city jointly. This treaty was kept for a short time, but finally Theodorich treacherously seized Odovaker at a banquet to which he had invited him, and had him put to death. He then won over to him all his enemies, and from that time on ruled over Goths and Italians unopposed. Theodorich never assumed the name or dignity of emperor, being content to be known as king, as the barbarians call their rulers. In fact, however, the subjects bore the same relation to him as to an emperor. He dispensed justice with a strong hand, and rigidly enforced the law and kept peace. In his time the land was protected from the attacks of neighboring barbarians, and his might and his wisdom were famous far and wide. He allowed his subjects neither to suffer nor to commit wrongs; his own followers were given only the lands which Odovaker had taken for his supporters. Thus Theodorich, although he bore the title of a tyrant, was in fact a righteous emperor. . . . He loved the Goths and the Italians equally, recognizing no difference between them contrary as this may seem to human nature. . . . After a reign of thirty-seven years, he died lamented by all his people.

36. Cassiodorus on Theodoric and Christian Society

Variae Epistolae, 1:9, 2:29; 3:7; 4:18, condensed transl. T. Hodgkin, *The Letters of Cassiodorus* (London: Oxford University Press, 1886), pp. 149, 186–87, 201, 244–45.

KING THEODORIC TO EUSTORGIUS,
BISHOP OF MILAN

'You will be glad to hear that we are satisfied that the Bishop of Augusta [Turin or Aosta] has been falsely accused of betrayal of his country. He is therefore to be restored to his previous rank. His accusers, as they are themselves of the clerical order, are not punished by us, but sent to your Holiness to be dealt with according to the ecclesiastical tradition.'

.   .   .   .   .

KING THEODORIC TO ADILA,
SENATOR AND COMES

'We wish to protect all our subjects, but especially the Church, because by so doing we earn the favour of Heaven. Therefore, in accordance with the petition of the blessed Eustorgius, Bishop of Milan, we desire you to accord all necessary protection to the men and farms belonging to the Milanese Church in Sicily: always understanding, however, that they are not to refuse to plead in answer to any public or private suit that may be brought against them. They are to be protected from wrong, but are not themselves to deviate from the path of justice.'

KING THEODORIC TO THE VENERABLE
JANUARIUS, BISHOP OF SALONA

'The lamentable petition of John says that you have taken sixty tuns of oil from him, and never paid him for them. It is especially important that preachers of righteousness should be righteous themselves. We cannot suppose that God is ignorant whence come the offerings which we make before Him [and He must therefore hate robbery for a burnt offering]. Pray enquire into this matter, and if the complaint be well founded remedy it promptly. You who preach to us our duty in great things should not be caught tripping in little ones.'

KING THEODORIC TO ANNAS,
SENATOR AND COMES

'Enquire if the story which is told us be true, namely that the Presbyter Laurentius has been groping for fatal riches among human corpses. An odious inversion of his functions, that he who should preach peace to the living has been robbing the dead, and that hands which have been touched with the oil of consecration should have been grasping at unholy gains, instead of distributing his own honestly acquired substance to the poor. If after diligent examination you find that the charge is true, you must make him disgorge the gold. As for punishment, for the sake of the honour of the priesthood we leave that to a higher Power.'

C. CLOVIS, THE CHURCH, AND THE RISE OF THE ORTHODOX FRANKS

37. Gregory of Tours on Clovis, the Vase of Soissons, and the Conversion and Baptism by St. Remy

Hist. Ecc. Franc., 2:27, 29–31, trans. Robinson, *REH*, II, pp. 51–55.

[The history of the Franks was written about a century after the time of Clovis by Gregory, bishop of Tours. The following extracts give some notion of this valuable source, upon which a great part of our knowledge of the Merovingian period rests.]

At this time [A.D. 486] the army of Clovis pillaged many churches, for he was still sunk in the errors of idolatry. The soldiers had borne away from a church, with all the other ornaments of the holy ministry, a vase of marvelous size and beauty. The bishop of this church sent messengers to the king, begging that if the church might not recover any other of the holy vessels, at least this one might be restored. The king, hearing these things, replied to the messenger: "Follow thou us to Soissons, for there all things that have been acquired are to be divided. If the lot shall give me this vase, I will do what the bishop desires."

When he had reached Soissons, and all the booty had been placed in the midst of the army, the king pointed to this vase, and said: "I ask you, O most valiant warriors, not

200

V-2. The Baptism of Clovis.
*Master of St. Gilles, late 15th
century, Franco-Flemish.*

to refuse to me the vase in addition to my rightful part." Those of discerning mind among his men answered, "O glorious king, all things which we see are thine, and we ourselves are subject to thy power; now do what seems pleasing to thee, for none is strong enough to resist thee." When they had thus spoken one of the soldiers, impetuous, envious, and vain, raised his battle-ax aloft and crushed the vase with it, crying, "Thou shalt receive nothing of this unless a just lot give it to thee." At this all were stupefied.

The king bore his injury with the calmness of patience, and when he had received the crushed vase he gave it to the bishop's messenger; but he cherished a hidden wound in his breast. When a year had passed he or-dered the whole army to come fully equipped to the Campus Martius and show their arms in brilliant array. But when he had reviewed them all he came to the breaker of the vase, and said to him, "No one bears his arms so clumsily as thou; for neither thy spear, nor thy sword, nor thy ax is ready for use." And seizing his ax, he cast it to the ground. And when the soldier had bent a little to pick it up the king raised his hands and crushed his head with his own ax. "Thus," he said, "didst thou to the vase at Soissons."

[Clovis took to wife Clotilde, daughter of the king of the Burgundians. Now Clotilde was a Christian. When her first son was born] she wished to consecrate him by bap-tism, and begged her husband unceasingly, saying, "The gods whom thou honorest are nothing; they cannot help themselves nor others; for they are carved from stone, or from wood, or from some metal. The names which you have given them were of men, not of gods,—like Saturn, who is said to have escaped by flight, to avoid being deprived of his power by his son; and like Jupiter himself, foul perpetrator of all uncleanness. . . . What power have Mars and Mercury ever had? They are endowed with magical arts rather than divine power.

"The God who should be worshipped is he who by his word created from nothingness the heavens and the earth, the sea and all that in them is; he who made the sun to shine and adorned the sky with stars; who filled the waters with creeping things, the land with animals, the air with winged creatures; by whose bounty the earth is glad with crops, the trees with fruit, the vines with grapes; by whose hand the human race was created; whose bounty has ordained that all things should give homage and service to man, whom he created."

But when the queen had said these things, the mind of Clovis was not stirred to believe. He answered: "By the will of our gods all things are created and produced. Evidently your god can do nothing, and it is not even proved that he belongs to the race of gods."

Meantime the faithful queen presented her son for baptism. She had the church adorned with tapestry, seeking to attract by this splendor him whom her exhortations had not moved. But the child whom they called Ingomer, after he had been born again through baptism, died in his white baptismal robe. Then the king reproached the queen bitterly. "If the child had been consecrated in the name of my gods he would be alive still. But now, because he is baptized in the name of your god, he cannot live.". . .

After this another son was born to him, and called in baptism Clodomir. He fell very ill. Then the king said: "Because he, like his brother, was baptized in the name of Christ, he must soon die." But his mother prayed, and by God's will the child recovered.

The queen unceasingly urged the king to acknowledge the true God, and forsake idols. But he could not in any wise be brought to believe until a war broke out with the Alemanni. Then he was by necessity compelled to confess what he had before wilfully denied.

It happened that the two armies were in battle, and there was great slaughter. Clovis' army was near to utter destruction. He saw the danger; his heart was stirred; he was moved to tears, and he raised his eyes to heaven, saying: "Jesus Christ, whom Clotilde declares to be the son of the living God, who it is said givest aid to the oppressed, and victory to those who put their hope in thee, I beseech the glory of thy aid. If thou shalt grant me victory over these enemies and I test that power which people consecrated to thy name say they have proved concerning thee, I will believe in thee and be baptized in thy name. For I have called upon my gods, but, as I have proved, they are far removed from my aid. So I believe that they have no power, for they do not succor those who serve them. Now I call upon thee, and I long to believe in thee—all the more that I may escape my enemies."

When he had said these things, the Alemanni turned their backs and began to flee. When they saw that their king was killed, they submitted to the sway of Clovis, saying: "We wish that no more people should perish. Now we are thine." When the king had forbidden further war, and praised his soldiers, he told the queen how he had won the victory by calling on the name of Christ.

Then the queen sent to the blessed Remigius, bishop of the city of Rheims, praying him to bring to the king the gospel of salvation. The priest, little by little and secretly, led him to believe in the true God, maker of heaven and earth, and to forsake idols, which could not help him nor anybody else.

But the king said: "Willingly will I hear thee, O father; but one thing is in the way— that the people who follow me are not content to leave their gods. I will go and speak to them according to thy word."

When he came among them, the power of God went before him, and before he had spoken all the people cried out together: "We cast off mortal gods, O righteous king, and we are ready to follow the God whom Remigius tells us is immortal."

These things were told to the bishop. He was filled with joy, and ordered the font to be prepared. The streets were shaded with embroidered hangings; the churches were adorned with white tapestries, the baptistery was set in order, the odor of balsam spread around, candles gleamed, and all the temple of the baptistery was filled with divine odor. . . . Then the king confessed the God omnipotent in the Trinity, and was baptized in the name of the Father, and of the Son, and of the Holy Ghost, and was anointed with the sacred chrism with the sign of the cross of Christ. Of his army there were baptized more than three thousand.

IV. Mohammed (570–632) and the Challenge of Islam to the Pope and to the Franks

A. THE KORAN AND MONOTHEISM

38. The Chapter of Unity

Surah 112, trans. E. H. Palmer, *The Qur'An* [*Sacred Books of the East*, ed. F. M. Mueller, Vol. IX] (Oxford: Clarendon Press, 1900), II, p. 344.

In the name of the merciful and compassionate God, say:

"He is God alone!
God the Eternal.
He begets not and is not begotten!
Nor is there like unto Him any one."

B. THE KORAN ON MUSLIMS, JEWS, AND CHRISTIANS

39. Unity versus Trinity; Christ only a Prophet

Surah 5, trans. Palmer, *Q*, I, pp. 107–8; 113–14.

Verily, those who believe and those who are Jews, and the Sabaeans, and the Christians, whosoever believes in God and the last day and does what is right, there is no fear for them, nor shall they grieve.

They misbelieve who say, "Verily, God is the Messiah, the son of Mary"; but the Messiah said, "O Children of Israel, worship God, my Lord and your Lord." Verily he who associates aught with God, God hath forbidden him paradise, and his resort is the fire, and the unjust shall have none to help them.

They misbelieve who say, "Verily, God is the third of three"; for there is no God but one, and if they do not desist from what they say, there shall touch those who misbelieve amongst them grievous woe.

Will they not turn toward God and ask pardon of Him? for God is forgiving and merciful.

The Messiah, the son of Mary, is only a prophet; prophets before him have passed away: and His mother was a confessor.

When God said, "O Jesus, son of Mary! remember my favors towards thee and towards thy mother, when I aided thee with the Holy Ghost, till thou didst speak to men in the cradle and when grown up.

"And when I taught thee the Book and wisdom and the law and the gospel; when thou didst create of clay, as it were, the likeness of a bird, by my power, and didst blow thereon, it became a bird; and thou didst heal the blind from birth, and the leprous by my permission; and when thou didst bring forth the dead by my permission; and when I did ward off the children of Israel from thee, and when thou didst come to them with manifest signs, and those who misbelieved among them said: 'This is naught but obvious magic.'

"And when I inspired the Apostles that they should believe in Him and in my Apostle, they said, 'We believe; do thou bear witness that we are resigned.'"

And when God said, "O Jesus, son of Mary! is it thou who dost say to men, take me and my mother for two gods, beside God?" He said: "I celebrate thy praise! what ails me that I should say what I have no right to? If I had said it, Thou wouldest have known it; Thou knowest what is in my soul, but I know not what is in Thy soul; verily Thou art one who knoweth the unseen. I never told them save what Thou didst bid me, 'Worship God, my Lord and your Lord,' and I was a witness against them so long as I was among them, but when Thou didst take me away to Thyself Thou wert the watcher over them, for Thou art witness over all.". . .

40. Jesus, Son of Mary, but the Apostle of God and of His Word

Surah 4, trans. Palmer, Q, I, pp. 93–95.

The people of the Book will ask thee to bring down for them a book from heaven; but they asked Moses a greater thing than that, for they said, "Show us God openly"; but the thunderbolt caught them in their injustice. Then they took a calf, after what had come to them of manifest signs; but we pardoned that, and gave Moses obvious authority. And we held over them the mountain at their compact, and said to them, "Enter ye the door adoring," and we said to them, "Transgress not on the Sabbath day," and we took from them a rigid compact.

But for that they broke their compact, and for their misbelief in God's signs, and for their killing the prophets undeservedly, and for their saying, "Our hearts are uncircumcised"—nay, God hath stamped on them their misbelief, so that they cannot believe, except a few—and for their misbelief, and for their saying about Mary a mighty calumny, and for their saying, "Verily we have killed the Messiah, Jesus the son of Mary, the apostle of God," but they did not kill Him, and they did not crucify Him, but a similitude was made for them. And verily, those who differ about Him are in doubt concerning Him; they have no knowledge concerning Him, but only follow an opinion. They did not kill Him, for sure! nay God raised Him up unto Himself; for God is mighty and wise! . . .

O ye people of the Book! do not exceed in your religion, nor say against God save the truth. The Messiah, Jesus, the son of Mary, is but the apostle of God and His Word, which He cast into Mary and a spirit from Him; believe then in God and His apostles, and say not "Three." Have done! it were better for you. God is only one God, celebrated be His praise that He should beget a Son!

V. The Conversion of Germany, the Decline of the Merovingians, and the Rise of the Carolingian Church

A. BONIFACE AND THE CONVERSION OF GERMANY (719–754)

41. Commissioned by Pope Gregory II for the German Mission (719)

S. Bon, et Lulli epist. 4, trans. Robinson, REH, I, p. 105.

Gregory, servant of the servants of God, to the devout priest Boniface:

Knowing that thou hast from childhood been devoted to sacred letters, and that thou hast labored to reveal to unbelieving people the mystery of faith, . . . we decree in the name of the indivisible Trinity, through the unshaken authority of Peter, chief of the apostles, whose doctrine it is our charge to teach, and whose holy see is in our keeping, that, since thou seemest to glow with the salvation-bringing fire which our Lord came to send upon the earth, thou shalt hasten to whatsoever tribes are lingering in the error of unbelief, and shalt institute the rites of the kingdom of God. . . . And we desire thee to establish the discipline of the sacraments, according to the observance of our holy apostolic see.

42. Appointed Presiding Bishop in Germany (722)

Trans. Robinson, *REH*, I, pp. 105–6.

Gregory, pope, to our well-beloved bishops established in Bavaria and Alemannia:
. . . It is fitting that ye recognize our brother and fellow-bishop, Boniface, as our representative, and that ye receive him with due honor in the name of Christ. And ye shall maintain the ministry of the Church with the Catholic faith according to the custom and precepts of the holy Catholic Apostolic Church; . . . And ye shall abhor the rites of the heathen, and the teaching of those coming from Britain and of false heretical priests. . . .

43. Boniface's Oath (722) to Pope Gregory III (715–731)

Ep. 8, trans. Robinson, *REH*, I, p. 106.

I, Boniface, bishop by the grace of God, promise to you, the blessed Peter, chief of the apostles, and to thy vicar, the blessed Pope Gregory, and to his successors, by the Father and the Son and the Holy Ghost, the indivisible Trinity, and by this thy most holy body, that, God helping me, I will maintain all the belief and the purity of the holy Catholic faith, and I will remain steadfast in the unity of this faith in which the whole salvation of Christians lies, as is established without doubt.

I will in no wise oppose the unity of the one universal Church, no matter who may seek to persuade me. But as I have said, I will maintain my faith and purity and union with thee and the benefits of thy Church, to whom God has given the power to loose and to bind, and with thy vicar and his successors, in all things. And if it comes to my knowledge that priests have turned from the ancient practices of the holy fathers, I will have no intercourse nor connection with them; but rather, if I can restrain them, I will. If I cannot, I will at once faithfully make known the whole matter to my apostolic lord.

44. Destruction of the Saxon Oak

Willibald, *Vita Bon.* (c. 786), 6, trans. Robinson, *REH*, pp. 106–7.

Many of the people of Hesse were converted [by Boniface] to the Catholic faith and confirmed by the grace of the spirit: and they received the laying on of hands. But some there were, not yet strong of soul, who refused to accept wholly the teachings of the true faith. Some men sacrificed secretly, some even openly, to trees and springs. Some secretly practiced divining, soothsaying, and incantations, and some openly. But others, who were of sounder mind, cast aside all heathen profanation and did none of these things; and it was with the advice and consent of these men that Boniface sought to fell a certain tree of great size, at Geismar, and called, in the ancient speech of the region, the oak of Jove [i.e. Thor].

The man of God was surrounded by the servants of God. When he would cut down the tree, behold a great throng of pagans who were there cursed him bitterly among themselves because he was the enemy of their gods. And when he had cut into the trunk a little way, a breeze sent by God stirred overhead, and suddenly the branching top of the tree was broken off, and the oak in all its huge bulk fell to the ground. And it was broken into four parts, as if by the divine will, so that the trunk was divided into four huge sections without any effort of the brethren who stood by. When the

pagans who had cursed did see this, they
left off cursing and, believing, blessed God.
Then the most holy priest took counsel with
the brethren: and he built from the wood of
the tree an oratory, and dedicated it to the
holy apostle Peter.

B. THE FRUIT OF BONIFACE'S WORK AND THE CAREER OF PEPIN III IN ALLIANCE WITH THE POPE

45. Pepin's Coronation (751/52)

Einhard, *Annales, ThM*, No. 6, pp. 37–38.

Anno 749. Burchard, bishop of Würz-
burg, and Fulrad, priest and chaplain, were
sent [by Pepin] to pope Zacharias to ask
his advice in regard to the kings who were
then ruling in France, who had the title of
king but no real royal authority. The pope
replied by these ambassadors that it would
be better that he who actually had the
power should be called king.

750 [751]. In this year Pepin was named
king of the Franks with the sanction of
the pope, and in the city of Soissons he
was anointed with the holy oil by the hands
of Boniface, archbishop and martyr of
blessed memory, and was raised to the
throne after the custom of the Franks. But
Childerich, who had the name of king, was
shorn of his locks and sent into a monastery.

753. . . . In this year pope Stephen
came to Pepin at Kiersy, to urge him to defend the Roman church from the attacks of
the Lombards.

754. And after pope Stephen had received a promise from king Pepin that he
would defend the Roman church, he
anointed the king and his two sons, Karl and
Karlmann, with the holy oil. And the pope
remained that winter in France.

46. Pepin Promises to Help the Pope (754/56)

Lib. Pont. *ThM*, No. 44, pp. 103–4.

When the king learned of the approach
of the blessed pope, he hastened to meet
him, accompanied by his wife and sons and
nobles, and sent his son Charles and certain
of the nobles nearly one hundred miles in

advance to meet the pope. He himself, however, received the pope about three miles
from his palace of Pontico, dismounting and
prostrating himself with his wife and sons
and nobles, and accompanying the pope a
little distance on foot by his saddle as if he
were his esquire. Thus the pope proceeded
to the palace with the king, giving glory and
praise to God in a loud voice, with hymns
and spiritual songs. This was on the sixth
day of the month of January, on the most
holy festival of the Epiphany of our Lord
Jesus Christ. And when they were seated in
the palace the pope began to beseech the
king with tears to make a treaty with St.
Peter and the Roman state and to assume
the protection of their interests. And the
king assured the pope on his oath that he
would strive with all his powers to obey his
prayers and admonitions and to restore the
exarchate of Ravenna and the rights and
territories of the Roman state, as the pope
wished. . . .

The aforesaid king Pepin, after receiving
the admonitions and the prayers of the pope,
took leave of him and proceeded to the
place called Kiersy, and called together
there all the lords of his kingdom, and by
repeating to them the holy admonitions of
the pope he persuaded them to agree to fulfil his promise to the pope.

47. Pepin's Donation of the Papal States (756) to the Pope, Stephen II (752–757)

Trans. *ThM*, No. 45, pp. 104–5.

The most Christian king of the Franks
[Pepin] despatched his counsellor Fulrad,
venerable abbot and priest, to receive these
cities, and then he himself straightway returned to France with his army. The aforesaid Fulrad met the representatives of King
Aistulf at Ravenna, and went with them
through the various cities of the Pentapolis
and of Emilia, receiving their submission
and taking hostages from each and bearing
away with him their chief men and the keys
of their gates. Then he went to Rome, and
placed the keys of Ravenna and of the other
cities of the exarchate along with the grant
of them which the king had made, in the

confession of St. Peter, thus handing them over to the apostle of God [Peter] and to his vicar the holy pope and to all his successors to be held and controlled forever. These are the cities: Ravenna, Rimini, Pesaro, Conca, Fano, Cesena, Sinigaglia, Forlimpopoli, Forli with the fortress of Sussubium, Montefeltre, Acerreagium, Monte Lucati, Serra, San Marino, Bobbio, Urbino, Cagli, Lucioli, Gubbio, Comacle; and also the city of Narni, which in former years had been taken from the duchy of Spoleto by the Romans.

VI. Charlemagne (768–814), His Caesaropapism and the Church

A. CHARLEMAGNE'S WARS, THE PAPACY, AND THE EMPIRE

48. Einhard on Charlemagne's Character and Achievements

Vita Karoli Magn., trans. *ThM*, No. 7, pp. 39–40; 43–45.

Then Karl returned to the attack which he had been making upon the Saxons and which had been interrupted by the Lombard invasion. This was the longest and most severe of all his wars, for the Saxons, being barbarians and pagans like most of the tribes in Germany, were bound by the laws neither of humanity nor of religion. For a long time there had been continual disturbances along the border, since there was no natural barrier marking the boundary between the two races, except in a few places where there were heavier forests or mountains. So the Franks and the Saxons were accustomed to make almost daily raids on the territory of each other, burning, devastating, and slaying. Finally the Franks determined to put an end to this condition of affairs by conquering the Saxons. In this way that war was begun which was waged continually for thirty-three years, and which was characterized by the most violent animosity on both sides, although the Saxons suffered the greater damage. The final conquest of the Saxons would have been accomplished sooner but for their treachery. It is hard to tell how often they broke faith; surrendering to the king and accepting his terms,

giving hostages and promising to accept the Christian faith and abandon their idols, and then breaking out into revolt again. This happened in almost every year of that war, but the determination of the king could not be overcome by the difficulties of the undertaking nor by the treachery of the Saxons. He never allowed a revolt to go unpunished, but immediately led or sent an army into their territory to avenge it. Finally after all the warriors had been overthrown or forced to surrender to the king, he transplanted some ten thousand men with their wives and children, from their home on the Elbe, to Gaul and Germany, distributing them through these provinces. Thus they were brought to accept the terms of the king, agreeing to abandon their pagan faith and accept Christianity, and to be united to the Franks; and this war which had dragged on through so many years was brought to an end. . . .

The glory of his reign was also greatly enhanced by his alliances and friendships with foreign kings and peoples. Thus Aldefonso, king of Gallicia and Asturia, was his ally, and spoke of himself by letters and ambassadors as the man of Karl. The kings of the Scots also were wont to address him as master, calling themselves his subjects and servants, of which expressions there are evidences in letters still existing which they have written to him. He was also in close relations with Aaron [Haroun-al-Raschid], king of the Persians, who ruled almost all of the east outside of India, and who always expressed the greatest friendship and admiration for Karl. On one occasion, when Karl sent an embassy with gifts for the holy sepulchre of our Lord and Saviour, he not only permitted them to fulfil their mission, but even made a present of that holy spot to Karl, to rule as his own. And when the embassy of Karl returned, it was accompanied by ambassadors from Aaron, bearing presents of fine robes, spices, and other eastern treasures. A few years before he sent to Karl at his request an elephant which was the only one he at that time possessed. The emperors of Constantinople, Nicephorus, Michael, and Leo, were his friends and allies and sent many embassies to him. Even when they suspected him of desiring to seize their empire, because he took the title of emperor, they nevertheless entered into alliance with him, to avoid a rupture.

He was very eloquent and could express himself clearly on any subject. He spoke foreign languages besides his own tongue, and was so proficient in Latin that he used it as easily as his own language. Greek he could understand better than he could speak. . . . He was devoted to the study of the liberal arts and was a munificent patron of learned men. Grammar he learned from Peter, an aged deacon of Pisa; in the other studies his chief instructor was Alcuin, a Saxon from England, also a deacon, and the most learned man of his time. With him he studied rhetoric, dialectic, and especially astronomy. . . . He tried also to learn to write, keeping tablets under the pillow of his couch to practise on in his leisure hours. But he never succeeded very well, because he began too late in life.

His last visit to Rome was made because the Romans had attacked and injured pope Leo, tearing out his eyes and tongue, and had thus forced the pope to call on the king for aid. And having come to Rome to restore the church which had greatly suffered during the strife, he remained there all winter. It was during this time that he received the title of emperor and Augustus, to which he was at first so averse, that he was wont to say that he would never have entered the church on that day, although it was a great feast day [Christmas], if he had foreseen the plan of the pope. But his great patience and magnanimity finally overcame the envy and hatred of the Roman emperors [of the east], who were indignant at his receiving the title. This he did by sending them frequent embassies and addressing them in his letters as brothers.

After he became emperor he undertook a revision of the laws of his empire, which were very defective, for the Franks had two laws [Salic and Ripuarian] differing in many points from one another. But he was never able to do more than to complete the various laws with a few additional sections and cause all the unwritten laws to be put into writing. He also wrote down for preser-

vation the ancient German songs, in which the wars and adventures of old heroes are celebrated. He began also to make a grammar of his native tongue. . . .

49. Charles' Manifesto to Pope Leo III (795/96–816) on Spiritual and Temporal Powers (796)

Ep. ad Leo III, trans. ThM, No. 47, p. 107.

Karl, by the grace of God king of the Franks and Lombards, and patricius of the Romans, to his holiness, pope Leo, greeting. . . . Just as I entered into an agreement with the most holy father, your predecessor, so also I desire to make with you an inviolable treaty of mutual fidelity and love; that, on the one hand, you shall pray for me and give me the apostolic benediction, and that, on the other, with the aid of God I will ever defend the most holy seat of the holy Roman church. For it is our part to defend the holy church of Christ from the attacks of pagans and infidels from without, and within to enforce the acceptance of the catholic faith. It is your part, most holy father, to aid us in the good fight by raising your hands to God as Moses did [Ex. 17:11], so that by your intercession the Christian people under the leadership of God may always and everywhere have the victory over the enemies of His holy name, and the name of our Lord Jesus Christ may be glorified throughout the world. Abide by the canonical law in all things and obey the precepts of the holy fathers always, that your life may be an example of sanctity to all, and your holy admonitions be observed by the whole world, and that your light may so shine before men that they may see your good works and glorify your father which is in heaven [Matt. 5:16]. May omnipotent God preserve your holiness unharmed through many years for the exalting of his holy church.

50. Pope Leo III's Coronation of Charles (800)

Liber Pont., 2:7, ed. Duchesne, trans. *ThM*, No. 8, p. 48.

After this, on Christmas day, all gathered together in the aforesaid church of St. Peter and the venerable pope crowned Karl with

his own hands with a magnificent crown.
Then all the Romans, inspired by God and
by St. Peter, keeper of the keys of heaven,
and recognizing the value of Karl's protection and the love which he bore the holy
Roman church and the pope, shouted in a
loud voice: "Long life and victory to Karl,
the pious Augustus crowned of God, the
great and peace-bringing emperor." The
people, calling on the names of all the saints,
shouted this three times, before the holy
confession of St. Peter, and thus he was
made emperor of the Romans by all. Then
the pope anointed Karl and his son with the
holy oil.

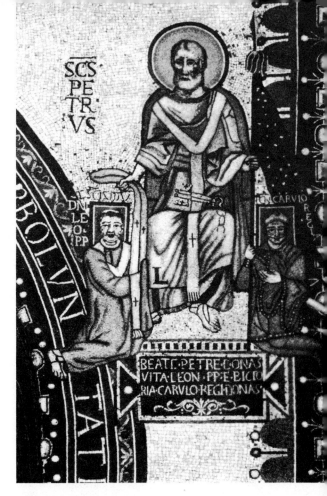

V-4. St. Peter Giving the Pallium to Pope Leo
III and the Standard to Charlemagne. *Mosaic of
the 8th century, Piazza S. Giovanni in Laterano, Rome.*

B. CHARLES AS LEGISLATOR FOR CHURCH AND SOCIETY

51. *Regulations Concerning the Churches and Worship Among the Conquered Saxons* (775–790)

*Cap. de Part. Saxoniae, 1, 4, 5, 6, 8, trans. PTR,
VI, (5), p. 2.*

First, concerning the greater chapters it
has been enacted.

It was pleasing to all that the churches of
Christ, which are now being built in Saxony
and consecrated to God, should not have
less, but greater and more illustrious honor,
than the fanes of the idols had had.

4. If any one, out of contempt for Christianity, shall have despised the holy Lenten
fast and shall have eaten flesh, let him be
punished by death. But, nevertheless, let it
be taken into consideration by a priest, lest
perchance any one from necessity has been
led to eat flesh.

5. If any one shall have killed a bishop
or priest or deacon, let him likewise be punished capitally.

6. If any one deceived by the devil shall
have believed, after the manner of the
pagans, that any man or woman is a witch
and eats men, and on this account shall have
burned the person, or shall have given the
person's flesh to others to eat, or shall have
eaten it himself, let him be punished by a
capital sentence.

8. If any one of the race of the Saxons
hereafter concealed among them shall have
wished to hide himself unbaptized, and shall

have scorned to come to baptism and shall
have wished to remain a pagan, let him be
punished by death.

52. *Churchmen Held Responsible for Re-form and for Learning and Teaching the Scriptures* (780–800)

*Ep. de Litteris Colendis, trans. PTR, VII, (5),
pp. 12–14.*

Charles, by the grace of God, King of
the Franks and Lombards and Patrician of
the Romans, to Abbot Baugulf and to all the
congregation, also the faithful committed to
you, we have directed a loving greeting by
our ambassadors in the name of omnipotent
God.

Be it known, therefore, to your devotion pleasing to God, that we, together with our faithful, have considered it to be useful that the bishoprics and monasteries entrusted by the favor of Christ to our control, in addition to the order of monastic life and the intercourse of holy religion, in the culture of letters also ought to be zealous in teaching those who by the gift of God are able to learn, according to the capacity of each individual, so that just as the observance of the rule imparts order and grace to honesty of morals, so also zeal in teaching and learning may do the same for sentences, so that those who desire to please God by living rightly should not neglect to please him also by speaking correctly. For it is written: "Either from thy words thou shalt be justified or from thy words thou shalt be condemned." For although correct conduct may be better than knowledge, nevertheless knowledge precedes conduct. Therefore, each one ought to study what he desires to accomplish, so that so much the more fully the mind may know what ought to be done, as the tongue hastens in the praises of omnipotent God without the hindrances of errors. For since errors should be shunned by all men, so much the more ought they to be avoided as far as possible by those who are chosen for this very purpose alone, so that they ought to be the especial servants of truth. For when in the years just passed letters were often written to us from several monasteries in which it was stated that the brethren who dwelt there offered up in our behalf sacred and pious prayers, we have recognized in most of these letters both correct thoughts and uncouth expressions; because what pious devotion dictated faithfully to the mind, the tongue, uneducated on account of the neglect of study, was not able to express in the letter without error. Whence it happened that we began to fear lest perchance, as the skill in writing was less, so also the wisdom for understanding the Holy Scriptures might be much less than it rightly ought to be. And we all know well that, although errors of speech are dangerous, far more dangerous are errors of the understanding. Therefore, we exhort you not only not to neglect the study of letters, but also with most humble mind, pleasing to God, to study earnestly in order that you may be able more easily and more correctly to penetrate the mysteries of the divine Scriptures. Since, moreover, images, tropes and similar figures are found in the sacred pages, no one doubts that each one in reading these will understand the spiritual sense more quickly if previously he shall have been fully instructed in the mastery of letters. Such men truly are to be chosen for this work as have both the will and the ability to learn and a desire to instruct others. And may this be done with a zeal as great as the earnestness with which we command it. For we desire you to be, as it is fitting that soldiers of the church should be, devout in mind, learned in discourse, chaste in conduct and eloquent in speech, so that whosoever shall seek to see you out of reverence for God, or on account of your reputation for holy conduct, just as he is edified by your appearance, may also be instructed by your wisdom, which he has learned from your reading or singing, and may go away joyfully giving thanks to omnipotent God. Do not neglect, therefore, if you wish to have our favor, to send copies of this letter to all your suffragans and fellow-bishops and to all the monasteries. [And let no monk hold courts outside of his monastery or go to the judicial and other public assemblies. Farewell. (*Legens valeat.*)]

53. The Liberal Arts Fostered and the Collection of Suitable Liturgical Lessons Authorized for Reading in the Churches (786–800)

Karoli Epistola Generalis, trans. PTR, VI, (5), pp. 14–15.

Charles, confiding in the aid of God, King of the Franks and Lombards, and Patrician of the Romans, to the religious lectors subject to our power.

Since the divine clemency always guards us at home and abroad, in the issues of war or in the tranquility of peace, though human insignificance is in no way able to pay back His benefits, nevertheless, because our God is inestimable in His mercy, He approves benignly the goodwill of those devoted to His service. Therefore, because we take care constantly to improve the condition of our churches, we have striven with watchful zeal to advance the cause of learning, which has been almost forgotten by the negligence of our ancestors; and, by our example, also we invite those whom we can to master the study of the liberal arts. Accordingly, God aiding us in all things, we have already corrected carefully all the books of the Old and New Testaments, corrupted by the ignorance of the copyists.

Incited, moreover, by the example of our father Pepin, of venerated memory, who by his zeal decorated all the churches of the Gauls with the songs of the Roman church, we are careful by our skill to make these churches illustrious by a series of excellent lectionaries. Finally, because we have found the lectionaries for the nocturnal offices, compiled by the fruitless labor of certain ones, in spite of their correct intention, unsuitable because they were written without the words of their authors and were full of an infinite number of errors, we cannot suffer in our days discordant solecisms to glide into the sacred lessons among the holy offices, and we purpose to improve these lessons. And we have entrusted this work to Paul the deacon, our friend and client. We have directed him to peruse carefully the sayings of the catholic fathers and to choose, so to speak, from the most broad meadows of their writings certain flowers, and from the most useful to form, as it were, a single garland. He, desiring to obey devoutly our highness, has read through the treatises and sermons of the different catholic fathers, has chosen from each the best, and has presented to us in two volumes lessons suitable for the whole year and for each separate festival, and free from error. We have examined the text of all these with our wisdom, we have established these volumes by our authority, and we deliver them to your religion to be read in the churches of Christ.

54. The Secular Priesthood and Monastic Life to Be Fittingly Observed; Schools for Training of the Ministry and Reform of Worship to Be Set up

Admonitio Generalis (789), 72, trans. *PTR*, VI, (5), p. 15.

And we also demand of your holiness that the ministers of the altar of God shall adorn their ministry by good manners, and likewise the other orders who observe a rule and the congregations of monks. We implore them to lead a just and fitting life, just as God Himself commanded in the Gospel. "Let your light so shine before men that they may see your good works and glorify your Father which is in heaven," so that by their example many may be led to serve God; and let them join and associate to themselves not only children of servile condition, but also sons of free men. And let schools be established in which boys may learn to read. Correct carefully the Psalms, the signs in writing (*notas*), the songs, the calendar, the grammar, in each monastery or bishopric, and the catholic books; because often some desire to pray to God properly, but they pray badly because of the incorrect books. And do not permit your boys to corrupt them in reading or writing. If there is need of writing the Gospel, Psalter and Missal, let men of mature age do the writing with all diligence.

55. Carl's Clerical and Lay Messengers (Missi Dominici) Dispatched Throughout the Realm to Oversee Justice and Christian Conduct (802?)

Leges 2, i, 33, trans. *ThM*, No. 9, pp. 49–51.

1. Concerning the representatives sent out by the emperor. The most serene and Christian emperor, Karl, chose certain of the ablest and wisest men among his nobles, archbishops, bishops, abbots, and pious laymen, and sent them out through his realm, and through these, his representatives, he gave his people rules to guide them in living justly. He ordered these men to investigate and to report to him any inequality or injustice that might appear in the law as then constituted, that he might undertake its correction. He ordered that no one should dare to change the prescribed law by any trickery or fraud, or to pervert the course of justice for his own ends, as many were wont to do, or to deal unjustly with the churches of God, with the poor or the widows and orphans, or with any Christian man. But he commanded all men to live righteously according to the precepts of God, and to remain each in his own station and calling; the

regular clergy to observe the rules of monastic life without thought of gain, nuns to keep diligent watch over their lives, laymen to keep the law justly without fraud, and all, finally, to live together in perfect peace and charity. And he ordered his *missi*, as they desired to win the favor of Almighty God and keep the faith which they had promised him, to inquire diligently into every case where any man complained that he had been dealt with unjustly by anyone, and in the fear of God to render justice to all, to the holy churches of God, to the poor, to widows and orphans, and to the whole people. And if any case arises which they can not correct and bring to justice with the aid of the local counts, they are to make a clear report of it to the emperor. They are not to be hindered in the doing of justice by the flattery or bribery of anyone, by their partiality for their own friends, or by the fear of powerful men.

2. The oath of fidelity to the emperor. He has also commanded that every man in his kingdom, clergyman or layman, who has already taken the oath of fidelity to him as king, shall now renew it to him as emperor; and that all persons over twelve years of age who have not yet taken the oath shall do so now. The nature and extent of the promise should be made known to all, for it includes not only, as some think, a promise of fidelity to the emperor for this life, and an engagement not to bring any enemy into the kingdom nor to take part in or conceal any infidelity to him, but includes all the following:

3. First, that each one shall strive with all his mind and strength on his own account to serve God according to the commandments and according to his own promise, for the emperor is not able to give the necessary care and oversight to all his people.

4. Second, that no one shall ever wrongfully claim, take, or conceal anything that belongs to the emperor, such as lands or slaves, by perjury or fraud, or through partiality or bribery; and that no one shall take or conceal fugitive serfs from the royal lands, by perjury or fraud. . . .

5. That no one shall do any violence or harm to the holy churches of God, to widows and orphans, or to strangers; for the emperor, after God and his saints, is constituted their special protector. . . .

56. General Laws Governing the Missi's Administration, under the Emperor, of Secular and Regular Clergy, People and Churches (802)

Cap. Missorum 10, 11, 13, 15–17, 19–20, trans. *PTR*, VI, (5), pp. 18–22.

10. That bishops and priests shall live according to the canons and shall teach others to do the same.

11. That bishops, abbots, abbesses, who are in charge of others, with the greatest veneration shall strive to surpass their subjects in this diligence and shall not oppress their subjects with a harsh rule or tyranny, but with sincere love shall carefully guard the flock committed to them with mercy and charity or by the examples of good works.

13. That bishops, abbots and abbesses shall have advocates, vicars and *centenarii* who know the law and love justice, who are pacific and merciful, so that through these greater profit or advantage may accrue to the holy church of God; because we are entirely unwilling to have in the monasteries harmful and greedy provosts and advocates, from whom greater blasphemy or injury may arise for us. But they shall be such as the canonical or regular institution orders them to be, submissive to the will of God and always ready to render justice to all, fully observing the law without malicious fraud, always exercising a just judgment in the case of all, such provosts indeed as the holy rule teaches that they should be. And let them wholly observe this, that they shall in no way deviate from the canonical or regular norm, but shall exhibit humility in all things. If, moreover, they shall have presumed to do otherwise, let them feel the discipline of the rule; and if they shall have been unwilling to amend their ways, they shall be removed from the provostship, and those who are more worthy shall be appointed in their places.

15. We will and command in every way that abbots and monks shall be subject to their bishops in all humility and obedience, just as is commanded by the canonical constitution. And all the churches and basilicas

shall remain in the defense and power of the church. And no one shall dare to divide or to cast lots concerning the property of the basilicas. And what has once been offered shall not be taken back, and shall be sanctified and shall be claimed as legal property. But if any one shall have presumed to do otherwise he shall pay and make good our ban. And the monks shall be corrected by the bishops of their province; but if they do not amend their ways then the archbishop shall summon them to the synod; and if even then they shall not have amended their ways, then they shall come together with their bishop to our presence.

16. Concerning choosing men for ordination, just as the lord emperor had formerly granted it, by the law of the Franks, to the bishops and abbots, so he has also now confirmed it; nevertheless, in this manner, so that neither a bishop nor an abbot in a monastery shall prefer the more worthless to the better, and he shall not desire to advance any one before his betters on account of relationship or any flattery, and that he shall not lead such an one to us to be ordained when he has a better concealed and kept back; we are in no way willing that this should be done, because it seems to be a mockery and deceit of us. But in the monasteries men of such a character are to be prepared for ordination that reward and profit may accrue both to us and to those who recommend them.

17. Moreover, that the monks shall live firmly and strictly in accordance with the rule, because we know that any one whose goodwill is lukewarm is displeasing to God, as John bears witness in the Apocalypse: "I would that thou wert cold or hot. So then, because thou art lukerwarm, and neither cold nor hot, I will spue thee out of my mouth." Let them in no way usurp to themselves secular business. They shall not have leave to go outside of their monastery at all, unless compelled by a very great necessity; but nevertheless the bishops, in whose diocese they shall be, shall take care in every way that they do not get accustomed to wandering outside of the monastery. But if it shall be necessary for any one to go outside in obedience to a command, and this shall be done with the counsel and consent of the bishop, persons of such character shall be sent out with a certificate, that there may be no suspicion of evil in them and that no evil report may arise from them. For the property and business outside of the monastery the abbot, with the permission and counsel of the bishop, shall ordain who shall provide, not a monk, but another of the faithful. Let them wholly shun secular gain or a desire for worldly affairs, because avarice or a desire for this world ought to be shunned by all Christians, but especially by those who seem to have renounced the world and its lusts. Let no one presume in any way to incite strifes and controversies, either within or outside of the monastery. But if any one shall have presumed to do so, he shall be corrected by the most severe discipline of the rule and in such a manner that others shall fear to commit such actions. Let them entirely shun drunkenness and feasting, because it is known to all that from these, men are especially polluted by lust. For a most pernicious rumor has come to our ears that many in the monasteries have already been detected in fornication and in abomination and uncleanness. It especially saddens and disturbs us that it can be said, without a great mistake, that some of the monks are understood to be sodomites, so that whereas the greatest hope of salvation to all Christians is believed to arise from the life and chastity of the monks, damage has been incurred instead. Therefore, we also ask and urge that henceforth all shall most earnestly strive with all diligence to preserve themselves from these evils, so that never again such a report shall be brought to our ears. And let this be known to all, that we in no way dare to consent to those evils in any other place in our whole kingdom; so much the less, indeed, in the persons of those whom we desire to be examples of chastity and moral purity. Certainly, if any such report shall have come to our ears in the future, we shall inflict such a penalty, not only on the guilty but also on those who have consented to such deeds, that no Christian who shall have heard of it will ever dare in the future to perpetrate such acts.

19. That no bishops, abbots, priests, deacons, or other members of the clergy shall presume to have dogs for hunting, or

V-5 (above) and V-6 (right). Hagia Sophia. *Anthemius of Tralles and Isidorus of Miletus, 532–537* A.D. *Istanbul (Constantinople).*

hawks, falcons and sparrow-hawks, but each shall observe fully the canons or rule of his order. If any one shall presume to do so, let him know that he shall lose his office. And in addition he shall suffer such punishment for it that the others will be afraid to usurp such things for themselves.

20. That abbesses, together with their nuns, shall live within the cloisters in concord and watchfully, and shall never presume to go outside of their cloisters. But if the abbesses wish to send any nuns out of the cloisters, they shall not do this without the consent and advice of their bishops. Likewise, also, when there ought to be any ordinations or receptions in the monasteries, they shall previously discuss these fully with their bishops; and the bishops shall announce to the archbishop what seems the safer or more useful way, and with his advice they shall perform what ought to be done.

57. *Clerical and Lay Examination (803, 802–813)*

Cap. Missorum, trans. *PTR,* VI, (5), pp. 15–16.

Ch. 2. Priests shall not be ordained without an examination. And excommunications shall not be ordered at random and without cause.

VII. Justinian, an Earlier Caesaropapist (527–565); His Patronage of Art and Letters and His Compilation of Laws on the Church and Society Compared with Those of Charles

58. *Exemptions and Privileges of Physicians, Professors, and Their Families*

Code, Bk. X, Tit. LII, No. 6, trans. S. P. Scott, *The Civil Law* (Cincinnati: The Central Trust Co., 1932), XV, p. 149. Grateful acknowledgment of permission to reprint Items 58 and 59 is made to The Central Trust Company (Executor of the Estate of Samuel P. Scott, de-

ceased), The Estate of Elizabeth W. Scott, deceased, and the Jefferson Medical College of Philadelphia, the copyright owners of *The Civil Law.*

6. *The Emerpor Constantine to Volusianus*

We order that physicians, *archiatri*, grammarians, and other professors of letters, as well as doctors of the law, together with their wives and children, and any property which they may possess in their own cities, shall be exempt from every function, and every kind of service, civil as well as public; and shall not be required to entertain guests in a province; nor perform any labor; nor be compelled to appear in court; nor be deprived of their property; nor be produced before any tribunal; nor suffer any injury; and if anyone should molest them, he shall be punished as the judge may decide.

We order that rewards and salaries shall be paid to them by which they may the more readily perfect themselves in their liberal studies and arts above mentioned.

Published at Sirmium, on the *Kalends* of August, during the Consulate of Crispus and Constantine, 321.

59. *Letters, Christian Doctrine, and the Selection of Ecclesiasts*

Novels, Tit. VI, Sixth New Constitution, First Collection, Chap. IV, trans. Scott, *CL,* XVI, p. 35.

After having, in conformity with the sacred canons, disposed of the preceding matters relating to bishops, We now decree, in compliance with the same canons, that no one can be ordained an ecclesiastic until after a careful examination, and that the candidate must be of good character, and by all means conversant with letters, and proficient in the doctrines of the Church. For We are unwilling for persons who are ignorant of letters to be ordained under any circumstances, that is to say, as clerks, priests, deacons, readers of the service, or of ecclesiastical or canonical books.

60. *Justinian, the Arts, and the Building of Hagia Sophia* (537)

Procopius, Buildings, 1:1, trans. H. B. Dewing and G. Downey. Reprinted by permission of the publishers from *Procopius,* Vol. VII, pp. 11–13 (Cambridge, Mass.: Harvard University Press, 1940).

And by way of shewing that it was not against the Emperor alone that they had taken up arms, but no less against God himself, unholy wretches that they were, they had the hardihood to fire the Church of the Christians, which the people of Byzantium call "Sophia," an epithet which they have most appropriately invented for God, by which they call His temple; and God permitted them to accomplish this impiety, foreseeing into what an object of beauty this shrine was destined to be transformed. So the whole church at that time lay a charred mass of ruins. But the Emperor Justinian built not long afterwards a church so finely shaped, that if anyone had enquired of the Christians before the burning if it would be their wish that the church should be destroyed and one like this should take its place, shewing them some sort of model of the building we now see, it seems to me that they would have prayed that they might see their church destroyed forthwith, in order that the building might be converted into its present form. At any rate the Emperor, disregarding all questions of expense, eagerly pressed on to begin the work of construction, and began to gather all the artisans from the whole world. And Anthemius of Tralles, the most learned man in the skilled craft which is known as the art of building, not only of all his contemporaries, but also when compared with those who had lived long before him, ministered to the Emperor's enthusiasm, duly regulating the tasks of the various artisans, and preparing in advance designs of the future construction; and associated with him was another master-builder, Isidorus by name, a Milesian by birth, a man who was intelligent and worthy to assist the Emperor Justinian. Indeed this also was an indication of the honour in which God held the Emperor, that He had already provided the men who would be most serviceable to him in the tasks which were waiting to be carried out. And one might with good reason marvel at the discernment of the Emperor himself, in that out of the whole world he was able to select the men who were most suitable for the most important of his enterprises.

So the church has become a spectacle of marvellous beauty, overwhelming to those who see it, but to those who know it by hearsay altogether incredible. For it soars to a height to match the sky, and as if surging up from amongst the other buildings it stands on high and looks down upon the remainder of the city, adorning it, because it is a part of it, but glorying in its own beauty, because, though a part of the city and dominating it, it at the same time towers above it to such a height that the whole city is viewed from there as from a watch-tower. Both its breadth and its length have been so carefully proportioned, that it may not improperly be said to be exceedingly long and at the same time unusually broad. And it exults in an indescribable beauty.

SUGGESTED READINGS

Arragon, R. F., *The Transition from the Ancient to the Medieval World.* New York: Holt, Rinehart & Winston, Inc., 1936.

Duckett, E. S., *Alcuin, Friend of Charlemagne.* New York: The Macmillan Co., 1951.

———, *The Gateway to the Middle Ages.* New York: The Macmillan Co., 1938.

———, *Anglo-Saxon Saints and Scholars.* New York: The Macmillan Co., 1947.

Dudden, F. H., *Gregory the Great,* 2 vols. New York: Longmans, Green & Co., Inc., 1905.

Giles, E., *Documents Illustrating Papal Authority.* London: SPCK, 1952.

Hitti, P. K., *History of the Arabs,* 3rd ed. New York: The Macmillan Co., 1946.

Jalland, T. G., *The Church and the Papacy.* Naperville, Illinois: Alec R. Allenson, Inc., 1944.

Kidd, B. J., *The Roman Primacy to A.D. 461.* New York: The Macmillan Co., 1936.

Laistner, M. L. W., *Thought and Letters in Western Europe—A.D. 500–900.* London: Methuen & Co., Ltd., 1931.

Levison, W., *England and the Continent in the Eighth Century.* New York: Oxford University Press, 1946.

Lot, F., *The End of the Ancient World and the Beginning of the Middle Ages.* New York: Alfred A. Knopf, Inc., 1931.

McCracken, G. E. and A. Cabaniss, *Early Medieval Theology,* Library of Christian Classics, Vol. IX. Philadelphia: Westminster Press, 1957.

McNeill, J. T., *Makers of Christianity.* New York: Holt, Rinehart & Winston, Inc., 1934.

Pirenne, H., *Mohammed and Charlemagne,* trans. B. Miall. New York: W. W. Norton & Co., Inc., 1939.

Shotwell, J. T. and L. R. Loomis, *The See of Peter.* New York: Columbia University Press, 1927.

Swift, E. H., *Hagia Sophia.* New York: Columbia University Press, 1940.

CHRONOLOGY

218

Illustration, page 220: **Knightly Armor, 13th Century.** *National Museum, Florence.*

VI

The Church, the Papacy,

and the

Economic-Social Milieu;

Feudalism, Investiture Struggle,

Crusades, Towns, and Trade

From its earliest years the Church had
known the embarrassment of preaching freedom from material
possessions while welcoming the support of earthly
goods. Through the centuries, Christian social theorists continued
to extol varying forms of communal living.
Actually, the earliest Christian possession of all
things in common was little more than shared consumption.
There was scant regard for cooperative production.
During its first millennium, the Church exhibited a variety of
monastic experiments of a semi-communal

nature. Matching its numerical growth and social influence, however, the Church came to reflect precisely the economy of the world around and within it. Being *in* the world but not *of* it, suggested a poignant declaration of independence from the world's power to coerce the spirit. Such was scarcely a realistic description of the Church's operation within the social structure.

With the passage of time, Christian institutions gained in influence and their protests against accommodation to earthly standards gathered weight. Even so, church organization approximated ever more closely the very outlines of structural rigidity that Christian idealists most deplored. To study the prophetic utterances of such leaders concerning the Church's worldliness is seldom to gain a balanced picture of the Church or of the world. Light is thus cast, to be sure, upon the inevitable involvement of Christians in their environing social order. Christian social critics never allowed the Church to become wholly domesticated on earth. They clamored ceaselessly for a recognition of the Christian life as a pilgrimage to heaven. Nothing they could do, however, including their most ingenious sublimation of Jesus' hard-headed teachings, could obviate one fact. Christians were in the *world*, even as the world was in *them*. Furthermore, the Christ had never offered hope for their extrication from their human social obligations. That a higher loyalty came first, yes! But, that a diminishing complicity in human affairs followed logically from this, no!

What the Christian ethic clearly demanded, and what recurring sages and saints unerringly pointed out, was something else again. Christians must be left in the world to handle its goods in stewardship for the divine Lord, without ever becoming possessed by a sense of possessiveness. Some of the subtlest competition among monastic theorists ranged over old questions in ever new guise. Ought the apprentice to perfection scorn the flesh, the world, and the goods of earthly life as if they had no genuine worth? Or, ought he utilize, humbly and gladly, every good of the human economy within the perspective of varying means graduated to the one true end? The monas-

tic orders had a checkered history of alternating rigor, laxity, and reformation. The persistence of this phenomenon sprang partly from genuine Christian puzzlement over the true nature and practice of a valid renunciation. If specialists in the higher Christian stewardship were unsure of their ground, how could the lowly practitioner of Christian dedication be expected to find his way? Suppose it were conceded that gospel poverty in its more subtle ramifications was a counsel for experts in perfection. Would this make true poverty of spirit any less requisite upon all genuine Christians? Could a special, dedicated group wash out the stains of human acquisitiveness for all? Without any consciously studied intention of doing so, the Church came increasingly to practice the implications of just such an institutional vicariousness.

In a sense, monks had the supreme commission. They were to transcend obvious victories over sheerly material dispossession with continuously waged struggles against the more insidious lures of spiritual acquisitiveness. Nonetheless, the Christian Church continued to apply two kinds of mutually re-enforcing pressures. It asked temporal powers to recognize the Church's prior claim to interpret and administer—through whatever intermediaries—the sole ownership by the divine of all human resources. Simultaneously, the Church claimed a superior disinterestedness where all its earthly manipulations were concerned. These, apparently, were guaranteed by its prosecuting an ultimately spiritual vocation. Not strangely, this might sometimes appear, in historical retrospect, to have been just another way of the Church's "eating its cake and having it too." Some there were, even in the Middle Ages, who thought it specious for the hierarchy to flaunt virtuously its unworldly disregard for economic power, even while it pressed most vigorously its wardship of all human business. Rarely, if ever, in the long centuries, did the Church seriously propose withdrawal from secular affairs. Customarily, it simply called spiritual all activities, however secular, that it felt called upon to touch.

Even in monasticism—perhaps one should

say especially there—poverty was more apparent than real. Original Benedictinism removed possession from the individual, only to lodge it the more firmly in the fraternal corporation. The much later Franciscan radicalism was carefully revised in accord with spiritual worldly wisdom before being approved for a society. Francis had never proposed his band for other than a little group of voluntarily poor men, and then with its main emphasis on other than merely economic non-acquisitiveness. But the hierarchy on earth of God's heavenly will proceeded consistently and devotedly to strengthen its claim, however indirect, upon every resource of the divine bounty. This was in the governing of renunciatory communities as well as of everything else beyond them. Renunciatory groups, the later Franciscans among them, proceeded to make a mockery of spiritual poverty with their consolidated wealthiness, both spiritual and temporal.

If, therefore, the medieval Church held lands, this was because in all good conscience it prayed for and, if necessary, fought for their acquisition and maintenance. To cluck one's tongue in mock surprise that the Church was drawn into temporal affairs is to compound many little intellectual dishonesties into one great hypocrisy. The more roughhewn the economy in which the Church lived, the more tense it became over its spiritual leadership. This uneasiness became progressively greater as the Church prosecuted its claim to lead the van of heavenly colonists deployed on earth for their return journey to heaven. Since God had deliberately created humanity to reach heaven by way of earth, how could the involvements of the human order be stigmatized as wholly evil or extraneous concerns?

For the Church to exist at all, it had to exist on earth and in the social order for however short or long a time God might choose to have it there! The Church, therefore, could not claim to be made up of, and to be dealing with, "Christian" men while it deliberated the fate of "other" men. For the Church, there were no "other" men, no men truly human who were not potentially Christian. There were no men, created by God, who existed beyond the Church's leading them into heaven or their lapsing from it into hell! With all of these, the Church lived in a given economy, at a stated time, after the pattern of income from lands and/or the increase from commerce, trade, and a moneyed economy. Whenever the Church dared speak from this living context to any or all of these people, it generalized hopelessly or prophesied pertinently in terms of its involved awareness of obligations both divine and human.

The documents in this chapter are not envisaged as an automatic clarification of all that matters in understanding the Church's precarious balance in society. No attempt is made to explain in a few words all that really counted in feudalism or in the rise of a proto-capitalistic society. A few suggestions are offered for alert inquiry into the complicated structure of feudal agrarianism and, latterly, its coexistence with a new urbanism. This is not to labor some useless technicality while the Church's spiritual testimony goes unregarded. It is, rather, a consideration of the everyday existence that impinged upon the Church and which the Church, in turn, helped to fashion.

It is a truism that few, if any, of the Church's institutional forms originated with her. To seek originality of this kind is to overlook the source of truly important differences in spirit. In an almost irritating fashion, the Church from its very inception employed services so old, in bearings so novel, as to make clear precedence of ideas and spiritual genius maddeningly difficult. How much of Judaistic form is there in Christianity's repudiation of Judaistic legalism? How much of pre-Christian dualism is there in Christian asceticism? How alike and how different are the pre-Christian and Christian species of the monastic genius? Patently, Christianity did not inaugurate even the larger part of the transformations it helped bring into truly original relief.

Feudalism was not introduced by Christian theorists or social scientists. From almost its very beginning, however, Christianity lived in a Roman society that had in it the potentialities for later feudal development. These feudal components did not wait upon the emergence of Germanic tribal eccentricities. They stemmed rather from the society of the later Roman empire. Man-to-man interdependence with mutual supports proffered by both the strong and the weak helped resolve the exigencies of precarious livelihood. Long, complicated experiments sought to surmount the tenuousness of landholding, breadwinning, and taxpaying in whatever kind. The end sought was the conscious advantage of little, peasant, worker-farmers and big, risk-taking, property holders. Something akin to contractual reciprocity came to seal the pledge given, each to the other, by small farmers and the great landed gentry. The former gave their little holdings to great farmer lords for enhanced economic security. The latter gained, in return, a clique with an ultimately identical welfare at stake. Individuals without land were likewise wrought into a pattern of privileged dependence under a protecting, and no less profiting, lord. Transplanted into this Roman extemporizing was a later Germanic potential. Tribal loyalties provided a following of warriors after battle-tested chiefs in a comradeship of food provision and armed exploits. Under Gothic improvisation, private troops might actually be rewarded by the lord, not only with armed prestige and plunder, but also in the bestowal of lands.

Under Charlemagne, one sees a kind of medieval feudalism in embryo that was to flourish under his successors. Actually, feudalism was a spirit of compromising adaptivity as well as a *modus vivendi* that grew with the particular exigencies of specific eras and locales. Seen in its usually romanticized outlines, feudalism focused the mutuality of lords and vassals. No less important, however, was the day-by-day association in mutual concord of the seigneur with his serfs and villeins on the great manorial estates. Feudalism as such registered the dual character of personal and landed tenure.

Actually, feudalism in the large was a highly extemporized and often unsystematic way of living for the Church and for other institutions. It sought a form of local order in lieu of stronger centralized governments that were rapidly collapsing. Even in Merovingian, as later in Carolingian, days the king had sometimes delegated administrative powers to "counts" or royal companions. Charlemagne found some "dukes" ruling ostensibly in the royal interest but with a wary eye upon ducal sovereignty. His *missi* (or official messengers) temporarily brought such ambitious men into line with his regal prerogatives. Later, with the decay of Carolingian centrality, these dukes resumed and expanded their former arrogation of royal powers. Weakened kings legalized accomplished facts with face-saving gestures. They recognized these counts and others as holders of their lands by virtue of royal services, military in the main and tax-wise on occasion. Feudalism was in virtually full operation wherever local suzerainty was secured at the price of stipulated services and desultory payments to the king, and where justice, financial collections, and armed retainers were supplied at the count's initiative.

In the following source readings, the workings of feudalism are observed, however briefly, as they universalized the relations of church and society within the localism of given periods and eras; also as these relationships of local character fell into a network pulling together ever larger geographical potentials. The lord, then, bound under his seigneury his pledged vassals. The vassal usually acknowledged a combination of personal and landed dependence upon his lord. Having given his oath of fidelity, he received from the lord a grant of land. The vassal, having commended himself to his lord in personal dependence, would become fused into the lord's companionship. In fully developed feudalism, certain specific immunities once granted the Church by the king, along with non-interference by his agents, became general in their application to other lords. These men, at once both lords and vassals, themselves held virtual immunity for their own administration, once it was regularized by tenurial and personal dependence upon other lords.

The terms "benefice" and "fief" recalled a one-time distinction in usage. They came, later, to imply virtual interchangeability. The benefice was originally granted by a monarch with lifetime tenure, for stated services and with utilization of land and products only. Then, as in later feudalism, the lord retained "eminent domain." The "benefice," having become hereditary under the Carolingians, came to be called a "fief." The term "benefice," connoting ecclesiastical tenure, was almost identical with "fief" in common parlance.

Lords, vassals (themselves lords to other vassals), benefice, fief, immunity, heredity of function—these were the stock-in-trade of feudalism. The practice of subinfeudation implied the simultaneous registration of all feudal contractors as both lords and vassals for identical grants of land. In other words, a given vassal granted to the vassals of his own lordship, parts of the land which he held in fief from his own suzerain. With the theoretical exception of the king on top, and the landless knight at the base of the feudal structure, all "were at the same time vassals of their own suzerains and suzerains of their own vassals." Within the manorial society on the lord's estates were grouped the manor house, peasant village, church, and other accoutrements of a self-sustaining, landed economy.

In all of this, as previously implied, the Church was thoroughly feudalized. This was true, however much it might attempt to surmount feudal limitations. Churchmen did try to mitigate the sharp realities of human injustice with divinely invoked comfort. It would be folly to attempt here even the most elementary digest of such analyses of the church in feudal society as those by J. W. Thompson, J. T. McNeill, M. Bloch, and others. What is indispensable is that the reader be forewarned against any supercilious surprise at the Church's economic-social articulation with institutional feudalism. Likewise requisite is the preparation for the matter-of-factness with which churchmen lived and improvised Christian leadership without complete capitulation to their age.

It was into this elastic, yet jealously constraining, social framework—with all its imprisoning privileges and graduated obligations—that the Church from the tenth through the fourteenth century found itself thrust. For the Church to live was to live in the world—this feudal world. Churchmen, whether popes, bishops, monks, or priests, administered lands for the Church, directly or indirectly. In this crazy patchwork of feudal disorder, put together on the spot, the Church held fiefs in vassalage from other lords, both spiritual and temporal. In turn, it exercised lordship over its own vassals. Serfs and villeins worked in virtual though varying bondage on its feudal manors. Feudal taxes, dues, aids, escheats, services, justice, and military forces were exacted from, and by, the officials of the Church. True, the Church's own laws were jealously guarded. These might forbid participation of the clergy in the outright manipulation of secular business, the workings of secular courts, and the downright shedding of blood. On occasion, however, the hierarchy, whether secular or monastic, did engage in some or all of these forbidden activities.

Even where Christian exemptions from direct social participation were preserved in a gentleman's agreement with secular officers, churchmen fulfilled the spirit, and often the letter, of feudal contract. They provided, from the serfs, vassals, and secular leaders under their feudal lordship, the labor, financial provisions, and warlike operations necessary to buttress their loyalty to, and protection by, their own seigneurial overlords. They got, for instance, the military aid from other lords and vassals that their own rescue from foreign marauders and internecine private war required. Throughout all this, the Church made its own contribution to the orderly chaos which it continued to extenuate and excoriate by turns. The Church might, and did, deplore wars, even just wars. It did strive honestly to limit warfare by special peace offensives and half-realistic compromises termed "truces of God." Still, it continued to altercate the feudal complexity with its own strife-producing exactions. Though their own existence was wedged firmly into their special feudal corners, Christian bishops and abbots sought, often vicariously, to diminish the hard lot of serfs and villeins on their estates. Similarly, they tried to suffuse the artificial chivalry of feudal knighthood and its endless amours with the elevated ideals and practices of Christian brotherhood and charity. The leavening of this-worldly institutions with other-worldly judgments and standards was as observable to the seeing eye as it was hidden from the average gaze.

That there were, in good standing, both sacrificial men of God and warrior bishops without scruple, is clearly evident to competent historical observers. By a haphazardly evolved pattern of feudal substitutes, the Church managed to extend and protect its secular parish holdings, as well as its monastic lands and other corporate investments. By any of the contemporary social standards the Church was wealthy by choice and always working harder to become more so. The folk literature and the trustworthy chronicler agree in attributing both self-sacrificing service and shrewdly calculating rapacity to bishops, abbots, and every other rank in the hierarchy. Official Christian rationalizing of sub-Christian practices coexisted, moreover, with the most penitential and prophetic summons to reformation and Christian social ministry. Purely secular officials reciprocated with a tongue-in-cheek piety liberally moistened with cynicism. Their consideration for Christian institutions mixed genuine respect for holy men of evangelical life with political maneuvering guaranteed to match or exceed that of the shrewdest, most unprincipled, church functionary.

The Church's chief glory was its consistent self-scrutiny and its penitential call to inner reform. Remorselessly and systematically it took to itself the basic responsibility, under God, for the recreant purposes and rebellious activities of all humanity. It is not strange, however, that at least some of these reform attempts served mainly to implant Christian hypocrisy and social injustice even more deeply within the feudal order. Such seems the penalty for projecting Christian social idealism into the very maw of political realism. The Church was, apparently, aware of the even graver sin of not confronting society with Christian ultimatums.

Feudal custom was stereotyped and protected by the Church at every level and in every area. The capacity of churchmen for both elastic improvising and death-engendering rigor was illustrated dramatically at several well-publicized points. These involved, simultaneously, the pervasive example of the secular clergy, the self-styled vocational perfection of the regulars, and the power-laden policies of the papal administration. The monastic life must have seemed to some medieval Christians a vicarious last hope for redeeming the helplessness of countless peasants, those ground under the systematic financial exactions of the hierarchy. From the concentrated prayer life of the monks might come at least some spiritual alleviation for the brutal economic pressures accompanying the papacy's administration of sacramental graces.

When the papacy, in the person of men like Gregory VII, sought reforms with which to purify the clergy as well as to buttress the Church's feudal appointment and investiture, it was to these same monks that the head of the hierarchy turned. To be sure this might seem somewhat like opening graves to find pallbearers. For the monastic orders, however fully pledged to renunciation of the world, had a way of joining field to field and of adding feudal dependency to feudal dependency, until they sometimes symbolized feudal aggrandizement itself. Nevertheless, it was to Cluny, so vigorous in her pristine Benedictinism, and to her far-flung dependencies that Hildebrand looked for reform energies and feudal support. The Cluniacs, of course, were only one reform movement out of many. Their reputation for spiritual rigorism and cultic regularity had, however, been particularly well earned. So had their later ingenuity for creating a self-sustaining and ever-widening feudal absolutism under the mother house. Already in Hildebrand's day, scores of houses in feudal dependence upon Cluny constituted a landed hierarchy worthy to challenge or to abet the papacy's own.

For Hildebrand to mount church-wide reform was for him to seek complete spiritual control of those presented for ecclesiastical appointment. In the medieval operation of unity within duality, this desire of a churchman to rule the affairs of ecclesiasts must have seemed as fair as the instinct of earthly rulers to guard the rights of temporality. Pope Gregory VII and Emperor Henry IV both made obeisance before this hoary euphemism of balanced rights and powers. Herein lay the difficulty. The theory never quite worked in actual practice. For the Church to have spiritual priority was, for Hildebrand at least, to assert the antecedent rights of spirituals to predispose the readily granted prerogatives of temporals. As some historians have insisted, Hildebrand was not propounding radical theories of papal power. His letters make it perfectly clear, however, that for the Church to carry out the mandates of the spiritual it must have a reserved right to order the temporal. As he stated it, this never amounted to any violation of secular prerogatives. As Christ's representative on earth, he was merely accepting the responsible direction of all human leaders to implement God's will.

The emperor did not take issue with this theory. Like a good Christian, he echoed it. He was not such a fool, however, as to believe that, after feudal church lords had hand-picked their own vassals, his prerogatives would still be untouched. From the vantage ground of the modern observer, both Gregory VII and Henry IV proceeded with feudal honesty and considerable awareness of certain absurd impracticalities already built into their mutual protestations. Perhaps they knew what they dared not admit; namely, that their claims were mutually overlapping and realistically incapable of completely harmonious operation. It was hardly in the nature of the medieval view, however, to admit or even to conceive the possibility of such an imbalance of spiritual and temporal powers. Some recent historians have self-righteously pointed out the inner self-contradiction in the Church's claim to control spiritual concerns alone, while, in fact, coveting temporal endowments altogether foreign to Christian idealism. It has been insinuated that lay investiture of church offices as well as temporal feudatories could have been avoided quite simply. What would have been necessary to guarantee this would have been merely the Church's renunciation of all but spiritual claims. This, however, is at least as specious as the assumption that the emperor never attempted to prostitute the spiritual vocation of churchmen so that he could exploit their earthly *savoir faire*.

Hildebrand began his reforming action with assumptions theoretically acceptable to his own day, at least, and worked his way up to a practicing radicalism that was to be violently contested then and afterwards. He assumed, from later canonical interpretations of earlier Christian councils, the mandate of the papal *curia* to enforce an unmarried clergy as normative in Christian tradition. This was, for the majority of western clerics in his time, about as indefensible in practice as it was hyper-legalistic in conception. It was almost as ridiculous as—though far more serious than—a modern attempt to enforce nineteenth-century legislation on horseless carriages against metropolitan traffic in the twentieth.

The immediate effect of Hildebrand's deeply-convinced action was to make virtual prostitutes by the thousands out of the innocent wives of bewildered and angry little clergymen. Owing to support derived from earlier monastic canonists like the redoubtable Peter Damian—a perfect blend of the demonic and the saintly by the pope's own admission—the program of reform had a sensational impact. To many souls so unfairly caught in the legalistic toils of a churning papal idealism, this must have seemed an inhumane blow; human dignity was pitilessly allowed to lie just where it fell. The pope, of course, could not have been unaware of how this would affect the liberation of the Church's landed wealth. Heretofore, it had been alienable by the heirs of a married clergy. The pope also raised a great hue and cry over simoniacal deals in church livings. All such were reminders of the shady electioneering of Simon Magus. The pontiff, with admirable staff support from church lawyers and feudal politicians, inveighed against all lay investiture of church officials. The emperor, sensing his own feudal prerogatives to be in mortal jeopardy, promptly engaged the issue. Reverberations from the ensuing struggle have never ceased. The

227

opening salvos of both parties echoed down through the useful but hardly profound clarifications of double investiture by the Concordat of Worms. They sounded forth periodically thereafter. The spokesmen of spiritual and temporal authority continued to obscure the realism of one patent fact, i.e., that these powers intersected by nature, and no amount of dedicated cooperation or political double talk could wholly alleviate their inevitable and recurrent collision.

The pope and the emperor ran a close race in the rhetorical display of injured innocence. Each invoked the divine witness to his purity of intent. Henry led off by officially resenting Hildebrand's platform as self-advertised feudal duplicity and a violation of spiritual trust. Hildebrand countered first with long-suffering, ecclesiastical self-restraint. This was followed by a resort to his administrative control over sacramental graces. He next placed the emperor outside the benediction of the Church's saving ministry, thereby freeing his feudal minions from further vassalage. Henry made a dramatic capitulation born out of equal, and perhaps superior, political finesse. He bowed to the pope's heavenly prerogatives and maneuvered him into the role of sacramental forgiveness, however distasteful. Henry thereby restored himself to the exercise of full feudal rights.

The struggle seesawed in tragi-comic relief for years. Hildebrand died in exile from Rome, like the brave and dedicated battler for the Lord he felt himself to be. He swallowed his lump of self-pity with an expiring vote of confidence in the Lord's will and His ultimate triumph over the ephemeral victories of kings and emperors.

Here, then, was one outreach of the feudal controversy. Hildebrand had not scrupled to corral every center of Italian heretical disaffection for the papal offensive against foreign bishops. Cluny in all her spiritual and economic might was his most irreplaceable ally. Together they countered the emperor's feudal right to nominate German ecclesiasts to Italian bishoprics. This was held to be contrary to the spiritual welfare of their immediate feudal overlord, the pope. Just as the medieval mind could not countenance

any complete severance of the spiritual and the temporal, so the controversy did not provide any clear winner or loser. This was a prime example of how the Church could not permit itself to be counted out of temporal affairs. No more could it afford a full victory in defense of them—if its own soul was to be saved.

When the scene shifted to the crusading era nothing really fundamental was changed. People had been going on pilgrimages in ever increasing numbers for a long time. This was true well before Urban II publicized the threat to Christian integrity implicit in infidel tenure of the Holy Land. Gregory VII, himself, had a crusade in his long-range plans. What the first papal crusade did—no less or more than that against the Albigensian heretics later—was to bring up to date the old papal claim. This presumed to arrange the eternal destinies of the faithful by supervising their spiritual and temporal activities for the legal and theological ends of the hierarchy. Urban II was himself a graduate of Cluniac instruction in spiritual reform and feudal strategy. Eugenius III was a product of Cistercian influence, who galvanized the powers of his old teacher Bernard for the second crusade. For the moment Urban's power plays operated from a formation mixing genuine unction and shrewd feudal generalship. He proposed to invoke divine sanction for the transplantation and unhindered expansion abroad of feudal competitors at home. Frustrating exhaustion of Christian energies in self-annihilating private wars could then be transmuted with devastating effect and full ecclesiastical blessing into an attack upon Islam.

Pope Urban II advanced his plans with fine oversimplification for laymen of legal technicalities in the plan of salvation. These he did not bother to clarify fully. If crusaders deduced from his promises that he had powers of whose limits he alone was well aware, this need not spoil his main point. He was the divinely appointed guardian of God's judgments and mercies. The practiced exploitation of human motives for the ends of hierarchical propaganda was, in his eyes, thoroughly justified. Was not what he willed the will of God for the repression of infidelity and the propagation of Christian faith? His hearers within the clergy and among the populace, both noble and peasant, vowed it to be so. *Deus volt!*

The pope felt empowered to allocate all human forces under the divine mandate for unlimited Christian expansion. Who can proffer lightly any cynical demurrer to the predominating play of religious dedication on the part of crusaders, high placed or low born? The gamut of motives rampant in Urban's address was eloquently and variedly reported by contemporary chronicles. Like the letters and sermons of Bernard and the feeble maledictions of Innocent III against the Christian rape of Constantinople, these create wonderment for the modern student. It is much easier to be nobly detached in one's judgments of medieval ethics than it is to be critical of equally gross deviations of a modern stamp. The piety of the sainted King Louis IX, who crusaded so courageously to so little avail, makes fascinating reading. So does the ironical coup of the impious Frederick II, whose gains were repudiated by the Church as those of an excommunicate. There is pathos in the letters, poems, caricatures, and consecrated prayers of the little and the great who suffered and died far from home.

The early textual editions of the French Academy were the forerunners of new crusading histories. The later editions and translations of sources for the collaborative production of a crusading corpus have recently flowered in numerous publications. The published notes of R. Alphandery, the brilliant one-man history of S. Runciman, and K. Setton's slowly emerging American history of the crusades lead to a steadily clarifying picture. One sees also what Evans' *Records of Civilization* clearly documents. These enormous dislocations of previously land-locked hordes from western Christendom were fraught with staggering significance for the human spirit. The political and social histories of earlier generations could not suffice for the analysis of motivations as subtle as those here presented. Alphandery touched the heart of the matter, as did some of the studies of the Bernardine centenaries.

The social leverage of the crusaders, with all their more obvious, cultural attachments, was fundamentally derived from the postulates of Christian eschatology and Messianism. These doctrinal fulcrums operated for princes of the Church, feudal lords, and humble bearers of the cross alike. There was a common psychology that pervaded papal propaganda and the strange magnetism of Bernard's sermonic exhortation. It was also basic in the frenzies of the Children's Crusade. This arose from highly varied applications of Christian teaching on the impending Kingdom and the last days.

Bernard preached the necessity of the crusaders' helping to bring in that Kingdom by taking the cross. When he did so, he obviously anticipated no signal and immediate answer of the Divine such as many humble Christians looked for. The failure of the Second Crusade, much of which he bitterly repudiated and accepted by turns as his own responsibility, has its most poignant lesson here. Even he could not homiletize Christian social responsibility with sufficient popular effect to consolidate the masses, without running the risk of confusing for them the deeper spiritual ends to be served. In a sense, it was his fault that they could have thought he meant what they interpreted him to say. They were convinced that they had a contract with God to fight a war for a material kingdom. Possession was to be miraculously given them at Jerusalem. This was a far cry from Bernard's more spiritualized conceptions. Their military service to his spiritual cause was intended to register their humble resignation to the divine will which was to be done on earth as in heaven. Bernard struggled vainly against popular sycophants and misguided idealists who preached their own versions of apocalyptic crisis. Innocent III, also, with all his dexterity in handling human potential, was subsequently no proof against human greed and angry violence following upon frustration and disillusionment. The interplay of the noblest and the vilest in human experience has seldom had stronger annotation than was supplied in the crusading era.

Strictly speaking, the crusades are not to be thought of as purely tangible forces that proceeded from specific causes with set purposes to preannounced objectives. They were more like a carrier wave or an electronic oscillation than they were comparable to institutions erected out of causes that in turn summoned forth itemized results. In the blaze of religious fervor that accompanied them, and in a sense gave rise to them, there eventuated a new mobility. This mobility challenged the old, static, feudal order with a new and terrifying flexibility. It was precisely this flexibility that Christian programmists had the least experience in handling. This, however, they were compelled to become most adept at controlling, if their ministry in the ensuing period was to be effective. Every shipload of feudal chieftains and peasant infantrymen that set out by sea learned unlimited new ways of encountering death. These came amid wholly unexpected, valorous exploits by the enemy. The Church was not content to preach the crusades or to recruit lay officers and men. It also supplied clerical authorities on logistics, psychological warfare, and the coordination of allied military strategy. On the Church also there devolved with frightening urgency the necessity of devising the most effective ways of raising fluid capital out of feudal resources. This she was expected to do without imperiling the old theological casuistries about property, usufruct, money, and usury. Hers was a mandate for exploiting "execrable" Jewry and its age-old sagacity in stretching nonexistent wealth into enviable affluence. All of this was for the ends of Christian salvation uncompromised by filthy lucre. Such demands imposed cruel strains on church leaders.

To call the roll of the major crusades themselves is to publicize some of the noblest adventures of the human genus. It is to salute many of the nameless greats among the little men of history. This roll call cannot ignore queens of the royal houses. Nor can it pass by equally influential women of more sensational, if less socially approved, connections. The accounts of magnanimous Saracens, as well as their unmentionable compatriots, can no more be avoided than the exploits of Frankish greatness and the

shameful chronicles of their occasional smallness.

The crusades are one long dithyramb of frustration for those who sailed, drowned, burned, and otherwise perished under the clear blessing of heaven and the bewildering victories of the infidel. Not until the days of World Wars I and II were the exploits of men thus far transplanted to be surpassed. The battle of personnel and supplies that they waged was recounted by their own chroniclers in terms of divine glory and despairing human honor. The accounts of Ambroise spoke the language of a soldier's heartache, as did those of the later Ernie Pyle.

In all of this, the Church both led and followed. It suggested most of the plans that failed to work. To it can be credited few of the saving innovations that were forced upon it. These came, it believed, by divine fortuitousness. What confronted it then and later was the timelessness of feudal conservatism and the angry eruptions of unanticipated change. The Church smarted with Bernard over the failure of the Second Crusade. It also burned with shame for the indignities of Christians at the sack of Constantinople. No less galling was the incapacity of Christians on the field to forget their disunities in the face of the Saracen threat. Confronting these ecclesiasts was the need to counter the little man's growing suspicion of all churchly apothegms; his simply not caring who preached, so long as no more than platitudes were at stake. In drafting the answer to that challenge, the Mendicants were to have first place.

I. Feudal Institutions, Church Lands, and Christian Society

A. FEUDAL COMMENDATION, BENEFICES, FIEFS

1. Form for Feudal Commendation

Formulae Turonenses, No. 43, p. 158, trans. ThM, No. 182, pp. 343–44.

To my great lord, (name), I, (name). Since, as was well known, I had not wherewith to feed and clothe myself, I came to you and told you my wish, to commend myself to you and to put myself under your protection. I have now done so, on the condition that you shall supply me with food and clothing as far as I shall merit by my services, and that as long as I live I shall perform such services for you as are becoming to a free-man, and shall never have the right to with-draw from your power and protection, but shall remain under them all the days of my life. It is agreed that if either of us shall try to break this compact he shall pay—solidi, and the compact shall still hold. It is also agreed that two copies of this letter shall be made and signed by us, which also has been done.

2. Form for a Gift of Land to a Monastery to Be Received Back by the Giver as a Benefice

Marculf, II, No. 3, pp. 74ff., trans. *ThM*, No. 184, pp. 345–46.

. . . I, (name), and my wife, (name), in the name of the Lord, give by this letter of gift, and transfer from our ownership to the ownership and authority of the monastery of (name), over which the venerable abbot (name) presides, and which was founded in the honor of (name) by (name) in the county of (name), the following villas (name), situated in the county of (name), with all the lands, houses, buildings, tenants, slaves, vineyards, woods, fields, pastures, meadows, streams, and all other belongings and dependencies, and all things movable and immovable which are found in the said villas now or may be added later; in order that under the protection of Christ they may be used for the support and maintenance of the monks who dwell in the aforesaid mon-astery. We do this on the condition that as long as either of us shall live we may possess the aforesaid villas, without prejudice to the ownership of the monastery and without dim-inution of the value of them, except that we shall be allowed to emancipate any of the slaves that dwell on the lands for the salva-

tion of our souls. After the death of both of us, the aforesaid villas with any additions or improvements which may have been made, shall return immediately to the possession of the said monastery and the said abbot and his successors, without undertaking any judi-cial process or obtaining the consent of the heirs.

3. A Fief Granted by a Count to a Bishop (1167)

Brussel, *Usage des fiefs*, I, 3, note, trans. *PTR*, IV, 3 (i), pp. 15–16.

In the name of the Holy and Undivided Trinity, Amen. I, Louis, by the grace of God, king of the French, make known to all pres-ent as well as to come, that at Mante in our presence, Count Henry of Champagne con-ceded the fief of Savigny to Bartholomew, bishop of Beauvais, and his successors. And for that fief the said bishop has made prom-ise and engagement for one knight and jus-tice and service to Count Henry; and he has also agreed that the bishops who shall come after him will do likewise. In order that this may be understood and known to posterity we have caused the present charter to be corroborated by our seal; done at Mante, in the year of the Incarnate Word 1167; pres-ent in our palace those whose names and seals are appended: seal of count Thiebault, our steward; seal of Guy, the butler; seal of Matthew, the chamberlain; seal of Ralph, the constable. Given by the hand of Hugh, the chancellor.

B. HOMAGE-FEALTY; COMPLICATING FEUDAL ALLEGIANCE AND SUB-INFEUDATION

4. Homage and the Confusion of Feudal Relations

Tabularium campania, cited by Du Cange, *Glossarium, Ligius*, trans. *ThM*, No. 213, pp. 364–65.

I, John of Toul, make known that I am the liege man of the lady Beatrice, countess of Troyes, and of her son, Theobald, count of Champagne, against every creature, living or dead, saving my allegiance to lord Enjorand of Coucy, lord John of Arcis, and the count of Grandpré. If it should happen that the count of Grandpré should be at war with the countess and count of Champagne on his own quarrel, I will aid the count of Grandpré in my own person, and will send to the count and the countess of Champagne the knights whose service I owe to them for the fief which I hold of them. But if the count of Grandpré shall make war on the countess and the count of Champagne on behalf of his friends and not in his own quarrel, I will aid in my own person the countess and count of Champagne, and will send one knight to the count of Grandpré for the service which I owe him for the fief which I hold of him, but I will not go myself into the territory of the count of Grandpré to make war on him.

5. Sub-Infeudation Illustrated from the English Hundred Rolls (1279)

Rotuli Hundredorum, II, 862, 673, and 681ff., trans. *PTR*, IV, 3 (iii), pp. 22–23.

Robert de Romeny holds one knight's fee in the vill of Steepleton for homage and his service from William de Leybourne, and he shall pay scutage, when it runs, for one shield, viz., forty shillings; and William de Leybourne holds from the countess of Albemarle, and the countess from the lord king *in capite*.

Roger of St. Germain holds one messuage from Robert of Bedford on the service of paying 3d. to the aforesaid Robert, from whom he holds and of paying 6d. to Richard Hylchester in place of the said Robert, who holds from him. And the said Richard holds from Alan de Chartres, and pays him 2d. a year and Alan from William the Butler, and the same William from lord Gilbert de Neville, and the same Gilbert from the lady Devorguilla de Balliol, and Devorguilla from the king of Scotland, and the same king from the king of England. Sir Adam de Cretinges holds and accounts in the vill of Stoughton, for four knights' fees from the bishop of Lincoln, and the bishop from the king. The same Adam holds by homage and scutage, when it runs, and has in demesne 13 score acres of arable land and 3 messuages of 2 acres, and 40 acres of woods and 7 acres of meadow and 10 acres of separable pasture.

11 villains, each with a virgate of 20 acres, a house and some meadow, and each performing certain weekly works, ploughing, etc.

16 cottars, each with a cottage and a rood of land, and each paying 12d. a year and performing certain labor.

1 cottar with a half acre, and 2 with houses only.

Sir Anselm de Gyse holds and accounts for two knights' fees, from the same Adam for half a mark a year and for scutage when it happens; and he has in his garden, with a house and vineyard, 6 acres of land; and of arable land 13 score acres, and in meadows 7 acres, and in separable pasture 10 acres and in woods 8 acres.

6 villains, each with 20 acres, etc., as above.

The prior of Bissemede holds one knight's fee from the said Anselm and pays to him scutage when it happens. The same prior has in his garden with the house 8 acres, and 5 score acres of arable land, and 8 acres of woods and 8 acres of meadow, and 6 acres of separable pasture.

5 free tenants with a total of 63¼ acres of arable land, etc.

3 villains with a total of 1¼ virgates.

5 cottars each with a cottage.

Geoffrey, son of Everard of Stoughton holds half a knight's fee from the said Anselm for homage and foreign service, and has in demesne 6 score acres of arable land, and in garden with a messuage one acre and a half and 4 acres of woods and 2 acres of separable pasture.

1 free holder with 6 acres.

William Schohisfoot holds the twelfth part of one knight's fee from the aforesaid Anselm for homage and foreign service, and has in garden with the house one acre and a half, and in arable land 20 acres, and 3 acres of meadow; and he ought to have common with his beasts in the meadow which is called Mora.

William Dingle holds from the said William one acre and a half of land, and pays annually 1d.

Various free and villein tenants holding immediately and mediately from Sir Adam de Cretinges.

C. THE UPPER SIDE OF FEUDALISM: MUTUAL DUTIES OF ECCLESIASTICAL VASSALS AND THEIR LORDS

6. Bishop Fulbert of Chartres Discourses on Feudal Reciprocity (1020)

Recueil des Hist. des Gaules et de la France, X, 463, trans. *PTR,* IV, 3 (iv), pp. 23–24.

To William most glorious duke of the Aquitanians, bishop Fulbert the favor of his prayers.

Asked to write something concerning the form of fealty, I have noted briefly for you on the authority of the books the things which follow. He who swears fealty to his lord ought always to have these six things in memory; what is harmless, safe, honorable, useful, easy, practicable. Harmless, that is to say that he should not be injurious to his lord in his body; safe, that he should not be injurious to him in his secrets or in the defences through which he is able to be secure; honorable, that he should not be injurious to him in his justice or in other matters that pertain to his honor; useful, that he should not be injurious to him in his possessions; easy or practicable, that that good which his lord is able to do easily, he make not difficult, nor that which is practicable he make impossible to him.

However, that the faithful vassal should avoid these injuries is proper, but not for this does he deserve his holding; for it is not sufficient to abstain from evil, unless what is good is done also. It remains, therefore, that in the same six things mentioned above he should faithfully counsel and aid his lord, if he wishes to be looked upon as worthy of his benefice and to be safe concerning the fealty which he has sworn.

The lord also ought to act toward his faithful vassal reciprocally in all these things. And if he does not do this he will be justly considered guilty of bad faith, just as the former, if he should be detected in the avoidance of or the doing of or the consenting to them, would be perfidious and perjured.

I would have written to you at greater length, if I had not been occupied with many other things, including the rebuilding of our city and church which was lately entirely consumed in a great fire; from which loss though we could not for a while be diverted, yet by the hope of the comfort of God and of you we breathe again.

7. William, Bishop of Auxerre, Acknowledges His Feudal Military Obligations

Quantin, *Rec. de Pieces du XIII siècle,* No. 116, p. 53, trans. *PTR,* IV, 3 (vii), pp. 29–30.

William, by the grace of God bishop of Auxerre to all who shall see these presents, greeting in the Lord. Know that we acknowledge that we owe to our lord Philip, illustrious king of the French, military service, as is the common service of bishops and barons; and this for the future we will perform through our knights, as others. For the same lord king has released our person from the service of the army so long as we live.

D. THE CHURCH, FEUDAL SOCIETY, AND JUSTICE

8. Crimes, the Judgment of God, and the Ordeal of Barley Bread

M. G. L. L., V, pp. 599ff., *Ordines judiciorum Dei,* p. 691, trans. *ThM,* No. 238, p. 409.

(1) First the priest prepares himself with the deacon, and then blesses the water; and the deacon prepares the barley flour which he mixes with the holy water and bakes, both of them saying during the process the seven penitential psalms, the litany, and the following prayers [certain prayers follow].

(2) Prayer over the bread. O God, who didst reveal the wood of the true cross on Mount Calvary, where Christ was betrayed by Judas (for God gave over his Son to be betrayed by Judas), reveal to us by the judgment of the barley bread whatever we ask in thy name.

(3) After the bread is baked the priest shall take it and place it behind the altar and shall say the mass for that day. After the mass he shall mark the bread with the sign of the cross, and shall place an iron rod

in the centre of the cross, with a hook at the top to suspend it by. The priest shall keep this bread by him and use it until it spoils. When anyone is accused of theft, or fornication, or homicide, and is brought before the priest, the priest shall take the bread and give it to two Christian men, and they shall hang it by the hook between them, and the priest shall say the following adjuration. And if the man is guilty, the bread will revolve around; if he is not guilty, the bread will not move at all.

(4) Adjuration over the barley bread. I adjure thee, barley bread, by God the omnipotent Father, etc., that if this man or woman has committed, consented to, or had any part in this crime, thou shalt turn around in a circle; if he is not guilty, thou shall not move at all. I adjure thee, barley bread, by the Mother of God, by the prophet Hosea, and the prophet Jonah, who prophesied unto Nineveh, by Lazarus, whom God raised from the dead, by the blind man, to whom the Lord restored his sight, by all the monks and canons and all laymen, by all women, and by all the inhabitants of heaven and earth, forever and ever, amen.

9. The "Saxon Mirror" (c. 1225–1275), Roman Law, and Feudal Christian Courts

Eike von Repgow, *Sachsenspiegel,* trans. ThM, No. 231, pp. 392, 394, 396.

I, 2. Every Christian man who has attained his majority is bound to attend the ecclesiastical court in the bishopric in which he lives three times a year. Three classes of people are exempt from this: The *Schoeffenbar* free shall attend the court of the bishop; the *Pfleghaften* shall attend the court of the *praepositus* of the cathedral, and the *Landsassen* shall attend the court of the archpriests.

They shall also all attend the civil courts. The *Schoeffenbar* free shall attend the burggrave's court [also called the advocate's court] every eighteen weeks. In it judgment is given under the king's ban. If a court is called to meet after the close of the regular court, all the *Pfleghaften* shall attend it to try all cases involving misdeeds. This attendance is all that the judge may require from them.

The *Pfleghaften* shall attend the court of the *Schultheiss* which is held every six weeks, to try cases concerning their possessions.

The *Landsassen* who have no property shall attend the court of the *Gograf* which is held every six weeks. In the courts of the *Gograf* and of the burggrave the *Bauermeister* shall make complaint of all whose duty it is to attend the court but do not do so. And he shall ask an investigation about all cases which involve bloody wounds, abusive speech, the drawing of swords in a threatening manner, and all kinds of misdeeds, provided no suit has been entered about them.

II, 13. A thief shall be hung. If a theft takes place by day in a villa [village] and the object stolen is worth less than three shillings, the *Bauermeister* may pass judgment on the thief the same day. He may punish him in his hair and skin, or fine him three shillings. This is the highest sum for which the *Bauermeister* may try [i.e., not more than three shillings]. But he cannot try the case the next day. But in cases involving money, or movable goods, or false weights and measures, and cheating in the sale of victuals, he may assess higher fines. Murderers, and all who steal horses from the plow, or grain from the mill, or rob churches or cemeteries, and all who are guilty of treason, or arson, or who make gain out of information entrusted to them by their lord, shall be broken on the wheel.

If anyone beats, seizes, or robs another, or burns his house, or does violence to a woman, or breaks the peace, or is taken in adultery, he shall have his head cut off. Whoever conceals a thief or stolen property or aids a thief in any way, shall be punished as a thief. Heretics, witches, and poisoners shall be burnt.

If a judge refuses to punish a crime, he shall be punished as if guilty of it himself. No one is bound to attend his court or submit to his judgment if he has refused to grant him justice.

III, 60. The emperor enfeoffs all ecclesiastical princes with their fiefs—using the sceptre as a symbol, and all secular princes with their *Fahnlehen* using a flag as a symbol. A *Fahnlehen* must not be vacant a year and a day. Wherever the king is, the mint and tolls of that place are surrendered to him during his stay there. And the local court is closed because he is the judge [and the local judge merely represents him]. While he is present all cases must be tried before him. The first time the king comes into the land [*i.e.*, after his election], all prisoners must be brought before him, and he shall decide whether they shall be set free or tried. . . .

II. Feudal Investiture of Church Offices and Feudal Reform

A. REFORM PROGRAMS OF POPE NICHOLAS II (1058–1061) AND GREGORY VII (1073–1085)

10. Papal Election Decree of Nicholas II (1059)

Scheffer-Boichorst, pp. 14ff., Doebere, III, No. 4a., trans. *ThM*, No. 59, pp. 128–30.

In the name of the Lord God, our Saviour Jesus Christ, in the 1059th year from his incarnation, in the month of April, in the 12th indiction, in the presence of the holy gospels, the most reverend and blessed apostolic pope Nicholas presiding in the Lateran patriarchal basilica which is called the church of Constantine, the most reverend archbishops, bishops, and abbots, and the venerable presbyters and deacons also being present, the same venerable pontiff by his apostolic authority decreed thus concerning the election of the pope: "Most beloved brothers and fellow-bishops, you know, since it is not hidden even from the humbler members, how after the death of our predecessor, Stephen of blessed memory, this apostolic seat, which by the will of God I now serve, suffered many evils, how indeed it was subjected to many serious attacks from the simoniacal money-changers, so that the column of the living God seemed about to topple, and the skiff of the supreme fisherman [Peter] was nearly wrecked by the tumultuous storms. Therefore, if it pleases you, we ought now, with the aid of God, prudently to take measures to prevent future misfortunes, and to provide for the state of the church in the future, lest those evils, again appearing,

which God forbid, should prevail against it. Therefore, fortified by the authority of our predecessors and the other holy fathers, we decide and declare:

1. On the death of a pontiff of the universal Roman church, first, the cardinal bishops, with the most diligent consideration, shall elect a successor; then they shall call in the other cardinal clergy [to ratify their choice], and finally the rest of the clergy and the people shall express their consent to the new election.

2. In order that the disease of venality may not have any opportunity to spread, the devout clergy shall be the leaders in electing the pontiff, and the others shall acquiesce. And surely this order of election is right and lawful, if we consider either the rules or the practice of various fathers, or if we recall that decree of our predecessor, St. Leo, for he says: 'By no means can it be allowed that those should be ranked as bishops who have not been elected by the clergy, and demanded by the people, and consecrated by their fellow-bishops of the province with the consent of the metropolitan.' But since the apostolic seat is above all the churches in the earth, and therefore can have no metropolitan over it, without doubt the cardinal bishops perform in it the office of the metropolitan, in that they advance the elected prelate to the apostolic dignity [that is, choose, consecrate, and enthrone him].

3. The pope shall be elected from the church in Rome, if a suitable person can be found in it, but if not, he is to be taken from another church.

4. In the papal election—in accordance with the right which we have already conceded to Henry and to those of his successors who may obtain the same right from the apostolic see—due honor and reverence shall be shown our beloved son, Henry, king and emperor elect [that is, the rights of Henry shall be respected].

5. But if the wickedness of depraved and iniquitous men shall so prevail that a pure, genuine, and free election cannot be held in this city, the cardinal bishops with the clergy and a few laymen shall have the right to elect the pontiff wherever they shall deem most fitting.

6. But if after an election any disturbance of war or any malicious attempt of men shall prevail so that he who is elected cannot be enthroned according to custom in the papal chair, the pope elect shall nevertheless exercise the right of ruling the holy Roman church, and of disposing of all its revenues, as we know St. Gregory did before his consecration.

But if anyone, actuated by rebellion or presumption or any other motive, shall be elected or ordained or enthroned in a manner contrary to this our decree, promulgated by the authority of the synod, he with his counsellors, supporters, and followers shall be expelled from the holy church of God by the authority of God and the holy apostles Peter and Paul, and shall be subjected to perpetual anathema as Antichrist and the enemy and destroyer of all Christianity; nor shall he ever be granted a further hearing in the case, but he shall be deposed without appeal from every ecclesiastical rank which he may have held formerly.

11. Gregory VII on Prohibition of Simony and Marriage of the Clergy (1074)

Siegebert of Gembloux, M. G. S. S., VI, 362, trans. *ThM*, No. 60, p. 134.

Pope Gregory [VII] held a synod in which he anathematized all who were guilty of simony. He also forbade all clergy who were married to say mass, and all laymen were forbidden to be present when such a married priest should officiate. In this he seemed to many to act contrary to the decisions of the holy fathers who have declared that the sacraments of the church are neither made more effective by the good qualities, nor less effective by the sins, of the officiating priest, because it is the Holy Spirit who makes them effective.

12. Gregory VII on Celibacy of the Clergy (1074)

Corpus Juris Canonici, Dist. LXXXI, C. 15, trans. *ThM*, No. 62, p. 135.

If there are any priests, deacons, or subdeacons who are married, by the power of omnipotent God and the authority of St. Peter we forbid them to enter a church until they repent and mend their ways. But if any remain with their wives, no one shall dare hear them [when they officiate in the church], because their benediction is turned into a curse, and their prayer into a sin. For the Lord says through the prophet, "I will curse your blessings" [Mal. 2:2]. Whoever shall refuse to obey this most salutary command shall be guilty of the sin of idolatry. For Samuel says: "For rebellion is as the sin of witchcraft, and stubbornness is

as iniquity and idolatry" [1 Sam. 15:23]. Whoever therefore asserts that he is a Christian but refuses to obey the apostolic see, is guilty of paganism.

13. The "Dictates" of the Pope (c. 1075–c. 1090), from the Hildebrandine Platform

Dictatus Papae, Jaffe, II, 174 (Doeberl III, 6), trans. *ThM*, No. 65, pp. 136–39.

1. That the Roman church was established by God alone.
2. That the Roman pontiff alone is rightly called universal.
3. That he alone has the power to depose and reinstate bishops.
4. That his legate, even if he be of lower ecclesiastical rank, presides over bishops in council, and has the power to give sentence of deposition against them.
5. That the pope has the power to depose those who are absent [*i.e.*, without giving them a hearing].
6. That, among other things, we ought not to remain in the same house with those whom he has excommunicated.
7. That he alone has the right, according to the necessity of the occasion, to make new laws, to create new bishoprics, to make a monastery of a chapter of canons, and *vice versa*, and either to divide a rich bishopric or to unite several poor ones.
8. That he alone may use the imperial insignia.
9. That all princes shall kiss the foot of the pope alone.
10. That his name alone is to be recited in the churches.
11. That the name applied to him belongs to him alone.
12. That he has the power to depose emperors.
13. That he has the right to transfer bishops from one see to another when it becomes necessary.
14. That he has the right to ordain as a cleric anyone from any part of the church whatsoever.
15. That anyone ordained by him may rule [as bishop] over another church, but cannot serve [as priest] in it, and that such

a cleric may not receive a higher rank from any other bishop.

16. That no general synod may be called without his order.

17. That no action of a synod and no book shall be regarded as canonical without his authority.

18. That his decree can be annulled by no one, and that he can annul the decrees of anyone.

19. That he can be judged by no one.

20. That no one shall dare to condemn a person who has appealed to the apostolic seat.

21. That the important cases of any church whatsoever shall be referred to the Roman church [that is, to the pope].

22. That the Roman church has never erred and will never err to all eternity, according to the testimony of the holy scriptures.

23. That the Roman pontiff who has been canonically ordained is made holy by the merits of St. Peter, according to the testimony of St. Ennodius, bishop of Pavia, which is confirmed by many of the holy fathers, as is shown by the decrees of the blessed pope Symmachus.

24. That by his command or permission subjects may accuse their rulers.

25. That he can depose and reinstate bishops without the calling of a synod.

26. That no one can be regarded as catholic who does not agree with the Roman church.

27. That he has the power to absolve subjects from their oath of fidelity to wicked rulers.

B. THE STRUGGLE OF GREGORY VII (1073–1085) AND EMPEROR HENRY IV (1056–1106) OVER SECULAR INVESTITURE OF CHURCH OFFICIALS

14. The Deposition of Gregory VII by Henry IV (1076)

M. G. L. L., fol. II, pp. 47ff. (Doeberl III, 8b), trans. *ThM*, No. 75, pp. 151–52.

Henry, king not by usurpation, but by the holy ordination of God, to Hildebrand, not pope, but false monk.

This is the salutation which you deserve, for you have never held any office in the church without making it a source of confusion and a curse to Christian men instead of an honor and a blessing. To mention only the most obvious cases out of many, you have not only dared to touch the Lord's anointed, the archbishops, bishops, and priests; but you have scorned them and abused them, as if they were ignorant servants not fit to know what their master was doing. This you have done to gain favor with the vulgar crowd. You have declared that the bishops know nothing and that you know everything; but if you have such great wisdom you have used it not to build but to destroy. Therefore we believe that St. Gregory, whose name you have presumed to take, had you in mind when he said: "The heart of the prelate is puffed up by the abundance of subjects, and he thinks himself more powerful than all others." All this we have endured because of our respect for the papal office, but you have mistaken our humility for fear, and have dared to make an attack upon the royal and imperial authority which we received from God. You have even threatened to take it away, as if we had received it from you, and as if the empire and kingdom were in your disposal and not in the disposal of God. Our Lord Jesus Christ has called us to the government of the empire, but he never called you to the rule of the church. This is the way you have gained advancement in the church: through craft you have obtained wealth; through wealth you have obtained favor; through favor, the power of the sword; and through the power of the sword, the papal seat, which is the seat of peace; and then from the seat of peace you have expelled peace. For you have incited subjects to rebel against their prelates by teaching them to despise the bishops, their rightful rulers. You have given to laymen the authority over priests, whereby they condemn and depose those whom the bishops have put over them to teach them. You have attacked me, who, unworthy as I am, have yet been anointed to rule among the anointed of God, and who, according to the teaching of the fathers, can be judged by no one save God alone, and can be deposed for no crime except infidelity. For the holy fathers in the time of the apostate Julian did not presume to pronounce sentence of deposition against him, but left him to be judged and condemned by God. St. Peter himself said: "Fear God, honor the king" [1 Pet. 2:17]. But you, who fear not God, have dishonored me, whom He hath established. St. Paul, who said that even an angel from heaven should be accursed who taught any other than the true doctrine, did not make an exception in your favor, to permit you to teach false doctrines. For he says: "But though we, or an angel from heaven, preach any other gospel unto you than that which we have preached unto you, let him be accursed" [Gal. 1:8]. Come down, then, from that apostolic seat which you have obtained by violence; for you have been declared accursed by St. Paul for your false doctrines and have been condemned by us and our bishops for your evil rule. Let another ascend the throne of St. Peter, one who will not use religion as a cloak of violence, but will teach the life-giving doctrine of that prince of the apostles. I, Henry, king by the grace of God, with all my bishops, say unto you: "Come down, come down, and be accursed through all the ages."

15. Gregory VII's First Deposition and Excommunication of Henry IV (1076)

Gregory VII, *Reg.* III, 10a, trans. *ThM*, No. 77, pp. 155–56.

St. Peter, prince of the apostles, incline thine ear unto me, I beseech thee, and hear me, thy servant, whom thou hast nourished from mine infancy and hast delivered from mine enemies that hate me for my fidelity to thee. Thou art my witness, as are also my mistress, the mother of God, and St. Paul thy brother, and all the other saints, that thy holy Roman church called me to its government against my own will, and that I did not gain thy throne by violence; that I would rather have ended my days in exile than have obtained thy place by fraud or for worldly ambition. It is not by my efforts, but by thy grace, that I am set to rule over the Christian world which was specially

intrusted to thee by Christ. It is by thy grace and as thy representative that God has given to me the power to bind and to loose in heaven and in earth. Confident of my integrity and authority, I now declare in the name of omnipotent God, the Father, Son, and Holy Spirit, that Henry, son of the emperor Henry, is deprived of his kingdom of Germany and Italy; I do this by thy authority and in defence of the honor of thy church, because he has rebelled against it.[*] He has refused to obey as a Christian should, he has not returned to God from whom he had wandered, he has had dealings with excommunicated persons, he has done many iniquities, he has despised the warnings which, as thou art witness, I sent to him for his salvation, he has cut himself off from thy church, and has attempted to rend it asunder; therefore, by thy authority, I place him under the curse. It is in thy name that I curse him, that all people may know that thou art Peter, and upon thy rock the Son of the living God has built his church, and the gates of hell shall not prevail against it.

16. Gregory VII Reports Henry IV's Penance at Canossa (1077)

Reg. IV, 12, 12a., trans. *ThM*, No. 80, pp. 158–59.

Gregory, bishop, servant of the servants of God, to all the archbishops, bishops, dukes, counts, and other princes of the German kingdom, defenders of the Christian faith, greeting and apostolic benediction.

Since you have made common cause with us and shared our perils in the recent controversy, we have thought it only right that you should be informed of the recent course of events, how king Henry came to Italy to do penance, and how we were led to grant him absolution.

According to the agreement made with your representatives we had come to Lombardy and were there awaiting those whom you were to send to escort us into your land. But after the time set was already passed, we received word that it was at that time

* He who attempts to destroy the honor of the church should be deprived of such honor as he may have held.—Ed.

238

impossible to send an escort, because of many obstacles that stood in the way, and we were greatly exercised at this and in grave doubt as to what we ought to do. In the meantime we learned that the king was approaching. Now before he entered Italy he had sent to us and had offered to make complete satisfaction for his fault, promising to reform and henceforth to obey us in all things, provided we would give him our absolution and blessing. We hesitated for some time, taking occasion in the course of the negotiations to reprove him sharply for his former sins. Finally he came in person to Canossa, where we were staying, bringing with him only a small retinue and manifesting no hostile intentions. Once arrived, he presented himself at the gate of the castle, barefoot and clad only in wretched woollen garments, beseeching us with tears to grant him absolution and forgiveness. This he continued to do for three days, until all those about us were moved to compassion at his plight and interceded for him with tears and prayers. Indeed, they marvelled at our hardness of heart, some even complaining that our action savored rather of heartless tyranny than of chastening severity. At length his persistent declarations of repentance and the supplications of all who were there with us overcame our reluctance, and we removed the excommunication from him and received him again into the bosom of the holy mother church. But first he took the oath which we have subjoined to this letter, the abbot of Cluny, the countess Matilda, the countess Adelaide, and many other ecclesiastic and secular princes going surety for him. Now that this arrangement has been reached to the common advantage of the church and the empire, we purpose coming to visit you in your own land as soon as possible. For, as you will perceive from the conditions stated in the oath, the matter is not to be regarded as settled until we have held consultation with you. Therefore we urge you to maintain that fidelity and love of justice which first prompted your action. We have not bound ourself to anything, except that we assured the king that he might depend upon us to aid him in everything that looked to his salvation and honor.

C. THE INCONCLUSIVE COMPROMISE OVER SPIRITUAL AND TEMPORAL INVESTITURE

17. Pope Calixtus II's Commitment: Concordat of Worms (1122)

M. G. L. L., fol. II, 75ff., trans. *ThM*, No. 85, p. 165.

Calixtus, bishop, servant of the servants of God, to his beloved son, Henry, by the grace of God emperor of the Romans, Augustus.

We hereby grant that in Germany the elections of the bishops and abbots who hold directly from the crown shall be held in your presence, such elections to be conducted canonically and without simony or other illegality. In the case of disputed elections you shall have the right to decide between the parties, after consulting with the archbishop of the province and his fellow-bishops. You shall confer the regalia of the office upon the bishop or abbot elect by giving him the sceptre, and this shall be done freely without exacting any payment from him; the bishop or abbot elect on his part shall perform all the duties that go with the holding of the regalia.

In other parts of the empire the bishops shall receive the regalia from you in the same manner within six months of their consecration, and shall in like manner perform all the duties that go with them. The undoubted rights of the Roman church, however, are not to be regarded as prejudiced by this concession. If at any time you shall have occasion to complain of the carrying out of these provisions, I will undertake to satisfy your grievances as far as shall be consistent with my office. Finally, I hereby make a true and lasting peace with you and with all of your followers, including those who supported you in the recent controversy.

18. Henry IV's Promise: the Same

M. G. L. L., fol. II, 76, trans. *ThM*, No. 86, pp. 165–66.

In the name of the holy and undivided Trinity.

For the love of God and his holy church and of pope Calixtus, and for the salvation

239

of my soul, I, Henry, by the grace of God, emperor of the Romans, Augustus, hereby surrender to God and his apostles, Sts. Peter and Paul, and to the holy Catholic church, all investiture by ring and staff. I agree that elections and consecrations shall be conducted canonically and shall be free from all interference. I surrender also the possessions and regalia of St. Peter which have been seized by me during this quarrel, or by my father in his lifetime, and which are now in my possession, and I promise to aid the church to recover such as are held by any other persons. I restore also the possessions of all other churches and princes, clerical or secular, which have been taken away during the course of this quarrel, which I have, and promise to aid them to recover such as are held by any other persons.

Finally, I make true and lasting peace with pope Calixtus and with the holy Roman church and with all who are or have ever been of his party. I will aid the Roman church whenever my help is asked, and will do justice in all matters in regard to which the church may have occasion to make complaint.

All these things have been done with the consent and advice of the princes whose names are written below: Adelbert, archbishop of Mainz; Frederick, archbishop of Cologne, etc.

III. The English Church as a Pawn in the Feudal Game

19. *The Decline of the English Church and Clergy at the Time of the Norman Conquest* (*1066*)

William of Malmesbury, *De gestis regum Anglorum*, 3:241ff., trans. Robinson, *REH*, I, pp. 226–28.

This was a fatal day to England, and melancholy havoc was wrought in our dear country during the change of its lords. For it had long before adopted the manners of the Angles, which had indeed altered with the times; for in the first years of their arrival they were barbarians in their look and manner, warlike in their usages, heathens in their rites.

After embracing the faith of Christ, by de-

grees and, in process of time, in consequence of the peace which they enjoyed, they relegated arms to a secondary place and gave their whole attention to religion. I am not speaking of the poor, the meanness of whose fortune often restrains them from overstepping the bounds of justice; I omit, too, men of ecclesiastical rank, whom sometimes respect for their profession and sometimes the fear of shame suffers not to deviate from the true path; I speak of princes, who from the greatness of their power might have full liberty to indulge in pleasure. Some of these in their own country, and others at Rome, changing their habit, obtained a heavenly kingdom and a saintly intercourse. Many others during their whole lives devoted themselves in outward appearance to worldly affairs, but in order that they might exhaust their treasures on the poor or divide them amongst monasteries.

What shall I say of the multitudes of bishops, hermits, and abbots? Does not the whole island blaze with such numerous relics of its own people that you can scarcely pass a village of any consequence but you hear the name of some new saint? And of how many more has all remembrance perished through the want of records?

Nevertheless, the attention to literature and religion had gradually decreased for several years before the arrival of the Normans. The clergy, contented with a little confused learning, could scarcely stammer out the words of the sacraments; and a person who understood grammar was an object of wonder and astonishment. The monks mocked the rule of their order by fine vestments and the use of every kind of food. The nobility, given up to luxury and wantonness, went not to church in the morning after the manner of Christians, but merely, in a careless manner, heard matins and masses from a hurrying priest in their chambers, amid the blandishments of their wives. The commonalty, left unprotected, became a prey to the most powerful, who amassed fortunes, either by seizing on their property or by selling their persons into foreign countries; although it is characteristic of this people to be more inclined to reveling than to the accumulation of wealth. . . .

Drinking in parties was an universal practice, in which occupation they passed entire nights as well as days. They consumed their whole substance in mean and despicable houses, unlike the Normans and French, who live frugally in noble and splendid mansions. The vices attendant on drunkenness, which enervate the human mind, followed; hence it came about that when they engaged William, with more rashness and precipitate fury than military skill, they doomed themselves and their country to slavery by a single, and that an easy, victory. For nothing is less effective than rashness; and what begins with violence quickly ceases or is repelled.

20. Statutes of William the Conqueror Involving Feudal Society and the Church

Stubbs, *Charters*, pp. 83–85, trans., Ernest F. Henderson, *Select Documents of the Middle Ages* (London: G. Bell & Sons, Ltd., 1896), pp. 7–8.

Here is shown what William the king of the English, together with his princes, has established since the Conquest of England.

1. Firstly that, above all things, he wishes one God to be venerated throughout his whole kingdom, one faith of Christ always to be kept inviolate, peace and security to be observed between the English, and the Normans.

2. We decree also that every free man shall affirm by a compact and an oath that, within and without England, he desires to be faithful to king William, to preserve with him his lands and his honour with all fidelity, and first to defend him against his enemies.

3. I will, moreover, that all the men whom I have brought with me, or who have come after me, shall be in my peace and quiet. And if one of them shall be slain, the lord of his murderer shall seize him within five days, if he can; but if not, he shall begin to pay to me forty-six marks of silver as long as his possessions shall hold out. But when the possessions of the lord of that man are at an end, the whole hundred in which the slaying took place shall pay in common what remains.

4. And every Frenchman who, in the time of my relative king Edward, was a sharer in England of the customs of the English, shall pay according to the law of the English what they themselves call "onhlote" and "anscote." This decree has been confirmed in the city of Gloucester.

5. We forbid also that any live cattle be sold or bought for money except within the cities, and this before three faithful witnesses; nor even anything old without a surety and warrant. But if he do otherwise he shall pay, and shall afterwards pay a fine.

6. It was also decreed there that if a Frenchman summon an Englishman for perjury or murder, theft, homicide, or "ran" —as the English call evident rape which can not be denied—the Englishmen shall defend himself as he prefers, either through the ordeal of iron, or through wager of battle. But if the Englishman be infirm he shall find another who will do it for him. If one of them shall be vanquished he shall pay a fine of forty shillings to the king. If an Englishman summon a Frenchman, and be unwilling to prove his charge by judgment or by wager of battle, I will, nevertheless, that the Frenchman purge himself by an informal oath.

7. This also I command and will, that all shall hold and keep the law of Edward the king with regard to their lands, and with regard to all their possessions, those provisions being added which I have made for the utility of the English people.

8. Every man who wishes to be considered a freeman shall have a surety, that his surety may hold him and hand him over to justice if he offend in any way. And if any such one escape, his sureties shall see to it that, without making difficulties, they pay what is charged against him, and that they clear themselves of having known of any fraud in the matter of his escape. The hundred and county shall be made to answer as our predecessors decreed. And those that ought of right to come, and are unwilling to appear, shall be summoned once; and if a second time they are unwilling to appear, one ox shall be taken from them and they shall be summoned a third time. And if they do not come the third time, another ox shall be taken: but if they do not come the fourth

time there shall be forfeited from the goods
of that man who was unwilling to come,
the extent of the charge against him—
"ceap-geld" as it is called,—and besides this
a fine to the king.

9.   I forbid any one to sell a man beyond
the limits of the country, under penalty of a
fine in full to me.

10.   I forbid that any one be killed or
hung for any fault, but his eyes shall be torn
out or his testicles cut off. And this command shall not be violated under penalty
of a fine in full to me.

IV. Pilgrimage and Crusade; Papal Propaganda and Social Susceptibility

A. POPE URBAN II (1088–1099), THE FIRST CRUSADE (1096–1099) AND MILITARY-MONASTIC ORDERS

21. The Pope's Address at the Council of Clermont (1095)

Fulcher of Chartres, Bongars, *Gesta Dei per Francos*, I, 382ff., trans. ThM, No. 279, pp. 514–17.

Most beloved brethren: Urged by necessity,
I, Urban, by the permission of God chief bishop
and prelate over the whole world, have come
into these parts as an ambassador with a divine
admonition to you, the servants of God. I hoped
to find you as faithful and as zealous in the
service of God as I had supposed you to be. But
if there is in you any deformity or crookedness
contrary to God's law, with divine help I will
do my best to remove it. For God has put you
as stewards over his family to minister to it.
Happy indeed will you be if he finds you faithful in your stewardship. You are called shepherds; see that you do not act as hirelings. But
be true shepherds, with your crooks always in
your hands. Do not go to sleep, but guard on
all sides the flock committed to you. For if
through your carelessness or negligence a wolf
carries away one of your sheep, you will surely
lose the reward laid up for you with God. And
after you have been bitterly scourged with re-
morse for your faults, you will be fiercely overwhelmed in hell, the abode of death. For according to the gospel you are the salt of the
earth [Matt. 5:13]. But if you fall short in your
duty, how, it may be asked, can it be salted?

O how great the need of salting! It is indeed
necessary for you to correct with the salt of wisdom this foolish people which is so devoted to
the pleasures of this world, lest the Lord, when
He may wish to speak to them, find them putre-
fied by their sins, unsalted and stinking. For if
He shall find worms, that is, sins, in them, because you have been negligent in your duty, He
will command them as worthless to be thrown
into the abyss of unclean things. And because
you cannot restore to Him His great loss, He
will surely condemn you and drive you from His
loving presence. But the man who applies this
salt should be prudent, provident, modest,
learned, peaceable, watchful, pious, just, equitable, and pure. For how can the ignorant teach
others? How can the licentious make others
modest? And how can the impure make others
pure? If anyone hates peace, how can he
make others peaceable? Or if anyone has soiled
his hands with baseness, how can he cleanse
the impurities of another? We read also that
if the blind lead the blind, both will fall into
the ditch [Matt. 15:14]. But first correct yourselves, in order that, free from blame, you may
be able to correct those who are subject to you.
If you wish to be the friends of God, gladly
do the things which you know will please Him.
You must especially let all matters that pertain
to the church be controlled by the law of the
church. And be careful that simony does not
take root among you, lest both those who buy
and those who sell [church offices] be beaten
with the scourges of the Lord through narrow
streets and driven into the place of destruction
and confusion. Keep the church and the clergy
in all its grades entirely free from the secular
power. See that the tithes that belong to God
are faithfully paid from all the produce of the
land; let them not be sold or withheld. If anyone seizes a bishop let him be treated as an out-
law. If anyone seizes or robs monks, or clergymen, or nuns, or their servants, or pilgrims, or
merchants, let him be anathema [that is, cursed].
Let robbers and incendiaries and all their accomplices be expelled from the church and
anathematized. If a man who does not give a
part of his goods as alms is punished with the
damnation of hell, how shoud he be punished
who robs another of his goods? For thus it happened to the rich man in the gospel [Luke
16:19]; for he was not punished because he had
stolen the goods of another, but because he had
not used well the things which were his.

You have seen for a long time the great disorder in the world caused by these crimes. It is
so bad in some of your provinces, I am told, and

you are so weak in the administration of justice, that one can hardly go along the road by day or night without being attacked by robbers; and whether at home or abroad, one is in danger of being despoiled either by force or fraud. Therefor it is necessary to reenact the truce, as it is commonly called, which was proclaimed a long time ago by our holy fathers. I exhort and demand that you, each, try hard to have the truce kept in your diocese. And if anyone shall be led by his cupidity or arrogance to break this truce, by the authority of God and with the sanction of this council he shall be anathematized.

After these and various other matters had been attended to, all who were present, clergy and people, gave thanks to God and agreed to the pope's proposition. They all faithfully promised to keep the decrees. Then the pope said that in another part of the world Christianity was suffereing from a state of affairs that was worse than the one just mentioned. He continued:

Although, O sons of God, you have promised more firmly than ever to keep the peace among yourselves and to preserve the rights of the church, there remains still an important work for you to do. Freshly quickened by the divine correction, you must apply the strength of your righteousness to another matter which concerns you as well as God. For your brethren who live in the east are in urgent need of your help, and you must hasten to give them the aid which has often been promised them. For, as the most of you have heard, the Turks and Arabs have attacked them and have conquered the territory of Romania [the Greek empire] as far west as the shore of the Mediterranean and the Hellespont, which is called the Arm of St. George. They have occupied more and more of the lands of those Christians, and have overcome them in seven battles. They have killed and captured many, and have destroyed the churches and devastated the empire. If you permit them to continue thus for awhile with impunity, the faithful of God will be much more widely attacked by them. On this account I, or rather the Lord, beseech you as Christ's heralds to publish this everywhere and to persuade all people of whatever rank, foot-soldiers and knights, poor and rich, to carry aid promptly to those Christians and to destroy that vile race from the lands of our friends. I say this to those who are present, it is meant also for those who are absent. Moreover, Christ commands it.

All who die by the way, whether by land or by sea, or in battle against the pagans, shall have immediate remission of sins. This I grant them through the power of God with which I am invested. O what a disgrace if such a despised and base race, which worships demons, should conquer a people which has the faith of omnipotent God and is made glorious with the name of Christ! With what reproaches will the Lord overwhelm us if you do not aid those who, with us, profess the Christian religion! Let those who have been accustomed unjustly to wage private warfare against the faithful now go against the infidels and end with victory this war which should have been begun long ago. Let those who, for a long time, have been robbers, now become knights. Let those who have been fighting against their brothers and relatives now fight in a proper way against the barbarians. Let those who have been serving as mercenaries for small pay now obtain the eternal reward. Let those who have been wearing themselves out in both body and soul now work for a double honor. Behold! on this side, will be the sorrowful and poor, on that, the rich; on this side, the enemies of the Lord, on that, his friends. Let those who go not put off the journey, but rent their lands and collect money for their expenses; and as soon as winter is over and spring comes, let them eagerly set out on the way with God as their guide.

22. The Truce of God and Crusaders' Indulgences (cf. Item 21 above)

Council of Clermont, Mansi, XX, 816, trans. *ThM*, No. 281, pp. 521–22.

1. It was decreed that monks, clergymen, women, and whatever they may have with them, shall be under the protection of the peace all the time [that is, shall never be attacked]. On three days of the week, that is, Monday, Tuesday, and Wednesday, an act of violence committed by one person against another shall not be regarded as a violation of the peace [truce]. But on the remaining four days of the week if anyone does an injury to another, he shall be held to be a violator of the holy peace [truce], and he shall be punished as has been decreed.

2. If anyone out of devotion alone and not for honor or gain sets out for Jerusalem to free the church of God, the journey shall be regarded as the equivalent of all penance.

23. Fulcher's Account of the Start of the Crusade

Recueil, III, 325, Bongars, I, 385, trans. *PTR*, I, 2 (v), pp. 22–23.

Such then was the immense assemblage which set out from the West. Gradually along the march, and from day to day, the army grew by the addition of other armies, coming from every direction and composed of innumerable people. Thus one saw an infinite multitude, speaking different languages and come from divers countries. All did not, however, come together into a single army until we had reached the city of Nicaea. What shall I add? The isles of the sea and the kingdoms of the whole earth were moved by God, so that one might believe fulfilled the prophecy of David, who said in the Psalm: "All nations whom Thou hast made shall come and worship before Thee, O Lord; and shall glorify Thy name," and that all those who reached the holy places afterwards said justly: "We will worship where His feet have stood." Concerning this journey we read very many other predictions in the prophets, which it would be tedious to recall.

Oh, how great was the grief, how deep the sighs, what weeping, what lamentations among the friends, when the husband left the wife so dear to him, his children also, and all his possessions of any kind, father, mother, brethren or kindred! And yet in spite of these floods of tears which those who remained shed for their friends about to depart, and in their very presence, the latter did not suffer their courage to fail, and, out of love for the Lord, in no way hesitated to leave all that they held most precious, believing without doubt that they would gain that hundredfold in receiving the recompense which God has promised to those who love Him.

Then the husband announced to his wife the time of his return, assuring her that if he lived by God's grace he would return to her. He commended her to the Lord, gave her a kiss, and, weeping, promised to return. But the latter, who feared that she would never see him again, overcome with grief, was unable to stand, fell lifeless to the ground, and

wept over her dear one whom she was losing in life, as if he were already dead. He then, as if he had no pity—and nevertheless he was filled with pity—and was not moved by the grief of any friends—and yet he was secretly moved—departed with a firm purpose. The sadness was for those who remained, and the joy for those who departed. What more can we say? "This is the Lord's doings, and it is marvelous in our eyes."

24. The Crusades and the Origin of the Templars (1119)

William of Tyre, 12:7, Bongars, *Gesta Dei per Francos*, pp. 819ff., trans. *ThM*, No. 265a, pp. 493–94.

In the same year [1118–19] certain nobles of knightly rank, devout, religious, and God-fearing, devoting themselves to the service of Christ, made their vows to the patriarch [of Jerusalem] and declared that they wished to live forever in chastity, obedience, and poverty, according to the rule of regular canons. Chief of these were Hugo de Payens and Geoffrey of St. Omer. Since they had neither a church nor a house, the king of Jerusalem gave them a temporary residence in the palace which stands on the west side of the temple. The canons of the temple granted them, on certain conditions, the open space around the aforesaid palace for the erection of their necessary buildings, and the king, the nobles, the patriarch, and the bishops, each from his own possessions, gave them lands for their support. The patriarch and bishops ordered that for the forgiveness of their sins their first vow should be to protect the roads and especially the pilgrims against robbers and marauders. For the first nine years after their order was founded they wore the ordinary dress of a layman, making use of such clothing as the people, for the salvation of their souls, gave them. But in their ninth year a council was held at Troyes [1128] in France at which were present the archbishops of Rheims and Sens with their suffragans, the cardinal bishop of Albano, papal legate, and the abbots of Citeaux, Clairvaux, and Pontigny, and many others. At this council a rule was established for them, and, at the direction of the pope, Honorius III, and of the patriarch of Jerusalem, Stephen, white robes were appointed for their dress. Up to their ninth year they had only nine members, but then their number began to increase and their possessions to multiply. Afterward, in the time of Eugene III, in order that their appearance might be more striking, they all, knights as well as the other members of a lower grade, who were called serving men, began to sew crosses of red cloth on their robes. Their order grew with great rapidity, and now [about 1180] they have 300 knights in their house, clothed in white mantles, besides the serving men, whose number is almost infinite. They are said to have immense possessions both here [in Palestine] and beyond the sea [in Europe]. There is not a province in the whole Christian world which has not given property to this order, so that they may be said to have possessions equal to those of kings. Since they dwelt in a palace at the side of the temple they were called "Brothers of the army of the temple." For a long time they were steadfast in their purpose and were true to their vows, but then they forgot their humility, which is the guardian of all virtues, and rebelled against the patriarch of Jerusalem who had assisted in the establishment of their order and had given them their first lands, and refused him the obedience which their predecessors had shown him. They also made themselves very obnoxious to the churches by seizing their tithes and first-fruits and plundering their possessions.

B. POPE EUGENIUS III (1145–1153), BERNARD OF CLAIRVAUX (1090–1153) AND THE SECOND CRUSADE (1147–1149)

25. The Pope Announces the Crusade (1145)

MPL 180:1064ff., trans. *ThM*, No. 284, pp. 525–29.

Eugene, bishop, servant of the servants of God, to his most beloved son, Louis, the illustrious and glorious king of the Franks, and to his beloved sons, the princes, and to all the faithful in God in Gaul, greeting and apostolic benediction.

VI-1. A Knight Templar.

From the history of our predecessors we learn how much they labored for the deliverance of the oriental church. For, in order to deliver it, our predecessor, Urban II, of blessed memory, sounded, as it were, a trumpet, and called together the sons of the holy Roman church from all parts of the world. At his voice, people from beyond the mountains, and especially the bravest and strongest warriors of the Franks and of Italy were inflamed with the ardor of love and came together. So a great army was collected which, with the aid of God, and not without great loss of life, freed from the filth of the pagans that city in which our Saviour died for us and left his glorious tomb as a memorial of his suffering for us. And they took many other cities which, for the sake of brevity, we omit. By the grace of God and the zeal of your fathers in defending them, these cities have, up to this time, remained in the hands of the Christians, and Christianity has been spread in those parts, and other cities have been valiantly taken from the infidels. But now, because of our sins and the sins of the people in the east (we cannot say it without great sorrow and weeping), the city of Edessa, or Rohais, as we call it, which was the only Christian city in those parts when the pagans held that country, has been taken by the enemies of the cross of Christ, and many Christian fortresses have been seized by them. The archbishop of Edessa and his clergy and many other Christians have been killed there. The relics of the saints have been trampled under foot by the infidels and scattered. You know as well as we how great a danger is threatening the church and the whole Christian world. If you bravely defend those things which the courage of your fathers acquired, it will be the greatest proof of your nobility and worth. But if not, it will be shown that you have less bravery than your fathers. Therefore we exhort, ask, command, and for the remission of your sins, we order all of you, and especially the nobles and the more powerful, to arm yourselves manfully to defend the oriental church, and to attack the infidels and to liberate the thousands of your brethren who are now their captives, that the dignity of the Christian name may be increased, and your reputation for courage, which is praised throughout the world, may remain unimpaired. Take for your example that Mattathias, who, to preserve the laws of his country, did not hesitate to expose himself, his children, and his relatives to death, and to leave all that he possessed in this world. And finally, by the divine aid, after many labors, he and his family triumphed over his enemies [1 Maccabees 2:1ff.].

Wishing, therefore, to provide for your welfare as well as to relieve the church in the east, we grant to those who, in a spirit of devotion, shall determine to accomplish this holy and necessary work, by the authority of God conferred on us, the same remission of sins as our predecessor, Pope Urban, granted. And we decree that their wives and children, their goods and possessions, shall be under the protection of the holy church, of ourselves, and of the archbishops, bishops, and other prelates of the church of God. And until they return, or their death is known, we forbid by our apostolic authority any lawsuit to be brought against them about any of the property of which they were in peaceful possession when they took the cross. Moreover, since those who fight for the Lord should not have their minds set on fine clothing, or personal decoration, or [hunting] dogs, or falcons, or other things which savor of worldliness, we urge you to take care that those who undertake so holy a journey shall not deck themselves out with gay clothing and furs, or with

VI-2. Mailed Conflict. Hortus Deliciarum

gold and silver weapons, but that they shall try to supply themselves with such arms, horses, and other things as will aid them to defeat the infidels.

If any are in debt but with a pure intention set out on this holy journey, they shall not pay the interest already due; and if they or others are pledged to pay the interest, by our apostolic authority we absolve them from their oath or pledge. If their relatives or the lords on whose fiefs they live cannot or will not lend them the money [necessary for the journey], they may pawn their lands and other possessions to churches, to clergymen, or to others, without the consent of the lords or their fiefs. In accordance with the grant of our predecessor and by the authority of omnipotent God, and of St. Peter, prince of the apostles, which authority is vested in us, we grant such remission of sins and absolution that whoever shall devoutly undertake and complete so holy a journey, or shall have died while on the way, shall have absolution for all his sins which he shall have confessed with a humble and contrite heart, and he shall receive the reward of eternal life from God the rewarder of all.

26. Bernard Supports the Crusade (1146)

Ep. 363:1–6, MPL 182:564ff., trans. S. J. Eales, Life and Works of Saint Bernard (London: John Hodges, 1889), II, pp. 906–910.

To the Lords and very dear Fathers, the Archbishops and Bishops, with the whole Clergy and the faithful people of Eastern France and Bavaria: Bernard, called Abbot of Clairvaux, desires that they may abound in the spirit of strength:

I write to you with respect to a matter which concerns the service of Christ, in whom is our salvation. This I say in order that the Lord's authority may excuse the unworthiness of the person who speaks; let the consideration of its usefulness to yourselves also excuse the faults of my address. I, indeed, am of small account; but I have no small love for you all, in the bowels of Jesus Christ. This, now, is my reason for writing to you, that I may thus approach you as a whole. I would rather do so by word of mouth, if the opportunity, as well as the will, were afforded me.

Behold, brethren, now is the accepted time, now is the day of salvation. The earth also is moved and has trembled, because the God of heaven has begun to destroy the land which is his: his, I say, in which the word of the Father was taught, and where he dwelt for more than thirty years, a man among men; his, for he enlightened it with miracles, he consecrated it with his own blood; in it appeared the first fruits of his resurrection. And now, for our sins, the enemies of the Cross have raised blaspheming heads, ravaging with the edge of the sword the land of promise. For they are almost on the point, if there be not One to withstand them, of bursting into the very city of the living God, of overturning the sanctuaries of our redemption, of polluting the holy places of the spotless Lamb with purple blood. Alas! they rage against the very shrine of the Christian faith with blasphemous mouths, and would enter and trample down the very couch on which, for us, our Life lay down to sleep in death.

What are you going to do then, O brave men? What are you doing, O servants of the Cross? Will you give what is holy to the dogs, and cast your pearls before swine? How many sinners there, confessing their sins with tears, have obtained pardon, after the defilement of the heathen had been purged by the swords of your fathers! The wicked man sees and is grieved; he gnashes with his teeth, and consumes away. He prepares the instruments of sin, and will leave no sign or trace of so great piety, if ever (which God forbid!) he gain possession of this holiest of holy places. Verily that would be an irremediable grief to all time, and irrecoverable loss, a vast disgrace to this most graceless generation, and an everlasting shame.

What are we then to think, brethren? Is the Lord's arm shortened so that it cannot save, because he calls his weak creatures to guard and restore his heritage? Can he not send more than twelve legions of angels, or merely speak the word, and the land shall be set free? It is altogether in his power to effect what he wishes; but I tell you, the Lord, your God, is trying you. He looks upon the sons of men to see if there be any to understand, and seek, and bewail his error. For the Lord hath pity upon his people, and provides a sure remedy for those that are afflicted.

Think what care he uses for your salvation, and wonder. Behold the abyss of his love, and trust him, O ye sinners. He wills not your death, but that you may turn and live; for now he seeks occasion, not against you, but for your benefit. What opportunity of salvation has God not tried and sought out, when the Almighty deigns to summon to his service murderers, robbers, adulterers, perjurers, and those guilty of other crimes, as if they were a people that dealt righteously? Doubt him not, O sinners; God is kind. If he willed to punish you, he not only would not seek your service, but would not accept it when offered.

Again I say, weigh the riches of the goodness of the Highest God; hear his plan of mercy. He makes, or feigns, a need for himself, while he desires to help you in your necessity. He wills to be held a debtor, that he may give pay to those that fight for him, pardon of sins, and everlasting glory. Therefore I may call it a highly favored generation which has happened upon a time so full of indulgence; upon which has come that acceptable year of the Lord, a very jubilee; for this blessing is spread over the whole world, and all fly eagerly to the sign of life.

Since, therefore, your land is fruitful in brave men, and is known to be full of robust youth, since your praise is in the whole world, and the fame of your valor has filled the entire earth, gird up your loins manfully, and take up arms in zeal for the Christian name. Let not your former warlike skill cease, but only that spirit of hatred in which you are accustomed to strike down and kill one another and in turn be overcome yourselves. How dire a madness goads those wretched men, when kinsmen strike each other's bodies with the sword, perchance causing the soul also to perish! But he does not escape who triumphs; the sword shall go through his own soul also, when he thinks to have slain his enemy only. To enter such a combat is madness, not valor: it is not to be ascribed to bravery, but rather to foolishness.

But now, O brave knight, now, O warlike hero, here is a battle you may fight without danger, where it is glory to conquer and gain to die. If you are a prudent merchant, if you are a desirer of this world, behold I show you some great bargains; see that you lose them not. Take the sign of the cross, and you shall gain pardon for every sin that you confess with a contrite heart. The material itself, being bought, is worth little; but if it be placed on a devout shoulder, it is, without doubt, worth no less than the kingdom of God. Therefore they have done well who have already taken the heavenly sign: well and wisely also will the rest do, if they hasten to lay upon their shoulders, like the first, the sign of salvation.

Besides, brethren, I warn you, and not only I, but God's apostle, "Believe not every spirit." We have heard and rejoice that the zeal of God abounds in you, but it behooves no mind to be wanting in wisdom. The Jews must not be persecuted, slaughtered, nor even driven out. Inquire of the pages of Holy Writ. I know what is written in the Psalms as prophecy about the Jews. "God hath commanded me," says the Church, 'Slay them not, lest my people forget.'"

V. The Crusades in the Era of Pope Innocent III (1198–1216)

A. THE FOURTH CRUSADE (1202–1204) AND THE CRUSADERS' SACK OF CONSTANTINOPLE (1204)

27. An Account of the Sack and the Desecration of Hagia Sophia

Nicetas, Alexii Ducae Imperium, 3–4, *Rec. des hist. des Croisades, hist. grec.*, I, 397, trans. PTR, III, 1 (v, 3), pp. 15–16.

3. . . . How shall I begin to tell of the deeds wrought by these nefarious men! Alas, the images, which ought to have been adored, were trodden under foot! Alas, the relics of the holy martyrs were thrown into unclean places! Then was seen what one shudders to hear, namely, the divine body and blood of Christ was spilled upon the ground or thrown about. They snatched

248

VI-3. Siege of a Walled City. Hortus Deliciarum

the precious reliquaries, thrust into their bosoms the ornaments which these contained, and used the broken remnants for pans and drinking cups,—precursors of Antichrist, authors and heralds of his nefarious deeds which we momentarily expect. Manifestly, indeed, by that race then, just as formerly, Christ was robbed and insulted and His garments were divided by lot; only one thing was lacking, that His side, pierced by a spear, should pour rivers of divine blood on the ground.

Nor can the violation of the Great Church be listened to with equanimity. For the sacred altar, formed of all kinds of precious materials and admired by the whole world, was broken into bits and distributed among the soldiers, as was all the other sacred wealth of so great and infinite splendor.

When the sacred vases and utensils of unsurpassable art and grace and rare material, and the fine silver, wrought with gold, which encircled the screen of the tribunal and the ambo, of admirable workmanship, and the door and many other ornaments, were to be borne away as booty, mules and saddled horses were led to the very sanctuary of the temple. Some of these which were unable to keep their footing on the splendid and slippery pavement, were stabbed when they fell, so that the sacred pavement was polluted with blood and filth.

4. Nay more, a certain harlot, a sharer in their guilt, a minister of the furies, a servant of the demons, a worker of incantations and poisonings, insulting Christ, sat in the patriarch's seat, singing an obscene song and dancing frequently. Nor, indeed, were these crimes committed and others left undone, on the ground that these were of lesser guilt, the others of greater. But with one consent all the most heinous sins and crimes were committed by all with equal zeal. Could those, who showed so great madness against God Himself, have spared the honorable matrons and maidens or the virgins consecrated to God?

Nothing was more difficult and laborious than to soften by prayers, to render benevolent, these wrathful barbarians, vomiting forth bile at every unpleasing word, so that nothing failed to inflame their fury. Whoever attempted it was derided as insane and a man of intemperate language. Often they drew their daggers against any one who opposed them at all or hindered their demands.

No one was without a share in the grief. In the alleys, in the streets, in the temples, complaints, weeping, lamentations, grief, the groaning of men, the shrieks of women, wounds, rape, captivity, the separation of those most closely united. Nobles wandered about ignominiously, those of venerable age in tears, the rich in poverty. Thus it was in the streets, on the corners, in the temple, in the dens, for no place remained unassailed or defended the suppliants. All places everywhere were filled full of all kinds of crime. Oh, immortal God, how great the afflictions of the men, how great the distress!

28. Abbot Martin's Theft of Relics

Gunther, *Hist. Constant.*, 19, Riant, Exuriae, I, 104ff., trans. *PTR*, III, 1 (v, 4), pp. 16–18.

While the victors were rapidly plundering the conquered city, which was theirs by right of conquest, the abbot Martin began to cogitate about his own share of the booty, and lest he alone should remain empty-handed, while all the others became rich, he resolved to seize upon plunder with his own sacred hands. But, since he thought it not meet to handle any booty of worldly things with those sacred hands, he began to plan how he might secure some portion of the relics of the saints, of which he knew there was a great quantity in the city.

Accordingly, having a presentiment of some great result, he took with him one of his two chaplains and went to a church which was held in great reverence because in it the mother of the most famous emperor Manuel had a noble grave, which seemed of importance to the Greeks, but ours held for naught. There a very great amount of money brought in from all the surrounding country was stored, and also precious relics which the vain hope of security had caused them to bring in from the neighboring churches and monasteries. Those whom the Greeks had driven out, had told us of this before the capture of the city. When many pilgrims broke into this church and some were eagerly engaged in stealing gold and silver, others precious stones, Martin, thinking it unbecoming to commit sacrilege except in a holy cause, sought a more retired spot where the very sanctity of the place seemed to promise that what he desired might be found.

There he found an aged man of agreeable countenance, having a long and hoary beard, a priest, but very unlike our priests in his dress. Thinking him a layman, the abbot, though inwardly calm, threatened him with a very ferocious voice, saying: "Come, perfidious old man, show me the most powerful relics you have, or you shall die immediately." The latter, terrified by the sound rather than the words, since he heard but did not understand what was said, and knowing that Martin could not speak Greek, began in the *Romana lingua*, of which he knew a little, to entreat Martin and by soft words to turn away the latter's wrath, which in truth did not exist. In reply, the abbot succeeded in getting out a few words of the same language, sufficient to make the old man understand what he wanted. The latter, observing Martin's face and dress, and thinking it more tolerable that a religious man should handle the sacred relics with fear and reverence, than that worldly men should, perchance, pollute them with their worldly hands, opened a chest bound with iron and showed the desired treasure, which was more grateful and pleasing to Martin than all the royal wealth of Greece. The abbot hastily and eagerly thrust in both hands and working quickly, filled with the fruits of the sacrilege both his own and his chaplain's bosom. He wisely concealed what seemed the most valuable and departed without opposition.

Moreover what and how worthy of veneration those relics which the holy robber appropriated were, is told more fully at the end of this work. When he was hastening to his vessel, so stuffed full, if I may use the expression, those who knew and loved him, saw him from their ships as they were themselves hastening to the booty, and inquired joyfully whether he had stolen anything, or with what he was so loaded down as he walked. With a joyful countenance, as always, and with pleasant words he said: "We have done well." To which they replied: "Thanks be to God."

29. *The Pope and the IV Lateran Council Project a Crusade (1215)*

Bull. Rom., III, i, 173ff., trans. *ThM,* No. 288, pp. 538–44.

Since we earnestly desire to liberate the holy land from the hands of the wicked, we have consulted wise men who fully understand the present situation. And at the advice of the holy council we decree that all crusaders who shall determine to go by sea shall assemble in the kingdom of Sicily a year from the first of next June. They may gather at their convenience either at Brindisi, Messina, or in any other place on either side of the strait. If the Lord permits, we shall also be there in order that the Christian army may, with our advice and aid, be well organized, and set out with the divine benediction and papal blessing.

1. Those who determine to go by land shall be ready at the same date, and they shall keep us informed of their plans in order that we may send them a suitable legate to counsel and aid them.

2. All clergymen of whatever rank, who go on the crusade, shall diligently devote themselves to prayer and exhortation, by word and example teaching the crusaders always to have the fear and the love of God before their eyes and not to say or do anything to offend the divine majesty. Even if they sometimes fall into sin, they shall rise again by true penitence. They shall show humility of heart and of body, and observe moderation in their way of living and in their dress. They shall altogether avoid dissensions and rivalries, and shun hatred and envy. Thus, equipped with spiritual and material arms, they shall fight more securely against the enemies of the faith, not resting on their own power but hoping in the divine strength.

3. These clergymen shall receive all the income of their benefices for three years, just as if they were residing in them, and, if it is necessary, they may pawn their benefices for the same length of time.

4. In order that this holy undertaking may not be prevented or delayed, we earnestly command all prelates, each in his own locality, to urge and insist that all who have taken the cross fulfil their vows to the Lord. And, if necessary, they may compel them to do so, in spite of all their subterfuges, by putting their persons under excommunication and their lands under the interdict. We except, however, those who may find some real hindrance in the way, on account of which we may decide that their vow may be commuted or put off.

5. In addition to these things, that nothing relating to Christ's business may be neglected, we command patriarchs, archbishops, bishops, abbots, and all others who have the care of souls, zealously to preach the crusade to those who are under their charge, by the Father, Son, and Holy Spirit, one only true eternal God, beseeching kings, dukes, princes, marquises, counts, barons, and other magnates, as well as the communes of cities, villages, and towns, that those who do not go in person to aid the holy land may, in proportion to their wealth, furnish a suitable number of fighting men and provide for their necessary expenses for three years. This they shall do for the remission of their sins according to the terms published in our general letter, and, for the sake of greater clearness, repeated below. Not only those who give their own ships, but also those who shall try to build ships for this purpose, shall have a share in this remission of sins.

6. If any shall be found so ungrateful to the Lord as to refuse, we warn them that they must answer for it to us before the terrible judge on the last day. Let all such consider with what conscience and what security they will be able to make their confession before the only begotten Son of God, Jesus Christ, into whose hands the Father has given all things, if, in this matter which so peculiarly concerns them, they refuse to obey him who was crucified for sinners, by whose favor and goodness they live and are sustained, nay, more, by whose blood they are redeemed.

7. Lest we should seem to put on other men's shoulders burdens so heavy that we would not so much as put a finger to them,

like those who say, but do not, we give 30,-000 pounds out of our savings for this work, and besides the passage-money which we give all crusaders from Rome and the surrounding country, we also give 3,000 silver marks which are left in our hands from the gifts of certain Christians, the rest having been spent for the benefit of the holy land by the patriarchs of Jerusalem and the masters of the Templars and the Hospitallers.

8. Since we wish all other prelates and clergy to have a share in this meritorious work and its reward, we, with the approval of the council, decree that all the clergy of whatever rank shall, for three years, give the twentieth of the income of their churches to the aid of the holy land, and for the collection of it we shall appoint certain persons. We except from this tax certain monks and also those who shall take the cross and go in person on the crusade.

9. Moreover, we and our brethren, the cardinals of the holy Roman church, will pay a tenth of our incomes; and let all know that they must faithfully do this. For any cardinal who shall knowingly commit any fraud in this matter shall incur the sentence of excommunication.

10. Now, because it is only just that those who devote themselves to the service of the heavenly ruler should enjoy some special prerogative, and since it is a little more than a year until the time set for going, we decree that all who have taken the cross shall be free from all collections, taxes, and other burdens. As soon as they take the cross we receive them and their possessions under the protection of St. Peter and of ourselves, so that archbishops, bishops, and other prelates are entrusted with their defence, and besides, other protectors shall be specially appointed to defend them. And until they return or their death shall be certainly known, their possessions shall not be molested. And if anyone shall act contrary to this he shall be restrained by ecclesiastical censure.

11. If any of those who go on the crusade are bound by oath to pay interest, their creditors, under threat of ecclesiastical censure, shall be compelled to free them from their oath and from the payment of the interest. If anyone compels them to pay the interest, he shall be forced to pay it back to them. We order the secular authorities to compel the Jews to remit the interest to all crusaders, and until they do remit it they shall have no intercourse with Christians. If any are not able for the present to pay their debts to Jews, the secular authorities shall secure an extension of time for them, so that after they have set out on the journey until their return or their death is certainly known, they shall not be disturbed about the interest. The Jews shall be compelled, after deducting the necessary expenses, to apply the income which they receive in the meantime from the property which they hold in pawn, toward the payment of the debt; since a favor of this kind, which defers the payment but does not cancel the debt, does not seem to cause much loss. Moreover, all prelates must know that they will be severely punished if they are lax in securing justice for crusaders or their families.

12. Since corsairs and pirates greatly impede the work by taking and robbing those who are going to, or returning from, the holy land, we excommunicate all who aid and protect them. Under the threat of anathema we forbid anyone knowingly to have anything to do with them in buying or selling, and we command all rulers of cities and other places to prevent them from practising this iniquity. Otherwise, since not to interfere with the wicked is the same as to aid them, and since he who does not prevent a manifest crime is suspected of having a secret share in it, we command all prelates to exercise ecclesiastical severity against their persons and lands.

13. Besides, we excommunicate and anathematize those false and impious Christians who, against Christ and the Christian people, furnish the Saracens with arms, irons, and timbers for their galleys. If any who sell galleys or ships to the Saracens, or accept positions on their piratical craft, or give them aid, counsel, or support with regard to their [war] machines to the disadvantages of the holy land, we decree that they shall be punished with the loss of all their goods, and they shall be the slaves of

those who capture them. We command that this decree be published anew every Sunday and Christian feast day in all the maritime cities, and the bosom of the church shall not be opened to offenders against it unless, for the support of the holy land, they give all that they have gained from such a damnable business, and as much more from their possessions, so that they shall be justly punished for their crimes. But if they cannot pay, they shall be punished in some other way, in order that by their punishment others may be prevented from impudently attempting things of the same sort.

14.   We forbid all Christians for the next four years to send their ships, or permit them to be sent, to lands inhabited by Saracens, in order that a larger supply of vessels may be on hand for those who wish to go to the aid of the holy land, and also that the Saracens may be deprived of that aid which they have been accustomed to get from this.

15.   Although tournaments have been prohibited by many councils under the general threat of punishment, we forbid them for three years under the threat of excommunication, because the crusade is hindered by them.

16.   Since, for the accomplishment of this work, it is necessary that Christian princes and peoples live in peace, and in order that the clergy may be able to make peace between all who are quarreling, or persuade them to make an inviolable truce, with the approval of the holy universal council we decree that a general peace shall be observed in the whole world for at least four years. And those who shall refuse to observe this peace shall be compelled to do so by excommunication of their persons and interdict on their lands, unless they have been so malicious in inflicting injuries on others that they themselves do not deserve the protection of such a peace. If they disregard the censure of the church, the ecclesiastical authorities shall invoke the secular power against them as disturbers of the business of Christ.

17.   Trusting, therefore, in the mercy of omnipotent God and the authority of Saint Peter and Paul, and by the authority to bind and loose, which God has given us, to all who shall personally and at their own expense go on this crusade we grant full pardon of their sins, which they shall repent and confess, and, besides, when the just shall receive their reward we promise them eternal salvation. And to those who shall not go in person, but nevertheless at their own expense and in proportion to their wealth and rank shall send suitable men, and likewise to those who go in person but at the expense of others, we grant the full pardon of their sins. All who shall give a fitting part of their wealth to the aid of the holy land shall, in proportion to their gifts and according to the degree of their devotion, have a share in this forgiveness. This universal council wishes to aid in the salvation of all who piously set out on this work, and therefore grants them in common the benefit of all its merits. Amen.

Given at the Lateran, 19 kal. Jan., year 18 of our pontificate.

30. *Jacques de Vitry on the Franciscans*

Hist. orient. 2:32. Quoted in *St. Francis of Assisi: The Legends and Lauds,* trans. N. Wydenbruck, ed. Otto Karrer, © 1948, Sheed & Ward, Inc., New York [also Sheed & Ward, Ltd., London], pp. 89–90. Used by permission.

"For some time I was at the Papal Court (of Pope Honorius III at Perugia), where I saw much that distressed me. Everybody was so preoccupied with secular and temporal matters, pertaining to kings and kingdoms, to disputes and lawsuits, that one could hardly speak of spiritual things.

"One solace, however, I have found in these parts. Great numbers of men and women, many of them worldly and wealthy, have forsaken everything for Christ and abandoned the world. They are called Brothers Minor, and the Pope and the Cardinals hold them in great esteem. They do not trouble at all about temporal things, but strive every day with fervent longing and vehement zeal to save souls which are in danger, detaching them from the world and guiding them. Already by the grace of God they have reaped a rich harvest, gaining many souls. . . .

"They live according to the tenets of the primitive church, of which it is written 'the multitude of them that believed were of one heart and of one soul' (Acts iv. 32). In daytime they go out into the towns and villages, so as to harvest souls by active work, at night they return to the hermitage or some solitary retreat and practise meditation.

"The women immure themselves in divers hospices near the towns; they accept no gifts, but live by the work of their hands. It distresses and perturbs them when clerics and laymen honour them more than they desire.

"The men of the order meet once a year with great spiritual gain, at an appointed place, so that they can rejoice in God and eat together, take counsel with good men and promulgate their holy institutions, which are confirmed by the Pope. Then they disperse again for a year and go to Lombardy, Tuscany, Apulia and Sicily. Even the Pope's secretary, Brother Nicolas, a holy and religious man, left the court so as to join them, but he was called back by the Pope, to whom he is indispensable. . . ."

VI. Emperor Frederick II (1215–1250) and the Sixth Crusade (1228–1229)

A. FREDERICK TELLS OF HIS TREATY WITH THE SULTAN OF BABYLON

31. Letter to Henry II of England (1279)

Trans. from Roger of Wendover, Bohn ed., II, 522–24 (RS II, 365ff., via *PTR*, I, 4 (vi, 1), pp. 24–27.

Frederic, by the grace of God, the august emperor of the Romans, king of Jerusalem and Sicily, to his well-beloved friend Henry, king of the English, health and sincere affection.

Let all rejoice and exult in the Lord, and let those who are correct in heart glorify Him, who, to make known His power, does not make boast of horses and chariots, but has now gained glory for Himself, in the scarcity of His soldiers, that all may know and understand that He is glorious in His majesty, terrible in His magnificence, and wonderful in His plans on the sons of men, changing seasons at will, and bringing the hearts of different nations together; for in these few days, by a miracle rather than by strength, that business has been brought to a conclusion, which for a length of time past many chiefs and rulers of the world amongst the multitude of nations, have never been

able till now to accomplish by force, however great, nor by fear.

Not, therefore, to keep you in suspense by a long account, we wish to inform your holiness, that we, firmly putting our trust in God, and believing that Jesus Christ, His Son, in whose service we have so devotedly exposed our bodies and lives, would not abandon us in these unknown and distant countries, but would at least give us wholesome advice and assistance for His honor, praise, and glory, boldly in the name set forth from Acre on the fifteenth day of the month of November last past and arrived safely at Joppa, intending to rebuild the castle at that place with proper strength, that afterwards the approach of the holy city of Jerusalem might be not only easier, but also shorter and more safe for us as well as for all Christians. When, therefore, we were, in the confidence of our trust in God, engaged at Joppa, and superintending the building of the castle and the cause of Christ, as necessity required and as was our duty, and whilst all our pilgrims were busily engaged in these matters, several messengers often passed to and fro between us and the sultan of Babylon; for he and another sultan, called Xaphat, his brother, were with a large army at the city of Gaza, distant about one day's journey from us; in another direction, in the city of Sichen, which is commonly called Neapolis, and situated in the plains, the sultan of Damascus, his nephew, was staying with an immense number of knights and soldiers also about a day's journey from us and the Christians.

And whilst the treaty was in progress between the parties on either side of the restoration of the Holy Land, at length Jesus Christ, the Son of God, beholding from on high our devoted endurance and patient devotion to His cause, in His merciful compassion of us, at length brought it about that the sultan of Babylon restored to us the holy city, the place where the feet of Christ trod, and where the true worshippers adore the Father in spirit and in truth. But that we may inform you of the particulars of this surrender each as they happened, be it known to you that not only is the body of the aforesaid city restored to us, but also the whole of the country extending from thence to the sea-coast near the castle of Joppa, so that for the future pilgrims will have free passage and a safe return to and from the sepulchre; provided, however, that the Saracens of that part of the country, since they hold the temple in great veneration, may come there as often as they choose in the character of pilgrims, to worship according to their custom, and that we shall henceforth permit them to come, however, only as many as we may choose to allow, and without arms, nor are they to dwell in the city, but outside, and as soon as they have paid their devotions they are to depart.

Moreover, the city of Bethlehem is restored to us, and all the country between Jerusalem and that city; as also the city of Nazareth, and all the country between Acre and that city; the whole of the district of Turon, which is very extensive, and very advantageous to the Christians; the city of Sidon, too, is given up to us with the whole plain and its appurtenances, which will be the more acceptable to the Christians the more advantageous it has till now appeared to be to the Saracens, especially as there is a good harbor there, and from there great quantities of arms and necessaries might be carried to the city of Damascus, and often from Damascus to Babylon. And although according to our treaty we are allowed to rebuild the city of Jerusalem in as good state as it has ever been, and also the castles of Joppa, Cesarea, Sidon, and that of St. Mary of the Teutonic order, which the brothers of that order have begun to build in the mountainous district of Acre, and which it has never been allowed the Christians to do during any former truce; nevertheless the sultan is not allowed, till the end of the truce between him and us, which is agreed on for ten years, to repair or rebuild any fortresses or castles.

And so on Sunday, the eighteenth day of February last past, which is the day on which Christ, the Son of God, rose from the dead, and which, in memory of His resurrection, is solemnly cherished and kept holy by all Christians in general throughout the world, this treaty of peace was confirmed by oath between us. Truly then on us and on all does that day seem to have shone favorably, in which the angels sing in praise of God, "Glory to God on high, and on earth peace, and good-will toward men." And in acknowledgment of such great kindness and of such an honor, which, beyond our deserts and contrary to the opinion of many, God has mercifully conferred on us, to the lasting renown of His compassion, and that in His holy place we might personally offer to Him the burnt offering of our lips, be it known to you that on the seventeenth day of the month of March of this second indiction, we, in company with all the pilgrims who had with us faithfully followed Christ, the Son of God, entered the holy city of Jerusalem, and after worshipping at the holy sepulchre, we, as being a Catholic emperor, on the following day, wore the crown, which Almighty God provided for us from the throne of His majesty, when of His especial grace, He exalted us on high amongst the princes of the world; so that whilst we have supported the honor of this high dignity, which belongs to us by right of sovereignty, it is more and more evident to all that the hand of the Lord hath done all this; and since His mercies are over all His works, let the worshippers of the orthodox faith henceforth know and relate it far and wide throughout the world, that He, who is blessed for ever, has visited and redeemed His people, and has raised up the horn of salvation for us in the house of His servant David.

And before we leave the city of Jerusalem, we have determined magnificently to rebuild it, and its towers and walls, and we intend so to arrange matters that, during our absence, there shall be no less care and diligence used in the business, than if we were present in person. In order that this our present letter may be full of exultation throughout, and so a happy end correspond with its happy beginning, and rejoice your royal mind, we wish it to be known to you our ally, that the said sultan is bound to restore to us all those captives whom he did not in accordance with the treaty made between him and the Christians deliver up at the time when he lost Damietta some time since, and also the others who have been since taken.

Given at the holy city of Jerusalem, on the seventeenth day of the month of March, in the year of our Lord one thousand two hundred and twenty-nine.

B. THE PATRIARCH OF JERUSALEM EXCORIATES FREDERICK II

32. *Gerold to All the Faithful* (*1229*)

Rolls Series, Matt. Paris, *Chron. maj.* 3:179–184, trans. *PTR*, I, 4 (vi, 2), pp. 27–31.

Gerold, patriarch of Jerusalem, to all the faithful—greeting.

If it should be fully known how astonishing, nay rather, deplorable, the conduct of the emperor has been in the eastern lands from beginning to end, to the great detriment of the cause of Jesus Christ and to the great injury of the Christian faith, from the sole of his foot to the top of his head no common sense would be found in him. For he came, excommunicated, without money and followed by scarcely forty knights, and hoped to maintain himself by spoiling the inhabitants of Syria. He first came to Cyprus and there most discourteously seized that nobleman J. [John] of Ibelin and his sons, whom he had invited to his table under pretext of speaking of the affairs of the Holy Land. Next the king, whom he had invited to meet him, he retained almost as a captive. He thus by violence and fraud got possession of the kingdom.

After these achievements he passed over into Syria. Although in the beginning he promised to do marvels, and although in the presence of the foolish he boasted loudly, he immediately sent to the sultan of Babylon to demand peace. This conduct rendered him despicable in the eyes of the sultan and his subjects, especially after they had discovered that he was not at the head of a numerous army, which might have to some extent added weight to his words. Under the pretext of defending Joppa, he marched with the Christian army towards that city, in order to be nearer the sultan and in order to be able more easily to treat of peace or obtain a truce. What more shall I say? After long and mysterious conferences, and without having consulted any one who lived in the country, he suddenly announced one day that he had made peace with the sultan. No one saw the text of the peace or truce when the emperor took the oath to observe the articles which were agreed upon. Moreover, you will be able to see clearly how great the malice was and how fraudulent the tenor of certain articles of the truce which we have decided to send to you. The emperor, for giving credit to his word, wished as a guarantee only the word of the sultan, which he obtained. For he said, among other things, that the holy city was surrendered to him.

He went thither with the Christian army on the eve of the Sunday when *"Oculi mei"* is sung [third Sunday in Lent]. The Sunday following, without any fitting ceremony and although excommunicated, in the chapel of the sepulchre of our Lord, to the manifest prejudice of his honor and of the imperial dignity, he put the diadem upon his forehead, although the Saracens still held the temple of the Lord and Solomon's temple, and although they proclaimed publicly as before the law of Mohammed—to the great confusion and chagrin of the pilgrims.

This same prince, who had previously very often promised to fortify Jerusalem, departed in secrecy from the city at dawn on the following Monday. The Hospitalers and the Templars promised solemnly and earnestly to aid him with all their forces and their advice, if he wanted to fortify the city, as he had promised. But the emperor, who did not care to set affairs right, and who saw that there was no certainty in what had been done, and that the city in the state in which it had been surrendered to him could be neither defended nor fortified, was content with the name of surrender, and on the same day hastened with his family to Joppa. The pilgrims who had entered Jerusalem with the emperor, witnessing his departure, were unwilling to remain behind.

The following Sunday when *"Laetare Jerusalem"* is sung [fourth Sunday in Lent], he arrived at Acre. There in order to seduce the people and to obtain their favor, he granted them a certain privilege. God knows the motive which made him act thus, and his subsequent conduct will make it known. As, moreover, the passage was near, and as all pilgrims, humble and great, after having visited the Holy Sepulchre, were preparing to withdraw, as if they had accomplished their pilgrimage, because no truce had been concluded with the sultan of Damascus, we, seeing that the holy land was already deserted and abandoned by the pilgrims, in our council formed the plan of retaining soldiers, for the common good, by means of the alms given by the king of France of holy memory.

When the emperor heard of this, he said to us that he was astonished at this, since he had concluded a truce with the sultan of Babylon. We replied to him that the knife was still in the wound, since there was not a truce or peace with the sultan of Damascus, nephew of the aforesaid sultan and opposed to him, adding that even if the sultan of Babylon was unwilling, the former could still do us much harm. The emperor replied, saying that no soldiers ought to be retained in his kingdom without his advice and consent, as he was now king of Jerusalem. We answered to that, that in the matter in question, as well as in all of a similar nature, we were very sorry not to be able, without endangering the salvation of our souls, to obey his wishes, because he was excommunicated. The emperor made no response to us, but on the following day he caused the pilgrims who inhabited the city to be assembled outside by the public crier, and by special messengers he also convoked the prelates and the monks.

Addressing them in person, he began to complain bitterly of us, by heaping up false accusations. Then turning his remarks to the venerable master of the Templars he publicly attempted to tarnish severely the reputation of the latter, by various vain speeches, seeking thus to throw upon others the responsibility for his own faults which were now manifest, and adding at last, that we were maintaining troops with the purpose of injuring him. After that he ordered all foreign soldiers, of all nations, if they valued their lives and property, not to remain in the land from that day on, and ordered count Thomas, whom he intended to leave as bailiff of the country, to punish with stripes any one who was found lingering, in order that the punishment of one might serve as an example to many. After doing all this he withdrew, and would listen to no excuse or answers to the charges which he had so shamefully made. He determined immediately to post some cross-bowmen at the gates of the city, ordering them to allow the Templars to go out but not to return. Next he fortified with cross-bows the churches and other elevated positions, and especially those which commanded the communications between the Templars and ourselves. And you may be sure that he never showed as much animosity and hatred against Saracens.

For our part, seeing his manifest wickedness, we assembled all the prelates and all the pilgrims, and menaced with excommunication all those who should aid the emperor with their advice or their services against the Church, the Templars, the other monks of the holy land, or the pilgrims.

The emperor was more and more irritated, and immediately caused all the passages to be guarded more strictly, refused to allow any kind of provisions to be brought to us or to the members of our party, and placed everywhere cross-bowmen and archers, who attacked severely us, the Templars and the pilgrims. Finally to fill the measure of his malice, he caused some Dominicans and Minorites who had come on Palm Sunday to the proper places to announce the Word of God, to be torn from the pulpit, to be thrown down and dragged along the ground and whipped throughout the city, as if they had been robbers. Then seeing that he did not obtain what he had hoped from the above-mentioned siege, he treated of peace. We replied to him that we would not hear of peace until he sent away the cross-bowmen and other troops, until he had returned our property to us, until finally he had restored all things to the condition and freedom in which they were on that day when he entered Jerusalem. He finally ordered what we wanted to be done, but it was not executed. Therefore we placed the city under interdict.

The emperor, realizing that his wickedness could have no success, was unwilling to remain any longer in the country. And, as if he would have liked to ruin everything, he ordered the cross-bows and engines of war, which for a long time had been kept at Acre for the defense of the Holy Land, to be secretly carried onto his vessels. He also sent away several of them to the sultan of Babylon, as his dear friend. He sent a troop of soldiers to Cyprus to levy heavy contributions of money there, and, what appeared to us more astonishing, he destroyed the galleys which he was not able to take with him. Having learned this, we resolved to reproach him with it, but shunning the remonstrance and the correction, he entered a galley secretly, by an obscure way, on the day of the Apostles St. Philip and St. James, and hastened to reach the island of Cyprus, without saying adieu to any one, leaving Joppa destitute; and may he never return!

Very soon the bailiffs of the above-mentioned sultan shut off all departure from Jerusalem for the Christian poor and the Syrians, and many pilgrims died thus on the road.

This is what the emperor did, to the detriment of the Holy Land and of his own soul, as well as many other things which are known and which we leave to others to relate. May the merciful God deign to soften the results! Farewell.

C. SALIMBENE OF PARMA SUMMARIZES FREDERICK'S EVIL CAREER

33. *Frederick II, His Excommunication, Crusade, and Death*

Chron. From *The Portable Medieval Reader,* ed. James Bruce Ross and Mary Martin McLaughlin, pp. 364–66. © 1949, The Viking Press, Inc., New York, and reprinted with their permission.

To these ten misfortunes of the Emperor Frederick we can add two more, so that we shall have twelve: first, that he was excommunicated by Pope Gregory IX; and second, that the Church tried to take away from him the kingdom of Sicily. And he was not without blame in this, for when the Church sent him across the sea to recover the Holy Land, he made a peace with the Saracens without advantage for the Christians. Moreover, he had the name of Mohammed publicly chanted in the church of God, as we have set

down in another chronicle, where we described the twelve crimes of Frederick. . . .

That Frederick who was once emperor died in 1250 A.D., in Apulia, in the little city which is called Fiorentino, which is about ten miles from the Saracen city of Nocera. And because of the very great stench of corruption which came from his body, he could not be carried to Palermo, where the sepulchres of the kings of Sicily are, and where they are buried.

The reasons for the failure to bury this king in the tombs of the kings of Sicily are manifold. The first was the fulfilment of the Scriptures, whence Isaiah: "Thou shalt not be joined with them in burial, because thou hast destroyed thy land and slain thy people." . . . The second was that such a great stench came from his body that it could not be endured. . . . The third reason was that his son Manfred, who was called prince, concealed his death, because he wanted to seize the kingdom of Sicily and Apulia, before his brother Conrad should come from Germany. Hence it was that many believed that he had not died, although he really had; and thus was fulfilled the Sibylline prophecy: "It will be said among the people, 'He lives' and 'He does not live,'" and this happened because his death was hidden. . . .

But know you that Frederick always delighted in having strife with the Church, and that he many times fought her, who had nourished, protected, and exalted him. Of faith in God he had none. He was a crafty man, wily, avaricious, lustful, malicious, and wrathful.

And yet at times he was a worthy man, when he wanted to prove his goodness and his generosity; then he was friendly, merry, full of sweetness and diligence. He could read, write, and sing, and make songs and music. He was a handsome, well-formed man, but only of middle height. I have seen him, and once I loved him, for he wrote on my behalf to Brother Elias, the minister general of the Franciscan order, to send me back to my father. He knew how to speak many and various languages. And, to put it briefly, had he been a good Catholic, and loved God, the Church, and his own soul, he would have had as his equals few emperors in the world. But since, as it is written, a little leaven leaveneth the lump, so he destroyed all his good qualities through this, that he persecuted the Church of God, which he would not have done, if he had loved God and his own soul. . . . So he was deposed from the imperial office, and died an evil death. . . .

VII. St. Louis (IX): The Virtues and Limitations of a Crusading Feudal King (1226–1270)

A. A BATTLE REPORT FROM THE SEVENTH CRUSADE (1248–1254)

34. A Knight Writes from Damietta (1249)

Rolls Series, Matt. Paris, *Chron.* Jam. 6:155ff., trans. *PTR*, I, 4 (viii, 1), pp. 35–40.

To his dear half-brother and well-beloved friend, master B. of Chartres, student at Paris, Guy, a knight of the household of the viscount of Melun, greeting and a ready will to do his pleasure.

Because we know that you are uneasy about the state of the Holy Land and our lord, the king of France, and that you are interested in the general welfare of the church as well as the fate of many relatives and friends who are fighting for Christ under the king's orders, therefore, we think we ought to give you exact information as to the events of which a report has doubtless already reached you.

After a council held for that purpose, we departed from Cyprus for the East. The plan was to attack Alexandria, but after a few days a sudden tempest drove us over a wide expanse of the sea. Many of our vessels were driven apart and scattered. The sultan of Cairo and other Saracen princes, informed by spies that we intended to attack Alexandria, had assembled an infinite multitude of armed men from Cairo, Babylon, Damietta and Alexandria, and awaited us in order to put us, while exhausted, to the sword. One night we were borne over the waves by a violent tempest. Toward morning the sky cleared, the storm abated, and our scattered vessels came together safely. An experienced pilot who knew all the coast in this part of the sea and many idioms, and who was a faithful guide, was sent to the masthead, in order that he might tell us if he saw land and knew where we were. After he had carefully and sorrowfully examined all the surrounding country, he cried out terrified, "God help us, God help us, who alone is able; we are before Damietta."

Indeed all of us could see the land. Other pilots on other vessels had already made the same observation, and they began to approach each other. Our lord, the king, assured of our position, with undaunted spirit, endeavored to reanimate and console his men. "My friends and faithful soldiers," said he to them, "we shall be invincible if we are inseparable in our love of one another. It is not without the divine permission that we have been brought here so quickly. I am neither the king of France nor the holy church, you are both. I am only a man whose life will end like other men's when it shall please God. Everything is in our favor, whatever may happen to us. If we are conquered, we shall be martyrs; if we triumph, the glory of God will be exalted thereby— that of all France, yea, even of Christianity, will be exalted thereby. Certainly it would be foolish to believe that God, who foresees all, has incited me in vain. This is His cause, we shall conquer for Christ, He will triumph in us, He will give the glory, the honor and the blessing not unto us, but unto His name."

In the meantime our assembled vessels approached the land. The inhabitants of Damietta and of the neighboring shores could view our fleet of 1500 vessels, without counting those still at a distance and which numbered 150. In our times no one, we believe, had ever seen such a numerous fleet of vessels. The inhabitants of Damietta, astonished and frightened beyond expression, sent four good galleys, with well-skilled sailors, to examine and ascertain who we were and what we wanted. The latter having approached near enough to distinguish our vessels, hesitated, stopped, and, as if certain of what they had to report, made ready to return to their own party; but our galleys with the fast boats got behind them and hemmed them in, so that they were com-

VI-4. Knight of the Latter Part of the 13th Century.

blinded them. Accordingly, three hostile galleys were soon sunk. We saved, however, a few enemies. The fourth galley got away very much damaged. By exquisite tortures we extracted the truth from the sailors who fell alive into our hands, and learned that the citizens of Damietta had left the city and awaited us at Alexandria. The enemies who succeeded in escaping and whose galley was put to flight, some mortally wounded, uttering frightful cries, went to tell the multitude of Saracens who were waiting on the shore, that the sea was covered with a fleet which was drawing near, that the king of France was coming in hostile guise with an infinite number of barons, that the Christians were 10,000 to one, and that they caused fire, stones, and clouds of dust to rain down. "However," they added "while they are still fatigued from the labor of the sea, if your lives and your homes are dear to you, hasten to kill them, or at least to repulse them vigorously until our soldiers return. We alone have escaped with difficulty to warn you. We have recognized the ensigns of the enemy. See how furiously they rush upon us, equally ready to fight on land or sea."

In consequence of this speech, fear and distrust seized the enemy. All of our men, assured of the truth, conceived the greatest hopes. In emulation of one another they leaped from their vessels into the barks; the water was too shallow along the shore, the barks and the small vessels could not reach the land. Several warriors, by the express order of the king, cast themselves into the sea. The water was up to their waists. Immediately began a very cruel combat. The first crusaders were promptly followed by others and the whole force of infidels was scattered. We lost only a single man by the enemy's fire. Two or three others, too eager for the combat, threw themselves into the water too quickly and owed their deaths to themselves rather than to others. The Saracens giving way, retired into their city, fleeing shamefully and with great loss. Great numbers of them were mutilated or mortally wounded.

We would have followed them closely, but our chiefs, fearing an ambuscade, held us back. While we were fighting some slaves

pelled, in spite of their unwillingness, to approach our ships.

Our men, seeing the firmness of the king and his immovable resolution, prepared, according to his orders, for a naval combat. The king commanded to seize these mariners and all whom they met, and ordered us afterward to land and take possession of the country. We then, by means of our mangonels which hurled from a distance five or six stones at once, began to discharge at them fire-darts, stones, and bottles filled with lime, made to be shot from a bow, or small sticks like arrows. The darts pierced the mariners and their vessels, the stones crushed them, the lime flying out of the broken bottles and captives broke their chains, for the gaolers had also gone out to fight us. Only the women, children and the sick had remained in the city. These slaves and captives, full of joy, rushed to meet us, applauding our king and his army, and crying "Blessed is he who cometh in the name of the Lord." These events happened on Friday the day of our Lord's Passion; we drew from it a favorable augury. The king disembarked joyfully and safely, as well as the rest of the Christian army. We rested until the next day, when, with the aid and under the guidance of slaves who knew the country and the roads, we got possession of what remained to be captured of the land and shore. But during the night the Saracens, who had discovered that the captives had escaped, had killed those who remained. They thus made of them glorious martyrs of Christ, to their own damnation.

In the darkness of the following night and on Sunday morning, as they lacked weapons and troops, the Saracens seeing the multitude of the Christians who were landing, their courage and firmness, and the sudden desolation of their own city, lacking leaders, superiors and persons to incite them, as well as destitute of strength and weapons for fighting, departed, taking their women and children and carrying off everything movable. They fled from the other side of the city by little gates which they had made long before. Some escaped by land, others by sea, abandoning their city filled with supplies of all kinds. That same day at nine o'clock, two captives who escaped by chance from the hands of the Saracens, came to tell us what had happened. The king, no longer fearing an ambuscade, entered the city before three o'clock without hindrance and without shedding blood. Of all who entered only Hugo Brun, earl of March, was severely wounded. He lost too much blood from his wounds to survive, for he was careless of his life, because of the reproaches which had been inflicted upon him, and rashly rushed into the midst of the enemy. He had been stationed in the front rank, at his own request, because he knew that he was an object of suspicion.

I must not forget to say that the Saracens, after having determined to flee, hurled at us a great quantity of Greek fire, which was very injurious to us, because it was carried by a wind which blew from the city. But this wind, suddenly changing, carried the fire back upon Damietta, where it burned several persons and fortresses. It would have consumed more property, if the slaves who had been left had not extinguished it by a process which they knew, and by the will of God, who did not wish that we should take possession of a city which had been burnt to the ground.

The king, having then entered the city in the midst of cries of joy, went immediately into the temple of the Saracens to pray and thank God, whom he regarded as the author of what had taken place. Before eating, all the Christians, weeping sweet and sacred tears of joy, and led by the legate, solemnly sang that hymn of the angels, the *Te Deum Laudamus*. Then the mass of the blessed Virgin was celebrated in the place where the Christians in ancient times had been wont to celebrate mass and to ring the bells, and which they had now cleansed and sprinkled with holy water. In this place, four days before, as the captives told us, the foul Mohammed had been worshiped with abominable sacrifices, loud shouts and the noise of trumpets. We found in the city an infinite quantity of food, arms, engines, precious clothing, vases, golden and silver utensils and other things. In addition we had our provisions, of which we had plenty, and other dear and necessary objects brought from our vessels.

By the divine goodness, the Christian army, like a pond which is greatly swollen by the torrents pouring in, was added to each day by some soldiers from the lands of lord Ville-Hardouin and some Templars and Hospitalers, besides pilgrims newly arrived, so that we were, by God's grace, largely reinforced. The Templars and Hospitalers did not want to believe in such a triumph. In fact, nothing that had happened was credible. All seemed miraculous, especially the Greek fire which the wind carried back onto the heads of those who hurled it against us. A similar miracle formerly took place at Antioch. A few infidels were converted to Jesus Christ and up to the present time have remained with us.

We, instructed by the past, will in the future exercise much prudence and circumspection in our actions. We have with us faithful Orientals upon whom we can count. They know all the country and the dangers which it offers; they have been baptized with true devotion. While we write, our chiefs are considering what it is necessary to do. The question is whether to proceed to Alexandria or Babylon and Cairo. We do not know what will be decided. We shall inform you of the result, if our lives are spared. The sultan of Babylon, having learned what has taken place, has proposed to us a general engagement for the morrow of St. John the Baptist's day, and in a place which the two armies shall choose, in order, as he says, that fortune may decide for the men of the East or the men of the West, that is between the Christians and themselves, and that the party to whom fate shall give the victory, may glory in it, and the conquered may humbly yield. The king replied that he did not fear the enemy of Christ one day more than another and that he offered no time for rest, but that he defied him to-morrow and every day of his life, until he should take pity on his own soul and should turn to the Lord who wishes the whole world to be saved, and who opens the bosom of His mercy to all those who turn to Him.

We tell you these things in this letter through our kinsman Guiscard. He seeks nothing else than that he may, at our expense, prepare himself for a professorship and have a fit lodging for at least two years.

We have learned nothing certain worth reporting about the Tartars. We can expect neither good faith from the perfidious, nor humanity from the inhuman, nor charity from the dogs, unless God, to whom nothing is impossible, works this miracle. It is He who has purged the Holy Land from the wicked Charismians. He has destroyed them and caused them to disappear entirely from under heaven. When we learn anything certain or remarkable of the Tartars, or others, we will send you word either by letter or by Roger de Montefagi, who is to return to France in the spring, to the lands of our lord the viscount, to collect money for us.

B. JOINVILLE WRITES ON ST. LOUIS, HIS CHARACTER, AND THE CRUSADES

35. The Crusaders, King Louis, and Saracen Bombardment with "Greek Fire" (see No. 34, above)

This and the following sections, 36–40, used by permission of the publishers. Joinville, *Vita*, from *The Life of Saint Louis*, by John of Joinville, trans. Rene Hague, ed. Natalis de Wailly, © 1955, Sheed & Ward, Inc., New York (also Sheed & Ward, Ltd., London), 43:203–208, pp. 74–75.

203. One night when we were on guard at the cat-castle they brought up an engine called a petrary; this was the first time they had done this, and they loaded the sling with Greek fire. When the good knight my Lord Walter of Ecurey, who was with me, saw it he said:

204. "My Lords, this is the worst danger we have yet had to face, for if they set fire to our cats and we stand fast we shall be burnt and lost: and if we leave the post we have been given to guard we shall be shamed. No one, then, but God alone can save us in this peril. My advice is, whenever they launch the fire, get down on hands and knees and pray to Our Lord to preserve us from this danger."

205. As soon as they sent over the first shot, we went on hands and knees as he showed us. The first shot went between our two cats and fell on the dam in front of us which the men had been making to block the stream. Our firemen were ready to put out the blaze, and as the Saracens were prevented from firing directly at them by the wings of the two shelters which the King had had built, they aimed up in the air so that their shots fell right down on them.

206. This is what Greek fire was like: it came straight at you, as big as a vinegar barrel, with a tail of fire behind it as long as a long spear. It made such a noise as it came that it seemed like the thunder of heaven; it looked like a dragon flying through the air. It gave so intense a light that in the camp you could see as clearly as by daylight in the great mass of flame which illuminated everything. Three times that night they bombarded us with Greek fire, and four times they fired it from the revolving crossbow.

207. Whenever our holy King heard that they were sending over Greek fire he would rise from his bed and hold up his hands to Our Lord, weeping, and saying, "Dear Lord God, hold my people safe." I do in truth believe that his prayers were of great help to us in our need. In the evening, when the Greek fire had been falling, he would send one of his chamberlains to know how we stood and whether the fire had done us any damage.

208. Once when they were thus bombarding us the fire fell on the river bank, close beside the cat which the men of my Lord of Courtenay were guarding. Up, then, came a knight they called the Albigensian and said to me, "Sir, unless you can give us some help, we shall all be burnt, for the Saracens have put over so many of their fire-bombs that it is like a tall hedge of fire moving on our turret." We jumped down and hurried across, and found that what he said was true. We put out the fire, but before it was extinguished the Saracens opened on us all from across the stream.

36. His Virtue and Love of God and People

Ibid., 3:20, pp. 26–27.

20. St. Louis loved God with his whole heart and it was on Him that he modelled his actions. This could be seen in that, as God died for the love of His people, so did the King more than once put his own body in danger of death for the love he bore his people; and this although, had he wished it, he might well have been excused. Of this I will tell you more later.

37. His True Faith and Piety

Ibid., 8:43, 44, p. 33.

43. As I shall tell you later, the holy King did all that lay in his power, whenever he spoke to me, to instil in me a firm faith in the Christian religion which God has given us. He said that our belief in the articles of faith should be so firm that neither for death nor for any hurt that might come to our persons should we be willing to transgress them in any way either by word or by deed. He

VI-5. St. Louis of France. *Giotto, Chiesa di S. Croce, Florence.*

said, too, that the Enemy is so subtle that when folk are dying he works with all his might to make them die with some doubt of the articles of our faith; for he sees that he cannot rob a man of the good works he has done and, what is more, that the man is lost to him if he dies in the true faith.

44. That is why we should be on our guard and watch against the trap; and when the Enemy sends such a temptation, we should say to him, "Be off! You shall not tempt me from my firm belief in all the articles of faith; even though you were to have all my limbs cut off, yet will I live and die in this mind." The man who does this beats the enemy with his own weapon, with the sword with which he was trying to kill him.

38. His Foundations and Endowments

Ibid., 139:688–690, 692, pp. 202–3.

688. Once the King asked me whether I washed the feet of the poor on Maundy Thursday. I told him no, it did not seem to me a good thing to do. He told me that I should not despise it, for God had done it. "You would, then, be most revolted at doing what the King of England does, who washes the feet of lepers and kisses them."

689. Before going to bed, he used to have his children brought to him and tell them stories of good kings and good emperors, telling them that they should take such men as examples. He told them stories, too, of wicked men of high estate, who, by their licentiousness and robberies and avarice, had lost their kingdoms. "I remind you of these things," he said, "so that you may be careful to avoid them and not incur the anger of God." He made them learn the Office of Our Lady and recite the day Hours to him, to accustom them to hearing the Office when they ruled their own possessions.

690. The King was so generous in almsgiving that wherever he went in his Kingdom he gave gifts to poor churches, to lazarhouses, almshouses and hospitals, and to poor gentlemen and gentlewomen. Every day he fed a crowd of poor, in addition to those who ate in his chamber; and often have I seen him with his own hand cut their bread and pour their drink. . . .

692. When any benefice of Holy Church fell in to the King, before bestowing it he consulted with worthy religious and laymen, and when he had heard their advice he gave the benefices in good faith and honestly and in accordance with the will of God. He refused to give any benefice to a cleric unless he resigned any other ecclesiastical benefices he held. In any town in his Kingdom in which he had not been before he visited the Friars Preachers and Grey Friars, if there were any there, to ask for their prayers.

39. His Charity

Ibid., 142:722, 725, pp. 209, 210.

722. In addition to all this, the King daily gave countless generous alms, to poor religious, to poor hospitals, to poor sick people, to other poor convents, to poor gentlemen and gentlewomen and girls, to fallen women, to poor widows and women in childbed, and to poor minstrels who from old age or sickness were unable to work or follow their trade. So we may well say that he was happier than Titus, the Emperor of Rome, of whom the old books tell us that he was greatly cast down and grieved on any day when he had done no act of charity. . . .

725. Soon afterwards he built another house outside Paris, on the road to St. Denis, which was called the House of the Daughters of God, and in this hostel he installed a large number of women who through poverty had abandoned themselves to the sins of the flesh, and gave them a revenue of four hundred pounds for their maintenance. In several places in his kingdom he built and endowed houses of Béguines and ordered that in them should be received women who wished to devote themselves to a life of chastity.

40. The Last, Fatal Crusade (the Eighth, 1270): Precepts to His Son on Individual, Ecclesiastical, and Social Responsibility

Ibid., 145:738–740, 742, 750, 751, pp. 213–15.

738. Of his expedition to Tunis I do not wish to give any account nor to say anything, since, thank God, I was not there, and I would not put in my book anything of which I am not certain. Let me confine myself, then, to speaking of our holy King and simply say that after arriving at Tunis before the castle of Carthage he succumbed to a dysentery of the belly (his eldest son Philip was sick with a quartan fever and the same dysentery as the King), which forced him to take to his bed, with the knowledge that soon he would have to pass from this world to the next.

739. Then he sent for my Lord Philip, his son, and bade him respect, as he would his will, all the precepts that he bequeathed to him. These precepts, which the King, it is said, wrote out with his own saintly hand, are set out below in the common tongue.

740. My dear son, my first precept is to set your heart on the love of God, for without that no man can be saved. Watch that you

do not do anything displeasing to God, that is to say, any mortal sin; you should rather suffer any sort of torment than commit a mortal sin. . . .

742. Be frequent in confession, and choose a worthy confessor who can teach you what you should do and what you should avoid; your behaviour should be such that your confessor and your friends may not be afraid to reprove you for your misdeeds. Attend devoutly and without irreverence at the service of Holy Church, praying to God with both your heart and your tongue, especially at Mass when the Consecration is made. Have a tender and compassionate heart for the poor, for the unhappy and unfortunate, and comfort and help them to the best of your power. . . .

750. Honour and love all persons of Holy Church, and watch that the gifts and alms that your predecessors have given them are not taken from them nor diminished. It is said of King Philip, my grandfather, that one of his Councillors once told him that the men of Holy Church were doing the King great wrong and injury by depriving him of his rights and diminishing his jurisdiction, and he was astonished that he should allow it. The good King answered that he certainly believed him, but that he took into ac-count the kindnesses and courtesies God had done him and would rather relinquish his rights than contend with the men of Holy Church.

751. Honour and revere your father and mother and keep their commands. Give the benefices of Holy Church to good men and of clean life, and in doing so take the advice of worthy and honest men.

VIII. The Church and Social Tension in the Crusading Period; the Transition from Agrarian Feudalism to Town Economy and Mercantilism

A. THE CHURCH AND FEUDAL-URBAN ECONOMY

41. *Early Grants of Market, Coinage, and Taxation Rights to a Church* (c. 952)

N. Schaten, *Annales Paderbornenses,* I, 295 (Neuhaus, 1693), trans. R. C. Cave and H. H. Coulson, *A Source Book for Medieval Economic History* (Milwaukee: The Bruce Publishing Co., 1936), p. 136, No. 13.

Otto the Great, A.D. 936–973, showed great favor to the Church as is illustrated by the grants he made bestowing counties and

VI-6. Investing a Knight with Arms, *c.* 1250.

duchies with temporal jurisdiction including rights of coinage, taxation, and markets.

In the name of the Holy and Indivisible Trinity, Otto, by the grace of God, King. Be it known to all our faithful, both present and future, that, at the intervention of the venerable bishop, Drugo, of the see of Osnabruck, we have granted a public market and the right to make money in the placed called Wyddenbrugge; for the redemption of our soul we have given to the same church whatever the fisc or royal power held there. Rights of coinage and taxation and other public rights, hitherto under our authority, we grant to the said bishop, or his successors [yet to be], and we firmly command that no judge exercise any authority to disturb him in these rights, or do him harm. And in order that the bishop and his successors may hold this from us and from our successors inviolably, and that it may be diligently adhered to by all people, we have ordered this charter to be sealed by the impression of our seal, confirming it with our own signature. The year of the Incarnation of the Lord 952, June twenty-eighth, in the sixteenth year of the reign of King Otto.

42. Archbishop Thurstan's Charter to Beverley (1130)

Stubbs, *Sel. Charters*, 131–32, trans. Cave and Coulson, *SBMEH*, pp. 203–4, No. 5.

The charter granted to Beverley was modeled on that of York and included the grant of a merchant gild with the same by-laws and customs as had been previously granted to York by King Henry I. The rent to be paid annually to the Archbishop was eighteen marks, a sum calculated to make up for the loss of revenue obtained by taxation of the citizens.

Thurstan, by the grace of God, Archbishop of York, to all the faithful of Christ, present and future, greeting and benediction, and the blessing of God.

Let it be known to you that I have granted and conceded on the advice of the chapter of York and Beverley, and with the counsel of my barons, and by my charter I have confirmed to the men of Beverley all the liberties and laws which the men of York have in their city.

Let it not be hidden from you that the lord Henry, our king, has granted to us the power to do these things, and that his charter has confirmed our statutes and our laws according to the form of the laws of the burgesses of York, saving the dignity and honor of God, of St. John, of us, and of our canons so that he might promote and exalt the honor of his almsgiving predecessors with all these free customs. I wish that my burgesses of Beverley might have their gild-house, and I grant and concede to them that they may carry out their statutes to the honor of God, of St. John, and of the cathedral chapter for the improvement of the town by the same laws and liberties as the men of York have in their gild.

I also grant a perpetual toll to them for eighteen marks annually; besides on the three feast days on which toll is due to us and to the cathedral chapter, *i.e.*, on the

VI-7. How a Mighty Knight Fought Earl Richard for His Lady's Sake.

feast of St. John the Confessor in May, and on the feast of the Translation of St. John, and on the feast of the Nativity of St. John the Baptist. On these three feasts I have freed all the burgesses of Beverley so that they are free and quit of all tax.

By the testimony of this charter I have granted to the same burgesses free entry and exit into and out of the town, in the plain, woods, marshes, roads, paths, and other thoroughfares, except in the meadows and cornfields; and this I grant and confirm as well and freely as ever any one can grant and confirm.

And know also that they are free and quit of all tax throughout the whole of Yorkshire, just as are the citizens of York. And I wish that if any one break this charter that he be anathema, as the custom of the church of St. John proclaims, and according as it is decreed in the church of St. John. Witnesses, etc.

43. Financial Embarrassments of a Monastery: Loans, Usury, Jews (1173)

Jocelin of Brakelond, *Chronica*, trans. Cave and Coulson, *SBMEH*, pp. 175–76, No. 7.

[This transaction violated the laws of the Church with respect to the pledge given in sacred vessels and vestments. The rate of interest, it will be seen, was 25 per cent per annum, a rate which was more than the monastery could afford. The protection afforded by the king to the Jews is shown by the message of the almoner summoning the abbot to answer for the financial embarrassment of his monastery and the transaction made with the Jew.]

Whence it happened that every monk who held office had his own seal, and of his own will contracted debts with Christian and Jews. Often the silk vestments and gold vessels and other ornaments of the church were pledged, without the sanction of the brethren. I saw a bond made to William Fitz-Isabel for 1040 pounds; but I knew neither the cause nor the origin of this. And I saw another bond made to Isaac, the son of Rabbi Joce, for 400 pounds, but I do not know why. And I saw a third bond made to

Benedict the Jew of Norwich, for 880 pounds; and this was the origin and cause of this debt. Our buttery was destroyed and William the sacristan undertook willy-nilly to restore it and he secretly borrowed from Benedict the Jew 40 marks at usury, and he gave him a bond sealed with a seal that used to hang near the shrine of St. Edmund, with which the gilds and fraternities were accustomed to seal, but which afterwards, but too late, to the joy of the monks, was broken. When that debt had increased to 100 pounds the Jew came with the letters from the lord king about the sacristan's debt; and then at length was revealed what had lain hidden from the abbot and the monks. Then the abbot was angry and wished to depose the sacristan, alleging the privilege of the lord Pope that he could depose the sacristan whenever he wished. But some one came to the abbot and, speaking for the sacristan, so prevailed upon the abbot that he allowed a bond to be given to Benedict the Jew for 400 pounds, to be repaid at the end of four years, namely for the 100 pounds to which it had already increased at usury, and for another 100 pounds that the same Jew had lent to the sacristan for the abbot's needs. And the sacristan undertook in full chapter to repay all the debt and a bond was made and sealed with the seal of the monks, but the abbot disagreed and did not apply his own seal since that debt did not apply to him. But at the end of four years the debt could not be repaid, and a new bond for 880 pounds was made, to be repaid at stated intervals, namely, 80 pounds a year. And the same Jew had several other bonds for smaller debts, and another bond which was for fourteen years, so that the sum of the debt owing to that Jew was 1200 pounds. And the almoner of the lord king indicated to the lord abbot that he should go to the king about such great debts.

44. A Papal License to Trade with the Saracens (1198)

MPL 214:493, trans. Cave and Coulson, *SBMEH*, pp. 104–5, No. 15.

[The eminence enjoyed by Venice in Mediterranean trade and the injury she suffered from the embargoes of Popes Gregory VIII and Innocent III on trade with the Saracens during the Crusades were sufficient to stimulate her to protest to such an extent that Pope Innocent III permitted her a limited trade in commodities produced in Europe.]

Besides the indulgence we have promised to those going at their own expense to the east, and besides the favor of apostolic protection granted to those helping that country, we have renewed the decree of the Lateran council which excommunicated those who presume to give arms, iron, or wood to the Saracens for their galleys, and which excommunicated those who act as helmsmen on their galleys and dhows, and which at the same time decreed that they should be deprived of their property for their transgressions by the secular arm and by the consuls of the cities, and that, if caught, they become the slaves of their captors. Following the example of Pope Gregory, our predecessor of pious memory, we have placed under sentence of excommunication all those who in future consort with the Saracens, directly or indirectly, or who attempt to give or send aid to them by sea, as long as the war between them and us shall last. But our beloved sons Andreas Donatus and Benedict Grilion, your messengers, recently came to the apostolic see and were at pains to explain to us that by this decree your city was suffering no small loss, for she is not devoted to agriculture but rather to shipping and to commerce. We, therefore, induced by the paternal affection we have for you, and commanding you under pain of anathema not to aid the Saracens by selling or giving to them or exchanging with them iron, flax, pitch, pointed stakes, ropes, arms, helmets, ships, and boards, or unfinished wood, do permit for the present, until we issue further orders, the taking of goods, other than those mentioned, to Egypt and Babylon, whenever necessary. We hope that in consideration of this kindness you will bear in mind the aiding of Jerusalem, taking care not to abuse the apostolic decree, for there is no doubt that whosoever violates his conscience in evading this order will incur the anger of God.

45. Money Taken in Usury to be Restored

Summa Theol., 2a, 2ae, Q. 78, a. 1, conclusion. The "Summa Theologica" of St. Thomas Aquinas, trans. by Fathers of the English Dominican Province, Part II (Second Part) (London: Burns, Oates, & Washbourne, Ltd.; New York: Benziger Brothers, Inc., 1918), p. 331.

Now money, according to the Philosopher (*Ethic.* v.: *Polit.* i.) was invented chiefly for the purpose of exchange: and consequently the proper and principal use of money is its consumption or alienation whereby it is sunk in exchange. Hence it is by its very nature unlawful to take payment for the use of money lent, which payment is known as usury: and just as a man is bound to restore other ill-gotten goods, so is he bound to restore the money which he has taken in usury.

46. Lenders May Enter into Agreement with Borrowers over Compensation for Losses Incurred

Ibid., a. 2, Rep. Obj. 1, p. 335.

Reply Obj. 1. A lender may without sin enter an agreement with the borrower for compensation for the loss he incurs of something he ought to have, for this is not to sell the use of money but to avoid a loss. It may also happen that the borrower avoids a greater loss than the lender incurs, wherefore the borrower may repay the lender with what he has gained. But the lender cannot enter an agreement for compensation, through the fact that he makes no profit out of his money: because he must not sell that which he has not yet and may be prevented in many ways from having.

47. Cases of Legitimate Borrowing from a Usurer under Necessity

Ibid., a. 4, Conclusion, p. 340.

Accordingly we must also answer to the question in point that it is by no means lawful to induce a man to lend under a condition of usury: yet it is lawful to borrow for usury from a man who is ready to do so and is a usurer by profession; provided the borrower have a good end in view, such as the relief of his own or another's need.

Alphandery, P., *La chrétienté et l'idée de croisade*. Paris: A. Michel, 1954.

Atiya, A. S., *The Crusade in the Later Middle Ages*. London: Methuen & Co., Ltd., 1938.

Boissonade, P., *Life and Work in Medieval Europe*, trans. E. Power. New York: Alfred A. Knopf, Inc., 1927.

Evans, J., *Monastic Life at Cluny 910–1157*. New York: Oxford University Press, Inc., 1931.

Hubert, M. J., trans., *Ambroise. The Crusade of Richard Lion-Heart* [Records of Civilization, 34]. New York: Columbia University Press, 1941.

Jarrett, Bede, *Social Theories of the Middle Ages 1200–1500*. Westminster, Maryland: Newman Press, 1942.

Krey, A. C., ed., *The First Crusade*. Princeton: Princeton University Press, 1921.

LaMonte, J., *The World of the Middle Ages*. New York: Appleton-Century-Crofts, Inc., 1949.

McGinty, E. M., *Fulcher of Chartres, Chronicle of the First Crusade*, Translations and Reprints. . . . Third Series, I. Philadelphia: University of Pennsylvania Press, 1941.

McNeal, E. H., trans., *Robert of Clari, The Conquest of Constantinople* [Records of Civilization, 23]. New York: Columbia University Press, 1936.

McNeill, J. T., "The Feudalization of the Church," in McNeill, *et al.*, *Environmental Factors in Christian History*. Chicago: University of Chicago Press, 1939, pp. 181–205.

MacDonald, A. J., *Hildebrand, A Life of Gregory VII*. London: Methuen & Co., Ltd., 1937.

Munro, D. C., *The Kingdom of the Crusaders*. New York: Appleton-Century-Crofts, Inc., 1935.

Newhall, R., *The Crusades*. New York: Holt, Rinehart & Winston, Inc., 1927.

Pirenne, H. *Medieval Cities*. Princeton: Princeton University Press, 1925.

———, *Economic and Social History of Medieval Europe*. New York: Harcourt, Brace & World, Inc., 1936.

Records of Civilization: Sources and Studies, ed., A. P. Evans. New York: Columbia University Press—especially, Robert of Clari, No. 23, 1926; Ambroise, No. 34, 1941; and William of Tyre, No. 35, 1943.

Robertson, H. M., *Aspects of the Rise of Economic Individualism*. Cambridge: Cambridge University Press, 1933.

Runciman, S., *A History of the Crusades*, 3 vols. Cambridge: Cambridge University Press, 1951–1954.

Setton, K., *A History of the Crusades*, Vol. I. Philadelphia: University of Pennsylvania Press, 1955.

Stephenson, C., *Medieval Feudalism*. Ithaca: Cornell University Press, 1942.

Thompson, J. W., *Economic and Social History of the Middle Ages 300–1300*. New York: Appleton-Century-Crofts, Inc., 1928.

———, *Feudal Germany*. Chicago: University of Chicago Press, 1928.

Throop, P., *Criticism of the Crusade*. Amsterdam: Swets & Zeitlinger, 1940.

CHRONOLOGY

1098	Crusaders take Antioch	1193	Death of Saladin
1099	Crusaders take Jerusalem	1195	Ambroise, poetical account of Crusade
1100–1118	Baldwin I, King of Jerusalem		
1122	Concordat of Worms	1202–1204	Fourth Crusade; capture of Constantinople (1204)
1144	Capture of Edessa by Mohammedans		
1145–1153	Pope Eugenius III	1204–1261	Latin Empire of Constantinople
1145	Pope Eugenius III proclaims a crusade	1208/09– 1226/29	Albigensian Crusade
1146	Bernard preaches second Crusade at Vezelay	1209	King John of England excommunicated
1147–1149	Second Crusade	1212	Children's Crusade (Origin of "Pied Piper"?)
1148	Crusaders defeated at Damascus; Normans take Tunis and Tripoli	1213	John submits to Pope; England and Ireland papal fiefs
1154	Seljuks take Damascus	1215	Magna Carta; Fourth Lateran
1160	Normans expelled from North Africa	1218–1221	Fifth Crusade
1174–1176	Saladin conquers Syria	1225	Third and lasting form of Magna Carta
1180–1183	Alexius II Comnenus		
1183	Peace of Constance; recognition of Lombard League	1226–1270	Louis IX, King of France
		1228–1229	Sixth Crusade
1187	Defeat of Latin army; loss of Jerusalem, etc.	1228	Frederick II lands at Acre
1189– 1192/93	Third Crusade	1229	Treaty between Frederick II and Sultan of Egypt; Frederick crowns himself King of Jerusalem
1190	Richard of England and Philip II of France on Third Crusade; Frederick Barbarossa drowned	1248–1254	Seventh Crusade
		1250	Capture of Louis IX
		1254	Louis IX returns to France
1191	Crusaders take Acre	1270	Eighth Crusade; death of Louis IX
1192	Richard captured; truce between Richard and Saladin; Richard to England (1194)	1348	Black Death
		1381	Peasants' Revolt

Great Founders and Leaders of the Orders. *Saints Francis, Benedict, Bernard, Romuald, Thomas Aquinas, and others. Fresco of Fra Angelico, R. Museo di S. Marco, Florence.*

VII

The Maturation of

Monasticism, Mendicancy, and

Mysticism

The Benedictine Rule was originally offered
as a spiritual guide to a small family of voluntary renunciants.
As such, it exhibited remarkable adaptability to
subsequent needs. Its moderation tempted those who adopted it
to flout its spirit in its very observance.
Throughout the ages, it retained a strange
capacity to evoke penitential re-examination and ever
new reformation. Contrasted with the quixotic
sensationalism of some Irish rules, the regimen of St. Benedict was
indeed oriented to realistic progress "in the
school of Christ's service." It was effective only when
its inner loyalties outran any outward urge
to exhibitionist disciplines and accomplishments.

The Benedictines had their share of abortive reformations. Virtually every century saw new perversions of old usages. Fresh graftings were unceasingly made on the parent stem. The chronological listings of typical monastic revivals suggest the poignantly resourceful career of tarnished yet refurbished reformations. Noble failure and renewed dedication characterized Benedictine congregations like those at Aniane, Cluny, and Hirschau. Other orders following the Benedictine Rule included the Camolduli, the Vallombrosians, the Grammontines, the Carthusians, the Cistercians, and the double order of Fontevrault. Many *coenobia* (or communal monasteries) of lesser known but not inferior dedication were traceable in varying degrees to the Benedictine inspiration and regulatory genius.

The developed power of the early medieval regulars found its greatest maturity in Benedictine revivals. The peculiar distinction of the Cluniacs for spiritual innovation and feudal politics has already been indicated. Perusing the more important passages of the original charter prepares one for the irony of Cluny's later denouement. Feudal complications were not avoided. The mother house and the powerful bishop of Rome paced each other in the fateful modification of pristine Benedictinism for the purposes of hierarchy.

Cluny gave the world a memorable lesson in the endlessly variable resourcefulness of Benedictine spirituality. She made of the Benedictine abbot a feudal lord of unprecedented power and magnificence. Obedience to him marked his rise in the mother house and his virtually unchecked absolutism throughout an ever-widening cluster of feudal dependencies. Subservient to the fiat of the mother cloister, these daughter houses exemplified the governmental regularities as well as the liturgical devotion and artistic panoplies so evident in Cluny herself. The Cluniacs in all their grandeur never forgot the respect accorded holy books and the reading of Divine Letters by St. Benedict. Their reputation for worldly grandeur did not include special distinction in scholarship. Their bitterest critics, especially their Benedictine associates, did not overlook Cluniac display in her libraries, her cultic ingeniousness, and the wide travels of her monks. These were noted as collectors of books, *objets d'art,* and architectural innovations. The famous twelfth-century church of the mother abbey was for a long time the pride of the West. Perhaps it helped precipitate a building program at Rome that was consummated in a new basilica for St. Peter's.

The Cluniacs may have studied all too few of the manuscripts they preserved. They were not social planners intent on reclaiming medieval agriculture—as some later Cistercians seemed bent on doing. In all of Cluny's frequently reported worldliness and susceptibility to deterioration, the memory of her early austerities was honored. The constantly reiterated centrality of Benedictine worship was observed. Cluny's glory through the centuries was the developing role of psalmody and liturgical vitality within the Benedictine community.

The Cistercians grounded their return to Benedictine purism in a positive distaste for what they regarded as Cluniac debasement of St. Benedict's intent. This famous argument over the best way of maintaining a virile spirit of renunciation within a flexible constitution was prophetic of Franciscan struggles yet to come. It should not be forgotten that the apparent acerbities of Cistercian and Cluniac contention over spiritual usages were not wholly condemnable as fraternal jealousy. It was at least partly attributable to a laudable concern over the circumstantial ambiguities and controversial validities of mutually cherished family honor. That the accents of liturgical simplicity in the early Cistercians could sound so foreign to the stresses of liturgical rhythm in the later Cluniacs is not entirely owing to the sincerity or dishonesty of either order. The strident protestations of evangelical poverty by the early Cistercians were no more unequivocal than those of the primitive Cluniacs. The social and cultural involvements of the later Cistercians were no less in need of reformation than those of the later Cluniacs. This may or may not be a valid evidence of Dr. Coulton's thesis concerning the cyclic morphology of monastic development. It certainly suggests one generalization. There is trouble ahead for the followers of any rule which places chief emphasis upon spiritual growth in grace, rather than sheerly legalistic observances. Such a community will be at least as susceptible to deterioration from the highest ideal as it will be tantalized by the demands of penitential renewal.

Even sympathetic historians must smile ruefully as they scan the self-righteous broadsides of Cistercian reformers indicting Cluniac decadence. Citeaux's vaunted humility circled back into her own face as a boomerang of pride. Benedict's disquisition, *Degrees of Humility and Pride,* never had a better commentary from proud humility than it received in Bernard's patronizing epistles to his friend Peter the Venerable. Peter must have helped effect many Cluniac purgations simply by enduring Bernard's humble belaborings. Cistercian shame and glory preceded Bernard, even as they outlived him. Robert of Molesme had been evicted by his monks for plaguing them with too much spiritual regularity. He was coerced by their papally abetted pressures into returning to them. They insisted that he share with them his new-found reputation for holiness at Citeaux. Stephen Harding, the Englishman, was to be the real genius in the adaptation of Benedictine resourcefulness to French reformation. Neither Robert, Bernard, nor Stephen deserves central casting in the drama that was played out at Citeaux, Clairvaux, and on many other stages. None of these constituted the Cistercian reform any more than did the rigid ascetics of early Cluny or the latitudinarian abbots of later Benedictinism. The chief potential for spiritual inspiration and perversion emerged, as so often before, from the abiding inexhaustibility of the Rule, itself. Regularly—and quite aside from any pun—the Rule elicited and rebuffed endless variations upon it. It repulsed all attempts to reduce it to a praiseworthy stereotype and to suck it dry into perpetual perfectedness.

The "Charter of Charity" (*Carta Caritatis*) was no less a work of genius than the mystical effusions of Clairvaux's abbot. Out of this valid recreation of old Benedictine customs grew a new pattern of governmental representation. Exemplified in it was an unprecedented sharing by mother and daughter houses of spiritual usages, disciplines, and yearnings. Together, they sought untrammeled spiritual regeneration. Only the hardiest critic would dare assay the full significance of this monastic constitution. Implicit in it was the potency for vigorous cross-fertilizations of medieval, constitutional monarchy. Nor may one presume to do more at this time than hint at the powers of liturgical and architectural reflorescence embodied in Cistercian renunciation. Its apparently restricted range of aesthetic sensibility and liturgical variety have prompted parallels between Cistercians and Puritans. However carefully hedged about, such comparisons are a disservice to both. Each fostered beneath its popular typings a vitality quite escaping the most edifying comparison.

The warm exchanges of Bernard and Peter were both animated and fraternal. There are far more winsome overtures to tolerant understanding in the former than are commonly stressed. Moreover, there are harder inflexibilities in the latter's soft-spoken rejoinders than are usually advertised. In their letters to each other, as in the *Apologia* here sampled, the velvet insistencies as well as the compassionate implacabilities of Benedict and the *Carta Caritatis* are faithfully reflected. Here is documentation in plenty for the quandary encountered throughout Christian history. How may the union of simple piety and dedicated beauty be preserved in the unaffectedness of genuine worship? Shall either disciplined asperities or aesthetic dedications be ruled automatic offenses against liturgical integrity? May either be enshrined as an uncontested winner over the other within the divine government of human variability? What true liturgy can fail to enshrine together the *ascesis* of the worshiper and the beauty of the Holy?

In company with the brilliant coruscations of Cluniac and Cistercian usages, the less colorful legislation of Lanfranc's *Constitutions* and the subtle humor of Jocelin's *Chronicle* may seem out of place. Not so! Perhaps among all the Cluniacs and Cistercians there are few cadences more movingly eloquent than the poetic austerities of the great scholar, teacher, and administrator, Lanfranc. Surely one can appreciate an occasional foil to Bernard's unrelieved sobersidedness in the penetrating sallies of Jocelin's astute reporting. Thomas Carlyle read Jocelin of Brakelond in the Latin. His respectful tributes to the Abbot Samson and his able chronicler are recorded in *Essays Past and Present*. Neither Jocelin nor Carlyle was given to sheer heroics. Both were fascinated by solid character in men and institutions. Jocelin's account transcends the significance of electioneering church politicians. It moves into the very heart of the age-old equilibrium held necessary between Christian contemplation and action.

What one can afford to ponder most seriously in Benedictine "Uses" and their reform penchants underlies each of the noble experiments selected for source reading. Benedict's spiritual descendants followed him in keeping loose-leaf observations on everyday routines. Discipline was fostered under stability of place and service. This *stabilitas loci* was at the heart of the Rule. An antidote was needed for much sarabaitic excess. Some cure had to be found for the doleful restlessness (*accidia*) of professional wanderers (*gyrovagi*). This was right at hand. For irresponsible change of scene and the *grand tour* to relieve *ennui*, Benedict proposed flexibility within stability. Relief from the obvious was not to be found in fleeing the usual. It was discovered in the solid researching of what undergirded and environed externals. Regularity within moderation and stability provided renewal and self-mastery. This was effected within the recreative disciplines of Divine Worship as it reconditioned human resourcefulness.

Yet tied up in the explicit packaging of implicit Benedictine freedom there lurked a nemesis. Contained in it was poison for the Church in a feudal age. Benedict's was a valuable essay—not a mere footnote—on Cassian's remedy for boredom. *Stabilitas loci* and *schola servitia* put Christ's student of the gospel to work as a loyal trooper of the guard. He learned while on regular duty right where he was. This had served very

well as a cure for individualistic, spiritual vagabondage in the sixth century. It played squarely into the hands of static, feudal localism in the twelfth and thirteenth. Keeping one's accustomed place and recapitulating via monastic conversion one's ascent and descent through the twelve degrees of humility and pride had their uses. This regimen might, however, reduce the entire spiritual equilibrium, too readily, to the fixed compound where the monk knelt, read, and labored.

Benedictine stability was not to be replaced by mendicant locomotion any more completely or suddenly than static feudalism was to bow out before urban mobility. Benedictines like Bernard got around quite a bit themselves. Irrevocably and disturbingly, however, the old feudal postulates became reset in the new fluidity of urban social movement. So, too, the earlier Benedictine stability was both blunted and renewed by the brash innovations of Augustinian, Franciscan, and Dominican mobility. The religious vocations were coming to include an increasing number of canons, both regular and secular. There were also the combined military and monastic orders. Everywhere one might encounter not only the noble but also the ridiculous precipitations that go with an age in flux.

The Franciscans had no corner on the ideal of evangelical poverty and spiritual self-giving. Perhaps they talked more about it, in terms more colorfully reminiscent of Jesus' disturbing actions, than did the Benedictines, for instance, or the Dominicans. The *Dominicanes*, almost literally the Lord's "watchdogs," made their main appeal in the name of the disciplined mind. Theirs was a constitution that ultimately rested upon evangelical preaching. Their offering was hardly less a matter of spiritual poverty than that of the Franciscans. The Minorites were scarcely less voluble as preachers than the Dominicans. The Dominicans were not long in dedicating their learning as a form of spiritual renunciation. Francis never actually got over his fright at seeing college professors bob up everywhere. He had a bad-tempered moment when he insinuated that the Lord could surely dispense with books and learned men, if and when it suited Him to do so.

The fact is that Francis was skeptical to the day of his death as to the value of formal education for his followers. He deplored its all-too-frequent display of self-important, patronizing theoretics. As such, it was the very antithesis of spiritual poverty. Nonetheless, the *Poverello* could not have been more responsible than he was for the call to true learning and self-examination as the way to genuine spiritual dedication. Without this intellectual activity, the fullest renunciation of one's total powers to the propagation of God's kingdom on earth as in heaven would have been impossible. The Dominicans knew this well. They had a point in saying that their training of the spirit to preach the gospel was merely another form of the Franciscan gospel of poverty.

Each of the two orders, the Franciscans, or "Friars Minor," and the Dominicans, or "Preachers," promptly began borrowing the other's hallmarks of distinctive emphasis. This happened with such rapidity that it confused the propaganda line of the monastic fraternities, within, as well as the competitive market in spirituality, without. The best that Pope Innocent III had recently been able to do was to inveigh against the hopelessly mounting tide of new orders with a strict dictum. These innovators were to take an already existing rule and adapt it to their specific needs. This satisfied no one, completely; not even the pontiff himself. Somewhat belatedly, he granted Francis oral permission for the limited exercise, in a trial period, of Jesus' highly elastic admonitions in the Sermon on the Mount. These, as Innocent reminded Francis, had never really been designed for such literal application as the "Little Poor Man" envisaged. Francis naïvely turned the pope's sophisticated inference with a sly reminder. The Holy Father would surely be the last to say that Christ's own rule of evangelical poverty was unworkable!

Francis piously implied that he was setting up no order at all—not even a counsel of perfection for anyone. With his own public avowal, he was merely honoring others like himself. He and they insisted on the duty they felt to embrace voluntary, gospel renunciation. This test of wills ended in a stalemate. Francis promised to try things out on a small scale. Innocent granted him the right to try and—as the pope seems privately to have prognosticated—the privilege of failing. In historical post-view the pope has been credited with realistic foresight and virtual endorsement of the *Poverello*. His surprise, had he lived, might have been great at the way in which the "Little Poor Man's" fancy caught the divine action at full tide.

In any event, Francis' poverty idealism from the very first was based on a hard-headed brand of stark realism. This was far removed from the popular identification of him later cherished in the public mind. Almost all of the fondest generalizations harbored by many modern critics and some historians miss the mark widely. He was not a visionary bent on organizing Jesus' literal actions into corporate demands for everybody. He contemplated no foundation to bind any not already committed. The use the hierarchy made of his voluntary association did not break his heart, as Sabatier once thought. Francis, the obedient son of the Church that he was, gladly made Catholic acquiescence to the hierarchy. This was the very evidence of spiritual renunciation that he had observed in Christ's humble descent into the hands of officiating priests at the altar. He insisted no less vigorously, however, in his last spiritual testament, upon the uncompromising character of evangelical poverty. Francis was no fool, even though many lesser men have made sport of the vagaries they erroneously attributed to him. Only in his most exuberant and undisciplined youthful fancies did he confuse true poverty with mere economic dispossession. He never provided a fully balanced critique of insidious wealth. Legend says that he once stowed away aboard a ship to avoid paying passage money. Still, he was more keenly aware than most people of the human temptation to duplicity and self-deception.

Actually, Francis' career of self-renouncing, social ministry was seldom one of antic arts or romantic feyness. He would not have been guilty of inflicting on the birds the modern commentaries usually associated with his preaching to the birds. He was an unreserved Catholic rooted in the Church's doctrines and committed with unrestricted ardor to her liturgy. Sentimental canonizations of him as "the Protestant saint" are possible only from the perspective of ignorance. He was as stubborn a renunciant and as realistic a visionary as most saints and mystics have usually been. He declared the Church's ancient doctrine of Christ's spiritual poverty. He stressed the realistic applicability of Biblical idealism, also the cosmic imminence and veritable inrupting into the present order of the community of God's Kingdom. He declared the Church to be the servant of God's burgeoning eternal society in the last days of the temporal world. The Church had proclaimed all this for a long time—with well-cushioned reservations, to be sure. Francis' stark avowal of it, out of practicing seriousness, startled sophisticated churchmen into common-sense resentment and near repudiation. The hierarchy quickly took the necessary measures to make reasonably safe Francis' reincarnation of old platitudes into new gospel explosiveness. The Church—and the world—never quite got over the salutary jolt thus administered.

Francis did not lay a finger upon the responsible privileges of rich men and ordered society. Nor did he kindle the poor into burning resentment and mordant attack upon holders of property. No stereotyped program was laid down for anyone—not even for those accepting the designation of the Lord's *pusillus grex*, his "little flock." To these, however, and to these alone, he proclaimed via Christ, himself, the glorious regularity of men newly set free. Theirs was the awesome, liberating responsibility, in the last times, of helping to lead all classes through the Church's open doorway into the beckoning eternal community. Is it strange that his watchword of peace in the midst of feudal and precapitalistic chaos was often misinterpreted? Need one be amazed that his sense of already existing comradeship with saints, angels, and all the worthies of the fatherland was startling to most; that his mystic confidence in the divine fellowship

shocked and even repelled some of his matter-of-fact kinsmen and compatriots?

In all of this, the populace sensed a more than passing relevance to Jesus' unconventional conduct. Well-wishers and caviling onlookers became alert to a novel personality in their midst. They began, forthwith, to fashion the legends of his spiritual eccentricity and invulnerability. Layers of plain, wide-eyed hearsay alternated with other tiers of hagiography and interlarded oral tradition to form a new deposit of folklore. Out of this and the creative cycles of vernacular imagery there was to be fabricated the rich tapestry of Giotto's fresco and mural eloquence. On a far different, yet not wholly removed, canvass the sources of Jesus' life and teachings had once begun to take soul and form. The empathetic response of Francis and his followers to their gospel Lord was re-echoed in the popular imagination. The similitude of Francis' life of poverty to Christ's experience of renunciation became a wellspring of vernacular art and literature. There was lasting truth in the exaggerated yet perceptive judgments of this folk sense. Permeating it was a realism that coursed through and beyond pedestrian fact.

Francis penetrated the consciousness of his age and entered into its prevailing moods. Even while re-enforcing the general outlines of the medieval world view, he inserted into its consciousness a freshness of vision that was breathtaking. He did not exploit the suppressed classes for some ulterior revolutionary program. He did remind these "little people," these *minuto populo*, that they, too, together with his own "little brethren," were true *minores*. They were the "least ones" to whom Christ had committed his eternal promises and his everlasting life. Within Francis' brotherhood none must ever be "prior." How could a "minor" ever have "priority"? To attribute downright ownership to a "poor brother" or to have one of these claim it was to evoke a compassionate gaze, perhaps an anguished outburst from the *Poverello*. On one occasion, a naïve brother speculatively touched a piece of money. Francis granted him the singular privilege of depositing it, while clenched between his teeth, on a steaming pile of redolent manure. Perhaps that would give him a protective coating against subliminal temptation!

So the friars broke down privileged *stabilitas* with wide-ranging phalanxes of unprivileged *mobilitas*. With spontaneously deployable regularity, they followed the people where they went. It has been suggested that with the scarcely less flexible Dominicans, the Franciscans exercised the combined functions of canons, monks, and friars. Theirs was the life expectancy of prophets, apostles, and teachers—yes, and of inquisitors! As Catherine of Siena once said of herself, everything that Francis did, he did *upon*, i.e., in terms of, the people. No hope or passion or lust or love of his did he fail to "take out" upon them. They were his life, and he was theirs. They, in turn, vented all that they were upon him. Not even in the later, poetic effusions of the legendary writings called the *Little Flowers*, or *Fioretti*, did Francis move unscathed through the world. In the candidly prosaic, yet imaginatively realistic, reporting of Celano and the *Three Companions*, Francis was forever getting into or out of trouble. Someone was always uncovering a new "poverty addict" reportedly more devoted than he. The *Poverello* was forever bolting forward in seething disbelief, only to check himself, in shamefaced, self-indictment over his pride. Periodically, he was catapulted in reverse from his flimsy, pitifully violated retreat with a cry, "Where's Francis?" and a shattering rejoinder "Why, in his cell!" "Whose cell? Certainly not Francis'." Not *his!* How dared such an acquisitive adjective infringe on his dispossession?

At the last, however, it was the Divinity Himself who finally "took out" everything at once upon poor Francis. Or so, at least, the historically foreshortened but no less prescient spiritual folklore was to insist. And while the ecstasies of Mt. Alvernia were being recorded, Francis was being transfixed with the very wounds of the self-dispossessed Christ himself. These were the Stigmata. His official biographer, Bonaventura, it was claimed, had once been cured in his youth by Francis' miraculous graces. When the learned Minister General wrote his philosophical-mystical treatises, he knew where to place the apex of contemplation. It was here on New Calvary—on Mt. Alvernia.

The story of the Dominicans is not essentially different from that of the Franciscans. Dominic may have been a less colorful, if more scholarly and stable, regular than his minorite contemporary. Yet, it is not accidental that many of the stories one order told about its founder were indignantly claimed by the other for its own. Each saint, it was said, propped up the tottering walls of St. John, Lateran. And what could be truer to the fact than this? Who can prove that Francis and Dominic did or did not meet in the flesh at the Fourth Lateran Council? More important than this by far was a verifiable truth—that their joint vocation was already hovering like a benediction over that assemblage. The Dominicans attested Francis' wedding to Lady Poverty. The Franciscans followed Dominic's sons to Paris, Oxford, Cambridge, and all the corridors of learning. They debated together and, sometimes, turned upon each other. Yet sooner or later each made the other's point in refutation of any who would violate true renunciation. Pope John XXII might welcome Dominican irritations over the Franciscans. Franciscans might blaze out at Dominicans. But who among the Franciscans could wash out the stains of fratricidal bloodshed spilled at the insistence of other Franciscans themselves from the veins of Franciscan poverty zealots?

Still, to the dialectician's halls, and to the prosecuting of heretical depravity, both orders went. Their bloody tracks led up to, and from, these halls of inquisition. They mounted new Alvernias and underwent fresh tortures at the hands of cruel Moslems as from other cross-shadowed infidels. Eventually, from the cudgelings of syllogistic debate there emerged the theologians, the political scientists, and above all, the preachers and missionaries who would convert the new world revealed by inquisition and crusade. From their combined ranks would rise the bulk of those contemplatives who would help record the inward stirrings of godly vision. Bernard of Clairvaux was one of the medieval glories of action and contemplation combined. He was father rather than child of Francis. Subsequently, much of his spirit was reborn in the *Pove-*

rello. Richard of St. Victor was learned beyond anything that his friend Bernard could endorse without reservation. His call was a far cry from Francis' own—or Dominic's, either. Yet Rachel and Leah alternated in Francis' dreams, also. The apex of Richard's fourth degree of violent love was to shake Francis into solitary communion with the Master and out again into social ministry like the Lord's own.

Meister Eckhart, though a Dominican, made some of Francis' points on the self-abnegating love of God as well as, if not better than, the *Poverello* ever did. John Tauler, another Dominican, was proof of the inwardness that no hierarchy could guarantee and that every preacher of the creed must entertain. Catherine of Siena's ambulatory "cell of self-knowledge" was the only domicile in which Francis and Dominic could long bide together in the converse of true learning. Jan van Ruysbroeck's indentification of Christ as the "treadling" in the mystical work entitled the *Sparkling Stone* celebrated one who was none other than the Lord of Francis and Dominic as well. The Flemish contemplative's "common life" had been the Friars' own. From its rich ground all had been sent down into the world's work of vicarious redemption. Such men were the creative improvisers that the church of the crusading era and of the new urbanism most needed. In them contemplation provided a new action at once inward and outward. Action both stimulated and was born of contemplation. The friars spoke a language of heartache and yearning that was the people's own.

I. Benedictine Monasticism and the Maturation of the "Regulars"

A. THE SETTING FOR THE CLUNIAC REVIVAL OF BENEDICTINE "REGULARITY"

1. The Foundation Charter of Cluny

Trans. E. F. Henderson from A. Bruel, *Recueil des Chartes de l'Abbaye de Cluny* (Paris, 1876), in *Select Documents of the Middle Ages* (London: G. Bell and Sons, Ltd., 1896), pp. 330–32.

Therefore be it known to all who live in the unity of the faith and who await the mercy of Christ, and to those who shall succeed them and who shall continue to exist until the end of the world, that, for the love of God and of our Saviour Jesus Christ, I hand over from my own rule to the holy apostles, Peter, namely, and Paul, the possessions over which I hold sway, the town of Cluny, namely, with the court and demesne manor, and the church in honour of St. Mary the mother of God and of St. Peter the prince of the apostles, together with all the things pertaining to it, the vills, indeed, the chapels, the serfs of both sexes, the vines, the fields, the meadows, the woods, the waters and their outlets, the mills, the incomes and revenues, what is cultivated and what is not, all in their entirety. Which things are situated in or about the country of Macon, each one surrounded by its own bounds. I give, moreover, all these things to the aforesaid apostles—I, William, and my wife Ingelberga—first for the love of God; then for the soul of my lord king Odo, of my father and my mother; for myself and my wife—for the salvation, namely, of our souls and bodies; . . . . I give these things, moreover, with this understanding, that in Cluny a regular monastery shall be constructed in honour of the holy apostles Peter and Paul, and that there the monks shall congregate and live according to the rule of St. Benedict, and that they shall possess, hold, have and order these same things unto all time. In such wise, however, that the venerable house of prayer which is there shall be faithfully frequented with vows and supplications, and that celestial converse shall be sought and striven after with all desire and with the deepest ardour; and also that there shall be sedulously directed to God prayers, beseechings and exhortations as well for me as for all, according to the order in which mention has been made of them above. And let the monks themselves, together with all the aforesaid possessions, be under the power and dominion of the abbot Berno, who, as long as he shall live, shall preside over them regularly according to his knowledge and ability. But after his death, those same monks shall have power and permission to elect any one of their order whom they please as abbot and rector, following

Ancien Benedictin de Cluni

VII-1. Ancient Benedictine of Cluny.

the will of God and the rule promulgated by St. Benedict,—in such wise that neither by the intervention of our own or of any other power may they be impeded from making a purely canonical election. . . . It has pleased us also to insert in this document that, from this day, those same monks there congregated shall be subject neither to our yoke, nor to that of our relatives, nor to the sway of the royal might, nor to that of any earthly power. And, through God and all his saints, and by the awful day of judgment, I warn and objure that no one of the secular princes, no count, no bishop whatever, not the pontiff of the aforesaid Roman see, shall invade the property of these servants of God, or alienate it, or diminish it, or exchange it, or give it as a benefice to any one, or constitute any prelate over them against their will.

B. MONASTIC CUSTOMS ACCORDING TO LANFRANC'S CONSTITUTIONS (C. 1080)

2. *Punishment for Careless Handling of the Lord's Body and Blood*

Decreta Lanfranci Monachis Cantauriensibus. Transmissa, Pars II, trans. David Knowles, *The Monastic Constitutions of Lanfranc* [Medieval Classics, gen. ed. V. H. Galbraith and R. A. B. Mynors] (New York: Oxford University Press, Inc., 1951), pp. 90–92. This and Item 3 are reprinted with grateful acknowledgment of permission granted by the original publishers, Thomas Nelson and Sons, Ltd., Edinburgh.

When for any reason there is such carelessness with regard to the body and blood of the Lord that it fall to the ground, or fall in such wise that it cannot be clearly seen where it has fallen, and whether any part of it has fallen to the ground, the matter shall be brought to the notice of abbot or prior as soon as possible, and he taking others with him shall go with speed to the place where the accident has happened. And if the body or blood of the Lord has fallen, or has been spilt, upon a stone or the earth or wood or mat or carpet or anything of that kind, the surface of the earth shall be taken up, that spot in the stone shall be scraped, and the part affected in the wood, matting, carpet or whatever it may be shall be cut out and thrown down the *sacrarium*. If the place where it fell cannot be accurately determined, and yet it is certain that it fell, a like procedure shall be accomplished in and around the spot where it is thought most likely that the particle or drops fell. Those responsible for the carelessness shall humbly beg pardon in the chapter next following; they shall be scourged on the bare flesh, and a penance, either of fasting or abstinence or corporal punishment or prayers or something of the kind shall be laid upon them. When they have returned to their places all the priests present shall rise and devoutly offer themselves for punishment. Then the president of the chapter shall keep seven of them, chosen at his discretion, for punishment, and order the others to be seated. When the chapter is over, all shall prostrate themselves and say the seven penitential psalms in the church, having begun to chant them on leaving the chapter-house; the psalms shall be followed by the *Pater noster* with the following chapters and collect: *Et ueniat super nos misericordia tua, Deus; Ne memineris iniquitatum nostrarum antiquarum; Dominus uobiscum; Oremus: Exaudi, Domine, preces nostras et confitentium tibi parce peccatis, ut quos conscientiae reatus accusat, indulgentia tuae miserationis absoluat,* or the collect *Deus, cui proprium est misereri semper,* or some other for the remission of sins.

If the blood of the Lord shall have fallen upon the corporal or some other clean cloth, and it be quite certain where it fell, that part of the cloth shall be washed in a chalice and the water of the first washing shall be received by the brethren, and that of the two following washings shall be thrown down the *sacrarium.* In the chapter next following, when pardon has been asked, those only who are responsible for the accident shall undergo the punishment set out above, but the brethren shall say in the church all the seven psalms with the chapters and collect as set out. If a death bill has been read that day in chapter they shall first chant the *Verba mea* on their way to the church, and afterwards the seven psalms as aforesaid. If in any other way a less serious accident occur with respect to this Sacrament, the brother responsible shall be punished more lightly at the discretion of the abbot or prior.

3. Community Usages on the Passing of a Sick Brother

Decreta, Pars II, trans. Knowles, *The Monastic Constitutions of Lanfranc,* pp. 122–24.

But if he seem not to be recovering, but rather to be coming nigh to death, as soon as sure indications of this make their appearance he shall never be left without two of the brethren who shall read to him day and night, while his senses remain, the narratives of the Passion and other parts of the gospels. When his senses fail, they shall recite the psalter without ceasing so long as he remains alive. And it shall be so arranged that when two go another pair shall replace them, and they shall say the regular hours there. When the sick man is in his agony and at the very point of death, if God so

wills, then the servant in charge shall unfold a sackcloth and lay on it ashes in the form of a cross from edge to edge of the sackcloth, and set the dying brother thereon. And then he shall sit by him, never leaving him, and watching carefully for the moment to come when he shall let the community know that he is passing.

When he sees him now in the agony of passing, he shall take the board in his hand and run to the door of the cloister and beat the board there with sharp and rapid blows until he is sure the community have heard. When they hear the sound, if they are at the High or Low Mass or a regular hour, a few brethren shall be told to remain in choir with the children and their masters, while all the rest run to the sick man, reciting the *Credo* in an ordinary tone of voice as they go. The brethren who remain, when they have finished the office, shall run in like manner, chanting the *Credo,* to the dying man. Wheresoever else they may be, and whatsoever they are doing when the sound of the alarm reaches them, they shall make no pretext for delay but run to the sick man, chanting the *Credo.* When they get there they shall complete the *Credo* together, and then chant the seven penitential psalms without the *Gloria;* then the priest shall add the chapter, 'Spare, O Lord, spare Thy servant, whom Thou didst deign to redeem with Thy precious blood; be not wroth with him for ever.' This shall be said thrice by the priest, and repeated each time by the whole community; then follows the ordinary litany, which should be prolonged or shortened as the brother's time of passing may demand. If, as sometimes happens, when the litany is finished he be not yet gone, the community shall depart, leaving a few brethren, as ordered, to recite the psalter from the beginning. When the time comes for the community to be recalled, they shall be called and shall come as above.

When the soul has left the body the bells shall be tolled thrice at short intervals, and the cantor shall begin the responsory *Subvenite sancti Dei.* When it is done, with its verse and the repeat, the priest shall add the prayer 'Set forth, O Christian soul.' When that is said they shall begin the commendation of the soul, and when the first collect *Tibi Domine commendamus* has been said the priest and community shall continue with what remains. Meanwhile the corpse shall be taken for washing by those of the same order as the dead man; that is, priests for a priest, deacons for a deacon and so forth, converses for a converse. A child's corpse shall however not be washed by children but by converses.

C. THE ORIGINS AND DEVELOPMENT OF THE CISTERCIAN ORDER (1098)

4. The Regulations of Stephen Harding and the Severity of the Early Order

William of Malmsbury, *Chronicle*, trans. J. A. Giles (London: Bohn, 1847).

In his time [Pope Urban II] began the Cistercian order, which is now both believed and asserted to be the surest road to heaven. To speak of this does not seem irrelevant to the work I have undertaken, since it redounds to the glory of England to have produced the distinguished man who was the author and promoter of that rule. To us he belonged, and in our schools passed the earlier part of his life. . . . He was named Harding, and born in England of no very illustrious parents. From his early years, he was a monk at Sherborne; but when secular desires had captivated his youth, he grew disgusted with the monastic garb, and went first to Scotland, and afterwards to France. Here, after some years' exercise in the liberal arts, he became awakened to the love of God. For, when manlier years had put away childish things, he went to Rome with a clerk who partook of his studies; neither the length and difficulty of the journey, nor the scantiness of their means of subsistence by the way, preventing them, both as they went and returned, from singing daily the whole psalter. Indeed the mind of this celebrated man was already meditating the design which soon after, by the grace of God, he attempted to put in execution. For returning into Burgundy, he was shorn at Molesmes, a new and magnificent monastery. Here he readily admitted the first elements of the order, as he had

VII-2. A Monk of Citeaux.

formerly seen them; but when additional matters were proposed for his observance, such as he had neither read in the rule nor seen elsewhere, he began, modestly and as became a monk, to ask the reason of them, saying, "By reason the supreme Creator has made all things; by reason He governs all things; by reason the fabric of the world revolves; by reason even the planets move; by reason the elements are directed; and by reason, and by due regulation, our nature ought to conduct itself. . . . See then that you bring reason, or at least authority, for what you devise; although no great credit should be given to what is merely supported by human reasons, because it may be combated with arguments equally forcible. Therefore from that rule [of St. Benedict], which, equally supported by reason and authority, appears as if dictated by the spirit

283

of all just persons, produce precedents, which if you fail to do in vain shall you profess his rule, whose regulations you disdain to comply with.". . .

Two of the fraternity, therefore, of equal faith and learning, were elected, who, by vicarious examination, were to discover the intention of the founder's rule; and when they had discovered it, to propound it to the rest. The abbat diligently endeavoured to induce the whole convent to give their concurrence, but . . . almost the whole of them refused to accept the new regulations, because they were attached to the old. Eighteen only, among whom was Harding, otherwise called Stephen, persevering in their holy determination, together with their abbat, left the monastery, declaring that the purity of the institution could not be preserved in a place where riches and gluttony warred against even the heart that was well inclined. They came therefore to Citeaux; a situation formerly covered with woods, but now so conspicuous from the abundant piety of its monks, that it is not undeservedly esteemed conscious of the Divinity Himself. Here, by the countenance of the archbishop of Vienne, who is now pope, they entered on a labour worthy to be remembered and venerated to the end of time.

Certainly many of their regulations seem severe, and more particularly these: they wear nothing made with furs or linen, nor even that finely spun linen garment, which we call Staminium; neither breeches, unless when sent on a journey, which at their return they wash and restore. They have two tunics with cowls, but no additional garment in winter, though, if they think fit, in summer they may lighten their garb. They sleep clad and girded, and never after matins return to their beds: but they so order the time of matins that it shall be light ere the lauds begin; so intent are they on their rule, that they think no jot or tittle of it should be disregarded. Directly after these hymns they sing the prime, after which they go out to work for stated hours. They complete whatever labour or service they have to perform by day without any other light. No one is ever absent from the daily services, or from complines, except the sick.

The cellarer and hospitaller, after complines, wait upon the guests, yet observing the strictest silence. The abbat allows himself no indulgence beyond the others— everywhere present, everywhere attending to his flock; except that he does not eat with the rest, because his table is with the strangers and the poor. Nevertheless, be he where he may, he is equally sparing of food and of speech; for never more than two dishes are served either to him or to his company; lard and meat never but to the sick. From the Ides of September till Easter, through regard for whatever festival, they do not take more than one meal a day, except on Sunday. They never leave the cloister but for the purpose of labour, nor do they ever speak, either there or elsewhere, save only to the abbat or prior. They pay unwearied attention to the canonical services, making no addition to them except the vigil for the defunct. They use in their divine service the Ambrosian chants and hymns, as far as they were able to learn them at Milan. While they bestow care on the stranger and the sick, they inflict intolerable mortifications on their own bodies, for the health of their souls. . . .

But to comprise briefly all things which are or can be said of them—the Cistercian monks at the present day are a model for all monks, a mirror for the diligent, a spur to the indolent.

5. *Stephen Harding and the Charter of Charity* (Carta Caritatis), *c. 1117*

Trans. based on J. M. Canivez, *Statuta Capitulorum Generalium Ordinis Cisterciensis* (Bibliothèque de la Revue d'histoire Ecclésiastique, Louvain, 1933), I, xxvi–xxxi. From *English Historical Documents 1042–1189*, eds. D. C. Douglas and G. W. Greenaway (New York: Oxford University Press, Inc., 1953). Reprinted by permission. Also by permission of Eyre & Spottiswoode (Publishers) Ltd., London. The passage is from the above, volume II, pp. 687–91.

Before the Cistercian abbeys began to flourish, the lord abbot, Stephen, and his monks ordained that abbeys were on no account to be established in the diocese of any bishop prior to his ratification and confirmation of the decree drawn up in writing between the abbey of Cîteaux and its daughter-houses, in order to avoid occasion of offence between the bishop and the monks. In this decree, therefore, the aforesaid brethren, guarding against possible dangers to their mutual peace, have made clear and established and handed down to later generations in what manner and by what agreement, nay rather, with what *love* the monks of their Order, though separated in body in abbeys in divers parts of the world, might be knit together inseparably in spirit. Moreover, they were of opinion that this decree should be called the "Charter of Love," because it casts off the burden of all exactions, pursues love alone and promotes the welfare of souls in things human and divine.

I. Inasmuch as we are known to be servants of the One True King, Lord and Master, albeit unprofitable, we therefore make no claim for worldly advantage of temporal gain on our abbots and brother monks, whom in divers places devotion to God shall call through us, the most wretched of men, to live under regular discipline. For, in our desire for their profit and that of all sons of holy Church, we are not disposed to lay any burden upon them or to effect anything calculated to diminish their substance, lest in striving to grow rich at their expense, we may not escape the sin of avarice, which is declared by the apostle to be servitude to idols.

II. Nevertheless we desire for love's sake to retain the cure of their souls, so that if they shall essay to swerve from their sacred purpose and the observance of the holy Rule —which God forbid—they may through our solicitude return to righteousness of life.

III. We will therefore and command them to observe the Rule of St. Benedict in all things as it is observed in the new monastery. Let the monks put no other interpretation upon the holy Rule but what the holy fathers, our predecessors, namely the monks of the new minster, have understood and maintained; and as we today understand and uphold it, so let them do also.

IV. And inasmuch as we receive in our cloister all the monks of their houses who come to us, and they likewise receive ours in theirs, so it seems good to us and in accordance with our will that they should maintain the customary ceremonial, chants and all books necessary for the canonical offices, both by day and by night, and for the Mass, after the form of the customs and books of the new minster, so that there be no discord in our worship, but that we may all dwell in one love and under one rule and with like customs.

V. No church or person of our Order shall presume to solicit from anyone a privilege contrary to the common customs of the Order, or in any wise retain it, if it has been granted.

VI. When the abbot of the new minster shall come on a visitation to one of these houses, let the abbot of the place recognize the church of the new minster as his mother-church and give place to him in all the precincts of the monastery, and let the visiting abbot take the place of the abbot of that house, so long as he remains there.

VII-3. Brother of the Cistercian Conversi.

VII. Except that he shall not take his meals in the guest-room, but in the refectory with the brethren, that discipline may be preserved, unless the abbot of the house be absent. Likewise let it be done in the case of all abbots of our Order who may chance to come on a visit. But if several shall come at the same time, and the abbot of the house be absent, let the abbot senior in rank take his meals in the guest-room. An exception shall also be made that the abbot of the house shall, even when a greater abbot is present, bless his own novices after the regular term of probation.

VIII. But let the abbot of the new minster be careful not to presume in any wise to conduct or order the affairs of the house he is visiting, or meddle in them, against the will of the abbot or the brethren.

IX. But if he learn that the precepts of the Rule or of our Order are transgressed in the said house, let him be diligent to correct the brethren lovingly, and with the advice and in the presence of the abbot. Even if the abbot be absent, he shall nevertheless correct what he has found wrong therein.

X. Once a year let the abbot of the mother-church visit all the houses of his foundation either in person or through one of his co-abbots. And if he shall visit the brethren more often, let them the more rejoice.

XI. Moreover, let the abbey of Cîteaux be visited by the four primary abbots, namely of La Ferté, Pontigny, Clairvaux and Morimond, together in person on such a day as they may choose, except that appointed for the holding of the annual chapter, unless perchance one of them be prevented by grievous sickness.

XII. When any abbot of our Order shall come to the new minster, let fitting reverence be shown to him; let him occupy the abbot's stall and take his meals in the guest-room if the abbot be absent. But if the abbot be present, let him do none of these things, but let him dine in the refectory. Let the prior of the abbey take charge of its affairs.

XIII. Between abbeys having no direct relationship with each other, this shall be the rule. Let every abbot give place to his co-abbot within the precincts of his monastery, that the saying may be fulfilled, "in honour preferring one another." If two or more abbots shall come to the monastery, the superior in rank shall take precedence of the others. But let them all take their meals together in the refectory, except the abbot of the house, as stated above. But whenever they meet on other occasions, they shall maintain their rank in accordance with the seniority of their abbeys, so, that he whose church is of older foundation, shall take precedence of the others. Whenever they take their seats together, let each humble himself before the others.

XIV. But when any of our churches has by God's grace so increased that it is able to establish a new house, let the two houses maintain the same relationship between them as obtains between us and our brethren, except that they shall not hold an annual chapter among themselves.

XV. But all the abbots of our Order shall without fail attend each year the general chapter at Cîteaux, with the sole exception of those detained by bodily infirmity. The latter, however, ought to appoint a suitable delegate, by whom the reason for their absence may be reported to the chapter. An exception may also be made for those who dwell in distant lands; let them attend at the intervals appointed for them in the chapter. But if, and when, on any other occasion any abbot shall presume to absent himself from our general chapter, let him crave pardon for his fault at the chapter held in the following year; let his absence not be passed over without serious attention being paid to it.

XVI. In this general chapter let the abbots take measures for the salvation of their souls, and if anything in the observance of the holy Rule or of the Order ought to be amended or supplemented, let them ordain it and re-establish the bond of peace and charity among themselves.

XVII. But if any abbot be found remiss in keeping the Rule, or too intent upon worldly affairs or in any way corrupt or wicked, let him be charged with the offence in the chapter, albeit in all charity. Let the accused crave pardon and perform the penance laid on him for his fault. Such a charge, however, may not be brought except by an abbot.

XVIII. If perchance any dispute shall arise between certain abbots, or an offence be charged against one of them so grave as to merit suspension or deposition, the decision of the chapter shall be observed without question.

XIX. But if, by reason of a difference of opinion, the case shall result in discord, the judgment of the abbot of Cîteaux and of those of sounder and more appropriate counsel shall be inflexibly upheld, precaution being taken that none of those personally involved in the case shall take part in the judgment.

XX. Should any church fall into extreme poverty, let the abbot of that house take pains to inform the whole chapter of the fact. Thereupon the abbots, one and all inflamed with an ardent fire of love, shall hasten to relieve that church from its poverty, so far as they are able, out of the resources bestowed upon them by God.

XXI. If any house of our Order become bereft of its abbot, let the abbot of the house from which it sprung, take every care for its governance, until a new abbot shall be elected. Moreover, on the day appointed for the election, let the abbots of the daughter-houses of that house be summoned, and let them and the monks of that house elect an abbot with the advice and assent of the abbot of the mother-house.

XXII. When the house of Cîteaux, the mother of us all, shall be bereft of its abbot, let the four primary abbots, namely those of La Ferté, Pontigny, Clairvaux and Morimond, make provision for it, and let the responsibility for the abbey rest upon them, until a new abbot be elected and appointed.

XXIII. A day having been fixed and named for the election of an abbot of Cîteaux, let a summons be conveyed with at least fifteen days' notice to the abbots of the houses sprung from Cîteaux and to such others as the aforesaid abbots and the monks of Cîteaux shall deem suitable and, being assembled in the name of the Lord, let the abbots and the monks of Cîteaux elect an abbot.

XXIV. It is permissible for any monk to be raised to the office of abbot of the mother-church of our Order, not only those of her daughter-churches, but also, in case of necessity for their abbots to be free to do so. But no member of another Order may be elected abbot, even as it is not permissible for one of us to be appointed to another monastery which is not of our Order.

XXV. Should any abbot beg leave of his father, the abbot of the house from which his own has sprung, to be relieved of the burden of his office on the pretext of his incapacity or through faint-heartedness, let the father-abbot have a care lest he assent to his request too readily and without a reasonable cause and urgent need. But if the necessity be very great, let the father-abbot do nothing in the matter of his own initiative, but let him summon certain other abbots of our Order and by their advice act in the way they have agreed upon.

XXVI. If any abbot become notorious for contempt of the holy Rule or as a transgressor of the Order or an accessory to the faults of the brethren committed to his charge, let the abbot of the mother-church, either in person or through his prior, or in whatever way is more convenient, exhort him on four occasions to mend his ways. But if he will neither suffer correction nor yield of his own accord, let a sufficient number of the abbots of our congregation be gathered together, and let them remove the transgressor of the holy Rule from his office; after which another more worthy of it may be elected by the monks of that church with the advice and goodwill of the greater abbot and in co-operation with the abbots and those who are related to it, as stated above.

XXVII. But if—which God forbid—the deposed abbot or his monks shall be contumacious and rebellious, and will not acquiesce in the sentence, let them be subject to excommunication by the abbot of the mother-church and his co-abbots, and thereafter coerced by him according as he thinks fit and is able.

XXVIII. Arising out of this, should any one of those so condemned come to himself again and desire to arise from the death of the soul and return to his mother, let him be received as a penitent son. For except for this occasion, which should always be avoided as far as possible, let no abbot retain a monk belonging to any other abbot of our Order without his assent; also let none bring his monks to dwell in the house of any other without his permission.

XXIX. In like manner if—which God forbid—the abbots of our Order shall discover that our mother-church of Cîteaux is becoming lukewarm in its sacred purpose, or is departing from the observance of the holy Rule, let them admonish the abbot of that house four times through the four primary abbots, namely those of La Ferté, Pontigny, Clairvaux and Morimond, in the name of the other abbots of the Order, to amend his life and take pains to amend that of others, and let them diligently fulfil in his case the remaining precepts prescribed for the other abbots, when they are intolerant of correction. But if he will not yield of his own accord, they may neither depose him nor condemn him as contumacious, until they come to depose him from his office as an unprofitable steward, either in the general chapter or—if perchance it be already known that the chapter is not due for summons—in another assembly specially convened for the abbots of the daughter-houses of Cîteaux and some of the others; whereupon both the said abbots and the monks of Cîteaux shall take care to elect a suitable abbot in his place. But if the former abbot and the monks of Cîteaux shall contumaciously resist, let them not forbear to strike them with the sword of excommunication.

XXX. Should any such transgressor afterwards come to his senses and, in the desire to save his soul, take refuge in one of our four primary churches, whether at La Ferté, or Pontigny, or Clairvaux, or Morimond, let him be received as an inmate and co-partner in the abbey in accordance with the Rule, until such time as he be justly reconciled with his own church, whereupon he may be restored thither. In the meantime the annual chapter of the abbots shall not be held at Cîteaux, but wheresoever the above-named four abbots shall previously have appointed.

6. Bernard the Cistercian Criticizes Cluniac Usages

Apologia, viii–xiii, trans. G. G. Coulton, *Life in the Middle Ages* (New York: Cambridge University Press, 1930, 1954), IV, pp. 169–74.

I marvel how monks could grow accustomed to such intemperance in eating and drinking, clothing and bedding, riding abroad and building, that, wheresoever these things are wrought most busily and with most pleasure and expense, there Religion is thought to be best kept. For behold! spare living is taken for covetousness, sobriety for austerity, silence for melancholy; while, on the other hand, men rebaptize laxity as "discretion," waste as "liberality," garrulousness as "affability," giggling as "jollity," effeminacy in clothing and bedding as "neatness." . . . Who, in those first days when the monastic Order began, would have believed that monks would ever come to such sloth? . . . Dish after dish is set on the table; and instead of the mere flesh-meat from which men abstain, they receive twofold in mighty fishes. Though thou have eaten thy fill of the first course, yet when thou comest to the second thou shalt seem not even to have tasted the first; for all is dressed with such care and art in the kitchen that, though thou hast swallowed four or five dishes, the first are no hindrance to the last, nor doth satiety lessen thine appetite. . . . For (to say nothing of the rest) who may tell of the eggs alone, in how many ways they are tossed and vexed, how busily they are turned and turned again, beaten to froth or hard-boiled or minced, now fried and now baked, now stuffed and now mixed, or again brought up one by one? . . . What shall I say of water-drinking, when watered wine is on no account admitted? All of us, forsooth, in virtue of our monkish profession, have infirm stomachs, and are justified in not neglecting the Apostle's salutary advice as to "drinking wine"; yet (I know not why) we omit that word "little" wherewith he begins. . . . Men seek for their garments, not the most useful stuff they may find, but the most delicately woven. . . . "Yet," sayest thou, "Religion is not in the dress, but in the heart." Well said. But thou, when thou wilt buy a frock, thou goest from city to city, scourest the markets, searchest the fairs from booth to booth, scannest the merchants' shops, turnest over each man's store, unrollest vast bales of cloth, touchest with thy fingers, bringest close to thine eyes, holdest up to the sunlight, and rejectest whatsoever is seen to be too coarse or too slight; on the other hand, whatsoever taketh thee with its purity and gloss, that thou seekest to buy forthwith at any price: I ask thee, therefore, doest thou this from thy heart, or in mere simplicity? . . . Yet I marvel, since the Rule saith that all faults of the Disciple concern the Master, and our Lord through His prophet threateneth to require the blood of such as die in their sins at the hands of their Pastors—I marvel how our Abbots suffer such things to be done; unless it be perchance (if I may risk the word) that no man confidently rebuketh that wherein he trusteth not himself to be without blame. . . . I lie, if I have not seen an Abbot with a train of sixty horses and more; on seeing such pass by, thou wouldst say that they are not fathers of monasteries but lords of castles, not rulers of souls but princes of provinces. . . .

But these are small things; I will pass on to matters greater in themselves, yet seeming smaller because they are more usual. I say naught of the vast height of your churches, their immoderate length, their superfluous breadth, the costly polishings, the curious carvings and paintings which attract the worshipper's gaze and hinder his attention, and seem to me in some sort a revival of the ancient Jewish rites. Let this pass, however: say that this is done for God's honour. But I, as a monk, ask of my brother monks as the pagan [poet Persius] asked of his fellow-pagans: "Tell me, O Pontiffs" (quoth he) "what doeth this gold in the sanctuary?" So say I, "Tell me, ye poor men" (for I break the verse to keep the sense) "tell me, ye poor (if, indeed, ye be poor), what doeth this gold in *your* sanctuary?" And indeed the bishops have an excuse which monks have not; for we know that they, being debtors both to the wise and the unwise, and unable to excite the devotion of carnal folk by spiritual things, do so by bodily adornments.

But we [monks] who have now come forth from the people; we who have left all the precious and beautiful things of the world for Christ's sake; who have counted but dung, that we may win Christ, all things fair to see or soothing to hear, sweet to smell, delightful to taste, or pleasant to touch—in a word, all bodily delights—whose devotion, pray, do we monks intend to excite by these things? What profit, I say, do we expect therefrom? The admiration of fools, or the oblations of the simple? Or, since we are scattered among the nations, have we perchance learnt their works and do we yet serve their graven images? To speak plainly, doth the root of all this lie in covetousness, which is idolatry, and do we seek not profit, but a gift? If thou askest: "How?" I say: "In a strange fashion." For money is so artfully scattered that it may multiply; it is expended that it may give increase, and prodigality giveth birth to plenty: for at the very sight of these costly yet marvellous vanities men are more kindled to offer gifts than to pray. Thus wealth is drawn up by ropes of wealth, thus money bringeth money; for I know not how it is that, wheresoever more abundant wealth is seen, there do men offer more freely. Their eyes are feasted with relics cased in gold, and their purse-strings are loosed. They are shown a most comely image of some saint, whom they think all the more saintly that he is the more gaudily painted. Men run to kiss him, and are invited to give; there is more admiration for his comeliness than veneration for his sanctity. Hence the church is adorned with gemmed crowns of light—nay, with lustres like cartwheels, girt all round with lamps, but no less brilliant with the precious stones that stud them. Moreover we see candelabra standing like trees of massive bronze, fashioned with marvellous subtlety of art, and glistening no less brightly with gems than with the lights they carry. What, think you, is the purpose of all this? The compunction of penitents, or the admiration of beholders? O vanity of vanities, yet no more vain than insane! The church is resplendent in her walls, beggarly in her poor; she clothes her stones in gold, and leaves her sons naked; the rich man's eye is fed at the expense of the indigent. The curious find their delight here, yet the needy find no relief. Do we not revere at least the images of the Saints, which swarm even in the inlaid pavement whereon we tread? Men spit oftentimes in an Angel's face; often, again, the countenance of some Saint is ground under the heel of a passer-by. And if he spare not these sacred images, why not even the fair colours? Why dost thou make that so fair which will soon be made so foul? Why lavish bright hues upon that which must needs be trodden under foot? What avail these comely forms in places where they are defiled with customary dust? And, lastly, what are such things as these to you poor men, you monks, you spiritual folk? Unless perchance here also ye may answer the poet's question in the words of the Psalmist: "Lord, I have loved the habitation of Thy House, and the place where Thine honour dwelleth." I grant it, then, let us suffer even this to be done in the church; for, though it be harmful to vain and covetous folk, yet not so to the simple and devout. But in the cloister, under the eyes of the Brethren who read there, what profit is there in those ridiculous monsters, in that marvellous and deformed comeliness, that comely deformity? To what purpose are those unclean apes, those fierce lions, those monstrous centaurs, those half-men, those striped tigers, those fighting knights, those hunters winding their horns? Many bodies are there seen under one head, or again, many heads to a single body. Here is a four-footed beast with a serpent's tail; there, a fish with a beast's head. Here again the forepart of a horse trails half a goat behind it, or a horned beast bears the hinder quarters of a horse. In short, so many and so marvellous are the varieties of divers shapes on every hand, that we are more tempted to read in the marble than in our books, and to spend the whole day in wondering at these things rather than in meditating the law of God. For God's sake, if men are not ashamed of these follies, why at least do they not shrink from the expense?

The abundance of my matter suggested much more for me to add; but from this I am distracted both by my own anxious business and by the too hasty departure of Brother Oger [the bearer of this letter]. . . . This is my opinion of your Order and mine; nor can any man testify more truly than you, and those who know me as you do, that I am wont to say these things not about you but to your faces. What in your Order is laudable, that I praise and publish abroad; what is reprehensible, I am wont to persuade you and my other friends to amend. This is no detraction, but rather attraction: wherefore I wholly pray and beseech you to do the same by me. Farewell.

D. AN ACCOUNT OF DAILY LIFE IN A
TWELFTH-CENTURY MONASTERY,
BURY SAINT EDMUND

7. How Electioneering Monks Talked out of Turn

Chronica Jocelini de Brakelonda, trans. H. E. Butler, *The Chronicle of Jocelin of Brakelond* (New York: Oxford University Press, Inc., 1949), pp. 11–15. This passage and Item 8 from the foregoing work [Medieval Texts, gen. eds. V. H. Galbraith and R. A. B. Mynors] is reprinted with grateful acknowledgment of permission granted by the original publishers, Thomas Nelson and Sons, Ltd., Edinburgh.

While the abbacy was vacant, we often besought God and his holy martyr, St. Edmund, as was meet and right, to give us a fitting shepherd for our Church, thrice every week prostrating ourselves in the choir after leaving the chapter house, and singing the seven penitential psalms; and some there were who, if they had known who was to be our Abbot, would not have prayed so devoutly. As to the choice of an Abbot, should the King grant us a free election, divers persons spoke in divers manners, some in public, some in private, and every man had his own opinion. And one said of another, 'That brother is a good monk, a person worthy of approval: he knows much concerning the Rule and the customs of the Church; though he be not so perfect a philosopher as certain others he might well fill the office of Abbot. Abbot Ording was an illiterate man, and yet he was a good Abbot and ruled this house wisely; moreover, we read in the Fables that it proved better for the frogs to choose a log for their king, in whom they could trust, than a serpent who hissed venomously and after hissing devoured his subjects.' To this another made answer, 'How may that be? How can he, a man who has no knowledge of letters, preach a sermon in Chapter, or on feast days to the people? How shall he who does not understand the Scriptures, have knowledge how to bind and how to loose? seeing that "the rule of souls is the art of arts and the science of sciences." God forbid that a dumb image should be set up in the Church of St. Edmund, where it is known that there are many men of learning and of industry.' Again another said of yet another, 'That brother is literate, eloquent and prudent, strict in his observance of the Rule; he has greatly loved the Convent, and has endured many ills for the possessions of the Church; he is worthy to be made Abbot.' And another replied, 'From all good clerks, O Lord deliver us; that it may please Thee to preserve us from all Norfolk barrators, we beseech Thee to hear us.' Again one said of a certain brother, 'That brother is a good manager, as is proved by the performance of his tasks and by the offices that he has filled so well, and the buildings and repairs that he has made. He knows how to work hard and to defend our house, and he is something of a clerk, though "much learning maketh him not mad." He is worthy to be Abbot.' The other made answer, 'God forbid that a man who cannot read or sing or celebrate the holy offices, a wicked man and unjust, a flayer of the poor—God forbid that such an one should be made Abbot!' Again a certain brother said of someone, 'that brother is a kindly man, affable and amiable, peaceful and composed, bountiful and generous, a literate man and eloquent, a very proper man in aspect and bearing, who is loved by many both within and without. And such a man, God willing, might be made Abbot to the great honour of the Church.' The other made answer, 'Nay; it would be an onus rather than an honour to have such a man; for he is over nice about his food and drink, thinks it a virtue to sleep long, knows how to spend much and gain little, snores when others keep vigil, would always be in the midst of abundance and gives no thought to the debts that grow from day to day, nor to the expenditure, how it may be met; hating

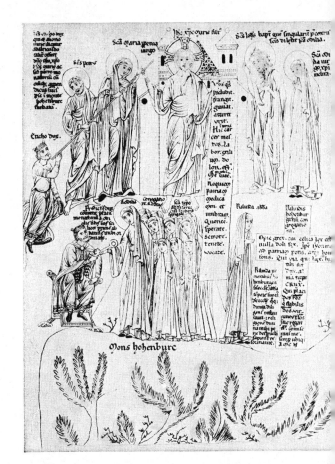

VII-4. Duke Eticho Founds the Monastery of Hohenburg. *The Duke, St. Peter, the Virgin, and Christ. Nuns of the Congregation, the Abbess, etc.* Hortus Deliciarum.

all toil and anxiety and caring for naught, provided that one day go and another come, —a man that loves and cherishes flatterers and liars, and himself says one thing and does another. From such a ruler may the Lord defend us!' Again one said of his comrade, 'That man is wiser almost than any of us, both in the things of the world and the things of the Church: a man of great wisdom, strict in observance of the Rule, literate and eloquent and personable in bearing. Such a ruler would beseem our Church.' Another replied, 'True, if only he were of sound and approved repute. But his reputation is deemed unsound, perhaps truly, perhaps falsely. And though he be a wise man, humble in Chapter, devout in the singing of

Psalms, and strict in the cloister, while he is in cloister, yet, if he chances to hold any office, he is apt to be disdainful, scorning monks and loving men of the world more than he should; and if he should happen to be angry, he will not say a word in answer to any of the brethren, not even if he be asked a question.' And in truth I heard another brother condemned by certain persons, because he had an impediment in his speech, wherefore it was said of him that he had draff or paste in his mouth, when he was called upon to speak. And I indeed, being a young man, 'understood as a child and spoke as a child,' and I said that I would not agree to any man being made Abbot, unless he knew something of dialectic and could distinguish between false argument and true. Again another, who thought himself wise, said, 'May God Almighty give us for our shepherd one who is a fool and ignorant, so that he will have to ask us to help him!' And I heard indeed that a certain man who was industrious and literate and of noble birth, was condemned by certain of our seniors because he was a novice, while the novices said of the seniors that they were decrepit old men, unfit to rule the Abbey. And so, many men said many things, and each of them 'was fully persuaded in his own mind.' I once saw Samson the sub-sacrist sitting by at gatherings of this kind at the time of blood-letting, when the cloister monks are wont to reveal the secrets of their hearts, each to each, and to confer with one another—I saw him sitting by and smiling, without a word, and noting the words of each; and I heard him repeat some of the aforesaid opinions after twenty years had passed. And as he listened, I used to reply to those who passed judgment after this fashion, saying that if we had to wait to elect an Abbot until we found someone who was free of all blame and without spot, we should never find such an one, since no one lives wholly without censure, and 'naught is in all things blest.' On one occasion I could not contain my spirit, but blurted out what I thought, thinking that I spoke to faithful ears, and I said that a certain brother was unworthy to be Abbot, though he had loved me and conferred many benefits upon me;

and said I thought another worthy to be made Abbot, and named a man whom I loved less. And behold! one of the sons of Belial revealed what I had said to my benefactor and friend: for which cause to this very day I have never either by prayer or gift been able to recover his favour to the full. What I have said I have said, and

The word once spoken flieth past recall.

One thing remains, that for the future I should be on my guard and, if I live long enough to see the abbacy vacant once again, I shall take care what I say on the matter, and to whom and when I say it, lest I should offend God by lying or man by speaking out of season. It will, however, if I last till then, be my counsel that we should choose one who is not too good a monk or too good a clerk, nor yet too ignorant or too weak, lest, if he know too much, he should be too confident in himself and his opinions and disdain others, or, if he be too stupid, should be a reproach to the rest of us. I know who said 'The middle way is safest,' and 'How blest are they who hold the middle path.' Or perhaps it will be wiser to say nothing at all, so that I may say in my heart, 'He that is able to receive, let him receive it.'

8. The Balance of Contemplation and Action in the Administration of Abbot Samson

Chronica, trans. Butler, *The Chronicle of Jocelin of Brakelond*, pp. 39–41.

Abbot Samson was of middle height, and almost entirely bald; his face was neither round nor long, his nose prominent, his lips thick, his eyes clear as crystal and of penetrating glance; his hearing of the sharpest; his eyebrows grew long and were often clipped; a slight cold made him soon grow hoarse. On the day of his election he was forty-seven years old, and had been a monk for seventeen. He had a few white hairs in a red beard and a very few in the hair of his head, which was black and rather curly; but within fourteen years of his election he was white as snow. He was a man of extreme sobriety, never given to sloth, extremely strong and ever ready to go either on horse-

VII-5. The Cistercian Abbey of Fontenay, 13th Century. *Left to right: church, cloister, dormitory, refectory, mill, forge, etc.*

back or on foot, until old age prevailed and tempered his eagerness. When he heard of the capture of the Cross and the fall of Jerusalem, he began to wear drawers of haircloth, and a shirt of hair instead of wool, and to abstain from flesh and meat; none the less he desired that meat should be placed before him when he sat at table, that so our alms might be increased. He preferred fresh milk and honey and the like to any other food. He hated liars and drunkards and wordy fellows, since virtue loves itself and hates its opposite. He condemned those who murmur at their food and drink, especially if they were monks, and preserved the old way of life that he had followed as a cloister monk; but he had this virtue, that he never liked to have a dish changed when it had once been placed before him. When I was a novice, I wished to try if this were true and, chancing to be a server in the refectory, I thought in my heart that I would place before him a dish, which displeased all the rest, on a platter that was very black and broken. And when he saw this, he was as one that saw not. But after a time I repented that I had done this, and forthwith seizing the platter, I changed both dish and platter for the better and carried them away; but he was angry and vexed and took the improvement ill. He was eloquent both in French and Latin, having re-

gard rather to the sense of what he had to say than to ornaments of speech. He read English perfectly, and used to preach in English to the people, but in the speech of Norfolk, where he was born and bred, and to this end he ordered a pulpit to be set up in the church for the benefit of his hearers and as an ornament to the church. The Abbot seemed also to love the active life better than the contemplative; he had more praise for good obedientiaries than for good cloister monks; and rarely did he approve of any man solely for his knowledge of literature, unless he were also wise in worldly affairs. And when he heard of any prelate that he grew faint beneath the burden of his pastoral cares and turned anchorite, he did not praise him for so doing.

II. Franciscan Renunciation and Apostolic Poverty

9. *Francis and the Official Rule of 1223*

Bullarium Romanum, III, i, 229ff., trans. *ThM*, No. 269, pp. 499–504.

1. This is the rule and life of the Minor Brothers, namely, to observe the holy gospel of our Lord Jesus Christ by living in obedience, in poverty, and in chastity. Brother Francis promises obedience and reverence

VII-6. Pope Innocent III Approving Francis'
Rule. *Giotto, Upper Church of St. Francis.*

to pope Honorius and to his successors who
shall be canonically elected, and to the
Roman Church. The other brothers are
bound to obey brother Francis, and his successors.

2. If any, wishing to adopt this life, come
to our brothers [to ask admission], they
shall be sent to the provincial ministers, who
alone have the right to receive others into
the order. The provincial ministers shall
carefully examine them in the catholic faith
and the sacraments of the church. And if
they believe all these and faithfully confess
them and promise to observe them to the
end of life, and if they have no wives, or if
they have wives, and the wives have either
already entered a monastery, or have received permission to do so, and they have
already taken the vow of chastity with the
permission of the bishop of the diocese [in
which they live], and their wives are of
such an age that no suspicion can rise
against them, let the provincial ministers
repeat to them the word of the holy gospel,
to go and sell all their goods and give to the

poor [Matt. 19:21]. But if they are not able
to do so, their good will is sufficient for
them. And the brothers and provincial ministers shall not be solicitous about the temporal possessions of those who wish to enter
the order; but let them do with their possessions whatever the Lord may put into
their minds to do. Nevertheless, if they ask
the advice of the brothers, the provincial
ministers may send them to God-fearing
men, at whose advice they may give their
possessions to the poor. Then the ministers
shall give them the dress of a novice,
namely: two robes without a hood, a girdle,
trousers, a hood with a cape reaching to the
girdle. But the ministers may add to these if
they think it necessary. After the year of
probation is ended they shall be received
into obedience [that is, into the order], by
promising to observe this rule and life forever. And according to the command of the
pope they shall never be permitted to leave
the order and give up this life and form of
religion. For according to the holy gospel
no one who puts his hand to the plough and
looks back is fit for the kingdom of God
[Luke 9:62]. And after they have promised
obedience, those who wish may have one
robe with a hood and one without a hood.
Those who must may wear shoes, and all the
brothers shall wear common clothes, and
they shall have God's blessing if they patch
them with coarse cloth and pieces of other
kinds of cloth. But I warn and exhort them
not to despise nor judge other men who
wear fine and gay clothing, and have deli-
cious foods and drinks. But rather let each
one judge and despise himself.

3. The clerical brothers shall perform
the divine office according to the rite of the
holy Roman church, except the psalter, from
which they may have breviaries. The lay
brothers shall say 24 Paternosters at matins,
5 at lauds, 7 each at primes, terces, sexts,
and nones, 12 at vespers, 7 at completorium,
and prayers for the dead. And they shall
fast from All Saints' day [November 1] to
Christmas. They may observe or not, as they
choose, the holy Lent which begins at
epiphany [January 6] and lasts for 40 days,
and which our Lord consecrated by his holy
fasts. Those who keep it shall be blessed of

the Lord, but those who do not wish to keep it are not bound to do so. But they shall all observe the other Lent [that is, from Ash-Wednesday to Easter]. The rest of the time the brothers are bound to fast only on Fridays. But in times of manifest necessity they shall not fast. But I counsel, warn, and exhort my brothers in the Lord Jesus Christ that when they go out into the world they shall not be quarrelsome or contentious, nor judge others. But they shall be gentle, peaceable, and kind, mild and humble, and virtuous in speech, as is becoming to all. They shall not ride on horseback unless compelled by manifest necessity or infirmity to do so. When they enter a house they shall say, "Peace be to this house." According to the holy gospel, they may eat of whatever food is set before them.

4. I strictly forbid all the brothers to accept money or property either in person or through another. Nevertheless, for the needs of the sick, and for clothing the other brothers, the ministers and guardians may, as they see that necessity requires, provide through spiritual friends, according to the locality, season, and the degree of cold which may be expected in the region where they live. But, as has been said, they shall never receive money or property.

5. Those brothers to whom the Lord has given the ability to work shall work faithfully and devotedly, so that idleness, which is the enemy of the soul, may be excluded and not extinguish the spirit of prayer and devotion to which all temporal things should be subservient. As the price of their labors they may receive things that are necessary for themselves and the brothers, but not money or property. And they shall humbly receive what is given them, as is becoming to the servants of God and to those who practise the most holy poverty.

6. The brothers shall have nothing of their own, neither house, nor land, nor anything, but as pilgrims and strangers in this world, serving the Lord in poverty and humility, let them confidently go asking alms. Nor let them be ashamed of this, for the Lord made himself poor for us in this world. This is the highest pitch of poverty which has made you, my dearest brothers, heirs and kings of the kingdom of heaven, which has made you poor in goods, and exalted you in virtues. Let this be your portion, which leads into the land of the living. Cling wholly to this, my most beloved brothers, and you shall wish to have in this world nothing else than the name of the Lord Jesus Christ. And wherever they are, if they find brothers, let them show themselves to be of the same household, and each one may securely make known to the other his need. For if a mother loves and nourishes her child, how much more diligently should one nourish and love one's spiritual brother? And if any of them fall ill, the other brothers should serve them as they would wish to be served.

7. If any brother is tempted by the devil and commits a mortal sin, he should go as quickly as possible to the provincial minister, as the brothers have determined that recourse shall be had to the provincial ministers for such sins. If the provincial minister is a priest, he shall mercifully prescribe the penance for him. If he is not a priest, he shall, as may seem best to him, have some priest of the order prescribe the penance. And they shall guard against being angry or irritated about it, because anger and irritation hinder love in themselves and in others.

8. All the brothers must have one of their number as their general minister and servant of the whole brotherhood, and they must obey him. At his death the provincial ministers and guardians shall elect his successor at the chapter held at Pentecost, at which time all the provincial ministers must always come together at whatever place the general minister may order. And this chapter must be held once every three years, or more or less frequently, as the general minister may think best. And if at any time it shall be clear to the provincial ministers and guardians that the general minister is not able to perform the duties of his office and does not serve the best interests of the brothers, the aforesaid brothers, to whom the right of election is given, must, in the name of the Lord, elect another as general minister. After the chapter at Pentecost, the provincial ministers and guardians may, each in his own province, if it seems best to

them, once in the same year, convoke the brothers to a provincial chapter.

9. If a bishop forbids the brothers to preach in his diocese, they shall obey him. And no brother shall preach to the people unless the general minister of the brotherhood has examined and approved him and given him the right to preach. I also warn the brothers that in their sermons their words shall be chaste and well chosen for the profit and edification of the people. They shall speak to them of vices and virtues, punishment and glory, with brevity of speech, because the Lord made the word shortened over the earth [Rom. 9:28].

10. The ministers and servants shall visit and admonish their brothers and humbly and lovingly correct them. They shall not put any command upon them that would be against their soul and this rule. And the brothers who are subject must remember that for God's sake they have given up their own wills. Wherefore I command them to obey their ministers in all the things which they have promised the Lord to observe and which shall not be contrary to their souls and this rule. And whenever brothers know and recognize that they cannot observe this rule, let them go to their ministers, and the ministers shall lovingly and kindly receive them and treat them in such a way that the brothers may speak to them freely and treat them as lords speak to, and treat, their servants. For the ministers ought to be the servants of all the brothers. I warn and exhort the brothers in the Lord Jesus Christ to guard against all arrogance, pride, envy, avarice, care, and solicitude for this world, detraction, and murmuring. And those who cannot read need not be anxious to learn. But above all things let them desire to have the spirit of the Lord and his holy works, to pray always to God with a pure heart, and to have humility, and patience in persecution and in infirmity, and to love those who persecute us and reproach us and blame us. For the Lord says, "Love your enemies, and pray for those who persecute and speak evil of you" [cf. Matt. 5:44]. "Blessed are they who suffer persecution for righteousness' sake, for theirs is the kingdom of heaven" [Matt. 5:10]. He that endureth to the end shall be saved [Matt. 10:22].

11. I strictly forbid all the brothers to have any association or conversation with women that may cause suspicion. And let them not enter nunneries, except those which the pope has given them special permission to enter. Let them not be intimate friends of men or women, lest on this account scandal arise among the brothers or about brothers.

12. If any of the brothers shall be divinely inspired to go among Saracens and other infidels they must get the permission to go from their provincial minister, who shall give his consent only to those who he sees are suitable to be sent. In addition, I command the ministers to ask the pope to assign them a cardinal of the holy Roman church, who shall be the guide, protector, and corrector of the brotherhood, in order that, being always in subjection and at the feet of the holy church, and steadfast in the catholic faith, they may observe poverty, humility, and the holy gospel of our Lord Jesus Christ, as we have firmly promised to do. Let no man dare act contrary to this confirmation. If anyone should, etc.

10. Francis' Last Will and Spiritual Testament of 1226

Bull. Rom., III, i, 231ff., trans. ThM, No. 270, pp. 504–7.

1. While I was still in my sins, the Lord enabled me to begin to do penance in the following manner: It seemed to me bitterly unpleasant to see lepers, but the Lord led me among them and gave me pity for them. And when I left them, that which had been bitter to me was turned into sweetness of soul and body. And a short time afterward I left the world [that is, began the religious life].

2. And the Lord gave me such faith in churches that I knelt in simplicity and said, "We adore thee, most holy Lord Jesus Christ, and all thy churches which are in the world, and we bless thee because thou hast redeemed the world through thy holy cross."

3. Afterward the Lord gave, and still gives me, such faith in priests who live according to the form of the holy Roman church, because of their clerical character, that if they should persecute me I would still have recourse to them. And if I were as

VII-7. Allegory of St. Francis' Betrothal to Lady Poverty. *Giotto, Lower Church of St. Francis.*

wise as Solomon and should find a poor priest in this world, I would not preach against his will in his church. And I wish to fear, love, and honor all priests as my lords. I am unwilling to think of sins in them, because I discern in them the Son of God, and they are my lords. And on this account, I wish to perceive in this world nothing of the most high Son of God except his most holy body and his most holy blood which they [the priests] receive in the sacraments, and they alone administer to others.

4. And these most holy mysteries I wish to honor and venerate above all things, and to put them up in honorable places.

5. And his most holy names and words, wherever I shall find them, in improper places, I wish to collect, and I ask that they be collected and put up in honorable places.

6. We ought to honor and venerate all theologians, who minister to us the divine word, as those who minister to us the spirit of life.

7. And afterward the Lord gave me brothers [that is, followers], and no one showed me what I ought to do, but the Lord himself revealed to me that I ought to live according to the form of the holy gospel, and I caused it to be written in a few simple words.

8. And the pope confirmed the rule. And those who came to adopt this life gave all they had to the poor. And we were content with one robe, mended within and without, and those who wished had a girdle and trousers.

9. We said the office as other clergymen, the laymen said Paternosters, and we gladly remained in the churches and we were simple and obedient.

10. And I labored with my hands, and I wish to labor. And I wish all my brothers to engage in some honest work. And those who do not know how, shall learn; not because of the desire to receive wages for their labor, but to set a good example and to escape idleness.

11. And when the wages for our labors are not given us, let us go to the table of the Lord and ask alms from door to door.

12. The Lord revealed to me this salutation that we should use it: "May the Lord give thee peace."

13. The brothers shall guard against receiving the churches and dwellings which are built for us, unless, as becomes the holy poverty which we have promised to observe in our rule, they always live there as pilgrims and strangers.

14. By their oath of obedience I firmly

forbid the brothers, wherever they are, to ask for a letter from the papal court, either themselves or through another, in order to secure a church or any position, either in the hope of securing a place to preach, or because of persecution which they may suffer. But wherever they shall not be received, they shall flee to another place to do penance with the blessing of the Lord.

15. And I earnestly wish to obey the general minister of this brotherhood, and that guardian whom he may put over me. And I wish to be so entirely in his hands and so subject to his control that I cannot go, or do anything, contrary to his will, because he is my lord.

16. And although I am simple and infirm, I wish always to have a clergyman who may perform the office for me as is contained in the rule. And all other brothers are bound by their oaths to obey the guardians, and perform the office according to the rule.

17. And if any do not perform the office according to the rule, but wish to change it in some way, or if there are any who are not catholic, all the brothers are bound by their oath of obedience to report all such, wherever they may find them, to the nearest guardian. And the guardian must watch them night and day, as a man in chains, so that they cannot escape, until he delivers them into the hands of the general minister. And the general minister shall send them with brothers who shall guard them night and day, as a man in chains, until they deliver them to the cardinal bishop of Ostia, who is the protector and corrector of this brotherhood.

18. And the brothers shall not say that this is another rule, because it is only a reminder, an admonition, an exhortation, and my testament, which I, your poor brother, Franciscus, make for you, my dear brothers, that we wholly observe the rule which we have promised to the Lord.

19. And the general minister and all the other ministers and guardians are bound by their oath of obedience not to add to, or take from, these words. But they shall always have this writing in addition to the rule, and in all the chapters when they read the rule they shall also read this. I strictly forbid all the brothers, clerical and lay, to put glosses

[explanations] into the rule or this testament in order to change the simple meaning of their words. But as the Lord enabled me to say and to write the rule and these words simply and plainly, so you shall understand them simply and plainly and without gloss. And with holy works you shall observe them to the end.

20. And whoever shall observe them shall be filled in heaven with the blessing of the most high heavenly Father, and in the earth he shall be filled with the benedictions of His Son, with the most holy Spirit, the Paraclete, and with all the virtues of heaven and of all the saints. And I, your poor brother and servant, Franciscus, as far as I can, confirm to you, within and without, that most holy benediction. Amen.

III. Western Mysticism and Its Maturation of the Contemplative Tradition

A. BERNARD OF CLAIRVAUX (1090–1153) AND THE DIVINE ELICITATION

11. The Soul Seeking God Is Anticipated by Him

(*Cantica Canticorum* 3:1, Serm. 84, trans. S. J. Eales, *Cantica Canticorum, Eighty-Six Sermons on the Song of Solomon* (London: Elliot Stock, 1895), pp. 511–15.

It is a great good to seek God. I think that, among all the blessings of the soul, there is none greater than this. It is the first of the gifts of God; the last degree of the soul's progress. By no virtue is it preceded; to none does it give place. To what virtue is that added which is not preceded by any? And to which should that give way which is the consummation of all virtues? For what virtue can be ascribed to him who is not seeking God, or what limit prescribed to one who is seeking him? *Seek his face evermore,* says the psalmist; nor do I think that when a soul has found him, it will cease from seeking. God is sought, not by the movement of the feet, but by the desires of the heart; and when a soul has been so happy as to find him, that sacred desire is not extinguished, but, on the contrary, is increased. Is the consummation of the joy the extinction of the desire? It is rather to it as oil poured upon a flame; for desire is, as it were, a flame. This is, indeed, the case. The joy will be fulfilled; but the fulfilment will not be the ending of the desire, nor therefore of the seeking. But think, if you can, of this earnest love of seeking God as being without any deprivation of him, and of the desire for him as without anxiety or trouble of mind. His presence excludes the one, and the abundance of his graces prevents the other.

2. But now observe why I have made these introductory remarks. It is that every soul among you that is seeking God should know that it has been anticipated by him, and has been sought by him before it began to seek him. For without this knowledge it might be that out of a great blessing might arise great harm, if, when it has been filled with the good gifts of the Lord, it treats those gifts as if they had not been received from him, and so does not render to God the glory of them. It is, doubtless, in this way that some who appeared very great before men, because of the graces which had been conferred upon them, were counted as the least before God, inasmuch as they did not render back to him the glory which was due on their account. But in saying this I have used inadequate terms. To spare you, I have spoken of "greatest" and of "least," but I have not thus expressed my thought in all its force. I will make clearer the distinction which I have tried to mark. I ought to have said that he who is the best of men becomes in this way the worst. For it is a thing certain and without doubt that such a person becomes as blamable as he before was praiseworthy, if he ascribe to himself the praise of that which was excellent in him. For this is one of the worst of crimes. Someone will perhaps say, "God forbid that I should be of that mind; I fully recognize that by the grace of God I am what I am; but suppose that a person should try to take for himself a little spark of glory for the grace that he has received, is he, therefore, a thief and a robber?" Let one who speaks thus listen to the words: *Out of thine own mouth will I judge thee, thou wicked servant.* For what can be more wicked than the servant usurping to himself the glory which belongs to his Lord?

3. *By night on my bed I sought him whom my soul loveth.* The soul seeks the Word, but it had been previously sought by the Word. For otherwise, when it had been once driven out or cast forth from the presence of the Word, it would have returned no more to obtain the sight of the good things it had lost if it had not been sought by the Word. Our soul, if abandoned to itself, is a spirit which goes to and fro, but does not return. Listen to a fugitive and wandering soul, and learn what it complains of, and what it seeks: *I have gone astray like a lost sheep: seek thy servant.* O man, dost thou desire to return? But if that depends upon thy own will, why dost thou entreat help? Why dost thou ask for from another what thou hast in abundance in thy own self? It is plain that he does desire this, and is not able to perform it; he is a spirit which goes to and fro, and returns not; though he who has not even the wish to return is farther removed still. Yet I would not say that the soul which longs to return, and desires to be sought, is wholly exposed and abandoned. For from whence comes this willingness which is in it? It comes, if I do not mistake, from its having been already sought and visited by the Word; nor is that visitation fruitless, since it has so worked in the soul as to produce that good will without which a return would not be possible. But it does not suffice to be sought once only, so great is the langour of the soul, and so great the difficulty of the return. What if the will of a soul is to return? The will lies inoperative if it be not supported by the power to do so. For, *To will is present with me,* says the apostle, *but how to perform that which is good I find not.* What is it, then, that the psalmist seeks in the passage that I have quoted? He plainly seeks nothing else than to be sought: which he would not seek if he had not been sought; and yet again, which he would not seek if he had been sought sufficiently. This latter grace, indeed, is what he entreats: *Seek thy servant;* that is, that what it has been granted to him to desire it may be granted to him also perfectly to attain, according to the good pleasure of God.

4. Yet it does not seem to me that the present passage is capable of being applied to a soul such as this, which has not attained

the second grace, and, though desiring to approach Him whom she loves, has not the ability to do so. For how can the words which follow be made to apply to such a soul; namely, that she rises and goes about the city in the streets, and in the broad ways seeks her Beloved, seeing that she herself needs to be sought? Let her do this as she is able; only let her remember that, as she was first loved, so she was first sought; and to that she owes it that she herself loves and is engaged in seeking. Let us, too, pray, beloved, that those mercies may speedily anticipate us, for we are brought into extreme need of them. But I do not say this of you all; for I know that very many of you are walking in the love wherewith Christ hath loved us, and are seeking him in simplicity of heart. But there are some (I say it with sorrow) who have not yet given us any mark of this saving and preventing grace being in them, and therefore no sign of their salvation; they are men who love their own selves, not the Lord, and seek their own interests, not those of Jesus Christ.

5. *I have sought*, says the bride, *him whom my soul loveth*. It is to this that the goodness of Him who has anticipated you in seeking you and loving you first—it is to this that his goodness is calling and arousing you. You would not seek him at all, O soul, nor love him at all, if you had not been first sought and first loved. You have been anticipated by a twofold benediction, that of love and of seeking. The love is the cause of the seeking; the seeking is the fruit and the clear proof of the love. You have been loved, so that you might not fear that you were sought for to be punished; you were sought for, that you might not complain that you were loved to no purpose. Each of these two great and unmistakable favors has given you courage, has removed shyness and timidity, has touched your feelings, and disposed you to return. Hence arises that zeal and ardor in seeking Him whom thy soul loveth; because, just as you were not able to seek him, until you had first been sought, so now that you have been sought, you are not able to do otherwise than seek him.

6. Again, never forget whence it is that you have come hither. And that I may ap-ply the better to myself what has been said (which is the safer course), is it not thou, O my soul, who, having left thy first Bridegroom, by whose side all had been well with thee, hast broken the faith first pledged to him, and gone after others? And now that thou hast sinned with them to the full, and art perhaps fallen into contempt with them, dost thou impudently and with effrontery desire to return to him to whom thou hast behaved with so much pride and insolence? What? when thou art fit only to hide thyself, dost thou seek the light, and though more deserving of correction than favor, dare to run unto the Bridegroom? Wonderful it will be if you do not find a judge to condemn you instead of a husband to receive you. Happy is he who shall hear his soul replying to these reproaches: I do not fear because I love, and also I am loved; nor could I have loved unless He had first loved me. Let those fear who have no love; but for the soul that loves there is nothing to be feared. How can those who have no love do otherwise than be under constant apprehension of injury? But because I love, I no more doubt that I am loved than I doubt of my own love; nor can I possibly fear his countenance whose affection for me I have assuredly felt. In what have I felt it, do you inquire? In this: that not only has he sought me, unhappy as I am, but has caused me to seek him, and to feel sure of succeeding in my search. Why should I not respond to him in his search to whom in his affection I respond? Why should he be angry at my seeking him, who, when I showed contempt for him, forgave it? He sought me when I contemned him; why should he contemn me when I seek him? Benign and gentle is the Spirit of the Word, and gentle is his greeting to me; he makes me aware of his kindness toward me; he whispers to me and convinces me of the earnest love of the Word for me, which cannot be hidden from him. For he searches the deep things of God, and knows that the divine thoughts are thoughts of peace and not purposes of vengeance. How can I be otherwise than encouraged to seek him who have had experience of his clemency, and am persuaded of his reconciliation with me?

7. My brethren, to think seriously of these truths is to be sought by the Word; to be persuaded of them is to be found by him. But not all are capable of receiving that Word. What shall we do for the little children among us—I mean those who are still in the stage of beginners (*incipientes*), and yet are far from being without understanding (*insipientes*), since they possess already the beginning of wisdom, being subject one to the other in the fear of Christ? How, I say, shall we cause them to believe that the spiritual life of the bride is marked by such experiences as these, since they know nothing as yet of such feelings themselves? But I send them to one to whom they cannot refuse credence. Let them read in a book [of Scripture] that which they fail to discern in the heart of a fellow man, and therefore will not believe. For it is written in one of the prophets: *If a man put away his wife, and she go from him, and become another man's, shall he return unto her again? shall not that land be greatly polluted? but thou hast played the harlot with many lovers, yet return again to me, saith the Lord.* They are the words of the Lord, and it is not permitted to doubt or hesitate. Let them believe what they have not experienced, that by the merit of their faith they may one day attain the fruit of experience. I think that now it has been sufficiently explained what it is to be sought by the Word, and how this is necessary, not for the Word but for the soul, so that the soul that has experienced this knows him both more fully and more happily. It remains to be treated of in the next discourse how souls that thirst for Christ seek him by whom they have been sought; or rather that we should learn that from her who is brought before us in these verses as seeking Him whom her soul loveth, him who is the Bridegroom of the soul, Jesus Christ our Lord, who is above all, God blessed forever. Amen.

B. RICHARD OF ST. VICTOR (C. 1123–1173) AND THE CONTEMPLATIVE VISION

12. Discretion and Contemplation, the Twin Offspring of Reason

Benj. Min., 71, trans. Clare Kirchberger, *Richard of Saint Victor: Selected Writings on Con-templation* (London: Faber and Faber Ltd.; New York: Harper & Brothers, 1957), p. 109.

By Joseph the soul is carefully taught and eventually it is brought to full self-knowledge, just as by his half-brother Benjamin, it is at length brought to the contemplation of God. For as by Joseph we understand the grace of discretion, so by Benjamin we understand the grace of contemplation. Both are born of the same mother for both the knowledge of God and of oneself are perceived by reason. Benjamin is born long after Joseph. For the soul which has been long exercised in self-knowledge and is not yet fully taught cannot be raised up to the knowledge of God. In vain does the eye of the heart which is not yet fit to see itself, try to see God. First man must learn to know his own invisible nature before he presumes to approach the invisible things of God. . . .

13. The Soul in Self-Knowledge Raised to the Contemplation of God

Benj. Min., 72, trans. Kirchberger, *Selected Writings*, pp. 109–10.

The rational soul truly finds in itself the chief and principal mirror for seeing God. If the invisible things of God are clearly seen, being understood by the things that are made, where, I ask, are the traces of knowledge distinctly impressed to be found, but in this image of God (in the soul)? Man is made after the likeness of God we read and believe, and therefore as long as we walk by faith and not by sight and as long as we still see in a glass darkly, we cannot find a better mirror for seeing Him in the imagination so to say, than the rational spirit. Let him who desires to see God wipe his mirror and cleanse his heart. The true Joseph ceases not from holding, wiping and inspecting his mirror incessantly. He must hold it up, lest by his affections he tend downwards, falling to the earth; wipe it, lest it become soiled by the dust of foolish desires; inspect it, lest it reflect the vain efforts to which his intention is turned. But when the mirror has been cleansed and examined for a long time carefully, a brightness of the divine light begins to shine through to him and a great beam of illumination not known hitherto, appears before his eyes. It was this light which enlightened the eyes of him who said: 'The light of thy countenance is sealed upon us, O Lord, thou hast given gladness in my heart.' Therefore by the sight of this light, which is wonderful in itself, the soul is marvellously enflamed and given the power to see the light which is above itself. I say, from this vision it conceives a flame of desire to see God and it takes courage. So the mind burning already with the desire of this vision, if it hopes for its desires may now know that it has conceived Benjamin. It conceives in hope, it bears with desire and the greater the desire, the nearer is the birth.

14. The Four-fold Thirst of the Soul for God

De Quatuor Gradibus Violentiae Caritatis, trans. Kirchberger, *Selected Writings,* pp. 223–24.

Let us go deeper and speak more openly. In the first degree the soul thirsts for God, in the second she thirsts to go to God, in the third she thirsts to be in God, in the fourth she thirsts in God's way. She thirsts for God when she desires to experience what that inward sweetness is that inebriates the mind of man, when he begins to taste and see how sweet the Lord is. She thirsts for God when she desires to be raised above herself by the grace of contemplation and to see the Lord in all His beauty, that she may truly say: 'For I have seen the Lord face to face, and my life is preserved.' She thirsts in God, when in ecstasy she desires to pass over into God altogether, so that having wholly forgotten herself she may truly say: 'Whether in the body or out of the body I cannot tell.' She thirsts in God's way when, by her own will I do not mean in temporal matters only but also in spiritual things, the soul reserves nothing for her own will but commits all things to God, never thinking about herself but about the things of Jesus Christ, so that she may say: 'I came not to do my own will but the will of the Father which is in heaven.' In the first degree, God enters into the soul and she turns inward into herself. In the second, she ascends above herself and is lifted up to God. In the third the soul, lifted up to God passes over al-

together into Him. In the fourth the soul goes forth on God's behalf and descends below herself. In the first she enters into herself, in the second she goes forth from herself. In the first she reaches her own life, in the third she reaches God. In the first she goes forth on her own behalf, in the fourth she goes forth because of her neighbour. In the first she enters in by meditation, in the second she ascends by contemplation, in the third she is led into jubilation, in the fourth she goes out by compassion. In the first degree a spiritual feeling sweeter than honey enters into her soul and inebriates her with its sweetness, so that she has honey and milk on her tongue and her lips distil the honeycomb. Those who have felt this will give forth a memorial of abundant sweetness, for the mouth speaketh out of the abundance of the heart. This is the first consolation which they who renounce the world receive at first and it generally confirms them in their good intention. This is the heavenly food which is wont to refresh those who go forth from Egypt and feed them in the wilderness; this is the hidden manna which no man knoweth who hath not received it. This is that spiritual sweetness and inward delight which is the milk and food of those who are as newborn babes and which brings them gradually to the strength of full grown men.

C. MEISTER ECKHART (C. 1260–1328) ON "ABGESCHIEDENHEIT" AND THE TRUE POSSESSION OF GOD

15. Inner Solitude, Self-abnegating Love for God, and Permeation by the Divine Presence

Die Reden der Unterscheidung (Talks of Instruction), 6, trans. R. B. Blakney, *Meister Eckhart: A Modern Translation* (New York: Harper & Brothers, 1941), pp. 7–10.

I was asked this question: "Some people withdraw from society and prefer to be alone; their peace of mind depends on it; wouldn't it be better for them to be in the church?" I replied, No! And you shall see why.

Those who do well do well wherever they are, and in whatever company, and those who do badly do badly wherever they are, and in whatever company. But if a man does well, God is really in him, and with him everywhere, on the streets and among people just as much as in church, or a desert place, or a cell. If he really has God, and only God, then nothing disturbs him. Why?

Because he has *only* God and thinks only God and everything is nothing but God to him. He discloses God in every act, in every place. The whole business of his person adds up to God. His actions are due only to Him who is the author of them and not to himself, since he is merely the agent. If we mean God and only God, then it is He who does what we do and nothing can disturb him—neither company nor place. Thus, neither can any person disturb him, for he thinks of nothing, is looking for nothing, and relishes nothing but God, who is one with him by perfect devotion. Furthermore, since God cannot be distracted by the numbers of things, neither can the person, for he is one in One, in which all divided things are gathered up to unity and there undifferentiated.

One ought to keep hold of God in everything and accustom his mind to retain God always among his feelings, thought, and loves. Take care how you think of God. As you think of him in church or closet, think of him everywhere. Take him with you among the crowds and turmoil of the alien world. As I have said so often, speaking of uniformity, we do not mean that one should regard all deeds, places, and people as interchangeable. That would be a great mistake; for it is better to pray than to spin and the church ranks above the street. You should, however, maintain the same mind, the same trust, and the same earnestness toward God in all your doings. Believe me, if you keep this kind of evenness, nothing can separate you from God-consciousness.

On the other hand, the person who is not conscious of God's presence, but who must always be going out to get him from this and that, who has to seek him by special methods, as by means of some activity, person, or place—such people have not attained God. It can easily happen that they are disturbed, for they have not God and they do not seek, think, and love only him, and therefore, not only will evil company be to them a stumbling block, but good company as well—not only the street, but the church; not only bad deeds and words, but good ones as well. The difficulty lies within the man, for whom God has not yet become everything. If God were everything, the man would get along well wherever he went and among whatever people, for he would possess God and no one could rob him or disturb his work.

Of what does this true possession of God consist, when one really has him? It depends on the heart and an inner, intellectual return to God and not on steady contemplation by a given method. It is impossible to keep such a method in mind, or at least difficult, and even then it is not best. We ought not to have or let ourselves be satisfied with the god we have thought of, for when the thought slips the mind, that god slips with it. What we want is rather the reality of God, exalted far above any human thought or creature. Then God will not vanish unless one turns away from him of his own accord.

When one takes God as he is divine, having the reality of God within him, God sheds light on everything. Everything will taste like God and reflect him. God will shine in him all the time. He will have the disinterest, renunciation, and spiritual vision of his beloved, ever-present Lord. He will be like one athirst with a real thirst; he cannot help drinking even though he thinks of other things. Wherever he is, with whomsoever he may be, whatever his purpose or thoughts or occupation—the idea of the Drink will not depart as long as the thirst endures; and the greater the thirst the more lively, deepseated, present, and steady the idea of the Drink will be. Or suppose one loves something with all that is in him, so that nothing else can move him or give pleasure, and he cares for that alone, looking for nothing more; then wherever he is or with whomsoever he may be, whatever he tries or does, that Something he loves will not be extinguished from his mind. He will see it everywhere, and the stronger his love grows for it the more vivid it will be. A person like this never thinks of resting because he is never tired.

The more he regards everything as divine —more divine than it is of itself—the more God will be pleased with him. To be sure, this requires effort and love, a careful cultivation of the spiritual life, and a watchful, honest, active oversight of all one's mental attitudes toward things and people. It is not to be learned by world-flight, running away from things, turning solitary and going apart from the world. Rather, one must learn an inner solitude, wherever or with whomsoever he may be. He must learn to penetrate things and find God there, to get a strong impression of God firmly fixed in his mind.

It is like learning to write. To acquire this art, one must practice much, however disagreeable or difficult it may be, however impossible it may seem. Practicing earnestly and often, one learns to write, acquires the art. To be sure, each letter must first be considered separately and accurately, reproduced over and over again; but once having acquired skill, one need not pay any attention to the reproduction [of the letters] or even think of them. He will write fluently and freely whether it be penmanship or some bold work, in which his art appears. It is sufficient for the writer to know that he is using his skill and since he does not always have to think of it, he does his work by means of it.

So a man should shine with the divine Presence without having to work at it. He should get the essence out of things and let the things themselves alone. That requires at first attentiveness and exact impressions, as with the student and his art. So one must be permeated with divine Presence, informed with the forms of beloved God who is within him, so that he may radiate that Presence without working at it.

D. JOHN TAULER (C. 1294–1361) ON MAN'S UNRESPONSIVENESS TO GOD'S INWARD WORD

16. Spiritual Deafness

Second Sermon for the Twelfth Sunday after Trinity, Reprinted from pp. 494–97 of *The Sermons and Conferences of John Tauler of the Order of Preachers*, trans. . . . by the Very Rev. Walter Elliott of the Paulist Fathers. Published by the Apostolic Mission House, Brookland Station, Washington D. C., 1910. Reproduced with the gracious permission of the Superior General, the Very Rev. William A. Michell, C. S. P.

And they bring to Him one deaf and dumb; and they besought Him that He would lay His hand upon him. And taking him from the multitude apart, He put His fingers into his ears, and spitting, He touched his tongue. And looking up to heaven, He groaned, and said to him: Ephpheta, which is, Be thou opened. And immediately his ears were opened, and the string of his tongue was loosed, and he spoke right. . . . He hath done all things well; He hath made both the deaf to hear, and the dumb to speak.—Mark vii, 32–37.

We are to inquire to-day into man's spiritual deafness. Since our first parents lent a willing ear to the voice of Satan, we are all deaf to the voice of the eternal Word of God within our souls. And yet we know full well that this divine Word is indescribably close to our souls, closer than our own thoughts, or our very nature to our conscious existence. Within our inmost souls dwells that divine Word, and He addresses us without ceasing. Man hears Him not, for he is afflicted with great deafness. Nor is this a blameless state of deafness, for we are like one to whom something is spoken, and who stops his ears lest he shall hear what it is. We are worse; we have done this so much that at last we have lost knowledge of ourselves, and are become dumb, that is to say, wholly stupid. Ask a worldly man about his interior life, and he is dumb—he knows not if there be any such a life. And the cause of it is that the enemy has crept into that soul, which has hearkened to him, and thus has become deaf and dumb.

Now how does Satan insinuate himself into the soul? Thou shalt detect him in all blameworthy conduct; his guidance is in all the deceit of this world, all inordinate love of created things, such as honors and riches, relatives and friends, and also self love in all its forms. Under cover of any of these does he insinuate himself into thy soul, for he is ever on the watch to take advantage of thy inclination to evil. Sometimes he urges thee to shun a certain pain that thou shouldst manfully bear; again, to seek forbidden joys, whispering inwardly in thy ear, showing pictures before the eyes of thy soul, all that thou mayst shut eyes and ears and soul to the eternal Word. If we but instantly turn away from the enemy's allurements, his temptations are easily overcome. If, on the contrary, one dallies with the tempter, gazes upon his pictures, listens to his suggestions, then he is nigh to destruction; the temptation is grown very heavy. Resist instantly, turn from him instantly, and thou art close to a victory. Soon thy deafness shall be cured, and thou shalt hear the inner voice of the eternal Word.

This deafness afflicts not only people living in the world but also those called to a spiritual life, but who permit their souls to be occupied by love and enjoyment of created things. This is well known to the devil, who tells them things calculated to gratify their inclinations. Some are made deaf by their infatuation for their self-chosen devotional customs and outward observances, which link them strongly to creatures in a spirit of proprietorship. The clatter of all this hinders the soul from hearing the inner voice of the eternal Word. We know well, of course, that we must have approved spiritual exercises and follow them earnestly; and yet without a feeling of proprietorship. Such are devout prayers to God as well as holy meditation, by means of which our sluggish nature is aroused; we are heartened to our work, and we are drawn inward to the Spirit; but never with an obstinate sense of ownership, and always looking inward to God in the depths of our souls. We should not imitate some men, who persist to their very deaths in certain external pious practices and use them in a wholly externized spirit, never seeking to go beyond this. If God wishes to speak to them, the ears of their souls are always preoccupied by other voices. Children, there are so many cases of this sort of spiritual deafness, that at the end of all things we shall be amazed at the revelation of it.

Now God's word is never spoken in any man's ears of whom it may not be said "If any one love Me, he will keep My word" (John xiv:23). St. Gregory explains this:

"Wouldst thou know if thou lovest God? Take note of thy conduct when thou art tried. What dost thou do when pain comes on thee, or contradiction, or any other distress from round about thee? And how dost thou bear thyself in time of interior distress, when thy mental anguish is so sharp that thou knowest not whither to turn for relief? What is thy bearing in sudden storms of adversity; when beset with difficulties all unforeseen? If thou shalt rest quiet in these visitations, thy soul resting in peace, without any outburst of impatience, with no fault of word or act or even motion, then without doubt thou lovest God truly." On the heart that truly loves, neither outward pain nor pleasure can make any impression. One may give to thee, one may take from thee, if only thy Beloved abide with thee, it is all one to thee, and thou restest in interior peace. Thy outward man weeps—that thou canst not help; the inner man rests content with God's holy will. But if, alas, thou canst not stand this test, then art thou deaf—the divine Word will not be heard by thee.

Another test: art thou full of thanksgiving to God for the manifold favors He has conferred on thee, and on all mankind, and on all creatures in earth and heaven and never ceases to confer? And art thou especially thankful for the unspeakable gift of His Son's holy humanity? Again, thy universal spiritual exercise should be sincere love of all mankind, not only the members of thy own community, but all priests and monks and nuns and sisters, and all humanity besides, of whatever state or condition; and this love should be active, and by no means confined in practice to thy own community, as far as lies in thy power. This universal love is of inestimable benefit; for whosoever are real enlightened friends of God, their hearts are melted with affection for all men living and dead. Had we no such lovers of mankind among us, our lot would be evil indeed. Furthermore, thou shouldst also show thy love by outward works, by making gifts, by speaking words of comfort and counsel, in so far as thy own real necessities will permit. And if thou art unable to give outward help, at least excite thy heart to say in all truth, that thou wouldst do so if it were within thy power. Here then are thy plain signs for true love, and they will show that thy heart is not deaf.

And now comes our Lord to a man deaf and dumb, and He spiritually putteth His finger in his ears, and anoints his tongue with His holy spittal, and immediately the man's soul can hear and can speak. O children, wonderful words might be said of this act of our Lord; we content ourselves with naming the seven gifts of the Holy Ghost, which thus enter the soul and are granted when it hearkens to God in very truth.

First is the spirit of fear, which is given us that we may renounce all self-will, all self-conceit. It teaches us to fly from every evil thing. After that is granted the gift of piety, making us tender-hearted, hindering all rash judgment, rendering us yielding and kindly towards all. The third touch of the Lord's finger is the gift of knowledge, giving us an interior lesson of divine experience, and guiding us to know the inner ways of union with God's holy will. The fourth is divine fortitude, by which the soul is so strengthened as to be able easily to suffer all pain for God's sake, and courageously to undertake all heavy tasks in His honor. The fifth is holy counsel, making all who receive it lovable men, and acceptable guides to others. And now come two touches of the divine finger that are deep and strong, namely, understanding and wisdom; but as to these, one can more easily feel the worth of them than he can describe them. May God grant that our ears may thus be opened to His truth, and that we may ever hearken to His eternal Word. *Amen.*

E. CATHERINE OF SIENA (1347–1380) AND HER "DIALOGUE"; THE TREATISE OF DIVINE PROVIDENCE AND THE CELL OF SELF-KNOWLEDGE

17. Self-Love Cast out by Self-Knowledge; The Soul that Loves God Loves Her Neighbor; Man Cannot Help Making an Act of Love

Dial. 7, trans. A. Thorold, *The Dialogue of the Seraphic Virgin Catherine of Siena . . .* (Westminster, Md.: The Newman Press, 1944), pp. 43–47.

7. How Virtues Are Accomplished by Means of Our Neighbor, and How It Is that

Virtues Differ to Such an Extent in Creatures

I have told thee how all sins are accomplished by means of thy neighbor, through the principles which I exposed to thee, that is, because men are deprived of the affection of love, which gives light to every virtue. In the same way self-love, which destroys charity and affection toward the neighbor, is the principle and foundation of every evil. All scandals, hatred, cruelty, and every sort of trouble proceed from this perverse root of self-love, which has poisoned the entire world, and weakened the mystical body of the holy church, and the universal body of the believers in the Christian religion; and, therefore, I said to thee, that it was in the neighbor, that is to say, in the love of him, that all virtues were founded; and, truly, indeed did I say to thee, that charity gives life to all the virtues, because no virtue can be obtained without charity, which is the pure love of me.

Wherefore, when the soul knows herself, as we have said above, she finds humility and hatred of her own sensual passion, for she learns the perverse law, which is bound up in her members, and which ever fights against the spirit. And, therefore, arising with hatred of her own sensuality, crushing it under the heel of reason, with great earnestness, she discovers in herself the bounty of my goodness, through the many benefits which she has received from me, all of which she considers again in herself. She attributes to me, through humility, the knowledge which she has obtained of herself, knowing that, by my grace, I have drawn her out of darkness and lifted her up into the light of true knowledge. When she has recognized my goodness, she loves it without any medium, and yet at the same time with a medium, that is to say, without the medium of herself or of any advantage accruing to herself, and with the medium of virtue, which she has conceived through love of me, because she sees that in no other way can she become grateful and acceptable to me but by conceiving hatred of sin and love of virtue; and, when she has thus conceived by the affection of love, she immediately is delivered of fruit for her neighbor, because in no other way can she act out the truth she has conceived in herself, but, loving me in truth, in the same truth she serves her neighbor.

And it cannot be otherwise, because love of me and of her neighbor are one and the same thing, and so far as the soul loves me she loves her neighbor, because love toward him issues from me. This is the means which I have given you, that you may exercise and prove your virtue therewith; because, inasmuch as you can do me no profit, you should do it to your neighbor. This proves that you possess me by grace in your soul, producing much fruit for your neighbor and making prayers to me, seeking with sweet and amorous desire my honor and the salvation of souls. The soul, enamored of my truth, never ceases to serve the whole world in general, and more or less in a particular case according to the disposition of the recipient and the ardent desire of the donor, as I have shown above, when I declared to thee that the endurance of suffering alone, without desire, was not sufficient to punish a fault.

When she has discovered the advantage of this unitive love in me, by means of which she truly loves herself, extending her desire for the salvation of the whole world, thus coming to the aid of its neediness, she strives, inasmuch as she has done good to herself by the conception of virtue, from which she has drawn the life of grace, to fix her eye on the needs of her neighbor in particular. Wherefore, when she has discovered, through the affection of love, the state of all rational creatures in general, she helps those who are at hand, according to the various graces which I have entrusted to her to administer; one she helps with doctrine, that is, with words, giving sincere counsel without any respect of persons; another with the example of a good life, and this indeed all give to their neighbor, the edification of a holy and honorable life. These are the virtues, and many others, too many to enumerate, which are brought forth in the love of the neighbor; but, although I have given them in such a different way—that is to say, not all to one, but to one one virtue, and to another another—it so happens that it is impossible to have one, without having them all, because all the virtues are bound together. Wherefore, learn that in many cases I give one virtue, to be as it were the chief of the others; that is to say, to one I will give principally love, to another justice, to another humility, to one a lively faith, to another prudence or temperance or patience, to another fortitude. These, and many other virtues, I place, indifferently, in the souls of many creatures; it happens, therefore, that the particular one so placed in the soul becomes the principal object of its virtue; the soul disposing herself, for her chief conversation, to this rather than to other virtues, and, by the effect of this virtue, the soul draws to herself all the other virtues, which, as has been said, are all bound together in the affection of love; and so with many gifts and graces of virtue, and not

only in the case of spiritual things but also of temporal. I use the word 'temporal' for the things necessary to the physical life of man; all these I have given indifferently, and I have not placed them all in one soul, in order that man should, perforce, have material for love of his fellow. I could easily have created men possessed of all that they should need both for body and soul, but I wish that one should have need of the other, and that they should be my ministers to administer the graces and the gifts that they have received from me. Whether man will or no, he cannot help making an act of love. It is true, however, that that act, unless made through love of me, profits him nothing so far as grace is concerned. See, then, that I have made men my ministers, and placed them in diverse stations and various ranks, in order that they may make use of the virtue of love.

Wherefore, I show you that in my house are many mansions, and that I wish for no other thing than love, for in the love of me is fulfilled and completed the love of the neighbor, and the law observed. For he only can be of use in his state of life who is bound to me with this love.

F. JAN VAN RUYSBROECK (1293–1381) AND "THE SPARKLING STONE": OUR LORD, JESUS CHRIST "A SHINING FORTH OF THE ETERNAL LIGHT"

18. Though One with God, We Must Eternally Remain Other than God

Sparkling Stone, 10, trans. C. A. Wynschenk Dom, John of Ruysbroeck, The Adornment of the Spiritual Marriage, The Sparkling Stone, The Book of Supreme Truth, ed. Evelyn Underhill (London: John M. Watkins, 1916, 1951), pp. 208–12. This and the following item, 19, are reproduced with the gracious permission of the original publishers, J. M. Dent and Sons, Ltd., London, 1916.

Though I have said before that we are one with God, and this is taught us by Holy Writ, yet now I will say that we must eternally remain other than God, and distinct from Him, and this too is taught us by Holy Writ. And we must understand and feel both within us, if all is to be right with us.

And therefore I say further: that from the Face of God, or from our highest feeling, a brightness shines upon the face of our inward being, which teaches us the truth of love and of all virtues: and especially are we taught in this brightness to feel God and ourselves in four ways. First, we feel God in His grace; and when we apprehend this, we cannot remain idle. For like as the sun, by its splendour and its heat, enlightens and gladdens and makes fruitful the whole world, so God does to us through His grace: He enlightens and gladdens and makes fruitful all men who desire to obey Him. If, however, we would feel God within us, and have the fire of His love ever more burning within us, we must, of our own free will, help to kindle it in four ways: We must abide within ourselves, united with the fire through inwardness. And we must go forth from ourselves towards all good men with loyalty and brotherly love. And we must go beneath ourselves in penance, betaking ourselves to all good works, and resisting our inordinate lusts. And we must ascend above ourselves with the flame of this fire, through devotion, and thanksgiving, and praise, and fervent prayer, and must ever cleave to God with an upright intention and with sensible love. And thereby God continues to dwell in us with His grace; for in these four ways is comprehended every exercise which we can do with the reason, and in some wise, but without this exercise no one can please God. And he who is most perfect in this exercise, is nearest to God. And therefore it is needful for all men; and above it none can rise save the contemplative men. And thus, in this first way, we feel God within us through His grace, if we wish to belong to Him.

Secondly: when we possess the God-seeing life, we feel ourselves to be living *in* God; and from out of that life in which we feel God in ourselves, there shines forth upon the face of our inward being a brightness which enlightens our reason, and is an intermediary between ourselves and God. And if we with our enlightened reason abide within ourselves in this brightness, we feel that our created life incessantly immerses itself in its eternal life. But when we follow the brightness above reason with a simple sight, and with a willing leaning out of ourselves, toward our highest life, there we experience the transformation of our whole selves in God; and thereby we feel ourselves to be wholly enwrapped in God.

And, after this, there follows the third way of feeling; namely, that we feel ourselves to be one *with* God; for, through the transformation in God, we feel ourselves to be swallowed up in the fathomless abyss of our eternal blessedness, wherein we can nevermore find any distinction between ourselves and God. And this is our highest feeling, which we cannot experience in any other way than in the immersion in love. And therefore, so soon as we are uplifted and drawn into our highest feeling, all our powers stand idle in an essential fruition; but our powers do not pass away into nothingness, for then we should lose our created being. And as long as we stand idle, with an inclined spirit, and with open eyes, but without reflection, so long we can contemplate and have fruition. But, at the very moment in which we seek to prove and to comprehend what it is that we feel, we fall back into reason, and there we find a distinction and an otherness between ourselves and God, and find God outside ourselves in incomprehensibility.

And hence the fourth way of distinction; which is, that we feel God *and* ourselves. Hereby we now find ourselves standing in the Presence of God; and the truth which we receive from the Face of God teaches us that God would be wholly ours and that He wills us to be wholly His. And in that same moment in which we feel that God would be wholly ours, there arises within us a gaping and eager craving which is so hungry and so deep and so empty that, even though God gave all that He could give, if he gave not Himself, we should not be appeased. For, whilst we feel that He has given Himself and yielded Himself to our untrammeled craving, that we may taste of Him in every way that we can desire—and of this we learn the truth in His sight—yet all that we taste, against all that we lack, is but like to a single drop of water against the whole sea: and this makes our spirit burst forth in fury and in the heat and the restlessness of love. For the more we taste, the greater our craving and our hunger; for the one is the cause of the other. And thus it comes about that we struggle in vain. For we feed upon His Immensity, which we cannot devour, and we yearn after His Infinity, which we cannot attain: and so we cannot enter into God nor can God enter into us, for in the untamed fury of love we are not able to renounce ourselves. And therefore the heat is so unmeasured that the exercise of love between ourselves and God flashes to and fro like the lightning in the sky; and yet we cannot be consumed in its ardour. And in this storm of love our activity is above reason and wayless; for love longs for that which is impossible to it, and reason teaches that love is in the right, but reason can neither counsel love nor dissuade her. For as long as we inwardly perceive that God would be ours, the goodness of God touches our eager craving: and therefrom springs the wildness of love, for the touch which pours forth from God stirs up this wildness, and demands our activity, that is, that we should love eternal love. But the inward-drawing touch draws us out of ourselves, and calls us to be melted and noughted in the Unity. And in this inward-drawing touch, we feel that God wills us to be His; and therefore, we must renounce ourselves and leave Him to work our blessedness. But where He touches us by the outpouring touch, He leaves us to ourselves, and makes us free, and sets us in His Presence, and teaches us to pray in the spirit and to ask in freedom, and shows us His incomprehensible riches in such manifold ways as we are able to grasp. For everything that we can conceive, wherein is consolation and joy, this we find in Him without measure. And therefore, when our feeling shows us that He with all these riches would be ours and dwell in us for ever more, then all the powers of the soul open themselves, and especially the desirous power; for all the rivers of the grace of God pour forth, and the more we taste of them, the more we long to taste; and the more we long to taste, the more deeply we press into contact with Him; and the more deeply we press into contact with God, the more the flood of His sweetness flows through us and over us; and the more we are thus drenched and flooded, the better we feel and know that the sweet-

ness of God is incomprehensible and unfathomable. And therefore the prophet says: "O taste, and see that the Lord is sweet." But he does not say how sweet He is, for God's sweetness is without measure; and therefore we can neither grasp it nor swallow it. And this is also testified by the bride of God in the Song of Songs, where she says: "I sat down under his shadow, with great delight, and his fruit was sweet to my taste."

19. The "Common Life" which Proceeds from the Contemplation and Fruition of God

Sparkling Stone, 14, trans. C. A. Wynschenk Dom, *The Sparkling Stone,* pp. 220–21.

The man who is sent down by God from these heights into the world is full of truth and rich in all virtues. And he seeks not his own but the glory of Him Who has sent him. And hence he is just and truthful in all things, and he possesses a rich and a generous ground, which is set in the richness of God: and therefore he must always spend himself on those who have need of him; for the living fount of the Holy Ghost, which is his wealth, can never be spent. And he is a living and willing instrument of God, with which God works whatsoever He wills and howsoever He wills; and these works he reckons not as his own, but gives all the glory to God. And so he remains ready and willing to do in the virtues all that God commands, and strong and courageous in suffering and enduring all that God allows to befall him. And by this he possesses a universal life, for he is ready alike for contemplation and for action, and is perfect in both of them. And none can have this universal life save the God-seeing man; and none can contemplate and enjoy God save he who has within himself the six points, ordered as I have described heretofore. And therefore, all those are deceived who fancy themselves to be contemplative, and yet inordinately love, practice, or possess, some creaturely thing; or who fancy that they enjoy God before they are empty of images, or that they rest before they enjoy. All such are deceived; for we must make ourselves fit for God with an open heart, with a peaceful conscience, with naked contemplation, without hypocrisy, in sincerity and truth. And then we shall mount up from virtue unto virtue, and shall see God, and shall enjoy Him, and in Him shall become one with Him, in the way which I have shown to you. That this be done in all of us, so help us God. Amen.

SUGGESTED READINGS

Bennett, R. F., *The Early Dominicans*. Cambridge: Cambridge University Press, 1937.

Butler, E. C., *Benedictine Monachism*. New York: Longmans, Green & Co., 1919.

——, *Western Mysticism*, 2nd ed. New York: E. P. Dutton, 1926.

Huber, R. M., *A Documented History of the Franciscan Order (1182–1517)*. Milwaukee: Nowing Publishing Apostolate, 1944.

Jones, R. M., *The Flowering of Mysticism*. New York: The Macmillan Co., 1939.

McNeill, J. T., *A History of the Cure of Souls*. New York: Harper & Brothers, 1951.

Petry, R. C., *Francis of Assisi*. Durham, North Carolina: Duke University Press, 1941.

——, ed., *Late Medieval Mysticism*, Library of Christian Classics, Vol. XIII. Philadelphia: Westminster Press, 1957.

Pourrat, P., *Christian Spirituality in the Middle Ages*, Vols. I and II. London: Burns, Oates and Washbourne, Ltd., 1924.

Scudder, V. D., *The Franciscan Adventure*. London: J. M. Dent & Sons, Ltd., 1931.

Williams, W. W., *Studies in St. Bernard of Clairvaux*. London: SPCK, 1927.

Workman, H. B., *Evolution of the Monastic Ideal*. London: Epworth Press, 1913.

CHRONOLOGY

910	*Cluny founded*
960–980	*Plays of Hrotswitha*
990–1021	*Aelfric, Abbot of Eynsham*
994–1048	*Odilo, Abbot of Cluny*
1012	*Camaldulians founded by Romuald of Ravenna (d. 1027)*
1038	*Vallombrosians founded by John Gualbert*
1049–1109	*Hugh, Abbot of Cluny*
1076	*Grandmont founded by Stephen of Thiers*
1084/86	*Carthusians founded by Bruno of Cologne*
1090–1153	*Bernard of Clairvaux*
1098	*Citeaux and Cistercians founded by Robert of Molesme*
c. 1099/1101	*Fontevrault, Double Order founded by Robert of Arbrissel*
1101	*Death of Raoul Ardent*
1109	*Death of Anselm, monk of Bec, and Archbishop of Canterbury*
c. 1110	*St. Victor founded by William of Champeaux*
1115	*Clairvaux founded by Bernard*
1117/19	*Cistercian Charter of Charity*
1118	*Order of Templars founded*
1120/24	*Premonstratensians founded by Norbert of Xanten*
1122–1152	*Suger, Abbot of St. Denys*
1122–1156	*Peter the Venerable, Abbot of Cluny*
1121/24	*Death of Guibert of Nogent*
1146/47	*Gilbertines made an order by Eugenius III*
c. 1150	*Bernard of Cluny's (Morval's) Contempt of the World*
1156	*Carmelites founded by Berthold of Calabria*
1170	*Birth of Dominic*
1173	*Jocelin of Brakelond enters St. Edmund; later author of Chronicle*
1179	*Death of Hildegarde of Bingen, Benedictine mystic*
1182	*Birth of Francis of Assisi*
1190	*Order of German Hospitalers*
1195–1231	*Anthony of Padua, Franciscan preacher*
1198	*Teutonic order evolved from Hospitalers*
1210	*Franciscans founded*
1212	*St. Clare and the Clarisses*
1215	*First Franciscan chapter general; Fourth Lateran Council; Magna Carta*

Illustration, page 312: Bust of St. Frederick. *Silver, parcel-gilt reliquary. Elijas Scerpswert, Utrecht, 1362.*

VIII

Innocent III, the Hierarchy, and

the Sacramental Church;

Heresy, Inquisition, and the

Preaching of the Faith

The medieval Church reached its peak
under Innocent III. He was of a noble Roman family. Before he
was thirty, he had studied the arts, canon and
Roman law, and theology at Paris and Bologna. His scholarly
perspective and contemplative proclivities
were joined in early devotional and liturgical
treatises. Such predilections also figured in his preparation
for ecclesiastical preferments. These were belatedly
realized after stinging rebuffs of fortune. Elevated at last with family
assistance to the coveted papacy, he wasted no
time in establishing his pontifical ambitions. In two
ordination sermons he fixed the tone of
subsequent utterances calling for universal papal supremacy.

Innocent's pontificate was characterized by his passion for power and by his indefatigable activity, including a voluminous correspondence. Noteworthy, also, were his unlimited interventions in episcopal, royal, imperial, and secular affairs. He brought bishops throughout the West into a tight, if unwilling, dependency under his hierarchical fiat. He gave new definition and scope to the cumulative offices of the hierarchy. These he centralized under papal control. His knowledge of both Roman and canon law and his astute administrative sense enabled him to exploit the fullest resources of papal courts, treasuries, and taxation systems. He made them unprecedented instruments of papal monarchialism and curial exaction. He assumed the full doctrinal and juridical implications of his vicarage, not only of Peter but also of Christ. Like Gregory VII, he drew upon the Church's eschatological prerogatives and her full spiritual initiative for the operation of the sacramental treasury. He sought thereby to control the immortal destinies of all men, and to rule both temporal and spiritual powers with unparalleled conclusiveness. His liturgical and theological discernment together with his legislative and judicial perspicacity provided him with a near throttle-hold upon the political balance of power. Seldom before or since has one man's successful will to dominate supplied such a vivid commentary on mixed motivation. In him, divine vocation and earthly opportunism clamored in disciplined accord. Under him, monastic energies were both critically rechanneled and potentially recodified. His was the hegemony of the sacramental charism. To him belonged the interpretation of eucharistic theology and liturgical canonics. The self examining and reforming ecclesiology of a preaching, teaching, missionizing, heresy-hunting, crusading heirarchy was coordinated by him. His reform passions were breathed into the subconscious respiration of the Christian populace itself.

Gregory VII and Boniface VIII rashly jousted with temporal force where it had the advantage of superior logistics and a restless society. Innocent's sagacious marshaling of material power frequently pitted temporal greats against each other upon battlefields and timetables of his own choosing. That he would have come out so well later under the shifting balance of the spiritual and temporal is debatable. One can scarcely imagine his attempting so much, with so little, so suddenly, as did Gregory VII before him and Boniface VIII after him. His paper work and staff concentrations were, for one thing, laid out on pin-pointed maps vastly transcending theirs. His reform projects moved with gargantuan resolve through the councils called to expedite his wishes. In his administration, specialized attention was given to almost every implication of sacramental theology, relic significance and delimitation, penitential discipline, Mariological controversy, financial improvisation, and systematized propaganda resourcefulness.

This entire chapter of readings bears the mark of the man who brought his feudal lordship down sharply over the reluctant vassalage of King John. That sovereign was appropriately dubbed "Lackland." There is no need to labor the many other instances of the pope's feudal absolutism, exercised over temporal and ecclesiastical lords alike. They were all vassals to his suzerainty. That the independent views of Runnymede barons were a voice from another era requires no argument. Innocent's letters did not overlook the threat, though even he could not stay the trend.

Innocent III as well as Peter Lombard had produced orderly considerations of the sacraments in their operating, liturgical context. Short passages from the Lombard's classic *Sentences* indicate how the sacraments were moving out of disorderly controversy into numbered orderliness and clarified character. What the IVth Lateran was to do by way of them was significant indeed. If ever a general council reflected papal initiative, it was the IVth Lateran. In the very first canon, the centuries came down to an ecclesiological synthesis that was Innocent's own. Here was an essay on the hierarchical church in comparison with which the *Dictatus papae* of Hildebrand's curia seems desultory and naive at best. Boniface VIII's *Unam sanctam*, with all its bluster, says far less.

For this canon and the ones that depend upon it show what the Church is; where its sacraments blaze, heal, and burn; and to what lengths of searing demolition the papal offensive against the Albigensian heretics will go. Here it is made plain how pervasively the pope intends to employ education throughout his earthly domain. Clearly, the growing abuse of relics is to be met head on. How, and wherewith, each little priest and great prince of the Church shall help realize the soteriological fulfillment of the ages under Christ's vicar, is boldly anticipated. Every Jew is, finally, to be surrounded and exploited into conversion or assimilation. All infidels are to be driven by the cross into the bowels of the earth, or to hell, or heaven. Crusading, preaching, and missionizing Christians will bring their sheaves at last into that earthly kingdom that will be offered up by the pontiff under the Spirit to God the Father and His Son in heaven.

One must admire the temerity of Innocent's pronouncements in the IVth Lateran on church unity, sacramental life, and social action. By the side of these, the ecumenical setting provided by Eugenius IV for the doctrine of the Church and sacraments was almost an anticlimax. It was little more than a draughtsman's reviewing a blueprint with the Master Architect. To the IVth Lateran, with its 412 bishops, 800 abbots, and countless priors, not to mention innumerable ecclesiasts and seculars to match, Innocent revealed his twin passions. He would strive to deliver the Holy Land from the unbeliever and reform the universal Church of the faithful. The fulfillment of all this he would not live to see. Many of his plans would follow strange detours with results that would do him little credit. Neither during his life nor after his death would all of his enterprises redound to his glory. In his young ward, later Frederick II, he had nurtured a viper whose serpentine ways belied papal foresight. Papal protestations had been made against the shameful debacle of the Fourth Crusade. These had not cleared his name of obloquy or cleansed his spirit from the charges of duplicity in his headship of the Latin empire. His all-too-human plans in 1215 for a glorious crusading victory would swiftly fade.

Nonetheless, in the year before his death the pontiff could with inspiring countenance limn the outlines of his most cherished reforms. He would, he vowed, convoke a general council to exterminate vices, cause virtues to flourish, redress wrongs, reform morals, destroy heresies, fortify the faith, terminate disputes, establish peace, protect liberty, win princes and people to the liberation of the Holy Land and, finally, promulgate wise ordinances for the higher and lower clergy. The tone was fulsome. The content was no less that of deep conviction and Christian dedication. If the execution was not fully consummated, neither was it wanting in noble explication.

History, of course, is never the doings of great men, only—if, indeed, it is ever chiefly theirs. Nor, perchance, is the limit of the Church's advance fixed by their colossal ability to distort the most noble potentialities of humble humanity. In all of this chapter, Innocent is constantly reflected and transcended by lesser men. The record implicit in this book is not so much his as theirs. To be sure his speeches carry farther with more practiced reverberation than their voiceless hopes can command.

This chapter attempts, in part, to make amends to little men, little parishes, little priests and clerks, little peasants and serfs, for the neglect into which their history has fallen. It was their humble and oft-exploited Christianity which constituted the base upon which the pyramiding hierarchy reared itself into its papal apex. The papal curia and hierarchy claimed to record the heavenly mandate and to reproduce the divinely authorized revelation. The historian must reflect upon this claim. He would do well, also, not to overlook an equally pertinent imprint of time. Without the great mass of the faithful no hierarchs could ever have achieved an eminence from which to proclaim their revelations.

There is plentiful evidence that in technical fact the church that mattered as an edifice of power was the ruling priesthood, the hierarchy. The clergy had long patronized the laity, while purporting to serve them. As a consequence the ancient equation of true greatness with humble service had often been obscured. The human yearnings and the daily miseries of the diminutive, feudalized Christian called for something more than the self-advertised, saving nobilities of ecclesiastical lordship. The pitiful supplications of humanity's massive "littleness" necessitated concentrated "leastness" that humble priests alone could supply. With all his thralldom, in common with the people, to the behemoth of grinding administration, the little priest did serve the little Christian. Somehow, serving through and beyond the hierarchy, he brought the divine graciousness he could neither originate nor contain into the communicating mouths and hearts of the *minuto populo.*

Nothing should prompt foolish disparagement of the medieval hierarchy. Already implicit in earliest Christianity, it fully explicated its medieval claims to be the indispensable agency of salvation. It was the self-confessed soul of the *Corpus Christianum,* the life protoplasm of the whole body of Christians. The sacraments, it said, had been instituted by Christ, who was the head of his church. To his vicar, the pope, he had committed their legal and spiritual administration, under priestly validation and hierarchical ordination. It was their saving graces, infused into man's life on earth, that were to transcend this natural order with a guarantee of supernatural beatitude in heaven.

The workings of sacramental life and the articulating hierarchy were not predicated solely upon the invulnerable ordination of popes, bishops, and ecclesiastical princes. They were as conclusively based upon the daily ministrations of the major and minor priesthood. Priests, with their deacons and sub-deacons, especially bore the brunt of sacramental efficacy. Here was the nub of salvation. At this junction block of time and eternity, the graciousness of the heavenly hierarchy was distributed in orderly gradation. This descended through the Church's earthly hierarchs, from the highest to the lowest. Through the humblest priest, the fullest energies of heaven were finally transfused into the veins of earth's humblest Christian. This was the saving institution that Innocent served in ruling and ruled in serving. He reiterated an ancient claim to be *servus servorum Dei*—"Servant of the servants of God." To the humble, at least, his serving must have seemed mostly ruling. It was his peculiar service to see that all whom he ruled, served God through him.

A considerable portion of this chapter's source texts is devoted to the complicated, sometimes appalling, often heart-warming vocation of little priests. Whether in feudal villages or in the new towns, the priest turned the key in God's lock. The upper hierarchs authorized his action and kept track of his operations. Still, it was he who typified and vivified the Church for the people. The passages that mark his comings and goings are not showpieces of piety or cynical exposés. They are simply a cross section of the paths which priests and people used together during their Christian pilgrimage. Presumably, the average priest thought little, read with difficulty, spoke officially in a language few including himself really understood, and wrote nothing at all. The people let all such exercises strictly alone. The typical reflections of little priests and their people must obviously be reported, therefore, from the responsible deliberations of more instructed analysts. This both complicates and oversimplifies, as it doubltless distorts, the picture at times. Having made realistic allowance for all such factors, the historian may, nonetheless, gather useful insights from contemporary documents and the distillations of oral tradition. The supplementing of these historical deductions will be further elucidated in Chapter IX. The outline titles and sub-titles of the present chapter set forth both chronologically and thematically these gleanings of the poor man's history. Here, again, the appended chronologies are not to prompt the reader's subconscious rebellion but to suggest the close warp and woof of historical data in realistic fidelity. No convenient summary, however careful and useful, should obviate

316

the recourse to such clarifying complexities.

There is benefit in observing both the ideal and the practice of the priestly function as Theodulph of Orleans reported it. Lanfranc was a later but no less dedicated scholar and bishop. Peter of Blois could contemplate the miseries of a wicked priest from the vantage ground of consecrated, parish responsibility. Francis made a few words go a long way in clarifying what a good Catholic must be and do. He placed in realistic perspective the awesome rite of the mass and the duties of all Christians who assisted at its celebration. No priest, however bad, could undo the workings of God's grace beyond all human deserts. Each priest was the channel of mercies that were quite immune to his unworthiness in their saving operation.

Robert Grosseteste was a language scholar, philosopher, gospel preacher, and administrator. He was the able bishop of Lincoln, the largest Catholic diocese of thirteenth-century England. In his official directions for parish life he included homely admonitions to corpulent mothers not to "overlay" their sleeping infants during the night. He utilized the new mendicant orders in his program of diocesan evangelism. He reactivated the time-honored, but generally lapsed, provision for visiting and disciplining cathedral clergy, monasteries, and parish communities. He was not a popular bishop. Nor did his fearless castigations of nepotistic papal appointments and nominations of unqualified foreigners to English church offices make him beloved of Roman pontiffs. The bent of his fearless if sometimes undiplomatic reform projects is well worth noting.

Not only his but other episcopal constitutions and visitation records are invaluable aids to understanding the life of little priests and little people. These visitation queries and their official replies are not fully objective, to be sure. Nor are popularity polls, civic ratings, and political platforms. Yet they do not completely falsify popular reaction, though the whole truth is not in them.

Something else, however, is even more valuable in viewing the medieval "common life" than Grosseteste's direction for archdeacons, rural deans, and synodical assemblies. Likewise transcended are the admirable records of diocesan pastoral life and pious measures for popular instruction of good archbishops like Peckham. John Myrcs' manual and similar ones for colloquial indoctrination of naive priests and parishioners are fascinating, "grass-roots" history of the highest order.

The source texts offer all too little material from a medieval group that was influential out of all proportion to its numbers. The Jews do come into focus at different times here, and in relation to such provisions as those of the IVth Lateran.

The texts of this chapter put a premium on accounts of the Church's battle for survival against the heresies. The Church was not quite the despicable big bully of all dissenters from its heirarchy that it has sometimes been pictured as being. The bulk of the heterodox were lumped together in the minds of churchmen as attackers of the hierarchy. This predominated for them over any considerations of dualism as such, manifestly serious though such doctrinal aberrations were. In many cases, the dualistic threat to Christian integrity was purveyed by organized counter-hierarchs. These called themselves the "good Christians." They held themselves to be the self-renouncing exemplars of the true church and hierarchy. They warred valiantly against the false Roman church and its illicit priesthood. The Roman Catholic hierarchy had itself chiefly to blame that its institutional wealth and often undisciplined priesthood so often gave the lie to its claims of sacrificial ministry. The heresiarchs, for their part, made considerable headway in lax parishes with their ascetic regimen, their "spiritualized" sacraments, and their challenging "evangelical" example.

The principal documents here translated and edited feature the "neo-Manichaean" heresies. The Church was not squeamish in lumping most opponents of the Catholic hierarchy under blanket designations. For instance, many medieval chroniclers and even some learned churchmen saw nothing actually dishonest in coupling Waldensian and Catharist dissent as basically and temperamentally equivalent. Both were, in their developed careers, dissenters from the Roman ecclesiology, sacramental system,

317

and hierarchical organization. Historically viewed, their central affirmations and negations were worlds apart. This, however, did not alter their Catholic opponents' view of the danger they posed to Catholic institutions. No more do the protagonists of democracy consistently disentangle the ideological eccentricities of socialists, nihilists, communists, Marxists, and many others. What counts is what they purportedly subvert—in this case, democracy.

Modern Roman Catholic scholars are quite aware of oversimplifications in the frequent medieval confusion of Waldensians and Albigensians. Recently edited documents give good reason to believe that Peter Waldo and his earliest associates were quite Roman in their profession of Catholic faith and life. That they later gravitated from disillusionment over the Church's decadent working ecclesiology into a Catharist vortex of dissent is by no means impossible. What is incontrovertible, however, is that the Waldensians, in their earliest protestations of Catholic loyalty, were as rigorous in their evangelical renunciation as the Church was lax. They were as non-dualistic to begin with as they were dedicated, ere long, to their own evangelical hierarchy in preference to the worldliness of Roman hierarchs. A note of spiritual independence soon crept into their manifestos of what makes a true church, true priests, and true believers. By and by they were as dissident from the Roman Catholic hierarchs and corporation as were the dualistic Catharists—though still for quite different reasons.

The Church's battle with heresy in the Middle Ages represented a significant interaction of altercating factors. From the earliest Christian centuries dualistic groups had become hopelessly entangled with anti-Christian folk legends. Cosmological myths and seriously countenanced ethical concerns were intertwined. In Bulgaria and Roumania, for example, social and political animus against harsh Byzantine overlords was rife. This disaffection together with a dualistic worldview was woven into the tenor of the very nursery rhymes on which babies were crooned to sleep at their mothers' breasts. The centers of the wool markets and the weavers' guilds in Western Europe were a link with the ports of entry from the East. A chain of Eastern importations bound together both heretical dualism and near-Eastern produce. The ancient geographic concentrations of spiritual heterodoxy and the new mercantile outlets for a new economy were welded into a solid front of religious skepticism and social restlessness. Along the waterfronts and within the textile workers' quarters, febrile stirrings of Persian dualism, gospel idealism, oriental occultism, and anticlerical revolution were spawned and disseminated.

It was with the powers and principalities of port towns and guild laborers that the mendicant preacher had to deal. The challenges confronting him there were no less demanding of doctrinal competence than the shrewd deviations of Manichaean leaders under inquisitorial scrutiny. Fearful bands of the faithful might touch off pogroms against Jews or precipitate lynchings of Catharists and other compromisers of godly society. As the Roman Empire followed the populace in its attacks upon early Christians, so the hunting-down of heretics was precipitated by popular fear and indignation. Local and episcopal inquisition followed popular agitation. They preceded papal action. Canonically, the Church committed to the secular arm the responsibility for executing the sentences it imposed. Pious kings like Louis IX and heterodox emperors such as Frederick II fulminated alike against the dangerous disrupters of society. In southern France, the Albigensians were deeply ensconced with noble support from Raymond of Toulouse. The Church's campaign against them was not finished without the near devastation of an entire population and its economy. Seeing the rising challenge of such heretics long before while on tour with the bishop of Osma, Dominic had envisioned his apostolate of gospel teaching. His disciples, with those of Francis, were to bear the burden of heretical detection. But—of greater import still—theirs was to be a counteroffensive in preaching sound doctrine and evangelical dedication. This, alone, would guarantee the Church's victory, if it ever came. The voices of true credo must come from faithful Christians tutored under well-informed preaching. The faithful must be redeemed from social skepticism and antihierarchical cynicism by mendicant social vicariousness.

The preaching manuals and the sermons of the mendicants show the friars' bent for adapting Catholic teaching to popular indoctrination. The passages from missionary tracts and narratives show something of the challenge of the new world that the crusading era brought. They reveal the serious flexibility of the Preaching Order and of the Friars Minor. In such diverse testimonies as those of Francis, Roger Bacon, Thomas Aquinas, and Ramon Lull a fresh insight into an old truth was apparent. Not by military might alone would the Church become victor over heretic and infidel. In the gospel charter of Franciscan poverty and in the early constitution of Dominican preaching there lay the answer. It was not enough to preach to the faithful alone. The unfaithful must be confronted with the gospel, also. They must be confounded and converted out of the gospel. They must be saved for and to the gospel. It was Lull's unusually documented credo that this should and must be done. For it he gave a spiritual witness sealed with a martyr's blood. In due season others would do likewise.

I. Innocent III and the Apogee of Pontificial Power

A. POPE INNOCENT III ACCEPTS THE VASSALAGE OF JOHN (LACKLAND), KING OF ENGLAND (1214)

1. King John Renders Homage and Fealty to the Pope

Ep. 67, "Rex Regum," trans. C. R. Cheney and W. H. Semple, *Selected Letters of Pope Innocent III Concerning England (1198–1216)* [Medieval Texts, gen. eds. V. H. Galbraith and R. A. B. Mynors] (Edinburgh: Thomas Nelson and Sons, Ltd., 1953), pp. 177–82. Grateful acknowledgment for permission to use the material quoted is accorded to the publishers, Thomas Nelson and Sons, Ltd.

Innocent, Bishop, servant of the servants of God, to his well-beloved son in Christ, John illustrious king of the English, and to his legitimate free-born heirs for ever.

The King of kings and Lord of lords, Jesus Christ, a priest for ever after the order of Melchisedech, has so established in the Church His kingdom and His priesthood that the one is a kingdom of priests and the other a royal priesthood, as is testified by Moses in the Law and by Peter in his Epistle; and over all He has set one whom He has appointed as His Vicar on earth, so that, as every knee is bowed to Jesus, of things in heaven, and things in earth, and things under the earth, so all men should obey His Vicar and strive that there may be one fold and one shepherd. All secular kings for the sake of God so venerate this Vicar, that unless they seek to serve him devotedly they doubt if they are reigning properly. To this, dearly beloved son, you have paid wise attention; and by the merciful inspiration of Him in whose hand are the hearts of kings which He turns whithersoever He wills, you have decided to submit in a temporal sense yourself and your kingdom to him to whom you knew them to be spiritually subject, so that kingdom and priesthood, like body and soul, for the great good and profit of each, might be united in the single person of Christ's Vicar. He has deigned to work this wonder, who being alpha and omega has caused the end to fulfil the beginning and the beginning to anticipate the end, so that those provinces which from of old have had the Holy Roman Church as their proper teacher in spiritual matters should now in temporal things also have her as their peculiar sovereign. You, whom God has chosen as a suitable minister to effect this, by a devout and spontaneous act of will and on the general advice of your barons have offered and yielded, in the form of an annual payment of a thousand marks, yourself and your kingdoms of England and Ireland, with all their rights and appurtenances, to God and to SS Peter and Paul His apostles and to the Holy Roman Church and to us and our successors, to be our right and our property— as is stated in your official letter attested by a golden seal, the literal tenor of which is as follows:

John, by the grace of God king of England, lord of Ireland, duke of Normandy and Aquitaine, count of Anjou, to all the faithful of Christ who may see this charter, greeting in the Lord.

By this charter attested by our golden seal we wish it to be known to you all that, having in many things offended God and Holy Church our mother and being therefore in the utmost need of divine mercy and possessing nothing but ourselves and our kingdoms that we can worthily offer as due amends to God and the Church, we desire to humble ourselves for the sake of Him who for us humbled Himself even unto death; and inspired by the grace of the Holy Spirit—not induced by force nor compelled by fear, but of our own good and spontaneous will and on the general advice of our barons—we offer and freely yield to God, and to SS Peter and Paul His apostles, and to the Holy Roman Church our mother, and to our lord Pope Innocent III and his catholic successors, the whole kingdom of England and the whole kingdom of Ireland with all their rights and appurtenances for the remission of our sins and the sins of our whole family, both the living and the dead. And now, receiving back these kingdoms from God and the Roman Church and holding them as feudatory vassal, in the presence of our venerable father, lord Nicholas, bishop of Tusculum, legate of the Apostolic See, and of Pandulf, subdeacon and member of household to our lord the Pope, we have pledged and sworn our fealty henceforth to our lord aforesaid, Pope Innocent, and to his catholic successors, and to the Roman Church, in the terms hereinunder stated; and we have publicly paid liege homage for the said kingdoms to God, and to the Holy Apostles Peter and Paul, and to the Roman Church, and to our lord aforesaid, Pope Innocent III, at the hands of the said legate who accepts our homage in place and instead of our said lord, the Pope; and we bind in perpetuity our successors and legitimate heirs that without question they must similarly render fealty and acknowledge homage to the Supreme Pontiff holding office at the time and to the Roman Church. As a token of this our perpetual offering and concession we will and decree that out of the proper and special revenues of our said kingdoms, in lieu of all service and payment which we should render for them, the Roman Church is to receive annually, without prejudice to the payment of Peter's pence, one thousand marks sterling—five hundred at the feast of St Michael and five hundred at Easter—that is, seven hundred for the kingdom of England and three hundred for the kingdom of Ireland, subject to the maintenance for us and our heirs of our jurisdiction, privileges, and regalities. Desiring all these terms, exactly as stated, to be forever ratified and valid, we bind ourselves and our successors not to contravene them; and if we or any of our successors shall presume to contravene them, then, no matter who he be, unless on due warning he come to his senses, let him lose the title to the kingdom, and let this document of our offer and concession remain ever valid.

I, John, by grace of God king of England and lord of Ireland, will from this hour henceforward be faithful to God and Saint Peter and the Roman Church and my lord Pope Innocent III and his catholic successors. I will not take part in deed, word, agreement, or plan whereby they should lose life or limb or be treacherously taken prisoners; any injury to them, if aware of it, I will prevent and will check if I can; and otherwise, I will notify them as soon as possible, or inform a person whom I can trust without fail to tell them; any counsel they have entrusted to me either personally or by envoys or by letter I will keep secret, nor will I wittingly divulge it to anyone to their disadvantage. I will help in maintaining and defending, to the utmost of my power, against all men, the patrimony of Saint Peter, and particularly the kingdom of England and the kingdom of Ireland. So help me God and the Holy Gospels of God whereon I swear.

To prevent any questioning of these terms at any time in the future, and for the greater surety of our offer and concession, we have caused this charter to be made and to be sealed with our golden seal; and as tribute for this the first year we pay a thousand marks sterling to the Roman Church by the hand of the said legate.

Witnessed by his lordship Stephen archbishop of Canterbury, and by their lordships William bishop of London, Peter bishop of Winchester, Eustace bishop of Ely, and Hugh bishop of Lincoln, and by our Chancellor, Walter de Gray, our brother William earl of Salisbury, Ranulf earl of Chester, William Marshal earl of Pembroke, William earl of Ferrers, Saer earl of Winchester, Robert de Ros, William Briwerre, Peter FitzHerbert, Matthew FitzHerbert, and Brian de Lisle our steward.

By the hand of Master Richard Marsh archdeacon of Richmond and Northumberland, at St Paul's London, the third of October A.D. 1213, in the fifteenth year of our reign.

This offer and concession so piously and wisely made we regard as acceptable and valid, and we take under the protection of Saint Peter and of ourselves your person and the persons of your heirs together with the said kingdoms and their appurtenances and all other goods which are now reasonably held or may in future be so held: to you and to your heirs, according to the terms set out above and by the general advice of our brethren, we grant the said kingdoms in fief and confirm them by this privilege, on condition that any of your heirs on receiving the crown will publicly acknowledge this as a fief held of the Supreme Pontiff and of the Roman Church, and will take an oath of fealty to them. Let no man, therefore, have power to infringe this document of our concession and confirmation, or presume to oppose it. If any man dare to do so, let him know that he will incur the anger of Almighty God and of SS Peter and Paul, His apostles.

VIII-1. The Mass of St. Martin of Tours. Franco-Rhenish Master.

II. The Hierarchical Church and the Sacramental System

A. PETER LOMBARD (1160/64) AND THE SEVEN SACRAMENTS

2. What a Sacrament Is

Lib. sent., IV, Dist. 1 (II), trans. E. F. Rogers, *Peter Lombard and the Sacramental System* (New York, 1917), p. 79. Grateful acknowledgment is made to the translator for the right to reprint Items 2–5.

II. WHAT A SACRAMENT IS

"A sacrament is the sign of a sacred thing (res)." However, a *sacred mystery* is also called a sacrament, as the sacrament of divinity, so that a sacrament may be the *sign of something sacred,* and the *sacred thing signified;* but now we are considering a sacrament as a *sign.*—So, "A sacrament is the visible form of an invisible grace."

3. What a Sign Is

Ibid., IV, Dist., 1 (III), trans. Rogers, *PL,* p. 79.

III. WHAT A SIGN IS

"But a sign, is the thing (res) behind the form which it wears to the senses, which brings by means of itself something else to our minds."

4. Of the Sacrament of the Altar

Ibid., IV, Dist. VIII (I), trans. Rogers, *PL,* p. 119.

I. OF THE SACRAMENT OF THE ALTAR

"After the sacrament of baptism and of confirmation, follows the sacrament of the Eucharist. Through baptism we are cleansed, through the Eucharist, we are perfected in what is good." Baptism extinguishes the fire of sins, the Eucharist restores us spiritually. Wherefore it is well called the Eucharist, that is, good grace, because in this sacrament not only is there increase of virtue and grace, but he who is the fount and source of all grace is received entire.

5. Of the Manner of Conversion

Ibid., IV, Dist. XI (I), trans. Rogers, *PL,* p. 134.

I. OF THE MANNER OF CONVERSION

But if anyone asks what the nature of that conversion is, whether of form, or of substance, or of some other sort; I am not able to define. I know however that it is not of form, because the appearances of the things remain what they were before, and the taste and the weight. To some it seems to be a change of substance, for they say that substance is so converted into substance, that the latter becomes the former in essence. With this opinion the foregoing authorities seem to agree.

But others make the following objection to this opinion: if the substance of bread, they say, or of wine is converted in substance into the body or blood of Christ, a substance is daily made the body or blood of Christ, which previously was not; and today there is a body of Christ, which yesterday was not; and daily the body of Christ is increased and formed of material, of which at its conception it was not made.—To these we can reply as follows: that the body of Christ is not said to be made by the divine words in the sense that the very body formed when the Virgin conceived is formed again, but that the substance of bread or wine which formerly was not the body or blood of Christ, is, by the divine words, made his body and blood. And therefore priests are said to make the body and blood of Christ, because by their ministry the substance of bread is made the flesh, and the substance of wine is made the blood of Christ; yet nothing is added to his body or blood, nor is the body or blood of Christ increased.

B. INNOCENT III AND THE IV LATERAN COUNCIL (1215); THE CHURCH AND THE SACRAMENTS

6. (Canon I) The Creed, The Church, The Sacraments, and Transubstantiation

Trans., H. J. Schroeder, *Disciplinary Decrees of the General Councils* (St. Louis, Mo.: B. Herder Book Co., 1937), pp. 237–39.

We firmly believe and openly confess that there is only one true God, eternal and immense, omnipotent, unchangeable, incomprehensible, and ineffable, Father, Son, and Holy Ghost; three Persons indeed but one essence, substance, or nature absolutely simple; the Father (proceeding) from no one, but the Son from the Father only, and the Holy Ghost equally from both, always without beginning and end. The Father begetting, the Son begotten, and the Holy Ghost proceeding; consubstantial and co-equal, co-omnipotent and coeternal, the one principle of the universe, Creator of all things invisible and visible, spiritual and corporeal, who from the beginning of time and by His omnipotent power made from nothing creatures both spiritual and corporeal, angelic, namely, and mundane, and then human, as it were, common, composed of spirit and body. The devil and the other demons were indeed created by God good by nature but they became bad through themselves; man, however, sinned at the suggestion of the devil. This Holy Trinity in its common essence undivided and in personal properties divided, through Moses, the holy prophets, and other servants gave to the human race at the most opportune intervals of time the doctrine of salvation.

And finally, Jesus Christ, the only begotten Son of God made flesh by the entire Trinity, conceived with the co-operation of the Holy Ghost of Mary ever Virgin, made true man, composed of a rational soul and human flesh, one Person in two natures, pointed out more clearly the way of life. Who according to His divinity is immortal and impassible, according to His humanity was made passible and mortal, suffered on the cross for the salvation of the human race, and being dead descended into hell, rose from the dead, and ascended into heaven. But He descended in soul, arose in flesh, and ascended equally in both; He will come at the end of the world to judge the living and the dead and will render to the reprobate and to the elect according to their works. Who all shall rise with their own bodies which they now have that they may receive according to their merits, whether good or bad, the latter eternal punishment with the devil, the former eternal glory with Christ.

There is one Universal Church of the faithful, outside of which there is absolutely no salvation. In which there is the same priest and sacrifice, Jesus Christ, whose body and blood are truly contained in the sacrament of the altar under the forms of bread and wine; the bread being changed (*transsubstantiatis*) by divine power into the body, and the wine into the blood, so that to realize the mystery of unity we may receive of Him what He has received of us. And this sacrament no one can effect except the priest who has been duly ordained in accordance with the keys of the Church, which Jesus Christ Himself gave to the Apostles and their successors.

But the sacrament of baptism, which by the invocation of each Person of the Trinity, namely, of the Father, Son, and Holy Ghost, is effected in water, duly conferred on children and adults in the form prescribed by the Church by anyone whatsoever, leads to salvation. And should anyone after the reception of baptism have fallen into sin, by true repentance he can always be restored. Not only virgins and those practicing chastity, but also those united in marriage, through the right faith and through works pleasing to God, can merit eternal salvation.

7. (*Canon 21*) *Confession, Reception of the Eucharist, and Penance*

Trans. Schroeder, *Disciplinary Decrees*, pp. 259–60.

All the faithful of both sexes shall after they have reached the age of discretion faithfully confess all their sins at least once a year to their own (parish) priest and perform to the best of their ability the penance imposed, receiving reverently at least at Easter the sacrament of the Eucharist, unless perchance at the advice of their own priest they may for a good reason abstain for a time from its reception; otherwise they shall be cut off from the Church (excommunicated) during life and deprived of Christian burial in death. Wherefore, let this salutary decree be published frequently in the churches, that no one may find in the plea of ignorance a shadow of excuse. But if anyone for a good reason should wish to confess his sins to another priest, let him first

seek and obtain permission from his own (parish) priest, since otherwise he (the other priest) cannot loose or bind him.

Let the priest be discreet and cautious that he may pour wine and oil into the wounds of the one injured after the manner of a skilful physician, carefully inquiring into the circumstances of the sinner and the sin, from the nature of which he may understand what kind of advice to give and what remedy to apply, making use of different experiments to heal the sick one. But let him exercise the greatest precaution that he does not in any degree by word, sign, or any other manner make known the sinner, but should he need more prudent counsel, let him seek it cautiously without any mention of the person. He who dares to reveal a sin confided to him in the tribunal of penance, we decree that he be not only deposed from the sacerdotal office but also relegated to a monastery of strict observance to do penance for the remainder of his life.

8. (*Canon 62*) *On the Abuse and the Validation of Relics*

Trans. Schroeder, *Disciplinary Decrees*, pp. 286–87. See also Chap. IX, Items 78–80, 88.

From the fact that some expose for sale and exhibit promiscuously the relics of saints, great injury is sustained by the Christian religion. That this may not occur hereafter, we ordain in the present decree that in the future old relics may not be exhibited outside of a vessel or exposed for sale. And let no one presume to venerate publicly new ones unless they have been approved by the Roman pontiff. In the future prelates shall not permit those who come to their churches *causa venerationis* to be deceived by worthless fabrications or false documents as has been done in many places for the sake of gain. We forbid also that seekers (*quaestores*) of alms, some of whom, misrepresenting themselves, preach certain abuses, be admitted, unless they exhibit genuine letters either of the Apostolic See or of the diocesan bishop, in which case they may not preach anything to the people but what is contained in those letters.

9. The True Body and Blood of Christ Contained under Double Species in One Sacrament

Breviloq., 6:9 (1), trans. E. E. Nemmers, *Breviloquium by St. Bonaventura* (St. Louis, Mo.: B. Herder Book Co., 1946), pp. 196–97.

1. As to the sacrament of the Eucharist, this must be held: that in this sacrament not only is the true body and blood of Christ signified but it is actually contained under the double species, namely, bread and wine, in one and not a twofold sacrament. This occurs after the consecration by the priest which is completed by saying over the bread the vocal form instituted by our Lord: This is My body; and over the wine: This is the chalice of My blood. When these words are spoken by a priest with the proper intention, each element is transubstantiated in substance into the body and blood of Jesus Christ even though the sensible species remain. The entire Christ is wholly contained in each of them, not in a circumscribed manner, but sacramentally. These words also show us that anyone worthily receiving the bread, not only sacramentally but through faith and charity by spiritual digestion becomes more a part of the mystical body of Christ and is in himself remade and cleansed. But he who approaches unworthily eats and drinks his own judgment, not discerning the most holy body of Christ.

10. Under Each Species Is the One Christ: The Body Hidden, the Accidents Existing Without Their Subject

Breviloq., 6:9 (5), trans. Nemmers, *Breviloquium*, pp. 199–200.

5. Because the blessed and glorious body of Christ cannot be divided into its parts and cannot be separated from the soul or from the highest divinity, hence under each species there is the one, entire, and indivisible Christ, namely, body, soul, and God. Hence in each is the one and most simple sacrament containing the entire Christ. And because every part of the species signifies the body of Christ, the whole body so exists in the whole species and it is in any part of it, whether it be undivided or separated. Hence the body is not there as circumscribed, as occupying space, as having position, as perceptible through any corporeal and human sense, but it is hidden from all sense so that faith may have its place and merit. That we may not perceive Him directly, these accidents, although they exist without their subject, have every function which they had previously as long as they contain within themselves the body of Christ and this is as long as they exist with their natural properties and are fit for eating.

11. An Account of the Seven Sacraments Written for the Armenians (1438)

"Exultate Deo" (1439), trans. from H. Denzinger, *Enchiridion symbolorum et definitionum*, pp. 201ff. (28 ed. [Friburg: Herder, 1952], Nos. 695–702, pp. 253–59), by Robinson, *REH*, I, pp. 348–54.

We have drawn up in the briefest form a statement of the truth concerning the seven sacraments, so that the Armenians, now and in future generations, may more easily be instructed therein.

There are seven sacraments under the new law: that is to say, baptism, confirmation, the mass, penance, extreme unction, ordination, and matrimony. These differ essentially from the sacraments of the old law; for the latter do not confer grace, but only typify that grace which can be given by the passion of Christ alone. But these our sacraments both contain grace and confer it upon all who receive them worthily.

The first five sacraments are intended to secure the spiritual perfection of every man individually; the last two are ordained for the governance and increase of the Church. For through baptism we are born again of the spirit; through confirmation we grow in grace and are strengthened in the faith; and when we have been born again and strengthened we are fed by the divine food of the mass; but if, through sin, we bring sickness upon our souls, we are made spiritually whole by penance; and by extreme unction we are healed, both spiritually and corporeally, according as our souls have need; by ordination the Church is governed and multiplied spiritually; by matrimony it is materially increased.

To effect these sacraments three things are necessary: the things [or symbols], that is, the "material"; the words, that is, the "form"; and the person of the "ministrant," who administers the sacrament with the intention of carrying out what the Church effects through him. If any of these things be lacking, the sacrament is not accomplished.

Three of these sacraments—baptism, confirmation, and ordination—impress indelibly upon the soul a character, a certain spiritual sign, distinct from all others; so they are not repeated for the same person. The other four do not imprint a character upon the soul, and admit of repetition.

Holy baptism holds the first place among all the sacraments because it is the gate of spiritual life; for by it we are made members of Christ and of the body of the Church. Since through the first man death entered into the world, unless we are born again of water, and of the spirit, we cannot, so saith Truth, enter into the kingdom of heaven. The material of this sacrament is water, real and natural—it matters nothing whether it be cold or warm. Now the form is: "I baptize thee in the name of the Father, and of the Son, and of the Holy Ghost." . . .

The ministrant of this sacrament is the priest, for baptism belongs to his office. But in case of necessity not only a priest or deacon may baptize, but a layman or a woman—nay, even a pagan or a heretic, provided he use the form of the Church and intend to do what the Church effects. The efficacy of this sacrament is the remission of all sin, original sin and actual, and of all penalties incurred through this guilt. Therefore no satisfaction for past sin should be imposed on those who are baptized; but if they die before they commit any sin, they shall straightway attain the kingdom of heaven and the sight of God.

The second sacrament is confirmation. The material is the chrism made from oil,

VIII-2. Baptism of Richard Beauchamp.

which signifies purity of conscience, and from balsam, which signifies the odor of fair fame; and it must be blessed by the bishop. The form is: "I sign thee with the sign of the cross and confirm thee with the chrism of salvation, in the name of the Father, and of the Son, and of the Holy Ghost." The proper ministrant of this sacrament is the bishop. While a simple priest avails to perform the other anointings, this one none can confer save the bishop only; for it is written of the apostles alone that by the laying on of hands they gave the Holy Ghost, and the bishops hold the office of the apostles. We read in the Acts of the Apostles, when the apostles who were at Jerusalem heard how Samaria had received the word of God, they sent to them Peter and John; who, when they were come, prayed that they might receive the Holy Ghost; for as yet it was fallen upon none of them,—they were only baptized in the name of the Lord Jesus. Then they laid hands upon them and they received the Holy Ghost. Now, in place of this

VIII-3. Confirmation.

VIII-4. Communion.

laying on of hands, confirmation is given in the Church. Yet we read that sometimes, for reasonable and urgent cause, by dispensation from the Holy See, a simple priest has been permitted to administer confirmation with a chrism prepared by a bishop.

In this sacrament the Holy Ghost is given to strengthen us, as it was given to the apostles on the day of Pentecost, that the Christian may confess boldly the name of Christ. And therefore he is confirmed upon the brow, the seat of shame, that he may never blush to confess the name of Christ

and especially his cross, which is a stumbling-block to the Jews and foolishness to the Gentiles, according to the apostle. Therefore he is signed with the sign of the cross.

The third sacrament is the eucharist. The material is wheaten bread and wine of the grape, which before consecration should be mixed very sparingly with water; because, according to the testimony of the holy fathers and doctors of the Church set forth in former times in disputation, it is believed that the Lord himself instituted this sacrament with wine mixed with water, and also because this corresponds with the accounts of our Lord's passion. For the holy Pope Alexander, fifth from the blessed Peter, says, "In the offerings of sacred things made to God during the solemnization of the mass, only bread and wine mixed with water are offered up. Neither wine alone nor water alone may be offered up in the cup of the Lord, but both mixed, since it is written that both blood and water flowed from Christ's side."

Moreover the mixing of water with the wine fitly signifies the efficacy of this sacrament, namely, the union of Christian people with Christ, for water signifies "people," according to the passage in the Apocalypse which says, "many waters, many people." And Julius, second pope after the blessed Sylvester, says: "According to the provisions of the canons the cup of the Lord should be offered filled with wine mixed with water, because a people is signified by the water,

and in the wine is manifested the blood of Christ. Therefore when the wine and water are mixed in the cup the people are joined to Christ, and the host of the faithful is united with him in whom they believe."

Since, therefore, the holy Roman Church, instructed by the most blessed apostles Peter and Paul, together with all the other churches of the Greeks and Latins in which glowed the light of sanctity and of doctrine, has from the beginning of the nascent Church observed this custom and still observes it, it is quite unseemly that any region whatever should depart from this universal and rational observance. We decree, therefore, that the Armenians likewise shall conform themselves with the whole Christian world, and that their priests shall mix a little water with the wine in the cup of oblation.

The form of this sacrament is furnished by the words of the Saviour when he instituted

VIII-5. Priests Hearing Confession before Lent. *Priests seated, heads covered, holding rods or wands. Penitents kneeling. Papal indulgences or licenses on walls. Altar, Reredos of Crucifixion, Crucifix.*

327

VIII-6. Unction: Death of Richard Beauchamp.

sacrament for the spiritual life. By it we recall the beloved memory of our Saviour; by it we are withheld from evil, and strengthened in good, and go forward to renewed growth in virtues and graces.

The fourth sacrament is penance. The material, as we may say, consists in the acts of penitence, which are divided into three parts. The first of these is contrition of the heart, wherein the sinner must grieve for the sins he has committed, with the resolve to commit no further sins. Second comes confession with the mouth, to which it pertains that the sinner should make confession to his priest of all the sins he holds in his memory. The third is satisfaction for sins according to the judgment of the priest, and this is made chiefly by prayer, fasting, and almsgiving. The form of this sacrament consists in the words of absolution which the priest speaks when he says, "I absolve thee," etc.; and the minister of this sacrament is the priest, who has authority to absolve either regularly or by the commission of a superior. The benefit of this sacrament is absolution from sins.

The fifth sacrament is extreme unction, and the material is oil of the olive, blessed by a bishop. This sacrament shall not be given to any except the sick who are in fear

it, and the priest, speaking in the person of Christ, consummates this sacrament. By virtue of these words, the substance of the bread is turned into the body of Christ and the substance of the wine into his blood. This is accomplished in such wise that the whole Christ is altogether present under the semblance of the bread and altogether under the semblance of the wine. Moreover, after the consecrated host and the consecrated wine have been divided, the whole Christ is present in any part of them. The benefit effected by this sacrament in the souls of those who receive it worthily is the union of man with Christ. And since, through grace, man is made one body with Christ and united in his members, it follows that through this sacrament grace is increased in those who partake of it worthily. Every effect of material food and drink upon the physical life, in nourishment, growth, and pleasure, is wrought by this

VIII-7. Order of a Priest.

of death. They shall be anointed in the following places: the eyes on account of the sight, the ears on account of the hearing, the nostrils on account of smell, the mouth on account of taste and speech, the hands on account of touch, the feet on account of walking, and the loins as the seat of pleasure. The form of this sacrament is as follows: "Through this holy unction and his most tender compassion, the Lord grants thee forgiveness for whatever sins thou hast committed by the sight,"—and in the same way for the other members. The minister of this sacrament is a priest. The benefit is even the healing of the mind and, so far as is expedient, of the body also. Of this sacrament the blessed apostle James says: "Is any sick among you? Let him call for the elders of the church and let them pray over him, anointing him with oil in the name of the Lord: and the prayer of faith shall save the sick, and the Lord shall raise him up; and if he have committed sins, they shall be forgiven him."

The sixth sacrament is ordination. The material for the priesthood is the cup with the wine and the paten with the bread; for the deaconate, the books of the Gospel; for the subdeaconate, an empty cup placed upon an empty paten; and in like manner, other offices are conferred by giving to the candidates those things which pertain to their secular ministrations. The form for priests is this: "Receive the power to offer sacrifice in the Church for the living and the dead, in the name of the Father, and of the Son, and of the Holy Ghost." And so for each order the proper form shall be used, as fully stated in the Roman pontifical. The regular minister of this sacrament is a bishop; the benefit, growth in grace, to the end that whosoever is ordained may be a worthy minister.

The seventh sacrament is matrimony, the type of the union of Christ and the Church, according to the apostle, who saith, "This is a great mystery; but I speak concerning Christ and the church." The efficient cause of marriage is regularly the mutual consent uttered aloud on the spot. These advantages are to be ascribed to marriage: first, the begetting of children and their bringing up in

VIII-8. Marriage.

the worship of the Lord; secondly, the fidelity that husband and wife should each maintain toward the other; thirdly, the indissoluble character of marriage, for this typifies the indissoluble union of Christ and the Church. Although for the cause of adultery separation is permissible, for no other cause may marriage be infringed, since the bond of marriage once legitimately contracted is perpetual.

III. The Priesthood and the Pastoral Functions of the Hierarchy

A. THEODULF OF ORLEANS (760–821) AND THE EPISCOPAL CURE OF SOULS

12. Bishops, Mass-Priests, and the Government of Souls

Capitula, 1 (In English translation from an old Saxon rendering of the Tenth Century), From J. Johnson, *A Collection of the Laws and Canons of the Church of England* (Oxford: John Henry Parker, 1850), I, pp. 452–53.

1. Ye ought to know and always to bear in mind that the care of God's people is

without doubt intrusted with us and the government of their souls; that we shall justly be punished at dooms-day for all those that perish through our neglect; and that we are to receive the reward of eternal life for them that we have gained to God with our example and doctrine. To us it is said by our Lord, "ye are the salt of the earth." If then Christian people are God's meat, and we the salt; then shall the people by the divine assistance by our means be with pleasure enjoyed by God. And ye ought to know, that your order is the second after ours and the next to us. As the bishops are in the stead of the Apostles in the assembly of the saints; so are the mass-priests in the stead of Christ's disciples. The bishops have the order of Aaron, the mass-priests the order of his sons; for it behoves you always to be mindful how high the dignity of the order [is,] and the consecration, and the anointing of your hand, which ye received from the bishop when ye took orders; that ye may never forfeit so high a favour, and never defile, by sinning, the hands that have been anointed with so holy an unction; but that ye keep your heart and body in purity, give all people an example to live well, and teach those over whom ye are, the right way to the kingdom of heaven.

B. BISHOP LANFRANC (1005–1085) AND HIS WINCHESTER CANONS (1071)

13. Canons Governing the Hierarchy, Priestly Integrity and the Liturgy

Trans. Johnson, *Laws and Canons*, II, pp. 8–9.

1. That no one be allowed to preside in two bishoprics.
2. That no one be ordained by means of simoniacal heresy.
3. That foreign clergymen be not received without commendatory letters.
4. That ordinations be performed at the certain seasons.
5. Of altars, that they be of stone.
6. That the sacrifice be not of beer, or water alone, but of wine mixed with water only.
7. Of baptism, that it be celebrated at Easter and Whitsuntide only, except there be danger of death.
8. That masses be not celebrated in churches, before they have been consecrated by bishops.
9. That the corpses of the dead be not buried in churches.
10. That the bells be not tolled at celebrating in the time of the secret.
11. That bishops only give penance for gross crimes.
12. That monks who have thrown off their habit be neither admitted into the army nor into any convent of clerks, but be esteemed excommunicate.

VIII-9. Bishop and Donor. *Painted limestone statue by French Sc., 15th century, Burgundian School.*

13. That every bishop celebrate a synod once a year.

14. That tithes be paid by all.

15. That clergymen either live chastely, or desist from their office.

16. That chalices be not of wax or wood.

C. PETER OF BLOIS (1204/1212) ON THE AWFUL RESPONSIBILITY OF THE PRIESTHOOD

14. The Misery of a Wicked Priest

Serm. 56, "On the Priesthood," trans. J. M. Neale, *Mediaeval Preachers and Mediaeval Preaching* (London: J. & C. Mozley, 1856), pp. 208–9.

Certainly a devout and prudent Priest, while he stands at the Divine table, will think of nothing else but "Jesus Christ, and Him crucified" (I Cor. 2:2). He will set before the eyes of his heart the humility of Christ, the patience of Christ, His Passion and sorrows; the reproaches of Christ—the spittings, the scourging, the spear, the Cross, the Death; he devoutly and solicitously recalls and crucifies himself in the memory of the Lord's Passion. . . . O how awful, how perilous a thing, my brethren, is the administration of your office! because ye shall have to answer not only for your own souls, but for the souls committed to your charge, when the Day of tremendous Judgment shall come! And how shall he keep another man's conscience whose own is not kept? For conscience is an abyss—a most obscure night: and what, then, of the wretched Priest who has undertaken this night, and to whom they cry, "Watchman, what of the day? Watchman, what of the night" (cf. Isa. 21:11)? What is that most wretched Priest to do who feels himself loaded with sins, implicated with cares, infected with the filthiness of carnal desires, blind, bowed down, weak, straitened by a thousand difficulties, anxious through a thousand necessities, miserable with a thousand troubles, precipitate to vices, weak to virtues? What shall he do—the son of grief—the son of eternal misery—who neither kindles the fire of love in himself, nor in others? Surely he is prepared for the fuel and the consumption of fire! "A fire is kindled in the fury of

the Lord" (cf. Jer. 15:14); and it shall burn even to the nethermost hell. A place is appointed for him with everlasting burnings; the worm is prepared which dieth not,—smoke, vapour, and the vehemence of storms; horror, and a deep shade; the weight of chains of repentance that bind, that burn, and that consume not! From which may that Fire deliver us Who consumes not, but consummates—which devours not, but enlightens every man that cometh into the world. May He illuminate us to give the knowledge of salvation unto His people; Who liveth and reigneth ever with the Father and the Holy Ghost, God to all ages of ages.

D. FRANCIS OF ASSISI (1182–1226) ON TRUE CATHOLICS, THE PRIESTHOOD, AND THE LITURGY

15. Confession and Communion

Ep. 1, trans. P. Robinson, *The Writings of Saint Francis of Assisi* (Philadelphia: Dolphin Press, 1905, 1906), pp. 98–103.

We ought indeed to confess all our sins to a priest and receive from him the Body and Blood of our Lord Jesus Christ. He who does not eat His Flesh and does not drink His Blood cannot enter into the Kingdom of God. Let him, however, eat and drink worthily, because he who receives unworthily "eateth and drinketh judgment to himself, not discerning the Body of the Lord" (I Cor. 11:29),—that is, not discerning it from other foods.

16. Reverence for Catholic Life, the Body and Blood of Christ, and for Priests

Ep. 1, trans. Robinson, *loc. cit.*

We ought also to fast and to abstain from vices and sins and from superfluity of food and drink, and to be Catholics. We ought also to visit Churches frequently and to reverence clerics not only for themselves, if they are sinners, but on account of their office and administration of the most holy Body and Blood of our Lord Jesus Christ, which they sacrifice on the altar and receive and administer to others. And let us all know for certain that no one can be saved except by the Blood of our Lord Jesus Christ

VIII-10. Philip the Good Assisting at Mass.

and by the holy words of the Lord which clerics say and announce and distribute and they alone administer and not others. But religious especially, who have renounced the world, are bound to do more and greater things, but "not to leave the other undone" (Luke 11:42).

E. ROBERT GROSSETESTE (1175–1253) AND THE ADMINISTRATION OF THE DIOCESE OF LINCOLN (1235–1253)

17. On the Bishop's Exercise of the Visitation Right and of the Gospel Pastorate

Propositio de visitatione diocesia suae, trans. F. S. Stevenson, *Robert Grosseteste, Bishop of Lincoln* (London: Macmillan & Company, Ltd., 1899), pp. 130–31. Acknowledgement of permission to reprint Items 17 and 18 is made to Macmillan & Company, Ltd., London, and St. Martin's Press, Inc., New York.

In his "Propositio de visitatione diocesia suae" Grosseteste, describing his "new and unaccustomed proceedings," says:

As soon as I was made Bishop I considered myself to be the overseer and pastor of souls, and therefore I held it necessary, lest the blood of the sheep should be required at my hands at the last judgment, to visit the sheep committed to me with diligence, as the Scripture orders and commands. Wherefore, at the commencement of my episcopate, I began to go round through the several archdeaconries, and in them through the several rural deaneries, causing the clergy of each deanery to be called together on a certain day and in a certain place, and the people to be warned that, at the same time, they should be present with the children to be confirmed and in order to hear the word of God and to confess. When clergy and people were assembled, I myself was accustomed to preach the word of God to the clergy, and some friar, either Preacher or Minor, to the people. Four friars were employed at the same time in hearing confessions and enjoining penances; and when the children had been confirmed, on that and the following day, I and my clerks gave our attention to inquiries, corrections, and reformations, such as belong to the office of inquiry. In my first circuit of this kind, some came to me to find fault with these proceedings, saying, 'My Lord, you are doing a new and unaccustomed thing.' To whom I answered, 'Every new thing which instructs and advances a man is a new thing fraught with blessing'; nor could I suppose at that time that on account of this my visitation any mischief would afterwards befall those placed under me.

VIII-11. Clerks Bearing the Gospel, Mitre and Cross. *Fragment of a Monument, Arnolfo di Lipo, Basilica di S. Giovanni in Laterano.*

VIII-12. Consecration of Archbishop Thomas Becket.

333

18. On Ecclesiastical Abuses and the Sad State of the Papal Curia; Decline of Gospel Teaching and the Pastoral Ministry

Memorandum (1250), Stevenson, *Robert Grosseteste*, pp. 286–88.

. . . And "although all pastors in common but one in the first pastor Christ, and all represent Him and occupy His place, yet, by a special prerogative, those who preside in this most holy See are peculiarly the representatives and vicars of Christ, as the cardinals represent the apostles, and other pastors those first fathers." All these ought incessantly to labour for the coming of God's kingdom. Such is the theory but what are the facts? Part of the world is in a state of unbelief, part has been severed by schism, and of the remainder a considerable portion is a prey to heresy and vice; and the cause is to be found in the lack of good pastors, the multiplication of bad pastors, and the restrictions placed upon the pastoral power. Then follows a fierce denunciation of the covetousness, the avarice, and the immorality of the clergy. "As the life of the pastors is the book of the laity, it is manifest that such as these are the preachers of all errors and wickednesses. They are in truth teachers of heresy, inasmuch as the word of action is stronger than the word of speech: they are worse than those who practise abominations, for they defile the soul."

"But what," he continues, "is the first cause and origin of these great evils? I fear to speak it, but yet I dare not be silent, lest I should merit the reproach of the prophet, 'Woe is me, because I have held my peace!' The cause, the fountain, the origin of all this, is this Roman Court, not only because it does not put to flight these evils and purge away these abominations, when it alone has the power to do so, and is pledged most fully in that sense; but still more because by its dispensations, provisions, and collations to the pastoral care, it appoints in the full light of the sun men such as I have described, not pastors, but destroyers of men; and, that it may provide for the likelihood of some one person, it hands over to the jaws of death many thousands of souls, for the life of each one of which the Son of God was willing to be condemned to a most shameful death. He who does not hinder this when he can is involved in the same crime; and the crime is greater in proportion as he who commits it is more highly placed, and the cause of evil is worse than its effect. Nor let any one say that this Court acts thus for the common advantage of the Church. This common advantage was studied by the holy fathers who endured suffering on this account; it can never be advanced by that which is unlawful or evil. Woe to those who say, Let us do evil that good may come! The work of the pastoral cure does not consist alone in administering the sacraments, repeating the canonical hours, and celebrating masses—and even these offices are seldom performed by mercenaries—but in the teaching of the living truth, the condemnation of vice, the punishment of it when necessary, and this but rarely can the mercenaries dare to do. It consists also in feeding the hungry, giving drink to the thirsty, clothing the naked, receiving guests, visiting the sick and those in prison, especially those who belong to the parish and have a claim on the endowment of the Church. These duties cannot be performed by deputies or hirelings, especially as they scarce receive out of the goods of the Church enough to support their own lives. This bad use of their office is greatly to be lamented in the case of the seculars, but in their case, at any rate, there is always the possibility that others of a better mind may follow them. When, however, parish churches are appropriated to religious houses, these evils are made permanent. Those who preside in this See are in a special degree the representatives of Christ, and in that character are bound to exhibit the works of Christ, and to that extent are entitled to be obeyed in all things. If, however, through favouritism or on other grounds they command what is opposed to the precepts and will of Christ, they separate themselves from Christ and from the conception of what a Pope should be; they are guilty of apostasy themselves and a cause of apostasy in others. God forbid that such should be the case in this See! Let its occupants, therefore, take heed lest they do or enjoin anything which is at variance with the will of Christ."

F. VISITATION QUERIES OF 1253 APROPOS CLERICAL AND LAY LIFE

19. Selections and Summarizations of Visitation Questions

Annales de Burton, p. 307, trans. E. L. Cutts, *Parish Priests and Their People in the Middle Ages in England* (London: SPCK, 1898), pp. 281–85.

1, 2, 3, 4 are about sensual sins on the part of the laity. 5. Whether any laymen are drunkards, or habitually frequent taverns, or practise usury of any kind. 6. Receive the free land of any church to farm. 7. Or receive in their fee the tithes of any church. 8. Whether rents assigned to lights or other specified uses of the church are converted to the use of the rector or vicar. 9. Whether any layman is compelled to communicate and offer after mass on Easter Day. 10. Whether any layman or other of whatever condition or reputation (*famae*) *perierit conscio rectore vel vicario loci*. 11. Whether any layman is notably proud, or envious, or avaricious, or slothful, or malicious, or gluttonous, or luxurious [the seven deadly sins]. 12. Whether any layman causes markets, or plays or pleas (*placita peculiaria*) to be held in sacred places, and whether these things have been prohibited on the part of the bishop. 13. Whether any laymen have played at "Rams" (*elevaverint arietes*), or caused scotales to be held, or have contended for precedence with their banners in their visitation of the mother church. 14. Whether any layman or woman entertain as a guest the concubine of any man of whatever condition, and keep a bad house. 15. Whether any sick person has lacked any sacrament from negligence of the priest lawfully called. 16. Whether any layman or other of whatever condition have died intestate, or without partaking of the sacraments, by the negligence of the priest or rector. 17. Whether any churches remain to be dedicated, or any have been destroyed without license from the bishop, since the Council of London. 18. Whether Jews dwell anywhere where they have not been used to dwell. 19. Whether any laymen have clandestinely contracted marriage in cases forbidden by law or without banns. 20. Whether the laity insist upon (*sunt pertinaces ut stent*) standing in the chancel with the clergy. 21. Whether any layman causes Divine service to be celebrated in any chapel without licence from the bishop. 22. In what way lay servants and representatives of parsons, abbots, priors, prioresses, and other parsons and religious persons, behave in their granges, mansions, and possessions. 23. Let diligent inquiry be made concerning the taxation of every church, and how much the rector of every church has given to the subsidy of the Lord Pope. 24. Whether any rectors or vicars or priests are very illiterate (*enormiter illiterati*). 25. Whether the sacrament of the Eucharist is everywhere carried to the sick with due reverence, and is kept in a proper manner. 26. Whether any of the aforesaid or others in sacred orders are incontinent, and in what kind of incontinence. 27. Whether the incontinent have been corrected by the archdeacon of the place, and how often and in what manner. 28. Whether any convicted or confessing incontinence have bound themselves to resignation of their benefices or other canonical punishment if they relapse, and whether any after so binding themselves have relapsed. 29. Whether any men beneficed or in sacred orders are married (*uxorati*). 30. Whether any clerics frequent the churches of nuns without reasonable cause. 31. Whether any of the clerks in holy orders keep (*tenent*) any woman related to him, or any concerning whom evil suspicions may arise. 32. Whether any are drunken, frequenters of taverns, or traders, or usurers, or fighters or wrestlers, or notorious for any vice. 33. Whether any are farmers, giving and receiving churches or vicarages to farm without the licence of the bishop. 34. Whether any are viscounts (high sheriffs) or secular judges, or hold baily-wicks (stewardships) for laymen, for which office they are obliged to give account (*unde obligentur eisdem ad ratiocinia*). 35. Whether any rectors make a bargain with their annual priests (*cum sacerdotibus annuis*) that, besides the stipend received from the rector, they may receive annualia and tricennalia from others. . . . 39. Whether any carry weapons, or have not the tonsure, and fitting habit. 40. Whether any one has more than one cure of souls without dispensation. . . . 43. Whether deacons hear confessions or minister other sacraments committed to priests only. 44. Whether any rector or vicar does not reside on his benefice. . . . 49. Whether cartings are done (*fiant cariagia*) on the Lord's days or festivals, and by whom. . . . 62. Concerning the life and proper conduct of archdeacons, deans, and clerics who minister in churches, and concerning the agents and servants of parsons and others. 63. Whether any anchorite has been made without the assent of the bishop. 64. Whether any monks or religious dwell in their granges or possessions, and how the monks behave there in spiritual things, and what is their reputation. 65. Whether the dean and others have entered into a confederacy during the vacancy of the see to the prejudice of the incoming bishop. 66. Whether any archdeacons have received more for procuration than they ought to receive according to the new consititution.

G. THE REPLIES OF THE "TESTES SYNODALES," OR "QUEST MEN," ON THE EXAMINATION OF THE PASTORAL CHARACTER AND FUNCTION

20. *Diocese of Exeter, Bishop Stapledon's Visitation* (1301)

Register, pp. 194, 130, 111, 109, trans. Cutts, *Parish Priests*, pp. 285–89.

Branscombe.—Thomas the Vicar conducts himself well in all things, and preaches willingly (*libenter*), and diligently does all things which belong to the office of a priest.

Culmstock.—William the Vicar is a man of good life and honest conversation, and his clerk likewise, and well instructs his parishioners. In the visitation of the sick and baptizing the children, and in all things which belong to his office, they know nothing to be found fault with in him, with the exception that he makes too little pause between the matins and mass on festival days.

Colyton.—Sir Robert the Vicar is a good man (*probus homo*), and preaches to them so far as he knows (*quatenus novit*), but not *sufficienter*, as it seems to them. They say also that his predecessors were accustomed to call the friars to instruct them about their souls' salvation, but he does not care for them; and if by chance they come he does not receive them, nor give them entertainment (*viatica*); whereof they pray that he may be admonished. Item, all the chaplains and clerks of the church live *honeste et continentes*.

Colebrook.—Hugh de Coppelestone and other trust-worthy men of the parish, lawfully requisitioned and examined, say that Sir William the Vicar preaches after his own fashion (*suo modo*); also he expounds to them the Gospels on the Lord's Days so far as he knows (*quatenus novit*); but concerning the Articles of the Faith, the Commandments of the Decalogue, and the mortal sins, he does not teach them much. And he does not say his matins with note on the more solemn days, and only celebrates on the week days every other day. He is defamed of incontinency with Lucia de la Stubbe, a married woman (*conjugata*). All his houses, except the hall and chamber, which were in a good state at his coming, are now falling to pieces and threatening to come down, and could not be made good for a hundred shillings. Also his gate is so far from the hall, which he has lately lengthened, that one calling without is not heard in the hall, which is dangerous for the sick parishioners.

St. Mary Church.—The parishioners have some complaints to make about business matters between themselves and the vicar, but finally testify that he preaches well and exercises his office laudably in all things when he is present; but that he is often absent, and stays at Moreton sometimes for fifteen days, sometimes for eight, so that they have not a chaplain, unless when Sir Walter, the chaplain of the archdeacon, is present, or some one can by chance be obtained from some other place.

Dawlash.—In Bishop Stapledon's Visitation, in 1301, the *synodales* say that the vicar, who has the reputation of being a good man, does not reside in person, but has in his place Sir Adam, a chaplain, who conducts himself *bene et honeste,* and teaches them excellently in spiritual matters. But Randulphus the chaplain has had his concubine for ten years or more, and, often corrected for it (*saepius inde correptus*), remains incorrigible. The clerk of the church is *continens et honestus.*

H. ARCHBISHOP PECKHAM († 1292) AND HIS CONSTITUTIONS ON CLERICAL RESPONSIBILITY (CANON 10 OF THE PROVINCIAL SYNOD OF LAMBETH, 1281)

21. *On the Ignorance of Priests; Pastoral Delinquency in Instruction and Preaching*

Trans. Cutts, *Parish Priests,* pp. 216–17.

The ignorance of priests precipitates the people into the pit of error, and the foolishness or rudeness of clerks, who ought to instruct the minds of the faithful in the Catholic faith, sometimes tends rather to error than to doctrine. Also some blind preachers do not always visit the places which most need the light of truth, as the prophet witnesses, who says, "The children seek for bread, and there is no one to break it to them;" and another prophet cries, "The poor and needy ask for water, and their tongue is parched." For the remedy of such mischiefs we ordain that every priest who presides over a people do four times a year, that is, once in each quarter of the year, on one or more festival days, either by himself or by another, expound to the people in popular language without any fanciful subtlety, the 14 Articles of Faith, the 10 Commandments of the Lord, the 2 Evangelical Precepts of Charity, the 7 Works of Mercy, the 7 Deadly Sins with their progeny, the 7 Principal Virtues, and the 7 Sacraments of Grace. And in order that no one may excuse himself from this on account of igno-

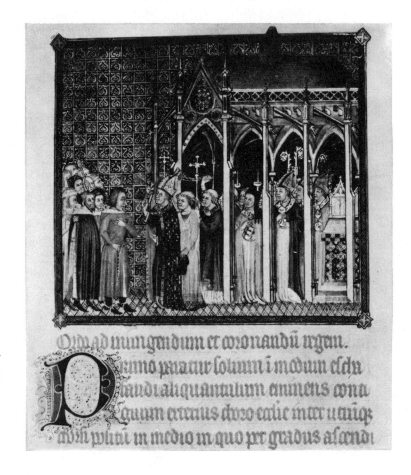

VIII-13. Procession of Bishops with Cross Bearer, Thurifer, Holy Water, Priests, and Canons.

rance, though all ministers of the Church ought to know them, we have here with great brevity summed them up.

Of the Articles of Faith.—Seven of them concern the mystery of the Trinity; four of these belong to the essence of the Godhead, and the other three relate to His works. The first is the unity of the Divine Essence in three Persons of the Indivisible Trinity agreeably to this part of the Creed, "*I believe in one God.*" The second is to believe God the Father, begotten of none. The third is to believe the Son the only begotten, and God. The fourth is to believe the Holy Ghost to be God, neither begotten nor unbegotten, but proceeding both from the Father and the Son. The fifth article is to believe in the creation of Heaven and Earth (that is, of every visible and invisible creature) by the whole and undivided Trinity.

The sixth is the Sanctification of the Church by the Holy Ghost, and by the Sacraments of Grace, and by all those things in which the Christian Church communicates. By which is understood that the Church, with its Sacraments and discipline, is, through the Holy Ghost, sufficient for the salvation of every sinner; and that outside the Church there is no salvation. The seventh article is the consummation of the Church in eternal glory by a true resurrection of body and soul; and on the contrary is understood the eternal damnation of the lost.

22. On the Priestly Administration of the Seven Sacraments

Trans. Cutts, *Parish Priests*, p. 222.

There are Seven Sacraments of the Church, the power of administering which is committed to the clergy. Five of these Sacraments ought to be received by all Christians in general; that is, Baptism, Confirmation, Penance, the Holy Eucharist, and Extreme Unction, which last is only for one who seems to be in danger of death; it should be given, if it may be, before a man is so far spent as to lose the use of his reason; but if he happens to be seized by a frenzy, or suffer from any alienation of mind, this Sacrament ought nevertheless to be ad-

ministered to him, provided he gave signs of a religious disposition before his mind was disturbed. Under such qualifications Extreme Unction is believed to be beneficial to the sick person provided he is predestinated (*predestinationis filius*), and either procures him a lucid interval or some spiritual advantage. The other two Sacraments are Order and Matrimony. The first belongs to the perfect, but the second in the time of the New Testament belongs to the imperfect only, and yet we believe that, by the virtue of the sacrament, it conveys grace, if it is contracted with a sincere mind.

I. JOHN MYRC'S (MIRK'S) VERSIFIED "INSTRUCTIONS FOR PARISH PRIESTS" [C. 1420] (MODERNIZED BY CUTTS, "PARISH PRIESTS," FROM EARLY ENGLISH TEXT SOCIETY, 31 [1868].)

23. The Priest is to Bid Everyone Come to Confession and Communion

EETS, p. 8, Ll. 244–49, via Cutts, *op. cit.*, p. 235.

Teach them then with good intent
To beleve in that sacrament
What they receive in form of bread
It is God's body that suffered dead
Upon the holy rood tree,
To buy our sins and make us free.

24. He Is to Explain the Relationship of the Elements to Christ's Death on the Cross

EETS, p. 9, Ll. 260–64, via Cutts, *op. cit.*, p. 236.

Hast thou eaten any Sonday
Withouten holy bred? Say yea or nay;

But teach them all to 'lieve sudde
That it which is on the altar made
It is very God's blood
That He shed on the rood.

25. And to Teach the People the Following or Similar Words to Say at the Consecration

EETS, pp. 9–10, Ll. 290–303, via Cutts, *op. cit.*, p. 237.

Jesu, Lord, welcome thou be,
In forme of bred as I Thee see;

VIII-14. Six Knights Doing Penance at the Shrine of St. Edmund.

Jesu for thy holy name
Shield me to-day from sin and shame.
Shrift and housel, Lord, thou grant me bo
Ere that I shall hennes go,
And true contrycion of my sin
That I Lord never die therein.
And as thou wert of a may y'bore,
Suffer me never to be forelore;
But when that I shall hennes wend
Graunt me thi blysse withouten ende. Amen.

Teche them thus or some othere thynge,
To say at the holy sakerynge.

Welcome, Lord, in form of bread,
For me thou suffered hard deed?
As thou didst bear the crown of thorn
Suffer me not to be forlorn.

J. THE LAY-FOLKS MASS BOOK (DIFFERENT VERSIONS, TENTH TO FIFTEENTH CENTURY) FOR THE INSTRUCTION OF THE PEOPLE (MODERNIZED BY CUTTS, *op. cit.*)

26. *What the People Are to Be Instructed to Say at Consecration, Elevation, etc.*

Lay-Folks Mass Book, EETS, 71 (1868), Text B, p. 40, Ll. 428–37; Text C, p. 42, Ll. 241–44; Text C, p. 44, Ll. 257–68, via Cutts, *op. cit.*, p. 247.

Loved by Thou, king,
And blessed be Thou, king,
    Of all thy giftes good;
And thanked be Thou, king,
Jesu, all my joying,

That for me spilt Thy blood,
    And died upon the rood.
Thou give me grace to sing,
The song of thy loving.
Pater noster. Ave maria. Credo.

When the priest the elevation has made
He will spread his arms on-brade,
Then is the time to pray for the dead,
Father's soul, mother's soul, brother dear,
Sister's souls, sibmen, and other sere,
That us good would, or us good did,
Or any kindness unto us kyd.
And to all in purgatory pine
This mass be mede and medicine;
To all Christian souls holy
Grant Thy grace and Thy mercy;
Forgive them all their trespass,
Loose their bonds and let them pass
From all pine and care,
Into the joy lasting evermore. Amen.

27. *When and How They Are to Say the Lord's Prayer in English*

Lay-Folks Mass Book, Text B, p. 46, Ll. 496–505, via Cutts, *op. cit.*, p. 248.

Fader our, that is in heaven,
Blessed be Thy name to neven.
Come to us Thy kingdom.
In heaven and earth Thy will be done.
Our ilk-day bread grant us to-day,
And our misdeeds forgive us aye,
As we do them that trespass us
Right so have mercy upon us,
And lead us in no founding,
But shield us from all wicked thing. Amen.

VIII-15. Elevation at Mass.

28. Prayers for Peace and Charity at the Pax; Prayers for Grace on Having Heard the Mass; Prayer of Thanksgiving

EETS, Text B, p. 56, Ll. 584–86, 596–99; p. 58, Ll. 610–13, via Cutts, *op. cit.*, p. 248.

Jesu my King, I pray to Thee,
Bow down thine ears of pity,
And hear my prayer in this place.

We pray this mass us stand in stead
Of shrift and als of housel bread.
And Jesu, for Thy woundes five,
Teach us the way of right-wise live. Amen

God be thanked of all his works,
God be thanked for priests and clerks,
God be thanked for ilk a man.
And I thank God all I can, etc.

K. A FOURTEENTH-CENTURY ANONYMOUS POEM ON THE PRIESTHOOD

29. The Cock Symbolic of Priestly Vigilance

"*Multi sunt presbyteri*," trans. J. N. Neale, *Collected Hymns* (London, 1869, 1914), pp. 69ff.

Many are the Presbyters
Lacking information

Why the Cock on each church tow'r
Meetly finds his station;
Therefore I will now hereof
Tell the cause and reason,
If ye lend me patient ears
For a little season.

Cock, he is a marvellous
Bird of GOD'S creating,
Faithfully the Priestly life
In his ways relating:
Such a life as he must lead
Who a parish tendeth,
And his flock from jeopardy
Evermore defendeth.

From what point the wind his course
On the tower directeth,
To that point the cock his head
Manfully objecteth:
Thus the Priest, where'er he sees
Satan warfare waging,
Thither doth he turn himself
For his flock engaging.

Cock, he, more than other birds
Way through ether winging,
Heareth high above the clouds
Choirs Angelic singing;
Thus he warns us cast away
Evil word and doing,
Thoughts and joys of things above
Evermore ensuing.

On his head a royal crown,
Like a king, he beareth;
On his foot a shapely spur,
Like a knight, he weareth;
Waxeth golden more and more
As in age he groweth;
And the lion quakes with fear,
When by night he croweth.

L. TYPICAL AND ATYPICAL TEACHING ON INDULGENCES

30. The Orthodox Official View on the Mystic Treasury and Supererogation

Bishop Lyndwood's *Provinciale*, ed. 1679, pp. 336–37, trans. G. G. Coulton, *Social Life in*

Britain from the Conquest to the Reformation (Cambridge: Cambridge University Press, 1918), pp. 203–4.

The Mystic Treasury is that of the merits of the whole Church, and of those made perfect in the Church, and also of Christ Himself. For this Treasure is collected from the abundance of superfluous merits which many saints have paid and weighed out beyond the measure of what they owed, and from the tribulations by them endured, whereof the merit is so great as to exceed all the penalty [of sin] owed by any living man; and especially the passion and merits of Christ, the least drop of whose blood or sweat would suffice for the expiation of all the sins that ever were; for all they are as nothing in respect of this . . . ; and the other good works done by true believers, all which are laid up in the Casket and Treasure-house of the Church, the dispensation whereof is granted to all who have the care of Christ's Mystical Body, and the key of the whole Church militant; that is, generally, to the Supreme Pontiff, but locally also to the other Bishops in their dioceses and Archbishops in their provinces, provided only that they do not exceed the quantity limited by [Canon] law.

31. Disillusionment over Unwarranted Dependence upon Papal Indulgences

Thomas Gascoigne, *Loci e Libro Veritatem*, ed. Rogers, 1881, *passim*, trans. Coulton, *Social Life in Britain*, pp. 204–5.

(P. 86.) The sixth river of Babylonian confusion and destruction [of the Church] is the false faith which some men have in indulgences granted by the Pope, or by man; which [faith] is not of God, for such men have not what is required for such a pardon in God's sight [*here follow five pages setting forth the orthodox theory of indulgences after St Thomas Aquinas and other similar authorities; then he proceeds, p. 91*]: O! how often have I heard worldly men of carnal life say proudly, "I care not how often I implead men, or gain great wealth for my own enjoyment, or impoverish the widows and the destitute by cunning sleights and crafty tricks; for, however ill I may live, by visiting such-and-such a church and by offering money there I can get a plenary remission of guilt and penalty for my sins!" O how blind of soul are those who say such falsehoods! How is that man loosed from bonds, who is yet held in bonds? How is he loosed from sin, while he leaveth not his iniquity, nor doeth either in will or in deed the good works which he oweth to God? . . . The men of our times [*homines moderni*] say "We reck not of any sin; but we do whatsoever pleaseth us as though it were lawful; we have sinned, and no vengeance hath overtaken us; and, if we sin again, we need have no fear, for the Kingdom of God is nigh unto us, and Rome is even at our doors; for we can easily and quickly get us pardon for our guilt, and remission of all the penalty thereof, if we give money for a papal indulgence.". . . A certain doctor at Bâle wrote there a great discourse of papal indulgences, wherein he affirmeth that he hath found no indulgences granted and sealed, after the fashion that is used in these days of ours, within the first thousand years after Christ; nor hath he found described, in the writings of any saint, any indulgences after the fashion now used. . . . Sinners say nowadays, "I care not how many or what evils I do in God's sight; for I can easily and quickly get plenary remission of all guilt and penalty by an absolution and indulgence granted me by the Pope, whose written grant I have bought for 4d, or for 6d, or have won as a stake for a game of tennis [with the pardoner]." For these indulgence-mongers wander over the country and give a letter of pardon sometimes for 2d., sometimes for a good draught of wine or beer, sometimes as a stake for a game of tennis, or even for the hire of a harlot or for carnal love. For Pietro da Monte who, about the year 1440, collected immense sums for indulgences granted by Pope Eugenius, when he went on shipboard to leave England, said to Doctor Vincent Clement: "By God!" (quoth he) "Pope Eugenius shall never have one penny from these full money-bags, unless I first get his promissory letters granting me the Archbishopric of Milan!"

IV. Heresy and Inquisition; Persecution and Toleration of the Jews

A. TEXTS FROM MANICHAEAN DUALISM AS A BRIDGE FROM ANCIENT TO MEDIEVAL HERESY

32. The Light-Form and the Five Fathers; Salutation, Veneration, and Laying on of Hands

Trans. by the editor from *Manichäische Handschriften der Staatlichen Museen Berlin*, ed. C. Schmidt, Bd. I, *Kephalaia*, ed. H. Ibischer (Stuttgart: W. Kohlhammer, 1940), Kap. 7–8, pp. 35–36, 40–41, and D. Roché, *Études Manichéennes et Cathares* (Paris: Vega, 1952), pp. 178–79.

The first Father is the Father of Greatness, the Glorious and Extolled One . . . the first Eternal One, the Root of all Light. . . .

The second Father, who has come forth from the first, is the Image or Figure of the Kings of Light. . . .

The third Father, who has come forth from the second, is the Jesus of the Brightness, the Magnificent One. . . .

The fourth Father is the Light-Nous (Light-Mind, or Light-Spirit), the chosen of the whole church. . . .

But the fifth Father is the Light-Form which the elect and the catechumens receive when they renounce the world. The Light-Form reveals himself to every man who departs his body toward the image, toward the figure [or likeness] of the Apostle, together with the three great, shining angels who come with it, the one holding the scepter in his hand, the second bearing the Light-Clothing, the third holding the diadem, the garland, and the crown of light. These are the three angels of light which come with the Light-Form and which manifest themselves with it to the elect and to the catechumens. . . .

These five mysteries, these five signs are sprung from the Godhead. They have been proclaimed to the world by an apostle. . . . The Light-Nous who comes into the world comes in these varied types. With these five things he chooses his church. Before everything else he gives the greeting of peace to men. When a man receives the salutation of peace, and becomes a Son of Peace, he is selected a believer. When he receives the greeting of peace he takes the right hand [extended to him as a symbol of truth] and is enrolled among the righteous. The Light-Nous then draws him to himself and places him [where he will] in the church. Owing to [this ceremony of the] right hand, the man receives the kiss of love (*agape*) and becomes a Son of the church. He is venerated and he venerates the God of Truth as well as the holy church. . . . Finally—in conclusion to all of this—the right hand of grace is laid upon him and he receives the imposition of hands, he is ordained, established in truth, and consolidated in it for eternity. He goes toward the Light-Nous by means of these good signs, he becomes a perfected [or consecrated] man, venerating and praising the God of Truth. . . .

At the moment of the man's death, the Light-Form rises before him and leads him from the Darkness to the Light. The Light-Form comforts him with a kiss and with quiet courage in the face of the demons who destroy the body. By his outlook and appearance he calms the heart of the elect now departing from the body. The angel carrying the scepter gives him his right hand, reclaiming him from the abyss of his body, and receiving him with a loving kiss. Each soul reverences his saviour, which is the Light-Form.

B. BOGOMILISM IN RELATION TO MANICHAEAN DUALISM AND CATHARISM

33. The Treatise of a Former Bogomil against that Sect

Trans. by the editor from *Le traité contre les Bogomiles de Cosmas le prêtre*, trans. H. C. Puech *et* A. Vaillant [L'Institut d'Études Slaves, 21] (Paris: Imprim. Nationale, 1945), selections from pp. 55–64, 77.

On the outside, indeed, the heretics appear as sheep. They are gentle and humble, silent, rendered pale by their hypocritical fasting. They utter no vain words. . . . Outwardly they are scarcely to be distinguished from true Christians. But within they are ravishing wolves as the Lord said. . . . Like a wolf about to carry off a lamb they first bow and sigh and respond with humility.

They act like those knowing in advance what transpires in the heavens, and whenever they see a simple, ignorant man they sow the tares of their instruction, blaspheming the doctrines handed down to the holy churches. . . .

But to what shall I liken these men? . . . Is it with demons that I should compare them? But they are worse than the demons themselves. For the demons fear the cross of Christ. . . . The demons fear a likeness of the Lord painted on a board and the heretics do not venerate images but call them idols. The demons fear the relics of God's righteous ones and dare not approach the reliquaries where the treasure lies without a price paid to Christians to save them from all danger. . . . And the heretics turn away in derision, and they jeer at us when they see us prostrate ourselves before the relics, beseeching the aid of the saints. . . . Refusing to render praises to the saints, at the same time they insult the miracles of our Lord performed through the relics of the saints by the power of the Holy Spirit. And they insist that these miracles have not occurred according to God's will but that it is the devil who does this in order to seduce men. . . .

They pretend that it is not God who has made the heaven, earth, and the whole visible world. . . .

As for the cross of our Lord, here are the blasphemies that they utter: "Why adore it? It was on this that the Jews crucified the Son of God. The cross is rather the enemy of God." Furthermore, in teaching their followers to despise it instead of adoring it they say: "If some one had killed the son of a king with a piece of wood, would this wood be held dear by the king? The same thing is true for God where the cross is concerned."

What, indeed, do they say concerning holy communion? "The communion was not instituted by God's command, and the eucharist is not actually the body of Christ as you [Catholics] pretend, but simple nourishment like all the rest. For it was not Christ who instituted the mass, that is why we do not honor the communion.

[Addressing the heretics, the writer demands of them:]

How is it that you blaspheme the sacred rules transmitted to us by the holy apostles and by the Fathers inspired of God—I refer to the [divine] office and the other prayers composed by good Christians—and how can you say: "It was not the apostles who bequeathed us the liturgy and the communion, it was John Chrysostom"? But from the incarnation of Christ to the time of John Chrysostom, three hundred years elapsed. In all those years would the churches of God have remained without liturgy and without communion?

You [heretics] insult the priests and the entire religious hierarchy, treating geniune believing priests like blind Pharisees. Launching a whole series of injuries at them, you pursue them in full cry like dogs baying after a horseman.

They do not limit their blasphemies to earth but direct them also to the heavens, saying that it is by the devil's will that everything exists: the heavens, the sun, the stars, the air, the earth, man, churches, crosses; all that properly belonging to God they deliver up to the devil. . . .

They, themselves, give to the devil the name, Mammon. They call him the creator and ordainer of earthly things. They say that it was he who commanded men to take wives, to eat meat and to drink wine. Disparaging in a word all our human joys, they set themselves up as denizens of the heavens while they denominate as servants of Mammon the men who marry and live in the world. As for themselves, they repudiate all these joys with disgust; not practicing abstinence as we do, but pretending that these things are impure.

C. THE CATHARISTS AND ANTI-HIERARCHICAL PRACTICES, ACCORDING TO AN INQUISITOR'S GUIDE BOOK, BERNARD GUI'S "PRACTICE OF THE INQUISITION"

34. The New-Manichaeans and Their Current Errors

Practica Officii Inquisitiones heretice pravitatis, 5:1 (1), via G. Mollat, *Bernard Gui, Manuel de l'Inquisiteur* (Paris: Société d'Édition Les Belles Lettres, 1926), I, 10–14, trans. by the editor.

The sect, the heresy, and the devoted supporters of the Manichaeans recognize and confess two Gods or two Lords, namely, a benevolent God and a wicked God. They assert the creation of all visible and material things to be, not the work of God the heavenly Father—as they call the good God—but the work of the devil and of Satan, of the evil God; for they call him the malevolent God, God of this era and prince of this world. They posit, then, two creators, God and the devil, and two creations, one, that is, of invisible and immaterial things, the other of things visible and material.

Likewise they invent two churches: one benevolent which they declare to be their sect—this same they assert to be the church of Jesus Christ; the other, the malevolent which they declare to be the Roman church. This they impudently call the mother of fornications, the great Babylon, courtesan and sanctuary (*basilicam*) of the devil, synagogue of Satan. They despise and defame the entire (Roman) hierarchy, its orders, its organization and statutes; denominating as heretics and wayward ones all those who hold its faith, teaching that no one is able to be saved in the faith of the Roman church.

Furthermore, they declare useless and vain each and all of the sacraments of the Roman church of our Lord Jesus Christ, that is, the eucharist or sacrament of the altar, the baptism performed with material water, confirmation, order, extreme unction, penitence, and marriage between a man and a woman. And they apishly devise in the place of these sacraments others almost like them. Thus they replace the baptism of water with another baptism, this one spiritual, which they term the *consolamentum* of the Holy Spirit, when for example they receive anyone, well or sick, into their sect and their order by the laying on of hands according to their accursed rite.

In the place of the eucharistic bread consecrated as the body of Christ, they fabricate a kind of bread which they call blessed bread or the bread of holy prayer. At the beginning of their meal, while holding the bread in their hands, according to their rite they bless, break, and distribute it to their assistants and to their "believers" (*et credentibus suis*). [One recalls here the apostolic *agape*. Ed.]

As for the sacrament of penitence, they say that true penitence is observed by taking up and holding fast their sect and order. They assure those, sick or well, who enter into the said sect and order, that all their sins are forgiven. Such are declared absolved from all their sins without any other satisfaction and even without restitution, if indeed they have anything belonging to another; on the condition, however, of their serving that sect and order. Over these [recruits] they claim a power identical and equal to that exercised by Peter, Paul and the other apostles of our Lord Jesus Christ. They insist that the confession of sins made to the priests of the Roman church avails nothing for salvation, declaring that neither the pope nor anyone else in the Roman church has the power of absolving any one from his sins.

In substitution for the sacrament of marriage, the bodily union between a man and a woman, they invent a spiritual marriage between the soul and God, when, for example, the "perfect" heretics (*heretici perfecta* or *perfecti*) or the "consoled" ones (*consolati*) admit anyone to their sect and order.

Likewise, they deny the incarnation of our Lord Jesus Christ within [the womb of] Mary always virgin, holding that he took no true human body or actual human flesh, such as other men have by virtue of their human nature. They hold, further, that he did not actually suffer and die on the cross, that he did not rise from the dead, that he did not ascend into heaven with a body and human flesh, but that all of this was done in similitude or by way of resemblance (*in similitudine facta fuisse*).

Equally do they deny that the Blessed Virgin Mary was the veritable mother of our Lord Jesus Christ and that she was an actual woman in the flesh. The Virgin Mary, they say, is really their sect and their order, that is the true penitence, chaste and virginal, that generates the sons of God when they are initiated into this same sect and order.

They even deny the future resurrection of the human body and in lieu of this they predicate certain spiritual bodies and a certain interior man. It is in reference to this last and in this sense that the future resurrection is to be understood. . . .

35. The "Perfect" Heretics (Perfecti) and the "Believers" (Credenti); the Inquisition Focused on the Former

Practica, 5:1 (1), via Mollat, *Manuel,* I, 16, trans. by the editor.

Such "perfect" heretics (*perfecti*) as we now speak of, the inquisitors are in the habit of detaining for a long time and for numerous reasons. This is, first of all, to invite them more frequently to accept conversion, for their conversion is especially advantageous. The conversion of Manichaean *perfecti* is usually sincere, rarely feigned. When they are converted they lay bare everything, open up the whole truth, and reveal all their accomplices; whence follows great fruit. Likewise, so long as the "perfect" are detained, their "believers" and accomplices confess the more readily. They expose themselves and the rest, fearing denunciation by the "perfect" if these are converted. If, however, these same heretics (*perfecti*), after frequent and patient exhorting to conversion, refuse to return to the faith and appear obdurate, one shall pronounce sentence against them and relinquish them to the secular arm and tribunal.

36. The "Perfect," the "Believers," the Melioramentum, *and the* Covenensa

Trans. by the editor from *Practica,* 5:1 (2), via Mollat, *Manuel,* I, 20–22.

The "perfect" teach their "believers" to render them a mark of veneration which they call the *melioramentum,* but which we call adoration [One kind was that used here; another was employed during the ceremony of initiation. Ed.]. The believer kneels in the presence of the "perfect," bowing low on a stool or to the ground, his hands joined, three times bowing and rising in turn, each time saying, *Benedicite.* In the end he says: "Good Christians, give us the blessing of God and your own; pray the Lord for us that God may preserve us from the evil death and lead us to the good end or to the hands of faithful Christians." And the "perfect" replies, "Receive God's blessing and ours. May God bless you, snatch away your soul from the evil death and lead you to the good end."

By the evil death the "perfect" mean death in the faith of the Roman church; but by the good end and the hands of faithful Christians they understand the reception of the believers at the moment of death into their sect and order according to their rite. It is this that they call the good end. As to the aforesaid reverence, the "perfect" pretend that it is addressed, not to themselves, but to the Holy Spirit which, they say, dwells in them and by which they have been inducted into the sect and rank which they claim to hold.

Furthermore, they teach their "believers" to draw up a pact which they term the *covenensa,* according to which the believers are to be received at their death into the sect and order of the "perfect"; in keeping with which the "perfect" are enabled to initiate them in the course of an illness, even if the sick one has lost the power of speech and no longer possesses ordinary memory.

37. Further Teachings of the Catharists about Their Own and the Roman Church

Practica, 5:1 (4), trans. *PTR,* III, 6 (2), pp. 9–10.

It would take too long to describe in detail the manner in which these same Manichean heretics preach, and teach their followers, but it must be briefly considered here.

In the first place they usually say of themselves that they are good Christians, who do not swear, or lie, or speak evil of others; that they do not kill any man or animal nor anything having the breath of life, and that they hold the faith of the Lord Jesus Christ and His Gospel as Christ and His Apostles taught. They assert that they occupy the place of the apostles, and that on account of the above mentioned things those of the Roman Church, namely, the prelates, clerks and monks, persecute them, especially the Inquisitors of Heresy, and call them heretics, although they are good men and good Christians, and that they are persecuted just as Christ and his apostles were by the Pharisees.

They moreover talk to the laity of the evil lives of clerks and the prelates of the Roman Church, pointing out and setting forth their pride, cupidity, avarice and uncleanness of life and such other evils as they know. They invoke with their own interpretation and according to their abilities the authority of the Gospels and the Epistles against the condition of the prelates, churchmen and monks, whom they call Pharisees and false prophets, who say but do not.

Then they attack and vituperate, one after the other, all the sacraments of the church, especially the sacrament of the Eucharist, saying that it cannot contain the body of Christ, for had this been as great as the largest mountain Christians would have consumed it entirely before this. They assert that the host comes from straw, that it passes through the tails of horses, to wit, when the flour is cleaned by a sieve [of horse hair]. That moreover it passes through the body and comes to a vile end which, they say, could not happen if God were in it. Of baptism, they assert that water is material and corruptible, and is therefore the creation of the Evil Power and cannot sanctify the soul, but that the churchmen sell this water out of avarice, just as they sell earth for the burial of the dead, and oil to the sick when they anoint them, and as they sell the confession of sins as made to the priests. Hence, they claim that confession made to the priests of the Roman Church is useless, and that since the priests may be sinners, they cannot loose nor bind, and being unclean themselves, cannot make another clean. They assert, moreover, that the Cross of Christ should not be adored or venerated, because, as they urge, no one would venerate or adore the gallows upon which a father, relative or friend had been hung. They urge further that they who adore the cross ought for similar reasons to worship all thorns and lances, because as Christ's body was on the cross during the passion so was the crown of thorns on his head and the soldier's lance in his side. They proclaim many other scandalous things in regard to the sacraments. They, moreover, read from the Gospels and the Epistles in the vulgar tongue, applying and expounding them in their favor and against the condition of the Roman Church in a manner which it would take too long to describe in detail, but all that relates to this subject may be read more fully in the books they have written and infected, and may be learned from the confessions of such of their followers as have been converted.

D. QUESTIONS POSED FOR THE CATHARIST BELIEVERS BY THE INQUISITION ACCORDING TO GUI'S "PRACTICA"

38. *The Form of Interrogation*

Practica, 5:1 (5), trans. by the editor, via Mollat, *Manuel,* I, 26–30.

At first the inquisitor shall demand whether the one under examination has seen or known anywhere, one or more *perfecti;* knowing or believing them to be such by name or reputation; when he has seen them, how often, with whom, and when;

Whether he has had any close contact with them; when and how; and who brought about this intimate acquaintance;

Whether he has welcomed to his house one or more *perfecti;* who and which ones; also who brought them there; how long they stayed; who visited them there; who took them away; where they went;

Whether he has heard their preaching, also what they said and taught in the course of it;

Whether he adored them, or saw others adore them or manifest reverence for them according to heretical custom; and what was the manner of adoring them;

Whether he has eaten bread blessed by them, and the manner of blessing this bread;

Whether he has entered with them into the pact called the *covenensa,* whereby he expressed the desire to be received at the time of his death into their sect and order;

Whether he has greeted them or seen others greet them in heretical fashion, that is, by laying both hands on both cheeks of the *perfecti,* then bowing the head, facing each cheek of the "perfect" in turn and repeating three times: Benedicite—this being the manner of greeting observed by the "believers" in the presence of the "perfect," on the occasion of their arrival and departure;

Whether he has participated in the initiation of one of them, how this was carried out; what the names were of the heretics and other persons present; the location of the house where the sick person lay; the length of time required by the ceremony; the hour at which it took place; whether the one initiated bequeathed anything to the "perfect"; to whom and how much; and who executed the will; whether adoration was accorded the officiating "perfect"; whether the person initiated died of his illness; and, if so, where he was buried; and who brought heretics there or took them back;

Whether he believed that the person initiated into the heretical faith was able to be saved;

Likewise he should be interrogated as to what the heretics have said and taught in his presence against the faith and sacraments of the Roman church; what he has heard them say of the sacrament of the eucharist, of baptism and of marriage, of the confession of sins made to priests, of the adoration or veneration of the Holy Cross; and concerning others of their errors already described;

Whether he has considered the "perfect" to be good and sincere men, possessing and preserving good faith, good sect, good doctrine, capable with their believers of being saved in the midst of their faith and sect.

Likewise, for how long a time he was or has remained in the said belief;

When he began to participate in the belief;

Whether he continues in it presently;

When and why he withdrew from the belief;

Whether he has previously been called or cited before an inquisitor; when and why; whether he has confessed anything concerning the heresy; whether he has abjured the error in the presence of an inquisitor; whether he was reconciled or absolved;

Whether, since then, he has committed anything in the said heresy, what and in what manner, as above.

Whether he has known one or several "believers" or those in agreement with the views of the "perfect" or those harboring them;

Whether he has accompanied any heretic or heretics from place to place or has possessed any of their books;

Whether his parents have been "believers"; whether they have participated in the actions of the heretics or have been made to do penance for heretical acts.

E. CATHARIST VIEWS AND PRACTICES DESCRIBED BY A FORMER ADHERENT AND SUPPOSED BISHOP, RAYNIER SACCONI

39. *Some Commonly Held Opinions*

Summa de Catharis, ed. A. Dondaine, *Un traité neo-Manichéen du XIII⁰ siècle: Le Liber de duobus principiis* (Rome: Instituto Storico Domenicano di S. Sabina, 1939), pp. 64–65, trans. by the editor.

Opinions common to all Catharists are these: namely, that the devil made this world and all things in it. Likewise, that all of the sacraments of the Church, that is the sacrament of baptism with material water and all the other sacraments avail nothing for salvation; that these are not true sacraments of Christ and of his Church but are rather the deceptive, diabolical sacraments of the wicked church. These sacraments the heretics regard as inferior to their own. Another commonly entertained opinion of the Catharists is that all fleshly marriage has always been a mortal sin, and that in the future, one will not be punished more severely for adultery or incest than because of legitimate wedlock. Even now among them nothing is more harshly punished than this. Furthermore, all the Catharists deny the future resurrection of the flesh. Then, too, they believe it a mortal sin to eat flesh, eggs and cheese, even in cases of urgent necessity, because all of these are the result of sexual union. Moreover, that it is not lawful to take an oath under any circumstance, this being regarded a mortal sin. Likewise that secular powers sin mortally in punishing criminals and heretics. Again, that no one is able to be saved except by them. That all children even baptized ones will not be more lightly punished eternally than thieves and homicides. But from this some Albigensians dissent. . . . All deny purgatory.

40. Sacraments, Laying on of Hands, and Consolamentum

Summa, ibid., p. 65, trans. by the editor.

The Catharists . . . have four sacraments—though false and inane, illicit and sacrilegious. These are the laying on of hands, the blessing of bread, penitence, and order. . . . The imposition of hands is termed by them *consolamentum* and spiritual baptism, or baptism of the Holy Spirit, without which, according to them, neither is mortal sin to be forgiven, nor is the holy spirit given to anyone, except by them alone, and by them conferred. But certain Albigensians differ here. . . . It is commonly agreed among all Catharists that the said imposition of hands effects no remission of sins if those laying on hands are then in any mortal sin. But this laying on of hands is effected by two at least, not only by their prelates or even their subordinates but in cases of necessity by the Catharist [followers], themselves.

F. FRAGMENTS FROM EARLY CATHARIST RITUALS

41. A Passage from the Consolamentum

According to L. Clédat, *Rituel Cathare* (Paris, 1887), pp. 470a–482b and VI–XXVI, via D. Roché, *Études*, pp. 179–81 and Dondaine, pp. 37ff., trans. by the editor.

If a believer is in abstinence [a period of prolonged temperance and fasting] and the "Christians" are in agreement about delivering to him the prayer [the *Pater*], then let them wash their hands, and the believers also, if there be any present. And then let one of the "good men," the one who is after the elder, make three reverences to the elder, and then let him prepare a table, and then make three more reverences, after which let him put a cloth on the table; then after three more reverences let him put the book on the cloth. And then let him say: "Bless you, have pity on you." And then let the believer make his *melhoirer* or *melioramentum* [a prayer addressed to the Holy Spirit supposedly resident in the "perfect"] and take the book from the hand of the elder. This one must then admonish the "believer" and preach to him with suitable testimonies . . . and then let the elder say the Lord's prayer and let the believer say it after him. Then let the elder say, "We deliver this prayer to you so that you may receive it from God, from us, and from the church, in order that you may be able to hear it all the days of your life, day and night, alone and in company with others, and that you may never eat or drink without first saying this prayer. And if you fail of this, it is necessary that you do penitence for it." And the believer must then say: "I have received it from God and you and the church." Then he must make his *melhoirer* and give thanks. . . .

[Having taken the book from the hand of the elder and having been further admonished, preached to, instructed, and queried concerning his desire for the *consolamentum*, the believer expresses his willingness to keep the commandments and persevere unto eternal life. He is about to receive "this holy baptism by the laying on of hands, instituted by Jesus Christ. . . ."]

Then let one of the "good men" make his *melhoirer* with the "believer" in the direction of the elder and then let him say, "*Parcite nobis*—mercy on us. Good Christians we pray you for the love of God that you grant this blessing that God has given you to our friend here." Then let the believer make his *melhoirer* and let him say: "*Parcite nobis*. I ask pardon from God, from the church and from all of you, for all the sins that I have done, said, thought, or brought about." And let the "Christians" say: "May you be forgiven by God, by us, and by the church, and we pray God that he may forgive you." And then they should "console" him. And let the elder take the book and put it on his head, and let the other "good men" each place thereon his right hand. [Then they say the appropriate prayers: *gratia, parcias, adoremus* etc.] The elder then says in Latin: "Holy Father, receive thy servant into thy righteousness and bestow thy grace and thy Holy Spirit upon him." After the prayer, the gospel, etc., they are to give the kiss of peace, embracing each other together with the book. And if there are believers present they too give the kiss of peace, bestowing the kiss of peace with the book and with each other. [That is the minister gives the kiss of peace to the new "Christian," embracing him or, if it is a woman, touching her symbolically on one of her shoulders with the Gospel. The new "Christian" then passes on the kiss in like manner to his neighbor. Finally all the men give each other the fraternal embrace, and the women salute each other likewise.]

42. The Reception of Spiritual Baptism and the Consolamentum: Excerpts from another ancient Ritual

Fragmentum Ritualis, via Dondaine, *Un traité*, pp. 162f., 164f., trans. by the editor. See this ancient "Latin Ritual" paralleled with the "Roman Ritual" of Clédat, above, in Dondaine, *op. cit.*, pp. 37ff., especially pp. 40–43.

Whence you ought to understand that this is the cause of your appearing before the church of Jesus Christ, namely the occasion of receiving this holy baptism with the imposition of hands and the pardoning of your sins, by way of interrogation in good conscience made to God by good Christians. Whereupon you should know that even as you are temporally before the church where Father, Son and Holy Spirit dwell spiritually, likewise with your soul you ought, in the presence of Christ and the Holy Spirit, to be prepared to receive this holy ordinance of Jesus Christ. Just as you have received into your hands the book where the precepts of Christ are written as well as the counsels . . . so spiritually you ought to receive the law of Christ in the workings of your soul for observance throughout your life as it is written: "You shall love the Lord your God, with all your heart, soul, etc. . . . ."

It behooves you to be faithful and lawful in things both temporal and spiritual, for if you prove unfaithful in temporal matters we do not believe that you will be faithful in things spiritual, nor do we believe that you will be able to be saved. . . .

You should make this vow to God, that you will never eat knowingly or voluntarily,

cheese, milk, eggs, or the flesh of birds, reptiles, or any beast prohibited by the church.

Likewise by this righteousness of Christ it behooves you to endure famine, thirst, scandals, persecution and death, since you will be supported by all of these in the love of God and for your salvation.

CONCERNING THE OFFICE OF THE CONSOLAMENTUM

Then the minister takes the book from the hands of the believer and says: "John"—if that be his name—"are you willing to receive this holy baptism of Jesus Christ, as it is brought to remembrance, and to retain it throughout your whole life with purity of heart and mind and not fail for any reason?" And John replies: "I am, pray the good Lord for me that he may give me his grace." Then the minister says, "May the true Lord God grant you his grace for the receiving of this gift to his honor and to your salvation." Whereupon the believer stands with reverence before the minister and says as the elder has said, who will have been in the presence of the minister, who says: "I come before God and you and the church and your holy order for the receiving of pardon and mercy for all my sins which have been committed by me at any time up to the present. Also that you may pray God to forgive me my sins. May he bless and have mercy upon us." Then the minister responds: "Receive from God and us and the church and from its holy order as well as from its holy precepts and disciples pardon and mercy for all your sins committed at any time up to now so that God may mercifully forgive you and lead you to eternal life." And the believer says, "Amen, do unto us Lord according to thy word." Then the believer rises and places his hand on the little table in front of the minister. And the minister then places the book on the believer's head, and all the other ministers together with the rest of the Christians who are there place their right hands over his. And the believer says: "In the name of the Father, and the Son, and the Holy Spirit." And he who is in front of the minister says,

"Amen." And all the others say it in unison. . . .

G. THE WALDENSIAN TRANSITION FROM HIERARCHIAL ORTHODOXY AND LOYALTY TO ANTI-HIERARCHICAL HETERODOXY

43. A Portion of a Purported Profession of Faith by the Waldensians

Trans. by the editor from a text of MS Bibl. Nac. de Madrid, 1114, fol. 1ᵗᵃ-2ᵗᵃ via A. Dondaine, "Aux origines du Valdéisme: une profession de foi de Valdès," *Archivum Fratrum Praedicatorum*, XVI (Rome: Instituto Storico Domenicano di S. Sabina, 1946), Appendice, pp. 231–32.

In the name of the Father, Son, and Holy Spirit as well as the most blessed and ever Virgin Mary. It is evident to all the faithful that I, Waldo, and all my brethren, out of regard for the holy gospel, believe with the heart, understand with faith, confess with the mouth, and affirm in simple language that Father, Son, and Holy Spirit are three persons. [We hold] the entire three-fold deity to be one God: coessential, consubstantial, coeternal, coomnipotent, with each one in the trinity of persons being fully God, and with the entirety of three persons comprising one God. Furthermore, we believe with the heart and confess with the mouth that Father, Son, and Holy Spirit constitute one God who is creator, maker and governor and, in keeping with place and time, the ordainer of all things visible and invisible, heavenly and ethereal, aquatic and terrestrial. We believe one and the same God to be the author of the Old and the New Testament, that is of the law of Moses, of the prophets and of the apostles who, remaining in Trinity, as it is said, has created all things. . . . [Again] we believe and confess that the incarnation of Divinity was not accomplished in the Father or in the Holy Spirit but in the Son, so much so that he who was, in the Divinity of the Father, the Son of God, was true God of the Father. He was also true man by virtue of his mother, having true flesh from his mother's womb and a rational human soul, both natures, alike, being in him. [In other words] we believe that he was God and man, one person, one son, one Christ, one God with the Father and Holy Spirit, ruler

and author of all things, born of the Virgin Mary with true nativity of the flesh. He ate, drank and slept, resting from the fatigue of travel. Likewise he suffered with the true passion of his flesh, died with the true death of his body, rose with the true resurrection of his flesh and with the true resumption of the life in which thereafter he ate and drank. Thereupon he ascended into heaven, where he now sits at the right hand of the Father whence he shall come to judge the living and the dead. All of this we believe with the heart and confess with the mouth. Likewise we believe one catholic church, holy, apostolic, and unsullied (*immaculata*), outside of which no one can be saved. Then, too, we in no way deny that the sacraments which are celebrated in it are of incalculable as well as invisible strength (*virtute*) in conjunction with the Holy Spirit's working and are lawfully administered by a sinful priest so long as the church receives him. Neither do we detract from the ecclesiastical offices or from the blessings celebrated by them. . . . We firmly believe and simply affirm that, after consecration, the sacrifice of bread and wine is the Body and Blood of Jesus Christ, in which nothing more is accomplished by a good priest, or less by a bad one. . . . The true ecclesiastical orders, that is, the episcopal, presbyterial, and others below and above these, as well as everything read or sung in the church, we humbly join in praising and faithfully venerate. We believe that the devil was made, not by condition, but by free will. The taking-on of flesh (*perceptis*) we blame least of all. With the heart we believe and with the mouth we confess the resurrection of this flesh we bear about with us, and not of some other. We stoutly believe and affirm a future judgment with the reception of rewards and punishments for each according to deeds brought forth in this flesh. Alms, sacrifices and other things capable of procuring benefits for the faithful having departed this life we do not doubt. And because faith, according to the apostle James, "is dead without works," we have renounced the world and all that we have, according to the Lord's own counsel. We have bestowed all on the poor and have decided to become poor. . . .

We propose to serve the evangelical counsels just like the precepts. It is, however, our avowal of faith that all those remaining in the world and retaining their possessions while giving alms and other benefits in serving the Lord's precepts will be able to be saved. On account of your discretion in all things, we set it forth that if by chance any should come to your region declaring themselves to be of our number, you may be assured that they are none of ours if they hold not this faith.

44. Part of a Purported, Early Waldensian Attack on Anti-Hierarchical Heretics

Trans. by the editor from *Liber antiheresis,* via Dondaine, "Aux origines," *AFP, XVI. Ibid.,* pp. 232–35.

[Our adversaries, the diabolical (Catharist?) heretics say to us:]

"Yours clearly appears to us to be a new doctrine. But ours is no unformed belief, since it has been accepted from many predecessors and held by us long since. . . ." They say, "Your religion does not please us inasmuch as it is new and has existed but a short time since its beginnings." We say truly: "This is empty and silly talk . . . our way, though new to you, is ancient. . . ." They say, "We would like to know what this new doctrine is that is taught by you. It introduces certain new things to our ears. We wish to know what these might be. . . ." But we believe this to be truly new because the New Testament has confirmed it. We are able to support from the New Testament and other divine testimonies our entire faith which is the basis of salvation and the foundation of our way of life. . . .

But they stoutly insist: "Where was the church from the coming of the Saviour to your appearance? And who taught Waldo this way? Was it not from some "good man" (*ab aliquo bono homine*) that he accepted it, or from some patron (*patronus*) that he discovered it?" We reply truly: "The church of God always exists where there is an assembly of the faithful (*congregatio fidelium*) who hold the right faith and fulfill it with the practice of works. If you really want to know who taught him, know that it was by way of the grace of God given him from

heaven and the gospel voice saying 'Blessed are the poor in spirit for theirs is the kingdom of heaven' (Matt. 5:3). This voice, I say, instructed and taught him."

But they persist, saying: "From whom has he heard it? And who has told him out of the gospel so that he might know this to be the right way?" We reply: "From the bishops and priests." Whereupon they retort in derision: "Would it be those pharisees, cursed by God, who have taught you? How would you be able to receive good works from these men who are impure and do not themselves possess the Holy Spirit?" In reply, we say: "Although we have heard the word of God from the mouths of these men, it is not from them that we have received grace and good works, but from God who gives wisdom and understanding to those who fear him. . . . From him we believe that we have whatever good there is within us. However condemnable the life of the priest, whatever good he says should be preserved. Thus by our Lord's own testimony to his disturbed followers: 'Observe and do what they tell you but do not follow their example in doing the things that they do. The scribes and pharisees are seated in Moses' chair' (Matt. 23:32). . . ." Waldo has received from them the word of God and his companions strive to fulfill it. . . . In this we confess our way to be truly new, forasmuch as it is confirmable by the New Testament. Our faith and our works are justified by gospel reasons. If you ask why we are poor, we remind you of our having read that our Saviour and his apostles were poor. . . .

Certain it is with all your glorying in vain display your patrons were called heretics by our Lord Jesus Christ; but it is amazing how you have dared claim to follow the life of the apostles when you have rejected their faith, poverty, and works, except in a few cases. . . . Never, indeed, did your patrons draw the example for your life from any of the disciples of Christ, but rather they resisted all of your ancestors. But I will tell you—if God will permit me—from whom your patrons took their example and the errors of your life. . . . There were those called gnostics, who, among other excrement, contended for two gods, one good the other evil. And you have patrons similar to these. There was another, Manicheus by name, who asserted that all visible things were made by the devil; and there was another, named Tatian, who abominated flesh. And you have ·patrons like these. And many others whom it would take too long to enumerate. . . .

But tell me, what do you see in the [Roman] clergy? . . . Do you believe to be true what I have asserted about them? [*i.e.* the Roman tradition of their apostolic origin and descent]. I know for certain that you do not believe, but that you say: "It is not possible to believe that they in any way hold to the church of God, for they are simoniacs, homicides, adulterers, fornicators and consistently persecute the friends of God, which makes it incredible that they should be apostles." We say to you in reply: "If these be not credible as themselves holding to the church of God because they do not do the works of God, neither are you to be believed. For neither do you possess in the slightest, (either) the faith of the apostles, without which it is impossible to please God, or their works."

But they stubbornly retort: "You always hold against us the hand of that fornicating Roman church." But replying we say: "We hold no fornicating neither any other illicit hand. Nor do we excuse the improper acts of priests or of others, but rather in disapproval do we resist them. For which cause and from the hatred of the same we suffer many persecutions."

But we are determined not to desist on account of any living person from holding up our hands and preaching freely, according to the grace God has given us, the faith of God and the sacraments of the church, against you, the Jews, gentiles, and all sects who detract from these, until death overtakes us. . . .

45. A Purportedly Waldensian, Anti-Roman, Confession of Faith

Trans. by the editor from A. Monastier, *Histoire de l'Église Vaudoise* . . . (Paris, 1847), II, pp. 316ff.

1. We believe and firmly hold everything contained in the twelve articles of the

Symbol, called the Apostles (creed), regarding as heresy whatever is out of harmony and not in keeping with the said twelve articles.

4. We believe that there is one God, all powerful, all wise, all good, who by his bounty has created all things. . . .

7. That Christ is our life, truth, peace, justice, and pastor (shepherd), advocate, victim, and sacrificer (priest), having died for the salvation of all believers, and risen for our justification.

8. Likewise we firmly hold that there is no other mediator and advocate beyond God the Father, except Jesus Christ. But that the virgin Mary has been holy, humble, and full of grace, and, likewise, we believe concerning the other saints that they await, hopefully, in heaven the resurrection of their bodies at the judgment day.

10. We have always believed it an abomination that one may not approach God except by way of human inventions such as feasts and vigils of the saints, holy water, abstention from meat and other foods on certain days, and such things, principally masses.

12. We believe that the sacraments are signs or visible forms of invisible graces, holding it good that the faithful use these same signs or visible forms on occasion as they are able. However, we believe that the said faithful are able to be saved without receiving the said signs when they have neither the place nor the means of being able to use the said signs.

13. We have no other sacraments than baptism and the eucharist.

46. A Portion of an Anti-Roman Catechism Attributed to the Early Waldensians

Trans. by the editor from Monastier, *op. cit.,* II, pp. 301ff.

Question, Pastor. What is the foundation of the commandments by which one must enter into life, without which foundation one is incapable of following worthily or observing the commandments?

Answer, Child. The Lord Jesus Christ, of whom the Apostle says (I Cor. 3:11): No one is able to lay any other foundation. . . .

Q. This God in whom you believe, how do you adore and serve him?

A. By the adoration of prayers (*latria*) external and internal. Outwardly by bowing the knees, raising the hands, by inclining the body, by hymns, by spiritual songs, by fasts and by invocations. But inwardly, I adore with pious affection, by a will surrendered to everything He wishes, but I serve by faith, hope and charity, according to His commandments.

Q. Do you believe in the holy church?

A. No, for it is a creature, but I believe that it exists.

Q. What do you believe regarding the holy church?

A. I say that the church must be thought of in two ways: one in terms of its substance or nature, the other in terms of the ministry. As for its substance, the holy catholic (universal) church is made up of all God's elect, from the beginning to the end, who have, according to the grace of God by the merits of Christ, been gathered together by the Holy Spirit and previously ordained to eternal life, their number and names being known only to the one having chosen them. . . . But the church with regard to the ministry, comprises the ministers of Christ with the people submitted to them, profiting from the ministry of faith, hope and charity.

Q. By what mark do you recognize the church of Christ?

A. By proper ministers and by a people who participate in the truth together with them.

Q. But by what thing do you know worthy ministers?

A. By the true sense of the faith, by a holy doctrine, by an exemplary life, by the preaching of the Gospel, and by a proper administration of the sacraments.

Q. How do you detect false ministers?

A. By their fruits, by their blindness, by wicked conduct, by perverse teaching and by an improper administration of the sacraments.

Q. By what do you know blind ministers?

A. It is when, not apprehending the truth necessary to salvation, they guard human inventions. . . .

Q. By what may we know bad doctrine?

A. This is when it teaches against faith and hope; to wit, in the case of idolatry rendered variously to the creature whether rational or non-rational, sensible, visible, or invisible. For the Father, with his Son and Holy Spirit must be served, and not any creature whatever. But contrary to these, one attributes to man, to the work of his hands, or to his words or to his authority, in such wise that the man believing blindly, judges these things added by God and by a false religion and by the avaricious simony of priests.

Q. By what may one discern the improper administration of the sacraments?

A. This happens when the priests do not understand the mind of Christ and, not knowing his purpose in the sacraments, say that grace and truth are bound up with external ceremonies alone, thus leading men to receive these same sacraments without the truth of faith, hope and charity; and the Lord protects his followers from such false priests, saying: "Beware of false prophets. . . ."

Q. How many things belong to the minister?

A. Two, the preaching of the Gospel word and the sacraments.

Q. How many sacraments are there?

A. Two, namely baptism and the eucharist.

Q. What of the blessed virgin, for she is full of grace, according to the angel?

A. The blessed virgin was and is full of grace as regards her own need, but not as involving communication to others. For God's Son alone is full of grace in the sense of participation, as it is said of him, "and we receive grace on grace from his fullness."

Q. Do you not believe in the communion of saints?

A. I believe that there are two kinds of things in which the saints have communion with each other. The one kind is substantial, the other ministerial. They have communion in things substantial by the Holy Spirit in God, by the merits of Jesus Christ. But they have communion in ministerial or ecclesiastical things by virtue of the ministries duly performed, such as those effected by words, sacraments and prayers. I believe in both of these meanings of the communion of saints, the first being only in God, and in Jesus Christ, and in the Holy Spirit, spiritually; this taking place in the church of Christ.

H. TEMPORAL PROCESS AGAINST THE HERETIC

47. An Edict of St. Louis (IX) against the Heretics of Languedoc (1228)

Trans. *PTR*, III, 6 (6), p. 15.

Moreover, since the keys of the church are often despised in that country [Languedoc], we command that excommunicated persons shall be avoided according to the canonical provisions, and that if any one shall contumaciously remain in a state of excommunication for a year, he shall be forced by material means to return to the unity of the Church, in order that those who are not induced to leave their evil way by the law of God, may be brought back by temporal penalties. We therefore order that our bailiffs shall, after one year, seize all the property, both real and personal, or all such excommunicated persons. And on no account shall such property be in any way returned to such persons, until they have been absolved and have rendered satisfaction to the church, and then only by our special order.

I. THOMAS AQUINAS ON THE SPIRITUAL POWER, THE CHURCH, AND HERESY

48. Whether Heretics Are to Be Tolerated

Summa Theol. 2a, 2ae, Q. XI, a. 3, trans. *PTR*, III, 6 (8), 17f.

Proceeding to the third question. First. It would appear that heretics are to be tolerated, for the Apostle says (2 Tim. ii. 24), "The Lord's servant must be gentle, in meekness, correcting them that oppose themselves to the truth; if peradventure God may give them repentance unto the knowledge of the truth, and they may recover themselves out of the snare of the devil." But if heretics are not tolerated but delivered over to death, they are deprived of the opportunity of repentance. Hence, this would seem contrary to the precept of the Apostle.

Second. Moreover, that which is necessary in the Church must be tolerated. But heresies are necessary in the Church. For the Apostle says (I Corinthians xi. 19), "For there must also be heresies among you that

VIII-16. Punishment of Heretics.

they which are approved may be made manifest among you." Therefore, it would seem that heretics are to be tolerated.

Third. Moreover, the Lord commands his servants (Matthew xiii.), that they should let the tares grow until the harvest, which is the end of the world, as is explained in the Interlinear Glossa. But the tares signify the heretics according to the interpretation of the saints. Therefore heretics are to be tolerated.

But against this is to be urged the saying of the Apostle (Titus iii. 10), "A man that is heretical, after a first and second admonition, refuse, knowing that such a one is perverted."

I reply that heretics must be considered from two points of view, namely, as regards the heretic himself, and secondly, as regards the church. As for the heretics themselves, there is their sin for which they deserve not only to be separated from the Church by excommunication, but to be sent out of the world by death. It is, indeed, a much more serious offence to corrupt the faith, upon which depends the life of the soul, than to falsify coin, by means of which the temporal life is sustained. Hence, if counterfeiters and other malefactors are justly hurried to death by secular rulers, much the more may those who are convicted of heresy not only be excommunicated but justly put to a speedy death. But on the side of the Church, there is mercy looking for the conversion of the erring. She does not therefore condemn immediately, but only after a first and second admonition, as the Apostle teaches. Should the heretic still prove stubborn, the Church, no longer hoping for his conversion, shall provide for the safety of others by separating him from herself by a sentence of excommunication. She further relinquishes him to the secular judgment to be put out of the world by death. Jerome also says (on the passage in Galatians v.—"a little leaven;"), and it is stated in 24. qu. 3, cap. 16, "Foul flesh must be cut away, and mangy sheep must be kept from the fold lest the whole house be burned, the whole mass corrupted, the whole body be destroyed. Arius was but a spark in Alexandria, but since this spark was not promptly quenched, the whole world has been devastated by the flames."

As to the first argument, namely, that which relates to the meekness in which a heretic should be admonished a first and a second time, if, after that, he refuses to return he is looked upon as perverted, as appears from the authority of the Apostle above cited (in the argument beginning, *But against*).

As to the second argument, any advantage which may proceed from heretics is in no way intentional on their part, as, for example, the proof they furnish according to the Apostle of the constancy of the faithful, or, as Augustine says,—*Lib. I de gen., cont. Manich.* (Cap. I., about the middle) "Let us put away all slothfulness, carefully searching the holy Scriptures." Their intention is, on the contrary, to corrupt the faith, and this is most harmful. We should, therefore, give more weight to those conscious aims which would cut them off, rather than the unintentional good which would seem to countenance their toleration.

To the third argument we may reply, as it is written in the Decretals, 24, qu. 3, Cap. beginning, *It is to be observed that excommunication is one thing and extirpation another*. One is excommunicated with a view, as the Apostle says (I Cor. v. 5), "that the spirit may be saved in the day of the Lord." That heretics shall be totally extirpated by death is not however contrary to the command of God, for that command is to be understood as applying only in case the tares cannot be destroyed without destroying the wheat at the same time, as has been said in the preceding question, art. 8, argument 1, when we treated of heretics in common with infidels.

J. POPE NICHOLAS III AND HERESY (1280)

49. *His Bull Condemning Heretics*

Bullarium Romanum, III, ii, pp. 26ff., trans. ThM, No. 161, pp. 309–10.

Nicholas, etc. We hereby excommunicate and anathematize all heretics, the Cathari, Patareni, the Poor Men of Lyon, Passageni, Josepheni, the Arnoldists, Speronists, and all others by whatever name they may be called. (1) When condemned by the church, they shall be given over to the secular judge to be punished. Clergymen shall be degraded before being punished. (2) If any, after being seized, repent and wish to do proper penance, they shall be imprisoned for life. (3) We condemn as heretics all who believe the errors of heretics. (4) We decree that all who receive, defend, or aid heretics, shall be excommunicated. If anyone remains under excommunication a year and a day, he shall be proscribed. (5) He shall not be eligible to hold a public office, or to vote in the election of officials. (6) His word shall not be accepted. (7) He can not serve as a witness nor can he make a will. (8) He shall not succeed to an inheritance. (9) He cannot bring suit against anyone, but suit may be brought against him. (10) If he is a judge, his sentences shall be invalid, and he shall not be permitted to hear cases. (11) If he is an advocate, he shall not be permitted to perform the duties of his office. (12) If he is a notary, the documents which he draws up shall be invalid and condemned with him. (13) If he is a clergyman, he shall be deposed from his office and deprived of every benefice. (14) Those who associate with the excommunicated shall themselves be excommunicated and properly punished. (15) If those who are suspected of heresy can not prove their innocence, they shall be excommunicated. If they remain under the ban of excommunication a year, they shall be condemned as heretics. (16) They shall have no right of appeal. (17) If judges, advocates, or notaries serve them in an official way, they shall be deprived of their office. (18) The clergy shall not administer to them the sacraments, nor give them a part of the alms. If they do, they shall be deprived of their office and they can never be restored to it without the special permission of the pope. Whoever grants them Christian burial shall be excommunicated until he makes proper satisfaction. He shall not be absolved until he has with his own hands publicly dug up their bodies and cast them forth, and no one shall ever be buried in the same place. (19) We prohibit all laymen to discuss matters of the catholic

faith. If anyone does so, he shall be excommunicated. (20) Whoever knows of heretics, or those who are holding secret meetings, or those who do not conform in all respects to the orthodox faith, shall make it known to his confessor, or to someone else who will bring it to the knowledge of the bishop or the inquisitor. If he does not do so, he shall be excommunicated. (21) Heretics and all who receive, support, or aid them, and all their children to the second generation, shall not be admitted to an ecclesiastical office or benefice. If any such have been admitted, their admission is illegal and invalid. For we now deprive all such of their benefices forever, and they shall never be admitted to others. If parents with their children have been freed [from excommunication], and their parents afterwards return to the heresy, their children are, by their parents' act, again brought under excommunication.

K. JOHN WYCLIF AND HERESY

50. *He Replies to the Papal Condemnation*

Modernized from T. Arnold, *Select English Works of Wycliff*, III, 504–6, PTR, II, 5 (3), pp. 13–14.

I have joy fully to tell what I hold, to all true men that believe and especially to the Pope; for I suppose that if my faith be rightful and given of God, the Pope will gladly confirm it; and if my faith be error, the Pope will wisely amend it.

I suppose over this that the gospel of Christ be heart of the corps of God's law; for I believe that Jesus Christ, that gave in his own person this gospel, is very God and very man, and by this heart passes all other laws.

I suppose over this that the Pope be most obliged to the keeping of the gospel among all men that live here; for the Pope is highest vicar that Christ has here in earth. For moreness of Christ's vicar is not measured by worldly moreness, but by this, that this vicar follows more Christ by virtuous living; for thus teacheth the gospel, that this is the sentence of Christ.

And of this gospel I take as believe, that Christ for time that he walked here, was most poor man of all, both in spirit and in having; for Christ says that he had nought for to rest his head on. And Paul says that he was made needy for our love. And more poor might no man be, neither bodily nor in spirit. And thus Christ put from him all manner of worldly lordship. For the gospel of John telleth that when they would have made Christ king, he fled and hid him from them, for he would none such worldly highness.

And over this I take it as believe, that no man should follow the Pope, nor no saint that now is in heaven, but in as much as he follows Christ. For John and James erred when they coveted worldly highness; and Peter and Paul sinned also when they denied and blasphemed in Christ; but men should not follow them in this, for then they went from Jesus Christ. And this I take as wholesome counsel, that the Pope leave his worldly lordship to worldly lords, as Christ gave them,—and move speedily all his clerks to do so. For thus did Christ, and taught thus his disciples, till the fiend had blinded this world. And it seems to some men that clerks that dwell lastingly in this error against God's law, and flee to follow Christ in this, been open heretics, and their fautors been partners.

And if I err in this sentence, I will meekly be amended yea, by the death, if it be skillful, for that I hope were good to me. And if I might travel in mine own person, I would with good will go to the Pope. But God has needed me to the contrary, and taught me more obedience to God than to men. And I suppose of our Pope that he will not be Antichrist, and reverse Christ in this working, to the contrary of Christ's will; for if he summon against reason, by him or by any of his, and pursue this unskillful summoning, he is an open Antichrist. And merciful intent excused not Peter, that Christ should not clepe him Satan; so blind intent and wicked counsel excuses not the Pope here; but if he ask of true priests that they travel more than they may, he is not excused by reason of God, that he should not be Antichrist. For

our belief teaches us that our blessed God suffers us not to be tempted more than we may; how should a man ask such service? And therefore pray we to God for our pope Urban the sixth, that his old holy intent be not quenched by his enemies. And Christ, that may not lie, says that the enemies of a man been especially his home family; and this is sooth of men and fiends.

L. THE CHURCH, THE GREAT PLAGUE, AND POGROMS AGAINST THE JEW (1349)

51. Persecution, and Protection by the Pope at Avignon

Trans. J. R. Marcus, *The Jew in the Medieval World: A Source Book, 315–1791* (Cincinnati: The Sinai Press, 1938), pp. 45–46.

In the year 1349 there occurred the greatest epidemic that ever happened. Death went from one end of the earth to the other, on that side and this side of the sea, and it was greater among the Saracens than among the Christians. In some lands everyone died so that no one was left. Ships were also found on the sea laden with wares; the crew had all died and no one guided the ship. The Bishop of Marseilles and priests and monks and more than half of all the people there died with them. In other kingdoms and cities so many people perished that it would be horrible to describe. The pope at Avignon stopped all sessions of court, locked himself in a room, allowed no one to approach him and had a fire burning before him all the time. [This last was probably intended as some sort of disinfectant.] And from what this epidemic came, all wise teachers and physicians could only say that it was God's will. And as the plague was now here, so was it in other places, and lasted more than a whole year. This epidemic also came to Strasbourg in the summer of the above mentioned year, and it is estimated that about sixteen thousand people died.

In the matter of this plague the Jews throughout the world were reviled and accused in all lands of having caused it through the poison which they are said to

357

have put into the water and the wells—that is what they were accused of—and for this reason the Jews were burnt all the way from the Mediterranean into Germany, but not in Avignon, for the pope protected them there.

V. Medieval Credo and Preaching to the Faithful

A. JACQUES DE VITRY, POPULAR PREACHING, AND MEDIEVAL SERMON ILLUSTRATIONS ("EXEMPLA")

52. The Devil and the Careless Clergy

Sermones Vulgares, 19, Summarized by T. R. Crane, *The Exempla* . . . (London: Published for the Folk-Lore Society by David Nutt, 1890), p. 141.

A certain holy man, while in choir, saw the devil loaded down with a full sack. He adjured the devil to tell him what he was carrying, and the devil replied that the sack was full of the syllables and words and verses of the psalms abbreviated or omitted by the clergy during that service. "These I diligently preserve for their accusation."

53. The "Nosy" Fox and the "Heavy-Footed" Mule

Ibid., 33, via Crane, *Exempla*, p. 147.

A fox once went to a mule and said, "What kind of an animal are you; are you a horse or an ass?" The mule replied, "What is that to you! I am a creature of God's." The fox said, "I wish to learn your parentage," and persisted in her question. Then the mule said, "I am the descendant of the great war-horse of the King of Spain." The fox continued, "Who was your father, and who your mother?" The mule, displeased and angry, said, "You will find my pedigree written on the shoe of my right foot." When the fox drew near to read the letters, the mule raised his foot and kicked and killed the fox..

54. A Nun Fails to Cross Herself and Eats a Devil

Ibid., 130, via Crane, *Exempla*, p. 189.

Saint Gregory tells of a nun who ate lettuce without making the sign of the cross and swallowed a devil. When a holy man tried to exorcise him the devil said: "What fault is it of mine? I was sitting on the lettuce, and she did not cross herself, and so ate me too."

55. The Jester's Horse: "Let Us Bow Our Knees"

Ibid., 258, via Crane, *Exempla*, p. 244.

A jester taught his horse to fall down when he said: "Let us bow our knees," and to get up when he said, "Rise." He made much merriment by offering his horse for sale to a monk, or clerk, or other man, and when the would-be purchaser mounted the horse to try it, the owner waited until it reached a muddy spot, and then said: "Let us bow our knees," and down went horse and rider, and the horse would not get up again until the jester said: "Rise."

B. MENDICANT PREACHING MANUALS

56. Humbert of Romans on the Indispensability of Preaching

Trans. in W. M. Conlon, *Treatise on Preaching by Humbert of Romans* (Westminster, Maryland: The Newman Press, 1951), Chap. 1, sec. 2, pp. 9–10.

In conclusion, let us admire the usefulness and necessity of such an office, since without it the whole world would have remained plunged in the darkness of error; increasing sin would choke out virtue; the most dangerous famine, the famine of the bread of sound doctrine, would ravage the world; sin would deliver up to death innumerable victims; the privation of the saving waters of wisdom would cause an intolerable drought and a desolating dearth of all good; and, lastly, we would not find the way to salvation.

For all these reasons, God, seeing how necessary preaching is, has not ceased since the beginning of the world, and will not cease until the end of time, to send preachers. St. Gregory commenting on the Gospel of St. Matthew tells us: the householder who sends workers into his vineyard at the third, sixth and ninth hours, is a figure of God Who, from the beginning of the world until the end, does not cease to supply preachers for the faithful.

57. A Modern Condensation of a Passage from a Medieval Sermon Manual

T. Waleys, *De modo componendi sermones* . . . , via R. C. Petry, *Preaching in the Great Tradition* (Philadelphia: Westminster Press, 1950), pp. 60–61.

Let the preacher beware of subtracting from his effectiveness by harboring cherished personal sins. The praise of God and edification of neighbor, not ostentation, are the ends of his ministry. Proper modesty in deportment and gesture is indispensable. Good sense says: Be neither an immobile statue nor an animated caricature. Watch your language and capitalize good speech methods. An experienced preacher speaks and is warmly received. Another uses almost the same words and gets nowhere. Why? Reputation counts, of course, but not entirely. It's partly a matter of speech manners and the effective exploitation of language.

The manner of speech is scarcely less significant than its content. Speak not too loudly or too softly. Shout and offend the refined. Speak too low and fail to be heard. Now shouting, now whispering, you offend all. Clamor to the heavens and repel those nearest you. Speak too low and the distant auditors think you have secrets with a few. Discipline your delivery as to proper velocity, distinctness, and moderate pauses.

Don't foster the suspicion that you are preaching another's sermon and have not had

VIII-17. A Friar Preaching from a Wooden Pulpit.

VIII-18. A Dominican Preaching to a Mixed, Out-of-Doors Congregation.

time to assimilate it yourself. Don't recite like a child. Take care not to bombard people with words that have no meaning for them. Following Paul's advice, prefer five words with understanding to ten thousand in tongues. Ponder your words. If you don't, how can your hearers? Cultivate stylistic clarity; avoid prolixity and redundancy. Give digests, sometimes, rather than extensive quotations.

Speak to the heart, not just the ears, of Jerusalem. Avoid vain display and affectation.

Strive to please God, not men. Be careful of saying anything about those, especially, who are absent; avoid preaching against anyone unless the total welfare of church and people, or the culprit's own spiritual needs, demands it. When necessary, speak fearlessly. Speak the truth without dissimulation. Proclaim the Word of God with faithfulness.

Let inexperienced preachers try out voice and gestures before speaking; on trees and stones, preferably. Get your friends to criticize you. Watch your enunciation and voice timbre. Don't despair! Keep on practicing.

These preaching aids—*artes praedicandi* as they were called—constituted the beginning, not the conclusion, of the whole matter of preaching. But help they did. And they would still help, if we studied them.

C. SECTIONS FROM REPRESENTATIVE MEDI-EVAL SERMONS

57A. *A Scholastic Sermon (c. 1230) by a University of Paris Chancellor, reproduced in Chap. IX, Item 26. See also this chapter, Item 14.*

57B. *Bernard of Clairvaux (1090–1153) on the Soul's Being Anticipated by God, reproduced in Chap. VII, Item 11.*

57C. *John Tauler (c. 1294–1361) on Spiritual Deafness, reproduced in Chap. VII, Item 16.*

58. *Raoul Ardent († 1101) on Indolent Pastors and Straying Sheep*

Serm., *MPL* 155, pp. 1406ff., trans. Louise P. Smith for *No Uncertain Sound*, ed. R. C. Petry

VIII-19. Preaching.

(Philadelphia: Westminster Press, 1948), pp. 130–31, 134.

ON THE TRANSFIGURATION OF THE LORD

(A Sermon on the Epistle of St. Peter Which Is Read on That Holy Day)

I will endeavor that you frequently have the means after my decease, whereby you may keep a memory of these things . . . (II Pet. 1:12)

. . . But, my brethren, when I look at our lives and the lives of those under our direction, I find few (and this is lamentable) either true preachers or true sheep. For present-day pastors are neither themselves mindful of the Scriptures, nor do they make others mindful. They strive for worldly wealth. In aim and in deed, they show themselves to be not shepherds but hirelings (cf. John 10:11–14). They are not pastors in aim because they seek what is their own, not what is Christ's. Are there not today prelates who are in the Church, not in order to benefit souls, but in order that they themselves may be exalted, honored, and entertained? They do not ask in which church they can aid more souls, but in which church they can collect more money, find more opportunity for profitable selling. In act, they prove themselves not to be pastors, because they make no effort to feed the sheep by example or by word, but fatten themselves on their offerings. . . .

You see, brethren, what we have just read we can observe today. The fat we destroy by our bad example. Those weak in sin we do not strengthen with our advice. Those broken by tribulations we do not console with our counsel. Those astray in error we do not call back. Those lost in despair we do not seek. When an ass falls down, there is some one to raise it; when a soul perishes, there is none to care. What kind of pastor is he who is more concerned with the ills of his pig and donkey than with the trouble of a Christian soul?

If the pastors act like this, what do the sheep do? Certainly it is not strange if the members are afflicted in the affliction of the head. The duty of the sheep is to hear and obey. But today the sinful sheep are unwilling to hear their pastors. They merely say: "The priest preaches to extract the cash." Even if they listen, they are certainly not mindful of what they have heard. They do not wish to obey their pastor but to judge him. "Why," they say, "do you not do yourself what you preach?" *Thou that sayest men should not commit adultery, committest adultery: that men should not steal, stealest* (Rom. 2:22, 21). When two or three walk together to the forum or to a country-house, then they judge their pastor. They carp and condemn, heedless of the word which the Lord spoke: *The disciple is not above his master* (Luke 6:40). And this verse: *Whatsoever they shall say to you, observe and do, but according to their works do ye not* (Matt. 23:3).

These wicked sons incur the curse of Ham. When Noah was drunk and exposed himself, Ham mocked him; but Shem and Japheth, turning their eyes away, covered him again. When Noah woke, he cursed the seed of Ham, but Shem and Japheth he blessed (Gen. 9:21–27). My brethren, there is no pastor so perfect that he does not do something of which to be ashamed. But it is a bad son who mocks him and publicly repeats the evil tale. A good servant hides the sin of his master, conceals and excuses it. Consequently, the latter merits a blessing, the former, a curse.

And now, my brethren, because we both have sinned, let us both lament, let us both hasten to do penance. Let us, like good shepherds, endeavor to acquaint you with the Gospel teaching both by word and by example. And you also, like good sheep, endeavor constantly, by listening and obeying, to remember what you have heard.

. . . The fourth section follows. In this Peter praises prophecy and those who give heed to it, saying, *whereunto you do well to attend* (vs. 19). Here he condemns, on the other hand, those who are unwilling to pay attention to the reading of the Scriptures. There are many such today, even among officials of Holy Church, who scorn the Scriptures and pursue hawking, hunting, dice, sports, and idle amusements; who even despise the Holy Scriptures and pursue secular law, law-suits, and vain inventions. With these words the ordinary people also are blamed, because they prefer to hear

361

popular songs, banjos, and idle shows rather than the Holy Scripture.

59. A Sermon by Wyclif († 1384) on Vernacular Preaching

Serm. 133, *Writings of John Wickliff* (Philadelphia: Presbyterian Board of Education, N.D.), I, pp. 225–27.

CHRIST PREACHING AT NAZARETH
(Sermon CXXXIII)

And Jesus came to Nazareth, and went into the synagogue on the Sabbath day, &c. (Luke 4:16).

This gospel tells how Christ preached. *Jesus went out in power of the Spirit into Galilee* (Luke 4:14). True men hold as belief, that the Holy Ghost led Jesus withersoever he went, and in what deeds soever he did. *And fame went out through all the land of him; and Christ taught in their synagogues, and was magnified of them all. And Christ came to Nazareth, where he was nourished; and he entered, according to his custom on Saturday, into a synagogue* (vss. 14–16). And hereof Christian men take custom to preach on Sunday; for it comes to us for sabbath instead of Saturday, as Luke saith here. And so should priests follow Christ's example, preaching on the sabbath, that is Sunday.

And Christ rose up to read; and the book of Isaiah the prophet was given him to read. *As Christ turned the book, he found the place where it is written, The Spirit of the Lord is upon me; wherefore he anointed me to preach, he sent me to poor men.* And so the Holy Ghost *bade me preach to prisoners forgiveness, and to blind men sight; to lead broken men into remission, to preach the year that the Lord accepteth* (vss. 16–19). This preaching now is all disused and turned to pride and covetousness. For however men may please the people, and win them worship with money, that they preach, and put back the profit of the people's souls. This book was ordained of God to be read in this place; for all things that befell to Christ were ordained to come thus. And so men say that Christ had the office of all ministers in the church.

And Christ praised Isaiah much, and these things read by Christ have better

order than we can tell. For the Holy Ghost was on Christ, both in his body and in his soul, since Christ was both God and man, and by his manhood led of God. And therefore this Spirit anointed Christ with God's grace as fully as any man might be anointed. And thus Christ must needs preach to meek men that would take it. For this is the best deed that man doth here to his brethren. And so Christ preached to prisoners the forgiving of their sins; and to men blind in knowledge, sight to know the will of God; and to lead broken men in forgiveness of their travail. And Christ preached the year of our Lord that was acceptable by himself. For he made the year of jubilee; and the day of giving of mercy and bliss was preached of Christ. And so all these words sound mercy and comfort of Christ, to men that are in prison here, for old sins that they have done.

And when Christ had folded this book he gave it to the minister, and he sat down; and the eyes of all in the synagogue were looking to him. And Christ began to say to them, This day is this writing fulfilled in your eyes (vss. 20–21), on me; for Isaiah said these words as a man that prophesied of Christ. *And all men gave him witness, and all wondered at the words of grace that came forth of his mouth* (vs. 21). Of this deed of Christ men take that it is lawful for to write and afterward to read a sermon, for thus did Christ our Lord and Master; for if men may thus turn the people, what should hinder them to have this manner? Surely travail of the preacher, or the name of having of good understanding should not be the end of preaching, but profit to the souls of the people. And however this end cometh best, is most pleasing to God. And curious preaching of Latin is full far from this end, for many preach themselves, and fail to preach Jesus Christ; and so sermons do less good than they did in meek times.

60. Bernardine of Siena (1380–1444) on Preaching and the Mass

Ed. and trans. by D. N. Orlandi and H. J. Robinson, *Sermons* (Siena: Tipographia Sociale, 1920), pp. 5ff.

1. O how many of you here present this morning will say: I knew not what I

did, I thought I did well while rather I was doing evil; and remembering this sermon they will say to themselves: O now am I enlightened as to what I should do, addressing these words to God: "Verbum tuum lucerna mea est Thy word is my enlightenment" (Ps. 119:105; D. 118:105). And when thou art about to make some contract in thy business, thou wilt pause first to think, saying: what said Friar Bernardine of such matters? He told me, in such matters you must do thus or thus; that is evil, that is not commendable, but this is good, and this I wish to do. And in this wise it will befall thee merely because of the words which thou hast heard preached to thee. But tell me: what would become of this world, I mean of the Christian faith, if there were no preaching? Within a very little our faith would have perished, for we should believe nothing of that which we now believe. And because of this Holy Church hath ordered that every Sunday there shall be preaching,—much or little, but some preaching. And she hath ordered thee to go to hear Mass, and if of these two duties thou canst perform but one, that is either hear Mass or hear the preaching, thou shouldst rather lose Mass and hear the preaching; since the reason for this doth appear plainly, thou dost not so endanger thy soul by not hearing Mass as by not listening to the preaching. Canst thou not perceive and understand without further argument? For tell me, should you believe in the Blessed Sacrament of the Altar if this had not been preached in holy sermons? Thou hast learned to believe in the Mass only from preaching. More than this, however shouldst thou have known what sin is, if not from preaching? What wouldst thou know of hell, if there were no preaching? What wouldst thou know of any good work, or how thou shouldst perform it, if not from preaching, or what wouldst thou know of the glories of Heaven? All these things that thou knowest came to thee through the words heard by thine ears, and it is in this wise that thou comest by knowledge to faith, and that which thou knowest and which thou hast hath come all through the word of God. And this is a sovereign rule, that which we have of the faith of Jesus Christ hath come merely through preaching. And this

VIII-20. A Churchman Preaching in the Open Air. *From* L'ordinaire des Crestiens, *1494, Paris.*

faith will never perish while it shall be preached.

61. Bernardine on Business Ethics, the Guilds, and the University of Siena

Via Orlandi and Robinson, Sermons, pp. 194ff.

1. First above all I say that a business doth become unlawful with relation to the person engaged therein. For example, understand me: it is not lawful for me who am a friar, to hang a man, since that doth not belong to my art; that art belongeth to secular men. And so, I say, it is not permitted to any friar or priest. And thus, I would say, that neither to friar nor to priest is it permitted to do that which belongeth to secular men to do. The priest and the friar should attend to the offices of the church and to the salvation of souls. Nor should you who are seculars give offices to religious; nor moreover should religious either accept them, or seek them, or exercise them. Nor should a religious entangle himself in secular business, no! Hearken now, answer me, fellow citizens: you are preparing your urns; are you placing friars in charge there? If you are putting them there, put me there as well. You set yourselves to believe that your secular chamberlains of the Commune have stolen the money of the Commune, and for

this reason perchance you would have them friars. The friars perhaps will not steal? Oh, it is an evil sign when because of this you demand friars! O what a blessing is this, that you do suspect one another? I have told you, and I say it to you because of the words of Paul: entangle not religious with these businesses (Cf. II Tim. 2:4). Doth it not suffice that you go to the home of the devil out of your desire for these offices without that you should endeavour to drag us thither as well? They have no other words in their mouths than these: We trust them not.

9. From naught doth the Commune so profit as from the utility of the Guilds, and from merchandise which is bought and sold. Seldom are Guilds licensed which are harmful,—such as is one, that is, the snipping of cloth;—snipping of cloth does naught for

the common good. Moreover the Guild of poisons does naught for the common good. Whensoever a property doth sustain damage, or human beings, this can not be for the common good. Saith Scotus in his Commentary on the 4th. Book of Sentences, Dist. 15: that those things which a Commune can not dispense with are three: the Guild of Wool-weavers is one, the greatest utility doth result thereof to the common good. Likewise the Guild of Shoemaking. Such Guilds are maintained by merchants, who have wool and leather brought hither. Now in like manner as these two are necessary, so also is the University necessary; it is but little appreciated by those who have never studied aught. Never suffer it to depart from Siena, O Sienese, for you can not comprehend the profit and the honour which will

VIII-21. St. Francis Proposes the Trial by Fire to the Sultan. *Giotto, Upper Church of Assisi.*

accrue to you therefrom a short time from now. Consider Bologna, the fame thereof, and the utility and the honour. So will it befall you if you shall be able to maintain it, for therein are men fitted to bring you into renown everywhere. Since that you have the *Sapienza* here, extend its privilege to the merchants and throughout the Republic, because as I have told you, it is necessary and profitable to the common good, and is most pleasing to the Good Lord God. You may perceive even now that already there cometh forth from out of it a band of your citizens fitted for the doctor's degree. And as I say to the citizens, so do I say likewise to you who study: see to it that you become not such great simpletons. It is a thing which is pleasing to God.

VI. The Medieval Church, Christian Expansion, and Franciscan Missions

A. FRANCIS OF ASSISI (1182–1226) AND PREACHING MISSIONS ABROAD

62. *On Going Among the Saracens and Other Infidels*

Reg. 1:16, trans. by the editor from H. Boehmer, *Analekten zur Geschichte des Franciscus von Assisi* (Tuebingen: J. C. B. Mohr, 1904), pp. 14–15.

Of those going among the Saracens and other infidels.

The Lord says: "Behold I send you as sheep in the midst of wolves. Be ye therefore wise as serpents and simple as doves" (Matt. 10:16). Wherefore let those brethren desiring to go among the Saracens and other infidels proceed with the consent of their minister and servant. Let the minister grant them permission and not refuse them if he regards them suitable for sending; for he will be held answerable to the Lord if in this or in like matters he acts unwisely. The brethren who go have two courses of action open to them spiritually. According to the one they are not to precipitate arguments or controversies but to be subordinated "to every human creature for God's sake" (I Pet. 2:13); at the same time confessing themselves to be Christians. The other method is that, when they see it is pleasing to God, they proclaim God's Word so that they [the infidels] may believe in God Omnipotent, Father, Son and Holy Spirit, the Redeemer and Saviour Son, and that they be baptized and made Christians because, "unless a man be born again of water and the Holy Ghost, he cannot enter into the kingdom of God" (John 3:5). They may declare to them these and other things pleasing to God since the Lord says in the Gospel: "Everyone that shall confess Me before men, I will also confess him before My Father who is in heaven" (Matt. 10:32); and "he that shall be ashamed of Me and My words, of him the Son of Man shall be ashamed, when He shall come in His majesty and that of His Father, and of the holy angels" (Luke 9:36). And all the brethren, wherever they are, should remember that they have given themselves and surrendered their bodies to the Lord Jesus Christ; and out of love for him, they ought to expose their bodies to enemies, visible as well as invisible, because the Lord says, "Whosoever shall lose his life for my sake, shall save it" (Mark 8:35; Luke 9:24) in eternal life. "Blessed are they that suffer persecution for justice's sake, for theirs is the kingdom of heaven" (Matt. 5:10). "If they have persecuted Me, they will also persecute you" (John 15:20). If however they should persecute you in one city, flee to another (cf. Matt. 10:23). "Blessed are ye when they shall revile you, and persecute you, and speak all that is evil against you, untruly, for My sake" (Matt. 5:11–12). "Be glad in that day and rejoice, for your reward is great in heaven" (Luke 6:23). "I shall say to you, my friends, be not afraid of them who kill the body, and after that have no more that they can do" (Luke 12:4). "See that ye are not troubled" (Matt. 24:6). "In your patience you shall possess your souls" (Luke 21:19). "But he that shall persevere unto the end, he shall be saved" (Matt. 10:22).

VIII-22. Two Lay Missionaries of the 13th Century, the Brothers Matthew and Nicholas Polo, and Pope Gregory X. *From the* Livre des Merveilles.

B. JOHN OF CARPINI'S MISSION TO THE EAST (1246)

62A. *A Franciscan Among the Tartars, reproduced in Chap. IX, Item 37.*

C. THE FRANCISCAN JOHN OF MONTE CORVINO REPORTS ON MISSIONS TO CATHAY (1291–1305)

63. *Labors in Persia, India, and Cathay*

Trans. H. Yule, *Cathay and the Way Thither* (London: Printed for the Hakluyt Society, 1866), I, pp. 197–99.

I, Friar John of Monte Corvino, of the order of Minor Friars, departed from Tauris, a city of the Persians, in the year of the Lord 1291, and proceeded to India. And I remained in the country of India, wherein stands the church of St. Thomas the Apostle, for thirteen months, and in that region baptised in different places about one hundred persons. The companion of my journey was Friar Nicholas of Pistoia, of the order of Preachers, who died there, and was buried in the church aforesaid.

I proceeded on my further journey and made my way to Cathay, the realm of the Emperor of the Tartars who is called the Grand Cham. To him I presented the letter of our lord the Pope, and invited him to adopt the Catholic Faith of our Lord Jesus Christ, but he had grown too old in idolatry. However he bestows many kindnesses upon the Christians, and these two years past I am abiding with him.

The Nestorians, a certain body who profess to bear the christian name, but who deviate sadly from the christian religion, have grown so powerful in those parts that they will not allow a christian of another ritual to have ever so small a chapel, or to publish any doctrine different from their own.

To these regions there never came any one of the Apostles, nor yet of the Disciples. And so the Nestorians aforesaid, either directly or through others whom they bribed, have brought on me persecutions of the sharpest. For they got up stories that I was not sent by our lord the Pope, but was a great spy and impostor; and after a while they produced false witnesses who declared that there was indeed an envoy sent with presents of immense value for the emperor, but that I had murdered him in India, and stolen what he had in charge. And these intrigues and calumnies went on for some five years. And thus it came to pass that many a time I was dragged before the judgment seat with ignominy and threats of death. At last, by God's providence, the emperor, through the confessions of a certain individual, came to know my innocence and the malice of my adversaries; and he banished them with their wives and children.

In this mission I abode alone and without

VIII-23. The Brothers Polo Delivering Cross and Gospel to the Great Khan. *From the* Livre des Merveilles.

any associate for eleven years; but it is now going on for two years since I was joined by Friar Arnold, a German of the province of Cologne.

I have built a church in the city of Cambaliech, in which the king has his chief residence. This I completed six years ago; and I have built a bell-tower to it, and put three bells in it. I have baptised there, as well as I can estimate, up to this time some 6,000 persons; and if those charges against me of which I have spoken had not been made, I should have baptised more than 30,000. And I am often still engaged in baptising.

Also I have gradually bought one hundred and fifty boys, the children of pagan parents, and of ages varying from seven to eleven, who had never learned any religion. These boys I have baptised, and I have taught them Greek and Latin after our manner. Also I have written out Psalters for them, with thirty Hymnaries and two Breviaries. By help of these, eleven of the boys already know our service, and form a choir and take their weekly turn of duty as they do in convents, whether I am there or not. Many of the boys are also employed in writing out Psalters and other things suitable. His Majesty the Emperor moreover delights much to hear them chaunting. I have the bells rung at all the canonical hours, and with my congregation of babes and sucklings I perform divine service, and the chaunting we do by ear because I have no service book with the notes.

D. ROGER BACON († 1292/94) DEPLORES MISSIONS BY FORCE OF ARMS, ALONE

64. The Neglect of Languages and of Preaching to the Infidel

Opus Majus, 3:13, trans. R. B. Burke, *The Opus Majus of Roger Bacon* (Philadelphia: University of Pennsylvania Press; London: Oxford University Press, 1928), I, pp. 111–12.

. . . For there is no doubt but that all nations of unbelievers beyond Germany would have been converted long since but for the violence of the Teutonic Knights, because the race of pagans was frequently ready to receive the faith in peace after preaching. But the Teutonic Knights are unwilling to keep peace, because they wish to subdue those peoples and reduce them to slavery, and with subtle arguments many years ago deceived the Roman Church. The former fact is known, otherwise I should not state the latter. Moreover, the faith did not enter into this world by force of arms but through the simplicity of preaching, as is clear. And we have frequently heard and we are certain that many, although they were imperfectly acquainted with languages and had weak interpreters, yet made great progress by preaching and converted countless numbers to the Christian faith. Oh, how we should consider this matter and fear lest God may hold the Latins responsible because they are neglecting the languages so that in this way they neglect the preaching of the faith. For Christians are few, and the whole broad world is occupied by unbelievers; and there is no one to show them the truth.

E. RAMON LULL († 1315/16) AND HIS CHALLENGE TO CONVERSION OF THE INFIDEL

65. Lull's Plan for Language Teaching and the Conversion of Saracens, Tartars, and Jews

Blanquerna, Chap. 80: 3, 4, 11, 13, trans. E. A. Peers, *Blanquerna: A Thirteenth Century Romance, Translated from the Catalan of Ramon Lull* (London: Jarrolds Publishers, Ltd., 1925), pp. 325–26, 330–31.

3. After these words, the Pope and the Cardinals and the religious, to honour the glory of God, ordained that to all monks that had learning there should be assigned friars to teach divers languages, and that throughout the world there should be builded divers houses, which for their needs should be sufficiently provided and endowed, according to the manner of the monastery of Miramar, which is in the Island of Majorca. Right good seemed this ordinance to the Pope and to all the rest, and the Pope sent messengers through all the lands of the unbelievers to bring back certain of them to learn their language and that they at Rome might learn the tongues of these unbelievers, and that certain men should return with them to preach to the others in these lands, and that to those unbelievers that learned Latin, and gained a knowledge of the Holy Catholic Faith, should be given money and garments and palfreys, that they might praise the Christians, who when they had returned to their own lands would continue to assist and maintain them.

4. Of the whole world the Pope made twelve parts, and appointed to represent him twelve men, who should go each one throughout his part and learn of its estate, to the end that the Pope might know the estate of the whole world. It came to pass that those who went to the unbelievers brought from Alexandria and from Georgia and from India and Greece Christians who were monks, that they might dwell among us, and that their will might be united with the will

of our monks, and that during this union and relationship they might be instructed in divers manners concerning certain errors against the faith, and should then go and instruct those that were in their country. Wherefore the Pope sent also some of our monks to the monks aforesaid, and ordered that each year they should send to him a certain number of their friars, that they might dwell with us, and, while they dwelt among us, learn our language.

11. Throughout all the world went forth the fame of the holy life of the Pope and the great good which he did, and daily was valour increased and dishonour diminished. The good which came from the ordinance which the Pope had established illumined the whole world, and brought devotion to them that heard the ordinance recounted; and throughout all the world was sent in writing an account of the process of the making thereof. It chanced one day that the Pope had sent to a Saracen king a knight who was also a priest, and of the Order of Science and Chivalry. This knight by force of arms vanquished ten knights one after the other on different days, and after this he vanquished all the wise men of that land by his arguments, and proved to all that the Holy Catholic Faith was true. By messengers of such singular talent, and by many more, did the ordinance aforementioned, which was established by the Holy Apostolic Father, illumine the world.

13. In a certain land there were studying ten Jews and ten Saracens together with ten friars of religion; and when they had learned our holy law and our letters, the half of them were converted to our law, and they preached our law to other Jews, and to Saracens our holy Christian faith, in the presence of many that had not yet been converted, and thus did they daily and continually. And because the Papal Court did all that was in its power, and through the continuance of the disputation, and because truth has power over falsehood, God gave grace to all the Jews and Saracens of that country so that they were converted and baptized, and preached to others the Holy Faith. Wherefore the good and the honour which, through the Pope Blanquerna, was

done to the Christian Faith, can in no wise be recounted.

66. More Specific Suggestions for Conversion

Tractatus de modo convertendi infideles, 3, via Ramon Sugranyes de Franch, *Raymond Lulle Docteur des Missions, avec un choix de Textes traduits et annotés* (*Nouvelle Revue de Sciences Missionaire,* Supplementa V, 1954), pp. 134–35, trans. by the editor.

One will first draw up a list of various sects throughout the world that resist the Catholic faith, and he will apply himself by numerous studies to learn the language of the infidels. Such work will be entrusted only to the noblest and most devoted men, those ready to die for Christ, learned in philosophy and theology, and of well regulated habits. These will then be sent to preach and debate with the infidels. Let their practice of disputation display the requisite grounding together with the necessary arguments and it will be of such stature as to stave in the positions of the infidels as well as to counter their objections; sufficient also to buttress the appropriate doctrines and retorts of the faithful. These rudiments of argumentation are scattered throughout the passages of Holy Scripture and in many learned authors. It will be necessary that competent men compose treatises based on arguments of this kind and translate them into various tongues, so that the infidels may be able to study them and take cognizance of their errors. Books will likewise need to be written on the errors of schismatics, which will be rebutted with essential reasons, easy to find. Such works distributed to the supporters of schism will show them the truth on which Holy Church is established. The pope and his friars must labor zealously for this cause of union among the schismatics. How much easier this would make their victory over the Tartars and other peoples!

A center of study will be organized at Rome, the nucleus of the church. Another at Paris, where knowledge is honored more than anywhere else. A large number of students there abound who will thus be able to introduce themselves to the kind of methods, conceptions, and arguments which they will encounter among the infidels. One of these faculties of study will be set up in Spain owing to the Saracens found there, one at Genoa and another at Venice whose citizens often visit the Saracens and Tartars, especially; others in Prussia, in Hungary, at Haifa, in Armenia, at Taurus, and in various places favorable to the acquisition of different languages and to discussion with the infidels. Studies within the Latin environment are preferable to those carried on among the infidels for reasons of security, perseverance and control of the students. In these schools children will be equipped with a knowledge of infidel tongues and inculcated with the desire to die for Christ. The Saracens rear their young for devilish purposes and worldly conceits. What will be so strange about Christians' bringing up their young people for the cause of Christ, who went to death and the cross for us, who is ready to heap glory and blessing on his disciples who will follow in his footsteps, and who is also our judge?

The church will be able to congratulate itself upon having such missionaries, preachers, and controversialists who will accept death while witnessing to their faith. Lay people will there find the most beautiful confirmation of revealed truth, and the death they will confront will nerve them to live well. God will work miracles at their hands in a fashion calculated to recall the infidels to the way of truth. How blessed shall those be who will busy themselves in raising up such men!

Addison, J. T., *The Medieval Missionary*. International Missionary Council, 1936.

Baldwin, S., *The Organization of Medieval Christianity*. New York: Holt, Rinehart & Winston, Inc., 1929.

Coulton, G. G., *Inquisition and Liberty*. London, 1938.

Crump, A. G., and E. F. Jacob, eds., *The Legacy of the Middle Ages*. New York: Oxford University Press, Inc., 1926.

Deanesly, M., *The Lollard Bible*. Cambridge: Cambridge University Press, 1920.

Elliott-Binns, L. E., *Innocent III*. London: Methuen & Co., Ltd., 1932.

Emery, R. W., *Heresy and the Inquisition in Narbonne*. New York: Columbia University Press, 1941.

Hardy, E. R., *Militant in Earth*. New York: Oxford University Press, Inc., 1940.

Lagarde, A., *The Latin Church in the Middle Ages*, trans. A. Alexander. New York: Charles Scribner's Sons, 1915.

Latourette, K. S., *A History of the Expansion of Christianity*, Vol. II. New York: Harper & Brothers, 1938.

McDonnell, E. W., *The Beguines and Beghards in Medieval Culture*. New Brunswick, N. J.: Rutgers University Press, 1954.

Moorman, J. R. H., *Church Life in England in the Thirteenth Century*. Cambridge: Cambridge University Press, 1945.

Obolensky, D., *The Bogomils*. Cambridge: Cambridge University Press, 1948.

Owst, G. R., *Literature and Pulpit in Medieval England*. Cambridge: Cambridge University Press, 1933.

Packard, S., *Europe and the Church under Innocent III*. New York: Holt, Rinehart & Winston, Inc., 1927.

Petry, R. C., ed., *No Uncertain Sound*. Philadelphia: Westminster Press, 1948.

Smalley, R., *The Study of the Bible in the Middle Ages*. New York: Philosophical Library, Inc., 1952.

Smyth, C., *The Art of Preaching*. New York: The Macmillan Co., 1940.

Warner, H. J., *The Albigensian Heresy*, 2 vols. London: SPCK, 1922, 1928.

Illustration, page 372: **Music-making Angels.** *Oak carving by Meister van Spes Nostra.*

IX

Medieval Education, the Arts, and Christian Iconography; Symbolism, the Liturgy, and the Common Life

The very title of this chapter, as well as the whole bearing of its source readings, suggests an oft unappreciated fact. Christian emphasis has never been placed upon education as an academic discipline in itself. Nor has it fallen upon worship divorced from the intellectual assumptions of the praying and acting community. From the days of Jesus, the common life (*koinos bios*) and the fellowship of the spirit (*koinonia*) reflected living interpenetrations. These characterized a guild (*universitas*) or college (*collegium*) of prayer, thought, and action. A more recent tendency persists in deprecating intellectual regimen as somehow extraneous to the spirit of Christ's individual and religious ministrations.

An equally obdurate distortion finds in early Christianity a self-conscious substitution of Christian intellectual and social assumptions for all previously existing views and reformations. Actually, the records mirror Christian discipleship as a distinctive *koinonia*, or *communio*. In it, older elements of disciplined thought and invested action were inseparably related. These were nurtured in a continuously innovating community of experienced solidarity.

Within such a coherence of living forces, it was well-nigh impossible to conceive education as being either a self-validating objective or a new methodology. Liturgy could never have constituted the end purpose so long as the total mind as well as the disciplined heart of the worshiper remained partly unclaimed for consolidated being and acting. The cultivation of the arts as a thing foreign to Christians, or of dissociated, individual ends as the sole concern of the Master, makes little sense in Jesus' radical community of love. Total worship was lived out of the stark realities of a cosmic kingdom already in operation, one peremptorily levying upon temporal preoccupation for eternal ends. Individuals had no true existence apart from their incorporation into the eternal community of God's unearned graciousness. No sentimental affections of the heart or routine genuflections of the body had meaning aside from their integrity with the fully exercised loyalties of the disciplined mind. The difficulty of many later Christians in perceiving this arises from a considerable unawareness of any but the more recent vernacular usages attached to key words. Among these are "community," "society," and "individual." Sometimes bewilderment stems from a break in the linkage between concepts, active as well as contemplative, such as *koinonia* and *persona*.

The "common life" becomes, in Chapter IX, no preview of the vulgar debasements visited upon the average person. It is a historical prospectus for viewing the mutual exercise of shared resources. Out of this context comes the instruction and catechesis in living tradition, the "imaged" realities or "icons" lying back of obvious references, and the liturgy of living, thinking, acting worshipers. All worship, thought, and action converge in the *noblesse oblige* of the community.

To departmentalize for convenience the characteristic activities of education, the plastic arts, architecture, and liturgy is to guarantee that history will be distorted. Ease of gathering information will be purchased at the price of oversimplified reality. Neither in the ancient world nor in medieval perspective was there any vocabulary of isolated academic subjects such as the twentieth century employs. There was no self-conscious specialization in early Christian architecture, medieval iconography, thirteenth-century political science, or scholastic education. There was no division of worship in the second-century parish church and no faculty of church historians at the University of Paris.

It is often regarded good sport to stigmatize medieval education as struggling under the beguiling manipulations of the Church. Science sometimes masquerades as a violated yearning for objectivity dishonored at the hands of religious bigotry. Elements of truth in such pitiful caricatures are obvious. So is the joint tenure of noble ideals and pet hypocrisies fostered in the endless succession of "modern" world views. Churchmen tend to arrogate truth-seeking to Christian auspices. There is a superciliousness that belongs especially to that brand of science which is always crusading for nonsubjective fact. The modern desire to restrict fields of knowledge to modest feasibility is laudable in intent. Equally praiseworthy was the penchant of medieval life to unify every divergent longing of mind, spirit, and daily exigency into a viable search for universal meaning.

How this quest came to expression, given the earlier educational aims of the Graeco-Roman world, has been assayed by countless scholars. The researches of Rashdall, Haskins, Denifle, and many more are well known. At this point a frank restatement of commendable digests borrowed from d'Irsay and Delhaye is indispensable.

The cherished schools of the ancient Greek world left scant mark upon the succeeding ages. The Christian catechetical instruction of Hellenistic Alexandria did place in a new light the indisseverable Christian concerns with *kerygma, didascalia,* and *catechesis.* They embraced the whole man, the teaching church, and the living liturgy. These were inserted within the noble perspectives of Hellenic wisdom and moderation. There was, of course, no prototype here for medieval schools or the growth of public Christian education. One must be forewarned against finding anywhere in the middle era—even in the heyday of the monastic schools—anything like truly general education. Nevertheless, certain overtones and undercurrents of rhetoric, grammar, and dialectic were transmitted from the old Roman schools, together with traces of the ancient Greek grammarians. These filtered into the liberal tradition inherited by Christian instruction. The evanescent glories of Christian Africa in the days of Tertullian and Cyprian, like those of Cassiodorus' era on the Continent, were intermittently reinvigorated in later thought and action. The influence of Roman schools and Christian scholars was still to be discerned in the fading culture of fourth- and fifth-century Gaul. Quite divergent from the Greek spirit and the Roman perspective was the renascent emphasis placed by Christian teachers upon the liberal arts in the succeeding ages. Yet from the fourth to the eighth century there was formed a strange synthesis of Roman decadence, barbarian vigor, and a newly emerging Christian unity. A fresh Christian orientation in classical studies was to capitalize the ancient liberal tradition for the service of sacred letters. This was utilized by the Christian hierarchy and a theological sophistication still to come.

At the outset of the Middle Ages the *trivium* (grammar, logic, and rhetoric) was primary, with its logical and philological emphases. The Carolingian era was to see a resurgence of the *quadrivium* (arithmetic, music, geometry & astronomy), thanks to the revival of Graeco-Roman disciplines in the work of men like Theodulph of Orleans, Paul the Deacon, and Peter of Pisa. Rabanus Maurus was formed under Alcuin, with an awareness of Irish catholicity in learning. He injected into his episcopal and monastic

activities an impetus yet observable in the days of Lanfranc and Anselm.

Scholarly reservations about the nature and extent of monastic culture should not lead to the deprecation of all monastic contributions. The monasteries, on however restricted a scale and with whatever specialization, did cultivate the liberal arts from the sixth to the eleventh century. This was usually in communities stressing the primacy of worship and the ancillary value, at best, of scriptural reading and copying. These fitted into a further context of manual labor. Nevertheless, one cannot discount the liberalizing bent of Cassian's foundations in Gaul, the memory of Cassiodorus' Christian humanism at Vivarium, and the proud intellectual tradition of Irish monasticism.

The Irish returned ten-fold to the Continent their own earlier tutelage in the arts from Gaul and Britain. Widespread, indeed, were the contrasting, sometimes competing, and often mutually reinforcing blessings of Benedictine and Celtic monasticism. These were to be discerned until the latter half of the eleventh century. One may not deny to these *coenobia* a significant structuring of the *Cura* and the *Schola Animarum*. True— these were a far cry from Jesus' lakeside seminars and the catechetical schools of Clement and Origen, not to mention the rhetorical disciplines of Roman Africa. Nonetheless, these centers of Benedictine *stabilitas* and Irish *mobilitas* both served the *opus dei.* They preserved and extended within the primacy of the worshiping community the literacy of the common life. In Gaul, Britain, and Germany the monastic schools fostered the Church's clerical indoctrination. During the ninth and tenth centuries, especially, itinerants from Irish and Anglo-Saxon centers of liberal study dotted the Continent with missions for the joint "curing" and "schooling" of souls. Under Charlemagne's exuberant prodding and with Alcuin's direction at the palace school in Aachen, as by derivation from his later career at Tours, both monastic and episcopal outposts operated in a flurry of educational enthusiasm. Corbie, Fleury, Fulda, Reichenau, St. Gall, St. Maur, Ferrières, Lorsch, and many other abbeys became justly famous. Alcuin's students and their own disciples—like Rabanus Maurus, Walafrid Strabo, Servatus Lupus, and Notker Balbulus—became synonyms for cultural evangelism. Their names joined others, earlier and later, such as Aldhelm, Bede the Venerable, Paul the Deacon, Peter of Pisa, Theodulph of Orleans, Agobard, John Scotus Eriugena, Dungal, Donatus, Hincmar, Radbertus, Ratramnus, Liutprand, Bruno, Hroswitha, Gerbert, and Fulbert, on the distinguished service scroll of Christian culture.

From the sixth to the eleventh century monastic instruction was ascendant. Monks kept "inner" schools for the training of renunciants and "outer" schools for limited service beyond. With the early eleventh century one observes a rapid passage from monastic to episcopal leadership. In the secular and cathedral chapter schools there coursed the stream of liberal studies. These marked the influence of scholastic energies and the pre-university guilds. Monastic ties with general instruction were strained and broken. Delhaye's study of twelfth-century education shows it to have been under the virtual domination of clerks. Monks were increasingly suspicious of learning as something ill-befitting the monastic vocation. "Interior" schools at Benedictine abbeys quickly followed the few remaining "exterior" ones into near collapse.

The chief Benedictine reformations were centered at Cluny and Citeaux. Each, with its increasing dependencies, stressed distinctive variations upon the commonly inspired Benedictine priority of worship. The Cistercian usages evidenced hostility to all but the more innocuous forms of Benedictine reading and cultural interest. Even the library resources and artistic magnificence of Cluny showed little concern with basic education outside the range of cultic life. Contrasted with Peter Damian's snarling anti-intellectualism, Bernard's demurrers seem more charitable. To superficial observers, they are scarcely less a vote of no confidence in learning as a prime attribute of the true Benedictine. Beside them, the earlier stress of Lanfranc upon the union of piety and learning constituted a nostalgic reminder of bygone "liberality." Dunstan's purported friendship for the arts and Anselm's irenic scholarship nurtured in monastic and episcopal camaraderie moved into sad eclipse. Monks were now better known for their aspersions against culture and their call to a holy barbarism than they were remembered for their once eager receptivity to liberal learning. The bishops' schools, however, and those of the secular chapters, grew steadily.

II

In Northern France, the trivium flourished anew. In time, the Parisian masters laid the basis for the University of Paris and the quadrivium. The memories attaching to Theodore of Canterbury and the glorious era of Aldhelm and Bede, were revived, as were the glories of York and Aachen. Schools at Tours and Rheims ushered in the epoch of Gerbert of Aurillac (later Pope Sylvester II). At Chartres, which irradiated the eleventh and twelfth centuries, Gerbert's spiritual son Fulbert taught with distinction. The hour of destiny struck at Paris, notwithstanding. The earlier, abortive revivals under Chrodegang and Charlemagne were rechanneled into the later renaissance of Christian letters.

The liberal arts, intermittently emphasized in Gaul, England, and Ireland, now came with cumulative focus into the orbit of episcopal leadership. The great centers included Metz, Orleans, Liege, Laon, and Rheims, as well as Chartres and Paris. Grammar ceded its place gradually to dialectic. The liberal arts, once virtually an end in themselves for the Romans, functioned as the servants of philosophy. The method of disputation rose into ascendancy with procedures reminiscent of Cassian's *Collations*, or *Conferences*. When employed by Bernard of Chartres and Abelard of Paris, the "evening collation" became a powerful reagent, as passages from John of Salisbury's *Metalogicon* make clear.

The constituent elements of scholasticism were already observable in Anselm of Bec and Fulbert of Chartres. The twelfth century saw scholasticism flourish. The thirteenth witnesses its triumphant placement at the core of university procedure. D'Irsay stands in awe before the sweeping advance of this new philosophical realism. Out of it shines the clear influence of Aristotle and the pulsations of Neo-Platonic vitality brought together under Christian modification. Here was a dominant world view and a prevalent system of discourse and discussion, collectively and critically fostered. A unique flowering marked the triumphant course of scholasticism.

The Cathedral schools had flourished since the end of the eleventh century. Bishop William of Champeaux, with his strongly realistic philosophy, was later to be pitted against Abelard's nominalism. He, for example, helped create a pattern of influential action. Episcopal patronage elicited the rise of famous masters with their enthusiastic students grouped about them. Peter Lombard continued the tradition of episcopal leadership with his incipient *Summa*, the *Sentences*, as a valuable support. Whereas at Chartres, philosophy and liberal studies predominated, at Paris a new vogue for theology developed. Scholars from the world scene flocked thither; men like the Englishman Stephen Langton, the German Otto of Freising, and others, Danish, Swedish, and Italian. From the ancient director of studies, the *scholasticus*, there developed the chancellor, the chief functionary of the sponsoring bishop. Clustered about Notre Dame in the Ile de la Cité, at the end of the twelfth century, there grew up thriving centers of instruction in the arts, philosophy, theology, and law.

To the north, on Mt. St. Genevieve, masters had held forth since the eleventh century. Then followed Alberic of Rheims and the redoubtable Robert of Melun. The hero of the Left Bank was Abelard. He was a one-time student of Laon, an erstwhile apprentice in dialectic at Notre Dame, a hardy dissenter from his associates' views wherever he went. He was the proponent of a brand of conceptualism often regarded as sheer nominalism. In him, purportedly rationalistic propensities were joined to a dialectical subtlety that threatened the very existence of universals. Students lionized him, as in fact he did himself. His *History of My Misfortunes* is scarcely the work of a modest man. His *Yes and No*, however, is more than

the operation of a troublemaking propounder of blasphemous riddles and inner contradictions attributed to the most reverend Fathers. Cheap distortions were traceable to his scintillating methods. Even so, his most estimable students, like John of Salisbury, paid him high tribute. He had, together with men such as Bernard of Chartres, inspired their indefatigable search for true knowledge. On the Left Bank, meanwhile, his student, Arnold of Brescia—no light troublemaker himself—gathered his own following.

Holding high eminence in Paris, too, was the school of the Canons of St. Victor. William of Champeaux had retired there from the stinging attacks of Abelard. His school gave rise to the solid attainments of Hugh, Richard, and Adam. Hugh's *Summa of the Sentences* held its own with Peter Lombard's. The future of the abbey school, however, was to be notable chiefly within its own orbit of canonical liturgy and contemplative vocation. It had slight affinity with the university later to be developed at Paris.

III

Abelard's own brilliant—and often unprincipled—career of conquest left him far short of founding the university. The intellectual currents set in motion in the episcopal schools there and fostered by him, as well as by less spectacular teachers, are, however, not to be discounted. Finally, out of the guild of scholars and disciples there being wrought into a community of learning, the greatest of medieval universities arose. From it, the *Summas*—at once so dear to some scholastics and so reprobated by Roger Bacon—were to appear. In these, as in the collections of the canon law, the stamp of the *Sic et Non* would be apparent. Eventually, the great master *Summa* of Thomas Aquinas lent to Abelard's reconstructed method the grave endorsement of thrust, counterthrust, and concluding thesis. From the congeries of competing masters, gathered in tightly reinforcing conclave, came new instruction by, and for, the church universal. This was given not only at diocesan hands but also with growing papal patronage.

The poor clerks and scholars of each cathedral church received free instruction. Their goal was the license to teach anywhere, received at the chancellor's hands. As for curriculum, the liberal arts led into philosophy, and philosophy into theology.

The university organization was a matter of gradual, existential response to functional necessities. Papal privileges were accorded the universities, those corporations of masters and students. These served to remind society, generally, of the Church's leading role in schools, learning, and teaching. Collisions between students and townsmen resulted in Philip Augustus' provision, in 1200, for placing the entire *universitas* under the Church's jurisdiction. The bishop exercised administrative responsibility through his minion, the chancellor. The rights of this functionary to confer the license, though bestowed by the papacy in 1208, suffered steady incursion and attrition. His loss was reflected in the gains registered by the Masters. The corporation of teachers, as it became less and less dependent upon local ecclesiasts, moved gradually under the direct protection of the Holy See. The bishop of Paris, local synods, and the entire provincial hierarchy fought a steady delaying action against the growing autonomy of the educational corporation. This now gravitated to the Left Bank. The first official statutes of 1215 were provided the *studium* by the cardinal Robert de Courçon. This was the virtual foundation of the university's legal, organized life. Though the pull of philosophical sophistication was strong, the place of theology increased under the patronage of Pope Gregory IX. Of paramount concern was the fostering of the whole medieval world view and the comprehension of the universe, rather than the acquisition of facts. This was joined ideally, in theological perspective, to the professional needs of churchmen and to the credo of professing Christians.

The chancellor's powers continued in nominal though steadily enfeebled vigor until 1301. With the advent of the Mendicants, however, a definite rebalancing of churchly influence became apparent. The cathedral chapter, with the chancellor as a member, resented the friars and the growing prestige of ecclesiastical catholicity fostered at the expense of provincial hierarchs. As the chancellor's prerogatives declined, and as theology and law migrated to the Left Bank, the influence of the episcopal school lessened. The four nations of masters and students in the arts and in the four faculties increased steadily. Between 1221 and 1229 juridical status was accorded the university. As yet, *universitas* still meant a social entity, guild, or corporation: *universitas magistrorum et scholarium Parisius commorantium.* Here, then, was a growing confraternity of thought, purpose, and action. In its geographical and intellectual context of universality, this guild of study stood forth as the *studium generale.* Not until 1261 did the word "university" take on its modern connotation.

Between 1228 and 1231, however, events brought Paris university life and organization to a new definition. A "town and gown" row with tragic consequences, in 1229, resulted in a mass migration of masters and students. Some went to Orleans and Angers, others to Toulouse and even to England. Paris saw the suspension of her most lucrative source of fame. King Louis IX's renewal of privileges for the university made a tardy appearance. Pope Gregory IX hastened to the role of mediator as he sharply rebuked the lethargic discharge of duties by the Bishop of Paris. In his papal ardor, Gregory paid almost as fulsome a tribute to the university as did the florid sermon of Chancellor Philip. The mendicants rose in a steady crescendo of opportunity and leadership, exercised at Paris during the secession. By 1231 the émigrés had returned to Paris, "the true home of the bees," as the chancellor put it. Moreover, the privileges accorded them at papal behest constituted the university's "Magna Charta." The ecclesiastical jurisdiction thereby reasserted was papal, not diocesan. The chancellor lost, forthwith, all but the most nominal powers: the right of according the license. Prior to his granting this, he must have taken an oath to the fraternity of Masters.

The *studia generalia* that gave rise to the universities were more than populous centers of a ballooning curriculum. Not everything was taught there. Rather, people from everywhere came to slake together their thirst for the unity of total meaning. Contrary to the localized perspectives that made feudalism so disruptive, there came to birth in these great intellectual foundations the most universalizing propensities of the medieval spirit. The *universitas* that arose had little in common with twentieth-century educational grandiloquence or the passion for organizational programs. It was—not merely, but supremely—a society, a guild, a body dedicated in common to that truth-seeking which ranges beyond all parochial interests and all particularized delimitations. Thus the *studium generale* transcended the *studium particularis*. So, the *universitas societas magistrorum et disciplorumque* set the whole body of masters and students in associated quest for common ends. Theirs was the spur of that wholeness in truth which entails inevitable teaching by the one who learns. That teaching, alone, is vital which arises from the joyous communicativeness of perpetual learning. The masters were those whose search in learning prompted students to seek with them. The true student was one who learned that no one can study without teaching. Through, and sometimes in spite of, the much-abused collation and dialectical syllogism, medieval minds grew sharply communicative and critically wary. They did so, even without the truly advantageous disciplines of the much-vaunted, modern laboratory. Beyond all cavil, teachers and students did sometimes work together, as indubitably as their modern counterparts have been known to "go it alone."

In this realm of the newly utilized liberal arts, the philosopher and theologian supplied a reincarnation of the old *schola* and *cura animarum*. Within these guilds of the liberal arts, there ministered the scholastic servants of the common life. John of Salisbury's *Metalogicon* witnesses a deference for the liberalizing disciplines being brought into renewed currency from their old Roman provenance. His battle with the "Cornificians" betokens more than just another long, drawn-out contest by the friends of solid method and substance against loose-mouthed, grammarless popularizers. Hugh of St. Victor had also fought that discourag-

ing engagement. Heralded in the struggle, however, was a triumphant investment of dialectical philosophy that was to serve theology and the new scholasticism well.

Scholasticism itself was probably never quite the sterile encrustation of knowledge that later caricatures have made it. With all of its faults, it was one way of transcending uncorrelated enthusiasms and uncritical assumptions with a concerted, systematic manner of reflecting upon total reality. Here was vastly more than reason in chilly subservience to faith, or belief put before understanding; more, even, than philosophy sternly remanded to the role of theology's hand-maiden. The *consortium* of mature scholars and eager students refocused, with all their arguments over realism and nominalism, a perspective of total concern with all being, and knowing, and doing. This necessitated collaboration within controversy that caused the heart of honest inquiry to leap, alike, in the breast of an Abelard and a Thomas Aquinas.

The range of common scholastic dueling bound together such strange blends of reason and revelation as Roger Bacon and the "boys" at Paris he loved to pillory. United across the centuries were sermonic allegorizings like those of the thirteenth-century chancellor Philip and fourteenth-century decrees on the proper way of lecturing on the liberal arts. Such academic conditioning went beyond the codifying of a way of life for the descendants of Hugh's prudent scholar. It transcended John of Salisbury's critical "shaking out of the authors" that stood in need of "plucked tail-feathers." The common scholastic discipline embraced in its catholicizing range a wide array of conflicting yet reinforcing views and personalities. Native to its doctrinal passions and eschatological commitments were the *Sentences* of Lombard, the *Summas* of Thomas, the evangelical disciplines and liberating scholarship of Robert Grosseteste, the preaching treatises of the Dominican Humbert de Romans, and many more. Woven together in scholastic purview were, also, the whole fabric of documented statecraft and the waspy commentaries of publicists. Embodied within it were treatises on civic ethics, legal corporateness, and cultic solidarity. All of these disciplines have latterly been dispersed in the modern dichotomy of the secular and the religious. Feudalism, in its localizing self-interest, atomized medieval life. The universities, it is true, had their "nations," their competing faculties, and their syllogistic stereotypes. Yet, they helped direct all the ramifying interests and yearnings of the lowliest peasant and the lordliest academician into one spiritual rhythm of the common life. Implicit even in the learned treatises of the university theologian or canonist were the considerations of a frequently overlooked popular literacy. There was participation by the simple in the concerns of proud minds. This was made possible by the unlettered peasants' reading from the universal sign boards of realistic symbol and iconograhic instruction.

Scholasticism and university curriculum were not just a timetable of reason and revelation under scheduled rapprochement. Theirs was an intellectual and spiritual rendezvous with everyday ultimates and perplexities. The *studium* refreshed and ennobled the energies of the *imperium* and the eternal ministrations of the *sacerdotium*. Moderns may, along with a famous church historian, earnestly seek the keying of scholasticism to the problem of universals. The position of the extreme realists with their Platonic emphasis put universals into a class apart, prior to all individual objects—*ante rem*. Moderate realists, reminiscent of Aristotle, sought the reality of universals in connection with individual objects—*in re*. Nominalists, meanwhile, out of Stoic context, saw in universals merely abstract names or *nomens*. As such these had their only existence in thought, unlike the reality that lodged in individual objects—*post rem*. All such analyses, nonetheless, tend to drive underground the problem of the more comprehensive realism with which church-invested scholastics sought the earthiest microcosm under the scrutiny of the great macrocosm.

The Middle Ages had assembled a varied set of deductions and disciplines from an enormous range of world views. These generally orthodox assumptions drew upon the Eastern Fathers. They utilized the translations of, and commentaries upon, Neo-Platonic philosophers. There were artful adaptations of esoteric learning to parish worship and monastic liturgy. The hierarchical imagery and contemplative symbolism of the Pseudo-Dionysius were uncritically appropriated from the works of Hilduin and John Scotus Eriugena. The role of Denys, the supposed companion of St. Paul, was identified with the patron saint of France and the author of the *Mystical Theology*. In the mystical treatises of the Victorines and the new architecture of St. Denys and Chartres, as in the transition from the old Romanesque to the high Gothic era, a breath-taking synthesis was being effected from the stimuli of spiritual and cultural suggestion. Thus the more primitive liturgical revivals of Dunstan and even Lanfranc, together with the conflicting Benedictine usages of Cluny and Citeaux, jostled the Dionysian symbolism of Suger and the new iconography of the thirteenth-century cathedral. A revived Christian humanism was on the rise. Clearly, it was not unmindful of the Greeks and Romans, nor was it unprepared for the strange creativity of Joachim, Dante, and Nicholas Cusanus.

John of Salisbury's humanistic sensibilities and those of twelfth-century learning evidenced the human spirit's seeking to link the lowliest peasant and the highest potentate under the ecstatic leadings of divine commerce. The revival of Christian, humanistic learning under the mediating services of the Latin and Greek classics yielded a new lexicography and a new set of writing manuals (*Artes Dictaminis*). In addition, there existed a whole world of men, women, and children worshiping in literate context with a living Latin. The Church's official language was truly meant for them, even though they could scarcely utter a word or trace a line of it. Theirs was the strange literacy of an almost untutored laity. They followed a clergy seldom fully literate in the measurably effective invocation of Latin praises and supplications. Their literacy consisted in their knowing when and where to join in human response to the self-immolation of the Divine. It was this communication that the liturgical action achieved and described. They appropriated this in a continuity of hearing, seeing, tasting, smelling, and otherwise sensing, symbolically, what was common experience in and beyond words.

Actually, the words arranged in scholastic disputation were those placed in liturgical context, no less than those matching the symbolic universalism of the humblest layman. The higher scholasticism was the sending to school of the people themselves, and of the clergy, whether in university classroom or under diocesan instruction. They were obliged to learn what they and the people in common must know. Placed on varying levels of mediating instruction, the most benighted were catechized endlessly in the common perspectives of universal life. Frequently, they sensed impressionistically, without benefit of Latin instruction, what the Latin disquisitions of the universities and the Latin invocations of the priest were all about. Truly, the Christian tradition of liturgy, word, symbol, and the arts created the self-same preoccupation for learned and unlearned, with the self-same living creed.

For the medieval man, as for those in every era, there were many ways of reading. Certainly, there were many kinds of books. Not all of these were alike readable by all the people. Just the same, what was read in glass or stone by the laymen was referable to the most learned tomes of the scholastic. Joined to the subliminal yearnings of the mediating priest were the passionate desires of the learned systematizer of thought. He longed to pit his intricate assumptions against the savage over-simplifications of popular conception. The final test of scholastic training was not to exhaust itself in carefully protected theoretics. It was to project under keen debate the theorems governing human susceptibility to the ultimate. The truly learned man, then as in any age, was one who knew enough about ramifying ideas to exploit them when and where they were most applicable. The unusual flexibility which the friars cultivated in their university preparation was specifically directed to their avowed ministry among those customarily deemed illiterate. It is noteworthy that they succeeded in exciting very ordinary minds with some very recondite ideas.

Demonstrable in any age is the rueful discovery that writing and/or printing may not always lead to reading. Reading does not always stimulate a given kind of writing. Obviously, people may read and understand more than has ever been written. Perhaps it is a modern conceit to recall how few people could once read in the conventionally approved ways, when many conventionally adept at reading today cannot truly read at all! The burden of the latter portions of Chapter IX will be to sensitize the present-day reader to the multiple opportunities for reading and communicating by medieval people, who are often held to have been relatively incapable of doing either.

The scrutiny of medieval education is not even mainly conjecturable, therefore, on the basis of so-called schools and universities alone. Without the vast coding and decoding by the most varied instructors and learners in the common life, the specialized study of medieval education may well come to naught. The medieval man read most effectively in the parish church, in wood, glass, and stone. He stretched his eye-span in the natural museums of symbolic bird, beast, and rock. His textbook was in the language of icons, whether high-pitched on cathedral roof or low-swung in liturgical context. What was here read dealt with the very things communicated in Peter Lombard's *Sentences*, in Paris lecture halls, by the cathedral architect or parish builder, and in the guild market-place. In all of these cultural highways and byways, there was daily communication among all classes. Employed were all the propaganda devices of shrewd urbanites, as of rural folklorists and popular saintmakers.

People have always televised what most mattered to them. Their media have been the swirling colors of the raucous or mellifluous dance; smoke signals synchronized with beating drums; the hieroglyphics of wood, stone, and marble; or, perchance, the staccato suggestion of film strip and electronic conditioning. People have undoubtedly read more than they could see, in purely conventional wording; even when this was labored and diagrammed with preconceived conclusiveness. Without any sheerly vexatious demand that one look in all but the more obvious places where people normally read, one may simply call attention to the normalcy with which they seek more than the obvious.

Human beings as a whole—not just philosophers—may be taught to distrust what is too much in vogue by the shortsighted. Unhappily also, they may be permitted or even urged to accept as normal what has been sufficiently taken for granted by enough of their fellows. So it was in the Middle Ages. Nevertheless, in a way almost uniquely theirs, the passionately titillated conversations of the sophistics and the gossipy clackings of commoners were astoundingly tuned in to the same human basics of discussion.

As previously suggested, the pristine call of the mendicants was not necessarily debased by its subjection to scholastic criticism. Nor was the new, university-acquired wisdom of Franciscans and Dominicans ever tested more rigorously than when it went on tour among shrewd villagers and sardonic townspeople; or when it faced the cynical veterans of the crusades. A lot of learning was needed to bring great issues to as tense a pass in sermon and confession as the daily exigencies of birth, life, and death regularly did. In truth, college professors and the conventionally illiterate, alike, conceivably did both heavy and light reading in various kinds of literature. Theirs was a range of literacy transcending merely one category of books.

A great, encyclopedic "book of knowledge" for all medieval persons might reasonably be expected to start with a basic vocabulary and fundamental readings. Quite properly, these were combined in the cathedral or its local substitute. This effectively mirrored and interpreted the universal message extended to each. Within it, on its exterior, and indeed throughout its environing locality, the cathedral conveyed meanings suitable to every expression of hope, fear, hate, love, and joy. Such lines were to be perused in a veritable library of books engraved on altar stone, wooden crucifix, and pavement "graffiti." Recorded within

it were the images of remembered processional, chanting voices, and sweet incense. Ultimately, it was to the poets and story tellers, as to the painters, builders, and musicians, that medieval people went for their interpretation of their universe. To these same oracles, as well as to the philosophers, historical theologians, and church historians, the modern observer must also go.

IV

There is no need to annotate Panofsky's controversial thesis on the relation of art and scholasticism. He is his own best interpreter. Simson in his *Gothic Cathedral* serves to reinforce with reservations many of the same points Panofsky makes. "Wooden" scholasticism is not easily relegated to its "deserved" obscurity. Seldom "wooden," its vigor grows surprisingly, even in the modern world. In the strange synthesis of art and scholastic architecture emphasized by Panofsky, both Abelard and Thomas resound. Present also is Villard de Honnecourt. Scholastic *summas* and cathedral buttresses stand back to back. The stage properties of builders and musicians fit neatly—perhaps too neatly—into their places. Mirrors, books, organs—what matters the figure? All figures are to be read, even as books are designed to be reflecting mirrors.

V

Émile Mâle reminds us that the Middle Ages conceived art as instruction. All that man needed most to know for his daily pilgrimage and his eternal salvation was taught him quite effectively. It came out of God's great book, the world itself. This was mirrored most eloquently in the cathedral, the veritable "Bible of the Poor." The orderly range of St. Thomas' vast *Summa* was reflected and translated from the world of theological ideas. It was transliterated into the word of life that even the humblest peasant might comprehend.

Medieval art was indeed "eminently symbolical," as Mâle insists. Form was the spirit's embodiment. Artists no less than theologians were spiritualizers of matter. Liturgical teaching found its way regularly into the central motifs of cathedral iconography.

That is, the language and the writing of images, pictures, likenesses, or reflections were best read from this universal book, the cathedral. It was, itself, a reflection, an image, of the divine intent for man, written so that all might read. What was there written was no less vital, though it was infinitely more adaptable to the instruction of ordinary minds, than the text books of the scholastics. What this Bible said and what the theologians taught was the same content of salvation.

Iconography, then, as Bréhier suggests, is virtually image-writing. It is a study of figured representations, be they of an individual or of an epoch, whether of the symbols and dogmas of a doctrine or of a religion. The art historian today may think of iconography as an auxiliary science. The medieval artist's main concern, however, was the heart of iconography itself. He discerned, followed, and, at the same time, taught the rules of spiritual typology. He made possible the recognition and appropriation of the ideas symbolized by these types. Truly, works of religious art make no sense until one comprehends, not only the persons and scenes figured forth, but, much more, the dogmatic intent of their portrayers.

Art, then, for the Middle Ages was veritably an instruction. Medieval iconography was, according to Mâle, a sacred writing, a holy mathematics, a symbolic language. The representation of sacred subjects was an orderly science, the principles of which were never left to individual whimsy. This virtual theology of art was not abandoned to chance. Rather, it was transmitted by the Church to lay artists, sculptors, and builders. Naturally it was summoned out of venerable hierarchical tradition for the perpetuation of salvation's working in the hearts of all men. The artist then had to know how to read writing, and how to write writing, this holy writing. He must put a nimbus where it belonged, not where his fancy dictated. Place, symmetry, number—all were of prime significance. How the Church was oriented was the major concern, not of the town council, but of the liturgist and the ecclesiastical calendar. The lay architect was inducted into, and held responsible for, this secret knowledge. Then it was re-translated by him in foundation stones and human edification. He must not only know how to read, but he must help teach others to read, also, the language that symbol speaks.

This language, the language of Christian art, was spoken, recorded, and interpreted in figures. One must be able to see more than he saw; to read in, behind, and beyond the obvious representation, the ultimate edification. A judgment scene depicting foolish maidens on Jesus' left and wise ones on his right was not an exercise in judging popularity contests. These two groups symbolized the reprobate and the blessed elect. Such, then, were the general characteristics of medieval iconography—an inception into the art of medieval reading and writing, not forgetting arithmetic. The harmonics of this consecrated writing, arithmetic, and symbolism was celestial music itself. This came down to earth to help prepare men for the symphonic beatitude of heaven.

The medieval era of encyclopedias, summas, mirrors, and images of the world was itself mirrored forth in Vincent of Beauvais' *Speculum.* Here was in fact the four-fold *Mirror of the World,* as the cathedral reflected God's universe. The *Mirror of Nature* reflected all life as God had created it, with thrilling emphasis on the sixth day and the creation of man. The *Mirror of Knowledge* projected man's overweening passion for the wrong knowledge. It purveyed his fall and the right knowledge of his way back, that Christ's revelation supplied. It also celebrated the spirit of life that resides in learning and the seven gifts of the Holy Spirit that were relatable to the seven liberal arts. The *Moral Mirror,* actually not of Vincent's own authorship, reflected what was an abridgment of Thomas' *Summa.* Here was the way of knowledge that leads to virtue and the struggle of the vices with the virtues. The *Historical Mirror* focused the whole dramatic struggle of humanity itself. This was the story of God's people and of his Church. Here were depicted the Old Testament, the Gospels, the lives of the saints as these were told in the *Golden Legend,* the end of world history, and the Last Judgment. The cathedral was, indeed, the "Bible of the Poor." It guaranteed that the dogmas of the schools and the gracious benedictions of the liturgy would be forever referable in the mind's eye of the people to the whole saga of redemption.

VI

The bond that united the scholastic artists, builders, and musicians to the people was no imaginary lien. It is only logical that the man whose world view was diffused so magisterially throughout the entire Middle Ages should stand at the head of the source selections in this category. Augustine's book *On Music*, like those *On the Free Will* and *On Order*, is basic to the understanding of the whole middle era. The discerning appreciations of a modern composer, Hindemith, are merely suggested. The excellent résumé of Routley is gratefully borrowed in some detail. Augustine's *De Musica* is given in the cogent brevity of selected passages. From these, it should be apparent that he was using the term "music" in a universal sense, the sense appropriated by the Middle Ages and reflected in the source texts here. This musical concept in its most catholic outreach was cumulatively referable to the symphonic and aesthetic critiques of countless medieval writers. Such presuppositions of universal musical composition and order appear in Suger's architectural remodeling. They figure in Grosseteste's conception of the liberal arts, as they do in Villard de Honnecourt's abstract portraiture and "musical" churches. They are equally traceable in Roger Bacon's neo-scholastic disquisitions on music, the dance, and theology. Machaut's innovations in poetry, drama, and the *Ars Nova* are not wholly new cloth spun without subconscious awareness of the old fabrics. The liturgical incorporation of folk fertility in the *Dies Irae* and the *Play of Daniel* are obvious collaborations of things old and new.

It may seem nonsense to the twentieth century to think of theologians studying the theoretics of drama, music, and the dance. Presumably, these worthies are busy enough excoriating each of these artistic media or incorporating them into some jazz liturgy.

Architects are not expected to build "musical" churches "on the square." Some, like Frank Lloyd Wright, are not lightly forgiven for erecting museums "in the round." Machaut's was an easy fusion of motets, masses, and secular "round dances," together with his assistance at mass in bucolic chapels and his weekend house parties with feudal lords and ladies. Perhaps these will be put down by moderns to the advance stirrings of healthy Renaissance versatility. The revival of the twelfth-century *Play of Daniel*, by interested scholars, Noah Greenberg, the "Pro Musica," and the "Cloisters" of the Metropolitan Museum of Art played to an appreciative house. It later moved on to a New York church for an extended engagement as legitimate, ecclesiastical drama with authentic musical settings. The role of the modern "Museum of Art," thanks especially to the venerable New York "Metropolitan," has been vastly expanded and interpreted to validate contemporary man's continuity with his historic past. The sources here presented show the naturalness with which the Middle Ages interpreted the varying activities of everyday life; also, it is hoped, the artificiality of divorcing modern interests from their medieval backgrounds.

Patently, the Middle Ages did not limit its sportive pastimes to noblemen's gambling and the clandestine churchyard romps of the innocuous peasantry. Gaming propensities, like the penchant for acting, claimed people of all classes. Ecclesiastical dignitaries indulged in "moralized chess." Girls and boys enjoyed "hot cockles" and "frog in the middle." Noble and peasant played segregated, and sometimes integrated, parts in sacred drama. They likewise descended, on occasion, to public buffoonery all out of keeping with the sacred places within or near which their "plays" were held. Tapestries, for example, and the border illuminations of service books are excellent witnesses to the medieval passion for gaming, playing musical instruments, dancing, wrestling, fighting, acting, and otherwise documenting the human. Everywhere, unquestioned piety was coupled without apology to the most worldly antics of courting youths, the budgetary shrewdness of pantaloon-picking wives, and the wholly irrepressible cavorting of just plain folks.

The source texts in this chapter are interspersed with digests and paraphrases where translations are too long to provide full context. Carefully selected references to phonographic editions, both LP and Stereophonic, have been appended for supplementing the rise of the *Ars Nova,* the role of liturgical music and drama, and related aspects of the Christian arts. The bearing in an electronic age of such wide-ranging data as the *Schwann Long Playing Record Catalogue, The Oxford Companion to Music,* and the recorded histories of music preserved by RCA Victor and Deutsche Grammophon Gesellschaft is not to be scorned. Nor are the delights of music and audio-visual development in discs and tape. Sound-recording equipment also is hardly to be despised. Reputable journals such as the English *Gramophone,* the American *High Fidelity, The American Record Guide,* and numerous others are surely resources to be capitalized for the service of contemporary arts. They may even help prompt the resuscitation of just regard for the medieval counterparts of modern artistic media.

VII

Who, after all, is to say what is marginal and what is basic to a given culture? The Middle Ages made a unity, not only of the bordered illuminations and central text of its priceless manuscripts, but of its serious devotion and its human gambolings as well. Chapter IX gives a significant place to service books. Missals represented, however indirectly, an ever-growing force constantly at work to dissolve medieval illiteracy in its more obvious sense. This guidebook was written for priests in the living Latinity of the Church's eucharistic graces. It was mediated to the people through the audio-visual action of the altar. The Church's liturgy, of which the mass was the living testament, placed the vibrant unison of Scriptures, hierarchical laws, and devotional exercises within the universal tradition of all Christian peoples and all ages. Communicable to and by the people themselves, the living witness of the Divine was recovenanted in human devotion through the saving Church and her sacraments. The inexhaustible treasury of the centuries provided universally recapturable source readings in the faith. These were selected from the recurring cycles of the Church's calendar. They were mediated beyond the popular limits of the sacred language to the people's own sense perception, to their symbolic comprehension of ultimate reality.

Every priestly exhortation, however halting or eloquent, harked back to the beginnings of divinely ordered salvation and forward to the final beatitude. Each symbolic allusion, crude though it sometimes was, constituted an illustrated lecture in catechetics, credo, and Christian profession. Every sacerdotal gesture, all censings, and each prayerful intonation recalled the divine plan. Man's overweening lust for the wrong knowledge was redeemed to saving wisdom through Christ and his sacramental Church. This was celebrated in the Church's true drama—which was not a mere representation but an actual reenactment of Christ's living incarnation. That drama was supported by the variety and colors of ecclesiastical vestments, in sonorous processionals, with hymns and antiphons, and in countless other ways. There was thus achieved the vernacular documentation of the saving action that the Church's official language summoned forth.

And the people had their own important, if curtailed, opportunities for participation in the drama of salvation. In genuflection, resonant recitative, and audibly reinforcing as well as visually stimulating response, they brought their personal offering of confession, praise, and supplication. They read figuratively and symbolically between the lines that which they could not read literally. Their literacy was by no means wholly ineffectual, though it was only partial.

In the source texts a selection from the canon of the mass in Latin, according to the Use of York, is juxtaposed with its translation. Pertinent sections from a French vernacular commentary on the mass by Vignay are translated also. The irony of the custom by which the people came to obscure their own literate comprehension of the liturgy through short-circuiting devices is alluded to via Philip of Navarre.

The priest sometimes had other books beyond the missal. Sometimes, also, he could read them: breviaries, and the like. These, too, were written in the Church's language but mediated to the people. The prayers, sermonettes, and hymns deposited in the official manuals of the hierarchy found their way, together with popular expositions on the mass, into the popular consciousness. Employed on occasion were rhyming, mnemonic devices. It would be historically correct to say that, from the point of absolute relevance, the people and their priest, himself, knew and read the Church's books all too little. Usually they had precious few such books to read. And they could read too little of what they had. Yet, it would be no less tenable to insist that, in the very midst of palpable ignorance, error, and instructional lethargy on the part of the priesthood, the people were never wholly illiterate. The texts of Chapter VIII as well as of Chapter IX throw light on this conundrum. The people had at least a minimal spiritual literacy which the liturgy itself guaranteed against every incursion of technical illiteracy. Many of the emergency measures for the recouping of priestly and popular ignorance illustrated in the previous chapter come into renewed focus here. Further collections, not only of written texts, but also of Virgin lore and hagiographical tradition, are exemplified. The *legenda*, or readings in Lives of the Saints, are illustrated, not only as Voragine recorded them, but also as the people and the priest relayed them through vernacular, oral invention. Legends, miracle accounts, and Virgin stories are among the most endlessly embroidered and zestfully told tales that books have failed to hold inside covers. What is seen in the code books of legend and iconographic suggestion is indisseverable, alike, from Caesarius of Heisterbach's *Dialogues on Miracles* and the Merode altarpiece, to name but two popular media so closely allied to the *Golden Legend*.

Bibles were of course not wholly lacking or unread, as the researches of Deanesly and Smalley have helped to make clear. The limits of this knowledge in terms of popular apprehension are well known, however. The liturgy, itself, was a kind of Bible reading, to be sure. Still the Biblical motif is not wholly clarified, aside from the so-called "Bibles of the Rich" and the "Bibles of the Poor." Scholars and a few wealthy patrons had access to Bible texts. The poor had their iconographic as well as their liturgical Testaments. Pictures, however, here as elsewhere, played a large part for both rich and poor. The knowledge of the Bible like all other medieval literacy was a mediation, in immense variability, of images derived by the few from written suggestion. These were returned in terms of vernacular imagery to popular comprehension. Certainly there were "Bibles" which pictured for a handful the cardinal aspects of the Hebrew-Christian tradition. These were then re-focused through artistic media upon the spiritual retina of the people. As already noted, an iconographic treasury was at hand for constant reflection, stimulation, and interpretation.

Perhaps relic worship was not actually the religion of the Middle Ages as some cynical scholars have intimated. The heroic and often debasing role it played is not hard to decipher in its more obvious outlines. A sympathetic interpretation of its range and subtlety is always a necessary desideratum. The sources in several chapters show how vital was the part played by relics, whether in the spiritual life of a St. Louis or in the chicanery of lay, as well as priestly, connivance. That there were other spiritual resources in plenty upon which the people drew has already been demonstrated.

It is in the "Books of Hours" that the rich man's devotion took one of its most spectacular forms. This was by no means torn from Biblical context or from the life of the gentry and the lower classes. Here again the life of the ages, whether of Christ's day or of the thirteenth century, was woven into the very art and iconography of universal genre that the wealthy patron commissioned for artistic creation. The medieval artist and craftsman found here a cherished metier. The two *Books of Hours of the Duke of Berry* achieved by the Limbourg brothers figure brilliantly in such a connection. They unite the threads of human foible and holy living found in the *Golden Legend* and the Bible record. In these and similar Books of Hours, the careers of St. Jerome, St. Martin of Tours, and ultimately St. Louis were joined to the Church's divine calendar, her offices, and the whole panorama of human sinfulness, repentance, and salvation.

One such book places the good Louis and his career within its Lessons, Prayers, and Responses. Recoverable from its texts and illuminations is the story of the king's boyhood, his mature piety, and his sacrificial crusading. Especially, however, does it enshrine in its illuminations the story of how Louis built the Sainte Chapelle to house the sacred relics purchased and conveyed with such great expense from Constantinople. Adapted also from old painted wooden panels in an ancient monastery and transposed into the Gothic windows long since gone from Sainte Chapelle is a precious iconographic history. Recounted are Louis' boyhood, his coronation, and his bringing to Paris and the little Chapel built for holy relics the very crown of thorns the Christ once wore. Some of these same themes are wrought into the later *Hours of Jeanne d'Évreux* cherished by the Metropolitan Museum of Art in New York. So the edifying career of Louis was told in the offices and illuminated margins of devotional manuals as well as in the biography of his loyal seneschal, Joinville.

From other Missals, Breviaries, and Books of Hours, come the no less moving stories of Jerome, Martin, and Thomas à Becket. Martin has moved into various chapters of the source book with the stubborn persistence of a national, Christian hero. He sustains ineradicable pertinence to liturgy, sermonic exhortation, relic and miracle account, martyr consecration, monastic renunciation, and cathedral iconography.

In the *Rohan Book of Hours*, recently given a new, sumptuous edition by the National Library in Paris, a poignant documentation of medieval piety is preserved. The ineffable regard with which the Father gazes upon man in his judged mortality, and upon His Son lying in death upon the lap of the grieving Virgin-Mother, has been reproduced in our volume. Here, again, was a book that was read, not only by the rich who commissioned it, but also by the poor who never saw it—except, that is, as they perused it every day in their own sin-ridden lives for which the Virgin interceded with her world-redeeming Son.

The code by which the simplest people deciphered the underlying graphics of salvation's plan is suggested in numerous contemporary guide books. The rather naive, yet touching, manual erroneously attributed to the great symbolist and scholar, Hugh of St. Victor, leads off the texts on Church symbols. Because it is at once so sweeping and even reckless in its coverage of allegory, icons, and liturgy, its place is more than justified. The far more reputable work of Durandus is so extensive as to permit of only limited reproduction. Yet the systematic intent and method by which a good bishop and liturgist tried to tie together Christian realities for the more literate priest, and ultimately for humble people, may be clearly discerned from the few passages outlined. In this "Rationale," this "Breastplate of Judgment," this setting forth of the reasons for variation in the Divine Offices, a vast trajectory is described. Even the preface here sampled, when taken with the treatise of the Pseudo-Hugh, accents the role of rites, ordinances, sacraments, and the liberal arts. It observes the work of painters, mechanics, and handicraftsmen; also the wide swinging-pendulum of living symbolism, figures, and typologies. There is consideration of vestments, scriptural senses and interpretations, eucharistic life, and the liturgy itself.

In contrasting and reinforcing relief the Bestiaries and Lapidaries reflect the penchant for seeing the human as it peers forth in the non-human and even the inanimate. The virtuous and the vicious are here read in nature's open book, indexed always to the religious sensitivity pervading every level of perception and communication.

VIII

In the books of contemplative vision a wide gamut is run. The mystic Hildegarde was surely one of the most remarkable women of her age. Her dubious contributions to medicine, art, and literature should be put in a sympathetic frame of reference to her theological postulates. Only a suggestion of the wealth of her symbolic allusion has been here supplied.

Herrade of Landsberg's *Garden of Delights* is a treasury of testamental and patristic lore. Its distillation of the Church's iconographic tradition is proof positive of the intricate instruction being settled into the very crevices of the monastic world view. The invaluable plates of Straub and Keller, made from manuscripts destroyed in the Franco-Prussian War, constitute a great depository of knowledge about twelfth-century ethics, military science, building, Biblical study, doctrine, and much more. This seeming mélange is, indeed, a tightly knit corps of intelligence for all who would sense the living tradition of the liturgical church. The plates chosen are given with only such commentary as is needed to point the direction followed in the work.

With Joachim of Flore one of history's most puzzling characters is encountered. The summation of Bett is a lively hint of the seer's massive impact and momentum. The perils of over-simplification here are hazardous indeed. Joachim was the master craftsman of visionary exuberance and revelatory insight implanted in a mosaic of disciplined confusion. His categories of the ages suggest a concordance of discords reminiscent of Gratian's *Decretum*. The Calabrian pummels every Judaeo-Christian type and figure into near unrecognizability. Yet his fundamental eschatology and social orientation become ever more consistently directional, the more one fumes about his incorrigible contradictions. Apparently, he was trying neither to contradict the Church's high calling in the hierarchy-ridden present nor to help transmit its temporal outlines to the unstereotyped future. There was in him,

probably, neither stark repudiation of the institutional church nor verification of its growing claims. Rather, his gaze envisioned a world in transition to the eternal kingdom, one that would emphasize the life of true monastics living in fraternal conjunction with spiritualized lay people. This was to be the much discussed, "New Disposition."

By the side of Joachim, Eike of Repgow is tame, indeed. Yet in him, also, the transplanting of the ages of Biblical law and feudal custom into the demanding and fulfilling future is rightly discernible. Dr. Hertz has accorded him renewed stature as a social prophet and pioneer in constitutional government, even as Professor Kisch has demonstrated his Biblical awareness. Both his *Saxon Mirror* and *World Chronicle* have been drawn upon for Chapters VI, IX, and X. The reproduction from the Amira edition based upon the war-ravaged Dresden manuscript is almost self-explanatory.

With Dante the great Divine-human panorama is spread in kaleidoscopic array. The purpose of the sources and illustrations is chiefly to remind us of how the creative legends gathering about Joachim and the *Poverello* were caught up in the *Paradiso* and transmitted to the ages through the Giottesque imagery of the Church of St. Francis in Assisi.

IX

This Dantian book, with co-authorship by Giotto, leads naturally into the populous urbanism of a new world a'borning. In the miscellaneous picture books of Siena, Assisi, and Florence there is mirrored the travail of the centuries-old, feudal states. They were in labor with the new heirs of the spirit just as were Joachim, Francis, and Dante. The many books that the people themselves read and interlined with their own spiritual commentary confront us here with staggering variety and brilliance. Even the recent photographic and technical victories of such publishers as Skira, Thames and Hudson, Prentice-Hall (with Abrams), Fabbristampa (with Viking), and many others can but suggest the age-long pilgrimage that is here so gloriously recorded. Especial gratitude must go out to those great teaching-laboratories, like the Metropolitan Museum of Art, in which this story is placed in relief, not only for scholars, but also for the school children of our day.

X

Finally, by way of denouement, the *Ars Moriendi* sets down its threnody of the "waning Middle Ages." Again Mâle supplies one of the most cogent interpretations of the "art of dying." That art was, after all, only one of dying insofar as this constituted the anteroom to true living. The commentary on the plates follows Mâle, though an entire literature is implicit.

I. Education; The *Schola Animarum* and the *Cura Animarum;* the Liberal Arts; the Benedictine *Cenobium; Stabilitas Loci* and *Opus Dei;* the Literacy of the Common Life

A. BENEDICT OF NURSIA (C. 543/47/55) AND THE "SCHOLA SERVITIA"; THE LORD'S TROOP IN ACTION

1. Founding a School for the Lord's Service

Reg., Prol., trans. E. F. Henderson, *Select Documents of the Middle Ages* (London: G. Bell & Sons Ltd., 1896), p. 274.

Prologue. . . . we are about to found, therefore, a school for the Lord's service; in the organization of which we trust that we shall ordain nothing severe and nothing burdensome. But even if, the demands of justice dictating it, something a little irksome shall be the result, for the purpose of amending vices or preserving charity;—thou shalt not therefore, struck by fear, flee the way of salvation, which can not be entered upon except through a narrow entrance. But as one's way of life and one's faith progresses, the heart becomes broadened, and, with the unutterable sweetness of love, the way of the mandates of the Lord is traversed. Thus, never departing from His guidance, continuing in the monastery in His teaching until death, through patience we are made partakers in Christ's passion, in order that

we may merit to be companions in His kingdom.

B. CASSIODORUS († C. 573) ON SCRIBES AND THE LIBERAL ARTS

2. Spreading the Scriptures by Reading and Copying

Instit. 1:30, trans. L. W. Jones, *An Introduction to Divine and Human Readings by Cassiodorus Senator,* A. P. Evans, ed., "Records of Civilization," 40 (New York: Columbia University Press, 1946), p. 133.

1. I admit that among those of your tasks which require physical effort that of the scribe, if he writes correctly, appeals most to me; and it appeals, perhaps not without reason, for by reading the Divine Scriptures he wholesomely instructs his own mind and by copying the precepts of the Lord he spreads them far and wide. Happy his design, praiseworthy his zeal, to preach to men with the hand alone, to unleash tongues with the fingers, to give salvation silently to mortals, and to fight against the illicit temptations of the devil with pen and ink. Every word of the Lord written by the scribe is a wound inflicted on Satan. And so, though seated in one spot, with the dissemination of his work he travels through different provinces. The product of his toil is read in holy places; people hear the means by which they may turn themselves away from base desire and serve the Lord with heart undefiled. Though absent, he labors at his task.

3. Grammar the Foundation of Liberal Letters

Instit., 2, Praef., trans. Jones, *DHR,* pp. 143–44.

4. Let us now enter upon the beginning of the second volume, and let us attend with some care, for it is crowded with etymologies and full of a discussion of definitions. In this book we must speak first of the art of grammar, which is manifestly the source and foundation of liberal studies. The word "book" (*liber*) comes from the word "free" (*liber*); a book, in other words, is the bark of a tree, removed and freed—the bark on which the ancients used to write oracular

responses before the invention of papyrus. In view of this, therefore, we are permitted to make short books or extended ones, since we are allowed to limit the size of books in accordance with their nature, just as the bark encloses both tiny shoots and vast trees. We ought, moreover, as Varro says, to understand that the elements of all arts came into existence because of some usefulness. "Art" is so called because it limits (*artet*) and binds us with its rules; according to others this word is taken over from the Greek expression *apo tes aretes*, which means "from excellence," the term applied by well-spoken men to skill in every matter. Second, we must speak of the art of rhetoric, which is deemed very necessary and honorable because of the splendor and fullness of its eloquence, especially in civil questions. Third, we must speak of logic, which is called dialectic; according to the statements of secular teachers this study separates the true from the false by means of very subtle and concise reasoning. Fourth, we must speak of mathematics, which embraces four sciences, to wit, arithmetic, geometry, music, and astronomy.

C. POPE GREGORY I († 604) ON TEACHING AND EXEMPLIFYING PASTORAL CARE

4. On the Cure of Souls as the Art of Arts

Reg. Past., 1:1, reproduced in Chap. V, Item 30.

D. THEODORE ARCHBISHOP OF CANTERBURY († 668) AND THE LIBERAL TRADITION

5. Theodore as Preceptor of Britain

Bede, *Hist. Eccl.*, 4:1–2, trans. BEHE, pp. 170–73.

There was then in the Niridian monastery, which is not far from the city of Naples in Campania, an abbat, called Hadrian, by nation an African, well versed in holy writ, experienced in monastical and ecclesiastical discipline, and excellently skilled both in the Greek and Latin tongues. The pope, sending for him, commanded him to accept of the bishopric, and repair into Britain; he answered, that he was unworthy of so great

a dignity, but said he could name another, whose learning and age were fitter for the episcopal office. . . .

There was at that time in Rome, a monk, called Theodore, well known to Hadrian, born at Tarsus in Cilicia, a man well instructed in worldly and Divine literature, as also in Greek and Latin; of known probity of life, and venerable for age, being sixty-six years old. Hadrian offered him to the pope to be ordained bishop, and prevailed; . . . He was ordained by Pope Vitalian, in the year of our Lord 668, on Sunday, the 26th of March, and on the 27th of May was sent with Hadrian into Britain. . . . This was the first archbishop whom all the English church obeyed. And forasmuch as both of them were, as has been said before, well read both in sacred and in secular literature, they gathered a crowd of disciples, and there daily flowed from them rivers of knowledge to water the hearts of their hearers; and, together with the books of holy writ, they also taught them the arts of ecclesiastical poetry, astronomy, and arithmetic. A testimony of which is, that there are still living at this day some of their scholars, who are as well versed in the Greek and Latin tongues as in their own, in which they were born.

E. CHARLEMAGNE ADMONISHES THE CLERGY TO SET UP SCHOOLS FOR TRAINING THE CLERGY

5A. [See Chap. V, Item 54; also 52, 53, 57]

F. ALCUIN AT YORK AND AS MASTER OF CHARLEMAGNE'S PALACE SCHOOL

6. Alcuin Writes to Charles (795) Extolling Christian Learning

Trans. by the editor from *Ep.* 121 (796/97), E. Dummler, *Epistolae Karolini Aevi*, II, Monumenta Germaniae Historica Epistolarum Tomus IV, Berlin, 1894), pp. 177–78.

These are things which your most noble attention has not disregarded—how, throughout the pages of Holy Scripture, we are admonished to learn wisdom. Among things conducing to the happy life nothing is more sublime, nothing more joyous in its exercise, nothing more effective against vices, nothing more laudable in everything entailing dignity than this same wisdom. Likewise, according to the philosophers, nothing is more necessary to ruling people, nothing knits together better the components of a strong moral life than the glory of wisdom, the praise of instruction, and the accomplishments of learning. . . .

O Lord King, exhort the youths who are in your Excellency's palace to this research for knowledge and the daily pursuit of it with the fullest application of their flourishing prospects, so that they may be held worthy of attaining age with honor and may through wisdom be enabled to arrive at eternal bliss. Meanwhile, I shall, within the limits of my own modest ability, not be dilatory in sowing the seeds of wisdom among your servants in this area. In so doing I shall have in mind the passage: "In the morning sow your seed and in the evening withhold not your hand." In the morning, during a period of flourishing studies I sowed the seed in Britain. Now, in the evening as it were, and with the cooling blood of age, I do not cease to sow seed in France. . . . As Jerome put it in one place: "The old age of those having instructed their youth in honest arts and having meditated on the law of the Lord day and night becomes more learned with age, more expert with use, more wise with the passage of time, and it harvests the sweetest fruits from studies long past."

7. Alcuin Writes to Bishop Ethelbert (797) Enjoining Christian Schools

Ep. 88, trans. A. F. Leach, *Educational Charters and Documents 598–1909* (Cambridge: Cambridge University Press, 1911), p. 21.

ALCUIN ON HEXHAM SCHOOL (c. 797)

To the pastor of chief dignity, Ethelbert bishop, and all the congregation serving God in the church of St Andrew, Alcuin, client of your love, greeting in Christ. . . .

May the light of learning remain among you. . . . Teach the boys and young men diligently the learning of books in the way of God, that they may become worthy successors in your honours and intercessors for you. . . . He who does not sow neither shall he reap, and he who does not learn cannot

teach. And such a place without teachers shall not, or hardly, be saved. It is a great work of charity to feed the poor with food for the body, but a greater to fill the hungry soul with spiritual learning. As a careful shepherd provides the best pasture for his flock, so a good teacher should with all his zeal provide for his subjects the pasture of eternal life. For the increase of the flock is the glory of the shepherd, and the multitude of learned men is the safety of the world. I know that you, most holy fathers, know this well and will willingly carry it out.

G. BISHOP THEODULPH OF ORLEANS (C. 820/21) ADMINISTERS THE CAROLINGIAN BEQUEST OF CHRISTIAN LEARNING

8. Instruction by Priests at Episcopal Behest

Cap. 20, trans. G. E. McCracken and A. Cabaniss, eds., *Early Medieval Theology* [LCC, Vol. IX] (Philadelphia: Westminster Press; London: Student Christian Movement Press, 1957), p. 387.

Let the presbyters keep schools in the villages and hamlets, and if any of the faithful desires to entrust his small children to them to be taught their letters, let them not refuse to receive and teach them, but let them teach them with the greatest love, noticing what is written: "They, however, who shall be learned shall shine as the splendor of the firmament, and they who instruct many to righteousness shall shine as the stars forever and ever." When, therefore, they teach them, let them demand no fee for this instruction, nor take anything from them, except what the parents shall offer them freely through zeal for love.

H. POPE EUGENIUS (826) HOLDS BISHOPS RESPONSIBLE TO FOSTER SCHOOLS

9. Masters and Teachers to Inculcate the Liberal Arts

Decreti Prima Pars, Dist., 37, c. 12, trans. A. F. Leach, *Educational Charters and Documents*, p. 21.

Complaints have been made that in some places no masters nor endowment for a Grammar School is found. Therefore all bishops shall bestow all care and diligence, both for their subjects and for other places in which it shall be found necessary, to establish masters and teachers who shall assiduously teach grammar schools and the principles of the liberal arts, because in these chiefly the commandments of God are manifested and declared.

I. ALFRED THE GREAT (871–899/901) AND HIS PALACE SCHOOL

10. Alfred's Translation of Gregory's Pastoral Rule *as a Basis for Christian Instruction*

Trans. H. Sweet, *King Alfred's West-Saxon Version of Gregory's Pastoral Care* (London: EETS, Original Series 45, 1871), pp. 2–8.

King Alfred bids greet bishop Waerferth with his words lovingly and with friendship; and I let it be known to thee that it has very often come into my mind, what wise men there formerly were throughout England, both of sacred and secular orders; and how happy times there were then throughout England; and how the kings who had power over the nation in those days obeyed God and his ministers; and they preserved peace, morality, and order at home, and at the same time enlarged their territory abroad; and how they prospered both with war and with wisdom; and also the sacred orders how zealous they were both in teaching and learning, and in all the services they owed to God; and how foreigners came to this land in search of wisdom and instruction, and how we should now have to get them from abroad if we were to have them. So general was its decay in England that there were very few on this side of the Humber who could understand their rituals in English, or translate a letter from Latin into English; and I believe that there were not many beyond the Humber. There were so few of them that I cannot remember a single one south of the Thames when I came to the throne. Thanks be to God Almighty that we have any teachers among us now. . . . When I remembered all this, I won-dered extremely that the good and wise men who were formerly all over England, and had perfectly learnt all the books, did not wish to translate them into their own language. But again I soon answered myself and said: "They did not think that men would ever be so careless, and that learning would so decay; through that desire they abstained from it, and they wished that the wisdom in this land might increase with our knowledge of languages. Then I remembered how the law was first known in Hebrew, and again, when the Greeks had learnt it, they translated the whole of it into their own language, and all other books besides. And again the Romans, when they had learnt it, they translated the whole of it through learned interpreters into their own language. And also all other Christian nations translated a part of them into their own language. Therefore it seems better to me, if ye think so, for us also to translate some books which are most needful for all men to know into the language which we can all understand, and for you to do as we very easily can if we have tranquillity enough, that is that all the youth now in England of free men, who are rich enough to be able to devote themselves to it, be set to learn as long as they are not fit for any other occupation, until that they are well able to read English writing: and let those be afterwards taught more in the Latin language who are to continue learning and be promoted to a higher rank. When I remembered how the knowledge of Latin had formerly decayed throughout England, and yet many could read English writing, I began, among other various and manifold troubles of this kingdom, to translate into English the book which is called in Latin Pastoralis, and in English Shepherd's Book, sometimes word by word and sometimes according to the sense, as I had learnt it from Plegmund my archbishop, and Asser my bishop, and Grimbold my mass-priest, and John my mass-priest. And when I had learnt it as I could best understand it, and as I could most clearly interpret it, I translated it into English; and I will send a copy to every bishopric in my kingdom; . . .

II. The Transition from the Benedictine Community of *Cura* and *Schola Animarum* to the Pre-University Clerical Schools, Canons Regular, Secular Chapter, and Cathedral Schools; the Liberal Arts and Early Scholasticism

A. DUNSTAN (C. 909–988) AS A LINK BETWEEN READING IN THE BENEDICTINE COMMUNITY AND CATHEDRAL INSTRUCTION

11. The Monk Gervase Places Dunstan Next to King Alfred in Fostering the Liberal Arts

The History of the Arch-Bishops of Canterbury, trans. J. Stevenson, *The Church Historians of England* (London, 1858), V, i, p. 303.

Then the monastic order, which had so long been oppressed in the time of the wars, raised its head and flourished; for under Dunstan, that prince and protector of the monks, the lights of the saints shone in England just as the stars shine in the heavens. He gave a great impetus to the liberal arts throughout the entire island, second therein only to King Alfred.

B. PETER DAMIAN (1007–1072) ADVOCATES THE SEPARATION OF SCHOLARSHIP AND BENEDICTINE PIETY

12. He Opposes the Rule of Benedict to Secular Knowledge

De Perfectione Monachorum, XI, trans. P. McNulty, *St Peter Damian, Selected Writings on the Spiritual Life* (London: Faber and Faber Ltd.; New York: Harper & Brothers, 1959), p. 104.

Moreover (if I may speak angrily) those who follow the rabble of grammarians, who, forsaking spiritual studies, desire to learn all the follies of worldly skill, who, despising the rule of Benedict, love to apply themselves to the rules of Donatus; such as these are of that number. These men are bored by the intricacies of ecclesiastical teaching and long for worldly knowledge; this is like deserting the chaste spouse lying upon the bridal-couch of faith and consorting with the harlots of the stage.

C. BISHOP LANFRANC (1005–1085) REAFFIRMS THE CONTINUITY BETWEEN BENEDICTINE READING AND THE "OPUS DEI"

13. The Regula, *Books, and Monastic Liturgy*

Decreta Lanfranci, trans. D. Knowles, *The Monastic Constitutions of Lanfranc* (New York: Oxford University Press, 1951), p. 19. Reprinted by permission of the original publishers, Thomas Nelson and Sons, Ltd., Edinburgh. (See Chap. IV, No. 26, for cap. 38 of the Rule.)

Before the brethren go in to chapter, the librarian should have all the books save those that were given out for reading the previous year collected on a carpet in the chapter-house; last year's books should be carried in by those who have had them, and they are to be warned by the librarian in chapter the previous day of this. The passage from the Rule of St Benedict concerning the observance of Lent shall be read, and when a sermon has been made on this the librarian shall read out a list of the books which the brethren had the previous year. When each hears his name read out he shall return the book which was given to him to read, and anyone who is conscious that he has not read in full the book he received shall confess his fault prostrate and ask for pardon. Then the aforesaid librarian shall give to each of the brethren another book to read, and when the books have been distributed in order he shall at that same chapter write a list of the books and those who have received them.

D. ANSELM (1033–1109) LINKS THE MONASTIC BERCEAU AT BEC WITH THE CATHEDRAL (OF CANTERBURY), SCHOLASTIC REALISM, AND DEVOTION

14. Not "Understanding in Order to Believe"; but "Believing in Order to Understand"

Prosologion, 1, trans. E. R. Fairweather, *A Scholastic Miscellany: Anselm to Ockham* [LCC, Vol. X] (Philadelphia: Westminster

Press; London: Student Christian Movement Press, 1956), p. 73.

I acknowledge, O Lord, with thanksgiving, that thou hast created this thy image in me, so that, remembering thee, I may think of thee, may love thee. But this image is so effaced and worn away by my faults, it is so obscured by the smoke of my sins, that it cannot do what it was made to do, unless thou renew and reform it. I am not trying, O Lord, to penetrate thy loftiness, for I cannot begin to match my understanding with it, but I desire in some measure to understand thy truth, which my heart believes and loves. For I do not seek to understand in order to believe, but I believe in order to understand. For this too I believe, that "unless I believe, I shall not understand."

15. The Existence of God, "Than Which a Greater Cannot be Thought"

Pros., 2, trans. Fairweather, *Scholastic Miscellany*, pp. 73–74.

And so, O Lord, since thou givest understanding to faith, give me to understand—as far as thou knowest it to be good for me—that thou dost exist, as we believe, and that thou art what we believe thee to be. Now we believe that thou art a being than which none greater can be thought. Or can it be that there is no such being, since "the fool hath said in his heart, 'There is no God' "? But when this same fool hears what I am saying—"A being than which none greater can be thought"—he understands what he hears, and what he understands is in his understanding, even if he does not understand that it exists. For it is one thing for an object to be in the understanding, and another thing to understand that it exists. When a painter considers beforehand what he is going to paint, he has it in his understanding, but he does not suppose that what he has not yet painted already exists. But when he has painted it, he both has it in his understanding and understands that what he has now produced exists. Even the fool, then, must be convinced that a being than which none greater can be thought exists at least in his understanding, since when he hears this he understands it, and whatever is understood is in the understanding. But clearly that than which a greater cannot be thought cannot exist in the understanding alone. For if it is actually in the understanding alone, it can be thought of as existing also in reality, and this is greater. Therefore, if that than which a greater cannot be thought is in the understanding alone, this same thing than which a greater cannot be thought is that than which a greater can be thought. But obviously this is impossible. Without doubt, therefore, there exists, both in the understanding and in reality, something than which a greater cannot be thought.

E. HUGH († 1141/42) AND THE SCHOOL OF ST. VICTOR; THE LIBERAL ARTS; READING TEACHING, AND SYSTEMATIC STUDY; THE BIBLE, CANONICAL LIFE, AND THE LITURGY

16. The Humility of the Learner and the Discipline of the Scholar

Didascalicon, 3:13. From *The Portable Medieval Reader*, ed. James Bruce Ross and Mary Martin McLaughlin, pp. 584–86. © 1949 by The Viking Press, Inc., and reprinted by their permission.

The prudent scholar, therefore, hears everyone freely, reads everything, and rejects no book, no person, no doctrine. He seeks from all indifferently what he sees is lacking in himself; he considers not how much he may know, but how much he may not know. Hence the Platonic saying: "I prefer to learn modestly from another, rather than shamelessly to thrust forward my own knowledge." Why are you ashamed to learn and not ashamed to be ignorant? This is more shameful than that. Or why do you strive for the heights, when you are lying in the depths? Consider rather what your powers are strong enough to bear. He advances most suitably who proceeds in an orderly way. When some desire to make a great leap, they fall into the abyss. Do not, therefore, hasten too fast, and thus you will more quickly achieve wisdom. Learn gladly from everyone what you do not know, since humility can make that yours which nature made the possession of someone else. You will be wiser than everyone, if you will learn from everyone. Those who receive from everyone are richer than anyone. Finally, hold no knowledge cheap, since all knowledge is good. If there is time, scorn no writing, or at least read it, since if you gain nothing, you will lose nothing, especially as in my estimation there is no book which does not set forth something to be desired. If it is treated in an appropriate place and order, there is none which does not have something special, which the diligent reader has found nowhere else. The rarer it is, the more gratefully it should be enjoyed. Yet there is nothing good which is not made better.

If you cannot read everything, read that which is more useful. Even if you can read everything, the same amount of labor should not be expended on all. But some things are to be read so that they may not be unknown, and some so that they may not be unheard of, since sometimes we believe that of which we have not heard to be of greater importance, and a thing is more easily judged when its results are known. You can see now how necessary for you this humility is, that you may hold no knowledge cheap, and may learn freely from all. Likewise it behooves you not to despise others when you begin to know something. This vice of arrogance takes possession of some so that they contemplate their own knowledge too lovingly, and since they seem to themselves to be something, they think that others whom they do not know can neither be nor become such as they. Hence also these peddlers of trifles, boasting I do not know of what, accuse their ancestors of simplicity, and believe that wisdom was born with them, and will die with them. They say that in sermons the manner of speaking is so simple that it is not necessary to listen to teachers in these matters, that each of them can penetrate the secrets of truth well enough by his own intelligence. They turn up their noses and make wry mouths at the lecturers in divinity, and they do not understand that they do God an injury, whose words are simple indeed in the beauty of their expression, but they proclaim stupidities with deformed sense. I do not advise imitating such as these. For the good student should be humble and gentle, a stranger to senseless cares and the enticements of pleasure; he should be diligent and zealous, so that he may learn freely from all. He is never presumptuous about his own knowledge, he shuns the authors of perverse teaching like poison, he learns to consider a matter for a long time before he makes a judgment, he knows or seeks not how to seem learned, but to be truly learned, he loves the words of the wise when they have been understood, and he strives to keep them always before his eyes, as a mirror in front of his face. And if perchance his understanding does not have access to the more obscure things, he does not immediately burst out into vituperation, believing that nothing is good unless he himself can understand it. This is the humility of the students' discipline.

F. PETER ABELARD (1079–1142): THE RECAPITULATION OF ANSELMIC DEVOTION IN AN ATMOSPHERE OF SCHOLASTIC RATIONALISM

17. The Yes and No as a Prototype of Creative Inquiry, Canonical Polarity, and Thomistic Synthesis

Sic et non, reprinted by permission of the publishers from A. O. Norton, *Readings in the History of Education* (Cambridge, Mass.: Harvard University Press, 1909), pp. 19–20, 21.

In truth, constant or frequent questioning is the first key to wisdom; and it is, indeed, to the acquiring of this [habit of] questioning with absorbing eagerness that the famous philosopher, Aristotle, the most clear sighted of all, urges the studious when he says: "It is perhaps difficult to speak confidently in matters of this sort unless they have often been investigated. Indeed, to doubt in special cases will not be without advantage." For through doubting we come to inquiry and through inquiry we perceive the truth. As the Truth Himself says: "Seek and ye shall find, knock and it shall be opened unto you." And He also, instructing us by His own example, about the twelfth year of His life wished to be found sitting in the midst of the doctors, asking them questions, exhibiting to us by His asking of questions the appearance of a pupil, rather than, by preaching, that of a teacher, although there is in Him, nevertheless, the full and perfect wisdom of God.

Now when a number of quotations from [various] writings are introduced they spur on the reader and allure him into seeking the truth in proportion as the authority of the writing itself is commended. . . .

In accordance, then, with these forecasts it is our pleasure to collect different sayings of the holy Fathers as we planned, just as they have come to mind, suggesting (as they do) some questioning from their apparent disagreement, in order that they may stimulate tender readers to the utmost effort in seeking the truth and may make them keener as the result of their seeking. . . .

1. That faith is based upon reason, *et contra.*

6. That God is tripartite, *et contra.*

8. That in the Trinity it is not to be stated that there is more than one Eternal being, *et contra.*

14. That the Son is without beginning, *et contra.*

32. That to God all things are possible, *et non.*

56. That by sinning man lost free will, *et non.*

69. That the Son of God was predestinated, *et contra.*

79. That Christ was a deceiver, *et non.*

122. That everybody should be allowed to marry, *et contra.*

G. GRATIAN'S DECRETUM (C. 1150/60); THE ABELARDIAN PATTERN IN THE CONCORDANCE OF DISCORDANT CANONS

18. The Case for and against the Cultivation of Secular Learning by the Clergy

Decreta Prima Pars 37. *Ibid.*, pp. 64, 66, 67.

Also Rabanus on the Afflictions of the Church:

The blessed Jerome is beaten by an angel because he was reading the works of Cicero.

We read about the blessed Jerome that when he was reading the works (e) of Cicero he was chidden by an angel because,

being a Christian man, he was devoting himself to the productions of the pagans.

[The discussion which follows, to "Hence Bede," etc., p. 66, is attributed, in modern editions, to Gratian.]

Hence, too, the prodigal son in the Gospel is blamed because he would fain have filled his belly with the husks (f) which the swine did eat.

Hence, too, Origen understands by the flies and frogs with which the Egyptians were smitten, the empty garrulousness of the dialecticians and their sophistical arguments.

From all which instances it is gathered that knowledge of profane literature is not to be sought after by churchmen.

But, on the other hand * one reads that

IX-1. The Decretum of Gratian, MS. *c.* 1300.

Moses and Daniel were learnèd in all the wisdom of the Egyptians and Chaldeans.

One reads also that God ordered the sons of Israel to spoil (g) the Egyptians of their gold and silver; the moral interpretation of this teaches that should we find in the poets either the gold of wisdom or the silver of eloquence, we should turn it to the profit of useful learning. In Leviticus also we are ordered to offer up to God the first fruits of honey, that is, the sweetness of human eloquence. The Magi, too, offered three gifts, by which some would have us understand the three parts (h) of philosophy.

*Summary. From now on, Gratian shows that the clergy ought to be learned in profane knowledge. And this is shown from six considerations. The first is stated at the beginning. The second begins: "One reads also." The third begins: "In Leviticus." The fourth begins: "The Magi, too." The fifth begins: "Finally." The sixth begins: "Hence also Ambrose."

(e) Because he read them for pleasure not for instruction, as de conse. dist. V. non mediocriter.
(f) That is, with profane wisdom which fills but does not satisfy. (a)
(a) For as husks load the belly and fill it but do not satisfy, so also this wisdom does not free from spiritual hunger nor banish blindness. But it oppresses with the weight of sins and with the guilt of hell. Whoever therefore, for the removing of the blindness of ignorance seeks to learn other arts and knowledge desires to fill his belly, as it were, with husks. According to Hugo.
(g) Dan. I. a. Exodi III. & XI.
(h) I. e. Ethics, natural philosophy, rational philosophy.

H. JOHN OF SALISBURY († 1180) BISHOP OF CHARTRES; THE METALOGICON, AND THE ADVANCING ROLE OF THE SECULAR CHAPTER AND CATHEDRAL SCHOOLS

19. The Liberal Arts: the Trivium (Grammar, Dialectic, and Rhetoric) and the Quadrivium (Arithmetic, Geometry, Astronomy, and Music)

Metalogicon, 1:12, trans. D. D. McGarry, *The Metalogicon of John of Salisbury, A Twelfth-Century Defense of the Verbal and Logical Arts of the Trivium* (Berkeley: University of California Press; London: Cambridge University Press, 1955), pp. 36–37.

While there are many sorts of arts, the first to proffer their services to the natural abilities of those who philosophize are the liberal arts. All of the latter are included in the courses of the Trivium and Quadrivium. The liberal arts are said to have become so efficacious among our ancestors, who studied them diligently, that they enabled them to comprehend everything they read, elevated their understanding to all things, and empowered them to cut through the knots of all problems possible of solution. Those to whom the system of the Trivium has disclosed the significance of all words, or the rules of the Quadrivium have unveiled the secrets of all nature, do not need the help of a teacher in order to understand the meaning of books and to find the solutions of questions. They [the branches of learning included in the Trivium and Quadrivium] are called "arts" [either] because they delimit [artant] by rules and precepts; or from virtue, in Greek known as *ares*, which strengthens minds to apprehend the ways of wisdom; or from reason, called *arso* by the Greeks, which the arts nourish and cause to grow. They are called "liberal," either because the ancients took care to have their children instructed in them; or because their object is to effect man's liberation, so that, freed from cares, he may devote himself to wisdom. More often than not, they liberate us from cares incompatible with wisdom. They often even free us from worry about [material] necessities, so that the mind may have still greater liberty to apply itself to philosophy.

20. On the Intercommunion Among Those Reading, Lecturing, Learning, and Teaching

Metalogicon, 1:24, trans. McGarry, *MJS*, pp. 65–66.

One who aspires to become a philosopher should therefore apply himself to reading, learning, and meditation, as well as the performance of good works, lest the Lord become angry and take away what he seems to possess. The word "reading" is equivocal. It may refer either to the activity of teaching and being taught, or to the occupation of studying written things by oneself. Consequently, the former, the intercommunication between teacher and learner, may be termed (to use Quintilian's word) the "lecture"; the latter, or the scrutiny by the student, the "reading," simply so called. On the authority of the same Quintilian, "the teacher of grammar should, in lecturing, take care of such details as to have his students analyze verses into their parts of speech, and point out the nature of the metrical feet which are to be noted in poems. He should, furthermore, indicate and condemn whatever is barbarous, incongruous, or otherwise against the rules of composition." . . . Let him "shake out" the authors, and, without exciting ridicule, despoil them of their feathers, which (crow fashion) they have borrowed from the several branches of learning in order to bedeck their works and make them more colorful. One will more fully perceive and more lucidly explain the charming elegance of the authors in proportion to the breadth and thoroughness of his knowledge of various disciplines.

21. On the Teacher's Obligation to Exemplify Source-Studies; the Evening Collation; the Battle against the Cornificians

Metal. 1:24, trans. McGarry, *MJS*, pp. 67–71.

The fruit of the lecture on the authors is proportionate both to the capacity of the students and to the industrious diligence of the teacher. Bernard of Chartres, the greatest font of literary learning in Gaul in recent times, used to teach grammar in the following way. He would point out, in reading the authors, what was simple and according to rule. On the other hand, he would explain grammatical figures, rhetorical embellishment, and sophistical quibbling, as well as the relation of given passages to other studies. He would do so, however, without trying to teach everything at one time. On the contrary, he would dispense his instruction to his hearers gradually, in a manner commensurate with their powers of assimilation. And since diction is lustrous either because the words are well chosen, and the adjectives and verbs admirably suited to the nouns with which they are used, or because of the employment of metaphors, whereby speech is transferred to some beyond-the-ordinary meaning for sufficient reason, Bernard used to inculcate this in the minds of his hearers whenever he had the opportunity. In view of the fact that exercise both strengthens and sharpens our mind, Bernard would bend every effort to bring his students to imitate what they were hearing. . . . According to him, the works of distinguished authors suffice. As a matter of fact, to study everything that everyone, no matter how insignificant, has ever said, is either to be excessively humble and cautious, or overly vain and ostentatious. It also deters and stifles minds that would better be freed to go on to other things. That which preëmpts the place of something that is better is, for this reason, disadvantageous, and does not deserve to be called "good." To examine and pore over everything that has been written, regardless of whether it is worth reading, is as pointless as to fritter away one's time with old wives' tales. . . . A further feature of Bernard's method was to have his disciples compose prose and poetry every day, and exercise their faculties in mutual conferences, for nothing is more useful in introductory training than actually to accustom one's students to practice the art they are studying. Nothing serves better to foster the acquisition of eloquence and the attainment of knowledge than such conferences, which also have a salutary influence on practical conduct, provided that charity moderates enthusiasm, and that humility is not lost during progress in learning. A man cannot be the servant of both learning and carnal vice. My own instructors in grammar, William of Conches, and Richard, who is known as "the Bishop," a good man both in life and conversation, who now holds the office of archdeacon of Coutances, formerly used Bernard's method in training their disciples. But later, when popular opinion veered away from the truth, when men preferred to seem, rather than to be philosophers, and when professors of the arts were promising to impart the whole of philosophy in less than three or even two years, William and Richard were overwhelmed by the onslaught of the ignorant mob, and retired. Since then, less time and attention have been given to the study of grammar. As a result, we find men who profess all the arts, liberal and mechanical, but who are ignorant of this very first one [*i.e.,* grammar], without which it is futile to attempt to go on to the others. But while other studies may also contribute to "letters," grammar alone has the unique privilege of making one "lettered."

I. THE FOURTH LATERAN COUNCIL (1215) ON EPISCOPAL RESPONSIBILITY AND THE CATHEDRAL SCHOOLS

22. (*Canon 11*), Diocesan Schools, Masters, Theologians, and the Cura Animarum

Trans. H. J. Schroeder, *Disciplinary Decrees of the General Councils* (St. Louis and London: B. Herder Book Co., 1937), pp. 252–53.

Since there are some who, on account of the lack of necessary means, are unable to acquire an education or to meet opportunities for perfecting themselves, the Third Lateran Council in a salutary decree (18) provided that in every cathedral church a suitable benefice be assigned to a master who shall instruct *gratis* the clerics of that church and other poor students, by means of which benefice the material needs of the master might be relieved and to the students a way opened to knowledge. But, since in many churches this is not observed, we, confirming the aforesaid decree, add that, not only in every cathedral church but also in other churches where means are sufficient, a competent master be appointed by the prelate with his chapter, or elected by the greater and more discerning part of the chapter, who shall instruct *gratis* and to the best of his ability the clerics of those and other churches in the art of grammar and in other branches of knowledge. In addition to a master, let the metropolitan church have also a theologian, who shall instruct the priests and others in the Sacred Scriptures and in those things especially that pertain to the *cura animarum*. To each master let there be assigned by the chapter the revenue of one benefice, and to the theologian let as much be given by the metropolitan; not that they thereby become canons, but they shall enjoy the revenue only so long as they hold the office of instructor. If the metropolitan church cannot support two masters, then it shall provide for the theologian in the afore-

said manner, but for the one teaching grammar, let it see to it that a sufficiency is provided by another church of his city or diocese.

III. The *Studium Generale* and the *Universitas;* Guilds of the Liberal Arts and Scholastic Servants of the Common Life; the Mendicants and the New *Mobilitas*

A. THE STATUTES OF ROBERT DE COURÇON FOR PARIS (1215)

23. The Universitas of Masters and Scholars; the Arts and Theology; Lectures, Courses of Study, Student Life, Licenses

Chart. Univ. Paris. I, (20), 78, trans. *PTR,* II, (3), pp. 12–15.

R., servant of the cross of Christ, by the divine mercy cardinal priest with the title of St. Stephen in Monte Celio and legate of the apostolic seat, to all the masters and scholars at Paris—eternal safety in the Lord.

Let all know, that having been especially commanded by the lord pope to devote our energy effectively to the betterment of the condition of the students at Paris, and wishing by the advice of good men to provide for the tranquility of the students in the future, we have ordered and prescribed the following rules:

No one is to lecture at Paris in arts before he is twenty years old. He is to listen in arts at least six years, before he begins to lecture. He is to promise that he will lecture for at least two years, unless he is prevented by some good reason, which he ought to prove either in public or before the examiners. He must not be smirched by any infamy. When he is ready to lecture, each one is to be examined according to the form contained in the letter of lord P. bishop of Paris (in which is contained the peace established between the chancellor and the students by the judges appointed by the lord pope, approved and confirmed namely by the bishop and deacon of Troyes and by P. the bishop, and J. the chancellor of Paris).

The treatises of Aristotle on logic, both the

old and the new, are to be read in the schools in the regular and not in the extraordinary courses. The two Priscians, or at least the second, are also to be read in the schools in the regular courses. On the feast-days nothing is to be read except philosophy, rhetoric, *quadrivialia*, the Barbarisms, the Ethics, if one so chooses, and the fourth book of the Topics. The books of Aristotle on Metaphysics or Natural Philosophy, or the abridgements of these works, are not to be read, nor "the doctrine" of master David de Dinant, of the heretic Amalric, or of Maurice of Spain.

In the inceptions and meetings of the masters and in the confutations or arguments of the boys or youths there are to be no festivities. But they may call in some friends or associates, but only a few. We also advise that donations of garments and other things be made, as is customary or even to a greater extent, and especially to the poor. No master lecturing in arts is to wear anything except a cope, round and black and reaching to the heels—at least, when it is new. But he may well wear a pallium. He is not to wear under the round cope embroidered shoes and never any with long bands.

If any one of the students in arts or theology dies, half of the masters of arts are to go to the funeral, and the other half to the next funeral. They are not to withdraw until the burial is completed, unless they have some good reason. If any master of arts or theology dies, all the masters are to be present at the vigils, each one is to read the psalter or have it read. Each one is to remain in the church, where the vigils are celebrated, until midnight or later, unless prevented by some good reason. On the day when the master is buried, no one is to lecture or dispute.

We fully confirm to them the meadow of St. Germain in the condition in which it was adjudged to them.

Each master is to have jurisdiction over his scholars. No one is to receive either schools or a house without the consent of the occupant, if he is able to obtain it. No one is to receive a license from the chancellor or any one else through a gift of money, or furnishing a pledge or making an agree-

ment. Also, the masters and students can make among themselves or with others agreements and regulations, confirmed by a pledge, penalty or oath, about the following matters: namely, if a student is killed, mutilated or receives some outrageous injury and if justice is not done; for taxing the rent of *Hospitia;* concerning the dress, burial, lectures and disputations; in such a manner, however, that the university is not scattered nor destroyed on this account.

We decide concerning the theologians, that no one shall lecture at Paris before he is thirty-five years old, and not unless he has studied at least eight years, and has heard the books faithfully and in the schools. He is to listen in theology for five years, before he reads his own lectures in public. No one of them is to lecture before the third hour on the days when the masters lecture. No one is to be received at Paris for the important lectures or sermons unless he is of approved character and learning. There is to be no student at Paris who does not have a regular master.

In order moreover that these may be inviolably observed, all who presume contumaciously to violate these our statutes, unless they take care, within fifteen days from the date of the transgression, to correct their presumption in the presence of the university of masters and scholars, or in the presence of some appointed by the university, by the authority of the legation with which we are entrusted, we bind with the bond of excommunication.

Done in the year of grace 1215, in the month of August.

B. THE "GREAT DISPERSION" OF THE UNIVERSITY OF PARIS (1229)

24. A "Town and Gown" Row and Clerical Withdrawal to Angers and Orleans

Matthew Paris, *Chronica Majora*, 3:166–169, reprinted by permission of the publishers, from A. O. Norton, *op. cit.*, pp. 93–95.

In that same year, on the second and third holidays before Ash Wednesday, days when the clerks of the university have leisure for games, certain of the clerks went out of the City of Paris in the direction of Saint Marcel's; for a change of air and to have contests in their usual games. When they had reached the place and had amused themselves for some time in carrying on their games, they chanced to find in a certain tavern some excellent wine, pleasant to drink. And then, in the dispute that arose between the clerks who were drinking and the shop keepers, they began to exchange blows and to tear each other's hair, until some townsmen ran in and freed the shop keepers from the hands of the clerks; but when the clerks resisted they inflicted blows upon them and put them to flight, well and thoroughly pommelled. The latter, however, when they came back much battered into the city, roused their comrades to avenge them. So on the next day they came with swords and clubs to Saint Marcel's, and entering forcibly the house of a certain shop keeper, broke up all his wine casks and poured the wine out on the floor of the house. And, proceeding through the open squares, they attacked sharply whatever man or woman they came upon and left them half dead from the blows given them.

But the Prior of Saint Marcel's, as soon as he learned of this great injury done to his men, whom he was bound to defend, lodged a complaint with the Roman legate and the Bishop of Paris. And they went together in haste to the Queen, to whom the management of the realm had been committed at that time, and asked her to take measures for the punishment of such a wrong. But she, with a woman's forwardness, and impelled by mental excitement, immediately gave orders to the prefects of the city and to certain of her own ruffians [mercenary body-guard] with all speed to go out of the city, under arms, and to punish the authors of the violence, sparing no one. Now as these armed men, who were prone to act cruelly at every opportunity, left the gates of the city, they came upon a number of clerks busy just outside the city walls with games,—men who were entirely without fault in connection with the aforesaid violence, since those who had begun the riotous strife were men from the regions adjoining Flanders, whom we commonly call Picards. But, notwithstanding this, the police, rushing upon these men who they saw were unarmed and innocent, killed some, wounded others, and handled others mercilessly, battering them with the blows they inflicted on them. But some of them escaping by flight lay hid in dens and caverns. And among the wounded it was found that there were two clerks, rich and of great influence, who died, one of them being by race a man of Flanders, and the other of the Norman Nation.

But when the enormity of this transgression reached the ears of the Masters of the University they came together in the presence of the Queen and Legate, having first suspended entirely all lectures and debates, and strenuously demanded that justice be shown them for such a wrong. For it seemed to them disgraceful that so light an occasion as the transgression of certain contemptible little clerks should be taken to create prejudice against the whole university; but let him who was to blame in the transgression be the one to suffer the penalty.

But when finally every sort of justice had been refused them by the King and the Legate, as well as by the Bishop, there took place a universal withdrawal of the Masters and a scattering of the Scholars, the instruction of the Masters and the training of the pupils coming to an end, so that not one person of note out of them all remained in the city. And the city which was wont to boast of her clerks now remained bereft of them. . . . Thus withdrawing, the clerks betook themselves practically in a body to the larger cities in various districts. But the largest part of them chose the metropolitan city of Angers for their university instruction. Thus, then, withdrawing from the City of Paris, the nurse of Philosophy and the foster mother of Wisdom, the clerks execrated the Roman Legate and cursed the womanish arrogance of the Queen, nay, also, their infamous unanimity [in the matter]. . . .

At length, through the efforts of discreet persons, it was worked out that, certain things being done to meet the situation as required by the faults on both sides, peace was made up between the clerks and citizens and the whole body of scholars was recalled.

401

25. Promise of Academic Freedom and Scholarly Opportunities at the New Studium

Chart. Univ. Paris., I, 129–131, trans. L. Thorndike, *University Records and Life in the Middle Ages* [A. P. Evans, ed., "Records of Civilization," 38] (New York: Columbia University Press, 1944), pp. 33, 34–35.

To all Christ's faithful and especially to masters and scholars studying in any land who may see this letter, the university of masters and scholars of Toulouse, about to plant a new studium, wish continued good life with a blessed end. No undertaking has a stable foundation which is not firmly placed in Christ, the foundation of holy mother church. We therefore with this in mind are trying in Christ with all our might to lay the permanent foundation of a philosophic school at Toulouse, on which others may build with us whose good will is lighted to this by luminous rays of the Holy Spirit. . . .

Further, that ye may not bring hoes to sterile and uncultivated fields, the professors at Toulouse have, cleared away for you the weeds of the rude populace and thorns of sharp sterility and other obstacles. For here theologians inform their disciples in pulpits and the people at the crossroads, logicians train the tyros in the arts of Aristotle, grammarians fashion the tongues of the stammering on analogy, organists smooth the popular ears with the sweet-throated organ, decretists extol Justinian, and physicians teach Galen. Those who wish to scrutinize the bosom of nature to the inmost can hear here the books of Aristotle which were forbidden at Paris.

What then will you lack? Scholastic liberty? By no means, since tied to no one's apron strings you will enjoy your own liberty. Or do you fear the malice of the raging mob or the tyranny of an injurious prince? Fear not, since the liberality of the count of Toulouse affords us sufficient security both as to our salary and our servants coming to Toulouse and returning home. But if they suffer loss of their property through the hands of brigands in the domain of the count, he will pursue our malefactors with the forces of the capitol of Toulouse, the same as on behalf of citizens of Toulouse. To what has been said we add further that, as we hope truly, the lord legate will summon other theologians and decretists here to enlarge the university and will set a time which scholars ought to spend at Toulouse to receive the indulgence, if that prevaricator envious of the human race does not impede their stay, which God forbid, that henceforth they may magnify the place and the folk of Romanus, fighting by the salubrious triumphal mystery of the cross.

As for prices, what has already been said should reassure you and the fact that there is no fear of a failure of crops. On this point you may trust both report and the nuncio and these verses:

For a little, wine, for a little, bread is had;
For a little, meat, for a little, fish is bought.

The courtesy of the people should not be passed over. For here is seen that courtly good humor has struck a covenant with knighthood and clergy. So if you wish to marvel at more good things than we have mentioned, leave home behind, strap your knapsack on your back, and make your motto the words of Seneca: "I shall see all lands as mine, mine as of all; I shall so live that I shall know I am known to others; for to aim high and have enlarged ideas is characteristic of a noble soul."

26. A Scholastic Sermon by the Chancellor Philip Illustrating Professional Self-Consciousness and Social Responsibility

Trans. by the editor from the MS text, Avranches (bibl. de la ville), ms. lat. 132 fol. 340r° via M. M. Davy, *Les sermons universitaires Parisiens de 1230–1231* (Paris: J. Vrin, 1931), pp. 167ff., 168–69; 171–73.

[Theme] "And when the man shall go to sleep, mark the place wherein he sleepeth; and thou shalt go in, and lift up the clothes wherewith he is covered towards his feet, and shall lay thyself down there. . . ." (Ruth 3:4).

[Comparison of the Bees with Scholars] We read in the book, *On the Nature of Animals*, 5, (19), 5, that bees, though greatly loving the place where they gather honey, will, if some hostile person bestrews their beehive with an ill-smelling herb, leave that place because of the disagreeable odor and fly about through flowering regions until they find what they have been seeking. But they will long for the place they left. And it so happens, if a wise householder purifies and cleans that place by removing the bitterness of the herb, they will return to it.

[Protheme] Bees are likened to scholars of whom the book of Ecclesiasticus says (11:3): "The bee is small among flying things but her fruit hath the chiefest sweetness." Small in bodily size, that is, but great in natural capacity. Wherefore, if in fighting they discharge their sting, they die. Scholars ought, likewise, to shun the vain exercise of bodily powers, that is, they ought not to be fighters, for in stinging or wreaking vengeance, they die as much to the life of wisdom as to the life of grace. But they are fertile in mind; and just as the bees, admittedly puny in bodily size, work with an effectiveness comparable to other animals, surpassing them in penetration, so these (scholars).

[Division 1.] Bees, for example, construct hexagonal dwellings for themselves in which they make honeycombs containing honey and wax and these are likewise the entrance to sweetness as well as to honey and to light as well as to wax. These hexagonal houses, out of fitness and in keeping with their work, symbolize perfection. Honey refreshes the taste. Wax is a means of light as well as of vision. The scholars of Paris were occupying hexagonal houses as much as the bees, that is these houses were suitable for studies. They were making honeycombs in which they were caressing the affections and enlightening the intellect; because, as *Proverbs* says (16:24), "Well ordered words are as a honeycomb, sweet to the soul. . . ."

[Division 2.] But their place having been polluted with acrid herbs, and a hostile man, whoever he may be, having sowed it over with a vile plant, they have taken flight and flown about over other flowering areas in order to find rest. They yearn, nevertheless, after the place they left, with the hope that a good and wise householder, that is the supreme pontiff, may purge it from the bitterness of the vile smelling herb so that they may return to their former place. Happy the locality and happy the place that piously brings together these dispersed sons. Pious, I say, the ones of course who will nourish them and afterwards restore them to their mother.

[Division 3.] Because this is a sign that the cup of nourishment does not desire dispersion. But the one who would nourish them would not seek to retain them for herself as does Angers. . . . It would seem that Orleans among others would have received these sons, not so much out of envy as out of desire to help them, and rightly so, because among others she is a sister of the City of Paris. And we read in Exodus concerning Moses that, upon the boy's refusal to accept an Egyptian nurse, his own sister said to Pharaoh's daughter: "Would you like me to call a Hebrew woman capable of nursing the infant?" She said yes, and the sister called the child's own mother who nursed him.

[Division 4.] The one planning to retain the sons for herself is comparable to a woman who, having overlaid her own baby, seized another from the bosom of a concubine. When both came up for judgment before Solomon the guilty one said, "The (living) child is mine." The other denied this, saying, "He is mine." Solomon, in order to discover the real mother shrewdly proposed dividing the living child. But his true mother suggested that he be given to the other woman, for she was shaken to her very soul. But the one who was not the baby's mother said, "Give it to neither of us, but divide it." And the King said, "Give it to that one," indicating the baby's real mother. . . . Thus it is clear that the city demanding

403

dispersion and division is not the true mother of the child. . . .

[Part I, Consideration 1.] "And when the man shall go to sleep. . . ." We read in the book of Ruth (1:1) that Naomi under the exigency of famine migrated to the land of Moab. Having decided to go back she was accompanied by her daughter in law, Ruth, upon her return. At Naomi's suggestion, Ruth went into Boaz's field to gather grain. She found grace in Boaz's eyes and he said to her (2:8), "Daughter do not glean in any other field . . . I have charged my young men not to molest thee. . . ."

[Application 1.] By Naomi is meant the beautiful new moon. And this rightly signifies an honorable body of scholars whose beauty is marvelous because they live in the Holy Spirit and preserve integrity. As the book of Wisdom (4:1) says, "O how beautiful is the chaste generation with glory . . . ," and that of Numbers (24:5), "How beautiful are thy tabernacles O Jacob, and thy tents, O Israel!" The tabernacle of Jacob refers to those serving in liberal disciplines. The tents of Israel represent theologians carrying on studies in Divinity so that they may see God. The new moon is fittingly spoken of, for the new moon increases. So it behooves these to press on, not ceasing from the acquisition of knowledge until they come to perfect understanding, that is to the full moon. Moreover, the moon derives its light, not from itself, but from the sun. So these also ought to realize that they have the light of knowledge, not from themselves, but from him of whom James speaks (1:17), "Every best gift and every perfect gift, is from above, coming down from the Father of lights. . . ."

[Application 2.] This beautiful generation was a certain one in Bethlehem, that is in Paris, which is the house of bread. And it is extraordinary that, from this house of bread, by reason of the exigencies of famine, exile became necessary. Not a scarcity, that is, of material bread, not even of spiritual bread as the Word of God says in Amos (8:11), "I will send forth a famine unto the land; not a famine of bread, nor a thirst of water, but of hearing the word of the Lord." Rather a spiritual famine which concerns justice. This bread they would eat but it shall not be so, because the vigor of justice is lacking. Of which bread Matthew speaks (5:6), "Blessed are they that hunger . . . for they shall have their fill.". . .

[Consideration 2.] On account of this lack Naomi, that is this beautiful generation, migrated to the land of Moab. The land of Moab is the city of Angers. . . . When she decided to return to Bethlehem, that is when she heard that the famine had ceased and that God had given fertility to the land. . . .

[Application 1.] She has advance knowledge that this famine has ceased and that spiritual bread, that is the bread of justice abounds, because the king has decreed that fulness of justice should be manifested toward scholars and that they should be recalled to Bethlehem, that is to the house of bread at Paris, and that their liberties, piously granted them by King Philip of happy memory, should be freely and inviolably preserved.

[Application 2.] Naomi having heard this decided to return and by God's grace did return. Not only returned but multiplied because her daughter-in-law returned with her. Ruth means seeing. What pertains to Ruth, thus interpreted as seeing, if not knowledge? Not the knowledge of liberal disciplines but the knowledge of experience accrued to her during this journey. . . .

[Application 3.] Naomi therefore has returned with Ruth her daughter-in-law, and Ruth herself, that is the soul thus taught by experience, shall enter the field of Boaz, that is of Christ, that is at Paris, which field Christ cultivates by plowing the disciplines and sowing the word of doctrine. . . . And Ruth will hear the voice of Boaz, that is of Christ saying, "Daughter do not go to glean in any other field, and do not depart from this place." He does not wish that others should depart from his flowering, fertile field, that is, from Bethlehem, that is from the house of bread, that is, from Paris. "For I have charged my young men not to molest thee." This is indeed the precept of Christ by way of the voice of his steward, lest the scholars may be molested by anything injurious to them.

E. POPE GREGORY IX AND THE MAGNA CHARTA OF THE UNIVERSITY OF PARIS (1231)

27. *Statutes for the University; Functions of the Chancellor; Licensing; Lectures and Disputations; Academic Protocol; Courses of Study; Student Life and Property*

Chart. Univ. Paris., I, (79), 136, trans. *PTR*, II, (3), pp. 7–11.

Gregory, the bishop, servant of the servants of God, to his beloved sons, all the masters and students at Paris—greeting and apostolic benediction.

Paris, the mother of sciences, like another Cariath Sepher, a city of letters, stands forth illustrious, great indeed, but concerning herself she causes greater things to be desired, full of favor for the teachers and students. There, as in a special factory of wisdom, she has silver as the beginnings of her veins, and of gold is the spot in which according to law they flow together; from which the prudent mystics of eloquence fabricate golden necklaces inlaid with silver, and making collars ornamented with precious stones of inestimable value, adorn and decorate the spouse of Christ. There the iron is raised from the earth, because, when the earthly fragility is solidified by strength, the breastplate of faith, the sword of the spirit, and the other weapons of the Christian soldier, powerful against the brazen powers, are formed from it. And the stone melted by heat, is turned into brass, because the hearts of stone, enkindled by the fervor of the Holy Ghost, at times glow, burn and become sonorous, and by preaching herald the praises of Christ.

Accordingly, it is undoubtedly very displeasing to God and men that any one in the aforesaid city should strive in any way to disturb so illustrious grace, or should not oppose himself openly and with all his strength to any who do so. Wherefore, since we have diligently investigated the questions referred to us concerning a dissension which, through the instigation of the devil, has arisen there and greatly disturbed the university, we have decided, by the advice of our brethren, that these should be set at rest rather by precautionary measures, than by a judicial sentence.

Therefore, concerning the condition of the students and schools, we have decided that the following should be observed: each chancellor, appointed hereafter at Paris, at the time of his installation, in the presence of the bishop, or at the command of the latter in the chapter at Paris—two masters of the students having been summoned for this purpose and present in behalf of the university—shall swear that, in good faith, according to his conscience, he will not receive as professors of theology and canon law any but suitable men, at a suitable place and time, according to the condition of the city and the honor and glory of those branches of learning; and he will reject all who are unworthy without respect to persons or nations. Before licensing any one, during three months, dating from the time when the license is requested, the chancellor shall make diligent inquiries of all the masters of theology present in the city, and of all other honest and learned men through whom the truth can be ascertained, concerning the life knowledge, capacity, purpose, prospects and other qualities needful in such persons; and after the inquiries, in good faith and according to his conscience, he shall grant or deny the license to the candidate, as shall seem fitting and expedient. The masters of theology and canon law, when they begin to lecture, shall take a public oath that they will give true testimony on the above points. The chancellor shall also swear, that he will in no way reveal the advice of the masters, to their injury; the liberty and privileges being maintained in their full vigor for the canons at Paris, as they were in the beginning. Moreover, the chancellor shall promise to examine in good faith the masters in medicine and arts and in the other branches, to admit only the worthy and to reject the unworthy.

In other matters, because confusion easily creeps in where there is no order, we grant to you the right of making constitutions and ordinances regulating the manner and time of lectures and disputations, the costume to be worn, the burial of the dead; also concerning the bachelors, who are to lecture and at what hours, and on what they are to lecture; and concerning the prices of the lodgings or the interdiction of the same; and concerning a fit punishment for those who violate your constitutions or ordinances, by exclusion from your society. And if perchance, the assessment of the lodgings is taken from you, or anything else is lacking, or an injury or outrageous damage, such as death or the mutilation of a limb, is inflicted on one of you, unless through a suitable admonition satisfaction is rendered within fifteen days, you may suspend your lectures until you have received full satisfaction. And if it happens that any one of you is unlawfully imprisoned, unless the injury ceases on a remonstrance from you, you may, if you judge it expedient, suspend your lectures immediately.

We command, moreover, that the bishop of Paris shall so chastise the excesses of the guilty, that the honor of the student shall be preserved and evil deeds shall not remain unpunished. But in no way shall the innocent be seized on account of the guilty; nay rather, if a probable suspicion arises against any one, he shall be detained honorably and on giving suitable bail he shall be freed, without any exactions from the jailors. But if, perchance, such a crime has been committed that imprisonment is necessary, the bishop shall detain the criminal in his prison. The chancellor is forbidden to keep him in his prison. We also forbid holding a student for a debt contracted by another, since this is interdicted by canonical and legitimate sanctions. Neither the bishop, nor his officials nor the chancellor shall exact a pecuniary penalty for removing an excommunication or any other censure of any kind. Nor shall the chancellor demand from the masters who are licensed an oath, or obedience, or any pledge; nor shall he receive any emolument or promise for granting a license, but be content with the above-mentioned oath.

Also, the vacation in summer is not to exceed one month, and the bachelors, if they wish, can continue their lectures in vacation time. Moreover, we prohibit more expressly the students from carrying weapons in the city, and the university from protecting those who disturb the peace and study. And those who call themselves students, but do not frequent the schools, or acknowledge any master, are in no way to enjoy the liberties of the students.

Moreover, we order that the masters in arts shall always read one lecture on Priscian, and one book after the other in the regular courses. Those books on natural philosophy which for a certain reason were prohibited in a provincial council, are not to be used at Paris until they have been examined and purged of all suspicion of error. The masters and students in theology shall strive to exercise themselves laudably in the branch which they profess; they shall not show themselves philosophers, but they shall strive to become God's learned. And they shall not speak in the language of the people, confounding the sacred language with the profane. In the schools they shall dispute only on such questions as can be determined by theological books and the writings of the holy fathers.

Also, about the property of the scholars who die intestate or do not commit the arrangement of their affairs to others, we have determined to arrange thus: namely, that the bishop and one of the masters, whom the university shall appoint for this purpose, shall receive all the property of the defunct, and placing it in a suitable and safe spot, shall fix a certain date, before which his death can be announced in his native country, and those who ought to succeed to his property may come to Paris or send a suitable messenger. And if they come or send, the goods shall be restored to them, with the security which shall have been given. If no one appears, then the bishop and masters shall expend the property for the soul of the departed, as seems expedient; unless, perchance, the heirs shall have been prevented from coming by some good reason. In that case, the distribution shall be deferred to a fitting time.

Truly, because the masters and students, who harassed by damages and injuries, have taken a mutual oath to depart from Paris and have broken up the school, have seemed to be waging a contest not so much for their own benefit as for the common good; we, consulting the needs and advantages of the whole church, wish and command that after the privileges have been granted to the masters and students by our most dearly beloved son in Christ, the illustrious king of the French, and amends have been paid by the malefactors, they shall study at Paris and shall not be marked by any infamy or irregularity on account of their staying away or return.

It is not lawful for any man whatever to infringe this deed of our provision, constitution, concession, prohibition and inhibition or to act contrary to it, from rash presumption. If any one, however, should dare to attempt this, let him know that he incurs the wrath of almighty God and of the blessed Peter and Paul, his apostles.

Given at the Lateran, on the Ides of April, in the fifth year of our pontificate.

F. THE DOMINICAN, THOMAS AQUINAS, AND THE SCHOLASTIC SYNTHESIS (C. 1270)

28. The Scholastic Resolution of Abelardian Dialectic: the Theological Virtues and Man's Supernatural Beatitude

Summa Theol., 1a, 2ae, Q. 62, a. 1, trans. Fathers of the English Dominican Province, *The "Summa Theologica" of St. Thomas Aquinas* (London: Burns, Oates & Washbourne, Ltd.; New York: Benziger Brothers, Inc., 1915), pp. 146–48.

First Article

WHETHER THERE ARE ANY THEOLOGICAL VIRTUES?

We proceed thus to the First Article:—
Objection 1. It seems that there are not any theological virtues. For according to *Phys.* vi., *virtue is the disposition of a perfect thing to that which is best: and by perfect, I mean that which is disposed according to nature.* But that which is Divine is above man's nature. Therefore the theological virtues are not virtues of a man.

Obj. 2. Further, theological virtues are quasi-Divine virtues. But the Divine virtues are exemplars, as stated above (Q. LXI., A. 5), which are not in us but in God. Therefore the theological virtues are not virtues of man.

Obj. 3. Further, the theological virtues are so called because they direct us to God, Who is the first beginning and last end of all things. But by the very nature of his reason and will, man is directed to his first beginning and last end. Therefore there is no need for any habits of theological virtue, to direct the reason and will of God.

On the contrary, The precepts of the Law are about acts of virtue. Now the Divine Law contains precepts about the acts of faith, hope, and charity: for it is written (*Ecclus.* ii. 8, *seqq.*): *Ye that fear the Lord believe Him,* and again, *hope in Him,* and again, *love Him.* Therefore faith, hope, and charity are virtues directing us to God. Therefore they are theological virtues.

I answer that, Man is perfected by virtue, for those actions whereby he is directed to happiness, as was explained above (Q. V., A. 7). Now man's happiness is twofold, as was also stated above (*ibid.,* A. 5). One is proportionate to human nature, a happiness, to wit, which man can obtain by means of his natural principles. The other is a happiness surpassing man's nature, and which man can obtain by the power of God alone, by a kind of participation of the Godhead, about which it is written (2 Pet. i. 4) that by Christ we are made *partakers of the Divine Nature.* And because such happiness surpasses the capacity of human nature, man's natural principles which enable him to act well according to his capacity, do not suffice to direct man to this same happiness. Hence it is necessary for man to receive from God some additional principles, whereby he may be directed to supernatural happiness, even as he is directed to his connatural end, by means of his natural principles, albeit not without the Divine assistance. Such like principles are called *theological*

IX-2. The Triumph of St. Thomas and the Allegory of Medieval Learning. *Spanish Chapel, Church of Santa Maria Novella, Florence. Andrea Buonaiuti de Firenze.*

virtues: first, because their object is God, inasmuch as they direct us aright to God: secondly, because they are infused in us by God alone: thirdly, because these virtues are not made known to us, save by Divine revelation, contained in Holy Writ.

Reply Obj. 1. A certain nature may be ascribed to a certain thing in two ways. First, essentially; and thus these theological virtues surpass the nature of man. Secondly, by participation, as kindled wood partakes of the nature of the fire: and thus, after a fashion, man becomes a partaker of the Divine Nature, as stated above: so that these virtues are proportionate to man in respect of the Nature of which he is made a partaker.

Reply Obj. 2. These virtues are called Divine, not as though God were virtuous by reason of them, but because by them God makes us virtuous, and directs us to Himself. Hence they are not exemplar but exemplate virtues.

Reply Obj. 3. The reason and will are naturally directed to God, inasmuch as He is the beginning and end of nature, but in proportion to nature. But the reason and will, according to their nature, are not sufficiently directed to Him in so far as He is the object of supernatural happiness.

G. THE FRANCISCAN, ROGER BACON, SATIRIZES THE MENDICANT "BOYS" AT PARIS (1271)

29. *Mendicant Inadequacy in Theology, Philosophy, and Language Study; Teaching and "Summa Making" Without Adequate Formation in Source-Texts*

Compendium Studii Philosophiae, 425, trans. G. G. Coulton, *Life in the Middle Ages* (Cambridge: Cambridge University Press, 1930, 1954), II, pp. 59–60.

(p. 425.) The second principal cause of error in the present pursuit of wisdom is this: that for forty years past certain men have arisen in the universities who have created themselves masters and doctors in theology and philosophy, though they themselves have never learned anything of any account; nor will they or can they learn by reason of their position, as I will take care to show by argument, in all its length and breadth, within the compass of the following pages. And, albeit I grieve and pity these as much as I can, yet truth prevaileth over all, and therefore I will here expound at least some of those things which are done publicly and are known to all men, though few turn their hearts to regard either this or other profitable considerations, by reason of those causes of error which I here set forth, and whereby almost all men are basely blinded. These are boys who are inexperienced in the knowledge of themselves and of the world and of the learned languages, Greek and Hebrew, which (as I will prove later on) are necessary to study; they are ignorant also of all parts and sciences of the world's philosophy and of wisdom, when they so presumptuously enter upon the study of theology, which requireth all human wisdom, as the saints teach and as all wise men know. For, if truth be anywhere, here is she found: here, if anywhere, is falsehood condemned, as Augustine saith in his book *Of Christian Doctrine*. These are boys of the two Student-Orders, as Albert and Thomas and others, who in many cases enter those Orders at or below the age of twenty years. This is the common course, from the English sea to the furthest confines of Christendom, and more especially beyond the realm of France; so that in Aquitaine, Provence, Spain, Italy, Germany, Hungary, Denmark, and everywhere, boys are promiscuously received into the Orders from their tenth to their twentieth year; boys too young to be able to know anything worth knowing, even though they were not already possessed with the aforesaid causes of human error; wherefore, at their entrance into the Orders, they know nought that profiteth to theology. Many thousands become friars who cannot read their Psalter or their Donat; yet, immediately after their admission, they are set to study theology. Wherefore they must of necessity fail to reap any great profit, especially seeing that they have not taken lessons from others in philosophy since their entrance; and, most of all, because they have presumed in those Orders to enquire into philosophy by themselves and without teachers, so that they are become Masters in Theology and in Philosophy before being disciples. Wherefore infinite error reigneth among them, although for certain reasons this is not apparent, by the Devil's instigation and by God's permission. One cause of this appearance is that the Orders have the outward show of great holiness; wherefore it is probable to the world that men in so holy a state would not presume on such things

as they could not perform. Yet we see that all states are corrupted in this age, as I have discoursed in detail above. . . .

H. METHODS OF LECTURING IN THE LIBERAL ARTS AT PARIS (1355)

30. *Proper Method Prescribed upon Penalty of Suspension*

Chart. Univ. Paris., III, 39–40, trans. L. Thorndike, *University Records and Life in the Middle Ages* (New York: Columbia University Press, 1944), p. 237.

In the name of the Lord, amen. Two methods of lecturing on books in the liberal arts having been tried, the former masters of philosophy uttering their words rapidly so that the mind of the hearer can take them in but the hand cannot keep up with them, the latter speaking slowly until their listeners can catch up with them with the pen; having compared these by diligent examination, the former method is found the better. Wherefore, the consensus of opinion warns us that we imitate it in our lectures. We, therefore, all and each, masters of the faculty of arts, teaching and not teaching, convoked for this specially by the venerable man, master Albert of Bohemia, then rector of the university, at St. Julien le Pauvre, have decreed in this wise, that all lecturers, whether masters or scholars of the same faculty, whenever and wherever they chance to lecture on any text ordinarily or cursorily in the same faculty, or to dispute any question concerning it, or anything else by way of exposition, shall observe the former method of lecturing to the best of their ability, so speaking forsooth as if no one was taking notes before them, in the way that sermons and recommendations are made in the university and which the lectures in other faculties follow. Moreover, transgressors of this statute, if the lecturers are masters or scholars, we now deprive henceforth for a year from lecturing, honors, offices and other advantages of our faculty. Which if anyone violates, for the first relapse we double the penalty, for the second we quadruple it, and so on. Moreover, listeners who oppose the execution of this our statute by clamor, hissing, noise, throwing stones by themselves or by their servants and accomplices, or in any

IX-3. Charles V, King of France, Patron of the Sciences. *Upper left: Charles V receiving a MS. Right: King and Queen discuss their children. Lower left: University studies, master and hearers, including the king. Lower right: Professor lecturing to a class.*

other way, we deprive of and cut off from our society for a year, and for each relapse we increase the penalty double and quadruple as above.

IV. Gothic Architecture, Scholasticism and the *Summas* of the Common Life; Mental Habit, Order, Measure, Light; Aesthetics and Gothic Symbolism

A. PANOFSKY'S THESIS ON GOTHIC
ARCHITECTURE AND SCHOLASTICISM

31. The High Scholastic Summa *and the High Gothic Cathedral; Scholastic Habit, the Self-Explication of Architecture and the Self-Explication of Reason*

Reprinted by kind permission from E. Panofsky, *Gothic Architecture and Scholasticism* (Latrobe, Pa.: The Archabbey Press, 1951), pp. 44–50, 58–59.

Like the High Scholastic *Summa*, the High Gothic cathedral aimed, first of all, at "totality" and therefore tended to approximate, by synthesis as well as elimination, one perfect and final solution; we may therefore speak of *the* High Gothic plan or *the* High Gothic system with much more confidence than would be possible in any other period. In its imagery, the High Gothic cathedral sought to embody the whole of Christian knowledge, theological, moral, natural, and historical, with everything in its place and that which no longer found its place, suppressed. In structural design, it similarly sought to synthesize all major motifs handed down by separate channels and finally achieved an unparalleled balance between the basilica and the central plan type, suppressing all elements that might endanger this balance, such as the crypt, the galleries, and towers other than the two in front.

The second requirement of Scholastic writing, "arrangement according to a system of homologous parts and parts of parts," is most graphically expressed in the uniform division and subdivision of the whole structure. Instead of the Romanesque variety of western and eastern vaulting forms, often appearing in one and the same building (groin vaults, rib vaults, barrels, domes, and half-domes), we have the newly developed rib vault exclusively so that the vaults of even the apse, the chapels and the ambulatory no longer differ in kind from those of the nave and transept. Since Amiens, rounded surfaces were entirely eliminated, except, of course, for the webbing of the vaults. Instead of the contrast that normally existed between tripartite naves and undivided transepts (or quinquepartite naves and tripartite transepts) we have tripartition in both cases; and instead of the disparity (either in size, on in the type of covering, or in both) between the bays of the high nave and those of the side aisles, we have the "uniform *travée*," in which one rib-vaulted central bay connects with one rib-vaulted aisle bay on either side. The whole is thus composed of smallest units—one might almost speak of *articuli*—which are homologous in that they are all triangular in groundplan and in that each of these triangles shares its sides with its neighbors.

As a result of this homology we perceive what corresponds to the hierarchy of "logical levels" in a well-organized Scholastic treatise. Dividing the entire structure, as was customary in the period itself, into three main parts, the nave, the transept, and the chevet (which in turn comprises the fore-choir and the choir proper), and distinguishing, within these parts, between high nave and side-aisles on the one hand, and between apse, ambulatory, and hemicycle of chapels, on the other, we can observe analogous relations to obtain: first, between each central bay, the whole of the central nave, and the entire nave, transept or fore-choir, respectively; second, between each side aisle bay, the whole of each side aisle, and the entire nave, transept or fore-choir, respectively; third, between each sector of the apse, the whole apse, and the entire choir; fourth, between each section of the ambulatory, the whole ambulatory and the entire choir; and fifth, between each chapel, the whole hemicycle of chapels, and the entire choir.

It is not possible here—nor is it necessary —to describe how this principle of progressive divisibility (or, to look at it the other way, multiplicability) increasingly affected the entire edifice down to the smallest detail. At the height of the development, supports were divided and subdivided into main piers, major shafts, minor shafts, and still minor shafts; the tracery of windows, triforia, and blind arcades into primary, secondary, and tertiary mullions and profiles; ribs and arches into a series of moldings. It may be mentioned, however, that the very principle of homology that controls the whole process implies and accounts for the relative uniformity which distinguishes the High Gothic vocabulary from the Romanesque. All parts that are on the same "logical level" —and this is especially noticeable in those decorative and representational features which, in architecture, correspond to Thomas Aquinas's *similitudines*—came to be conceived of as members of one class, so that the enormous variety in, for instance,

the shape of canopies, the decoration of socles and archevaults, and, above all, the form of piers and capitals tended to be suppressed in favor of standard types admitting only of such variations as would occur in nature among individuals of one species. Even in the world of fashion the thirteenth century is distinguished by a reasonableness and uniformity (even as far as the difference between masculine and feminine costumes is concerned) which was equally foreign to the preceding and to the following period.

The theoretically illimited fractionization of the edifice is limited by what corresponds to the third requirement of Scholastic writing: "distinctness and deductive cogency." According to classic High Gothic standards the individual elements, while forming an indiscerptible whole, yet must proclaim their identity by remaining clearly separated from each other—the shafts from the wall or the core of the pier, the ribs from their neighbors, all vertical members from their arches; and there must be an unequivocal correlation between them. We must be able to tell which element belongs to which, from which results what might be called a "postulate of mutual inferability"— not in dimensions, as in classical architecture, but in conformation. . . .

We are faced neither with "rationalism" in a purely functionalistic sense nor with "illusion" in the sense of modern *l'art pour l'art* aesthetics. We are faced with what may be termed a "visual logic" illustrative of Thomas Aquinas's *nam et sensus ratio quaedam est.* A man imbued with the Scholastic habit would look upon the mode of architectural presentation, just as he looked upon the mode of literary presentation, from the point of view of *manifestatio.* He would have taken it for granted that the primary purpose of the many elements that compose a cathedral was to ensure stability, just as he took it for granted that the primary purpose of the many elements that constitute a *Summa* was to ensure validity.

But he would not have been satisfied had not the membrification of the edifice permitted him to re-experience the very processes of architectural composition just as the membrification of the *Summa* permitted

IX-4 and IX-5. Notre Dame of Paris, *Left: View from southeast, apse. Below: nave, 1163–c. 1200.*

him to re-experience the very processes of cogitation. To him, the panoply of shafts, ribs, buttresses, tracery, pinnacles, and crockets was a self-analysis and self-explication of architecture much as the customary apparatus of parts, distinctions, questions, and articles was, to him, a self-analysis and self-explication of reason.

B. SIMSON ON THE GOTHIC CATHEDRAL

32. *The Nature of Medieval Symbolism*

Reprinted by kind permission from Otto von Simson, *The Gothic Cathedral,* Bollingen Series XLVIII (Pantheon Books), Bollingen Foundation, New York, 1956, pp. xix–xx.

. . . it will be useful briefly to consider what distinguishes the medieval attitude toward art from our own.

The simplest way of defining this difference is to recall the changed meaning and function of the symbol. For us the symbol is an image that invests physical reality with poetical meaning. For medieval man, the physical world as we understand it has no reality except as a symbol. But even the term "symbol" is misleading. For us the symbol is the subjective creation of poetic fancy; for medieval man what we would call sym-

412

bol is the only objectively valid definition of reality. We find it necessary to suppress the symbolic instinct if we seek to understand the world as it is rather than as it seems. Medieval man conceived the symbolic instinct as the only reliable guide to such an understanding. Maximus the Confessor, a thinker we shall meet again later, actually defines what he calls "symbolic vision" as the ability to apprehend within the objects of sense perception the invisible reality of the intelligible that lays beyond them.

V. The Cathedral as the Four-Fold Mirror of the World and of the Common Life; Vincent de Beauvais' *Speculum Majus*

A. THE "SPECULUM NATURALE": CREATION AND NATURE

33. Catholic Lore; the Book of Creation and Its Beauties; the Universe, Its Creator, and Creatures

This and Item 34 are reprinted by permission of the publishers from H. O. Taylor, *The Mediaeval Mind*, Volume II (Cambridge, Mass.: Harvard University Press, 1949), pp. 346, 347, 348, 349–50, 350–51. This item, pp. 346–48.

"[Here are] certain flowers according to my modicum of faculty, gathered from every one I have been able to read, whether of our Catholic Doctors or the Gentile philosophers and poets. Especially have I drawn from them what seemed to pertain either to the building up of our dogma, or to moral instruction, or to the incitement of charity's devotion, or to the mystic exposition of divine Scripture, or to the manifest or symbolical explanation of its truth. Thus by one grand *opus* I would appease my studiousness, and perchance, by my labours, profit those who, like me, try to read as many books as possible, and cull their flowers. Indeed of making many books there is no end, and neither is the eye of the curious reader satisfied, nor the ear of the auditor.". . .

"Moreover I have diligently described the nature of things, which, I think, no one will deem useless, who, in the light of grace, has read of the power, wisdom and goodness of God, creator, ruler and preserver, in that same book of the Creation appointed for us to read.". . .

IX-6. Chartres Cathedral, Buttresses and Horizontal Sections after Goubert.

"Verily how great is even the humblest beauty of this world, and how pleasing to the eye of reason diligently considering not only the modes and numbers and orders of things, so decorously appointed throughout the universe, but also the revolving ages which are ceaselessly uncoiled through abatements and successions, and are marked by the death of what is born I confess, sinner as I am, with mind befouled in flesh, that I am moved with spiritual sweetness toward the creator and ruler of this world, and honour Him with greater veneration, when I behold at once the magnitude, and beauty and permanence of His creation. For the mind, lifting itself from the dunghill of its affections, and rising, as it is able, into the light of speculation, sees as from a height the greatness of the universe containing in itself infinite places filled with the divers orders of creatures."

413

B. THE "SPECULUM DOCTRINALE": KNOWLEDGE AND THE LIBERAL ARTS

34. The Sciences (Doctrinae); the Trivium; Practical and Speculative Sciences; the Arts and Sciences in Relation to Each Other

See Item 33, *ibid.*, pp. 349–51.

". . . in this second part, in like fashion we propose to treat of the plenary restitution of that destitute nature. . . . And since that restitution, or restoration, is effected and perfected by *doctrina* (imparted knowledge, science), this part not improperly is called the *Speculum doctrinale.* For of a surety everything pertaining to recovering or defending man's spiritual or temporal welfare (*salutem*) is embraced under *doctrina.* In this book, the sciences (*doctrinae*) and arts are treated thus: First concerning all of them in general, to wit, concerning their invention, origin and species; and concerning the method of acquiring them. Then concerning the singular arts and sciences in particular. And here first concerning those of the Trivium, which are devoted to language (grammar, rhetoric, logic); for without these, the others cannot be learned or communicated. Next concerning the practical ones (*practica*), because through them, the eyes of the mind being clarified, one ascends to the speculative (*theorica*). Then also concerning the mechanical ones; since, as they consist in making (*operatio*), they are joined by affinity to the *practica.* Finally concerning the speculative sciences (*theorica*), because the end and aim (*finis*) of all the rest is placed by the wise in them. And since (as Jerome says) one cannot know the power (*vis*) of the antidote unless the power of the poison first is understood, therefore to the *reparatio doctrinalis* of the human race, the subject of the book, something is prefixed as a brief epilogue from the former book, concerning the fall and misery of man, in which he still labours, as the penalty for his sin, in lamentable exile. . . .

"For the obtaining of these three remedies every art and every *disciplina* was invented. In order to gain Wisdom, *Theorica* was devised; and *Practica* for the sake of virtue; and for Need's sake, *Mechanica. Theorica* driving out ignorance, illuminates Wisdom; *Practica* shutting out vice, strengthens Virtue; *Mechanica* providing against penury, tempers the infirmities of the present life. *Theorica,* in all that is and that is not, chooses to investigate the true. *Practica* de-

IX-7. Grammar Teaching. *Chartres—west, right portal, archivolt.*

termines the correct way of living and the form of discipline, according to the institution of the virtues. *Mechanica,* occupied with fleeting things, strives to provide for the needs of the body. For the end and aim of all human actions and studies, which reason regulates, ought to look either to the reparation of the integrity of our nature or to alleviating the needs to which life is subjected. The integrity of our nature is repaired by Wisdom, to which *Theorica* relates, and by Virtue, which *Practica* cultivates. Need is alleviated by the administration of temporalities, to which *Mechanica* attends. Last found of all is Logic, source of eloquence, through which the wise who understand the aforesaid principal sciences and disciplines, may discourse upon them more correctly, truly and elegantly; more correctly, through Grammar; more truly, through Dialectic; more elegantly, through Rhetoric."

414

35. St. Martin According to the Legenda Aurea (November 11)

Trans. G. Ryan and H. Ripperger, *The Golden Legend of Jacobus de Voragine* (New York: Longmans, Green & Co., 1941), Part II, p. 674.

Of Martin, Saint Ambrose speaks as follows: 'The blessed Martin was found so perfect that he clothed Christ in the guise of a poor man, and the garment which the needy one received was put on by the Lord of the world! O happy gift, that clothed divinity! O glorious division of a cloak, that covered a soldier and the King together! O inestimable gift, that was found worthy to deck the Godhead!'

36. St. Thomas of Canterbury, the King of England, and the Golden Legend (December 29)

Trans. Ryan and Ripperger, *op. cit.*, Part I, p. 70.

And, in the same manner as in the past, he defended the rights of the Church, the king being unable to move him by pleading or by force. Then the king, seeing that he could not sway him, sent soldiers in arms after him; and these, entering the cathedral, loudly asked where the archbishop was. He came to meet them, and said: 'Here I am! What do you desire of me?' And they replied: 'We have come to kill thee; thy last hour has come!' Then he said to them: 'I am ready to die for God, and to defend justice, and to protect the liberties of the Church. But since you seek only me, I adjure you, by the almighty God, and under pain of anathema, to do no harm to any of my priests! As for me, I recommend the Church and I recommend myself to God, the Blessed Virgin, Dionysius, and to all the saints.' Having spoken these words, he bowed his venerable head to the sword of the wicked, and they sundered the top of his skull, scattering his brains upon the pavement of the temple. Thus Saint Thomas

IX-8. Saints: Martin of Tours, Jerome, Gregory the Great. *Chartres Cathedral, south portal (13th century), right bay, right side.*

died a martyr's death, in the year of the Lord 1174.

37. Hakluyt's version of Catholic Missions According to the Speculum Historiale

32:2, 20, trans. C. R. Beazley, ed., *The Texts and Versions of John De Plano Carpini and William de Rubruquis* (as printed for the first time by Hakluyt in 1598, together with some shorter pieces (London: Printed for the Hakluyt Society, 1903), No. 13, pp. 107, 128–29.

About this time also, Pope Innocentius the fourth sent Frier Ascelline being one of the order of the Praedicants, together with three other Friers (of the same authoritie whereunto they were called) consorted with him out of diuers Couens of their order, with letters Apostolicall vnto the Tartars

IX-9. St. Martin, Christ, and Baptism. *Chartres Cathedral*, Bay 24.

IX-10. St. Thomas Becket, His Life and Murder. *Chartres Cathedral, window.*

campe: wherein hee exhorted them to giue ouer their bloudie slaughter of mankinde, and to receiue the Christian faith. And I, in verie deede, receiued the relations concern-

IX-11. Last Judgment. *Bourges, west portal.*

ing the deedes of the Tartars onelie, (which, according to the congruence of times, I haue aboue inserted into this my woorke) from a Frier Minoritie, called Simon de Sanct. Quintin, who lately returned from the same voyage. And at the verie time also, there was a certaine other Frier Minorite, namely Frier Iohn de Plano Carpini, sent with certaine associates vnto the Tartars, who likewise (as himselfe witnesseth) abode and conuersed with them a yeere and three moneths at the least. For both he & one Frier Benedict a Polonian being of the same order, and a partaker of all his miserie and tribulation, receiued straight commaundement from the Pope, that both of them should diligently searche out all things that concerned the state of the Tartars. And therefore this Frier Iohn hath written a little Historie (which is come to our hands) of such things, as with his owne eyes hee sawe among the Tartars, or which he heard from diuers Christians worthy of credit, remaining there in captiuitie. Out of which historie I thought good by way of conclusion, to insert somewhat for the supply of those things which are wanting in the said Frier Simon.

. . . . .

Wherefore, the first saturday next after Ashwednesday, hauing about the Sunnes going downe, taken vp our place of rest, the armed Tartars came rushing vpon vs in vnciuil and horrible maner, being very inquisitiue of vs what maner of persons, or of what condition we were: & when we had answered them that we were the Popes Legates, receiuing some victuals at our handes, they immediatly departed. Moreouer in the morning rising and proceeding on our iourney, the chiefe of them which were in the guard met with vs, demaunding why, or for what intent and purpose we came thither: and what busines we had with them: Unto whom we answered, we are the legates of our lord the Pope, who is the father & lord of the Christians. He hath sent vs as well vnto your Emperour, as to your princes, and all other Tartars for this purpose, because it is his pleasure, that all Christians should be in league with the Tartars, and should haue peace with them. It is his desire also that they should become great or in fauour with God in heauen, therfore he admonisheth them aswel by vs, as by his own letters, to become Christians, and to embrace the faith of our Lord Iesu Christ, because they could not otherwise be saued. Moreouer, he giues thē to vnderstand, that he much marueileth at their mōstrous slaughters & massacres of mankind, & especially of Christians, but most of al of Hungariās, Mountaineirs, & Polonians, being al his subiects, hauing not iniuried them in ought, nor attempted to doe them iniurie. And because the Lord God is grieuously offended thereat, he aduiseth them from henceforth to beware of such dealing, & to repent them of that which they had done. He requesteth also, that they would write an answere vnto him, what they purpose to doe hereafter, and what their intention is. All which things being heard and vnderstood, the Tartars sayd that they would appoint vs poste horses and a guide vnto Corrensa.

D. THE (PSEUDO-VINCENT) "SPECULUM MORALIA"

38. *The* Summa Theologica *of Thomas Aquinas on Lust*

2a, 2ae, Q. 153, a. 4, concl., trans. Fathers of the English Dominican Province, The "Summa Theologica" of St. Thomas Aquinas (London: Burns, Oates, & Washbourne, Ltd.; New York: Benziger Brothers, Inc., 1915), p. 126.

I answer that, As stated above (Q. CXLVIII., A. 5; I.-II., Q. LXXXIV., AA, 3, 4), a capital vice is one that has a very desirable end, so that through desire for that end, a man proceeds to commit many sins, all of which are said to arise from that vice as from a principal vice. Now the end of lust is venereal pleasure, which is very great. Wherefore this pleasure is very desirable as regards the *sensitive* appetite, both on account of the intensity of the pleasure, and because suchlike concupiscence is connatural to man. Therefore it is evident that lust is a capital vice.

VI. The Literacy of the Artists, Builders and Musicians; Order, Measure and Light; Music, the Dance, and Theology; the Liturgy and the Common Life

A. AUGUSTINE ON MUSIC, "NUMEROSITAS," UNIVERSAL ORDER, AND THE ARTS

39. *His Concept of Musical Order Stated by a Modern Composer*

Reprinted by permission of the publishers from P. Hindemith, A Composer's World (Cambridge, Mass.: Harvard University Press, 1952), p. 4.

Musical order, as recognized and evaluated by our mind, is not an end in itself. It is an image of a higher order which we are permitted to perceive if we proceed one step further to the sixth degree on our scale of musical assimilation: if we put our enjoyment of such knowledge ("enjoyment, the weight of the soul!") into the side of the balance that tends towards the order of the heavens and towards the unification of our soul with the divine principle.

IX-12. Female Figure Symbolizing Lust. *St. Stephen, Auxerre.*

40. *Augustine's* De Musica

Analyzed and summarized by E. Routley, *The Church and Music* (London: Gerald Duckworth and Co., Ltd., 1950), pp. 57–59.

De Musica is written in six books, of which it is only the sixth which need engage our attention. The first five books are, as he explains at the beginning of the sixth, of a merely preparatory nature, written so that the import of the sixth can be made clear to those who have no special training. They deal with the principles of prosody, expounding the principles which lie behind the laws determining the use of short and long syllables in Latin verse. These principles he traces back to the quality of *numerositas,* and we are embarrassed at the outset by the fact that this word and its cognate *numeri,* which we shall continually be meeting, are strictly untranslatable. Music, he says, is the *ars bene modulandi* (the art of the well-ordered), and the quality of that which is *bene modulatus* is *numerositas.* The choice of this word indicates that Augustine accepts the connection which the Greeks established between music and mathematics; but he accepts it (as we may also accept it) not in the sense that music, like mathematics, is basically impersonal and unemotive (which is obviously wrong), but that both music and mathematics are exact forms of expression, matters of delicate adjustment, derived from precise knowledge.

Numerositas is, moreover, a quality of the whole universe, and music in exhibiting it shows itself to be in direct touch with ultimate reality and to be therefore a means of mediating that reality to the hearer. In this conception Augustine is still following closely the teaching which the school of Pythagoras had coined nearly a thousand years before. *Numerositas* is indeed very nearly a Latin translation of the Greek *harmonia.* This quality is diversified in the aesthetic level in certain movements which he calls *numeri,*—movements, as we shall see, which establish the faculty of apprehending music; they are found both in the music and in the hearer. If this explanation is at all adequate, we now ask the reader's permission to leave the word untranslated in the text. Augustine's thought can only be properly followed in the original language, and to translate this key word would be to mislead the reader far more seriously than to leave it as it stands.

The sixth book of *De Musica* opens with an apology for the lengthy treatment of prosody which has gone before. Augustine says that his purpose in the work is frankly to provide a gradual passage from devotion to art to devotion to God. He assumes that the properties of verse are well known to most people, but that the properties of abstract music are not so well known, and that he can reach his goal best by starting along a familiar road. But the transition from the study of prosody to the study of "music" is, as the superscription to Book VI declares, the transition from "the study of the mutable *numeri* which are in earthly things to the immutable *numeri* which are the property of immutable truth." Music is more like immutable truth than poetry, in as much as it is less bound up with matter and with created things. Augustine's declared purpose is:

to separate growing man, or men of any age, not violently but by degrees, from the carnal senses and carnal letters, to which it is so difficult for them not to be attached. Reason must lead them to attach themselves in love and without the interference of nature to the unchanging truth of the one God and Lord of all things who presides over human minds.

418

41. Augustine Defines Music

De Musica, 1:3 (4), trans. R. C. Taliaferro, *Augustine On Music* [*Writings of Saint Augustine*, II] (New York: Fathers of the Church, Inc., 1947), pp. 175–76.

M.   Music is the science of moving well. But that is because whatever moves and keeps harmoniously the measuring of times and intervals can already be said to move well. For it is already pleasing, and for this reason is already properly called mensuration. Yet it is possible for this harmony and measuring to please when they shouldn't. For example, if one should sing sweetly and dance gracefully, wishing thereby to be gay when the ocasion demanded gravity, such a person would in no way be using harmonious mensuration well. In other words, that person uses ill or improperly the motion at one time called good because of its harmony. And so it is one thing to mensurate, and another to mensurate well. For mensuration is thought to be proper to any singer whatever if only he does not err in those measurings of voice and sounds, but good mensuration to be proper to the liberal discipline, that is, to music. Now, even if the motion itself, because it is misplaced, does not seem to you good, even though you admit it is harmonious in construction, yet let us hold to our definition and keep it the same everywhere, not to have a merely verbal battle upset us where the thing itself is clear enough. And let us not bother whether music be described as the science of mensurating or as the science of mensurating well.

42. Augustine on Numerositas, *Numbers, and Harmony*

De Musica, 6:4 (7), trans. Taliaferro, *Augustine On Music*, p. 333.

M.   Why, then, do we hesitate to prefer sounding and corporeal numbers to those made by them, even though they are made in the soul which is better than the body? Because we are preferring numbers to numbers, producers to produced, not the body to the soul. For bodies are the better the more harmonious [*numerosiora*] they are by means of these numbers. But the soul is made better through lack of those numbers it receives through the body, when it turns away from the carnal senses and is reformed by the divine numbers of wisdom. So it is truly said in the Holy Scriptures, 'I have gone the rounds, to know and consider and seek wisdom and number.' And you are in no way to think this was said about those numbers shameful theaters resound with, but about those, I believe, the soul does not receive from the body, but receiving from God on high it rather impresses on the body. And what kind of thing this is, is not to be considered in this place.

43. On the Harmony of Things Celestial and Terrestrial

Ibid., 6:11 (29), p. 355.

(29)   Let's not, then, be envious of things inferior to ourselves, and let us, our Lord and God helping, order ourselves between those below us and those above us, so we are not troubled by lower, and take delight only in higher things. For delight is a kind of weight in the soul. Therefore, delight orders the soul. 'For where your treasure is, there will your heart be also.' Where delight, there the treasure; where the heart, there happiness or misery. But what are the higher things, if not those where the highest unchangeable undisturbed and eternal equality resides? Where there is no time, because there is no change, and from where times are made and ordered and changed, imitating eternity as they do when the turn of the heavens comes back to the same state, and the heavenly bodies to the same place, and in days and months and years and centuries and other revolutions of the stars obey the laws of equality, unity, and order. So terrestrial things are subject to celestial, and their time circuits join together in harmonious succession for a poem of the universe.

44. A Modern Résumé of the Augustinian Synthesis of Music, Architecture, and the Arts

Reprinted with kind permission from Otto von Simson, *The Gothic Cathedral*, Bollingen Series XLVIII (Pantheon Books), Bollingen Foundation, New York, 1956, pp. 22–23.

In the second book of his treatise *On Order*, Augustine describes how reason, in her quest for the blissful contemplation of things divine, turns to music and from music to what lies within the range of vision: beholding earth and heaven, she realizes that only beauty can ever satisfy her, in beauty figures, in figures proportion, and in proportion number.

2. The aesthetic implications are clear. Augustine was nearly as sensitive to architecture as he was to music. They are the only arts he seems to have fully enjoyed; and he recognized them even after his conversion, since he experienced the same transcendental element in both. For him, music and architecture are sisters, since both are children of number; they have equal dignity, inasmuch as architecture mirrors eternal harmony, as music echoes it.

Consistent with this view, Augustine uses architecture, as he does music, to show that number, as apparent in the simpler proportions that are based on the "perfect" ratios, is the source of all aesthetic perfection. And he uses the architect, as he does the musician, to prove that all artistic creation observes the laws of numbers. The architect, if he is a mere practitioner rather than a "scientist" of his art, may be unaware of the fact that he is instinctively applying mathematical rules. No beautiful edifice is conceivable, however, unless these rules have been applied and unless their presence is apparent to the observer.

45. Augustine's Own Summation on the Function of Numbers in the Human Artist and in the Divine Artificer

De Libero Arbitrio, 2:16 (42). The selection from Selections from Medieval Philosophers, Vol. I, pp. 59–60, ed. and trans. by Richard McKeon, is reprinted with the permission of Charles Scribner's Sons © 1929 Charles Scribner's Sons; renewal © 1957.

42. Look upon the sky and the earth and the sea and whatsoever flashes in them or above them or crawls beneath them or flies or swins; they have forms, because they have numbers: take that from them, they will be nothing. Therefore, from what are they, except from number: seeing that being pertains to them in so far as they are numbered? And human artificers too have numbers of all corporeal forms in art, to which they fit their works, and they move their hands and instruments in fashioning, until that which is formed outside is borne back to that light of numbers which is within, and until it can receive its consummation, so far as that is possible, and in order that by way of the interpreting sense it may please that internal judge who gazes upon the heavenly numbers. Ask in the next place, what moves the arms of the artificer himself; it will be a number, for they are moved likewise according to number. And if you withdraw work from the hands, and the intention of fashioning from the soul, and if the motion of the limbs be turned to delight, that will be called a dance. Ask then, what it is that pleases in a dance; number will answer you: Behold it is I. Now look upon the beauty of the formed body; numbers are held fast in place. Look upon the beauty of mobility in the body; numbers are poured forth in time. Go into the art whence these proceed; seek in it time and space; it never will be; nowhere will it be; nevertheless number lives in it: nor is its region of spaces nor its age of days; and yet when they who wish to make themselves artists apply themselves to learning the art, they move their body through places and times, and even their mind through times: certainly with the passage of time they become more skilled. Transcend then the mind of the artist too that you may see the eternal number; then wisdom will flash forth to you from the very interior seat and from the secret place itself of truth; and if that should beat back your still too languid glance, turn the eye of your mind into that way, where wisdom showed itself joyfully. But remember that you have broken the vision which you may seek forth again when you are stronger and sounder.

B. BOETHIUS (c. 480–524) ON THREE KINDS OF MUSIC

46. Universal, Human, and Instrumental Music

De Institutione Musica, 1:2. Reprinted from Source Readings in Music History Selected and Annotated by Oliver Strunk, pp. 84–85, by per-

mission of W. W. Norton & Company, Inc., ©
1950, together with Item 47. Published in London by Faber & Faber, Ltd.

A writer upon music should therefore state at the beginning how many kinds of music those who have investigated the subject are known to have recognized. There are three kinds: the first, the music of the universe; the second, human music; the third, instrumental music, as that of the cithara or the tibiae or the other instruments which serve for melody.

The first, the music of the universe, is especially to be studied in the combining of the elements and the variety of the seasons which are observed in the heavens. How indeed could the swift mechanism of the sky move silently in its course? And although this sound does not reach our ears (as must for many reasons be the case), the extremely rapid motion of such great bodies could not be altogether without sound, especially since the courses of the stars are joined together by such mutual adaptation that nothing more equally compacted or united could be imagined. For some are borne higher and others lower, and all are revolved with a just impulse, and from their different inequalities an established order of their courses may be deduced. For this reason an established order of modulation cannot be lacking in this celestial revolution.

Now unless a certain harmony united the differences and contrary powers of the four elements, how could they form a single body and mechanism? But all this diversity produces the variety of seasons and fruits, and thereby makes the year a unity. Wherefore if you could imagine any one of the factors which produce such a variety removed, all would perish, nor, so to speak, would they retain a vestige of consonance. And just as there is a measure of sound in low strings lest the lowness descend to inaudibility, and a measure of tenseness in high strings lest they be broken by the thinness of the sound, being too tense, and all is congruous and fitting, so we perceive that in the music of the universe nothing can be excessive and destroy some other part by its own excess, but each part brings its own contribution or aids others to bring theirs. For what winter binds, spring releases, summer heats, autumn ripens; and the seasons in turn bring forth their own fruits or help the others to bring forth theirs. These matters will be discussed more searchingly later on.

What human music is, anyone may understand by examining his own nature. For what is that which unites the incorporeal activity of the reason with the body, unless it be a certain mutual adaptation and as it were a tempering of low and high sounds into a single consonance? What else joins together the parts of the soul itself, which in the opinion of Aristotle is a joining to-

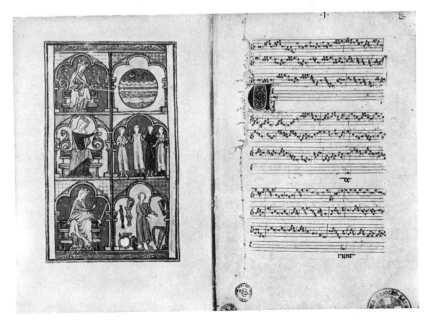

IX-13. Boethian Categories of Music: Universal, Human, and Instrumental.

gether of the rational and the irrational? What causes the blending of the body's elements or holds its parts together in established adaptation? But of this I shall treat later.

The third kind of music is that which is described as residing in certain instruments. This is produced by tension, as in strings, or by blowing, as in the tibiae or in those instruments activated by water, or by some kind of percussion, as in instruments which are struck upon certain bronze concavities, by which means various sounds are produced.

C. CASSIODORUS (C. 485–573) AND THE DISCIPLINE OF MUSIC

47. The Universe Founded and Governed by Music

Institutiones, 1:5 (2), *ibid.*, p. 88.

2. The discipline of music is diffused through all the actions of our life. First, it is found that if we perform the commandments of the Creator and with pure minds obey the rules he has laid down, every word we speak, every pulsation of our veins, is related by musical rhythms to the powers of harmony. Music indeed is the knowledge of apt modulation. If we live virtuously, we are constantly proved to be under its discipline, but when we commit injustice we are without music. The heavens and the earth, indeed all things in them which are directed by a higher power, share in this discipline of music, for Pythagoras attests that this universe was founded by and can be governed by music.

D. SUGER OF ST. DENIS († 1152) AND THE REBUILDING OF THE ABBEY CHURCH

48. The Johannine Gospel, the Martyr St. Denis, and the Neoplatonic Light Philosophy Commemorated in the Great Bronze Doors

De Administratione, 27. This and Items 49 and 50 reprinted with the kind permission of the publishers from the translation of E. Panofsky, ed. and tr., *Abbot Suger On the Abbey Church of St.-Denis and Its Art Treasures* (Princeton,

N. J.: Princeton University Press; London: Oxford University Press © 1946); this item, pp. 47, 49.

Bronze casters having been summoned and sculptors chosen, we set up the main doors on which are represented the Passion of the Saviour and His Resurrection, or rather Ascension, with great cost and much expenditure for their gilding as was fitting for the noble porch. Also [we set up] others, new ones on the right side and the old ones on the left beneath the Mosaic which, though contrary to modern custom, we ordered to be executed there and to be affixed to the tympanum of the portal. We also committed ourselves richly to elaborate the tower[s] and the upper crenelations of the front, both for the beauty of the church and, should circumstances require it, for practical purposes. Further we ordered the year of the consecration, lest it be forgotten, to be inscribed in copper-gilt letters in the following manner:

For the splendor of the church that has fostered
  and exalted him,
Suger has labored for the splendor of the church.
Giving thee a share of what is thine, O Martyr
  Denis,
He prays to thee to pray that he may obtain a
  share of Paradise.
The year was the One Thousand, One Hundred,
  and Fortieth
Year of the Word when [this structure] was
  consecrated.

The verses on the door, further, are these:

Whoever thou art, if thou seekest to extol the
  glory of these doors,
Marvel not at the gold and the expense but at
  the craftsmanship of the work.
Bright is the noble work; but, being nobly
  bright, the work
Should brighten the minds, so that they may
  travel, through the true lights,
To the True Light where Christ is the true door.
In what manner it be inherent in this world the
  golden door defines:
The dull mind rises to truth through that which
  is material
And, in seeing this light, is resurrected from its
  former submersion.

And on the lintel:

IX-14. Twelfth-Century Masonry and Working Costume. Hortus Deliciarum.

Receive, O stern Judge, the prayers of Thy Suger;
Grant that I be mercifully numbered among Thy own sheep.

49. *Sumptuous Receptacles for the Sacred Bodies of Patron Saints*

Ibid., 31, pp. 55, 57.

OF THE GOLDEN ALTAR FRONTAL IN
THE UPPER CHOIR

Into this panel, which stands in front of his most sacred body, we have put, according to our estimate, about forty-two marks of gold; [further] a multifarious wealth of precious gems, hyacinths, rubies, sapphires, emeralds and topazes, and also an array of different large pearls—[a wealth] as great as we had never anticipated to find. You could see how kings, princes, and many outstanding men, following our example, took the rings off the fingers of their hands and ordered, out of love for the Holy Martyrs, that the gold, stones, and precious pearls of the rings be put into that panel. Similarily archbishops and bishops deposited there the very rings of their investiture as though in a place of safety, and offered them devoutly to God and His Saints. And such a crowd of dealers in precious gems flocked in on us from diverse dominions and regions that we did not wish to buy any more than they hastened to sell, with everyone contributing donations. And the verses on this panel are these:

Great Denis, open the door of Paradise
And protect Suger through thy pious guardianship.
Mayest thou, who hast built a new dwelling for thyself through us,
Cause us to be received in the dwelling of Heaven,
And to be sated at the heavenly table instead of at the present one.
That which is signified pleases more than that which signifies.

Since it seemed proper to place the most sacred bodies of our Patron Saints in the upper vault as nobly as we could, and since one of the side-tablets of their most sacred sarcophagus had been torn off on some unknown occasion, we put back fifteen marks of gold and took pains to have gilded its rear side and its superstructure throughout, both below and above, with about forty ounces. Further we caused the actual receptacles of the holy bodies to be enclosed with gilded panels of cast copper and with polished stones, fixed close to the inner stone vaults, and also with continuous gates to hold off disturbances by crowds; in such a manner, however, that reverend persons, as was fitting, might be able to see them with great devotion and a flood of tears. On these sacred tombs, however, there are the following verses:

Where the Heavenly Host keeps watch, the ashes of the Saints

Are implored and bemoaned by the people, [and] the clergy sings in ten-voiced harmony.

To their spirits are submitted the prayers of the devout,

And if they please them their evil deeds are forgiven.

Here the bodies of the Saints are laid to rest in peace;

May they draw us after them, us who beseech them with fervent prayer.

This place exists as an outstanding asylum for those who come;

Here is safe refuge for the accused, here the avenger is powerless against them.

50. The Procession and Rites Accompanying the Translation of the Sacred Relics of the Patron Saints

De Consecratione, 7, *ibid.,* pp. 115, 117, 119, 121.

When the mysteries of the holy consecration had been performed in proper

IX-15. Abbey Church of St. Denis, Central Portal.

manner we proceeded to the translation of the sacred Relics and approached the ancient and venerable tombs of our Patron Saints; for thus far they had not been moved from their place. After prostrations, the pontiffs as well as our Lord the King, and all of us so far as we could in view of the narrowness of the room, inspected—when it had been opened—the venerable shrines, executed under King Dagobert, which contained their most sacred bodies dear to God; chanted and wept with immeasurable joy; and said, inviting a king as devout as humble:

Come, help thyself with thy own hands to carry hither our Lord, Apostle and Protector, so that we may revere the most sacred ashes, embrace the most sacred urns, rejoice throughout our lives at having received and held them. For these are the holy men who gave over their bodies as a testimony to God; who for our salvation, burning with the fire of charity, left their land and kin; who with apostolic authority taught the faith of Jesus Christ to all Gaul; who fought for Him like men; who, naked, conquered scourges and, fettered, [conquered] wild and famished beasts; who sustained, unscathed, extension on the rack and the fire of the furnace, and finally blissful decapitation by blunted axes. Onward, then, Most Christian King, let us receive him who will receive us, our blessed Denis, humbly entreating him to pray for us to Him who promised truthfully; the love and benevolence which thou hast will always obtain its end for whomsoever thou wilt pray.

Forthwith muscles are moved, arms are thrust out, so many and so important hands are extended that not even the seventh hand was able to reach the sacred shrines themselves. Therefore, our Lord the King himself, injecting himself into their midst, received the silver chasse of our special Patron from the hand of the bishops—I believe, from the hand of the Archbishops of Reims and Sens, the Bishop of Chartres and others —and led the way out as devoutly as nobly. A marvel to behold! never could anyone see such a procession, apart from that which had been seen on the occasion of the old consecration by the Heavenly Host: when the bodies of the holy martyrs and confessors, out of the draped tents and on the shoulders and necks of bishops, counts and barons, went forth to meet the most holy Denis and his Companions at the ivory door; when [those in the procession] proceeded through the cloisters with candlesticks, crosses and other festive ornaments and with many odes and hymns; when they carried their Patrons amicably yet, for joy, weepingly. No greater joy in the world could ever have exalted them.

When the [procession] had returned to the church and had ascended by the stairs to the upper altar, destined for the rest of the Saints (while the Relics of the Saints had been deposited on the old altar) the rites were performed at the new main altar which was to be consecrated in front of their new tomb; the consecration of this [new main altar] we entrusted to the Lord Archbishop of Reims, Samson. The rites were also splendidly and solemnly performed at the other twenty altars that were to be consecrated. . . .

After the consecration of the altars all these [dignitaries] performed a solemn celebration of Masses, both in the upper choir and in the crypt, so festively, so solemnly, so different and yet so concordantly, so close [to one another] and so joyfully that their song, delightful by its consonance and unified harmony, was deemed a symphony angelic rather than human; and that all exclaimed with heart and mouth:

Blessed be the glory of the Lord from His place. Blessed and *worthy of praise and exalted above all* be Thy name, Lord Jesus Christ, Whom God Thy Father has anointed the Highest Priest with the oil of exultation above Thy fellows. By this sacramental unction with the most holy chrism and by the susception of the most holy Eucharist, Thou uniformly conjoinest the material with the immaterial, the corporeal with the spiritual, the human with the Divine, and sacramentally reformest the purer ones to their original condition. By these and similar visible blessings, Thou invisibly restorest and miraculously transformest the present [state] into the Heavenly Kingdom. Thus, when Thou *shalt have delivered up the kingdom to God, even the Father,* mayest Thou powerfully and mercifully make us and the nature of the angels, Heaven and earth, into one State; Thou Who *livest and reignest* as God *for ever and ever.* Amen.

E. JOHN OF SALISBURY († 1180) ON THE ARTS AND MUSIC

51. *The Legitimate Uses of Music and Its Abuses in the Later Service of the Church*

Policraticus, 1:6, Reprinted with the kind permission of the publishers from J. P. Pike, trans. *Frivolities of Courtiers and Footprints of Philosophers; Being a Translation of the First, Second, and Third Books and Selections from the Seventh and Eighth Books of the Policraticus of John of Salisbury* (Minneapolis: The University of Minnesota Press, 1938; London: Oxford University Press), pp. 30, 32.

One should not slander music by charging it with being an ally of the frivolities of courtiers, although many frivolous individuals endeavor by its help to advance their own interests. Music is indeed one of the liberal arts and it has an honorable origin whether it claims Pythagoras, Moses, or Tubal, the father of those who play upon the harp, as the author of its being. Because of the great power exercised by it, its many forms, and the harmonies that serve it, it embraces the universe; that is to say, it reconciles the clashing and dissonant relations of all that exists and of all that is thought and expressed in words by a sort of ever varying but still harmonious law derived from its own symmetry. By it the phenomena of the heavens are ruled and the activities of the world and men are governed. Its instruments form and fashion conduct and, by a kind of miracle of nature, clothe with melodies and colorful forms of rhymes and measures the tone of the voice, whether expressed in words or not, and adorn them as with a robe of beauty.

To add our own testimony, the Fathers of the Church have highly praised music. Finally, by virtue of it the violence of the evil spirit is controlled, and thanks to it his power over his own subjects [40] is weakened. . . . The singing of love songs in the presence of men of eminence was once considered in bad taste, but now it is considered praiseworthy for men of greater eminence to sing and play love songs which they themselves with greater propriety call *stulticinia,* follies.

The very service of the Church is defiled,

425

in that before the face of the Lord, in the very sanctuary of sanctuaries, they, showing off [42] as it were, strive with the effeminate dalliance of wanton tones and musical phrasing to astound, enervate, and dwarf simple souls. When one hears the excessively caressing melodies of voices beginning, chiming in, carrying the air, dying away, rising again, and dominating, he may well believe that it is the song of the sirens and not the sound of men's voices; he may marvel at the flexibility of tone which neither the nightingale, the parrot, or any bird with greater range than these can rival. Such indeed is the ease of running up or down the scale, such the dividing or doubling of the notes and the repetitions of the phrases and their incorporation one by one; the high and very high notes are so tempered with low or somewhat low that one's very ears lose the ability to discriminate, and the mind, soothed by such sweetness, no longer has power to pass judgment upon what it hears. When this type of music is carried to the extreme it is more likely to stir lascivious sensations in the loins than devotion in the heart. But if it be kept within reasonable limits it frees the mind from care, banishes worry about things temporal, and by imparting joy and peace and by inspiring a deep love for God draws souls to association with the angels.

F. ADAM OF ST. VICTOR († c. 1175/85) AND HIS SEQUENCES

52. *Sequences for St. Stephen's Day*

Trans. J. M. Neale, *Medieval Hymns and Sequences* (London: J. Masters, 1851).

Yesterday, with exultation
Joined the world in celebration
    Of her promised Saviour's birth;
Yesterday the Angel nation
Poured the strains of jubilation
    O'er the Monarch born on earth.

But to-day, o'er death victorious,
By his faith and actions glorious,
    By his miracles renowned,
Dared the Deacon Protomartyr
Earthly life for heaven to barter,
    Faithful midst the faithless found.

. . . . .

Forward, champion, in thy quarrel!
Certain of a certain laurel,
    Holy Stephen, persevere!
Perjured witnesses confound,
Satan's synagogue astound
    By thy doctrine true and clear.

Lo! in heaven thy Witness liveth:
Bright and faithful proof he giveth
    Of his martyr's blamelessness:
Thou by name a 'Crown' impliest;
Meetly then in pangs thou diest
    For the Crown of Righteousness!

For a crown that fadeth never,
Bear the torturer's brief endeavour;
    Victory waits to end the strife:
Death shall be thy birth's beginning,
And life's losing be the winning
    Of the true and better life.

Whom the Holy Ghost endueth,
Whom celestial sight embueth,
    Stephen penetrates the skies;
There God's fullest glory views,
There his victor strength renews,
    For his near reward he sighs.

See, as Jewish foes invade thee,
See how Jesus stands to aid thee,
    Stands to guard his champion's death:
Cry that opened heaven is shown thee:
Cry that Jesus waits to own thee:
    Cry it with thy latest breath!

G. ROBERT GROSSETESTE (1175–1253) ON THE MINISTRY OF THE LIBERAL ARTS; MUSIC, ORDER AND LIGHT; GEOMETRY, LINES, ANGLES, AND FIGURES

53. *Without Geometry, Neither Science nor Beauty; without Music, Neither Proportion nor Knowledge*

A Free adaptation by the editor from *De artibus liberalibus*, as edited in L. Baur, *Die philosophischen Werke des Robert Grosseteste, Bischofs von Lincoln Beiträge zur Geschichte der Philosophie des Mittelalters*, IX (Münster i/W, 1912), pp. 1–7, and as analyzed in E. De Bruyne, *Études d'esthétique médiévale* (Brugge, 1946), III, pp. 145ff.

The core of Grosseteste's thought on proportions, universal harmony, and music may be reconstructed from his work, *On the Liberal Arts*, and from his treatise, *On Lines, Angles, and Figures*. He realistically assesses human frailty and finds in the liberal disciplines the regimen that purges errors and supplies defects. Maximal importance is attached to the consideration of lines, angles, and figures. The knowledge of natural philosophy is impossible without recourse to geometrical principles. Without geometry there is neither knowledge nor beauty. Likewise, where music is lacking proportion and knowledge are absent. When our concern is not only with the effects of bodily movement but also with the ordering of those movements themselves, we turn to music which is their harmonious organizer and governor (*modificatrix*). Music scrutinizes proportion in all movement. In the lilt of the song that is heard and in the swirling color of the dance that is seen, music amplifies the heart-beat of the universe. Musical inquiry, therefore, concerns itself with the proportions of the human voice and the rhythmic gesticulations of the human body, as well as the sounds and movements of other bodies. Attention is also levied upon musical instruments, their charming potentials with regard to sound and movement, and their relation, together with other musical media, to heavenly and non-celestial harmonies. That is, music inspires and records the heard melodies of our world. It also dictates and reproduces the language of astral spaces and times. From heavenly movements come earthly harmonies. Musical speculation is indispensable if the proportions of times and seasons as well as the make-up of the elements of this lower world are to be known, together with the composition of all other elements. Musical pleasure as well as the ethical effects of music are fit subjects for investigation. Music, no less than medicine, ministers to and orders the spirit of man. Its therapy serves body and mind alike. The soul follows the body in its passions. The body follows the soul in its actions. The wise man apprehends the concord that reigns between the physical and the psychical. The same proportions rule the rhythms of sounds and souls. The spirit of man expands in joy and shrivels in sorrow. He who can induce instrumental rhythms can strum upon man's heart strings. He can change the state of souls almost at will.

54. The Blending of Aesthetics, Harmony, and Light

Reprinted by kind permission from Otto von Simson, *The Gothic Cathedral*. Bollingen Series XLVIII (Pantheon Books), Bollingen Foundation, New York, 1956, pp. 198–99.

One may add that Grosseteste also offers the metaphysical confirmation of the Gothic tendency to blend the aesthetics of harmony and "musical" proportions with that of light. The beauty of light, he maintains, is due to its simplicity, by which light is, like unison in music, "ad se per aequalitatem concordissime proportionata" ("most harmoniously related to itself by the ratio of equality").

H. VILLARD DE HONNECOURT AND HIS "ALBUM" (C. 1250): ABSTRACT GEOMETRY, PORTRAITURE, MUSICAL CHURCHES, AND SCHOLASTIC ARCHITECTURE

55. The Gothic Builder and His Exposure to the Scholastic Point of View

From E. Panofsky, *Gothic Architecture and Scholasticism* (Latrobe, Pa.: The Archabbey Press, 1951), pp. 23–24.

It is not very probable that the builders of Gothic structures read Gilbert de la Porrée or Thomas Aquinas in the original. But they were exposed to the Scholastic point of view in innumerable other ways, quite apart from the fact that their own work automatically brought them into a working association with those who devised the liturgical and iconographic programs. They had gone to school; they listened to sermons; they could attend the public *disputationes de quolibet* which, dealing as they did with all imaginable questions of the day, had developed into social events not unlike our operas, concerts, or public lectures; and they could come into profitable contact with the learned on many other occasions. The very fact that neither the natural sciences nor the humanities nor even mathematics had evolved their special esoteric methods and terminologies kept the

IX-16. Tomb of Hugh Libergier († 1263). *Architect of St. Nicaise at Rheims, Rheims Cathedral.*

sheer abstractions, like the head in plate 35 [Fig. IX–20] of the *Album* which initiates his discussion of "portraiture." The character of facial details, coupled with the absence of relief or model, clearly indicates a process of reducing material forms in accord with general principles. Later sarcasms at his expense based on "unrealistic" lions and his defective drawings so lacking in "naturalness" and draughtsman's accuracy are quite beside the point. It is enough that his lines let one know or recognize what he was dealing with. His geometric schematizations, therefore, have a definitely abstract character. They follow rules and establish norms whose reality tolerates ramifications within recognized limits. Figure 38 [Fig. IX–21] of the *Album*, with its straight lines and squares, establishes an approximate character for the tracery of facial outlines, with variations from the ideal rectangle of the human body. What Honnecourt thinks as an artist is, moreover, perfectly in keeping with the philosophic premises of his contemporaries. His geometric postulates correspond to formal essences or to the quiddities of species. Just as those permit distinctive individuation so these allow for countless fluctuations.

whole of human knowledge within the range of the normal, non-specialized intellect; and —perhaps the most important point—the entire social system was rapidly changing toward an urban professionalism. Not as yet hardened into the later guild and "Bauhütten" systems, it provided a meeting ground where the priest and the layman, the poet and the lawyer, the scholar and the artisan could get together on terms of near-equality.

56. The Abstract Character of Portraiture and Geometry Schematized

A résumé by the editor. Cf. De Bruyne, *op. cit.*, pp. 256–57.

Villard designs from an intellectual rather than a visual outlook. Perspective is a matter of mind or idea. His "portraits" are

57. How to Make a Lectern or Reading Desk

Album, text for Pl. 13, fol. 7, adapted from R. Willis, *Facsimile of the Sketch-Book of Wilars de Honecort* (London: Parker, 1859), p. 45.

" 'Whoever desires to make a lectern to read the Gospel from, will see here the best form which I construct. Three serpents rest on the ground, and upon them is fixed a plank in the form of a trefoil. On this rest three serpents in a different direction, with columns of the same height as those serpents, and above is a triangle. Over all you see how perfect is the form of the lectern of which you have the portrait. In the middle of the three columns there must be a stem to carry the pummel upon which the eagle is placed.' "

428

58. Building a Church on the Square

Ibid., text for Pl. 28, fol. 14v, p. 80.

"This is a square church which was designed for the Cistercian Order."

59. The Church Laid out on the Square (Ad quadratum): the Ideal Musical Form of the Cistercian Church

De Bruyne, op. cit., III, 257 and I, 22–23 with permission from Simson, op. cit., p. 199.

[De Bruyne notes that the ideal form of the Cistercian church is musical. It follows the fundamental rules of Boethius' aesthetics. A remarkable unity pervades the initial proportions: 1:1 is the square; 2:4, the double square; 3:4 and 4:5, the first rectangle, parta altera longiores. Simson observes that the basic unit from which all proportions are drawn is the square bay of the side aisles.]

. . . . . .

And these proportions, as Professor de Bruyne observes, correspond in each case to the ratios of the musical consonances, the same ratios that, as we have seen, were actually employed by the Cistercian builders. Thus the length of the church is related to the transept in the ratio of the fifth (2:3). The octave ratio (1:2) determines the relations between side aisle and nave, length and width of the transept, and, we may assume on the basis of Cistercian practice, of the interior elevation as well. The 3:4 ratio of the choir evokes the musical fourth; the 4:5 ratio of nave and side aisles taken as a unit corresponds to the third; while the crossing, liturgically and aesthetically the center of the church, is based on the 1:1 ratio of unison, most perfect of consonances.

60. Scholastic Disputation and the Sic et non Applied to Architecture

Album, text for Pl. 29, fol. 15, adapted from Willis, Facsimile, p. 91; quoted from Panofsky, Gothic Architecture and Scholasticism, pp. 87–88.

"Istud bresbiteriu' invener't ulardus d'hunecort & petrus de corbeia ī̃ se disputando."

"Above is (the presbytery of) a church with

IX-17. Making a Lectern. Honnecourt's Album.

IX-18. Building a Church on the Square. Honnecourt's Album.

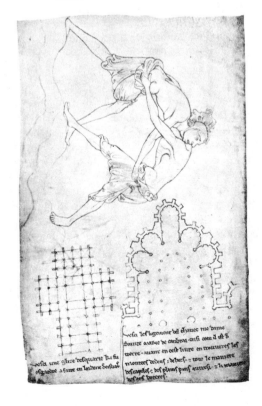

IX-19. Scholastic Disputation and the *Sic et Non.*
Honnecourt's Album.

a double circumscribing aisle, which Wilars de
Honecort and Peter de Corbie contrived together."

. . . . .

There is one scrap of evidence—well
known, to be sure, but not as yet considered
in this particular light—which shows that at
least some of the French thirteenth-century
architects did think and act in strictly Scholastic terms. In Villard de Honnecourt's
"Album" there is to be found the groundplan
of an "ideal" chevet which he and another
master, Pierre de Corbie, had devised, according to the slightly later inscription, *inter
se disputando.* Here, then, we have two
High Gothic architects discussing a *quaestio,*
and a third one referring to this discussion
by the specifically Scholastic term *disputare*
instead of *colloqui, deliberare,* or the like.
And what is the result of this *disputatio?* A

430

chevet which combines, as it were, all possible *Sics* with all possible *Nons.*

61. *The* Album *on Portraiture, Masonry,
and the Art of Geometry*

Album, text and commentary for Pl. 35, fol. 18,
adapted from M. Quicherat and R. Willis, *Facsimile,* pp. 109–110ff.

"Here begin the elements of portraiture."
"Here begin the powers of the lines of portraiture for facilitating work, as taught by the
art of geometry. On the other leaf will be those
of masonry."

. . . . .

This art of geometry has been admirably
characterized by M. Quicherat as follows:—

It would be extremely difficult to give a precise definition of this method, so arbitrary is it
in application. The process consists either in reducing human forms to simple lines, or in reducing the representations of human or animal figures to elementary forms, such as triangles or
squares set in juxtaposition. All this is done
without calculation or principle, so that geometry has no other office than to furnish the forms
and nomenclature of a very questionable ap-
proximation. The processes in question teach,
not a science of drawing, but a mere art of readily reproducing certain attitudes, by merely retaining in the memory the simple geometrical
figures which are respectively associated with
them. Thus, eye and hand would become the
slaves of habits which, because they dispense
with the study of nature, make drawing easy,
according to the boast of Wilars de Honecort.
The matière de portraiture is, in truth, a mere
routine, and the drawings are a set of patterns
for a certain number of selected subjects. But it
is remarkable that the peculiar attitudes and
aspects produced by this method are precisely
those which characterize the works of the painters and sculptors of the thirteenth century.

62. *The* Album *and Geometric Abstraction
Applied to the Human Head*

Album, text for Pl. 38, fol. 19v° from Willis,
Facsimile, p. 110, with brief editorial résumé
via De Bruyne, *Études esthétique,* III, p. 259;
cf. Simson, *Gothic Cathedral,* p. 198, n. 46.

"In these four pages are figures of the art of
geometry; but to understand them great attention must be given by any one who would comprehend the peculiar use of each."

. . . . .

In figure 38 [Fig. IX–21] of his *Album*, Honnecourt sets forth the basics of his plastic theory. The process of dimidiation, or of halving the square, gives him the fundamental geometry of the human head. The face is approximately three times as high and twice as wide as the nose. One length of the nose needs to be added for the skull and another for the neck. A reminder of the head drawn "according to true measure" and of the whole Villardian system is found in a head of Christ from a Rheims Cathedral window.

63. The Album *on the Flying Buttress of Rheims Cathedral*

Album, text for Pl. 64, fol. 32v° from Willis, *Facsimile*, p. 235.

This page gives the section of the apsidal wall of the Cathedral of Rheims above the level of the chapels, with a lateral view of the double flying-buttresses, and of the great isolated piers which receive them.

I. ROGER BACON († 1294) ON MUSIC, THE DANCE, AND THEOLOGY

64. A Free Editorial Adaptation from the Opus Tertium

Caps. 59–60, 71–74, with the aid of De Bruyne, *Études esthétique,* III, pp. 234–38, especially.

Roger Bacon followed Master Robert of Lincoln in much of his musical theory as well as at numerous other points. Bacon gives the *Quadrivium* the nod over the *Trivium*. Music is the fundamental art. Without it, Grammar and the other disciplines of the *Trivium* remain unknown. Bacon pursues both sonority and harmony. He rises to instrumental appeal. He vibrates to the chanting of human voices. In plastic music he sees as well as hears the language of gestures, the eloquence of bodily movement, the throbbing insinuations of the soul-intoxicating dance. Complete aesthetic delight waits upon the union of the aural and the visual. Theologians, especially, ought to know what is involved here. They should

IX-20. Elements of Portraiture and the Art of Geometry. *Honnecourt's* Album.

IX-21. Geometric Abstraction and the Human Head. *Honnecourt's* Album.

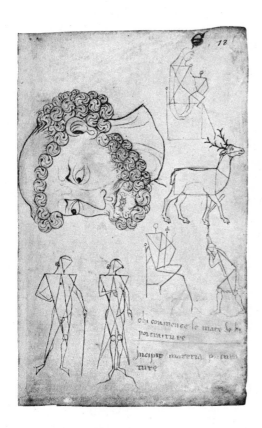

IX-22. Flying Buttresses of Rheims Cathedral.

virility of harmony as well as true suavity. Sheer sonics are anathema. Rustic clangor and the cult of cacophony are disparaged. Perish the sight and sound of "bumps" and "grinds"; also pelvic gyrations full of lubricity and slithering, gliding insinuations! Church and society invite the measured strength of sound that caresses the ears and sweetly elevates the mind to celestial things.

All too prevalent in Bacon's day were harmonic curiosities and sensuous effusiveness. He felt that integrity in music and liturgy was well-nigh gone. Denatured falsettos and male sopranos shamefully drowned out the virile harmonies of sacred music with their effeminate voices. Yet music remained richly potential for the edifying growth of the Christian people. No way ever had led to soul discipline more effectively than that coming through the ears. The church in her chants had a glorious heritage. The Holy Spirit, himself "Master of the Church," invited to enharmonic song. Under noble auspices music had been known to reform morals, quiet the inebriate, preserve health, cure the sick and conduce to restful slumber.

Bacon notes that music makes the spirit gay so that the whole body is comforted with the solace of the mind. In singing the entire nervous system is invigorated. All the veins are dilated so that corrupt vapors are exhaled and the restorative air is inspirited. Testimonies are legion apropos music's sleep-inducing powers and its exorcism of confused dreams.

seek out the reasons of things musical. Theoretical music must serve theological knowledge, that is, practical music. Music must serve the moral and the mystical life as well. Utter delight felt in the heart of man is a sudden and unpredictable ravishment springing out of the beauty of rhythms and meters. This ineffable experience invades the soul suddenly and transports it into the pure regions of truth and everlasting joy.

Roger has definite if unoriginal ideas on the subject of harmony. There are three kinds. The diatonic is spirited, hard, bold, fierce, savage. The chromatic is lascivious, dissolute, soft. The enharmonic is virile and steady, and the church's clear preference. The church and mature society rule out violence and womanish softness. They proscribe the ventral agitations of crude song. Nor can they condone the constricting influences of rude melody. They exalt the

J. POPE JOHN XXII AND THE NEW MUSIC (1325)

65. On the "Ars Nova" and the Prohibition of New Musical Devices; the Rules for Proper Musical Usage

Trans. E. Routley, *The Church and Music* (London: Gerald Duckworth & Co., Ltd., 1950), pp. 241–42.

The learned authority of the Fathers of the Church directs that in the observances of divine praise which we offer in the discharge of our rightful service we may require of the worshipper an alert mind, of the speaker uninterrupted discourse, and of the singers a modest demeanour which expresses itself in grave and serene music. The Lord's song in their mouths sounded graciously; indeed, when musicians so sing and utter their words that God is extolled in the heart and devotion to Him is kindled, the song cannot but be gracious. For this reason it is laid down that for the better devotion of the faithful there shall be psalmody in the church of God.

To this end, let priests and people sing the services of morning and evening, and the celebrations of the Mass, reverently, clearly, and to suitable music, finding their delight in good enunciation and their full satisfaction in musical propriety.

But there is a new school, whose disciples, observing with care the regularity of musical time-values, concern themselves with new devices, preferring their new inventions to the ancient songs of the church; by their practices the music of the liturgies is disordered with semibreves, minims, and even shorter notes. They break up the melodies with hockets, they embellish them with discants; sometimes they so force them out of shape with 'triples' and other music proper to profane occasions that the principles of the antiphonary and the gradual are wholly neglected. They forget on what they are building; they so disguise the melody that it becomes indistinguishable; indeed the multitude of notes is so confusing that the seemly rise and decorous fall of the plainsong melody, which should be the distinguishing feature of the music, is entirely obscured. They run and will not rest, they inebriate the ears without soothing them; the conduct of the singers is so appropriate to their matter that decent devotion is held in contempt and a reprehensible frivolity is paraded for admiration. Boethius is right when he says that the frivolous mind is either delighted by hearing frivolous music or by the habit of attending to it is emasculated and corrupted.

Therefore we and our brethren have long held that this required correction. We hasten to banish and eradicate this thing from the church of God. We will use all our power to destroy it. On the advice, then of our brethren we emphatically enjoin that from this time no one shall presume to make use of such material, or any similar material, in the offices we have mentioned, especially during the canonical hours or in celebrating the solemnities of the Mass. If any disobey he shall be punished according to this canon by eight days' suspension from office. This punishment shall be administered either by the ordinaries in the place where the offence was committed or, where it is not a matter involving deprivation of office, by their deputies; where deprivation is involved it shall be administered by the President or approved officer in whose hands the punishment of such offences and excesses shall be deemed to lie most fitly or by their deputies.

In this we do not mean to prohibit the use of harmony occasionally on festive days either in the celebration of the Mass or in the divine offices; we approve such harmony as follows the melody at the intervals, for example, of the octave, fifth, and fourth, and such harmony as may be supported by the simple chant of the church; but we prescribe this condition, that the integrity of the chant itself remain undamaged, and that no well-established piece of music is altered as under this authority. Such harmonies as fulfil these conditions we hold to be soothing to the ear, conducive to devotion, and a safeguard against inattention in the minds of those who sing psalms to God.

K. GUILLAUME DE MACHAUT († 1377) AND THE "NEW ART" (ARS NOVA); MUSIC, POETRY, AND THE CHURCH

66. An Editorial Résumé of Machaut's Contribution in Relation to His Age

Guillaume de Machaut (c. 1300–c. 1377) was priest and poet, scholar and musician. At one time he was a canon of Rheims Cathedral. One of the few outstanding composers of the fourteenth century, he was perhaps the first great one in the Western tradition. He served the colorful King John of Bohemia in secretarial capacity and chivalric adventures. The Duchess of Normandy and Charles V of Navarre also enjoyed his loyalty. He composed works both secular and sacred, presumably including a coronation mass for Charles V as well as the first in polyphonic form. He wrote both the words and the music for his own songs. Spiritually and materially he contributed to the New Art (*Ars Nova*) with its liberation in style from the old rhythmic modes and from the Old Art (*Ars Antiqua*). His own adventurous experience doubtless helped fit him for the espousal of the new music, the emergence of which the troubadours may well have facilitated.

Machaut won poetic distinction in a chivalric age. His "Remède de Fortune" opens a window into the morals and customs of fourteenth-century feudalism. The last part of it gives a participant's account of the dances in which he joined lords and fair ladies—his own lady love among them. One such dance took place in the open air in a kind of park, close by a château. In lieu of instruments the dancers provided accompaniment in turn, with Machaut intoning a kind of virelai. Rondeaus and other chansons were employed. In this bucolic round dance, the participants held hands as they moved in a circle, much as the accompanying plate shows them doing. Before repairing to the château to regale the company with adventurous amours, among others, Machaut stops

to participate in the mass at a beautiful sylvan chapel. Painted in gold by the hand of a master, the little chapel is tastefully elegant in its unsurpassed colors. Guillaume makes his devotions with due supplication for himself in the toils of love and for his dame. He prays that he may be found worthy for her service in everything touching the perfection of her honor in body and soul:

> That she might have held as reasonable
> My little service acceptable
> This was the end of my prayer.

The mass concluded, a trumpet is heard sounding. The chamberlain now gives the order to prepare the repast. The poet details the functions of each servant, how the valets prepare their masters, and the persiflage of an international company. The gentlemen meanwhile leave, removed their "corsets," and replaced them with more comfortable, loose-fitting apparel. The company is now gathered into the banquet hall. See Figs. IX–24 and IX–26. At meal's end an orchestra appears, as described by Machaut in Item 67—one of the most interesting, if all too brief, medieval accounts. To the sound of the music they do an "estampie"—a kind of "stomp"—in which the cadences are rhyth-

IX-23. A Round Dance. *Miniature from Guillaume de Machaut's* Remède de Fortune.

mically accented by the stamping of the feet. Then, grouped by twos and threes, the convivialists gather in a game room where they play, dance, and sing to the accompaniment of experienced musicians. This goes on until a knight comes to announce wine and spiced goodies. One eats and drinks and finally takes leave of his hostess in the afternoon.

In this long poem, the eyewitness account of chivalric life in its most fascinating, everyday course unfolds—including the role of the arts, music, and good living, à la mode. However sophisticated this churchman may be in his blending of the troubadour's art and the idiom of the *Ars Nova*, Machaut maintains a style all his own. The first extant setting for the text of the Mass written by one man is also his—the Mass of our Lady. One of his motets for the virgin is partly translated and illustrated in Item 68 and Fig. IX–25. His share in the fusing of devotion and the common life remarked throughout Chapter IX is further emphasized in recordings of his secular and ecclesiastical compositions catalogued in Schwann. In the *American Record Guide*, XXIV, 10 (June, 1958), pp. 922ff., there is an excellent, very readable article by John W. Barker, "The Ars Nova and the Late Middle Ages, A 'New Deal' in Old Music," with a critical evaluation of Machaut and his phonographic listings.

67. *Machaut and the Fourteenth-Century Orchestra*

Via the Remède de Fortune," *Oeuvres*, E. Hoepffner, ed. (Paris: Firmin Didot, 1911), from *The Portable Medieval Reader* ed. James Bruce Ross and Mary Martin McLaughlin (New York: The Viking Press, Inc., 1949), pp. 560–61. Reprinted by permission.

Afterwards all came into the hall which was not ugly or dull, where each was, in my opinion, honoured and served both with wine and meat as his body and appetite demanded. And there I took my sustenance by looking at the countenance, the condition, the carriage, and the bearing of her in whom is all my joy. But here come the musicians after eating, without mishap, combed and dressed up! There they made many different harmonies. For I saw there all in one circle viol, rebec, gittern, lute, micanon, citole, and the psaltery, harp, tabor, trumpets, nakers, organs, horns, more than ten pairs, bagpipes [*cornemuses*], flutes [*flajos*], bagpipes [*chevrettes*], krumhorns, cymbals, bells, timbrel, the Bohemian flute [*la flaüste brehaingne*], and the big German cornet, flutes [*flajos de saus*], flute [*fistule*], pipe, bagpipe [*muse d'Aussay*], little trumpet, buzines, panpipes, monochord where there is only one string, and bagpipe [*muse de blef*] all together. And certainly, it seems to me that such a melody was never seen or heard, for each of them, according to the tune of his instrument, without discord, viol, gittern, citole, harp, trumpet, horn, flute, pipe, bellows [?*souffle*], bagpipe, nakers, tabor, and whatever one can do with finger, feather, and bow, I have seen and heard on this floor.

68. *Machaut and His Motet on the Virgin*

Felix virgo-Inviolata genetrix . . . , Reprinted from *The Notation of Medieval Music* by Carl Parrish. By permission of W. W. Norton & Company, Inc. © 1957, pp. 217–18. Published in London by Faber and Faber, Ltd. Used by permission of Laurence Pollinger, Ltd., London.

Blessed virgin, mother of Christ,
Who brought joy to the unhappy world
By thy birth-giving,
    Sweetest one;
Thus thou didst destroy heresies
When thou hadst faith in the angel,
And bore a son,
    Purest one.
Implore thy son, most pious maid,
That he may drive away the many evils
And many torments
    Which we suffer;
For, from being the most favored people,
Most splendid light of light,
From the heights to the depths
    We have been led.
We are deprived of all good things,
We are pursued by the wicked,
Through whom we are subjected
    To the yoke of slavery.
For, as if blind, we stray,
Nor do we follow our guide,
But are diverted from paths
    Which are safe for us.

Source of grace and virtue,
Our only hope of safety, have pity on us,
For we are forsaken,
    And help us,
So that freed from guilt, and led into the right
    way,
And with our enemies destroyed,
    Peace with rejoicing may be with us.

Stainless mother,
Victress free from pride,
    Thou gavest birth gladly;
Keeper of the court of heaven
Who lends ear to the sorrowing,
    Star of the sea,
Who, as a mother, consoles
And prays for the fallen,
    Humbly;

Matchless fount of grace
Who rules over the angels,
    Swiftly
Prepare for us a safe journey,
And aid us valiantly,
    For we are dying.
We are assailed by enemies,
And we defend ourselves weakly,
    And we do not know
Whither we can turn,
Nor through whom we can be saved
    Unless through thee.
As, therefore we beg
That beneath thy wings we may abide;
    O turn us back towards thee.
For thee we long, sighing and lamenting.

L. THE "DIES IRAE" (OF THOMAS OF CELANO?); SEQUENCE FOR THE BURIAL OF THE DEAD; LATER USE IN CHERUBINI'S AND BERLIOZ' "REQUIEM"

69. *Day of Wrath! O Day of Mourning!*

Dies Irae, trans. Dr. W. J. Irons (1848).

Day of wrath! O Day of mourning!
See fulfilled the prophet's warning,
Heaven and earth in ashes burning!

O what fear man's bosom rendeth,
When from heaven the Judge descendeth,
On whose sentence all dependeth!

Woundrous sound the trumpet flingeth,
Through earth's sepulchres it ringeth,
All before the throne it bringeth!

Death is struck, and nature quaking,
All creation is awaking,
To its Judge an answer making!

Lo, the book, exactly worded!
Wherein all hath been recorded;
Thence shall judgment be awarded.

When the Judge his seat attaineth,
And each hidden deed arraigneth,
Nothing unavenged remaineth.

What shall I, frail man, be pleading,
Who for me be interceding,
When the just are mercy needing?

IX-24. Table Music. *Miniature from Guillaume de Machaut's* Remède de Fortune.

436

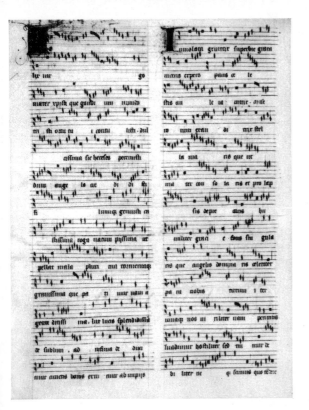

IX-25. **Notation and Text.** *Motet from* Felix Virgo *by Guillaume de Machaut.*

King of majesty tremendous,
Who dost free salvation send us,
Fount of pity! then befriend us!

Think! kind Jesu, my salvation
Caused thy wondrous incarnation;
Leave me not to reprobation!

Faint and weary thou hast sought me,
On the cross of suffering bought me;
Shall such grace be vainly brought me?

Righteous Judge! for sin's pollution
Grant thy gift of absolution,
Ere that day of retribution!

IX-26. **A Banquet, 1377.** *Miniature,* Grandes Chroniques de France.

IX-27 and IX-28. General Resurrection. *Top: Dead rising from their tombs; trumpeting angel followed by saints. Bottom: Bodies of dead disgorged by animals; angel rolling up the heavens like a scroll.* Hortus Deliciarum.

Guilty, now I pour my moaning,
All my shame with anguish owning;
Spare, O God, thy suppliant, groaning!

Thou the sinful woman savedst,
Thou the dying thief forgavest;
And to me a hope vouchsafest!

Worthless are my prayers and sighing,
Yet, good Lord, in grace complying,
Rescue me from fires undying!

With thy favored sheep, O place me!
Nor among the goats abase me;
But to thy right hand upraise me.

While the wicked are confounded,
Doomed to flames of woe unbounded,
Call me! with thy saints surrounded.

Low I kneel, with heart submission;
See, like ashes, my contrition;
Help me, in my last condition!

Ah! that Day of tears and mourning!
From the dust of earth returning,
Man for judgment must prepare him:
Spare, O God, in mercy, spare him!

Lord, all pitying, Jesus blest,
Grant them thine eternal rest!

M. MEDIEVAL LITURGY, MUSIC, DRAMA AND "THE PLAY OF DANIEL" AT BEAUVAIS

70. The Cloisters, Noah Greenberg, The New York Pro Musica, and The Play of Daniel

Selections from the original text with translations by Jean Misrahi. (New York: Oxford University Press, Inc. © 1959). Reprinted by permission. Original play reproduced at the Cloisters of The Metropolitan Museum of Art, New York, and incorporated in the record album for Decca recording, DL9402/Stereo 79402, p. 11.

Tunc projicient Danielem in lacum. Statimque Angelus tenens gladium comminabitur leoni-

bus ne tangant eum, et Daniel intrans lacum
dicet:

Hujus rei non sum reus;
Miserere mei Deus;
    eleyson.
Mitte, Deus, huc patronum
Qui refrenet vim leonum;
    eleyson.

Interea alius Angelus admonebit Abacuc prophe-
tam ut deferat prandium quod portabat mes-
soribus suis Danieli in lacum leonum, dicens:

Abacuc, tu senex pie,
Ad lacum Babyloniae
Danieli fer prandium;
Mandat tibi Rex omnium.

Cui Abacuc:

Novit Dei cognitio
Quod Babylonem nescio,
Neque lacus est cognitus
Quo Daniel est positus.

Tunc Angelus, apprehendens eum capillo capitis
sui, ducet ad lacum, et Abacuc Danieli offerens
prandium, dicet:

Surge, frater, ut cibum capias;
Tuas Deus vidit angustias;
Deus misit, da Deo gratias,
    Qui te fecit.

Et Daniel cibum accipiens dicet:

Recordatus es mei, Domine;
Accipiam in tuo nomie,
    Alleluia!

IX-29. Daniel and the Lion's Den. Roda Bible

IX-30. The Prophet Habakkuk "Flown in" by an
Angel to Feed Daniel in the Lion's Den.

Then they thrust Daniel into the pit. Immedi-
ately an angel holding a sword keeps the lions
at bay lest they touch him, and Daniel calls out
as he goes into the pit:

For this charge I am not guilty;
Have mercy on me, O God;
    eleyson.
Send, O God, a protector here
To restrain the lions' power;
    eleyson.

Meanwhile another angel brings a message to
Habacuc the prophet, to take the repast which
he was bringing to his reapers to Daniel in the
lions' den, saying:

Habacuc, O holy old man,
Take the meal to Daniel
In the den at Babylon;
The King of all commands you.

Habacuc answers him:

The omniscience of God knows well
That I know not Babylon,
Nor is the den known to me
In which Daniel has been placed.

Then the angel, taking him by the hair of his
head, leads him to the den, and Habacuc says
to Daniel as he offers him the repast:

IX-31. Play of Daniel from the 12th Century MS.

IX-32. A Concert in a Garden. *Tapestry motif, Gobelins Museum, Paris.*

Rise up, brother, and take the food;
God has seen your afflictions;
God has sent it, give thanks to God,
　　The God who made you.
And Daniel, taking the food, says:
O Lord, You have remembered me;
This food in Your name I accept.
　　Alleluia!

440

N. MUSIC, DRAMA, GAMES, DANCES, AND MANUSCRIPT MARGINALIA

71. *Editorial Notes to Accompany the Plates from the Metropolitan Museum of Art and others*

The aura of the dance, music, and art that is integral with the whole of Section VI

IX-33. The Game of Marionettes. Hortus Deliciarum

has the closest possible affinity with Section IX, especially Items 119–126. The unity of the common life stressed in the introduction is here galvanized by the pictures. Chuckling humor, no less than the earthy charm of childrens' games and dancing maidens, is coupled with the activities of shrewish wives. All is portrayed in intimate conjunction with the noblest aims of existence. Here the rhythms of the common life are appended via the marginalia to the devotions of the *Books of Hours* and other sacred pursuits.

The recordings listed at the end of this chapter help to make real the music—no less compounded of sacred and secular—that was characteristic of the Middle Ages. It is fitting that the Cloisters and other divisions of the Metropolitan Museum of Art in New York should be pivotal in their portrayals of the common life, whether in the *Bulletin* interpretations of the collections, in the collaborative staging of the *Play of Daniel,* or in the tapestries commented upon at length by the staff.

O. CESSOLI-VIGNAY-CAXTON AND THE MORALIZED GAME OF CHESS

72. *Feudal Manners and Chessmen Related to the Figure from the Glazier Collection*

Figure IX–37, reproduced from Mr. Glazier's magnificent MS of Jacobus de Cessolis, unites the medieval love of games and allegory. Chess was a favorite pastime. Interpreting the game symbolically, after the fashion of the "moralities," Cessolis built on what was originally a sermon. Life and society were symbolized by the game itself. Each rank or class, as well as every trade or profession, had its chess pieces. Here at the beginning, Jean de Vignay—the vernacular

IX-34. Game of Frog in the Middle, at Bottom of Annunciation Scene. *Frontispiece for the* Hours of the Virgin, *the letter "D" enclosing a picture of Queen Jeanne d'Évreux kneeling, reading a book. From a French MS., 1325–1328, by Jean Pucelle,* The Hours of Jeanne d'Évreux, *fol. 16.*

441

translator of this Latin work into French, as well as the author of the vernacular Commentary on the Mass in Item 74—wears the garb of a hospitaler. Chess pieces supply personifications of royalty, high ecclesiasts, monastics, feudal nobility, craftsmen, laborers, entertainers, and representatives of the common people.

VII. Illuminated Books: Missals, Breviaries, and Books of Hours; the Literacy of the Clergy and Laity; the Arts and the Common Life

A. MASS BOOKS; COMMENTARIES ON THE MASS; THE LITURGY AND THE COMMON LIFE

73. The Canon and Order of the Mass— York Use

The Lay Folks Mass Book, ed. T. F. Simmons, EETS, No. 71, pp. 104–15. (a) Prayers for the Acceptance of the Gifts or Oblations (Lat. and Eng.), ibid., pp. 104, 105.

IX-35. Proverb of the Dominating Woman Holding Her Husband's Pants. *Marginal drawing from* The Hours of Jeanne d'Évreux, *fol. 202*.

Junctis manibus sacerdos inclinet se dicens:

Te igitur clementissime Pater, per Iesum Christum Filium tuum Dominum nostrum supplices rogamus ac petimus:

Hic erigat se et osculetur altare, faciendo signum super calicem.

Uti accepta habeas et benedicas haec dona, haec munera, haec sancta sacrificia illibata, In primis quae tibi offerimus pro ecclesia tua sancta catholica, quam pacificare, custodire, adunare, et regere digneris toto orbe terrarum, [una cum famulo tuo Papa nostro N.] (1) et antistite nostro N. et rege nostro N. et omnibus orthodoxis, atque catholicae et apostolicae fidei cultoribus.

Let the priest with his hands together bow himself and say:

Thee therefore most merciful Father, through Jesus Christ, thy Son, our Lord, we humbly pray and beseech:

Here let him raise himself and kiss the altar, and making a cross over the chalice (let him say):

That thou wouldest hold accepted and bless these gifts, these offerings, these holy undefiled sacrifices, which first of all we offer to thee for thy holy catholic church, which do thou vouchsafe to keep in peace, to watch over, to knit together and govern, throughout the whole world, together with thy servant our Pope, and our Bishop N, and our King N, and all right believers, and maintainers of the Catholic and Apostolic faith.

442

(b) Presentation of the Oblations and the Institution (Changing of the Bread and Wine into the Body and Blood of Christ; the Two-fold Consecration or Institution, i.e., the Sacrifice complete), *ibid.*, pp. 107, 109.

This oblation therefore of our service as also of thy whole household, we beseech thee, O Lord, that having been reconciled thou wouldest accept; and wouldest order our days in thy peace, and ordain that we be delivered from eternal damnation and numbered with the flock of thine elect; through Christ our Lord. Amen.

Which oblation, do thou, we beseech thee, O God Almighty, vouchsafe to render altogether blessed, counted, reckoned, reasonable and acceptable, that it may be made unto us the Body and Blood of thy most beloved Son, our Lord Jesus Christ.

Pope Alexander appointed [the Qui pridie]. *With head bowed over the linen cloths (let him say) at taking up the host:*

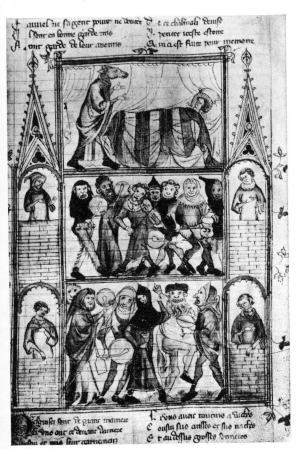

IX-36. The Masked Mummers. *Miniature from the MS. of Roman de Fauvel.*

IX-37. The Game of "Moralized Chess." *Jacobus de Cessolis,* Le jeu des échecs moralisé, *trans. from the Latin by Jean de Vignay, showing Jean de Vignay, himself, with personified chess pieces.*

Who on the day before he suffered took bread into his holy and most honoured hands, (*Here let him raise his eyes*) and with his eyes raised up towards heaven, unto Thee, O God, his Father almighty, giving thanks to Thee, he blessed and (*Here let him touch the host*) brake and gave to his disciples, saying, Take and eat ye all of this, for this is my Body. In like manner after supper, taking also this most excellent cup into his holy and most honoured hands, and likewise giving thanks unto Thee, he blessed and gave to his disciples, saying, Take and drink ye all of this, for this is the cup of my Blood, of the new and everlasting covenant, a mystery of faith, which shall be shed for you and for many for the remission of sins:

Here the priest covers the chalice with the corporasses.

443

IX-38. Consecration of the Host. Paten on South End of Altar. *Chalice in the middle; reredos with Crucifix. Priest elevates Host; clerk adjusts Priest's chasuble.*

IX-39. Consecration of the Chalice Elevated by Priest.

As often as ye do (*or* offer) these things; ye shall do them in memory of me.

Here the priest spreadeth abroad his arms after the manner of a cross.

Wherefore also we thy servants, O Lord, and also thy holy people, in memory as well of the blessed passion of the same Christ, thy Son, our Lord, as of his resurrection from the dead, and also of his glorious ascension into the heavens do offer unto thy excellent majesty, of thine own gifts, albeit given unto us,

Here let him draw back his arms and make the sign of the cross

a pure, a holy, and undefiled sacrifice, the holy bread of eternal life, and the cup of everlasting salvation; . . .

(*c*) The Sacrificial Banquet or Communion; Lord's Prayer, Fraction, Agnus Dei, Commixture, Pax, Reception or Communion by the Priest, *ibid.*, pp. 113, 115.

Here let him take the paten and kiss it: he makes a cross therewith on his face, [and] breast: from the crown of the head

down to the breast, on the right across to the left, saying:

Favourably give peace in our days, that we, being succoured by the help of thy merciful kindness, may both be free from sin, and safe from troubles;

And let him say:

Through the same, our Lord,

And let him break the Body into three pieces.

Jesus Christ thy Son, who liveth and reigneth with thee, in the unity of the Holy Ghost, God, world without end. Amen.

The peace of God be with you always.

And with thy spirit.

O Lamb of God, that takest away the sins of the world, have mercy upon us.

O Lamb of God, that takest away the sins of the world, have mercy upon us.

O Lamb of God, that takest away the sins of the world, grant us thy peace.

Let him put the third piece into the Blood and say:

May this all-holy mingling of the Body and Blood of our Lord Jesus Christ be unto

444

IX-40. The Fraction. *Priest breaks bread over chalice.*

us and to all that receive, health of mind and body, and a healthful preparation for laying hold on eternal life, through the same Christ our Lord. Amen.

Let him give (to himself) *to kiss the chalice and the corporasses, and* (that), *risen up, he might give the* Pax *to the ministers, saying:*

Receive the bond of peace and charity that ye may be meet for the most holy mysteries of God.

Let us pray.

O Lord, holy Father, Almighty everlasting God, grant us so to receive this Body and Blood of thy Son the Lord, our God, that we may be worthy thereby to obtain remission of all our sins and to be replenished by thy Holy Spirit; for thou art God, and beside thee, there is none other, but thou only, Who livest and reignest God, world without end. Amen.

THE PRIEST FOR HIMSELF

May the partaking of thy Body and Blood, O Lord Jesu Christ, which I unworthy, am daring to receive, come upon me neither unto judgment nor unto condemnation, but for thy pity's sake may it be profitable unto me for defence of soul and body; who with God the Father and the Holy Ghost livest and reignest God, world without end. Amen.

O Lord Jesu Christ, Son of the living God, who of the will of the Father, and with the co-operation of the Holy Ghost, hast by thy death given life to the world; Deliver me by this thy holy Body and Blood from all my iniquities, and from all that is evil in me; and make me to be obedient to thy commandments, and never suffer me to be for ever separated from thee; who with God the Father and the same Holy Spirit livest and reignest God, world without end. Amen.

At taking the Body.

The Body of our Lord Jesus Christ be unto me an everlasting medicine unto eternal life. Amen.

At receiving the Blood.

The Blood of our Lord Jesus Christ preserve me unto everlasting life. Amen.

At receiving the Body and Blood.

The Body and the Blood of our Lord Jesus Christ preserve my body and my soul unto everlasting life. Amen.

74. Vignay's Fourteenth-Century Commentary on the Mass

Selections trans. by the editor via *Exposition de la messe* from *La Legende Dorée* of Jean De Vignay. . . . Alcuin Club Collections, II (London: Longmans, Green and Co., Ltd., 1899), pp. 11–13.

Then the priest approaching the main consecration says, *Quam oblationem.* And he makes five signs of the cross on the bread and on the wine in remembrance of the five wounds of our Lord. The sense of the priest's prayer is: "Lord of our hearts, we pray that this offering may be made and consecrated, approved and confirmed by thee into a very reasonable host and into an acceptable sacrifice, so that this bread may be converted into the body and this wine turned into the blood of thy very dear child Who suffered great agony for us. . . ."

. . . All that the priest does by way of the consecration represents that which the Lord did in the midst of his disciples on the day

IX-41. Communion, the Host. *Priest preparing to receive the Host. Deacon is at right. Sub-deacon leans on north end of altar. Two of kneeling congregation hold books.*

of the Supper. Whereupon He took the bread and, giving thanks to God the Father, he blessed it and broke it and gave it to his disciples, saying, "Take and eat, this is my very own body." And the priest does the very same thing, except that here he does not break the bread into fragments but by way of signification bows to the one and to the other.

Then the priest wipes his three fingers on the corporal (the communion cloth) because he wishes to take this precious host most becomingly. And afterwards the priest takes it and raises his eyes above to give thanks to God, thereby teaching and signifying that when we undertake a good work we ought to elevate the eyes of our heart, as at the beginning here and chiefly in this good work. Thereupon he blesses the bread by making the sign of the Cross. He thereby signifies the blessed passion of our Lord on the blessed Cross. And then the priest repeats the words that our Lord said: "Take and eat, this is my very own body." He thus intones the five sacramental words: *Hoc est enim corpus meum.* Whereupon the bread is converted into the very body of Jesus Christ who died on the cross for us.

Following this our Lord at the Supper placed the wine before his disciples rendering thanks to God the Father. He blessed it and gave it to his disciples saying: "Take and drink for this is the chalice of my very

own blood which is the confirmation of the New and of the Old Testament and the mystery of the faith which will be spread abroad for you and for my people unto the remission of your sins. As often as you do this which I have shown you, do it in remembrance of me." Then the priest . . . takes the chalice, and raising his eyes above he blesses it and says: "Take and eat all. For this is the chalice of my own blood.". . .

As soon as the priest has said these words in Latin in memory of our Saviour, the wine is converted into the very blood of Christ that he shed for us on the tree of the cross.

And it is this which enables us to consider in this precious sacrament the nine marvelous miracles capable of being proved by likenesses of nature.

The first is that the substance of the bread and of the wine is changed into the substance of the very body and precious blood of Jesus Christ. And this is demonstrated for us according to a natural resemblance with nourishment. By bread and wine body and blood are built up in the creature much more strongly. Our Lord who is sovereign over nature is able by the strength of his words to bring about the conversion of the bread and the wine into his own body and his own precious blood. . . .

The third is that each day our Lord is parceled out and consumed without loss to. himself. That is to say, neither God nor the sacrament is diminished. For a natural reason, because if I have a candle capable of giving light, another may take of my light without in any way lessening mine. Also, each one is able to take this holy sacrament without in any way lessening it, but he who takes it unworthily, he lessens it for himself.

The fourth miracle is that the host of God is entirely contained in each part. The example of the mirror is pertinent here. For when it is cracked or broken, there appears in each part of the mirror the thing that is reflected.

The fifth miracle is that if this precious sacrament is taken by an evil creature the sacrament is not corrupted thereby. For we see that when the rays of the sun pass among refuse the sun is not soiled thereby. So it is when any creature has received the body of our Lord unworthily and when it considers what it has done in thus receiving its Saviour in such great filth as that wherein it is by reason of its sin. Then it conceives in bitterness of soul such great contrition that it returns to grace and is thereby purged of its sin.

The sixth miracle is that the body of Jesus Christ is a nourishment unto death for sinners. For the apostle Paul says that anyone eating it unworthily eats it to his own judgment. Just as good wine and meat are injurious to an ailing person so the body of Jesus Christ is harmful to (deliberate) sinners. . . .

The ninth miracle is that when the bread is changed into the body of our Lord Jesus Christ the accidents remain, that is to say, whiteness, roundness and taste. Nevertheless, this is really not bread, but the body of Christ, which is given under the species of bread; since it would be a matter of great horror for the priest to eat raw flesh or to drink blood.

75. *Philip Navarre on "Nice" Christians and the Mass*

An editorial note on *Les quatre âges de l'homme* (Paris: Firmin Didot, 1888), p. 78, and Ch. V. Langlois, *La vie en France au moyen âge.* . . . (Paris: Hachette, 1926), II, p. 231 and n. 2, also, p. 232.

The author indicts those silly, simpleminded (nice) Christians who "naively

(nicement) go to mass and naively depart." He is referring to a peculiar custom, once quite wisespread, of leaving the church immediately after the Gospel Lesson, letting the priest finish the mass alone. It was ludicrous indeed, for one ought to witness the elevation and remain at least "until the peace was given" and the priest had communicated. Then, only, might those present participate in the sacrament. Jacques de Vitry, the famous thirteenth-century preacher, was reported as saying that he once knew a knight who had never been present at a sermon. He was ignorant of what the holy sacrifice actually was. He assumed that one celebrated merely to take up an offering. The desire to escape before the collection was doubtless one reason for the development of the custom.

IX-42. Communion, the Chalice. *Paten rests on corporas. The chalice is in the Hand of the communicating priest. There are no clerks. Images of saints are on brackets.*

76. The Virgin Miraculously Substitutes for a Recreant Nun

Caesar of Heisterbach, *Dial.*, Dist. VII, cap. 34, trans. *PTR*, II, 4 (2), pp. 4–5.

Not many years ago, in a certain monastery of nuns, of which I do not know the name, there lived a virgin named Beatrix. She was beautiful in form, devout in mind, and most fervent in the service of the mother of God. As often as she could offer secretly to the Virgin special prayers and supplications, she held them for her dearest delight. Indeed, having been made custodian, she did this more devoutly because more freely.

A certain clerk, seeing and lusting after her, began to tempt her. When she spurned the words of lust, and on that account he insisted the more strenuously, the old serpent enkindled her breast so vehemently that she could not bear the flames of love. Therefore coming to the altar of the blessed Virgin, the patroness of the oratory, she spoke thus: "Mistress, I have served thee as devoutly as I could; behold, I resign thy keys to thee, I cannot longer withstand the temptations of the flesh." And, having placed the keys on the altar, she secretly followed the clerk.

When that wretched man had corrupted her, he abandoned her after a few days. Since she had no means of living and was ashamed to return to the convent, she became a harlot. After she had continued in that vice publicly for fifteen years, she came one day in a lay habit to the door of the monastery. She said to the doorkeeper, "Did you know Beatrix, formerly custodian of this oratory?" When the latter replied, "I knew her very well. For she is an honest and holy woman, and from infancy even to the present day she has remained in this monastery without fault." When she hearing the man's words, but not understanding them, wished to go away, the mother of mercy appeared in her well-known image and said to her, "During the fifteen years of thy absence, I have performed thy task; now return to thy place and do penance; for no one knows of thy departure." In fact, in the form and dress of that woman, the mother of God had performed the duties of custodian. Beatrix entered at once and returned thanks as long as she lived, revealing through confession what had been done for her.

77. The Virgin Punishes a Deprecator of Her Statue

Ibid., cap. 44, trans. *PTR*, II, 4 (3), p. 5.

In the chapel of the castle of Veldenz there is a certain ancient image of the blessed Virgin holding her son in her bosom. This image is, indeed, not very well made, but is endowed with great virtue. A certain matron of this castle, which is situated in the diocese of Trier, standing in the chapel one day looked at the image and despising the workmanship, said, "Why does this old rubbish stand here?"

The blessed Mary, the mother of mercy, not, as I think, complaining to her son of the woman who spoke so foolishly, but predicting the future penalty for the crime to a certain other matron, said, "Because that lady," designating her by name, "called me old rubbish, she shall always be wretched as long as she lives."

After a few days that lady was driven out by her own son from all her possessions and property, and up to the present day she begs wretchedly enough, suffering the punishment for her foolish speech. Behold how the blessed Virgin loves and honors those who love her, and punishes and humbles those who despise her.

78. The Feast of Relics Following upon the Feast of Thomas à Becket in the Sarum Missal

Collect and Secret, trans. F. E. Warren, *The Sarum Missal in English* (London: Alexander Moring, Ltd., 1911), Pt. II, p. 403. Reprinted by permission from the Receiver and Manager on behalf of the company.

COLLECT

Grant, we beseech thee, almighty God, that the merits of the mother of God, and ever-virgin Mary, and of thy saints whose

IX-43. Virgin and Child. *French wooden sculpture, painted and gilded. Late 13th century.*

relics are contained in this church, may protect us; so that through their prayers we may ever rejoice and praise thee in tranquillity and peace. Through etc.

SECRET

Merciful God, we beseech to regard with gracious look the gifts now offered to thy majesty, that they may be profitable to our salvation, through the prayers of those whose most holy relics are preserved in this church. Through etc.

79. *False Relics Ascribed to Thomas à Becket*

Caesar of Heisterbach, *Dial.*, Dist. VIII, cap. 70, trans. *PTR*, II, 4 (3), p. 14.

A certain knight loved most ardently the above-mentioned martyr, St. Thomas of Canterbury, and sought everywhere to obtain some relic of him. When a certain wily priest, in whose house he was staying, heard of this he said to him, "I have by me a bridle which St. Thomas used for a long time, and I have often experienced its virtues." When the knight heard this, and believed it, he joyfully paid the priest the money which the latter demanded and received the bridle with great devotion.

God truly, to whom nothing is impossible, wishing to reward the faith of the knight and for the honor of his martyr, deigned to work many miracles through the same bridle. The knight seeing this founded a church in honor of the martyr and in it he placed as a relic the bridle of that most wicked priest.

80. *Guibert De Nogent on the Abuse of Relics*

De Pignoribus Sanctorum I, ii, 6, *MPL* 156:621, trans. by the editor via J. Calmette, *Textes et documents d'histoire:* II, *Moyen âge* (Paris: Les Presses Universitaires De France, 1937), pp. 55–56. See also, Chap. VIII, Item 8.

A certain church, one of the most renowned, sought by employing a public spokesman to establish a fund-raising scheme for repairing damages to its building. This boaster exceeded all proper bounds in speaking of its relics. Bringing forward a box he said (I was there): "Know that in this reliquary there is a piece of bread that our Lord chewed with his own teeth. If this seems hard for you to believe, here is a person (he was referring to me) who possesses letters of unimpeachable testimony and who will, if necessary, attest the truth of what I have asserted." I confess that I blushed upon hearing it. And, save that the presence of those whom he seemed to hold as witnesses made me fearful of disturbing their peace rather than that of the speaker I would have been obliged to expose the falsehood. What shall I say, until certain monks, not to men-

IX-44. Merode Altarpiece: The Annunciation with Donors and St. Joseph. *Robert Campin, active 1406–1444.*

tion clerks, restraining this filthy gain, proclaim as heretical talk such as I have heard concerning our faith? It is a case of saying with Boethius: "I shall be reckoned a fool if I contend with fools."

C. THE VIRGIN AND THE MERODE ALTAR PIECE

81. *The Iconography of the Merode Altarpiece*

Reprinted with the kind permission of the Metropolitan Museum of Art, New York, from the article by Margaret B. Freeman, "The Iconography of the Merode Altarpiece," *The Metropolitan Museum of Art Bulletin*, XVI, 4 (Dec., 1957), pp. 130–37.

The iconography of the Merode altarpiece is something of a puzzle—a puzzle which has interested many people for a long time. As in almost all puzzles, some of the solutions are easy, some are more obscure, and, in this case, some remain undiscovered. The basic difficulty is that Robert Campin, rejoicing in the ability to reproduce the physical world in paint on a wooden panel, at the same time felt it important to endow his apparently natural world with as much spiritual meaning as possible. The question

is, as Erwin Panofsky says, "how we are to decide where the general . . . transfiguration of nature ends and actual specific symbolism begins." For instance, in the Annunciation scene of our painting, are the lions on the Virgin's bench meant to signify Christ, are they meant to suggest King Solomon's throne, a favorite Old Testament prototype of the Virgin Mary—or are they merely the kind of carved finial that could be seen on many a piece of medieval furniture because people liked lions? . . .

Mary herself was a good housekeeper. The floor is spotless, the bronze vessels well polished and the andirons free from rust. The author of *Speculum humanae salvationis* writes that when she dwelt in the temple, before being affianced to Joseph, "she washed the things that were there to be washed and cleaned what needed cleaning."

In our little painting Mary, her housework done, is comfortably seated on a cushion on the floor, engrossed in the book that she is reading. The book is carefully protected even from Mary's clean hands by a white cloth. Another book and a scroll lie on the table, suggesting that she is in need of a few reference works. The author of *Speculum* says that she "understood very well the books of the prophets and the Holy Scriptures. . . . In reading them and realizing their meaning she profited.". . .

The painter of our altarpiece has expressed the same idea in a more natural way. He has placed the Virgin Mary on the floor, not so that she may reach her texts more easily or because she, being young, enjoys sitting on the floor, but because this is the accepted position for the Virgin of Humility. Millard Meiss has pointed out that the conception is derived from Italy, where many a Madonna in similar posture has been clearly labeled "Our Lady of Humility." Campin has made Mary's humble position even more apparent by painting an elegantly carved bench behind her, equipped with a brilliant blue covering cloth and a cushion. . . .

In any case there is no doubt that other household objects introduced into the setting in a completely natural and disarming way are full of symbolism. The stalk of Madonna lilies, one of the most important accessories of Annunciation scenes from the fourteenth century on, is here rather casually arranged in a blue and white jug placed on the table as it would be in any home. The lily, of course, is first of all the symbol of Mary's purity. . . .

The shining bronze laver with the clean blue-bordered towel is also more than a normal bit of household equipment. It, too, is a symbol of Mary's purity. . . .

Of course this light which is entering Mary's chamber is more than ordinary sunlight; it is the light divine emanating from God. In many Annunciation scenes God himself is shown dispatching the dove, symbol of the Holy Ghost, on beams of light to the presence of Mary. It is undoubtedly significant that in our painting the beams of light number exactly seven. Interpreted as the seven gifts of the Holy Spirit, the beams of light become a substitute for the dove, the more familiar symbol of the Holy Ghost. Although God the Father is absent from our Annunciation and the Holy Ghost is suggested only by the seven rays of light, God the Son is very much in evidence as a tiny infant, gliding in on the beams of light. This rather literal way of expressing the mystery

of the Incarnation was frowned upon by the Church but had been popular in Italy and depicted elsewhere for over a century preceding our painting. The fact that the little Child carries a cross emphasizes the significance of the Annunciation: that God became Man to suffer and die in order to redeem mankind from the original sin of Adam. . . .

The walled garden itself, with its battlemented gate, is also a symbol of the virginity of Mary. The imagery was derived from the Song of Songs: "A garden enclosed is my sister, my spouse; a spring shut up, a fountain sealed.". . .

Joseph the Carpenter seems to specialize in mousetraps. One is on display at the open window and another, of a different design, rests completed on his workbench along with sundry tools of his trade. These mousetraps, as Meyer Schapiro has brilliantly demonstrated, are placed in the picture not solely because Campin enjoyed painting such contraptions but because he intended to convey, once again, a theological concept under the guise of familiar, everyday things. The interpretation is to be found in sermons by Saint Augustine, and following him, by Peter Lombard. It was firmly believed by the people of the late Middle Ages that the knowledge of the divinity of Christ must be kept from the devil, who was responsible for man's original sin, who made necessary the coming of God to earth in human form to suffer and die by way of atonement. The devil was never to know that Christ was more than man. Only thus could the archenemy be fooled and the original sin of Adam and Eve wiped out.

D. **BOOKS OF MEDIEVAL HAGIOGRAPHY; THE GOLDEN LEGEND; MISSALS, BREVIARIES, BOOKS OF HOURS, SERMONS**

82. St. Jerome, the Lion, and the Golden Legend (Sept. 30)

Reprinted by permission of the Publishers from *The Golden Legend of Jacobus de Voragine*, trans. G. Ryan and H. Ripperger (New York and London: Longmans, Green and Co. 1941), II, pp. 589–91.

One day, as evening was drawing on, and Jerome sat with the brethren to hear the sacred lessons, suddenly a lion came limping into the monastery. At the sight of him all the other monks fled, but Jerome went forward to meet him as a host his guest. The lion then showed him his wounded foot, whereupon he called the brothers and ordered them to wash the lion's feet and to dress his wound with care. When they did this, they found that the lion's pads were wounded by thorns. By their care, however, the foot was healed, and the lion, losing all his wildness, lived among them as a tame beast. Jerome judged from this that God had sent the lion not merely to have his foot healed, but to serve the monks; wherefore, after consulting the brethren, he put the lion in charge of the ass which carried wood from the grove to the monastery. Thereafter the beast cared for the ass as a shepherd for his sheep, constantly accompanying it to pasture, guarding it on all sides as it fed in the fields, and bringing it home at the same hour daily, when its work was done and it had fed. But once when the ass was in pasture and the lion was overcome with drowsiness, certain merchants who were passing that way with their camels saw the ass alone, and straightway stole it. Being roused from sleep, and not finding his companion, the lion ran roaring this way and that, and finally returned sadly to the doors of the monastery, nor dared to enter, as he used to do, for shame at having lost the ass. When the brothers saw that he came back later than was his wont, and without the ass, they thought that he had been forced by hunger to eat the ass; wherefore they refused to give him his customary portion of food, and said to him: 'Go and eat what is left of the little ass, and so have thy fill!' Yet they were reluctant to believe that the lion had done this wrong, and went into the pasture looking for traces of the ass; but finding none, they reported the matter to Jerome. At his behest they gave the ass's work to the lion, and loaded upon his back the wood which they cut; and this the beast bore patiently. And one day when he had finished his work, he went out to the pasture, running about and looking for his comrade; and all at once he saw the traders afar off, marching along with their loaded camels, and the ass walk-

ing in the lead; for it was common in that region, when camels were going on a long march, to have an ass lead them by a rope tied about his neck. When the lion recognized the ass, he uttered a tremendous roar, rushed upon the caravan, and put the men to flight. Then, still roaring frightfully, he beat his tail upon the earth, and forced the terrified camels, laden as they were, to go before him to the monastery. When the brethren saw this and related it to Jerome, he said: 'Beloved brothers, wash the feet of our guests and give them to eat, and further await the will of the Lord!' Then the lion ran happily about the monastery, as he had used to do, lying down in the path of each of the brethren, and wagging his tail, as if begging pardon for the wrong he had not done. But Jerome, foreseeing what was to come, said to the brothers: 'Go now, and make ready for the oncoming guests!' While he was yet speaking, a messenger came, announcing that certain guests had come to the door, and wished to see the abbot. He went to meet the merchants, who threw themselves at his feet, begging forgiveness for their fault; and he, lifting them up graciously, bade them take what was theirs, and leave what belonged to others. They then besought Jerome to accept a measure of oil, in return for his blessing; and after much urging, he consented. They promised further to give such a measure to the brethren annually, and to provide that it should be given by their heirs.

83. St. Martin, the Naked Beggar, and the Golden Legend (Nov. 11)

Ibid., pp. 663–64.

Martin comes from *Martem tenens*, one who sustains Mars, that is, one who wages war, namely against vice and sin. Or it is the same as *martyrum unus*, one of the martyrs, for he was a martyr, at least by desire, and by the mortification of his flesh. Or Martin is interpreted one who arouses to anger, or one who provokes, or one who dominates; for by the merit of his holiness he aroused the Devil to envy, provoked God to mercy, and dominated his body by continuous penances. For reason, or the spirit, should domi-

IX-45. St. Jerome. *A page from a French MS. of* The Golden Legend, *15th century.*

nate the flesh, says Dionysius in his letter to Demophilus, as the master dominates his servant, or the father his son, or an elder a frivolous youth.

The life of Saint Martin was written by Sulpicius Severus, a disciple of Saint Martin, whom Gennadius numbers among his illustrious men.

Martin was born in the town of Sabaria, in Pannonia, but was reared at Pavia in Italy, where his father was a tribune of soldiers. He himself served in the army under the Emperors Constantine and Julian, but against his will. For he was inspired by God from infancy, and when he was twelve years of age he fled to the church, maugre his parents' unwillingness, and asked to be received as a catechumen; and he would have become a hermit, had not the infirmity of his body forbidden him. But since the Caesars had decreed that the sons of veterans should take their fathers' places in the army, Martin was compelled to take arms when he reached the age of fifteen. He took with him only one serving-man, and Martin often waited upon him, and drew off his boots and polished them.

It chanced one winter day that Martin was passing through the gate of Amiens, and came upon a poor and almost naked beggar. The poor man had received no alms that day, and Martin considered that he was re-served to himself; wherefore he drew his sword, divided his cloak in two parts, gave one part to the beggar, and wrapped himself in the other. On the following night, in a vision, he saw Christ wearing the part of his cloak with which he had covered the beggar, and heard Him saying to the angels who surrounded Him: 'Martin, while yet a catechumen, has clothed Me with this garment!' Hence the holy man, not puffed up with pride, but acknowledging the goodness of God, had himself baptized. He nevertheless continued in the profession of arms for two years, at the insistence of his tribune, who in turn promised that when his term as tribune was completed, he would renounce the world.

84. St. Martin's Day and Fourteenth-Century Preaching

An editorial résumé based on a Sermon by Saint-Gilles (Nov. 17, 1230) after MS 338 nouv. acq. Lat. de la Bib. Nat. de Paris, fol. 43r°, via M. M. Davy, *Les sermons universitaires Parisiens de 1230–1231* (Paris: J. Vrin, 1931), pp. 277ff.

The preacher divides his sermon into four parts. I considers St. Martin's life as soldier, student, monk, and bishop. II deals with his works. Each aspect of his life suggests a specific labor. In brief résumé, St. Martin's example is capitalized insofar as

453

IX-46. St. Martin. *From the* Passionael, *printed by Henrick Eckert von Hamberch, Antwerp, 1505.*

he was fighter, scholar, contemplative and preacher. Clerks too have many battles to wage, chiefly those of words against heretics and the like. Even as St. Martin did, so ought scholars avoid laziness and be diligent in studying the Scriptures and the book of conscience. Out of this book—before God, all the saints, and the assembled people—they must read at the judgment. Martin's life in its monastic aspect was an inspiration to the praise of God and contemplation. As a bishop his chief work was preaching. He was a tireless sower of the gospel. The preacher calls for the emulation of that work. Unfortunately, there are those who, having received the seed of God's word, lose it forthwith and are unable to sow it. Seed and fruits as well are thereby lost. III sees Martin's life consummated as to longevity, innocence, poverty, and good deeds. IV evaluates the treasury he bequeathed out of

his military career behind the buckler of the faith and beneath the helmet of salvation, his student treasures of disciplined knowledge, his monastic bequest of heavenly consolations, his episcopal conservation of faithful souls.

85. St. Martin in the Sarum Missal

Trans. F. E. Warren, *The Sarum Missal in English* (London: Alexander Moring, Ltd., 1911), Pt. II, pp. 397–99. Reprinted by permission from the Receiver and Manager on behalf of the Company.

TRANSLATION AND ORDINATION OF ST. MARTIN

[July 4]

At Mass   *Office*

Therefore was there a covenant of peace made with him by the Lord, that he should be the chief of the sanctuary and of his people; and that he and his posterity should have the dignity of the priesthood for ever.

Ps. My song shall be alway of the loving-kindness of the Lord.

Collect

O God, who gavest the blessed Martin to be the minister of eternal salvation unto thy people; grant, we beseech thee, that he who was the performer of thy commands upon earth may ever deign to be our intercessor in heaven. Through etc. *Memory of the Visitation [of the B.V.M.] and of the apostles.*

Epistle. Ecclus. xliv. 16, 17, 19—23; xlv. 3, 7, 16.

Behold, a high priest . . . a sweet savour.

Gradual

I have found David my servant: with my holy oil have I anointed him. My hand shall hold him fast: and my arm shall strengthen him.

V. The enemy shall not be able to do him violence: the son of wickedness shall not hurt him.

Alleluya. V. The Lord chose thee to be a high priest among his people.

Sequence

Let the whole Church, in catholic peace united,

Proclaim the praise of Martin, priest of Christ,

And at his name let heretics flee pale.
In such a son rejoice, Pannonia;
Exult in such a scholar, Italy,
In holy strife each of Gaul's three divisions
Contends of which he should be held the
    bishop;
But let all joy alike to call him father:
His body rests in care of Tours alone.
Let Franks and Germans join in his ap-
    plause,
Clad in whose cloak the Lord himself was
    seen.
He in the parts of Egypt is renowned;
And by wise men of Greece, who count
    themselves
Inferior in gifts and skill to Martin:
For fevers he allays, and devils casts out,
And paralytic limbs restores to vigour.
By his prevailing prayer three dead are
    raised.
He impious rites destroys, and images
Unto the flames delivers, for Christ's glory;
With unclad arms the mysteries celebrat-
    ing,
He with a light from heaven is endued.
With eyes and hands, and his whole soul
    uplifted
To heaven, all things earthly he despises.
Of Christ he ever spake and righteousness,
And all which to true life doth appertain;
Therefore we all entreat thee, blessed
    Martin,
That as thou here hast many wonders
    shown us,
So by thy supplication thou would'st ever
Pour out on us the grace of Christ from
    heaven.

Gospel. St. Luke, xii. 32–34.
Fear not, little flock, . . . heart be also.

Offertory

My truth also and my mercy shall be with
him: and in my name shall his horn be
exalted.

Secret

We beseech thee, O Lord, that the intercession of thy blessed confessor and bishop
Martin may commend our gifts, and make us
always acceptable unto thy majesty. Through
etc.

Communion

Faithful and wise is that servant whom his
lord hath made ruler over his household, to
give them their portion of meat in due season.

Postcommunion

We beseech thee, O Lord, that the sacrament which we have received may be the
defence of our salvation, and that through
the intervening merits of thy blessed confessor and bishop Martin, it may be the absolution of all our sins. Through etc.

86. St. Louis of France in Ancient and Modern Missals (Aug. 25)

Reprinted by permission from F. X. Lasance
and W. R. Kelly, *The New Roman Missal*
(New York: Benziger Brothers, Inc., 1937), pp.
1172–73.

O God, Who didst take Thy blessed
confessor, Louis, from an earthly throne to
the glory of the heavenly kingdom, by his
merits and intercession we beseech Thee
that Thou make us to be associates of the
King of kings, Jesus Christ Thy Son. Who
with Thee. . . .

87. Saint Louis and the Breviary, Ancient and Modern

Lessons 4–6 from *The Roman Breviary*, Vol. II
(Summer) (London: William Blackwood and
Sons, 1879), p. 1239.

SECOND NOCTURN

Fourth Lesson

Lewis IX, King of France [was born on
the 25th day of April, in the year of our
Lord 1215]. At the age of twelve years he
lost his father. He was brought up under the
godly care of his mother, Blanche of Castile.
In the twentieth year of his reign he fell
grievously sick, and the thought then occurred to him of delivering Jerusalem out of
the hands of the Moslems. On his health being restored, he received a banner from the
Bishop of Paris, and crossed the sea [to
Egypt] with a very great army. In his first
battle he put the Saracens to flight, but, a
great number of the soldiers perishing by
disease, he was himself conquered and taken
prisoner.

The King afterwards entered into treaty with the Saracens, and he and his army departed in peace. He remained five years in the East, during which he redeemed great numbers of Christians from slavery among the unbelievers, and also brought many of the unbelievers themselves to believe in Christ. Moreover he rebuilt several cities of the Christians at his own cost. Meanwhile, his mother departed this life, whereby he was constrained to return home, where he gave himself up entirely to works of godliness.

Sixth Lesson

He built many monasteries, and charitable institutions for the poor. By his alms he relieved the needy, and often visited the sick, for whom he not only provided at his own cost, but waited on them with his own hands with such things as they wanted. He wore a plain dress and constantly chastised his body with hair-cloth and fasting. [In the year 1270] he crossed the sea [to Tunis] to make war again upon the Saracens. His camp was pitched in sight of the enemy, but he was seized with pestilence, and died uttering the words—"I will come into Thy house—I will worship toward Thy holy temple, and praise Thy Name." (Pss. v. 8; cxxxvii. 2.) His body was afterwards carried to Paris, and it is kept and honoured in the famous Abbey Church of St. Denys, but his head in the oratory called "La Sainte Chapelle." He was renowned for miracles, and Pope Boniface VIII enrolled his name among those of the Saints.

88. St. Louis on Relics, Ste. Chapelle, and the Books of Hours

An editorial note apropos A. Longnon's *Documents Parisiens sur l'iconographie de S. Louis* (Paris: H. Champion, 1882).

In 1237 Louis IX, King of France, came to the rescue of the financially embarrassed Latin Emperor of Constantinople. A large sum secured for St. Louis the purchase of the crown of thorns, presumably worn by Christ during his passion. Surmounting expensive complications and delays, the king finally received the precious relic in August

of 1239. Accompanying it humbly in majestic processionals, Louis escorted it to its temporary abode in the chapel of St. Nicholas. Later it was conveyed, together with some iron from the sacred lance, portions of the purple mantle, and splinters from the holy cross, to the lovely Ste. Chapelle. This Gothic masterpiece was uniquely designed and consummately erected to house the relics.

In Fig. IX–47, the crown of thorns is being carried to the chapel on the site of later Ste. Chapelle. The bishop leads with the king immediately following. The latter bears on his shoulders the poles of a device supporting a large gold crown on a cushion. Visible through three perforations in its border is the true crown of thorns, previously authenticated at Louis' direction. A bareheaded, and apparently barefooted, prince carries the rear supports of the great golden crown and its precious inner deposit. This picture of the translation and that of the crown's placement on the altar of Ste. Chapelle or its predecessor in Fig. IX–48 are taken from the *Book of Hours* of Jeanne II, daughter of Louis X (1314–1316) and Queen of Navarre. This private service and prayer book contains the Office or Hours of St. Louis. Lessons almost identical with the later ones of Item 87 are included.

E. BIBLES AND BOOKS OF DEVOTION FOR THE RICH AND THE POOR; PICTURE BOOKS OF THE COMMON LIFE

89. Editorial Commentary on the Figures

From H. O. Hassall, *The Holkham Bible Picture Book* (London: The Dropmore Press, Ltd., 1954).

In fol. 40 of BM, MS Add. 47682, reproduced in Fig. IX–49, the great of earth are seen in fratricidal combat. They fight in armor astride spotted horses. They may represent feudal worthies or rich merchants. London citizens and Norwich merchants had knightly rank. Commoners engage their fellow commoners on foot. They employ heavy arrow heads designed for war, not hunting.

In fol. 42ᵛ of the same MS, reproduced in Fig. IX–50, the Last Judgment is followed

IX-47. The Translation of the Crown of Thorns. *The Bishop, St. Louis, and others.*

IX-48. The Crown of Thorns on the Altar of Ste. Chapelle. *Crowned head of St. Louis. King at the altar with Queen just behind him.*

by torture for the damned and bliss for the elect. An angel invites nude souls into heaven, while other angels above the doorway give a musical salute. A baker and ale wife bearing their professional tools ride demons piggyback into hell. A man with tonsure is atop the shoulders of a demon who wheels damned souls on a barrow. Wheelbarrows were known to Europe at least as early as late thirteenth century.

90. Editorial Statements on the Relation of the Biblia Pauperum, *the* Bibles Moralisées, *and the* Speculum Humanae Salvationis, *to the* Holkham Bible

Bibles of the Poor, Moralized Bibles, and *The Mirror of Human Salvation* have already been related in Item 81 to the *Golden Legend* and *The Merode Altarpiece.* An example of a *moralized* Bible is found in Fig. IX–51. It shows Blanche of Castile with her son Louis IX of France. Hassall (*op. cit.,* pp. 42–45) cogently summarizes the relation of such works to the *Holkham Bible Picture Book.* The *Speculum* was composed by a Strasbourg Dominican. The *Biblia Pauperum* emanated from Germany. Both, like

the *Holkham Bible,* were educational in purpose and pitted "type" against "antitype," after the fashion contemporary in Bible studies. These books were directed to the laity. As Albert the Great remarked, pictures constituted the books of laymen. Actually the *Holkham Bible* was for the rich, not the poor. Such "long religious argument(s) with comic interludes," had definite affinity with stained glass windows and wall paintings. They were, however, intended for non-scholarly people who could read. Eventually they had wide distribution among these half-literates.

F. BOOKS OF HOURS: THE CHURCH'S CALENDAR AND SEASONS

91. The Tres Belles Heures *and the* Belles Heures *of the Duke of Berry and the Limbourg Brothers Related to the Plates —Editorial Comment*

The *Books of Hours* get their name from their chief divisions, containing the Hours (or Offices) of the Virgin—that is, services conducted by the clergy at canonical hours —together with the Hours of the Cross and of the Holy Ghost, etc.

457

IX-49. Fratricidal Conflict. Holkham Bible Picture Book.

IX-50. Last Judgment, Heaven and Hell. Holkham Bible.

The *Most Rich Hours* was created for Jean, the Duke of Berry, Prince of France (1340–1416), by the Limbourg Brothers, Pol, Jean, and Armand. This book of service and private devotion has been called "supreme beyond question amongst illuminated books." Begun around 1413, it was unfinished when the Duke died. The *Beautiful Hours* was illuminated by Pol, Herman and Jean Limbourg, c. 1410–1413. From this work, fol. 186ᵛ, is taken Fig. IX–53. See also this chapter, Item 82, as well as Fig. IX–45. Consult the sumptuous Cloisters-Metropolitan Museum of Art edition: *The Belles Heures of Jean, Duke of Berry, Prince of France* (New York, 1958).

92. The Rohan Book of Hours Related to those of the Limbourg Brothers—Editorial Comment

The *Rohan Book of Hours*, c. 1418–1425, probably owes some of its inspiration to the Limbourg brothers. It is distinctive in the "monumental scale of its illuminations" and original in its presentation of "narrative and symbolic scenes." Its stark emotion and realistic disdain for cheap edification is clearly registered in Fig. IX–54 on the "Defunct Man" and Fig. IX–55, the "Pieta." The Heavenly Father does not ignore but rather transcends the tragedy of man's sin even as he irradiates the Virgin's passionate, yet restrained agony.

In the "Dead Man Before His Judge" the corpse is naked. Man takes nothing out of this world. The scroll reads: "Into Thy hands I commend my spirit. . . ." The Lord is overwhelmingly majestic, yet filled with tenderness. He controls the world (orb) and wields the sword of justice. His vitality contrasts strikingly with the withered, distorted body of the dead man. The devil, having seized the soul of the defunct (in the likeness of a nude infant), is made to relinquish it to the rescuing archangel Michael.

In the "Pieta" the Virgin swoons in grief. She is borne up with difficulty by the almost reproachful St. John. God the Father lifts his hand in benediction. He does not cancel the agony of this tragic moment; yet his gaze

458

IX-51. Moralized Bible. *Blanche of Castile and Her Son, Louis IX (St. Louis).*

is not that of Divine remoteness but of Fatherly love.

93. *The Hours of St. Louis—Editorial Comment*

The office (or hours) of St. Louis already noted in Item 88 is included in the Cloisters-Metropolitan Museum of Art edition of *The Hours of Jeanne d'Evreux* (New York, 1957). Illuminated by Jean Pucelle, this lovely book was a gift to Jeanne from her husband, Charles IV of France. From this are drawn Figs. IX–56 and IX–57, as well as Figs. IX–34 and IX–35, showing on their margins children's games and the foibles of adults.

G. MANUALS OF SYMBOLISM, ALLEGORY, ICONOGRAPHY, LITURGY AND THE COMMON LIFE

94. *The Pseudo-Hugh of St. Victor on* The Mystical Mirror of the Church

Prol. and Chap. 1, trans. J. M. Neale in *The Symbolism of Churches and Church Ornaments,*

IX-52. Daniel Fed by Habakkuk. Speculum Humanae Salvationis.

a Translation of the First Book of the Rationale Divinorum Officiorum Written by William Durandus (Leeds: T. W. Green, 1843), Supplement, pp. 197–205.

Your love hath asked of me to treat of the Sacraments of the Church, and to set forth unto you their mystical sweetness. But since with the more willingness, because with the more ease and boldness, I do evolve (after my custom) points of Logick rather

IX-53. St. Jerome Pulls the Thorn from the Lion's Foot. *From a French MS, c. 1410–1413, by Pol, Jean, and Herman de Limbourg,* The Belles Heures of Jean, Duke of Berry, *fol. 186ᵛ.*

IX-54. Death of a Christian. Rohan Book of Hours.

IX-55. The Pietà. Rohan Book of Hours.

than of Theology; I began to doubt whether to withstand your admonition, or the rather to write. But when I presently remembered, how that every good thing when shared with others becometh more bright and beautiful when it is shared, I incontinently betook myself to my pen, having invoked the aid of "Him Who openeth and no man shutteth, and shutteth and no man openeth." Wherefore I have put into the lips of your understanding the Tractate which you did desire, flowing within with nectar like the honeycomb: and the same, because therein ye may see as in a mirrour what every thing in the church doth mystically denote, I have called "The Mystical Mirrour of a Church."

CHAPTER I. OF A CHURCH

The material church in which the people cometh together to praise God, signifieth the Holy Catholick Church, which is builded in the heavens of living stones. This is the Lord's House which is firmly builded. The "chief corner stone is Christ." *Upon* this, not *besides* this, is the "foundation of the Apostles and Prophets"; as it is written, "Her foundations are upon the holy hills." The walls builded thereon, be the Jews and Gentiles coming from the four quarters of the world unto Christ. All the stones be polished and squared; that is, all the Saints be pure and firm: the which also be placed so as to last for ever by the hands of the Chief Workman. Of these some be borne and do not bear, as the more simple folk in the Church; some be borne and do also bear, as the middling sort; others do only bear, and be not borne, save by Christ alone, Who is the single Corner stone. And in this House by how much any one doth differ from and excel others, by so much being the more humble doth he hold up more of the building. One charity doth join all together after the fashion of cement: and the living stones be bound together by the bond of peace. The Towers be the Preachers and the Prelates of the Church: who are her wards and defence. Whence saith the Bridegroom unto His Spouse in the Song of Songs: "Thy neck is like the Tower of David builded for an armoury." The cock which is placed thereon representeth Preachers. For the cock, in the deep watches of the night, divideth the hours thereof; with his song he arouseth the sleepers; he foretelleth the approach of day; but first he stirreth up himself to crow by the striking of his wings. Behold ye these things mystically: for not one is there without meaning. The sleepers be the children of this world, lying in sins. The cock is the company of preachers, which do preach sharply, do stir up the sleepers to cast away the works of darkness, crying, "Woe to the sleepers: awake thou that sleepest"; which also do foretell the coming of the light, when they preach of the Day of judgement and future glory. But wisely before they preach unto others do they rouse themselves by virtues from the sleep of sin, and do chasten their bodies. Whence saith the Apostle, "I keep under my body and bring it into subjection." The same also do turn themselves to meet the wind when they bravely do contend against and resist the rebellious by admonition and argument, lest they should seem to flee when the wolf cometh. The iron rod, upon which the cock sitteth, sheweth the straightforward speech of the preacher; that he doth not speak from the spirit of man, but according to the Scriptures of God: as it is said, "If any man speak, let him speak as the oracles of God." In that this rod is placed above the Cross, it is shown that the words of Scripture be consummated and confirmed by the Cross: whence our Lord said in His Passion, "It is finished." And His Title was indelibly written over Him. The ball (*tholus*) upon which the Cross is placed doth signify perfection by its roundness: since the Catholick Faith is to be preached and held perfectly and inviolably: *Which Faith, except a man do*

IX-56. St. Louis Miraculously Recovers His Lost Breviary. The Hours of Jeanne d'Évreux, *fol. 154ᵛ*.

IX-57. St. Louis Burying the Bones of the Crusaders. The Hours of Jeanne d'Évreux, *fol. 159ᵛ*.

keep whole and undefiled, without doubt he shall perish everlastingly. Or else the ball doth signify the world redeemed by the Price of the Cross: on which account the Cross is placed over it. The cock being set over the Cross signifieth that the preacher ought to make sure this point, that Christ redeemed the world by His Cross. The pinnacle and turret show the mind or life of a Prelate who tendeth unto things above.

461

IX-58. Iconography of the Church as the Image of the Vine and of the Mystic Wine Press. *The vine grows out of the ground. Angels on outer margin protect the fruit and good works of the righteous against demons. In the center, Christ treads grapes brought in baskets to the press by two groups: on the left, a pope, a bishop, monks, hermits, etc.; on the right, queens, women in religion and in the world. Turning the press is probably one of the elect saved by Christ's death. Below, probably Sts. Peter and Paul and First Martyr, Stephen, empty their baskets at Christ's feet. The wine press, itself, is the image of the Church in which are united the fruits of holiness. The press is also a symbol of the Cross. Christ, who died on the Cross alone, also treads the grapes alone—for man's salvation. At lower left, Christ crosses the closed circle to heal a leper, symbolic of reclaimed heretics and repentant souls. At right, Enoch and Elias preach to Jews and others on the Last Days and Safeguard the faithful against the wiles of AntiChrist.* Hortus Deliciarum.

The bells, by the voice of which the people is called together unto the church, typify also preachers: the which being necessary for many uses are called by many names. The clapper, which causeth the sound from the two sides of the bell, is the tongue of the preacher which causeth both Testaments to resound. The wodden frame, whence the bell hangeth, signifieth the Cross; the cramps, charity; by which charity the Preacher being fast bound to the Cross, boasteth, saying, "God forbid that I should glory save in the Cross of our Lord Jesus Christ." The rope is the life and humility of the preacher. Whence the Apostle saith, "He condescendeth towards others. Whether we exalt ourselves it is for God; whether we abase ourselves it is for you." The rings on the rope are perseverance and the crown of reward. The glazed windows of the church be the Holy Scriptures, which do ward off the wind and the rain, that is, do depel all hurtful things; and when they do transmit the brightness of the True Sun by day into the church, they do give light to them that be therein. These be wider within than without, because the sense mystical is more ample and more pre-eminent than the sense literal. These be frequented of preachers, "who do fly as a cloud and as the doves to the windows." Also by the windows the five senses of the body be signified: which ought to be narrow without, lest they should take in vanities, but should be wide within to receive spiritual good. The door is Christ: whence the Lord saith in the Evangele, "I am the Door." The pillars be Doctors; who do hold up spiritually the Temple of God by their Doctrine, as do the Evangelists also the Throne of God. These, for the harmony of divine eloquence, be called silver columns: according to that of the Song of Songs, "He made the pillars thereof of silver." The Stalls do denote the Contemplative: in whom God doth rest without offence. These, for that they do contemplate the highest divinity and glory of the eternal life, be compared unto gold; whence in the aforesaid Song of Songs it is said, "He made a golden bed." The Beams be such as spiritually sustain the Church: the Cielings such as adorn it and strengthen it; of the which (because they be not corrupted by vices) the Bride glorieth in the same Canticles, saying, "The beams of our house are cedar and our rafters of fir." For God hath built His Church of living stones and imperishable wood: according to that, "Solomon made himself a litter of the wood of Lebanon"; that is, Christ *of His Saints made white by chastity*. The Chancel, when lower than the body of the church, showeth mystically how great humility ought to be in the Clergy; according to the saying, "The greater thou art the more humble thyself." The Altar signifieth Christ, without Whom, no acceptable gift is offered unto the Father. Whence the Church uttereth Her prayers unto the Father *through* Christ. The vestments with which the Altar is adorned be the Saints, of whom the Prophet speaketh unto God, saying, "Thou shalt surely clothe Thee with them all as with an ornament." The steps by which we ascend unto the Altar, do spiritually denote the Apostles and Martyrs of Christ, who have shed their blood for the love of Him. The Bride in the Canticles saith, "The ascent unto it is purple, the midst thereof being paved with love." Furthermore, the fifteen virtues be expressed by the fifteen steps with which they went up unto the Temple of Solomon: and the same be shown by the Prophet in the fifteen continuous Psalms, which the righteous man hath disposed as steps or degrees in his heart. This is the ladder which Jacob saw; the top of which touched the heavens. The Lights of the church be they by whose doctrine the Church shineth as the sun and the moon: unto whom it is said by our Lord's voice, "Ye are the light of the world." They be also the examples of good works: whence He saith in His admonitions, "Let your light so shine before men." In that the church is adorned joyfully within but not without, is shown morally that its "glory is all from within." For although it be contemptible externally, yet doth it shine within in the soul, which is the abode of God: whence the Church saith, "I am black but comely." And again, "Yea I have a goodly heritage." Which the Prophet considering, saith, "Lord, I have loved the habitation of Thy House: and the place where Thine Honour dwelleth," which

place also Faith, Hope, and Charity, do spiritually adorn. The Cross of Triumph is placed in the middle of the church, because the Church loveth Her Redeemer in the middle of Her heart, and "the midst thereof is paved with love, for the daughters of Jerusalem." The which, as a sign of victory, let all who see say one and all, *Hail, salvation of the whole world; hail, life-giving Tree!* Wherefore, lest we should ever forget the love of God for us, "Who gave His only begotten Son" to redeem us His servants, the Church armeth Herself in Her bosom and forehead with this sign, signifying that the Mystery of the Cross must always be believed by us in our heart, and confessed openly with our mouth. The figure of which went before Her in Egypt. But when we cross ourselves from the forehead downwards, and then from the left to the right, we do set forth this mystery, that "God bowed the heavens and came down," to teach us to prefer things eternal unto things temporal. But by this Sign the army of the devil is overthrown; the Church triumpheth, "terrible as an army with banner. How dreadful is this place: this is none other but the house of God." And the Hymn saith, *The banners of the King come forth: The Cross unfolds its Mystery.* Round this do the heavenly legions rally. Of this it is written, "I saw the Holy City, New Jerusalem, coming down from God out of heaven."

For the Church is militant here; in Her home she doth reign: a part is in pilgrimage, a part in glory. That which is in pilgrimage, coming up from Her exile through the Desert, doth sigh for Her home, from the "waters of Babylon for the heavenly Jerusalem;" while the other part, continually seeing peace, doth hold perpetual festival. Thus the heavenly city of Jerusalem is called the *Vision of Peace.* How glorious is Her Kingdom, "glorious things are spoken of Thee, thou City of God." Her guardians be the citizens of Heaven, the legions of Angels, with the glorious company of the Apostles, the Prophets, and the Patriarchs, the armies of Martyrs robed in purple, the flowers of Virgins, the verdant quire of Confessors, compassed about with the universal assembly of all the Saints, chaste and glorified! And

463

this wondrous Court of Heaven is yet more wondrously adorned by that one incomparable jewel, the *Virgin Mother,* 'whose like there ne'er hath been, whose like there ne'er shall be.' But how great is the admiration of all in beholding the King Himself, and how harmonious be the songs in praise of Him; this is known to those alone, who have deserved to stand amongst the happy throng, and to behold the mystery of the Trinity, and the glory of Christ: Who is encircled by the angelick quires; upon Whom the angels desire continually to gaze. To behold this the Immortal King face to face, the Church below is preparing Herself: and while she keepeth here Her Feasts of time, she is remembering the Festivals of Her home and of eternity; in which the Bridegroom is hymned by angelical instruments. And all the Saints continually celebrating the day of great festivity "which the Lord hath made," cease not in their nuptial songs to laud the Eternal Bridegroom, the beautiful in form above the sons of men; Him who hath chosen the Church for Himself of His free mercy. Of whom, as He had seen Her from eternity, He saith, "I will get Me to the mountain of myrrh, and to the hill of frankincense and will speak unto my spouse." For whom, "He came forth as a Bridegroom out of His chamber and rejoiced as a Giant to run His course"; and He went forth from His Father, and returned unto His Father,—went forth indeed even unto Hades, returned unto the Throne of God—to make all His Elect, from the beginning even unto the end of the world, one kingdom in the vision of the Supreme Trinity: in which is glorified "one God world without end."

95. *William Durandus on Symbolism*

Rationale, Proeme, 1, 2, 4, 6, 9, 18, trans. J. M. Neale, *Symbolism of Churches,* pp. 3–8, 13–14.

Here beginneth the First Book of Gulielmus Durandus *his* Rationale *of the* Divine Offices.

THE PROEME

1. All things, as many as pertain to offices and matters ecclesiastical, be full of divine significations and mysteries, and overflow with a celestial sweetness: if so be that a man be diligent in his study of them, and know how to draw "honey from the rock, and oil from the hardest stone." But who "knoweth the ordinances of heaven, or can fix the reasons thereof upon the earth"? For he that prieth into their majesty, is overwhelmed by the glory of them. Of a truth "the well is deep, and I have nothing to draw with:" unless He giveth it unto me "Who giveth to all men liberally, and upbraideth not:" so that "while I journey through the mountains" I may "draw water with joy out of the wells of salvation." Wherefore, albeit of the things handed down from our forefathers, capable we are not to explain all, yet if among them there be any thing which is done without reason, it should forthwith be put away. Wherefore I, William, by the alone tender mercy of God, Bishop of the Holy Church which is in Mende, will knock diligently at the door, if so be that "the key of David" will open unto me: that the King may "bring me in to His Treasury," and shew unto me the heavenly pattern which was shewed unto Moses in the mount: so that I may learn those things which pertain to Rites Ecclesiastical, whereof they teach and what they signify: and that I may be able plainly to reveal and make manifest the reasons of them, by His help, "Who hath ordained strength out of the mouth of babes and sucklings: Whose Spirit bloweth where It listeth," dividing to "each severally as it will" to the praise and glory of the Trinity.

2. Sacraments we have received to be signs or figures, not in themselves virtues, but the significations of virtues, by which men are taught as by letters. Now of signs there be that are natural, and there be that are positive: concerning which, and also of the nature of a Sacrament, we shall speak hereafter.

. . . . . .

4. Now the Professors of the arts liberal, and of all other arts, seek how they may clothe, support, and adorn with causes and hidden reasons those things which be nakedly and without ornament therein set forth; painters moreover, and mechanics and handicraftsmen of what sort soever, study in every variety of their works to ren-

der and to have at hand probable reasons thereof. So, also, unseemly is it to the magistrate to be ignorant of this world's laws; and to the pleader to know nothing of the law, wherein he is exercised.

. . . . .

6. Furthermore, the symbolism which existeth in things and offices ecclesiastical, is often not seen, both because figures have departed, and now it is the time of truth; and also because we ought not to judaise. But, albeit those types of which the truth is made manifest have departed, yet even to this time manifold truth is concealed, which we see not; wherefore the Church useth figures. For so by white vestments we understand the beauty in which our souls shall be arrayed, or the glory of our immortality, which we cannot manifestly behold: and in the Mass, by the oblation on the Altar, the Passion of Christ is represented, that it be held in the memory more faithfully and more firmly.

. . . . .

9. Now, in Holy Scriptures there be divers senses: as historic, allegoric, tropologic, and anagogic. Whence, according to Boethius, all Divine authority ariseth from a sense either historical or allegorical or from both. And, according to S. Hierom, we ought to study Holy Scriptures in three ways:—firstly, according to the letter; secondly, after the allegory, that is, the spiritual meaning; thirdly, according to the blessedness of the future.

History is *things signified by words:* as when a plain relation is made how certain events took place: as when the children of Israel, after their deliverence from Egypt, made a Tabernacle to the Lord. And history is derived from ἱστορεῖν, which is to gesticulate: whence gesticulators, (that is, players) are called *histriones.*

. . . . .

18. This work is described as a Rationale. For as in the Breast Plate of Judgement which the Jewish High Priest wore was written manifestation and truth, so here the reasons of the variations in Divine Offices and their truths are set forth and manifested: which the Prelates and Priests of Churches ought faithfully to preserve in the shrine of their breasts: and as in the breast plate there was a stone by the splendour of which the children of Israel knew that God was well pleased with them: so also the pious reader who hath been taught the mysteries of the Divine Offices from the clearness of this work will know that God is favourably disposed towards us, unless we rashly incur His indignation by our offence and fault. The breast plate was woven of four colours and of gold: and here, as we said before, the principles on which are founded the variations in Ecclesiastical Offices, take the hues of four senses, the Historic, the Allegoric, the Tropologic, and the Anagogic, with Faith as the ground work.

H. THE PHYSICAL UNIVERSE AND THE SPIRITUAL WORLD: BESTIARIES AND LAPIDARIES

96. *"There is a beast, which has the name sawfish"*

Trans. G. C. Druce, *The Bestiary of Guillaume Le Clerc* (London: Headley Brothers, Ltd., Invicta Press, 1936), pp. 20–21.

There is a beast, which has the name sawfish
And which does not live on land,
But in the great ocean dwells.
This beast is not little,
But is very big bodied;
Great wings has this dumb beast.
When it sees on that sea
Ships and swift vessels sailing,
With the wind it fills its wings,
Towards the ship it sails swiftly.
The wind carries it over the waves
Which are salt and very deep,
So it goes sailing far
Until it can go no farther.
Then it falls back and gives up
And the sea swallows it up
And draws it down to the depths.
The mariners who sail the sea
Are not wishful to meet it,
For it is a great peril of the sea,
It often brings the ship to grief
When it is able to reach it.
This beast without doubt
Bears a very great meaning.
The sea, which is vast and deep,
Signifies this present world,

Which is very bad and bitter
And perillous like the sea.
They who go sailing on the sea
Signify good folk who be,
Who go voyaging through this world
And steer their ship straight on
Through the waves, through the storms,
Against the dangers and the winds.
This is the meaning to be understood:
They are the good folk, whom the beast
Cannot catch or cause to drown,
Who never cease to battle.
Through this world go sailing
The wise men, steering their ship
So straight that the fell adversary
Is not able to wreck them.
The beast, of which I have told you,
Which on the sea sails a short way,
Then gives up and sinks into the deep,
Signifies many who be
Who commence by doing well,
By serving God and loving him;
And when they come in danger
Of great comforts and of pleasures,
Of desires which are great,
And of the deceits of this world,
Then they give up steering straight;
Soon they suffer shipwreck
And fall into adversities,
Into sins, into wickedness
Which drag them down to the depths below,
Straight into the abode of hell.

IX-59. Bestiary, Sawfish.

97. *"Amethyst is of purple color. . . . Who-so bereth this stone shall have in him the more mind of God. . . ."*

Reprinted from *English Medieval Lapidaries* by Joan Evans (London: Oxford University Press, for the Early English Text Society [Original Series, 190], 1933 [for 1932]), p. 26, with the kind permission of the Honorary Secretary of the Society.

Amatist is of purpure colour & draweth to colour of blode newe shedde. The boke telleth vs that this stone is comfortable to hym that bereth hit when wylde beestis commen to hym, & hit is comfortable in all sorowes, & holdeth man in gode beleue & stronge. & as the boke of Moyses seith vs, he that bereth Amatist shal be welcome before kyng & prince, & deliuerly shal wirke in all crafte that he entermeth of, & holdeth man lowely. Who-so bereth this stone shal haue in hym the more mynde of God, & is ful graciouse. The scripture of diuinite seith vs that amatist is of purpure colour that the Iewys clothed inne oure lorde Ihesu Xrist in despite for he made hym kyng. Of that colour & for that cause kynges shulde clothe hem when thei holden high courtes. For Salamon seith vs that the clothyng of the colour of Amatist shulde remembre vs of the clothynge of purpure that god was clothed inne atte his deethe, where-inne the Iewys clothed hym in scornyng, & the lordeshippe of / angeles & the deethe of martyres.

VIII. Books of Contemplative Vision: The "Ages" of Church and World; New Spiritual Monastics; the Divine-Human "Comedy" and the Common Life

A. HILDEGARDE OF BINGEN (1098–1179) AND THE MYSTIC VISION

98. *The Vision of the Great Mountain with Many Windows and the Bright One Above*

Scivias, 1:1, trans. F. M. Steele, *The Life and Visions of St. Hildegarde* (London: Heath, Cranton and Ousley, Ltd., 1914), pp. 130–37.

Summary.—*Of the strength and stability of the eternity of the kingdom of GOD. Of the fear of the Lord. Of those who are poor in spirit. That the Virtues coming from GOD, fearing GOD, guard the poor in spirit. That the works of men are not able to be hidden from the knowledge of GOD. Solomon concerning this matter.*

I saw as it were a great mountain, having the colour of iron, and above it a certain One sitting, of such exceeding great brightness that His brilliancy dimmed my sight. And out of both sides of Him stretched a soft shadow, like a wing of wonderful length and breadth. And before Him, at the foot of this same mountain, stood a certain image full of eyes round about it, and because of the multitude of the eyes, I was unable to discern any human form about it. And before this last image was another of a child clothed in a pale vestment, with white shoes, and upon his head descended so much brightness, from Him Who sat upon the top of the mountain, that I was not worthy to look upon His face, except through Him Who sat above. Many living sparks fell down which flew round these images with great gentleness.

In this same mountain many little windows were to be discerned, in which appeared as it were heads of men, some pale and some white. And behold, He Who sat above the mountain called out in a very strong and most penetrating voice, saying:

O man! fragile dust of the dust of the earth, and ashes of ashes, cry aloud and say concerning the entrance into incorruptible salvation: Forasmuch as those who are learned and see the inner meaning of the Scriptures, but wish neither to tell it nor to preach it because they are blind and tepid in preserving the righteousness of God, open to them the lock of these mysteries, which they timid ones conceal in a hidden field without fruit. Therefore write at large from a fountain of abundance, and so overflow in mystical erudition, that they may tremble at the profusion of your irrigation, who wished you to be considered contemptible on account of Eve's transgression.

But thou dost not get this profound knowledge from men, for thou receivest it from above, from the tremendous and heavenly Judge, where in very clear light this serenity will shine strongly among the shining ones. Arise, therefore, cry aloud, and say: These things are manifested to thee by the strongest power of Divine help, because He Who governs every one of His creatures powerfully and benignly, pours forth Himself in the light of celestial illumination, upon those fearing Him and walking in His gentle love, in a spirit of humility, and leads those persevering in the way of righteousness, to the joys of the eternal vision.

IX-60. *Bestiaire D'Amour. Sailors land on the back of a whale, thinking it to be Land. It submerges, and they Drown. Fournival, 14th century MS.*

From whence also, as thou seest, this great mountain having an iron colour means the strength and stability of the eternity of the kingdom of God, which by no means of change or decay is able to be exterminated. And He Who sitting above in such light that the brightness of the vision blinded thee, shows in the kingdom of blessedness, Him Who, governing all the world in the splendour of perfect serenity, is incomprehensible to the minds of men in His heavenly divinity.

But from each side of Him a soft shadow, like a wing of wonderful length and breadth, is extended: which is both in admonishing and chastising a sweet and gentle protection, showing justly and lovingly an ineffable justice in the perseverance of true equity.

And before Him at the foot of the mountain was standing a certain image, full of eyes everywhere: because the gazing into the kingdom of God in humility before Him, fortified by the fear of the Lord, and with the clearness of a good and just intention, trains in men earnest endeavour and divine stability: thus thou wast not able to discern any human form in it by reason of its eyes, because He mitigates, by the sharpest glance of His inspection, all that forgetfulness of the justice of God, which men in weariness of spirit often feel, for human inquiry in its weakness cannot shake off His vigilance.

And before this image was another of the age of a child, in a white tunic, and it appeared to be shod with white shoes, because those who are poor in spirit follow in the preceding fear of the Lord, in as much as the fear of the Lord, in humble devotion, holds fast firmly the blessedness of poverty of spirit, which does not desire vainglory nor elation of heart, but loves simplicity and sobriety of mind, not attributing its good works to itself but to God, as it were in the pallor of subjection, like the garment of a white tunic, but following faithfully the innocent footsteps of the Son of God.

So much brightness descended upon His head from Him Who sat above the mountain, that thou wast not able to see His face, because the serenity of His visitation, Who governs every creature laudably, infuses the power and strength of His beatitude, so much that thou with thy weak and mortal regard wast not able to grasp His riches, and he who has divine riches submits himself humbly to poverty.

But because many living sparks go out from Him, Who sits above the mountain, and fly round those images with great gentleness, this means that divers and very strong virtues shining in great brilliancy come from Almighty God, and embrace ardently and comfort those who fear God truly, and who love poverty of spirit faithfully, and are surrounded by His help and guardianship. Then in this same mountain as it were many little windows were seen at which appeared men's faces, some pale and some white, because in the highest height of the deepest and clearest knowledge of God, the endeavours of men are neither able to be hidden nor concealed when they very often show in themselves earnestness and beauty, for sometimes men fatigued in heart and action sleep in disgrace, and sometimes roused up they watch in honour, as Solomon testifies according to My will saying: "The hand of the poor worketh extreme poverty, but the hand of the strong prepares riches' (*Prov. x.*).

For it is said that that man makes himself poor and weak, who is unwilling to do justice,

or to blot out iniquity or to remit debt, when he remains careless in the wonderful things of the works of blessedness. But he who works the works of salvation running in the way of truth, he obtains a fountain of glory, in which he prepares for himself, both in heaven and on earth, the most precious riches.

And whosoever has the knowledge of the Holy Spirit and the wings of faith, he will not transgress my admonition, but will perceive it, embracing it in the joy of his soul.

99. *Vision by the Soul of Living Light; a Starless Sky Seen Through a Luminous Mist*

Trans. by the editor from texts edited and collated in H. Liebschuetz, *Das allegorische Weltbild der Heiligen Hildegard von Bingen* (Leipzig/Berlin: Teubner, 1930), pp. 168–69, F. W. Wentzlaff-Eggebert, *Deutsche Mystik zwischen Mittelalter und Neuzeit* (Berlin: W. de Gruyter & Co., 1944), pp. 26–30, and J. Buehler, *Schriften der Heiligen Hildegard von Bingen* (Leipzig: Insel-Verlag, 1922), pp. 34–37.

Ever since the days of my childhood, when my bones, sinews and veins were not yet come to full strength, even until the present day, when I am more than seventy years old, I have joyously sustained the grace of this vision. Moreover, when God wills it, my soul launches itself in vision to the height of the firmament up through alternating layers of the ether. There it sometimes distributes itself among numerous peoples of the earth even though they be far from me in distant lands. And because I perceive these things thus in my soul, I behold them according to the shifting nuances of the clouds and of other creatures. But I do not hear these things with external [bodily] ears, nor with the deliberations of my heart, neither do I perceive them through any collaboration of my five senses. Rather, do I contemplate all these things in my soul, with my outer eyes wide open, in full watchfulness day and night, and without any of the deficiencies commonly associated with ecstasy.

The light that I see is wholly boundless, it is immeasurably brighter than a cloud which the sun suffuses. I see in it no height, length, or breadth. It is, in my parlance, the Shadow of the Living Light. And just as the sun, the earth, and the stars are reflected in water, so there are reconstructed for me in this light the writings, speech, virtues and manifold works of men.

And what I see and experience in this vision, I preserve long in memory so that, when I see and hear this light, I remember and simultaneously see, hear, recognize and, as it were, instantaneously learn what I know. But what I do not envision in this light, that I do not know, for I am untutored and I have only been taught to read letters in utter simplicity. And what I write down in the vision that I see and hear, I bring forth in unpolished Latin words as I hear it in contemplation. In the vision I am not taught to write as philosophers do. And the words of my vision are not the words which sound from the mouths of men, but are like a glittering flame and like a cloud moving in pure air.

The nature of this light I am unable to recognize, even as I am incapable of fully envisaging the sun's disk. In this same light I see, not often, but occasionally, another light which I term the Living Light. When and how I see this I am not able to make known. So long as I see it, every sorrow and all anguish is swept away from me; so that I am as an innocent young maiden and not as an old woman.

On account of recurring illness which I suffer, I sometimes experience a tedium of words and visions. But when my soul sees and tastes this Light, then, as I said before, I become so altered that all sadness and trouble are forgotten. And what I there see and hear in vision refreshes my soul like that drawn from a fountain, which however remains full and inexhaustible.

Under no condition does my soul want for that Light which I have called the Shadow of the Living Light. I see it as I behold the firmament without stars through a brilliantly lighted cloud or mist. I also see therein what I must often speak and know in order to answer those questioning me concerning the Living Light.

In apparition I also perceived what that first book of my visions, the Scivias (Know the Way) should be called, for it was specifically created in the way of the Living Light and not upon any other teaching. In true vision also I have written the book Scivias and all the others. . . .

B. HERRADE OF LANDSBERG AND HER GARDEN OF DELIGHTS ("HORTUS DELICIARUM")

100. Editorial Commentary on the "Ladder of the Virtues (Charity)"

Hortus Deliciarum, Pl. LVI, also pp. 43ff. and 34ff., as edited by A. Straub and G. Keller (Strasbourg: Schlesier and Schweikhardt, 1901). Publie aux Frais de La Société Pour La Conservation des Monuments Historiques d'Alsace.

This Ladder of the Virtues is, more accurately, the Ladder of Charity. The inscription at the upper left reads: "This ladder represents the ascent of the virtues and of the religious exercise of holiness by which one seeks to attain the crown of eternal life. Many at first set out to climb it but, wounded by devilish arrows they draw back in time. Diverted and enticed by earthly hindrances and desires they fall miserably." From the foot of the ladder the dragon rears himself in ambush against those attempting the ascent. A soldier and his lay, female companion, as well as a nun, a clerk, a monk, a recluse, and a hermit fall in turn before the arrows of demoniacal figures and their own sins. The first couple like others are subject to physical appetites, the soldier being dazzled, meanwhile, by the prospect of a beautiful horse and armor. The nun falls to the blandishments of a priest. Then a clerk is lured off the ladder by his waving girl friend. Farther up a monk is mesmerized by a basket full of gold. A recluse dreams of a soft bed. As for the hermit, he is enamored of his little garden. It is charity alone, thanks to angelic protection, who receives at the top of the ladder the Crown of Life from the Lord's own hand. The inscription at the head reads: "This personification of Virtue signifies all the saints and the elect who will be led with angelic protection to the celestial reward. And the virtue of charity, alone, comprising all the other virtues, will lead to the attainment of the crown of heavenly recompense." Those falling away perilously as herewith depicted may, however, be enabled by penitence and the Lord's help to remount the ladder and ascend to the summit of the virtues.

101. *Editorial Commentary on "Philosophy and the Liberal Arts"*

Ibid., Pl. XI[b18] and pp. 10–11.

In the center Philosophy rules as queen. From her golden crown issues three heads, labeled Ethics, Logic, and Physics. Socrates and Plato studiously face each other across reading desks placed at her feet. Next her bosom she holds a long band, reading: "The wise alone are able to do what they will." On the right one notes: "Seven well-springs of living water gush forth from Philosophy. These are called the Liberal Arts." And on the left: "The Holy Spirit is the originator of the seven liberal arts which are Grammar, Rhetoric, Dialectic, Music, Arithmetic, Geometry, and Astronomy." The circle environing Philosophy bears the legend: "I, Philosophy, with the art ruling all things that are, divide the subject arts into seven parts."

In the top circle is Grammar, her head veiled in white. She has a book in one hand

IX-61. Ladder of Charity. Hortus Deliciarum.

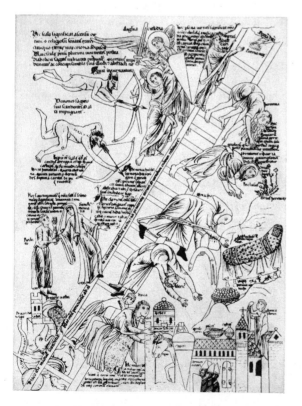

and disciplining switches in the other. Next right is Rhetoric holding a stylus and two writing tablets. Their black border betokens the care that should characterize a speaker preparing a discourse. Dialectic is engaged in lively conversation, as the gesturing right hand suggests. The left hand holds the head of a barking dog. This symbolizes the incessant cries elicited by disputation and the wariness with which the debater follows his opponent's line of argument. Music plays a kind of harp here called a zither. An old instrument called the *organistrum* and a lyre are at either side. Arithmetic has a counting device, a semicircular wand comprising a string of twenty-two black balls. Geometry bears a compass and surveying equipment. Astronomy scans the starry sky. In her hand is a closed box or bushel basket, probably suggesting the role of meteorology in agricultural labor.

In the circumference that embraces all of these are the words: "These exercises of the world Philosophy has investigated; having investigated, she has observed them; she has set them down in writing and has infused her children with them. Philosophy teaches by the study of the seven arts, examining thoroughly the elements and the innermost secrets of things."

Below and outside the circle are four poets and/or magicians. A raven hovers over each one seated at his desk and whispers malevolent inspiration in his ear. However receptive to philosophers of pagan antiquity, Herrade like her contemporaries drew the line at poets and magicians. Their purported inspiration by "the Spirit of the world" accented an age-long conflict between the liberal arts and authors, or literature proper.

C. JOACHIM OF FIORE AND THE "AGES," "STATES," AND "TIMES" OF THE WORLD AND CHURCH

102. *A Summary-Preview of Joachim's "Ages"*

Reprinted by permission of the publisher from H. Bett, *Joachim of Flora* (London: Methuen & Co., Ltd., 1931), pp. 44–47.

But amid all this nightmare of apocalyptic exegesis, Joachim never loses sight of his main conception—the three great dispensations which are respectively identified with God the Father, God the Son, and God the Holy Spirit. The first age reaches from Adam to Christ. It is initiated in Adam, fructified from Abraham to Zacharias, and consummated in Christ. During this age men live a carnal life: it is the age of those who marry and give in marriage. The second age reaches from Uzziah to the present time. It is initiated in Uzziah, fructified from Zacharias to the forty-second generation following, and consummated, therefore, in the year 1260. During this age men live a mixed life, between the flesh and the spirit; it is the age of clerics. The third age reaches from St. Benedict to the end of the world. It is initiated in St. Benedict, and fructified from the twenty-second generation after St. Benedict, i.e. about 1200, to the end of the dispensation. During this age men live a spiritual life; it is the age of monks. The three ages therefore overlap. The age of the Son begins to appear in the age of the Father, and reaches on into Joachim's own lifetime. The age of the Spirit begins to appear in the age of the Son, some centuries before Joachim's time, and reaches on to the end of the world. But the age of the Father ends with the birth of Christ, and the age of the Son ends with the final reign of the Spirit. The third age has a peculiar *donum Spiritus Sancti* which is especially a *donum contemplationis*. There is to be an *ordo contemplantium*, and the whole Church will be an *ecclesia contemplativa*. The three ages therefore represent a spiritual progress. Truth is revealed dimly in the first age of the Old Covenant, more clearly in the second age of the New Covenant, and fully and finally in the last age, the dispensation of the Spirit.

Joachim develops this idea of the three dispensations with almost a lyrical passion. The first period is the age of law, the second of grace, the third of love. The first is the age of mere slavery, the second of filial service, the third of liberty. The first age is ruled by the attributes of the Father, as power, dread, and faithfulness; the second by the attributes of the Son, as humility, truth, and wisdom; the third by the attributes of the

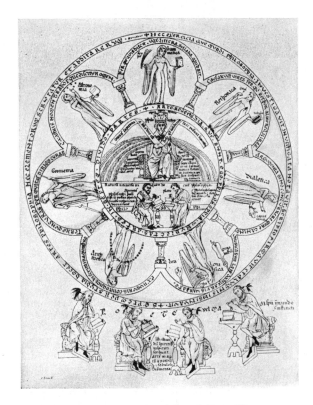

IX-62. Philosophy and the Liberal Arts. Hortus Deliciarum.

Spirit, as love, liberty and joy. The first period is therefore the age of fear and law and a life of labour; the second of wisdom and grace and a life of discipline; the third of love and happiness and a life of contemplation. The first is the age of babes, the second of the young, the third of the old. The first is a starry night, the second a grey dawn, the third the full day. The first is winter, the second spring, the third summer. The first is the rind, the second the stone, the third the kernel. The first bore nettles, the second roses, and the third shall bear lilies. The first is earth, the second water, the third fire. The first is Septuagesima, the second Lent, the third Easter. The first is the age of the married—*ordo conjugatorum*—which is an image of the Father, in His fatherly relation. The second is the age of clerics—*ordo clericorum*—which is an image of the Son, Who is the Word of God and the Wisdom of God, for it is the business of the clerical

IX-63. The Chariot of Lust. *A personified vice, dressed like a courtesan, flaunting violets and other flowers, is accompanied in her car by her corrupt female associates coated in mail: Amour, Lasciviousness, Beauty, Sloth, Voluptuousness, Garrulity, Indecency, Coquetry, and others—all ready for full onslaught against the Virtues (not shown) temporarily taken by surprise.* Hortus Deliciarum.

IX-64. The Chariot of Lust Overturned. *The Virtue, Temperance, arriving in the nick of time, raises the Cross against Lust. The horses bolt, and the chariot is upset. Lust is crushed under a millstone by Temperance, symbolic of Christ. Voluptuousness runs barefoot through a thorn bush. Amour abandons bow and quiver. Beauty drops girdle and jewelry. Lust and her accomplices, now dressed in long robes without armor and with hair unbound, are in stupefied, despairing rout before Temperance.*

472

order to speak and teach. The third is the age of monks—*ordo monachorum*—which is an image of the Holy Spirit, Who is Love, for those who despise the world are inflamed with the love of God, and led by the Spirit, as the Lord was when He was driven into the desert. It is thus the peculiar business of laymen to work, of clerics to teach, of monks to praise. The relative worth and exaltation of the three orders is shown by the fact that a layman may become a cleric, but a cleric cannot revert into a layman, and so a cleric may become a monk, but a monk cannot revert into a cleric. The three ages are thus ages respectively of work, of learning, and of praise. This is really a sacerdotal history of the world, beginning with the Levites, prolonged in the secular clergy, and fulfilled in the Benedictine Order as finally reformed under a more rigorous rule. It is in this sense a philosophy of history, conceived in terms of the monastic ideal, but representatively not confined to that precise form, because the Levites represent all who lived under the law of Moses, and the clerics represent all who live under the law of Christ, and the monks represent all who will live in ardent love under the Spirit.

103. Joachim, Salimbene and the Threefold State

Chronica, via G. G. Coulton, *From St. Francis to Dante* (London: Nutt, 1906), p. 151 (1261–240).

As Salimbene puts it (1261–240), "he divides the world into a threefold state; for in the first state the Father worked in mystery through the patriarchs and sons of the prophets, although the works of the Trinity are indivisible. In the second state the Son worked through the Apostles and other apostolic men; of which state He saith in John 'My Father worketh until now, and I work.' In the third state the Holy Ghost shall work through the Religious."

104. The Three "States" According to the Expositio

Trans. by the editor from the *Liber in Expositionem in Apocalipsam* (Venice, 1527), cap. 5.

The first of these three states [or orders] spoken of existed during the period of the law. Then the Lord's people, serving in lowliness like that of children, were under the elements of this world. They were as yet unable to attain that coming liberty of spirit referred to by the one who said, "If the Son liberates you, you will be free indeed." The second state was initiated under the Gospel. It remains to the present time with a certain liberty considered from the perspective of the past but not with that freedom to be characteristic of the future. Thus the Apostle says, "Now we know in part and we prophesy in part, but when that which is perfect is come that which is in part shall be done away." And in another place, "Where the spirit of the Lord is, there is liberty." Therefore, the third state will be ushered in toward the close of our present age; no longer under the veil of the letter but in the spirit of complete liberty. The first age which shone under the law of circumcision was begun with Adam. The second, refulgent under the Gospel was instituted by Uzziah. The third, permitting us to calculate the numbers of the generations was given by St. Benedict, the consummation of whose surpassing splendor is to be anticipated near the end. At that time Elias will be revealed and the unbelieving people of the Jews will be converted to the Lord. Then, also, the Holy Spirit will appear to cry in a loud voice in these words: "The Father and the Son have worked up to this time, and now I work." The letter of the former Testament seems with a certain propriety to pertain to the Father. The letter of the New Testament will pertain to the Son. Likewise the spiritual understanding proceeds beyond both Father and Son to the Holy Spirit. To return as it were to the order of the married which prevailed in the first age, this with a certain fittingness seems to pertain to the Father. The order of preachers (or clerks) who are in the second—likewise the order of monks having been established at the very end of the era—pertains to the Holy Spirit. And according to this, the first state is, in a manner of speaking, ascribed to the Father, the second to the Son, the third to the Holy Spirit. . . . From one perspective, it is possible to consider the ages of the world as being five in number; the fifth, proceeding in

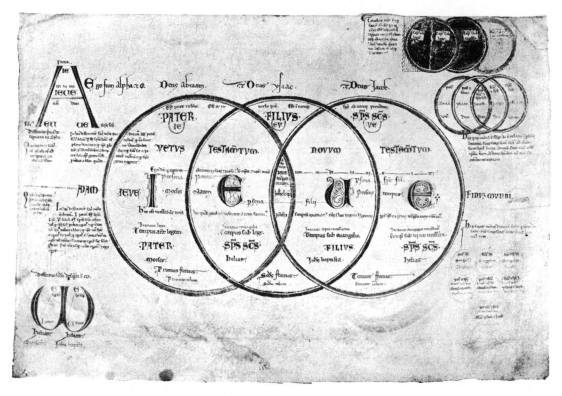

IX-65. Joachim and the Trinitarian Circles. Figure Book.

the heavenly country (*patria*) where duration of time does not exist, cannot readily be cast into these categories. The first refers to a time antedating the period of law. The second, that under law. The third, that under the Gospel. The fourth, under the spiritual intellect. The fifth consisting in the manifest vision of God. So, likewise, it behooves the elect of God to go on from virtue to virtue, to pass on from splendor to splendor, until they behold the God of Gods in Zion —from the natural law to the law of Moses; from the law of Moses to that of the Gospel; from that of the spiritual intellect to the true, eternal contemplation of God.

105. The Three "States" According to the Concordia

84, fol. 112, trans. by the editor with the aid of A. Rosenberg-R. Birchler, *Das Reich des Heiligen Geistes* (München-Planegg, 1954 [1955]), pp. 82–83, E. Benz, *Ecclesia Spiritualis* (Stuttgart: Kohlhammer, 1934), p. 9, and Bett, *Joachim*, p. 46.

The first state [or era] was that in which we were under law, the second when we were under grace, the third when we lived in anticipation of even richer grace; grace for grace he gave us says John (1:16), or faith for love and both together. The first state was in knowledge, the second in the power of wisdom, the third in the perfection of understanding. The first in the bondage of a slave, the second in the service of a son, the third in freedom. The first in vexation, the second in action; the third in contemplation. The first in fear, the second in faith, the third in love. The first under the condition of a slave, the second that of one free, the third that of a friend. The first the age of children, the second that of the young, the third that of the old. The first in starlight, the second in moonlight, the third in full daylight. The first in winter, the second in spring, the third in summer. The first bringing forth nettles, the second roses, the third lilies. The first producing grass, the second stalks, the third wheat. The first water, the second wine, the third oil. The first pertaining to Septuagesima, the second to Quadragesima, the third to Easter.

106. The "Months" After the Conception of Elizabeth

Trans. by the editor from the *Tractatus super quatuor Evangelia*, ed. E. Buonaiuti (Roma, 1930), I, 35, compared with Rosenberg-Birchler, *Das Reich*, pp. 93–94.

The first month after Elizabeth's conception signifies the time of the apostles, the second the time of the martyrs, the third the time of the doctors or teachers, the fourth the time of the virgins, the fifth the time of the Western monks. The sixth month, since the angel Gabriel was then sent to the Virgin, signifies the sixth time of the opening of the six seals according to the Apocalypse; the time in which the Virgin was to conceive and shortly after which the one conceiving in her old age (that is, Elizabeth) must give birth. . . . Accordingly, we maintain it is in this sixth time that it behooves the virginal, or rather the continent and contemplative, church to conceive. It is fitting that she have in the womb of her profession that holy people which, according to Daniel, is to be given the kingdom that is to rule supreme over everything under heaven. She will be delivered of this kingdom at the end of the age, so that the son of this chaste mother may at the same time escape the shadows of this world and be born in the Fatherland of eternal glory.

107. The Sixth and Seventh "Ages" or "Times" According to the Misterium Ecclesia

Trans. by the editor from L. Tondelli, M. Reeves, B. Hirsch-Reich, *Il libro delle figure dell' abate Gioachino da Fiore*, 2nd ed., Vol. II (Torino, 1953), "Transcrizione del testo delle tavole," Tavola 19, compared with Rosenberg-Birchler, *Das Reich*, pp. 98–99. This translation and the one following were made with the kind permission of Società Editrice Internazionale, Torino.

Therefore, the time of Quadragesima signifies the sixth age. Eastertime represents the seventh, of whom the Apostle says: "The Sabbath rest will be given to the people of God." And these two eras, namely the sixth and the seventh, stand in perfect contrast: to the sixth pertains labor, to the seventh rest. The one relates specifically to Christ, the other to the Holy Spirit. For Christ, in a particular way, inaugurated the sixth age; wherein, soon after its beginning, the Holy Spirit initiated the seventh, given in a two-fold way to the Apostles after the Lord's passion. So there were instituted in the church two orders and two ways of life: one with regard to those working, the other with respect to those contemplating; the one in the active, the other in the contemplative life. The active life, therefore, which pertains to the sixth age is properly ascribed to Christ who, having taken upon himself our mortal body, chose to preach, suffer, and die. The contemplative life, however, which looks to the Sabbath, is rightly attributed to the Holy Spirit which was always free and devoid of the efforts of labor. . . . Therefore, the active life refers to Peter, the contemplative to John; to Peter belongs laborious pain and sorrow, to John effortless tranquillity. But one day both Peter and John will be summoned, because both orders have been instituted together in the coming of the Lord and in the advent of the Holy Spirit. Observe, however, that these two, who set forth together, shall not finish their course at the same time; because Peter having died, John remains in this life. That transient life belonging to Peter shall be consummated in the sixth age, but that belonging to John will be rendered lasting and will become the seventh age in all its glory.

108. The Plan of the New Orders Pertaining to the Third State as a Preview of the Heavenly Jerusalem

Trans. by the editor from the *Dispositio novi ordinis* . . . after Tondelli, *Il libro*, "Transcrizione,". . . Tavola 12, and compared with H. Grundmann, *Neue Forschungen über Joachim von Fiore* (Marburg, 1950), and Rosenberg-Birchler, *Das Reich*, pp. 134ff. For literature and text see M. W. Bloomfield, "Joachim of Flora: A Critical Survey of the Canon, Teachings, Sources, Biography and Influence," *Traditio*, XIII (New York: Fordham University Press, 1957), pp. 249–309.

PAUL THE APOSTLE

For as the body is one, and hath many members. . . . so also is Christ (I Cor. 12:12). For the body also is not one member, but many. If the foot should say, because I am not the hand, I am not of the body; is it therefore not of the body? (I Cor. 12:14–15).

JOHN THE EVANGELIST

I John saw a door opened in heaven and behold a throne was set in heaven and round about the throne and in the midst of it were four living animals full of eyes before and behind. And the first animal was like a lion, the second like a calf, the third having the face as it were of a man, the fourth like an eagle flying (Apoc. 4:1–2; 6–7).

And he gave some apostles, and some prophets and other some evangelists, and other some pastors and doctors. For the perfecting of the saints, for the work of the ministry, for the edifying of the body of Christ: Until we all meet into the unity of the faith, and of the knowledge of the Son of God, unto a perfect man, unto the measure of the age of the fullness of Christ (Ephes. 4:11–13).

1. Oratory (House of Prayer) of the holy God-begotten Mary and of the Holy Jerusalem
   Dove. Spirit of Counsel. Nose. Seat of God.

This house will be the mother of all and in it will reside the spiritual father who will govern all, and whose government and will, all must obey. The brethren of this house will live according to order in all things so that their example of patience and sobriety may edify others. In fasting they will follow the Rule of the Cistercians. . . .

2. The Oratory of St. Peter and of all the Holy Apostles
   Lion. Spirit of Courage. Hand.

In this oratory will dwell the aged brethren and those of delicate health who, because of weak stomachs, are not able to sustain the full ardors of the Rule in fasting, yet who wish, insofar as they are able, to follow the Rule in all sincerity and by their simplicity and obedience to manifest proper reverence for it. . . .

3. The Oratory of St. Stephen and of all the Martyr Saints
   Calf. Spirit of Knowledge. Mouth.

In this oratory will be those brethren who are strong in obedience to outer works and who are not able to grow as much as is desirable in the perfection of spiritual discipline, or teaching. . . .

4. The Oratory of St. Paul and of all the holy Doctors of the Church
   Man. Spirit of Understanding. Ear.

In this oratory will be educated men or at least such as are still being instructed and who are docile before God. These are men longing and able to devote themselves more than the rest to spiritual reading. They are zealous for spiritual teaching more than anything else so that they may have the means of bringing forth things new and old. . . .

5. The Oratory of St. John the Evangelist and of all the Virgin Saints
   Eagle. Spirit of Wisdom. Eye.

In this oratory will be proved and perfected men who, by the stimulation of spiritual longing, wish to lead a quiet life. Each will have his own cell into which he may readily enter when he wishes to pray. This will be, not just where each one might wish it, but next the cloister, in keeping with the arrangement and will of the spiritual father who is over all. . . .

6. Oratory of St. John the Baptist and of all the Prophets
   Dog. Spirit of Devotion. Foot.

In this oratory will be gathered priests and clerks who wish to live continently and together but are not willing to renounce completely the eating of flesh and the wearing of warm clothing. . . .

7. The Oratory of St. Abraham the Patriarch and of all holy Patriarchs
   Sheep. Spirit of Fear. Body.
   "We are the people and the sheep of his pasture."

In this oratory will be assembled the married, with their sons and daughters under the common life, who associate with their wives more for the raising up of progeny than for pleasure. And at stated times or days they shall abstain from them by consent in order to devote themselves to prayer; taking into consideration the conditions of youth and age, in order that they may not be tempted by Satan. They shall have their own houses and shall guard themselves from all accusations. And they shall obey the master according to the ordering and will of the spiritual father. . . . They shall fast in winter on every holy day, except in cases of illness. They shall be covered with a simple cloak. Among these Christians there shall not come any idle ones who do not work for their bread. . . . Each one shall work at his own handicraft or trade, and individual craftsmen or artists shall have their own superiors. Whoever will not work according to his ability will be compelled by the master and denounced by all. Their way of life and clothing shall be simple, as befits Christians. Outlandish styles and dyed cloth shall not be found among them. Further, honest and reliable women will work wool and process it for the poor of Christ and they will be as mothers to the rest, instructing the adolescents and girls in the fear of the Lord. Those in this house will give tithes of all they possess to the clergy for the support of the poor and of strangers as well as of boys who study doctrine. . . . So that, if any have a superfluity while others have less than they need, according to the judgment of the spiritual father, the excess shall be taken from those having more and given to those having less; so that none may be in need among them, and thus everything will be in common.

D. EIKE OF REPGOW (C. 1180–C. 1235) AND HIS WORLD CHRONICLE

109. The Creation of Adam and Eve

> Items 109–112 trans. by Mr. Gerald Shinn in collaboration with the editor from the *Sächsische Weltchronik, Monumenta Germaniae Historica*, Script. II (Hannover, 1877), p. 67.

God made Adam as the last of His works in the first hour of the day. He created him from the earth in His likeness and gave him power over beasts, birds and fish. Then He placed him in Paradise. In the third hour, He made Eve from Adam's rib while he slept and gave her to him for his wife. In the sixth hour they both sinned because they ate the fruit that God had forbidden them. In the ninth hour God cast them out of Paradise and sent them into the world.

110. The Persecution of Diocletian

> *Ibid.*, pp. 113–14.

Diocletian and Maximian, like Nero, stirred up a persecution against Christianity. It was the greatest and the longest persecution, lasting ten years. In one month alone

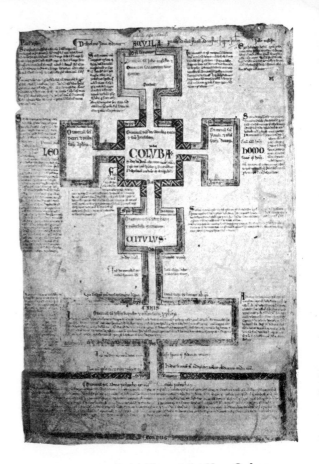

IX-66. Joachim and the Plan of the New Orders. Figure Book.

seventeen thousand men and women were martyred. Watchmen were posted by the doorways, in the street, in the market, by wells and by rivers; then, when anyone came along he was forced to confess whether he was a Christian or a heathen. The situation was so grave that the heathen seized the Christians, the servant his master, the father his son, brother his brother, just as Christ had said. Old men, who should have been honored, were seized and dragged through the streets like dogs. Then, for the amusement of the people, they were thrown to the lions and to the bears, which ripped them apart. Elderly maiden ladies and women, whom no one should rightly have touched, were dragged through the mire by the hair. There were men who denied that they were Christians. Still others killed themselves for fear that they might deny their shepherd. What reward God gave

IX-67. The Seven Ages of the World. *The Earthly Paradise. God the Father and Creator in Blessing.*

IX-68. Dante, *Divine Comedy. MS., 14th century, Florence.*

IX-69. Francis Renounces His Earthly Father before the Bishop. *Fresco, Giotto, Upper Church of St. Francis, Assisi.*

IX-70. Francis Supporting the Tottering Chapel of St. John Lateran in Innocent III's Dream. *Giotto, Upper Church of St. Francis.*

them, God only knows. It would have been better if they had worshiped the idol.

111. Justinian and His Laws

Ibid., p. 135.

In the five hundred and twenty-seventh year from the birth of our Lord, Justinian became emperor. He was thirty-eight years old. He greatly improved the empire in Rome and Constantinople. He conquered Persia, expelled the Goths from Lombardy, and reconquered Africa. He constructed [the church of] St. Sophia in Constantinople, which no one has surpassed. He decreed that no heretic might become a soldier. He also collected the laws from all books into one book, which is called the *Institutes*. He is the emperor who honored the rule of law more than any other.

112. The Coronation of Charlemagne

Ibid., p. 150.

In the year 801 from the birth of our Lord, Karl the Great became emperor at Rome—the seventy-third from Augustus. He ruled for fourteen years. It happened like this:

As King Karl stood before St. Peter's altar during the mass, in the holy days at Christmastide, Pope Leo set the crown on his head before he knew it. He was then proclaimed emperor and Augustus with great love over all the people. Pope Leo consecrated him emperor and honored him before the senators, even as men had done for the old emperors in times past, as soon as the token of honor was brought from Constantinople to Rome. After the coronation everyone knelt and bowed his head.

E. DANTE AND THE DIVINE COMEDY

113. The Paradiso *and Joachim of Fiore*

Canto XII, ll. 127–41. This item, together with 114 and 115 trans. J. D. Sinclair, *The Divine Comedy of Dante Alighieri*, III: *Para-*

diso (London: The Bodley Head, Ltd., 1946). This item, p. 181.

I am the living soul of Bonaventura of Bagnorea, who in great offices ever put last the left-hand care. Here are Illuminato and Augustine, who were among the first barefoot Poor Brothers that in the cord made themselves God's friends; Hugh of St Victor is here with them, and Peter the Bookworm, and Peter the Spaniard who shines below in twelve books; Nathan the prophet, and Chrysostom the Metropolitan, and Anselm, and that Donatus who deigned to set his hand to the first art; Rabanus is here, and beside me shines the Calabrian Abbot Joachim, who was endowed with a spirit of prophecy.

114. The Paradiso *of the Three Circles*

Ibid., Canto XXXIII, ll. 115–26, p. 485.

In the profound and clear ground of the lofty light appeared to me three circles of three colours and of the same extent, and the one seemed reflected by the other as rainbow by rainbow, and the third seemed fire breathed forth equally from the one and the other. O how scant is speech and how feeble to my conception! and this, to what I saw, is such that it is not enough to call it little. O Light Eternal, that alone abidest in Thyself, alone knowest Thyself, and, known to Thyself and knowing, lovest and smilest on Thyself!

115. The Paradiso, *Giotto, St. Francis, and Lady Poverty*

Ibid., Canto XI, ll. 58–63, 73–78, 85–117, pp. 165, 167, 169.

. . . for, still a youth, he ran into strife with his father for a lady to whom, as to death, none willingly unlocks the door, and before his spiritual court *et coram patre* he was joined to her, and thenceforth loved her better every day. . . . But, lest I proceed too darkly, take now Francis and Poverty for these lovers in all I have said. Their harmony and happy looks moved men to love and wonder and sweet contemplation and led them to holy thoughts, . . . Then that father and master went on his way with his lady and with that family which now was bound with the lowly cord; nor did cowardice of heart weigh down his brow for being Pietro Bernardone's son nor for appearing an object of wonder and contempt, but royally he opened his stern resolve to Innocent and had from him the first seal upon his order. When the company of Poor Brothers increased behind him whose wondrous life were better sung in heaven's glory, the holy purpose of this chief shepherd was encircled with a second crown by the Eternal Spirit through Honorius. And when, in thirst for martyrdom, he had preached Christ and them that followed Him in the proud presence of the Sultan, and, finding the people unripe for conversion and not being willing to remain for no purpose, he had returned to the harvest of the Italian fields, then, on the rough crag between Tiber and Arno, he received from Christ the last seal, which his members bore for two years. When He that had destined him to so much good was pleased to take him up to the reward he had won by making himself lowly, to his brothers, as to the rightful heirs, he commended his most dear lady and bade them love her faithfully; and from her bosom the glorious soul chose to set forth, returning to its kingdom, and for its body would have no other bier.

IX. Miscellaneous Open Picture Books of Gothic Painting: Frescoes, Murals, Wood, Glass, Stone, Pavement "Graffiti," Bronze, Marble, and Tapestry; the Cities of Assisi, Siena, and Florence

A. ASSISI: GIOTTO AND THE FRESCOES IN THE CHURCH OF ST. FRANCIS; EPISODES FROM THE "LIFE OF ST. FRANCIS" BY BONAVENTURA

116. Francis' Renunciation of His Earthly Father before the Bishop

Bon., 2:4. This, together with Items 117, and 118, is reprinted by permission of the publishers from *The Life of St. Francis* by Bona-

ventura, with an introduction by T. Okey, trans. E. Gurney Salter, [Everyman's Library, No. 485] (New York: E. P. Dutton & Co., Inc.; London: J. M. Dent & Sons, Ltd., 1910). This item, p. 313. See Fig. IX–69.

Yea more, as one drunk with wondrous fervour of spirit, he threw aside even his breeches, and stood up naked in the presence of all, saying unto his father, "Hitherto I have called thee my father on earth, but henceforth I can confidently say 'Our Father, Which art in heaven,' with Whom I have laid up my whole treasure, and on Whom I have set my whole trust and hope." The Bishop, seeing this, and marvelling at such exceeding fervour in the man of God, rose forthwith, and, weeping, put his arms round him; then, devout and kindly man as he was, covered him with the cloak wherewith he himself was clad, bidding his servants give him something to clothe his limbs withal, and there was brought unto him a mean and rough tunic of a farm-servant of the Bishop.

117. Francis, Pope Innocent III, and the Tottering Chapel

Ibid., Bon., 3:10, p. 321. See Fig. IX–70.

For in a dream he [Innocent] saw, as he recounted, the Lateran Basilica about to fall, when a little poor man, of mean stature and humble aspect, propped it with his own back, and thus saved it from falling. "Verily," saith he, "he it is that by his work and teaching shall sustain the Church of Christ." From this vision, he was filled with an especial devotion unto him, and in all ways disposed himself unto his supplication, and ever loved the servant of Christ with an especial affection. Then and there he granted his request, and promised at a later day to bestow yet more upon him. He sanctioned the Rule, and gave him a command to preach repentance, and made all the lay Brethren that had accompanied the servant of God wear narrow tonsures, that they might preach the word of God without hindrance.

118. *Francis, the Six-Winged Seraph, and the Sacred Stigmata*

Ibid., Bon., 13:3, pp. 384–85. See Fig. IX–71.

. . . he beheld a Seraph having six wings, flaming and resplendent, coming down from the heights of heaven. When in his flight most swift he had reached the space of air nigh the man of God, there appeared betwixt the wings the Figure of a Man crucified, having his hands and feet stretched forth in the shape of a Cross, and fastened unto a Cross. Two wings were raised above His head, twain were spread forth to fly, while twain hid His whole body. . . . Accordingly, as the vision disappeared, it left in his heart a wondrous glow, but on his flesh also it imprinted a no less wondrous likeness of its tokens. For forthwith there began to appear in his hands and feet the marks of the nails, even as he had just beheld them in that Figure of the Crucified.

IX-71. Francis Receiving the Stigmata. *Giotto, Upper Church of St. Francis.*

IX-72. (*Above*) Cathedral Interior, Siena. IX-73. (*Upper right*) Cathedral Pulpit, Siena. IX-74. (*Right, center*) Plan of Marble Pavement of Cathedral Adorned with "Graffiti," Siena. IX-75. (*Bottom right*) Allegory of Good Government, 1338–1340.

B. SIENA: THE CATHEDRAL, PALAZZA PUBBLICO, PIAZZA DEL CAMPO; STS. BERNARDINE AND CATHERINE

119. Commetary on the Interior of the Nave, Fig. IX–72

Figure IX–72 highlights ornamental intricacy and columns of strikingly alternate coloration, as well as figured pavement.

120. Commetary on the Pulpit by Niccoli Pisano, His Son Giovanni, etc., Fig. IX–73

This octagonal pulpit in Fig. IX–73 is rich in symbolism. It carries reliefs on the Liberal Arts, statuettes of the Apostles, scenes of Visitation and Nativity, Adoration of the Magi, Massacre of the Innocents, Crucifixion and Last Judgment. Animals and landscapes are realistically portrayed.

121. Commentary on the "Graffiti" of the Cathedral, Fig. IX–74

More than fifty of these designs adorn the 3000 square yards of pavement. Those under the dome shown in Fig. IX–74 include treatments of Moses receiving the Law, the Death of Absolom, the Slaughter of the Innocents, and many other Old Testament themes.

122. Commentary on A. Lorenzetti's Allegory of the Blessings of Good Government in the Palazzo Comunale, Fig. IX–75

This great fresco in Fig. IX–75, though now sadly deteriorated, is noteworthy for its

IX-77. Horse Race on Palio Day, Siena.

IX-76. St. Bernardine Preaching in the Piazza del Comune, Siena. *Painting by Pietro di Sano.*

strange blend of ethereality and realistic genre. The busy life of trade shares the limelight with girls doing a round dance. Critics marvel at the life of grandiose, poetic vision universalized in imaginary, yet none the less valid, realization of the everyday. The towered buildings and Duomo convey the sense of a walled medieval city. The ways of peace are set forth in scenes of buying, selling, and manufacturing, with craftsmen busily at work, and shops well filled. Merchants and country people alike bring in their produce. Outside, the hunt goes on; fields are worked and grain is harvested; cavaliers abound. Religion, music, and recreation are indisseverable.

123. Commentary on the Painting by Pietro di Sano of S. Bernardine's Preaching in the Piazza del Comune, Fig. IX–76

Bernardine, the Franciscan popular preacher, has been encountered in the sermons of Chapter VIII. This painting in Fig. IX–76, like the earlier passages, symbolizes his articulation with the common life and his being equally at home in cathedral or movable outdoor pulpit—as, indeed, in every other activity of his beloved Siena. Together with Catherine the great mystic, included in Chapter VII, he brought great fame to church and town.

124. Commentary on the Virgin and the Horse Race in the Piazzo del Campo on a Palio Day, Fig. IX–77

Figure IX–77 brings to focus the near indistinguishability of what the modern carefully differentiates as "sacred" and "secular." All the items and pictures attendant upon 120–125 emphasize the subtle nuances of the common life. In Item 124 and Fig. IX–77 this reaches its apogee. The *Palio* is Siena's main festival held in connection with the Feast of the Assumption. Each of ten wards, chosen by lot from seventeen, races its own horse—previously blessed by the Church—under its own distinctive colors. Medieval traditions of town and church are gaily reactivated. The winner of the race receives a banner, *i.e.* the *pallio* or *pallium*, bearing the Virgin's image. Palio Day is replete with medieval pageantry entailing costumes, standards, processions, and games in abundance. The profound and the lighthearted proclivities of humanity are set in joyous unison.

IX-78. Detail of East Doors (Gates of Paradise). *Isaac, Jacob, and Esau in gilt bronze. Baptistery, Florence, by Lorenzo Ghiberti.*

C. FLORENCE: THE BAPTISTERY AND THE CATHEDRAL MUSEUM

125. Commentary on the Bronze Door of the Baptistery, Fig. IX–78

Here in Fig. IX–78 the drama of the everyday in the medieval city is continued. This thematic treatment of Isaac, Jacob, and Esau from the "Gates of Paradise" doors has the rhythm of the medieval commune no less than that of the Old Testament.

126. Commentary on the Cantoria of Luca Della Robbia and Donatello

Donatello's artistry in Fig. IX–80 is full of life and jauntiness. Luca della Robbia's, in Fig. IX–79, surpasses it with his cherubic legions enveloped in strutting, joyous cacophony. The spirit bears the contagion of unarguable good humor.

IX-79. Cherubs with Cymbals. *Marble cantoria, c. 1435, by Luca della Robbia. Cathedral Museum, Florence.*

IX-80. Dancing and Singing Cherubs. *Marble cantoria, c. 1433–1439, by Donatello. Cathedral Museum, Florence.*

IX-81. The Dying Man Sees His Sins Reviewed. Ars Moriendi.

IX-82. The Dying Man Consoled. Ars Moriendi.

X. The Waning of the Middle Ages; The Dance of Death; The *Ars Moriendi;* Living and Dying in the Common Life

127. *The Dying Man Sees His Sins Pass in Review*

Editorial commentary on Vérard's *L'Art de bien vivre et de bien mourir* as reproduced in E. Mâle, *L'art religieux de la fin du moyen âge en France* (Paris: Librairie Armand Colin, 1931), is based on Figs. 213–218, pp. 382–387. The right to photograph and reproduce these figures has been granted most graciously by the publishers, Librairie Armand Colin. This item, Fig. 213, p. 382. See Fig. IX–81.

The *Art of Dying* made a rare impact upon fifteenth-century life and thought. The present drawings and commentary based upon those of Vérard trace the last hours of the dying man. His senses fail and his grip upon life inexorably slips away. Five temptations assailing him are depicted in the first five figures. Preparatory to this one, the demons have concealed from him the comforting presence of Christ and the Virgin. The devilishly inspired vision of pagans worshiping their idols is all too clear to him. Satanic doubts and angelic consolation will continue to alternate in his befogged consciousness. In this first drawing the dying man has reconstructed before his eyes his entire lifetime of sins. A list of these is flaunted before him. They are reincarnated before his horrified gaze. The woman of his amours, the man he deceived, the poor he rejected, even the freshly bleeding corpse of the man he murdered, haunt him in this picture. The demons screech out his impious record and the devil claims him for his own son in ironic denial of his heavenly patrimony.

128. *He Is Consoled by the Angels*

Ibid., Fig. 214, p. 383. See Fig. IX–82.

Here an angel from heaven comes to his rescue, accompanied by four saints. These are Peter, who three times denied his Lord —here symbolized by the rooster and the keys; Mary Magdalen, herself no mean sinner; Paul, represented as the rider unhorsed; and the "good" thief who repented on the cross. These are all examples of the lengths to which divine mercy is prepared to go. The dying man is admonished to resist despair. The slightest intimation of a contrite heart can wash out sins as numerous as drops of water in the ocean. Despair is the real enemy. God can deal with any crime so long as one does not, like Judas, count all as lost. Seeing the man's revived hope the demons temporarily admit defeat.

129. He Envisages the Theft of His Property Even as He Expires

Ibid., Fig. 215, p. 384. See Fig. IX–83.

The demons now concentrate on the task of deflecting the dying man's attention from God's salvation freely offered the repentant soul. His mind must be diverted to worldly preoccupations that can surely damn him. Presently, there pass before him in demonically inspired review the loved ones he must shortly leave. What will be the fate of wife and child? Thinking of his house, he sees it clearly with basement door forced open and the wine stores already being tippled by a worthless servant. A thief is leading the horse from its stable. These holdings were prized above God himself. What can stay their passing? Again the angel bolsters his sagging faith. He is confronted with a vision of Christ on the cross. He gave up everything, including His own life, as His followers must also. God's Providence will remember wife and child, later shown under the angel's protection.

130. He Banishes His Heirs

Ibid., Fig. 216, p. 385. See Fig. IX–84.

But the demons are not yet finished. They get his mind back on himself and rouse his self-pity over his sufferings. They prompt suspicion of his purportedly sympathetic attendants. After all they are interested in nothing save the earthly goods he will leave. The tortured man tosses his covers, upsets the table of glassware, and takes a good kick at a potential heir standing by

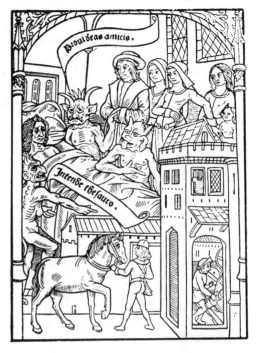

IX-83. The Dying Man Sees His Property Stolen. Ars Moriendi.

IX-84. The Dying Man Banishes His Heirs. Ars Moriendi.

487

IX-85. The Dying Man's Last Temptation. Ars Moriendi.

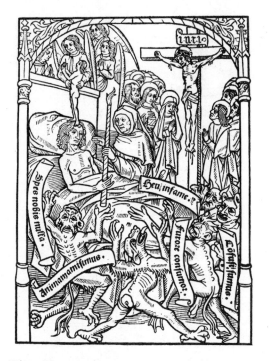

IX-86. The Dying Man's Soul Conducted to Heaven. Ars Moriendi.

the bed. The servant appears stunned. The angel will shortly counter by showing him martyrs like Stephen and Catherine, Christ included, who repulsed self-pity, remained faithful unto death and inherited the Kingdom.

131. His Last Temptation

Ibid., Fig. 217, p. 386. See Fig. IX–85.

The demons have one more try. They attack him at his most vulnerable point, his pride. Crowns laid on his bed remind him that he has been a pretty good fellow after all, unlike those long-time rascals who made their peace with God at the very last minute. He deserves the best, not the worst he is now experiencing. His resolve weakens. The angels come none too soon. They fix his gaze on those who have triumphed through humility. Little children and the Virgin herself followed that way. She and the Trinity appear forthwith. The Christian passes, suffering the last agonies of death as all must— but, triumphantly, his temptations forever stilled.

132. His Soul Is Conducted from His Body into Heaven

Ibid., Fig. 218, p. 387. See Fig. IX–86.

Now his soul is conducted from his body into heaven. Death has lost in its very winning. The awful struggle has delivered up a spirit to eternal rest and bliss. The priest, having heard his last confession, puts a wax candle in his hand. The howling demons are thwarted for good. The soul rises peacefully to the skies.

488

Monophonic and Stereophonic Discs, Stereophonic Tapes

Deutsche Grammophon Gesellschaft (DGG) has long maintained an "Archive Production" (ARC) division for twelve major "Research Periods" with attendant recordings of highest caliber. The first three periods emphasize, respectively, Gregorian Chant, the Central Middle Ages (1100–1350), and the Early Renaissance (1350–1500).

The History of Music in Sound, Vol. II: Early Medieval Music up to 1300 (RCA Victor, LM6015).

The Play of Daniel (XIIth cent.). Noah Greenberg, New York PMA (Decca 9402; Stereo 79402; Stereo Tape, St 7 9402).

de la Halle, Adam (c. 1240–1287), *XIIIth and XIVth Century Dances.* Cape, Brussels Pro Musica Antiqua (PMA) (DGG ARC-3002).

Music of the Middle Ages, Vol. IV. English Polyphony of the XIIIth and Early XIVth Century. Russell Oberlin, Chas. Bressler (Expériences Anonyme, EA-0024); XIVth and Early XVth Century (EA-31); Vol. VII, The Thirteenth Century, Russell Oberlin, Chas. Bressler (Expér-Anon., EA-35).

Choral Music of the XIIIth to XVIth Centuries. Franciscan "Laudi," etc. Quartetto Polifonico (London, LL995).

Machaut, Guillaume de (c. 1300–1377), *Mass: Notre Dame, and 10 Secular Works.* Cape, Brussels PMA (DGG, ARC–3032); *Motets, Ballades, Virelais and Rondeau.* Hunter, Coll. Music University of Illinois (West. 18166).

Dunstable, John (c. 1370–1453), *Six Motets.* Cape, Brussels PMA (DGG ARC-3052).

Dufay, Guillaume (c. 1400–1474). *Hymns, Choruses and Songs.* Chaboy, Boepple, Dessof Choir (Bach 582; Stereo 5008); *Sacred Songs.* Cape, Brussels PMA (DGG, ARC-3003); *Secular Works.* Cape, Brussels PMA (EMS-206); *Missa Caput.* Ambrosian Singers (Oiseau-Lyre, OL-50069); *Missa "L'homme arme."* Ensemble Voices and Trombones. Dir. R. Blanchard (Ducretet Thomson, 320 C 108).

Okeghem, Johannes (1430–1495), *Five Chansons.* Cape, Brussels PMA (DGG, ARC-3052).

Music of the Medieval Court and Country Side. Greenberg, New York PMA (Decca DL 9400).

Five Centuries of Spanish Song. Victoria de los Angeles. Side 1: Gothic Period (RCA Victor, LM-2144).

Spanish Music of the Renaissance. N. Greenberg, New York PMA (Decca D 9409; Stereo 79409).

Selected Recordings by Modern Composers Utilizing Medieval Themes

Berlioz, H., *Requiém: Grand-messe des Morts,* Op. 5 (Dies Irae Theme). Ch. Munch, Boston Sym. Orch. and New England Conser. Choir ([2] RCA Victor, LD-6077; Stereo, LDS-6077; Stereo Tape, FTC-7000).

Eliot, T. S., *Murder in the Cathedral* (Thomas à Becket). Robert Donat and Old Vic Co. ([2] Angel 35043/44).

Hindemith, P., *Noblissima Visione* (St. Francis of Assisi). Hindemith, Phila. Orch. (Angel 35490); *Mathis der Maler* (Grunewald Altar Piece and St. Anthony Theme). Stein-

berg, Pitts. Orch. (Cap. P 8364; Stereo SP 8364).

Honegger, A., *Jeanne d'Arc au Bûcher.* Ormandy, Phila. Orch., Temple U. Choir (2 Col. SL-178).

Orff, C., *Carmina Burana* (Medieval Student and Tavern Songs Adapted). Stokowski, Houston Orch. (Cap. PAR-8470; Stereo SPAR 8470).

Prokofieff, S., *Alexander Nevsky* (Crusaders' Theme). Reiner, Chicago Orch. (RCA Victor, LM 2395; Stereo LSC-2395).

Journals Listing and/or Reviewing Recorded Music

The American Record Guide (ARG) Incorporating *The American Tape Guide* (P. O. Box 319, Radio City Station, New York 19, N. Y.; reliable and suggestive).

The Gramophone (Gr.) (Subscription Dept., 379 Kenton Road, Kenton, Harrow, Middle-

sex, England; full, discriminating, British coverage of records).

High Fidelity (HF) (The Billboard Publishing Co., Great Barrington, Mass.; records, tapes, equipment reviews, monthly).

Saturday Review (SR) (Saturday Review, Inc.,

25 W. 45th St., New York; weekly with special monthly roundups).

Schwann Long Playing Record Catalogue (W. Schwann, Inc., Boston 16, Mass.); *Artist Issue*, 1960 (Indexed by orch., quartets, etc., conductors, vocal and instr. soloists, choral and operatic groups, etc.).

Representative Books and Special Articles Dealing With Music and Recordings

Barker, J. W., "Birth of an Art: The Origins of Polyphony," *ARG*, XXIV, 7 (Mar., 1958), 288–91, 329–30; "The Ars Nova and the Late Middle Ages: A 'New Deal' in Old Music," *ARG*, XXIV, 10 (June, 1958), 418–22, 436–37. Excellent settings for milieu of medieval music, with numerous evaluations of recordings listed earlier.

Gajard, Dom Jos., [Introductions, Commentaries, and Translations for] Gregorian Chant. Choir of the Monks of Saint Pierre de Solesmes. Prefaced to accompany Decca (London) Long Playing "FFRR" Records LXT 2704–08. See Schwann Catalogue under "Collections"—Choral—Gregorian Chant, Gajard, Solesmes; also *Artist Issue* 1960, Conductors—Gajard. Those reading French should consult Gajard's *Études Grégoriennes*, I (Abbaye Saint Pierre de Solesmes, Desclée and Co., Tournai, Belgium, 1954).

Harman, A., *Medieval and Early Renaissance Music* (Vol. I, *Man and His Music*). Fairlawn, N. J.: Essential Books, 1959.

Henakan, D., "A Listener's Guide to Paperbacks," *SR*, XLIV, 28 (July 15, 1961), 38–40. An unusual introduction to classical and current musical works in relation to recorded music. Wide selections of paperbacks include works by Percy Scholes, Alfred Einstein, P. Hindemith, A. Copland, Sir D. F. Tovey, Jacques Barzun, I. Stravinsky, and many others.

Hindemith, P., *A Composer's World*. Cambridge, Mass.: Harvard University Press, 1952. Significant treatment of Augustine's *De Musica* in the light of modern music.

Lang, P. H., *Music in Western Civilization*. New York: W. W. Norton & Company, Inc., 1941.

Scholes, Percy, *The Oxford Companion to Music*. New York: Oxford University Press, Inc., 9th ed., 1955 ['59, '60]. Uniquely fascinating feature articles, illustrations, glossaries. (See Ars Nova, Mass, History of Music, Hymns and Hymn Tunes, Liturgy, Minstrels, Troubadours, Plain Song, Church Music, Latin Hymns, Dies Irae, Requiem, etc.)

Representative, Discerning Reviews of Recordings and Books for the Medieval Period from XIIth to XVth century in *ARG*, XXVII, 7 (Mar., 1961), 558–60; *Gr.* XXXIX, 458 (July, 1961), 78 (Play of Daniel); *HF*, XI, 5 (May, 1961), 62–63; *HF*, X, 12 (Dec., 1960), 103 [Stereo Tape of Play of Daniel]; *HF*, XI, 4 (Apr., 1961), 139 [Stereo Tape of Berlioz, Requiem—cf. *ARG*, XXVII, 11 (July, 1961), 902]; *ARG*, XXVII, 6 (Feb., 1961), 505–06 on the French Ars Antiqua—Expér. Anon. EA-35; *ARG*, XXVII, 7 (March, 1961), 588–89—Review of A. Harman, *op. cit.*

SUGGESTED READINGS
Art and Literature

Bamm, P., (pseud. for Kurt Emmrich), *The Kingdoms of Christ*, trans. C. Holme. New York: McGraw-Hill Book Co., Inc., 1959.

Curtius, E. R., *European Literature and the Middle Ages*. New York: Pantheon Books Inc., 1953.

de Bruyne, E., *Études d'esthétique médiévale*, 3 vols. Bruges, Belgium: "De Tempel" Tempelhof, 1946).

Delaissé, L. M. J., *et al.*, *Miniatures Médiévales*. Geneva: Editions Des Deux-Mondes, 1959.

Ferguson, G., *Signs and Symbols in Christian Art*. New York: Oxford University Press, Inc., 1954.

Fletcher, Banister, *History of Architecture* (6th ed.). New York: Charles Scribner's Sons, 1921.

Janson, H. W., ed., *Key Monuments of the History of Art*. Englewood Cliffs, N. J.: Prentice-Hall, Inc., and New York: Harry N. Abrams, Inc., 1959.

Mâle, É., *Religious Art from the Twelfth to the Eighteenth Century*. New York: Pantheon Books, Inc., 1949.

————, *Religious Art in France in the Thirteenth Century*. New York: E. P. Dutton & Co., 1913.

Marucchi, L. and E. Micheletti, *A History of European Painting: Medieval Painting*, trans. H. E. Scott. New York: Viking Press, 1960.

van der Meer, F., *Atlas de la civilisation occidentale*. Amsterdam: Elsvier, 1952.

Morey, C. R., *Early Christian Art*. Princeton, N. J.: Princeton University Press, 1942.

————, *Medieval Art*. New York: W. W. Norton & Company, 1942.

Porcher, J., *The Rohan Book of Hours*. London: Faber & Faber, Ltd., 1959.

Rand, E. K., *Founders of the Middle Ages*.

Cambridge, Mass.: Harvard University Press, 1928.

Rice, Talbot, *The Art of Byzantium*, photos by M. Hirmer. New York: Thames and Hudson Publishers, Inc., 1959.

Robb, D. M. and J. J. Garrison, *Art in the Western World*. New York: Harper & Brothers, 1935.

Simson, O., *The Gothic Cathedral*. New York: Pantheon Books, Inc., 1956.

————. *Sacred Fortress: Byzantine Art and Statecraft in Ravenna*. Chicago: University of Chicago Press, 1948.

Taylor, H. O., *The Classical Heritage of the Middle Ages*, rev. ed. New York: The Macmillan Co., 1911.

Philosophy, Theology, and the Universities

Copleston, F. C., *A History of Philosophy*, Vols. II and III. London: Burns, Oates and Washbourne, Ltd., 1950, 1953.

d'Irsay, S., *Histoire des Universités*, Vol. I. Paris: Picard, 1933.

Delhaye, P., "L'organisation scolaire au XIIᵉ siècle," *Traditio*, V (1947), 211–68.

Fairweather, E. F., *A Scholastic Miscellany*, Library of Christian Classics, Vol. X. Philadelphia: Westminster Press, 1956.

Gilson, É., *History of Christian Philosophy in the Middle Ages*. New York: Random House, 1955.

Haskins, C. H., *The Renaissance of the Twelfth Century*. Cambridge, Mass.: Harvard University Press, 1927.

————, *The Rise of the Universities*. New York: Holt, Rinehart & Winston, Inc., 1923.

Leff, G., *Medieval Thought*. Baltimore: Penguin Books, Inc., 1958.

McGiffert, E. C., *A History of Christian Thought*, Vol. II. New York: Charles Scribner's Sons, 1932.

Rashdall, H., *The Universities of Europe in the Middle Ages*, rev. ed. by F. M. Powicke and A. B. Emden, 3 vols. New York: Oxford University Press, Inc., 1936.

Rait, R. S., *Life in the Medieval University*. Cambridge: Cambridge University Press, 1931.

Taylor, H. O., *The Medieval Mind*, 4th ed., 2 vols. Cambridge, Mass.: Harvard University Press, 1949.

Thompson, J. W., *The Literacy of the Laity*. Berkeley: University of California Press, 1939.

————, *The Medieval Library*. Chicago: University of Chicago Press, 1939.

Waddell, H., *Wandering Scholars*. Boston: Houghton Mifflin Co., 1927.

The Common Life in Village, Town, and Country

Holmes, U. T., Jr., *Daily Life in the Twelfth Century*. Madison: University of Wisconsin Press, 1952.

Huizinga, J., *The Waning of the Middle Ages*. London: Edward Arnold & Co., Ltd., 1954.

McCulloch, J. A., *Medieval Faith and Fable*. Boston: Marshall-Jones Co., 1932.

Painter, S., *Medieval Society*. Ithaca, N. Y.: Cornell University Press, 1951.

Power, E., *Medieval People*. Gloucester, Mass.: Peter Smith Publishers, 1937.

Rickert, E., *Chaucer's World*. New York: Columbia University Press, 1948.

Schevill, F., *History of Florence*. New York: Harcourt, Brace & World, Inc., 1936.

————, *Sienna: The Story of a Mediaeval Commune*. New York: Charles Scribner's Sons, 1909.

c. 480–524   Boethius—Consolation of Philosophy

c. 480–570   Cassiodorus—Tripartite History, Letters

c. 530/40–600   Fortunatus—Pange Lingua

538–593   Gregory of Tours—History of the Franks

540–604   Gregory the Great—Pastoral Rule, Dialogues, Morals, Letters

c. 560/70–636   Isidore of Seville—Etymologies, Works on the Priestly Office

602–690   Theodore of Tarsus—Greek scholar, Archbishop of Canterbury

c. 628–690   Benedict Biscop

c. 640–709   Aldhelm—Anglo-Saxon Scholar

c. 659   Death of Jonas of Bobbio—Life of Columban

c. 672/73–735   Bede the Venerable—Ecclesiastical History of England

c. 675–754   Winfrith (Boniface)—Apostle to the Germans

676–c. 750   John of Damascus—On the Orthodox Faith

c. 720–c. 800   Paul the Deacon—History of the Lombards

735–804   Alcuin—Head of Carolingian Palace School (790)

c. 760–821   Theodulph—Latinist, poet, Bishop of Orleans

c. 770–804   Einhard—Life of Charlemagne

c. 776–856   (H) Rabanus Maurus—Disciple of Alcuin at Tours, Abbot of Fulda, Archbishop of Mainz

c. 790–865   Paschasius Radbertus, Abbot of Corbie—On the Body and Blood of the Lord

c. 805–869   Gottschalk—Student of Maurus at Fulda, friend of Strabo

809–849   Walafrid Strabo—Disciple of Maurus

Fl. 810–25   Dungal—Irish monk, scholar, teacher at Pavia

c. 810–c. 880   John Scotus Eriugena—Translator of Pseudo-Dionysius

845–882   Hincmar, Archbishop of Rheims—Political and Ecclesiastical Treatises

† 862   Servatus Lupus—Disciple of Maurus, Abbot of Ferrières

† c. 868   Ratramnus of Corbie—Controversial works on Eucharist

871–899/901   Alfred, King of England—Translator of Gregory's Pastoral Rule and Dialogues (894), etc.

† 876   Donatus—Irish teacher, poet

884/87   Notker Balbulus of St. Gall—Gesta Karoli Magni

893   Asser's Life of Alfred

900   Of Symphonies—from the Scholia Enchiriadis

c. 909–988   St. Dunstan—Scholar Reformer, Archbishop of Canterbury (959/60)

920–972   Liutprand of Cremona

925–965   Bruno of Cologne—the Palatine School

932–c. 1002   Hroswitha of Gandersheim—Poems, dramas (c. 960–80)

942   Odilo, Abbot of Cluny—Enchiridia Musices

950–1003   Gerbert (Pope Sylvester II, 999–1003) Scholasticus of Rheims, Tours, etc.

960–1028   Fulbert—Pupil of Gerbert, and Master of the School of Chartres

995   Durham Cathedral begun

1000–1010   Songs of Roland

1005/08–1089   Lanfranc of Pavia—Teacher at Bec, Archbishop of Canterbury

1007–1072   Peter Damian—Scholar, monk, preacher, cardinal

1023   Death of Wulfstan—Sermons

1033–1109   Anselm of Aosta—Monk, teacher of Bec, Archbishop of Canterbury

1036   Death of Avicenna, Arab philosopher

1040–1116   Ivo of Chartres—Canonist

† 1048/50	Raoul Glaber, Chronicler
† 1050	Guido of Arezzo—Benedictine monk and author of musical tracts
1050–1133	Hildebert, Bishop of Mans—Poet, hymn writer
1052	Westminster Abbey begun
c. 1060–1130	Irnerius, Professor of law based on Justinian's Code (Bologna, 1105)
1063–1118	Cathedral of Pisa
1070–1121	William of Champeaux, Teacher at Paris, founder of St. Victor
1075–1145	Ordericus Vitalis—Ecclesiastical History
1079–1093	Winchester Cathedral
1079–1142	Peter Abelard—Teacher at Paris, History of My Misfortunes, Sic et Non
1080–1154	Gilbert de la Porrée
1083–1189	Ely Cathedral
c. 1085–1148	William of St. Thierry—Letters, Spiritual Treatises
1089–1130	Abbey Church of Cluny rebuilt
1090–1153	Bernard of Clairvaux, Sermons, Mystical Works
c. 1095–c. 1142/44	William of Malmesbury, English historian
1098–1179	Hildegarde of Bingen—Visions and Hymns
c. 1100–1160/64	Peter Lombard—Sentences (c. 1147/50)
1101	Death of Raoul Arden—Scholastic, teacher, preacher
1109–1115	Great Portal of Cluny
1110–1158	Otto of Freising—The Two Cities
1110/15–1180	John of Salisbury—Scholar, teacher, author of Policraticus, Metalogicon; sec. to Thomas Becket and Bishop of Chartres (1176–1180)
1114–1182	Gerard of Cremona—Tr. into Latin of Greek and Arabic authors
1121/24	Death of Guibert de Nogent—Autobiography
1126–1198	Averroes, Arab philosopher
1134–1150	West facade of Cathedral of Chartres; N. Tower, 1134; S. Tower, 1145
1137–1144	Abbey Church of St. Denys
1140–c. 1209	Walter Map—De Nugis Curialium
1141	Death of Hugh of St. Victor—Didascalicon (On Study and Teaching), On the Sacraments
1147–1233	Giraldus Cambrensis—Autobiography, etc.
c. 1150–1160	Gratian's Decretum
c. 1152	Death of Suger—History of Louis VI, Abbot of St. Denys
c. 1155	Bernard of Cluny (Morval)—On Contempt of the World
1162–1170	Thomas Becket, Archbishop of Canterbury
1163–1235	Notre Dame, Paris, built
1171	College des Dix-huit at University of Paris
1173	Death of Richard of St. Victor—Benjamin Major and Benjamin Minor
1173	Jocelin of Brakelond (Chronicle) enters monastery
1174	Choir of Canterbury Cathedral built by William of Sens
1175	University of Paris a definite guild; Latin translation of Avicenna
1175–1253	Robert Grosseteste—Author, scholar, teacher of Franciscans, Bishop of Lincoln (1235–1253)
c. 1180–1260	Jean de St. Gilles—Dominican scholar and preacher
1182–1226	Francis of Assisi
Fl. 1182	John Beleth, liturgist
† 1192	Adam of St. Victor—Liturgical hymns
1195–1231	Anthony of Padua, Franciscan preacher
1198	Death of Averroes
1200	University of Salerno
c. 1200	Emergence of Oxford (Beginnings as early as 1167/68)
† 1201	Roger Hovedon—Chronicler
1203	Death of Stephen of Tournai, Canonist; University of Siena founded
1204/1212	Death of Peter of Blois—Sermons, Mystical Treatise

493

1206–1280	Albertus Magnus, Dominican scholar and teacher of Thomas Aquinas
1209	Cambridge University founded
1209–1235	Nave of Lincoln Cathedral
1211–1241	Rheims Cathedral rebuilt
1215	Statutes of University of Paris
1218/20	Amiens Cathedral begun
1220–1258	Salisbury Cathedral built
1220–1272	Berthold of Regensburg, Franciscan preacher
1221	Dominicans at Oxford
1221–1274	Bonaventura—Franciscan Minister General, scholar
1222	University of Padua
1224	Franciscans at Oxford
1224	University of Naples founded by Frederick II
1225	Romance of the Rose by Guillaume de Loris
1225–1274	Thomas Aquinas, Dominican scholar—Summas
1226	Laon Cathedral completed
1228–1229-	Thomas of Celano
1244–1247	Lives of Francis; Dies Irae
1230	Bartholomew Anglicus—On the Properties of Things
1230–1298	Jacobus de Voragine—Dominican author of Golden Legend
1230–1306	Jacopone da Todi, Franciscan author of Lauds, Stabat Mater, etc.
1230	Caesarius of Heisterbach's Dialogue On Miracles
1237–1296	(William) Durandus of Mende, Dominican canonist, author of Symbolism of Churches
1240	Death of Jacques de Vitry, monastic preacher, cardinal, exempla collector
1245	Death of Alexander of Hales, Franciscan scholar and author of Summa
1249	University College, Oxford
1257/58	Collège de Sorbonne founded; University of Paris
1259	Death of Matthew Paris—Major Chronicle
1260	Chartres Cathedral conse-

	crated; Franco of Cologne—Musical theorist
1260–1328	Meister Eckhart, scholastic mystic, Dominican preacher and teacher
1261	Death of Stephen of Bourbon, Dominican writer of preaching manuals
1264	Death of Vincent de Beauvais, Dominican encyclopedist—Universal Mirror
1265–1321	Dante Alighieri—Divine Comedy, On Monarchy
1266–1337	Giotto, frescoes at Assisi, etc.
1270/1272	Death of Dominican Thomas Cantimpré, Works on Preaching
1274	Death of Robert de Sorbon, Scholar; Comparison of Paris Finals and Last Judgment
1275	Death of Raymond Pennafort, Dominican Decretalist and Master General
1277	Death of Humbert of Romans, Dominican general and author of Treatise on Preaching
c. 1289	Death of Franciscan Salimbene of Parma—Chronicle
1292	Death of John Peckham, Franciscan Archbishop of Canterbury
1292/94	Death of Roger Bacon, Franciscan scholar—Opus Majus (c. 1266)
1293–1381	Jan van Ruysbroeck—Dutch scholar and mystic
1294–1361	John Tauler, Dominican mystic and preacher
1304–1374	Petrarch, humanist
1306/16	Death of John of Paris—On the Power of Kings and Popes; Early Conciliarist
1308	Death of John Duns Scotus—Franciscan nominalist
1315/16	Death of Ramon Lull—Franciscan mystic, missionary, scholar
c. 1318	Marchetto da Padua—Musical theorist
1319	Jean de Muris—Musical theorist
1320	Nicole Bozon—Franciscan collector of preaching stories

c. 1320–1384 *John Wyclif—Oxford professor, reformer, translator of Scriptures, preacher*

c. 1331 *Death of Bernard of Gui—Dominican Inquisitor's Guide*

1340–1400 *Geoffrey Chaucer*

1340 *Death of Thomas Waleys—On Composition of Sermons*

1341 *Petrarch crowned Poet Laureate*

c. 1342 *Death of Marsilius of Padua—Author of Defensor Pacis (1324)*

1348 *University of Prague*

1349 *Death of William of Ockham, Commentary on the Sentences*

1350–1420 *Pierre D'Ailly—Educator, Chancellor of Paris, conciliarist*

Fl. 1360–1368 *John Bromyard—Cambridge Dominican and author of Preaching Summa*

1363–1429 *Jean Gerson—French scholar, mystic, University of Paris head, conciliar treatises, sermons*

1366 *Death of Henry Suso—Dominican preacher and mystic*

1377 *Death of Ludolph the Carthusian—Life of Christ; Guillaume de Machaut—Poet, composer*

c. 1380–1400 *German Theology—Mystical work influencing Luther*

1380–1444 *Bernardine of Siena—Franciscan scholar, canonist, and popular preacher*

1380–1471 *Thomas à Kempis—Compiler of Imitation of Christ*

1386 *Heidelberg University*

1387 *Chaucer begins Canterbury Tales*

1392 *Erfurt University*

1401–1464 *Nicholas of Cusa—Conciliar theorist (Catholic Concordance), mystic (Vision of God), bishop-reformer, preacher*

1405–1457 *Lorenzo Valla—Exposure of Donation of Constantine*

1409 *Leipzig University*

1415 *Death of John Hus—On the Church*

1419 *Death of Vincent Ferrer—Dominican preacher, Treatise on Spiritual Life*

1436–1517 *Cardinal Ximenes—Inquisitor General, Polyglot Bible*

1445/55–1536 *Lefèvre d'Étaples—Translation of New Testament*

1447 *Earliest datable printed book in Europe; Vatican Library founded*

1452–1498 *Girolamo Savonarola—Dominican preacher, prophet, reformer*

1453–1455 *Gutenberg and Fust print Mazarin Bible at Mainz*

1464/69–1536 *Erasmus—Praise of Folly, Greek New Testament (1516)*

1476 *Caxton's printing press*

The Girandola at the Castle of Sant'Angelo Celebrating the Anniversary of
the Election of a Pope.

X

The Late Medieval Papacy
and the Conciliar Epoch; Christian Revolution
and Reform; the Waning of
the Middle Ages

A distinctive characteristic of the Middle Ages was its passion for unity. The balance sought in the relations of the spiritual and the temporal was a paramount concern. Skepticism over the practicability of such an equilibrium was resented as the sheerest impiety. The Church's growing involvement in the social order was matched by its insistence upon spiritual rights in the temporal sphere. Its paternalizing of political activities was not to be interpreted as undue challenge to temporal powers. Royal and imperial authorities reciprocated with assertions of loyalty to spiritual precedence. Their declarations of worldly prerogatives were not to be held as being in any way prejudicial to those of the Church.

During the later centuries of the Middle Ages, the Church continued to bring its most cogent pressures upon the administration of the whole Christian commonwealth (*corpus Christianum*). Concurrently, new ambitions of rising nations like France, England, and many other feudal communities were definitely ascendant. Seemingly, the more infeasible the old unitary theories proved to be, the more the spiritual and temporal powers vied with each other in reasserting them.

With irritating consistency, the national legists and the Church's canonists indicted all defections from mutual consideration as the sole responsibility of the opposite party in this precarious balance. Each camp echoed the other's call to renewed probity and reformation. These were joined to a rising tide of interest in representative government. Such had never been wholly absent from the theorists of ecclesiastical administration or from the critiques of temporal authority. The older spiritual propulsions for representative unity in the councils were now environed by the newly enunciated thrust of a reinvigorated papacy. The gathering momentum of canonists and decretalists was steadily fashioning a new corporate personality for the papal institution. The nation's experts in Roman law grasped every opportunity to circumvent papal enlargement of its plenitude of power (*plenitudo potestatis*). There were extremists on both sides. The most fascinating exercises of political sagacity still paid lip-service, at least, to the equilibrium subscribed to alike by spirituals and temporals.

The canonists and theologians labored to validate the Church's total tradition of constitutional government in relation to the mounting absolutism of hierarchy and papacy. The task was not easy. Nevertheless, there emerged a fresh emphasis upon conciliar government. This was held to be true, both to the Church's integrity as the Body of Christ, and to her pre-eminent juridical status in the Divine-human order. Interest was reasserted in the Church's religious and social integrity. She was the whole society, guild, or body of the faithful (*congregatio, universitas fidelium*). Reforming churchmen called upon the *ecclesia* to be her true self. They admonished the hierarchy and papacy to realize their full heritage of corporate representativity and service. Impassioned reform pleas also emanated from supporters of the new role being envisaged by emperors, kings, and nations.

The brief text from Eike of Repgow restates the classic preoccupation with balanced spiritual and temporal powers. Contrasted with it, the grating presumptions of Boniface VIII seem rash bombast. Yet, Boniface was neither a fool nor a blustering coward, any more than was Philip IV or Edward I. Forces were here in a new imparity that would defy all efforts to restore the status quo. Perhaps the culminating bravado of Boniface was a sincere commentary on the mounting casuistry of his decretalists. No less cumulative and explosive were the intensified claims of the legists and publicists employed by the new national sovereigns.

Out of this tense background John of Paris appeared. He was a Dominican of theological acumen and sane, historical outlook. With studied calmness, he restated the old theorems of balanced forces in Christian unity, but his detachment belied his potentiality for later conciliar argument and jarring reform. Perhaps his was the most irenic presentation of conciliar thought before the Great Schism. The readings here chosen are from a limited context that does not give full relief to his views. Because of his pioneering influence, a somewhat lengthy survey will relate the sources excerpted to his larger thought. He helped prompt the turning away from old stereotypes of balanced powers to the scrutiny of ramifying authority within the hierarchy. He was to press consideration of the pope as universal dispensator, rather than outright possessor, of the Church's catholic authority. His emphasis fell upon the exercise of ecclesiastical prerogative by the council, as well as by the pope. Hierarchical authority was held derivable from the people, as well as from God. Papal deposability was actively considered.

For John of Paris, prelatial powers came from God directly and from the Christian people indirectly. This was by virtue of their being an electing and consenting body. Furthermore, the authority held in diffusion by the Church's membership equalled that lodged in papal concentration. The pope was declared to be in fact what he had once been in theory. He was the Church's principal servant, not its absolute sovereign. He was dispensator of all community goods held requisite to the exercise of right faith and conduct. As such, he was answerable to a council which was itself greater than the pope alone. Its precedence was registered in cases involving papal heresy. The council ruled also concerning any pontifical maladministration of church properties. It acted on all undue declarations regarding faith and heretical doctrine. Situations calling for papal deposition ought properly therefore to entail the action of a general council. After all, the ultimate authority of the Church resided in the universal *ecclesia*. This whole Christian people (*populus Christianus*) constituted the integral Body of Christ. It was under the Lord's headship, not that of Peter or of the pope. The pope was accurately denominated head of the Church only in the context of his priority among ministers. Properly speaking, Christ alone was its head in the truly maximal sense. Some later conciliarists were to get credit for saying more heatedly, but less well, what John of Paris had so calmly suggested.

Pierre DuBois' proposals, like John of Paris' theories, were probably evoked by the storm over the bulls of Boniface VIII. He combined barbed criticisms of the institutional church with some unoriginal platitudinizing. There were positive suggestions for ecclesiastical and social reform under the conciliar initiative of the Church. These were to be representative of its fully unitive catholicity. The passages quoted split earlier and later portions of the work, *On the Recovery of the Holy Land*.

Clement V's removal to Lyons (1305–1309) and to Avignon (1309–1314) inaugurated an era of papal dislocation from Rome and a new "Babylonian Captivity." Sometime between 1309 and 1317, perhaps, Dante penned his *On Monarchy*. His frustration over Florentine politics leading to his own exile and his disgust with the papal lawyers of Avignon were reflected in it. Of primary concern to him, however, were the growing pretensions to pontifical supremacy over imperial rights. His preoccupation with the old Roman Empire and its initiative in early Christian civilization was nostalgic and at times ludicrous. Chiefly, however, he sought true human peace under a concordance of godly powers, both imperial and papal. Each of these he held to be immediately derivable from God. His dependence upon Thomas Aquinas may sometimes have been exaggerated. Certain outlines of Aquinian eschatology are obvious.

The prince, no less directly than the pope —though in a degree and kind reflecting his temporal calling—is responsible, in his own unique way, for helping order the earthly commonwealth to celestial beatitude. The passages reproduced are necessarily inadequate to a balanced perspective on his whole work. Even here, however, the collaborative and distinctive elements in papal and imperial mutuality are clearly observable. The emperor of this world derives his power immediately from God, who is Prince of the entire universe. The pope has a definite spiritual supervision covering a wide range of man's temporal activities. The emperor also has his inviolable prerogatives, though in the spiritual sense they are still honorably inferior to those of the supreme pontiff. From the one divine artificer and end of human society, both pope and emperor draw their respective powers in divinized immediacy.

The Avignon papacy had in John XXII a shrewd authority on church law. From his canonical eminence he challenged the more idealistic interpretation of the Church's longstanding tradition of evangelical poverty. The newly oriented hierarchy was experiencing unprecedented financial drains. To recoup and expand its fortunes the pope devised a taxation system as sweeping as was his canonical attack upon Franciscan poverty idealism. The immediate reaction of publicists, legists, and Franciscan sympathizers outdid the broadsides of Dante against the *curia* and its decretalists. William of Ockham, himself a Franciscan, mounted a sharp counter-attack against the pope, with the opportunist assistance of the would-be emperor, Ludwig the Bavarian. William argued nobly, but vainly, for a realistic assessment of papal powers that would admit of their clearly fixed limits and the Christian duty of conciliar leadership. Any such plenitude of power as the pope rightfully held must not be granted to him as temporal domination. The peace that Dante and Marsilius of Padua sought could never come so long as exaggerated papal demands paralyzed the very soul of evangelical service.

Marsilius, however sympathetic with William's irenic arguments, far transcended Ockham's deferential challenge to papal leadership. The system of Marsilius was the creation of a medieval thinker, not the wholly modern divorcement from the Middle Ages it is sometimes pictured as being. His accentuated Aristotelianism and his seeming anticlerical animus supported Christian assumptions of truly medieval character. Nonetheless, he assailed the later centuries of cumulative papal rights as having had little or no basis in early Christian intent. He proposed shunting them into a severely restricted usefulness ancillary to representative popular government and conciliar decision. The sources provided can only hint at the fateful conclusions Marsilius drew from Greek philosophy and Biblical authority. These anticipated a subservient role for the ecclesiastical hierarchy under the human legislator and the general council of Christians. These texts will have served their purpose, however, if they lead on to studies and translations like those of Gewirth from the *Defender of Peace* (*Defensor Pacis*). On no account should the contribution made by Ockham be lost sight of against that of Marsilius. William confronted papal arrogance with the rigoristic logic of the Franciscan renunciatory spirit. It is no credit to his order or to the Church that his penetrating critique, like his intellectual honesty and his whole later career, was accorded disciplinary contempt. Baudry's later editing of his *Breviloquium*, and Brampton's earlier textual rescue of his *De Imperatorum et Pontificum Potestate* are invaluable aids. They constitute a commendable requiem for some of the "noblest assertions of intellectual integrity ever made."

The Great Schism brought shame and dismay to the entire *Corpus Christianum*. For the first time, an electoral body in full continuity, though with shifting constituency, had reversed itself into a dual election. Here was simultaneous backing of two different popes by the same responsible electorate. This was more than a case of true pope against antipope. That had occurred before, as it would again. But this had never been. Theoretically it could never be. But there it was! The "Manifesto" of the revolting cardinals is given in brief excerpt. Its complete translation in Ullmann advances little beyond this shocking announcement. The "Response" of its opponents is available in Ullmann also. With him we must conclude that the case made in the "Manifesto" is thin, indeed. The shock of these electors upon seeing how little the honest but irascible Urban VI was "their man" scarcely justifies their rationalization. That their first choice was made under coercion and was therefore invalid, and that their subsequent one constituted their only genuine election, seems unlikely at best.

Once precipitated, the Schism ramified in terrifying fashion. It elicited nationalistic jealousies that lined up with pressure groups under competing popes and curias. Now there were duplications of everything: popes, cardinalates, papal quarters and entourages, tax levies, building programs, and all the rest. Before the dual schism could be resolved, there would be a triple division to replace it.

Meanwhile, numerous voices had called upon the hierarchy to heal itself and upon the pope to return to Rome. Among these was one, Catherine of Siena, whose loyalty to the Church's hierarchy and whose sacrificial dedication to reform were no more to be doubted than the vigor of her criticism. Chapters usually omitted from modern editions of her *Dialogues* are almost unparalleled for their realistic indictment of the Church's hierarchy. Still, what could churchmen—even popes—do to silence concern so self-immolating as hers? At the close of his life, Gregory XI heeded her prophetic summons and returned to Rome. Soon bent on going back to Avignon, he died before he could start. This was the crisis that had its aftermath in the Great Schism.

John Wyclif was another critic of the Babylonian Captivity who, like Catherine, lived on into the time of schism. Unlike her, he castigated the hierarchy unmercifully. He did this, not so much out of suffering loyalty, as in studied defiance. The papacy and curia impressed him as being more comparable to antichrist than to Christ, the only true head of the Church. He gave unrestricted adherence to "Goddis lawe" in preference to the worldly clergy's "canon law." The mendicants, with whom he had apparently once sympathized, he came later to brand as "the pope's new orders," and as "private religionists." His sermonic powers in defense of the vernacular Bible have already been studied in Chapter VIII. In his considerable corpus of homiletic writings, the bent toward social criticism and the popular appeal that had repercussions in Lollard's preaching may be observed.

With Henry of Langenstein, the major appeal to conciliar action was launched at last. Definitely building upon Conrad of Gelnhausen, Henry's platform was self-explanatory. Gelnhausen had, in his *Letter of Concord*, differentiated between the universal church, or the whole *congregatio fidelium*, and the Roman church, made up of pope and cardinals. The latter was adjudged inferior to the former. Together, Conrad and Henry recapitulated John of Paris, William of Ockham, and Marsilius of Padua. The University of Paris had issued an early appeal for a general council. It was later to recommend conciliar action as one means of healing the schism. Nicholas of Clémanges, though personally loyal to Pope Benedict XIII, had, from his inside view of curial abuses, presented a sobering critique of the hierarchy and a call for reformation. He was to live into yet other eras of disillusionment characterized by conciliar failure.

In the treatises and sermons of Pierre d'Ailly and Jean Gerson, especially, the cumulative impact of conciliar theory and practice was increasingly felt. They are not to be perused to the exclusion of other vital conciliarists such as Filastre and Zabarella. Tierney's studies of the latter have shown his sizable contribution to Christian representative government. Still, the one-time university chancellor, bishop, and cardinal, Peter, with his former student and Paris successor, Jean Charlier, espoused conciliarism from its early trials through its most spectacular victories. Gerson never got to Pisa, though his writings assisted in making this council possible. D'Ailly helped guide both Pisa and Constance. At this last greatest convocation under conciliar principles, Gerson and D'Ailly perfected their earlier labors with new tracts, sermons, and behind-the-scenes negotiations. They doubtless inspired and expedited, more than any others, the train of operations that was consummated in the conciliar manifesto, "Sacrosancta." Together, as two of the most consecrated churchmen of their era, they helped secure, at least temporarily, the healing of the schism. They also joined efforts for promising but ephemeral reforms within the Church and curia. In the process, they, more than any others, capitalized the council for the suppression of heresy. The deaths of two dedicated Christians, Jerome of Prague and John Hus, were principally chargeable to these equally-devoted leaders. D'Ailly had often warned that if reformation were not given genuine priority, union and sound doctrine could not be long guaranteed. The honest if reactionary pocketing of reformation within revived papal absolutism, once Martin V became pope, made Master Peter's prophecy a sad truth. His conciliar propositions, recently translated by Professor Oakley, make sober reading alongside his friend Gerson's pronouncements.

Between Pisa and Constance, Niem's *De Modis* provided an outstanding synthesis of old and new conciliar arguments. So, also, John Hus's *On Simony* proceeded with concurrent Wyclifian propositions to independent if supporting conclusions. Hus gave fresh, Bohemian outlet to the reform instinct and to scholarly vernacular prophetism. Dr. Spinka's editorial researches and monographs, together with S. Harrison Thomson's work on Wyclif and Hus, help to establish the character of that genuine indebtedness Hus owed to Wyclif. They also clarify the unique contribution Hus made, over and beyond his English predecessor. The fuller evaluation of

Gerson's and D'Ailly's influence has had to wait upon recent works like those of Combes, Mourin, and Connolly. The old texts of Du Pin's *Opera* do scant justice to such giants of scholarship, mystical piety, and evangelical ardor as these. The studies of Czech, as well as of Latin, documents by men like Drs. Spinka and Thomson are only the prelude to proper appreciation for Hussite leaders and their catalytic influence on the conciliar epoch.

The last section of this book of readings attempts to relate the earlier tradition of episcopal visitation and diocesan reform, reviewed in Chapter VIII, with the fifteenth-century vicissitudes of conciliarism and diocesan supervision. Johann Busch and Nicholas of Cusa registered uncommonly significant attempts to reform the Church from within. The council of Constance, particularly, had put its collective finger upon the festering sores of curial, monastic, and parish corruption. The conciliar cure for the schism had had tragic repercussions. Its remedy for heretical depravity had been almost as virulent as the disease. Waiting upon papal initiative to implement promising reform measures had proved a form of conciliar cession to revived pontifical self-containment. The councils had gone on to barter away their heritage of reform unity and doctrinal reawakening. Their ecclesiastical and political opportunism interred their earlier idealism in a shallow grave of pope-baiting, nation-mongering, and conciliar degradation.

Nicholas of Cusa, one of the greatest minds and most versatile Christians of the fifteenth century, at one time summarized and backed conciliar principles to the fullest. The bearing of these may be discerned from the translated portions of his *De Concordantia, De auctoritate praesidendi in concilio, Epistolae*, and *De Pace Fidei*. Finally, he apparently became disillusioned, at least with the working cynicism of the later councils. He threw in his lot wholeheartedly with the papacy and its revival of visitation reform. It seems hypocritical to brand him a betrayer of conciliar ideals, especially in the light of the perversions that subsequent conciliarists tolerated and abetted.

One may feel shocked by the evolution and denouement of Cusa's conciliar principle. Nevertheless, the reforming integrity he drew from these was readapted to his own share in the ecumenical encounter with the Greeks, Hussites, and non-Christian peoples. They pervaded his catholic perspective upon the episcopal visitation in Germany. The spiritual honesty of Cusa receives new documentation from his letters analyzing the Bohemian rites, his eucharistic sermons, and his irenic interpretation of Christian liturgy in relation to the non-Christian cult.

Wyclif and Hus had entered a populous world of theological controversy and social unrest girded with the vernacular Bible and a renewed gospel ministry. They had exhibited reform improvisings of striking character. The Franciscan canonist and popular evangelist, Bernardine of Siena, was a reforming voice within the hierarchy. He was thoroughly alive to social discontent and the Church's responsibility for leadership on social issues. Cusa had few of the popularizing gifts of Wyclif and Hus, or of Bernardine, though he admired the Sienese preacher immensely. Yet his sensitivity to heretical and Christian lay movements within the Low Countries, Germany, and elsewhere, was no less perceptive than theirs. He had himself studied at Deventer under the once-vigorous Brethren of the Common Life, with whose reformation at Windesheim Johann Busch so manfully struggled. Nicholas' own sympathies with the Christian lay spirit and true Christian humanism were real. Their character has often been denatured and romanticized. Cusa labored within the Church at all times. He consistently supported and helped energize its hierarchy. This was the God-given instrumentality of that unitive reform which the recent councils had promised in vain. He invited exile and death itself if such proved to be the price of his reforming program.

The heroic dedications of Johann Busch and Nicholas Cusanus may seem at times a pitiful attempt to stay a collapsing order. The translations from Busch's *Chronicle*, like the reports from Cusa's visitation program summarized by Dr. Coulton, make fascinating but depressing copy. The Church at its entrenched levels of customary, vested inter-

X-1. St. Peter and the Bestowal of the Two Swords
on Pope and Emperor.

est had no intention of surrendering laxity
for reformation. Busch and Cusa narrowly
escaped with their lives from their monastic
visitations of "acquisitive brothers" and "irate
sisters." The resourcefulness of such men,
however, proclaims all the more the recur-
ringly tough yet resilient stubbornness of
Christian reform through the ages.

Out of such contexts in an already re-
shaped world of exploration, popular sounding boards, pamphleteering, and competing
world religions, Cusa attempted his Christian revival. Within it he sought the reunion
of contemplation and action, of the *cura* and
schola, animarum. In his day the pagan and
Christian Renaissance already challenged
one to the life of a new humanism. It was
part and parcel of Dante's *Convivio,* the classical revivals of Petrarch, the Christian
worldy-wiseness of Poggio and Bracciolini
and Pope Nicholas V, as well as the distant
thunderings of Gutenberg, Schaefer, and
Fust. The prophetic Biblical reforms and political fulminations of Savonorola were in the
offing. Rapidly copied manuscripts had long
carried sharp popular impact when coupled
pictorially with pamphleteering themes.
What these could become under the aegis of
the Florentine Dominican, Savonarola, and
the Wittenberg Augustinian, Luther, was a
tale of the waxing as well as the waning of
the Middle Ages. A new world was already
growing up within the old. The "idiot" that
Francis called himself and the philosopher

"idiot" that Cusa wrote about were quite different. Yet, they were referable, alike, to the
portentous modesty of little men and great
spirits rising to new dignity in Christian re-
nascence.

I. Representative Theories of Chris-
tian Unity and Duality in Spiritual
and Temporal Powers

A. EIKE OF REPGOW (C. 1180–C. 1235) AND THE TWO SWORDS

1. The Papal or Spiritual and the Imperial or Temporal

Sachsenspiegel, "Landrecht," 1:1, trans. Gerald
Shinn and the editor from K. von Amira, *Die
Dresdener Bilder Handschrift des Sachsenspie-
gels,* Erläuterungen, I, p. 4.

God has placed two swords in the world
for the protection of Christianity—the spiritual having been given to the pope and the
temporal to the king. When the pope goes
riding and mounts a white horse, the king
shall hold the stirrup for him in order that
the saddle may not slip. This signifies that
what the pope opposes but cannot overcome
with the spiritual law, the king shall overcome with the temporal law in obedience to
the pope. So, also, the spiritual power shall
aid the temporal, if it be necessary.

503

X-2. Boniface VIII Proclaiming the Jubilee Year of 1300. *Giotto, Chiesa di Giovanni in Laterano.*

B. POPE BONIFACE VIII (1294–1303) AND THE NEW NATIONAL POWERS

2. Protests against Unrestricted Taxation of the Clergy by Temporal Authorities

Clericis Laicos (1296), Tosti, Hist. de. Bon. VIII, I, pp. 395ff., trans. *ThM*, No. 162, pp. 311–13.

It is said that in times past laymen practiced great violence against the clergy, and our experience clearly shows that they are doing so at present, since they are not content to keep within the limits prescribed for them, but strive to do that which is prohibited and illegal. And they pay no attention to the fact that they are forbidden to exercise authority over the clergy and ecclesiastical persons and their possessions. But they are laying heavy burdens on bishops, churches, and clergy, both regular and secular, by taxing them, levying contributions on them, and extorting the half, or the tenth, or the twentieth, or some other part of their income and possessions. They are striving in many ways to reduce the clergy to servitude and to subject them to their own sway. And we grieve to say it, but some bishops and clergy, fearing where they should not, and seeking a temporary peace, and fearing more to offend man than God, submit, improvidently rather than rashly, to these abuses [and pay the sums demanded], without receiving the papal permission. Wishing to prevent these evils, with the counsel of our brethren, and by our apostolic authority, we decree that if any bishops or clergy, regular or secular, of any grade, condition, or rank, shall pay, or promise, or consent to pay to laymen any contributions, or taxes, or the tenth, or the twentieth, or the hundredth, or any other part of their income or of their possessions, or of their value, real or estimated, under the name of aid, or loan, or subvention, or subsidy, or gift, or under any other name or pretext, without the permission of the pope, they shall, by the very act, incur the sentence of excommunication. And we also decree that emperors, kings, princes, dukes, counts, barons, *podestà, capitanei,* and governors of cities, fortresses, and of all other places everywhere, by whatever names such governors may be called, and all other persons of whatever power, condition, or rank, who shall impose, demand, or receive such taxes, or shall seize, or cause to be seized, the property of churches or of the clergy, which has been deposited in sacred buildings, or shall receive such property after it has been seized, or shall give aid, counsel, or support in such things either openly or secretly, shall by that very act incur the sentence of excommunication. We also put under the interdict all communities which shall be culpable in such matters. And under the threat of deposition we strictly command all bishops and clergy, in accordance with their oath of obedience, not to submit to such taxes without the express permission of the pope. They shall not pay anything under the pretext that they had already promised or agreed to do so before the prohibition came to their knowledge. They shall not pay, nor shall the above-named laymen receive anything in any way. And if the ones shall pay, or the others receive anything, they shall by that very act fall under the sentence of excommunication. From this sentence of excommunication and interdict no one can be absolved except in the moment of death, without the authority and special permission of the pope. . . .

3. Both Swords in the Church's Power; One to Be Used by, the Other for, the Church

Unam Sanctam (1302), Raynaldus, anno 1302, sec. 13, *Rev. des. Quest. Hist.* 46, pp. 255f., *ThM,* No. 164, pp. 314–17.

The true faith compels us to believe that there is one holy catholic apostolic church, and this we firmly believe and plainly confess. And outside of her there is no salvation or remission of sins, as the Bridegroom says in the Song of Solomon: "My dove, my undefiled is but one; she is the only one of her mother, she is the choice one of her that bare her" [Song of Sol. 6:9]; which represents the one mystical body, whose head is Christ, but the head of Christ is God [I Cor. 11:3]. In this church there is "one Lord, one faith, one baptism" [Eph. 4:5]. For in the time of the flood there was only one ark, that of Noah, prefiguring the one church, and it was "finished above in one cubit" [Gen. 6:16], and had but one helmsman and master, namely, Noah. And we read that all things on the earth outside of this ark were destroyed. This church we venerate as the only one, since the Lord said by the prophet: "Deliver my soul from the sword; my darling from the power of the dog" [Ps. 22:20]. He prayed for his soul, that is, for himself, the head; and at the same time for the body; and he named his body, that is, the one church, because there is but one Bridegroom [cf. John 3:29], and because of the unity of the faith, of the sacraments, and of his love for the church. This is the seamless robe of the Lord which was not rent but parted by lot [John 19:23]. Therefore there is one body of the one and only church, and one head, not two heads, as if the church were a monster. And this head is Christ and his vicar, Peter and his successor; for the Lord himself said to Peter: "Feed my sheep" [John 21:16]. And he said "my sheep," in general, not these or those sheep in particular; from which it is clear that all were committed to him. If therefore Greeks or anyone else say that they are not subject to Peter and his successors, they thereby necessarily confess that they are not of the sheep of Christ. For the Lord says in the Gospel of John, that there is one fold and only one shepherd [John 10:16]. By the words of the gospel we are taught that the two swords, namely, the spiritual authority and the temporal are in the power of the church. For when the apostles said "Here are two swords" [Luke 22:38]—that is, in the church, since it was the apostles who were speaking—the Lord did not answer, "It is too much," but "It is enough." Whoever denies that the temporal sword is in the power of Peter does not properly understand the word of the Lord when he said: "Put up thy sword into the sheath" [John 18:11]. Both swords, therefore, the spiritual and the temporal, are in the power of the church. The former is to be used by the church, the latter for the church; the one by the hand of the priest, the other by the hand of kings and knights, but at the command and permission of the priest. Moreover, it is necessary for one sword to be under the other, and the temporal authority to be subjected to the spiritual; for the apostle says, "For there is no power but of God: and the powers that are ordained of God" [Rom. 13:1]; but they would not be ordained [*i.e.,* arranged or set in order; note the play on the words] unless one were subjected to the other, and, as it were, the lower made the higher by the other. For, according to St. Dionysius, it is a law of divinity that the lowest is made the highest through the intermediate. According to the law of the universe all things are not equally and directly reduced to order, but the lowest are fitted into their order through the intermediate, and the lower through the higher. And we must necessarily admit that the spiritual power surpasses any earthly power in dignity and honor, because spiritual things surpass temporal things. We clearly see that this is true from the paying of tithes, from the benediction, from the sanctification, from the receiving of the power, and from the governing of these things. For the truth itself declares that the spiritual power must establish the temporal power and pass judgment on it if it is not good. Thus the prophecy of Jeremiah concerning the church and the ecclesiastical power is fulfilled: "See, I have this day set thee over the nations and over the kingdoms, to root out, and to pull down, and to destroy, and to throw down, to build, and to plant" [Jer. 1:10]. Therefore if the temporal power errs, it will be judged by the spiritual power, and if the lower spiritual power errs, it will be judged by its superior. But if the highest spiritual power errs, it can not be judged by men, but by God alone. For the apostle says: "But he that is spiritual judgeth all things, yet he himself is judged of no man" [I Cor. 2:15]. Now this authority, although it is given to man and exercised through man, is not human, but divine. For it was given by the word of the Lord to Peter, and the rock was made firm to him and his successors, in Christ himself, whom he had confessed. For the Lord said to Peter: "Whatsoever thou shalt bind on earth shall be bound in heaven: and whatsoever thou shalt loose on earth shall be loosed in heaven" [Matt. 16:19]. Therefore whosoever resisteth this power thus ordained of God, resisteth the ordinance of God [Rom. 13:2], unless there are two principles (beginnings), as Manichaeus pretends there are. But this we judge to be false and heretical. For Moses says that, not in the beginnings, but in the beginning [note the play on words], God created the heaven and the earth [Gen. 1:1]. We therefore declare, say, and affirm that submission on the part of every man to the bishop of Rome is altogether necessary for his salvation.

C. JOHN OF PARIS (C. 1241/51–1306/16)
AND THE BALANCE OF THE SPIRITUAL AND THE TEMPORAL (1302–1303)

4. The Priest Greater than the Prince in Spiritual Affairs, the Prince Greater than the Priest in Temporal Affairs

De potestate regia et papali, 5. Reprinted from *Medieval Political Ideas* by Ewart Lewis, by permission of Alfred A. Knopf, Inc. Published in 1954 by Alfred A. Knopf, Inc. Vol. II, pp. 585–86.

From what has just been said, one can easily see which is first in dignity, the kingship or the priesthood. For what is later in time is customarily first in dignity, as the perfect in comparison with the imperfect, and the end in comparison with the means. And therefore we say that the priestly power is greater than the royal power and excels it in dignity, since we always find that to which belongs the ultimate end is more perfect than, and better than, and gives direction to that to which belongs the inferior end. Now the kingship is ordained for this purpose: that the associated multitude may live according to virtue. . . . And it is further ordained to a higher end, which is the enjoyment of God; and guidance to this end is the charge of Christ, Whose ministers and vicars are the priests. Therefore the priestly power is of greater dignity than the secular power. And this is commonly conceded. . . .

However, if the priest is, in an absolute sense, greater in dignity than the prince, it does not follow that he is the greater in all respects. For the lesser secular power is not related to the greater spiritual power as originating from it or being derived from it, as, for example, the power of a proconsul is related to the emperor, who is greater than he in all respects and from whom his power is derived. But it is like the power of the head of a household in comparison with the power of a commander of soldiers, neither one of which is derived from the other, but both of which are derived from some superior power. Therefore the secular power is greater than the spiritual in some repects: namely, in temporal affairs; and in regard to those affairs it is not subjected to the spiritual power in any way, since it does not owe its origin to the spiritual power, but both owe their origin immediately to one supreme power: namely, the divine; therefore the lower is not subjected completely to the higher but only in those respects in which the supreme power has subordinated it to the greater. For who would say that because a teacher of letters or instructor in morals ordains all the members of a household to a nobler end (namely, to the knowledge of truth), therefore a physician, who looks after the lower end (namely, the health of the body), should be subjected to him in the preparing of his medicines? For this is not fitting, since the head of the household, who established them both in the house, did not subordinate the physician to the tutor in this respect. Therefore the priest is greater than the prince in spiritual affairs and, conversely, the prince is greater than the priest in temporal affairs, although in an absolute sense the priest is the greater, inasmuch as the spiritual power is greater than the temporal. . . .

D. PIERRE DU BOIS AND CHRISTIAN REFORM (1305–1307)

5. The Recovery of the Holy Land through Unified Catholic Action; Conciliar Plans for Reforming the Church Universal

De recuperatione terrae sanctae, ed. C. V. Langlois (Paris: A Picard, 1891), from *The Portable Medieval Reader*, ed. James Bruce Ross and Mary Martin McLaughlin (New York: The Viking Press, Inc., © 1949), pp. 293–95, 296–98. Reprinted by permission.

To the end, therefore, that the Holy Land can be recovered, and having been recovered, can be held against so many and such great demons, who have followers, protectors, and helpers, the devout prayers of the universal Church seem necessary. And it does not seem possible to have them without a reformation of the condition of the universal Church, which is discussed below. Nor is it possible unless the whole commonwealth of Christians obedient to the Roman Church, bound together by the bond of peace, is united in such a way that Catholics would mutually desist from all warfare among themselves; so that if any should engage in war, out of this warfare and because of it, the recovery and defence of the Holy Land might be strengthened.

This could be accomplished thus. After a general council has been called, because of ardour for the deliverance of the Holy Land, the greatest royal experience will be able to request through the lord pope that the princes and prelates should agree and determine to the end that, when anyone whosoever says that he has suffered injuries according to the laws and customs of the kingdoms and regions, justice will be done, more quickly than is customary, by judges established in those places, and where they have

not been established, they should be, in the manner described below. No Catholic should rush to arms against Catholics; no one should shed the blood of a baptized Christian. Whoever wants to fight should strive to fight against the enemies of the Christian faith, of the Holy Land and the holy places of the Lord, not against brothers, seeking an occasion of bodily and spiritual perdition.

Those who should presume, moreover, to carry on warfare against their fellow Catholics, in defiance of this wholesome decision, by that act should incur the loss of all their goods, with everything which aids them in fighting—foodstuffs, arms, and other necessities of life or battle—and in ruling, in any way whatsoever. After the war has ended, those who survive, of whatever estate, condition, and sex, should be exiled forever from their lands and possessions, and, completely deprived, with all of their descendants, they should be sent to people the Holy Land. As much as will be necessary for their expenses and for making the journey should be given to them from the property of which they have been deprived, if they should be obedient and willingly intend to transfer themselves to the Holy Land. . . .

Just as, moreover, it is necessary and expedient that the harmonious and united temporal resources of the whole commonwealth of Catholics should be brought together for so great a recovery and preservation, so it will be necessary, by the devout prayers of the universal Church, to seek and obtain this great blessing of the recovery and maintenance of so great a peace, from Him from whom all good proceeds, who is God and the Lord of armies, who alone is the cause of peace and victory. For if the leaders of warfare and the fighting men entrusted to them should be confident in their own strength, and should think that this strength suffices to obtain and keep so great a victory, and to resist the evil spirits fighting against them, with their persuasions and temptations . . . it will not be possible in this way to recover and keep the Holy Land. For this reason, it seems expedient that the council should seek to reform and improve the condition of the Church Universal, so that the prelates both greater and lesser may abstain from that

507

which is forbidden by the holy fathers; that they may guard their precepts, commandments, and counsels, as they are understood, according to the saying of the prophet, "Depart from evil, and do good; seek peace and pursue it." And then, when the true peace of the heart has been attained, all Catholic prelates, with all the clergy and people committed to their care, should form one spiritual commonwealth, in order to approach what the apostle says, "And the multitude of them that believed were of one heart and one soul.". . .

If, indeed, it will seem good to strengthen the bonds of universal peace in the manner prescribed, it should be resolved, by agreement of the council of prelates and princes, that all prelates, of whatever rank, and also the secular knights in their own ranks, will firmly swear that they will observe, with all their strength, the covenants of this peace with its penalties, and that they will take care that it is observed, in every way in which they can. Thus anyone who will scorn or neglect to fulfill this oath, because of this, by the apostolic authority and that of the sacred council, will *ipso facto* incur sentence of major excommunication. Thus anyone who assails this covenant of peace in the future will be strongly attacked by all those knights of the spiritual and temporal army, with all their strength, so that he will not be able to resist. . . .

E. DANTE ALIGHIERI (1265–1321) ON HUMANITY'S TWO-FOLD DIRECTIVE (C. 1308–13)

6. The Pope to Lead Men to Life Eternal; the Emperor to Direct Mankind to Temporal Happiness

De Monarchia 3:16. Lewis, *op. cit.*, pp. 592–94.

Although it was shown in the preceding chapter . . . that the authority of the empire is not caused by the authority of the supreme pontiff, yet it was not altogether proved that it is immediately derived from God, unless as a consequence of that argument. For if it is not derived from the vicar of God it follows that it is derived from God. Therefore, to prove our proposition decisively, it must be manifestly proved that the emperor or monarch of the world is immediately related to the Prince of the universe, Who is God.

Now in order to understand this it should be known that man alone among beings holds a middle place between corruptibles and incorruptibles; wherefore he is rightly likened by philosophers to the horizon which is midway between the two hemispheres. For if man is considered in terms of his two essential parts, his soul and his body, he is corruptible if the body alone is considered, but incorruptible if the soul alone is considered. . . .

If, therefore man is something midway between the corruptible and the incorruptible, he must share both natures, since every mean smacks of the nature of the extremes. And since every nature is ordained to some ultimate end, it follows that there is a two-fold end for man: that, even as among all beings he alone partakes of corruptibility and incorruptibility, so he alone among all beings is ordained to two ultimate ends, of which one is his as he is corruptible, the other as he is incorruptible.

Therefore the ineffable Providence has set before man two ends to be pursued: namely, the beatitude of this life, which consists in the operation of his own virtue and is typified by the earthly paradise; and the beatitude of the life eternal, which consists in the enjoyment of the divine countenance, to which man's own virtue cannot ascend unless it is aided by divine light; and this is described for our understanding as the heavenly paradise.

To these beatitudes, as to diverse ends, man must come through diverse means. For we come to the first through philosophic teachings, if indeed we follow them by acting in accordance with the moral and intellectual virtues. But we come to the second through spiritual teachings which transcend the human reason, if indeed we follow them by acting in accordance with the theological virtues, faith, hope, and charity. Therefore these ends and means . . . would be frus-

X-3. Philip the Fair and His Council, 1322. *Miniature from the* Actes du Procès de Robert d'Artois.

trated by human greed, if men, straying like horses in their bestiality, were not restrained on the road with bit and rein.

And therefore man needed a twofold directive, corresponding to the twofold end: namely, the supreme pontiff, who would lead the human race to life eternal in accordance with revealed truth, and the emperor, who would direct mankind to temporal felicity in accordance with philosophic teachings. And since none, or few, and these only with great difficulty, can reach this harbour unless the waves of alluring desire are calmed and mankind rests freely in the tranquillity of peace, this is the mark at which the guardian of this world, who is called the Roman Prince, should especially aim: that mortals in their little space may freely live with peace. And

since the disposition of the world follows the inherent disposition of the heavens to move in circles, it is necessary, if useful lessons of liberty and peace, suitable to time and place, are to be applied by that guardian, that he be controlled by Him Who, foreknowing, contemplates the total disposition of the heavens. Moreover, this is none other than He Who has preordained it, so that through His control He in His providence may bind all things in their orders. But if this is so, God alone chooses, He alone confirms that guardian who has no superior. . . .

Thus, therefore, it appears that the authority of temporal monarchy flows into it directly, without any intermediary, from the fountain of universal authority. And this fountain, one in the citadel of its simplicity,

509

flows into many channels from its abundance of goodness.

And now I seem to have reached my intended goal. For I have revealed the truth which answers the question whether the office of monarch is necessary to the well-being of the world, and the question whether the Roman people rightfully claimed empire for itself, and the last question whether the authority of the monarch is derived from God immediately or through someone else. And the truth of the last question is not to be construed so narrowly that the Roman prince is not subject to the Roman pontiff in any respect, since mortal felicity is in a way ordained to immortal felicity. Therefore let Caesar pay to Peter the reverence which a first-born owes to his father, that, brightened by the light of paternal grace, he may shine more virtuously upon the whole earth, over which he has been set by Him alone who is the Governor of all spiritual and temporal things.

II. Early Conciliar Theorists and Political Reformers During the Avignon Papacy

A. MARSILIUS OF PADUA ON THE COMMUNITY OF BELIEVERS, THE COUNCIL AND THE LEGISLATOR

7. *Chief Authority for Determining the Bearing of Scripture Belongs Only to a General Council of Christians, or to Its More Weighty Part* (Pars valentior)

Defensor Pacis, Dict. II, cap. 20, ed. Prévité-Orton. *Ibid.*, pp. 392–93.

2. . . . I show that the principal authority, mediate or immediate, to determine [the meaning of ambiguous statements in the Holy Scripture] belongs only to a general council of Christians or its more weighty part, or to those to whom this authority may have been granted by the corporation of faithful Christians, as follows. All provinces or notable communities of the world should choose, in accordance with the determination of their human legislator or legislators and with regard to a due proportion, in quantity

X-4. Avignon and Papal Quarters. *Left to right: Belfry of Notre-Dame-des-Doms, Tower de la Campane, Entrance to Papal Palace, Clementine Chapel, Tower of Saint-Laurent.*

and quality, of the persons so chosen, faithful men, first priests and then laymen, qualified by the superior uprightness of their lives and their knowledge of divine law. These men, acting as judges in the first sense of the term [*i.e.*, as experts; cf. *dictio* 2, ch. 2, sec. 8] and representing the whole corporation of faithful people by the authority granted to them by the corporations, should come to a certain place which the majority of them choose as most appropriate. In this place they should, together, define those matters of divine law which have appeared doubtful and which it is useful, expedient, and necessary to determine, and also ordain other things, pertaining to the ritual of the church, or divine worship, which may add to the peace and tranquillity of the faithful. For it would be idle and disadvantageous to convene an inexpert multitude of the faithful to this assembly; disadvantageous, also, since they would be distracted from their necessary tasks for the sustenance of corporal life—a situation which would be burdensome and, perhaps, unbearable.

3. All the faithful are by divine law liable to this assembly, because of its purpose, but in different ways: for the priests are liable because it is their office to teach the law according to its true meaning and to further those things that contribute to its purity and truth, to condemn contrary errors, and to recall men from error by their exhortations, arguments, and reproofs. . . . However, after the priests and beyond the rest of the people, those who are learned in divine law are liable, for they ought to guide others and to meet with the priests, especially if they have been sufficiently required and commanded to do so, because 'to know the good and not to do it is a sin,' as it is written in James 4: [17]. Also, for the defining of other things, aside from divine law, for the common utility and peace of the faithful, those who have been appointed to this duty by the human legislator can and ought to participate in the council. Legislators have an obligation also: to choose suitable persons to compose the council, to provide them with temporal necessities, and, if need be, for the sake of the public utility, to compel the attendance of those suitable and chosen persons who may refuse to attend.

4. Moreover, that the said authority of defining and ordaining in the way we have described belongs only to the general council, and to no other individual or particular college, can be shown by the same reasoning and authoritative passages of Holy Scripture as we showed, in the twelfth chapter of *dictio* I and the seventeenth chapter of this *dictio*, to apply to legislation and to the secondary institution of ecclesiastical officers, changing only the minor premise of the argument: that is, substituting for the determining of law or the secondary institution of ecclesiastical officers the determining or defining of ambiguities in the Divine Law, together with the rest of the things to be ordained in regard to the ritual of the church, or divine worship. For it is particularly necessary that discretion and care be diligently maintained in these decisions, inasmuch as they are to be held by law and faith; and also in decisions which can profit or harm all the faithful.

8. Basic Conclusions of Marsilius on the General Council of Christians, the Bible, Ecclesiastical Offices and Community Welfare; the Council, not the Pope, the Supreme Authority Within the Church

Def. Pacis, Dict. III, cap. 2, Goldast, *Monarchia Sancti Romani Imperii,* II, 309ff., trans. ThM, No. 165, pp. 318–23.

Conclusion 1. The one divine canonical Scripture, the conclusions that necessarily follow from it, and the interpretation placed upon it by the common consent of Christians, are true, and belief in them is necessary to the salvation of those to whom they are made known.

2. The general council of Christians or its majority alone has the authority to define doubtful passages of the divine law, and to determine those that are to be regarded as articles of the Christian faith, belief in which is essential to salvation; and no partial council or single person of any position has the authority to decide these questions.

3. The gospels teach that no temporal punishment or penalty should be used to compel observance of divine commandments.

4. It is necessary to salvation to obey the commandments of the new divine law [the New Testament] and the conclusions that follow necessarily from it and the precepts of reason; but it is not necessary to salvation to obey all the commandments of the ancient law [the Old Testament].

5. No mortal has the right to dispense with the commands or prohibitions of the new divine law; but the general council and the Christian "legislator" alone have the right to prohibit things which are permitted by the new law, under penalties in this world or the next, and no partial council or single person of any position has that right.

6. The whole body of citizens or its majority alone is the human "legislator."

7. Decretals and decrees of the bishop of Rome, or of any other bishops or body of bishops, have no power to coerce anyone by

secular penalties or punishments, except by the authorization of the human "legislator."

8. The "legislator" alone or the one who rules by its authority has the power to dispense with human laws.

9. The elective principality or other office derives its authority from the election of the body having the right to elect, and not from the confirmation or approval of any other power.

10. The election of any prince or other official, especially one who has the coercive power, is determined solely by the expressed will of the "legislator."

11. There can be only one supreme ruling power in a state or kingdom.

12. The number and the qualifications of persons who hold state offices and all civil matters are to be determined solely by the Christian ruler according to the law or approved custom [of the state].

13. No prince, still more, no partial council or single person of any position, has full authority and control over other persons, laymen or clergy, without the authorization of the "legislator."

14. No bishop or priest has coercive authority or jurisdiction over any layman or clergyman, even if he is a heretic.

15. The prince who rules by the authority of the "legislator" has jurisdiction over the persons and possessions of every single mortal of every station, whether lay or clerical, and over every body of laymen or clergy.

16. No bishop or priest or body of bishops or priests has the authority to excommunicate anyone or to interdict the performance of divine services, without the authorization of the "legislator."

17. All bishops derive their authority in equal measure immediately from Christ, and it cannot be proved from the divine law that one bishop should be over or under another, in temporal or spiritual matters.

18. The other bishops, singly or in a body, have the same right by divine authority to excommunicate or otherwise exercise authority over the bishop of Rome, having obtained the consent of the "legislator," as the bishop of Rome has to excommunicate or control them.

19. No mortal has the authority to permit marriages that are prohibited by the divine law, especially by the New Testament. The right to permit marriages which are prohibited by human law belongs solely to the "legislator" or to the one who rules by its authority.

20. The right to legitimatize children born of illegitimate union so that they may receive inheritances, or other civil or ecclesiastical offices or benefits, belongs solely to the "legislator."

21. The "legislator" alone has the right to promote to ecclesiastical orders, and to judge of the qualifications of persons for these offices, by a coercive decision, and no priest or bishop has the right to promote anyone without its authority.

22. The prince who rules by the authority of the laws of Christians, has the right to determine the number of churches and temples, and the number of priests, deacons, and other clergy who shall serve in them.

23. "Separable" ecclesiastical offices may be conferred or taken away only by the authority of the "legislator"; the same is true of ecclesiastical benefices and other property devoted to pious purposes.

24. No bishop or body of bishops has the right to establish notaries or other civil officials.

25. No bishop or body of bishops may give permission to teach or practice in any profession or occupation, but this right belongs to the Christian "legislator" or to the one who rules by its authority.

26. In ecclesiastical offices and benefices those who have received consecration as deacons or priests, or have been otherwise irrevocably dedicated to God, should be preferred to those who have not been thus consecrated.

27. The human "legislator" has the right to use ecclesiastical temporalities for the common public good and defence, after the needs of the priests and clergy, the expenses of divine worship, and the necessities of the poor have been satisfied.

28. All properties established for pious purposes or for works of mercy, such as those that are left by will for the making of a crusade, the redeeming of captives, or the support of the poor, and similar purposes,

may be disposed of by the prince alone according to the decision of the "legislator" and the purpose of the testator or giver.

29. The Christian "legislator" alone has the right to forbid or permit the establishment of religious orders or houses.

30. The prince alone, acting in accordance with the laws of the "legislator," has the authority to condemn heretics, delinquents, and all others who should endure temporal punishment, to inflict bodily punishment upon them, and to exact fines from them.

31. No subject who is bound to another by a legal oath may be released from his obligation by any bishop or priest, unless the "legislator" has decided by a coercive decision that there is just cause for it.

32. The general council of all Christians alone has the authority to create a metropolitan bishop or church, and to reduce him or it from that position.

33. The Christian "legislator" or the one who rules by its authority over Christian states, alone has the right to convoke either a general or local council of priests, bishops, and other Christians, by coercive power; and no man may be compelled by threats of temporal or spiritual punishment to obey the decrees of a council convoked in any other way.

34. The general council of Christians or the Christian "legislator" alone has the authority to ordain fasts and other prohibitions of the use of food; the council or "legislator" alone may prohibit the practice of mechanical arts or teaching which divine law permits to be practiced on any day, and the "legislator" or the one who rules by its authority alone may constrain men to obey the prohibition by temporal penalties.

35. The general council of Christians alone has the authority to canonize anyone or to order anyone to be adored as a saint.

36. The general council of Christians alone has the authority to forbid the marriage of priests, bishops, and other clergy, and to make other laws concerning ecclesiastical discipline, and that council or the one to whom it delegates its authority alone may dispense with these laws.

37. It is always permitted to appeal to the "legislator" from a coercive decision rendered by a bishop or priest with the authorization of the "legislator."

38. Those who are pledged to observe complete poverty may not have in their possession any immovable property, unless it be with the fixed intention of selling it as soon as possible and giving the money to the poor; they may not have such rights in either movable or immovable property as would enable them, for example, to recover them by a coercive decision from any person who should take or try to take them away.

39. The people as a community and as individuals, according to their several means, are required by divine law to support the bishops and other clergy authorized by the gospel, so that they may have food and clothing and the other necessaries of life; but the people are not required to pay tithes or other taxes beyond the amount necessary for such support.

40. The Christian "legislator" or the one who rules by its authority has the right to compel bishops and other clergy who live in the province under its control and whom it supplies with the necessities of life, to perform divine services and administer the sacrament.

41. The bishop of Rome and any other ecclesiastical or spiritual minister may be advanced to a "separable" ecclesiastical office only by the Christian "legislator" or the one who rules by its authority, or by the general council of Christians; and they may be suspended from or deprived of office by the same authority.

B. WILLIAM OF OCKHAM († 1349) ON DELIMITATION OF PAPAL POWER AND THE ROLE OF THE GENERAL COUNCIL

9. *The Papal Plenitude not to Include Temporal Domination*

De imperatorum et pontificum potestate (1346/47), 1, ed. C. K. Brampton (Oxford, 1927). Lewis, *op. cit.*, pp. 607–8.

. . . When Christ constituted the blessed Peter head and prince of all believers, he did not give him such plenitude of power that he could regularly and by right do everything which was not contrary to di-

X-5. Palace of the Popes. *Chapel of Clement VI.*

vine or natural law, but assigned definite limits to his power, which he was not to transgress. That he did not give him such plenitude of power in temporals is proved by authority and by reason. For the apostle says in II Timothy 2:[4], 'Let no one fighting for God involve himself in secular affairs, that he may please Him Whose favour he has won.' Therefore, since the blessed Peter was not the least among the special soldiers of God, and particularly strove to please God, he ought not to involve himself in secular affairs, and thus his receiving from Christ such plenitude of power in temporals would have been to no purpose. Also, plenitude of power in temporals includes the power and domination of the kings of the gentiles; but Christ prohibited the power and domination of the kings of the gentiles to the blessed Peter and the other apostles, as appears in Luke 22:[25–26], Mark 10:[42–43], and Matthew 20:[25], where we read that Christ said these words, 'You know that the princes of the gentiles lord it over them, and those who are greater among them exercise authority; not so will it be among you, but whoever may wish to become greater among you will be your minister.' Therefore, on the contrary, Christ forbade to the apostles the aforesaid plenitude of power in temporals.

Further, no temporal lord has greater rightful power over his slave (taking the word 'slave' in its most precise sense) than that he can impose on him everything which is not contrary to divine law or the law of nature; wherefore, if Christ had given to the blessed Peter such plentitude of temporal power over all believers, He would have made all men his slaves in all respects, which is manifestly inconsistent with the liberty of the law of the gospel. . . . Moreover, even as Christ did not give the blessed Peter such plenitude of power in temporals, so also he did not grant him such plenitude of power in spirituals. For . . . the evangelic law is a law of less servitude than was the Mosaic

514

law, which the blessed Peter said, as we read in Acts 15:[10], was 'a yoke which neither he nor his fathers could bear.' If, however, the blessed Peter had received from Christ the aforesaid plenitude of power in spirituals, he would have received from Christ the authority to impose on the faithful more and heavier burdens, in regard to divine worship and in regard to vigils, fasts, and other spiritual matters, than were the burdens of the old law. Thus the law of the gospel would be a law of greater servitude than the law of Moses. Therefore . . . it can be seen that Christ, when He set the blessed Peter over all believers, set definite limits which he was not permitted to transgress.

10. Limitations on the Exercise of Powers Entrusted to Peter by Christ: a Pope Intervening in Temporals Puts His Sickle in Alien Corn

Ibid., 2, p. 608.

. . . We should now see what these limits are that the blessed Peter was not permitted to transgress and within which he was permitted to exercise the power entrusted him by Christ. . . .

In the first place, I think it should be maintained that the papal principate instituted by Christ in no way regularly includes temporals and secular affairs; and this is manifestly proved not only by the words of the apostle in II Timothy 2:[4], cited above, but also the blessed Peter, as we read in [*Decretum*], c. 29, C. II, q. I, told the blessed Pope Clement, 'You must indeed live blamelessly and strive with the utmost zeal to put aside all the affairs of this life: not to become a guarantor, nor an advocate in lawsuits, nor to be found involved in any sort of mundane business at all. For Christ wishes to ordain you today neither judge nor advocate in secular affairs.' And the blessed Bernard, writing to Pope Eugenius concerning the papal power, alludes to this, saying, 'You have power in regard to sins, not in regard to possessions. Because of the former, not the latter, you have received the keys of the kingdom of heaven: that you may exclude false witnesses, not possessors' [*De Consideratione*, bk. I, ch. 6].

If, therefore, the pope, except in case of necessity, intervenes in temporals, he is considered to put his sickle into another's harvest, unless he has received authority over such matters from the emperor or someone else. And indeed what he does in such matters is not valid, since 'those things that are done by a judge are null and void if they do not belong to his office' (ch. 26, bk. 5, tit. 12 *in Sexto*). . . .

X-6. Palace of the Popes. *Aile du Consistoire: Le Grand Tinel.*

11. When and How a General Council May Be Assembled Without Papal Authorization

Dialogus, ed. Goldast, pt. 1, bk. 6, ch. 84. *Ibid.*, pp. 399–402.

PUPIL: . . . Tell me first, in regard to the council: if the pope is a notorious heretic, and if the electors of the supreme pontiff share or unduly countenance his heretical depravity, and if there appears to be no other way to coerce the heretical pope, how or by whom ought a general council to be assembled?

TEACHER: They say that in this case any catholic who knows that the pope is a notorious heretic, or hears it publicly discussed that the pope is a notorious heretic, ought to be ready to assemble for a general council if it is expedient, and anyone, in so far as befits his rank, ought to exhort other catholics to assemble for a general council. However, this primarily concerns prelates and those learned in divine law. Secondarily, it concerns kings and princes and other public powers. In the third place, however, it concerns all catholics, men and women. Thus even catholic women, if they know the pope to be a heretic and the electors negligent in regard to the election of a supreme pontiff, ought, if it is expedient, to urge catholics to convene in a general council for the ordaining of the church; nay, more, even the women themselves ought to attend, if they can further the common good thereby.

PUPIL: This assertion amazes me. For it seems to contain three absurdities: first, that a general council ought to be called without the authorization of the pope; second, that kings and princes and other laymen ought to assemble for a general council; third, that women can and should take part in a general council. For it is clearly proved by the sacred canons that the first is absurd. For, as is maintained throughout di. 17 [of the *Decretum*], a general council cannot be convened without the authority of the supreme pontiff. For Pope Pelagius says [c. 5]: 'We are instructed again and again, by many papal and canonic and ecclesiastical rules, that councils may not be held without the licence of the Roman pontiff. . . .'

TEACHER: That a general council can be convened without the authority of the pope seems to be proved by several arguments. The first is as follows: a particular council can lawfully be convened without the authority of the pope to judge concerning the same true pope. Therefore, all the more, a general council can be convened to judge concerning a heretical pseudo-pope without his authority. The premise of this argument seems to be proved by two manifest examples. The first is that of the bishops who convened to inquire about the deed and idolatry of the blessed Marcellinus; their assembly was a particular council, convened without the authority of this same Pope Marcellinus. The second is that of the assembly which convened to judge and depose Pope John XXII; this assembly was only a particular and not a general council. All the more, therefore, a general council could be formed to judge concerning a heretical pope detected in notorious heresy.

PUPIL: This argument seems clearly to prove that a general council could be assembled without the authority of a false, heretical pope; but it does not prove that one could be convened without the authority of a true pope. Whence it also seems that if the pope is a heretic, a catholic pope ought to be elected before the general council is summoned.

TEACHER: It appears to some thinkers that the argument just given patently shows that a general council can be convoked without the authority of any pope whatever, true or false. For if it is lawful to hold a particular council without the authority of the pope for the purpose of inquiring or judging about a true pope, it is much more lawful to hold a general council during the vacancy of the apostolic see, without the authority of a pope, for the due coercion of a pseudo-pope, expecially if the pseudo-pope cannot otherwise be coerced. The former is lawful, as is proved by the two examples; therefore the latter ought also to be considered lawful.

The second argument is as follows: every people and every community and every body which can make law for itself without the consent or authority of anyone else can without the authority of anyone else elect certain persons to represent the whole community or body. But all the faithful are one body, as Paul says in Romans 12:[5], 'We, being many, are one body in Christ'; and they are one people and one community. Therefore they can elect certain persons to represent the whole body. Moreover, if men so elected come together at one time, they constitute a general council, since a general council seems to be nothing else than an assembly of certain men who represent the whole of Christendom. Therefore, a general council can be convened without the authority of anyone whatever who is not a catholic and a believer, and, consequently, without the authority of a heretical pope.

The third argument is as follows: the universal church, meeting together to ordain something, can be described as a general council. But the universal church might be reduced to a number so small that it could all assemble at the same time; for once, after the ascension of Christ, it was so small in number, and therefore it is not impossible that it might become so small again. Consequently, it is not impossible that the universal church might convene as a universal council even if there were no true pope. Thus it is not impossible that in the vacancy of the apostolic see the universal church might convene all at once. But the universal church does not have less power and authority when it is too numerous to convene all at once than when it can convene all at once. Therefore, whatever the universal church could do through itself . . . it can do through certain men elected from diverse parts of the church. Therefore, if we suppose that diverse parts of the universal church should elect men to convene to ordain something concerning the church of God, the men thus elected, meeting together, could be called a general council, regardless of the fact that there was no true pope. And thus when there is no true pope a general council can be assembled without the authority of the pope.

PUPIL: I somewhat understand this way of putting it, yet, that I may understand it better and thus more clearly arrive at the truth, tell me by what method, according to the opinion we have been discussing, a general council ought to be convened.

TEACHER: It is said that it would be reasonable to send, from each parish or community which could easily convene in one assembly, some person or persons to an episcopal council or to the parliament of the king or prince or of some other public power, and that this in turn should elect some persons to be sent to the general council; and the persons thus elected by episcopal councils or by the parliaments of secular powers can, when they convene in one place, be called a general council.

PUPIL: . . . Explain how those who hold this opinion answer the authorities in which it is manifestly asserted that a general council ought not to be assembled without the authority of the supreme pontiff.

TEACHER: They answer that as a rule a general council ought by no means to be assembled without the authority of the supreme pontiff. Yet this rule fails in a specific case: namely, when the pope has become a heretic and the electors of the supreme pontiff fail to elect a pope and provision for this situation cannot be made otherwise than through a general council of the church. Therefore they say that the authoritative statements of those supreme pontiffs who assert that a general council ought not to be assembled without the authority of the pope are by no means to be denied; but they are to be understood sensibly, that they may not be interpreted in any way that prejudices the Christian faith, which ought by all means to take precedence over even a catholic pope.

III. The Great Schism (1378–1417/55) and the Dissipation of Christian Unity

A. THE MANIFESTO OF THE REVOLTING CARDINALS (1378)

12. Clement VII Set up Against Urban VI

Baluzius, *Vitae Paparum Avenionensium*, I, 468ff., trans. ThM, No. 167, pp. 325–26.

. . . After the apostolic seat was made vacant by the death of our lord, pope Gregory XI, who died in March, we assembled in conclave for the election of a pope, as is the

X-7. Pope Gregory XI's Return from Avignon to Rome. *Hospital of St. Marie della Scala. Matteo di Giovanni.*

law and custom, in the papal palace, in which Gregory had died. . . . Officials of the city with a great multitude of the people, for the most part armed and called together for this purpose by the ringing of bells, surrounded the palace in a threatening manner and even entered it and almost filled it. To the terror caused by their presence they added threats that unless we should at once elect a Roman or an Italian they would kill us. They gave us no time to deliberate but compelled us unwillingly, through violence and fear, to elect an Italian without delay. In order to escape the danger which threatened us from such a mob, we elected Bartholomew, archbishop of Bari, thinking that he would have enough conscience not to accept the election, since every one knew that it was made under such wicked threats. But he was unmindful of his own salvation and burning with ambition, and so, to the great scandal of the clergy and of the Christian people, and contrary to the laws of the church, he accepted this election which was offered him, although not all the cardinals were present at the election, and it was ex-

torted from us by the threats and demands of the officials and people of the city. And although such an election is null and void, and the danger from the people still threatened us, he was enthroned and crowned, and called himself pope and apostolic. But according to the holy fathers and to the law of the church, he should be called apostate, anathema, Antichrist, and the mocker and destroyer of Christianity. . . .

B. JOHN WYCLIF "ON THE PASTORAL OFFICE" (1378), AND "ON THE CHURCH AND HER MEMBERS" (1384)

13. God's Law, the Vernacular Scriptures, and the Friars

Officio pastoralis, 2:2a, trans. in M. Spinka, ed., *Advocates of Reform* [LCC, Vol. XIV] (Philadelphia: Westminster Press; London, Student Christian Movement Press, 1953), pp. 49–51.

The friars with their followers say that it is heresy thus to write God's law in English and make it known to ignorant men. . . .

It seems first that the knowledge of God's

law should be taught in that language which is best known, because this knowledge is God's Word. When Christ says in the Gospel that both heaven and earth shall pass away but his words shall not pass away, he means by his "words" his knowledge. Thus God's knowledge is Holy Scripture that may in no wise be false. Also the Holy Spirit gave to the apostles at Pentecost knowledge to know all manner of languages to teach the people God's law thereby; and so God willed that the people be taught his law in divers tongues. But what man on God's behalf should reverse God's ordinance and his will? For this reason Saint Jerome labored and translated the Bible from divers tongues into Latin that it might after be translated into other tongues. Thus Christ and his apostles taught the people in that tongue that was best known to them. Why should men not do so now? And for this reason the authors of the new law who were apostles of Jesus Christ wrote their Gospels in divers tongues that were better known to the people. Also the worthy kingdom of France, notwithstanding all hindrances, has translated the Bible and the Gospels with other true sentences of doctors out of Latin into French. Why should not Englishmen do so? As the lords of England have the Bible in French, so would it not be against reason that they have it in English; for thus, with unity of knowledge, God's law would be better known and more believed, and there might be more agreement between kingdoms. In England the friars have taught the Lord's Prayer in the English language, as men see in the play of York, . . . and in many other counties. Since the Lord's Prayer is part of Matthew's Gospel, as clerks know, why may not all of the Gospel be turned into English as is this part? This is especially so since all Christian men, learned and ignorant, who should be saved might always follow Christ and know his teaching and his life. But the common people of England know it best in their mother tongue and thus it is the same thing to prevent such knowledge of the Gospel and to prevent Englishmen from following Christ and coming to heaven. I well know that there may be faults in unfaithful translating as there might have been many faults in turning from Hebrew into Greek and from Greek into Latin, and from one language into another. But let men live a good life, and let many study God's law, and when errors are found let them who reason well correct them. Some say that the friars and their followers labor in this cause for three reasons; God knows whether they be so. First, the friars would be thought so necessary to the Englishmen of our kingdom that solely in their knowledge lay the knowledge of God's law, and to tell the people God's law in whatever manner they please. And the second reason is: Friars would lead the people in teaching them God's law and thus they would teach some, hide some, and cut off some parts. For then faults in their life should be less known to the people and God's law should be less truly known both by clerks and by common people. The third cause that men notice consists in this, as they say: All these new orders are afraid that their sins should be known and how their entry into the Church had no divine sanction. Thus out of fear they do not desire that God's law be known in English, for they could not put heresy upon men if English told what they said. May God move lords and bishops to stand up for the knowing of his law.

14. The Three-Fold Church and God's Secret Election

The Church and Her Members, 1, put into Modern English by Thomas A. Schafer from T. Arnold, *Select English Works of John Wyclif* (Oxford: Clarendon Press, 1871), III, pp. 339–40. Used by permission of Mr. Thomas A. Schafer, together with Items 15–17.

Christ's Church is his Spouse, and is composed of three parts. The first part is in bliss with Christ, the head of the Church, and contains angels and blessed men who are now in heaven. The second part of the Church are saints in purgatory; these commit no additional sins, but purge their old sins. Many errors come from praying for these saints; and since they are all dead in body, Christ's words may be applied to them —let us serve Christ in our life, and "let the dead bury the dead." The third part of the Church is composed of true men that are living on earth, who shall afterwards be among the saved in heaven and who live here the lives of Christian men. The first part is called the victorious, the second is called the sleeping, and the third is called the fighting Church; and these three together make up the Church.

The head of the Church is Christ, who is both God and man. This Church is mother to each man that shall be saved; it contains no men as members except those that shall be saved. For, as Christ vouchsafes to call this Church his Spouse, so also he calls men cursed who are devils, as was Iscariot. And far be it from Christian men to grant that Christ has wedded the devil; since Paul says, in our belief, that Christ has no communion with Belial. And here we take it as a matter of belief that each member of holy Church shall be saved with Christ, as well as that each member of the devil shall be damned. Therefore, while we are fighting here, we know not whether we shall be saved, nor do we know whether we are members of holy Church. Just as it is God's will concerning these three parts of the Church, that we cannot distinguish them with certainty, so he wills it with good reason that we do not know whether we are of the Church. But in proportion as a man may hope that he shall be saved in bliss, so he should suppose that he is a limb of holy Church; and thus he should love holy Church and worship it as his mother.

And in view of this hope, which does not amount to belief, two sins should be put to flight: pride of men and covetousness, which men exercise on the ground that they are members of holy Church. For no pope that lives knows whether he is a member of the Church or whether he is a limb of the devil, destined to be damned with Lucifer. It is therefore a blind folly that men should fight for the pope more than they fight for the faith; for the many who do so are fighting for the devil. And we take this as the faith, or at least a truth consonant with the faith, that no man living knows whether he shall be saved or damned, although he may hope, short of belief, that he shall be saved in heaven. Although a man might have a direct teaching from God that he shall be saved in heaven, few or none have ever had; at any rate, put

such as that by themselves, for they would have no evidence to show that God has told them this.

The first belief that we should have is, that Christ is God and man: how he is self-existent in his Godhead, and how he lived here by his manhood. And thus are our hope and belief tempered in Christian men.

15. Christ's True Vicarage Contrasted With That of the Pope; Christ the Only Head of the Church

Ibid., 2, pp. 342–43.

For one may proclaim that he alone is Christ's vicar here on earth and that he has unique power to tax graces as he pleases. For, he may allege, Peter did the same after Christ, and many others after Peter; and besides, there needs to be one governor and one head in a community. But true men think that the devil fails at this point, goes unstable by two ways, and reverses God's law. The devil ought first to prove that this pope is Peter's vicar and therefore the vicar of Christ, in that he serves Christ. For the faith teaches that the choosing made by man is a false sign and insufficient to constitute Christ's vicar, but that the works of a man's life should constitute him a servant of Christ. And so Christ bids the Jews that they ought to believe on his works. Therefore, the true vicar of Christ should be the poorest man of all, and the meekest of all men, and the man of most labor in Christ's Church. (But choosing of cardinals and dividing of benefices and taking of new names are very far from such a portrait.) Thus lived Peter, after Christ; he sought no such names, nor to be head of holy Church, but how meekly he might serve it. Each apostle in his country wrought according to Christ's law, and none of them ever had need to come to Peter to be confirmed. But the only head of holy Church is Jesus Christ, who is here with us, who is ever in the midst of three that are gathered in his name.

That man is unreasonable who thinks that Clement in Peter's time was greater than John the evangelist or any apostle who lived at the same time. And if we can believe the records when they tell how Clement left his office and procured others to help him as Paul helped Peter, and how Peter meekly suffered Paul to rebuke him when he had erred, we may plainly see how these popes have fallen from Peter and how much more they have fallen from Christ, who might not err in anything. Do we suppose that Christ would cease preaching, or seal up offices of the Church, or that he would pass judgment on a matter of which he did not have first-hand knowledge, or make himself more than he was? All these things that the popes do teach us that they are Antichrists, for Christ himself might not take a name—unless it were meekness and truth.

If you say that Christ's Church must have a head here on earth, you say truly; for Christ is the head, who must be here with his Church until the day of doom, as well as everywhere by reason of his Godhead. For since the power of a king must be extended throughout all his realm, much more is the power of Christ shared with all his children. And if you say that Christ must needs have such a vicar here on earth, you deny Christ's power and place this devil above Christ. For the faith teaches us that no one can ground this vicar on Christ's law alone, but on the presumption of man. Such haughtiness of emperors has destroyed their empire; and God willing, these popes shall destroy themselves, yea, even here—for no doubt they shall be destroyed in hell by the judgment of Christ.

In fine, whatever argument men may bring forward which is based on Christ, Peter, or other good ground, it plainly militates against such a pope because of the great discrepancy between them. And when sound argument fails these men, they trust to human help and pretend hypocritically how good they are. But God curses, by Jeremiah, them that so trust in man.

16. Papal Misgovernment of the Church and the Decadence of the New Friar Orders

Ibid., 4, pp. 345–46.

Let us see further how this steward may err in the ordering of the Church; and let us begin with the friars, who were the last introduced. It is likely that Christ's priests, who were on hand when the monks came, had turned aside too much from Christ's law, and that at that time the monks lived better lives than they. But these monks stood only a while, and turned all the sooner to covetousness; and after the monks came the canons, and after the canons came the friars. It was because the previous lapse of the priests was so great, that these new orders came in. But as these new orders changed in clothing, books, and other rites, they also deviated in God's office from that which Christ bade his priests perform. Indeed, if the apostles were now alive and saw priests serving in the Church the way they do, they would not call them Christ's officers, but the officers of Antichrist.

We have reason to think that these new orders, added to all the old orders, are burdensome to the Church in the amount of worldly goods that they consume. For the number of priests brought in by Christ was sufficient for Christ's house—and now, for the same house, there are not only more of them than necessary, but they are worse; and the house is being diminished by them. Who can deny that the present number of these officers is too high? So it is, that this steward has filled the house with a new crop of idle servants to its harm. Paul teaches, as we believe, that they should not be a burden to the Church, and that they have no power but is to be used for its profit, not its harm. It seems, therefore,—and for good reason— that this steward exceeds his power but falls short in the governing of the Church. This he does by going against the rule that Christ has taught; and so he is not Christ's steward, but a steward of Antichrist. What man is there who cannot see that a steward of an earthly lord, who, when many servants have done amiss, not only lets them alone, but brings in new ones that have done worse in a little while, fails foully in his office? In like manner, servants upon servants have proved expensive to this house. And if it is true that at first their administration was good but at present is altogether other than that, it follows that the changing of these new idle servants would do additional harm to the house. That is the way things stand in the Church because of these new servants which have been brought into it.

17. The Pope's New Orders Opposed to God's Law

Ibid., 5, p. 350.

In addition, these sects impugn the gospel and also the old law; for they set more store by their own statute, though it be contrary to God's law, than they do by the law of the gospel; and so they love their order more than they do Christ. For example, though there be never so much need to go out and preach God's law, to defend our mother holy Church, yet their order does not allow them to do so, unless they have their prior's leave, even though God bids them do this very thing. And commonly these private priors hinder their fellows from going out. As a result, be they never so rich, the friars shall be of no help to their fleshly elders; for they have nothing that is properly their own but sin.

This is the error Christ reproves in the Pharisees, who strain out the gnat and swallow the camel; for they pay attention to a lesser matter and cause a greater evil. Also these Pharisees set much store by their fastings and other things which they have established; but to the keeping of God's commandments they pay not half so much attention. For example, he is considered apostate who leaves off his habit for a day; but for leaving off works of love he is not blamed at all. And so they blaspheme against God, and say that whoever dies in his habit shall never go to hell because of the holiness that is in the garment—whereby they reverse Christ's saying and sew an old patch on new cloth. For their order, they say, is gathered from the old law and the new; but they have built upon it new things that they keep as gospel. Hence they observe their own fasting and other rites that they keep more than they do the biddings of Christ, which are no "new commandments" to them.

522

IV. Reform Critiques and Early Appeals for a General Council to End the Schism

A. HENRY OF LANGENSTEIN: A LETTER ON BEHALF OF A COUNCIL OF PEACE (1381)

18. Three Ways of Ending the Schism; the General Council Endorsed

Epistola concilii pacis, 4, trans. in Spinka, *Advocates of Reform* [LCC, Vol. XIV], p. 110.

4. The Solution of These Disagreements Must Be Undertaken By a General Council

. . . Now, of this schismatic iniquity, which is hindering the action of divine grace by its venomous seed, I believe an end can be made by three ways that are open to men. The first is this: that anyone who is conscious of being a party to the above-mentioned crimes take it to heart and through penance reconcile himself to God. The second: that it be arranged throughout the circle of the Universal Church to make continual supplication for divine mercy publicly in fasting, weeping, and prayer. The third: that when these preparations have been carried out for the bestowal of the grace of the Holy Spirit, a general council be called in the name of Jesus Christ to purge his Church from the iniquities and various excesses, all too common at this time, and, after these causes have been removed, to tear up from the very roots the present division in the city of God which this befouling and monstrous schism has brought forth.

Here is a way of peace, a way oft trodden by our fathers before us, a way of salvation. The record of past events, which is the teacher of modern men, ought surely to move Christian kings and princes to undertake with the greatest enthusiasm this way which is pleasing to God and demand its execution without delay. History informs us that formerly, through the devotion, patronage, and encouragement of kings, in past emergencies of the Church provincial and general synods of bishops were in the providence of God frequently called and that they faithfully submitted themselves and their lawsuits, as well as the correction and emendation of their laws, to the holy judgment of their councils. This is evident from a wide consideration of the proceedings of the councils which have been recorded. . . .

19. The General Council the One Hope: Already Proposed by the University of Paris (1381)

Ibid., 13, p. 121.

Again, from what has been said above we conclude that it is clearer than the light of day that no other human way than that of a council has been found by which this schism can be completely settled and to this recourse must finally be made. Indeed, the party that rejects this way renders his case somewhat suspicious, just as a deceptive person seeks the corners and is afraid to come out into the light. Similarly, the party that takes refuge in a council in this way confirms his case. Thus, the party who is first to humble himself before a council would greatly justify himself, because he would thereby demonstrate that he had zeal toward God.

Again, we conclude that all the princes and the prelates and any others who resist and oppose this most reasonable and suitable way, trodden by and customary among the Fathers, do seriously and damnably sin and err. Such people clearly demonstrate that they are bound and blinded by damnable affections.

Therefore, after every covering and bond of sin, ambition, lust, and fear, etc., have been destroyed, all the faithful, under pain of incurring the divine displeasure, must strive with all their might to bring peace to the Church by this way.

Thus, on account of the above-mentioned reasons an answer to the question must be made in the affirmative.

It ought to add not a little weight to this part of the argument that the University of Paris, solemnly assembled in the Monastery of Saint Bernard of Paris, on the 20th day of May, 1381, unanimously decided through the four faculties, Theology, Canon Law, Medicine, and Arts, to uphold this view and intend, if permitted, to further it as far as possible by sending persuasive and hortatory letters and epistles to the princes, communities, and prelates.

20. Conciliar Procedure for Ending the Schism

Ibid., 14, pp. 125–26.

Moreover, the procedure leading up to and during such a council would be as follows: First, before the Church had assembled, it would be announced to the parties concerned, namely, Urban and his cardinals, or at least to those who took part in his election, that they should appear before the Church on a specified day, and in a particular city, with all their witnesses, reasons, defenses, and documents in readiness, without further procrastination. Secondly, when the prelates have come together, the patriarchs would take their places first, because they know their order, then the abbots would be seated; then the minor prelates and doctors of theology and of both Laws, admitted and elected according to the number agreeable to the council. Thirdly, according to the custom of the Fathers, after solemn invocation of the Holy Spirit had been made and prayers reverently poured out toward God that justice and truth might be made known, each party would be heard, before all the Fathers and in the presence of the other, adequately and at length, even to two or three replies. Fourthly, that when everything that each party had said had been written down and handed to each archbishop, and after each had discussed it at length with their clergy, the entire council, or the most capable deputies appointed by the council, would decide which articles, both how many and in what way, had been properly proved or semi-proved by each party. Fifthly, that, after everything from each party had been properly made known or proved and briefly summed up by the notaries, a definite judgment would be made from the council either in a resolution passed by all, or by certain people unanimously elected by all for this purpose.

It is necessary that one of the two contestants be pronounced pope or neither of them. If this latter were the case, no other means of assistance would remain except for all the former cardinals to assemble again and choose someone according as the Holy Spirit would direct them. The schism would then be ended. Here is a possible way, intelligible and free from danger, and undoubtedly the most reasonable. Therefore a reply must now be made to the reasons stated above that have been advanced against this way.

B. THE UNIVERSITY OF PARIS AND THE TRIPLE PROPOSAL FOR ENDING THE SCHISM (1393)

21. The Ways of Cession, Arbitration, and General Council

D'Achery, *Spicilegium*, I, 777f., trans. *ThM*, No. 168, pp. 326–27.

The first way. Now the first way to end the schism is that both parties should entirely renounce and resign all rights which they may have or claim to have to the papal office. . . .

The second way. But if both cling tenaciously to their rights and refuse to resign, as they have done up to now, we would propose the way of arbitration. That is, that they should together choose worthy and suitable men, or permit such to be chosen in a regular and canonical way, and these shall have the full power and authority to discuss the case and decide it, and if necessary and expedient, and approved by those who according to the canon law have the authority [that is, the cardinals,] they may also have the right to proceed to the election of a pope.

The third way. If the rival popes, after being urged in a brotherly and friendly manner, will not accept either of the above ways, there is a third way which we propose as an excellent remedy for this sacrilegious schism. We mean that the matter shall be left to a general council. This general council might be composed, according to canon law, only of prelates, or, since many of them are very illiterate, and many of them are bitter partisans of one or the other pope, there might be joined with the prelates an equal number of masters and doctors of theology and law from the faculties of approved universities. Or if this does not seem sufficient to anyone, there might be added besides one or more representatives from cathedral chapters and the chief monastic orders, in order that all decisions might be rendered only after most careful examination and mature deliberation.

C. NICHOLAS OF CLÉMANGES (1367–1437) ON THE FINANCIAL EXACTIONS OF THE PAPAL TREASURY ("CAMERA") [1401]

22. Ecclesiastical Luxury and Avarice; Excesses of Papal Revenue Collectors

De Ruina, 3 and 9, Von der Hardt, *Magnum Constantienae Concilium*, Tom. I, Pt. III, 7 and 11, trans. *PTR*, III, 6 (3), pp. 29–30.

CHAP. III. ON THE THREE VICES WHICH HAVE GIVEN RISE TO ALL THE OTHER ILLS IN THE CHURCH

After the great increase of worldly goods, the virtues of our ancestors being quite neglected, boundless avarice and blind ambition invaded the hearts of the churchmen. As a result, they were carried away by the glory of their position and the extent of their power and soon gave way to the degrading effects of luxury. Three most exacting and troublesome masters had now to be satisfied. *Luxury* demanded sundry gratifications, wine, sleep, banquets, music, debasing sports, courtesans and the like. *Display* required fine houses, castles, towers, palaces, rich and varied furniture, expensive clothes, horses, servants and the pomp of luxury. Lastly is *Avarice* which carefully brought together vast treasures to supply the demands of the above mentioned vices or, if these were otherwise provided for, to gratify the eye by the vain contemplation of the coins themselves.

So insatiable are these lords, and so imperious in their demands, that the Golden Age of Saturn, which we hear of in stories, should it now return, would hardly suffice to meet the demands. Since it is impossible, however rich the bishop and ample his revenue, to satisfy these rapacious harpies with that alone, he must cast about for other sources of income.

For carrying on these exactions and gathering the gains into the Camera, or Charybdis, as we may better call it, the popes appoint their *collectors* in every province, those, namely, whom they know to be most skillful in extracting money, owing to peculiar energy, diligence or harshness of temper, those in short who will neither spare nor except but would squeeze gold from a stone. To these the popes grant, moreover, the power of anathematizing any one, even prelates, and of expelling from the communion of the faithful, every one who does not, within a fixed period, satisfy their demands for money. What ills these collectors have caused, and the extent to which poor churches and people have been oppressed, are questions best omitted, as we could never hope to do the matter justice. From this source come the laments of the unhappy ministers of the church, which reach our ears, as they faint under the insupportable yoke, yea, perish of hunger. Hence come suspensions from divine service, interdicts from entering a church, and anathemas, a thousand fold intensified in severity. Such things were resorted to in the rarest instances by the fathers, and then only for the most horrible of crimes; for by these penalties, a man is separated from the companionship of the faithful and turned over to Satan. But now-a-days, these inflictions are so fallen in esteem, that they are used for the lightest offence, often for no offence at all, so they no longer bring terror, but are objects of contempt. To the same cause, is to be ascribed the ruin of numerous churches and monasteries and the levelling with the ground, in so many places, of sacred edifices, while the money which used to go for their restoration, is exhausted in paying these taxes. But it even happens, as some well know, that holy relics in not a few churches, crosses, chalices, feretories and other precious articles go to make up this tribute.

Who does not know how many abbots and other prelates, when they come to die, are, if they prove obnoxious to the papal camera on account of their poverty, refused a dignified funeral and even denied burial, except, perchance, in some field or garden or profane spot, where they are secretly disposed of. Priests, as we all can see, are forced by reason of their scanty means of support, to desert their parishes and their benefices and, in their hunger, seek their bread where they may, performing profane services for laymen. Some rich and hitherto prosperous churches have, indeed, been able to support this burden, but all are now exhausted and can no longer bear to be cheated of their revenue.

V. Jean Gerson (1363–1429), Pierre D'Ailly (1350–1420), and the Groundwork for the Council of Pisa (1409)

A. GERSON ON THE RIGHT OF THE GENERAL COUNCIL TO CONVENE WITHOUT PAPAL AUTHORITY (1408/9)

23. *The Church, Whose Head Is Christ, May Assemble Herself in a General Council to Procure a Vicar and Secure Unity*

Tract. De Unitate ecclesiastica (Opera, II, 113–118, Goldast, II, 1426ff.), Consid. 2. Lewis, op. cit., p. 403.

The essential unity of the church continues always in her relation to Christ her Bridegroom. For 'Christ is the Head of the church' [Ephesians 5:23], in Whom we are all one, according to the apostle, even if He has no vicar: that is, when His vicar is bodily or civilly dead or when there is no probability that Christians will ever show obedience to him or to his successors. Then the church, by divine and natural law, to which no positive law rightly understood offers any obstacle, can assemble herself in order to procure for herself, at a general council representing her, one certain vicar; and she can do this not only by the authority of the lord cardinals, but also by the assistance and aid of any prince or other Christian. For the mystical body of the church, most perfectly established by Christ, does not have less right and strength for the procuring of her own union than has any civil, mystical, or true natural body; for there is no provision in immediate and immutable divine or natural law that the church cannot congregate herself and unite herself without a pope or without any particular rank or college, in which death or error can, in a particular instance, occur.

24. Prevailing Conciliar Principles Summarized on the Eve of Pisa (1409)

Reprinted with the permission of the editors and translator from Francis Oakley, "The 'Propositiones Utiles' of Pierre D'Ailly: An Epitome of Conciliar Theory," *Church History*, XXIX, 4 (Dec., 1960), 399–402.

Some useful propositions for the ending of the present schism by way of a General Council

1. According to that saying: "Christ is head of the Church," and that other one: "We are all one body in Christ," the unity of the mystical body of the whole Christian Church depends fully and perfectly upon the unity of Christ, its head.

2. Although the Pope, inasmuch as he is the Vicar of Christ, can, in a certain way, be said to be the head of the Church, nevertheless the unity of the Church does not necessarily depend upon—or originate from—the unity of the Pope. This is clear from the first dictum and also because of the fact that the Church remains one even when there is no Pope—in accordance with that saying of the Canticles: "My dove is one," and that of the Symbol: "[I believe in . . .] one, holy, Catholic and Apostolic Church."

3. From Christ, the head, his mystical body which is the Church, originally and immediately has its power and authority, so that in order to conserve its own unity, it rightly has the power of assembling itself or a general council representing it. This is clear from that saying of Christ: "Wheresoever two or three will have gathered in my name, there I will be in the midst of them" —where, it should be observed, he does not say: "in the name of Peter," or "in the name of the Pope," but "in my name," giving to understand that wherever, and by whomsoever, the faithful may be gathered, provided that this is done in his name, that is, in the faith of Christ and for the safety of his own Church, he himself stands by them as director and infallible guide.

4. The mystical body of the Church has this power [i.e. of assembling in general council] not only by the authority of Christ, but also by the common natural law. This is clear because any natural body naturally resists its own division and partition, and, if it is an animate body, naturally summons up all its members and all its powers in order to preserve its own unity and to ward off its division—and, in a like way, any civil body, or civil community, or rightly ordained polity. And, therefore, the spiritual or mystical body of the Christian Church, which was ordered in the best way (for the ecclesiastical polity is described in the Canticles "as an army set in array"), is able to make use of the same means in order to conserve its unity, and to ward off any schismatical division as destructive of its well-ordered regime.

5. This same authority and authoritative power was made use of by the primitive Church. This is clear because in the Acts of the Apostles it is found that four general councils were assembled, and it does not say

X-8. Pierre D'Ailly, Cardinal of Cambrai.

PIERRE D'AILLI
Cardinal de Cambrai

that they were convoked on the authority of Peter alone, but by the common consent of the Church. And in one famous council at Jerusalem, it is not Peter but James, the bishop of that place, who is found to have presided and to have made known the decision.

6. After increases in the growing early Church, this aforementioned authority and power of convoking general councils was with reason limited and restricted, in such a way that it was permitted to no one to assemble councils of this sort without the authority of the Pope. This is clear from the common laws which are contained in the *Decretum* and *Decretales*. And the reason for this was both that the Apostolic See might be honored, and in order to forestall heretics and schismatics, who, at one time, used to manage by means of the power of secular princes, to call and assemble at pleasure, councils for the support of their own errors.

7. Such a limitation or restriction does not prevent this same authoritative power from remaining, always and absolutely, in the universal Church itself. This is clear, since positive laws cannot completely take away from the Church that power which belongs to it by divine and natural law.

8. Notwithstanding the limitation or restriction which we mentioned, the Church in certain cases can hold a general council without the authority of the Pope. This is clear from what has already been said, and, in addition, because that which was introduced for the good of the Church should not be observed to its hurt and grave peril. But this very limitation or restriction which, as was said, was introduced by the positive law for the good of the Church, in certain cases can most gravely prejudice it. And three cases, in particular, can be designated. In the first place, if, in the event of a vacancy in the [Apostolic] See, heresy or some other persecution of the Church were to appear, which ought to be counteracted by a general council. Secondly, if, in a case where necessity or manifest utility dictated the summoning of a council, the Pope were mad or heretical, or otherwise useless or lacking in this matter, or, if required to act on this, refused or culpably (*damnabiliter*) neglected to call a council. Thirdly, if there were several contenders for the Papacy so that the whole Church obeyed no single one of them, nor appeared at the call of any one or even of two of them at the same time—just as is the case in the present schism. In these and in similar cases, therefore, it is clear from what has been said that the Church can and should assemble a general council without the authority of the Pope.

9. The positive laws which commonly say that without the authority of the Pope it is not lawful to assemble a general council, should be interpreted in an equitable manner (*civiliter*)—that is, when a single Pope has been accepted peacefully by the Church, and, manifest utility coinciding, is capable and ready for the summoning of such a council. This is clear from what has been said and from Aristotle's teaching in the *Ethics* where he speaks of *epieikeia*.

10. For the settling of the present schism a general council can be assembled by the authority of the universal Church, without the authority of the Pope, and, indeed, against his wishes. And it can be convoked, not only by the Lords Cardinal, but also, on occasion, by any of the faithful whatsoever, who, if they are able, know how to help further, either by authoritative power or loving advice, the execution of so great a good. This is clear from what has been said, and also because in a case of necessity so great, all the faithful, and especially the greater and more powerful ones, should hasten to the aid of the Church, and attack the more quickly evils which are so evident. Moreover, arguments and authorities as much of divine as of human law could be cited, in addition to those already mentioned, but, if well grasped, the latter suffice, and on the basis of them could be erected some other propositions which would touch more particularly the council now called together at the city of Pisa. But these I will let be, since they follow so clearly from the above reasons, that if those are well understood, it will be unnecessary to expound them more fully.

Done at the city of Aix, on the first of January, fourteen hundred and nine, by Peter, bishop of Cambrai.

25. Holds Itself Competent to Try Popes

Raynaldus, anno 1409, sec. 71, trans. *ThM*, No. 169, pp. 327-28.

This holy and general council, representing the universal church, decrees and declares that the united college of cardinals was empowered to call the council, and that the power to call such a council belongs of right to the aforesaid holy college of cardinals, especially now when there is a detestable schism. The council further declared that this holy council, representing the universal church, caused both claimants of the papal throne to be cited in the gates and doors of the churches of Pisa to come and hear the final decision [in the matter of the schism] pronounced, or to give a good and sufficient reason why such sentence should not be rendered.

26. Vows to Reform the Church

Ibid., ThM, No. 170, p. 328.

We, each and all, bishops, priests, and deacons of the holy Roman church, congregated in the city of Pisa for the purpose of ending the schism and of restoring the unity of the church, on our word of honor promise God, the holy Roman church, and this holy council now collected here for the aforesaid purpose, that, if any one of us is elected pope, he shall continue the present council and not dissolve it, nor, so far as is in his power, permit it to be dissolved until, through it and with its advice, a proper, reasonable, and sufficient reformation of the universal church in its head and in its members shall have been accomplished.

VI. Conciliar Treatises of Reformers Between Pisa and Constance

A. DIETRICH OF NIEM († 1418) AND THE MANNER OF UNITING THE CHURCH (1410)

27. The Apostolic and Particular (Roman) Church Contrasted with the Universal Church; General Council and Reformation

De modis uniendi ac reformandi ecclesiae, trans. in Spinka, *op. cit.,* pp. 157-61.

DISCIPLE: The long desired and true union of the Church . . . could be brought about in three ways, especially when two or three are contending for the papacy as they are in fact doing at the present moment, namely, by the way of resignation and renunciation, or by the way of deposition and privation, or by the way of force, violence, and open attack.

In support of the first method, I put forward the following conclusions: Whenever any possible way by which that union may be secured is given, it ought to be accepted immediately by the true vicar of Christ; secondly, that whenever there is a question of the union of the Church, if no more clement way is found, the pope, under pain of committing mortal sin, is bound to accept this way. . . .

MASTER: Which way will be followed in the future general council?

DISCIPLE: Indeed, above all, advance must be made by the way of justice which is twofold: the way of recognition and reconciliation, and the way of resignation. Now, since everyone knows that the General Council of Pisa was holy and just, it is agreed that the deposition and deprivation of those two who were then and are now contending for the papacy were holy acts and that in this way the subsequent elections to the papacy of Alexander V and John XXIII were also just and honorable. Therefore, let the method that can better be carried out be upheld, namely, that these two, as deprived heretics, recognize their errors and together with their adherents be reconciled to and reincorporated in the Church. If these two cannot be drawn to bring about the unity of the Church by this method, then the way of resignation by all means shall be put into effect by having the true vicar of Christ resign, should this be necessary. . . .

MASTER: But what will become of the acts of these three up to that time?

DISCIPLE: This will actually be determined by the future council. However, it would seem to me that where anything, such as an official position or a benefice, is held, not by two, but only by one person, this should be tolerated for the sake of avoiding greater scandal. Wherever and however it is possible to give peace and union to the Church, this should be done by the council, proceeding at all times with mercy. Immediately at the end of five or six years, another general council should be held and, with God's help, a more extensive reformation of all things brought about.

MASTER: But in the event that none of these [rivals] should wish to resign at this general council, or if one should but another did not, what then?

DISCIPLE: In this situation neither the one who is willing should be favored, by having him remain pope, unless the Universal Church should agree to this and withdraw entirely from the other two; nor should the one who refuses be spared. The council and the Universal Church should withdraw from these three, as from those who destroy the unity of the Church. . . .

It would, however, be of little advantage to have one head if the members were not subject to the body. The Church will easily find one to assume the lordship of the papacy, but it will be difficult to reunite under the obedience of [one] head the members of the body of Christ, divided for so long a time. . . .

Those members are placed in different positions, some higher, some lower, in this holy mystical body. These are all to be led back to the unity of the Church in a twofold way: by obedience and by subtraction. By "obedience" I mean obedience to the one true universal and undoubted vicar of Christ; by "subtraction," the general withdrawal of obedience by common consent and unanimous desire from the two, or the three, rivals for the papacy who are scandalizing the whole Church. As I have already said, all Christians under pain of mortal sin are uniformly bound to carry out this withdrawal.

Supposing that the Universal Church, of which Christ is the head, should have no pope, still the believer who dies in love would be saved. For when two or more contend for the papacy, and when the Universal Church does not know which one is the true pope, to accept one or other as pope is neither an article of faith nor a deduction from it, nor is any faithful Christian bound to believe any one of them. For it is plain that such a person is not of the one holy Catholic Church but rather of the divided Apostolic Church.

Hence the apostles, in composing the Creed, did not say, "I believe the holy pope," or "the vicar of Christ." The universal Christian faith is not in the pope. He is an individual person and may fail. But they said, "I believe in the holy Catholic Church." And in order to define what the Church is, for the sake of the many who say and have said that the evil, however much they may be in the Apostolic Church, yet are not in the Catholic Church, [the apostles] said that it is "the communion of the saints." For it is certain that he who is in mortal sin is neither in the Church nor of the Church which is founded in love.

When there are in the Apostolic Church three popes who dispute over the papacy for their own ends and are in mortal sin, it is best to refuse obedience to such litigants and dividers of the body of Christ. For the faithful Christian is saved in the unity of the holy Catholic Church although he does not have the unity of the Apostolic Church. . . .

As a general council represents this Universal Church, I shall express my views on the summoning of such a council.

Elsewhere I have said that, when the reformation of the Universal Church and the case of the pope is discussed, . . . the summoning of a general council in no way belongs to the pope, even though he be the sole universal and undoubted pope. It does not even belong to him to preside as judge or to define anything having to do with the state of the Church. This [prerogative] belongs primarily to the bishops, cardinals, patriarchs, secular princes, communities, and the rest of the faithful. A man of ill report cannot and must not, from the point of view of what is right, be a judge, particularly in his own case, when, for the sake of the common welfare, the resignation and deprivation of a private individual's advantage and honor is the aim. Therefore, according to the example of the ancients, the bishops, the secular princes, the communities, and the ecclesiastics will summon [a council to meet] in some suitable, safe place, having the necessities of life in abundance, and will also summon to this [council] those contending for the papacy. . . . Out of the number [of prelates, cardinals, bishops, and temporal lords] some will be selected who could and ought to preside in this general council. But when there is a question of the reformation of any kingdom or province, of the removal of heresy and the defense of the faith, then it belongs to the pope and his cardinals to summon a council.

MASTER: Is not such a council in which the pope does not preside above the pope?

DISCIPLE: Certainly. It is superior in authority, dignity, and function. The pope himself is bound to obey such a council in all things. Such a council can limit the power of the pope. To such a council, as it represents the Church Universal, the keys of binding and loosing were granted. Such a council can take away the papal rights. From such a council no one can appeal. Such a council can elect, deprive, and depose the pope. Such a council can set up new laws, and destroy old ones. The constitutions, statutes, and regulations of such a council are immutable and cannot be set aside by any person inferior to the council.

The pope is not and has not been at any time able to make dispensations contrary to the canons passed by general councils unless a council has specifically granted this power to him for some important reason. The pope cannot change the acts of a council; indeed he cannot interpret them or make dispensations contrary to them since they are like the Gospels of Christ, which admit of no dispensation and over which no pope has jurisdiction. In this way there will be among the members the unity of the spirit in the bond of peace. . . .

Thus a general council, representing the Universal Church, if it desires to see a thorough union, if it desires to repress schism, if it wishes to bring an end to schism, if it wishes to exalt the Church, should before all else limit and define, according to the example of the holy Fathers who preceded us, the coercive and usurped power of the popes.

The said Lord Alexander V, before his election to the papacy, and while the holding of the said Council of Pisa was being discussed, fully agreed that this be done. He even used to speak to me of this, and with many philosophical, theological, and legal arguments exerted himself to bring about such a limitation. But when he was made

pope he did not strive to let it see the light. Indeed, many of the supreme pontiffs, in the course of time, have applied this coercive power contrary to God and justice by depriving lesser bishops of the power and authority bestowed upon them by God and the Church, who in the primitive Church were of equal power with the pope. . . . But now the Roman pope has reserved all ecclesiastical benefices. Now he has summoned all causes to his *curia*. Now he wishes that the granting of penance, the legitimization of clerics, and the holy ordination of anyone without distinction, be carried out at his *curia*. Those who are not able to obtain ordination in their own lands are easily ordained in that very *curia*. Now the monasteries of those orders in which monks used to live in religion in large numbers are given to the said cardinals *in commendam*. In each of these monasteries there is scarcely a tenth, or none at all, or only a few, of the monks that used formerly to live in them. Hence you will see some nephews or lay relations of the cardinals passing their time uselessly at that Roman *curia*, cleaving only to luxury and pleasure, and possessing enough pompous and costly clothes to satisfy even a great prince. But the poor religious out of whose income such pomp is produced are continually laboring at that *curia* in great penury, and the poor are not nourished from the patrimony of Jesus Christ, so uselessly squandered by others.

Thus let the holy Universal Council restore and reform the Church Universal according to the ancient laws. Let it limit the misused papal power contained in the *Decretum* and the *Decretals,* and the pretended power in the *Sext* and the *Clementines,* not to mention other papal constitutions. For Christ gave to Peter no other power than that of binding and loosing—of binding by means of penance and of loosing sins. He did not empower him to bestow benefices, to possess kingdoms, castles, and cities, nor to deprive emperors and kings [of their authority]. If Christ had in such a way conferred power on Peter, then Peter himself or Paul (which it is not right to say) gravely sinned or erred in that they did not deprive the Emperor Nero of his imperial power, whom they knew to be the worst and most savage persecutor of the Christians. . . .

Let the Universal Church put an end to all these and similar [abuses] in a general council and let her restore the former common law. Let not the bishops and clergy be deprived of their authority and the privileges granted to them by God and general councils. . . .

B. JOHN HUS († 1415) ON THE PAPACY AND SIMONY

28. *Three Ways in Which the Papacy May Be Simoniacal*

On Simony, 4, ibid., pp. 211–14.

Let us now inquire whether a pope may be a simoniac. It would appear that he cannot, since he is the lord of all the world, who by right takes whatever he wishes and does as he pleases; moreover, that he is the most holy father who cannot sin. But know that many popes were heretics or otherwise evil, and were deposed from the papacy. It would be a long story to write about such. Accordingly, have no doubt whether a pope can be a simoniac. If someone would defend him by saying that he cannot commit simony or other mortal sin, he would exalt him above Peter and the other apostles. As for the argument that he is the lord of all the world, who by right takes whatever he wishes and does as he pleases, the answer is that there is only one Lord of all the world who cannot sin and who has the right to rule the world and to do as he pleases, and that Lord is God the mighty One. Furthermore, as for the argument that the pope is the most holy father who cannot sin, I deny it; for it is our Father most holy, the Lord God, who alone cannot sin.

But perhaps you say, "In this world the pope is the most holy father." I answer that if you prove that he lives the most holy life, following Christ in His poverty, humility, meekness, and work, then I shall admit that he is most holy. But his manifest covetousness, pride, and other sins predispose men to believe that he is not the most holy father!

X-9. John Hus.

But you retort: "The whole world calls him the most holy father except yourself! Why should you be more worthy of belief?" Thereupon I answer that you exaggerate when you speak of "the whole world," since hardly perhaps one in a hundred acknowledges him as the bishop of Rome. But even though all men were to call him holy and the most holy, if his acts be contrary to Christ he is not holy, whether or not he is called so. For thus says the Lord, "O my people, they that call thee blessed deceive thee." For what else are they but flatterers who call people holy in order to get pay, and promise people holiness when they pay them! Likewise priests and clerics, desiring papal favor, call him the most holy. And he thinks it is as they say and approves that they address him so to his face and in writing! Woe to him that allows himself to be so deceived!

Furthermore, they put forth the excuse that he is most holy on account of his office. But the saints reply that office does not make a man holy, as is proved by the apostle

X-10. John Hus on His Way to Execution. *A sketch from the chronical of the Council of Constance by Ulrich von Richental.*

Judas and by the bishops and priests who murdered Christ. Moreover, the saints affirm that the worthier the office the greater the damnation of the incumbent if he be sinful. Accordingly, the saints acknowledge that priesthood and episcopacy are the worthiest offices on earth; but woe to him who should befoul them by a mortal sin! I know that the apostles, after Christ, were the most holy fathers on earth, and that they could in truth be so called; but they would not permit it. Moreover, if a pope lived in an apostolic manner, he likewise would be a holy father. But men should beware of flattering him, and he of pride, so that both would avoid sinning. For what avails it that a man be called holy when in the sight of God he is damned? What avails it to the Antichrist that he exalts himself above God when Christ shall hurl him into hell? And on the other hand, what harm if a man be reviled by the world, provided God praise him?

Asserting, therefore, that the pope may be a simoniac, let us see in what manner that may be. In the first place, he is such when he desires the papal dignity on account of emoluments and worldly esteem. For there is no estate in Christendom more liable to fall [than the papal]. For if he does not follow Christ and Peter in his manner of life more than others, he should be called the apostolic adversary rather than the apostolic successor. Therefore, everyone who runs after and strives for that dignity on account of material gain or worldly eminence is guilty of simony. But such a desire may be hid from men; therefore, if he neglects to perform his task properly, for the sake of the Christian communion, as Christ and Saint Peter have done, and if he seeks worldly goods and carnal life, he manifests to the people that he fell into the way of simony.

The second form of that kind of simony consists in the various regulations contrary to the law of God which the pope promulgates in order to secure material gain, even though not openly, but in such a manner that it could be interpreted as against the law of God. For is it not against God's order that he commands that his cooks, doormen, grooms, and couriers be accorded the first claim upon benefices of great dignity in lands the language of which they do not know? Or that the announcement of an appointment be withheld until the appointee first place the money on the board? And how many other such regulations there are!

The third form of papal simony is the appointment of bishops and priests for money. A proof of this is at present plainly to be seen in the payment of many thousand gulden for the archbishopric of Prague.

In these three forms the pope then may become a simoniac. But if any pope avoids simony and follows the Saviour in his manner of life, he has the right to make use of all things in the world, just as the apostles. For if anyone should prove holier than the pope, he has a better right, before God, [to the use of all things] than the pope, since he is a more beloved and worthier son of God, who is the King of all the world. Besides this right to the use of the world, he has likewise the right to serve the holy Church, and to order, teach, and direct it in accordance with the Word of God. But that is a different matter from the worldly rule in which men, particularly clerics, easily go astray. For the papal office, as well as the apostolic, consists in preaching the Word of God, in administering the sacraments, and in praying diligently to God on behalf of the people. To administer temporal possessions belongs to the lower estate, the secular. Consequently, the pope should observe that Christ and Peter did not meddle with ruling over worldly possessions. For to one who had said to him: "Master! bid my brother to divide the inheritance with me," Christ said, "Man, who made me a judge or a divider over you?" And again when another said to him, "I will follow whithersoever thou goest." And Jesus said unto him, "The foxes have holes and the birds of heaven have nests; but the Son of Man hath not where to lay his head." Furthermore, when Pilate told him, "Thine own nation and bishops delivered thee unto me; what hast thou done?" Jesus answered: "My kingdom is not of this world; if my kingdom were of this world, then would my servants fight that I should not be delivered to the Jews. But now is my kingdom not hence."

VII. The Council of Constance and Conciliar Utterances

A. CONSTANCE AND THE DECREE, "SACROSANCTA" (1415)

29. *Claims to Authority over the Pope, Himself*

von der Hardt, II, 98, trans. *ThM*, No. 171, pp. 328–29.

This holy synod of Constance, being a general council, and legally assembled in the Holy Spirit for the praise of God and for ending the present schism, and for the union and reformation of the church of God in its head and in its members, in order more easily, more securely, more completely, and more fully to bring about the union and reformation of the church of God, ordains, declares, and decrees as follows: And first it declares that this synod, legally assembled,

is a general council, and represents the catholic church militant and has its authority directly from Christ; and everybody, of whatever rank or dignity, including also the pope, is bound to obey this council in those things which pertain to the faith, to the ending of this schism, and to a general reformation of the church in its head and members. Likewise it declares that if anyone, of whatever rank, condition, or dignity, including also the pope, shall refuse to obey the commands, statutes, ordinances, or orders of this holy council, or of any other holy council properly assembled, in regard to the ending of the schism and to the reformation of the church, he shall be subject to the proper punishment; and unless he repents, he shall be duly punished; and if necessary, recourse shall be had to other aids of justice.

B. GERSON AND KEY TREATISES IN DEFENSE OF CONSTANCE (C. 1415)

30. *The Conciliar Position on the Right of Papal Deposition*

Libellus de auferibilitate papae ab ecclesia, Consid. 10 and 11 (*Opera*, II, 209ff., Goldast, II, 1411ff.). Reprinted from *Medieval Political Ideas* by Ewart Lewis, by permission of Alfred A. Knopf, Inc. Published in 1954 by Alfred A. Knopf, Inc. Vol. II, pp. 403–4, 404–5.

The vicarious spouse of the church is, in particular cases, removable from the church, either by her direct action or through the general council which represents her or by persons appointed by her for this purpose, regardless of whether or not the vicar himself consents to his abdication.

. . . Surely God gave the church no rank, no degree of dignity, no kind of ministry except for her edification and common utility. This appears in Ephesians 4:[11–12] and Corinthians 6 [I Corinthians 12:4–30]. Surely He gave these things for the peace of her 'in whose borders he made peace,' as the Psalmist says [Psalms 147:14]. And love brings this about; wherefore love is described by the apostle as 'the end of law' [I Timothy 1:5]. And on love Christ based the pastoral office: 'If thou lovest Me,' said Christ to Peter, 'feed My sheep' [John 21:17]. And who does not see that there could be many cases, some of which are involved in the present situation, in which the church would be not edified but destroyed, not united but scattered, not fed but devoured, if he who had been duly and canonically ordained the vicarious spouse of the church would not yield voluntarily, or would not be ejected against his will? And let no one wonder at what we say, as if it contradicted the commandment, 'Touch not My anointed' [Psalms 105:15]. In the same way it would be right for any individual, in case of violence attempted by a true pope against his chastity or life, to repel force with force, instigated by blameless self-defence, and thus he would have a lawful right to lay violent hands upon the pope or throw him into the sea. Why should it not likewise be lawful on occasion for the whole church to do the same, in her own defence and in the cautious repression of attempted violence?

The vicarious spouse of the church is in particular cases removable by a general council held without his consent or against his will.

Let us say first that regularly by divine law a general council ought not to be held if the pope does not call or approve it, if there is one and if there is no legitimate allegation against him. But general rules often undergo exceptions, even as in grammar, so also in morals, in which, especially, particular cases occur in infinitely variable ways: to which exceptions is ordained the higher law, the interpreter of the others, which Aristotle calls *epieikeia* in V *Ethics*, [ch. 10], and another, more divine, which he calls *gnome* in VI *Ethics*, [ch. 1]. Now this law always has place in the interpretation of other particular laws, where the reason and end of their institution is seen to fail. Now the end of all laws, not only human but also divine, is love, which works unity. If there is a case, therefore, in which the observation of any law would dissipate unity and be an obstacle to the public welfare, who, using reason, would say that it ought to hold? Doubtless no one would wish this to be done in his own case; how much more would all the community reasonably shun it!

But if anyone should ask by what authority a council of this sort is supported, or what authority it uses, seeing that it is, as it seems, headless without the pope, it should be answered that it uses the authority of Christ its Head and indefeasible Spouse; besides this, the authority of His laws both divine and natural, which grant this licence either to necessity or to manifest charity or to religious piety. For this we have a text, Mark 2:23, concerning the excuse of the disciples who wished to pluck grain on the sabbath and who were excused by the law of necessity, confirmed by the example of David, who ate consecrated bread.

31. What a General Council Is; Its Powers in Relation to the Papacy

Sermo Habitus XXI die Julii, 1415 (*Opera*, II, 274ff., Goldast, II, 1406ff.). *Ibid.*, pp. 407–8.

Now what is a general council? It has been described elsewhere, and I repeat: 'The general council is an assemblage, made by a lawful authority, to some place, from every hierarchic degree of the whole catholic church, at which no faithful person who demands to hear is excluded, for healthfully discussing and ordaining those things which concern the due regimen of the same church in faith and morals.' It could be deduced from this definition, together with the preceding statements, in what way the plenitude of papal power was granted by Christ in those things which are supernatural. In others also, which natural, canonical, and civil laws assign to it, as to a monarch, the papal power stands supreme and is concorded with the power of the council, which has been spoken of: because the papal power is included in the council, although this power is in the pope in one way, in the council in another way. Even as the keys were given to Peter in one way, and in another way to the church. Whence the council has, in many things which concern the pope, the authority to advise and recommend; the pope, the authority to exercise and execute. For the council could not of itself either absolve in the court of conscience, or ordain priests, or make the Body of Christ, or conquer the infidels with an armed hand; and so of many things; but it pertains to it to advise or recommend about things of this sort; and he who denies its dictate contumaciously denies the Holy Spirit, whose it is to direct the council itself in advising and recommending. Example in man, where the reason has the power to advise and recommend; the will, the exercise and execution.

32. Bill of Divorcement from Pope to Church and from Church to Pope

De potestate ecclesiastica et de origine juris et legum (*Opera*, II, 226ff., Goldast, II, 1384ff.), Consid. 7. *Ibid.*, p. 410.

Ecclesiastical power, considered respectively and, in a sense, materially, as assigned to particular subjects, can be called variable and removable in many instances. This is demonstrated daily, when changes are made through a new consecration or a new election or institution of ministers. Consequently, we can say the same thing in regard to the papal power, which is mutable and removable by natural death, as is obvious, or by civil death, namely, by deposition, at least in regard to his plenitude of jurisdiction. . . . Whence, as the pope can renounce the papacy and give a bill of divorcement to his bride, the church, even without guilt on her part, though he should not do this without cause, so the church can dismiss her vicarious spouse and give him a bill of divorcement, without guilt on his part but not without cause. . . .

33. Plenitude of Ecclesiastical Power and the General Council; How the Council Can Secure a Head for Itself

Ibid., Consid. 11. pp. 412, 413–14.

Ecclesiastical power in its fulness is in the church as in its end, and as in that which regulates the application and use of this sort of plenitude of ecclesiastical power, either directly or through a general council sufficiently representing it. It is clear, at any rate, that the plenitude of ecclesiastical power was given to Peter by Christ for the building of His church, as our definition sets forth, in conformity with the statement of the apostle. For this reason Augustine says, with certain others, that 'the keys of the church were given not to one, but to a unity,

X-11. Jean Gerson.

and that they were given to the church.' And this can fittingly be understood in the way which the consideration sets forth, because 'the keys of the church were given for the sake of the church and its unity as for the sake of an end.' Also this plenitude of ecclesiastical power can be said to be in the church or the council not only formally as in its end but also in two other ways: in respect of its assignment to particular persons, and in respect of the regulation of its use, if perchance it should be liable to be turned into abuse.

We can add to this consideration that the plenitude of ecclesiastical power, if it be considered in its breadth, is itself not in the pope alone, unless in a certain way, as being in his own way the source and origin of power. For this breadth of power embraces in itself other ecclesiastical powers collectively from the highest to the lowest. And the plenitude of ecclesiastical power of the pope is among them as an integral part in the whole, and thus it is not greater than or superior to the power of the whole church, as a part is not greater than the whole. If, on the other hand, this plenitude is considered in its height, then without any doubt the plenitude of ecclesiastic power of the pope is greater than and superior to the rest; but now that which is the rest can by no compact constitute a general council, according to what was said earlier, that a general council, as such, necessarily includes the papal authority, whether a pope exists or not; for if there is a pope and he is willing to do his duty in convoking a council, certainly it ought to be authorized by him. If, however, he pertinaciously refuses, to the destruction of the church, then action should be taken as if there were no pope; and the power of assembling itself remains in the church itself, and that of providing for itself, and that of ordaining concerning papal power, in the second and third ways, in respect to its allocation and its use; the situation corresponds to that of a chapter and a dean, or a university and its rector.

But the principal difficulty occurs h.. e: what, if the pope is dead or ejected, can this council do? It can, therefore, first constitute one pope for itself in the accustomed way through the election of the lord cardinals; or in another way through consensus; or through the way of the Holy Spirit, if there is reasonable hope that thus all can be brought to agree upon one candidate; or perchance through the awaiting of a divine miracle, as in the election of Matthew. And concerning this power of the council, that it can make one head for itself, there is no difficulty.

C. REFORM DEMANDS AND THE AGENDA OF CONSTANCE (1417)

34. Reforms Called for

von der Hardt, IV, 1452, trans. *ThM*, No. 172, pp. 329–30.

The holy council at Constance determined and decreed that before this holy council shall be dissolved, the future pope, by the grace of God soon to be elected, with the aid of this holy council, or of men appointed by each nation, shall reform the church in its head and in the Roman curia, in conformity to the right standard and good government of the church. And reforms shall be made in the following matters: 1. In the number, character, and nationality of the cardinals. 2. In papal reservations. 3. In annates, and in common services and little services. 4. In the granting of benefices and expectancies. 5. In determining what cases may be tried in the papal court. 6. In appeals to the papal court. 7. In the offices of the *cancellaria,* and of the penitentiary. 8. In the exemptions and incorporations made during the schism. 9. In the matter of commends. 10. In the confirmation of elections. 11. In the disposition of the income of churches, monasteries, and benefices during the time when they are vacant. 12. That no ecclesiastical property be alienated. 13. It shall be determined for what causes and how a pope may be disciplined and deposed. 14. A plan shall be devised for putting an end to simony. 15. In the matter of dispensations. 16. In the provision for the pope and cardinals. 17. In indulgences. 18. In assessing tithes.

35. The Conciliar Decree, Frequens

Ibid., 1435, No. 173, pp. 331–32.

A good way to till the field of the Lord is to hold general councils frequently, because by them the briers, thorns, and thistles of heresies, errors, and schisms are rooted out, abuses reformed, and the way of the Lord made more fruitful. But if general councils are not held, all these evils spread and flourish. We therefore decree by this perpetual edict, that general councils shall be held as follows: The first one shall be held five years after the close of this council, the second one seven years after the close of the first, and forever thereafter one shall be held every ten years. One month before the close of each council the pope, with the approval and consent of the council, shall fix the place for holding the next council. If the pope fails to name the place the council must do so.

VIII. The Conciliar Movement and Reform after Constance

A. JOHANN BUSCH (1428/29) AND THE UNREFORMED CLERGY

36. Monastic Visitation in the Low Countries; Attempted Reform at Windesheim

From "Autobiography of John Busch," *British Magazine*, XIX (1841).

The monastery of St. Martin, in Ludin-kerka, of our order, in Friesland, in the diocese of Utrecht, which was previously an abbey of our order, began to be reformed in the year 1428. Before its reformation there were but few priests there, and a great many converts—more than thirty or fifty—who had entered into an agreement with the converts of a neighbouring monastery of the Cistercian order, a mile off, that they would mutually help each other with a hundred armed men. The consequence was that they had subdued all that part of Friesland. A certain vassal, however, who lived in the town about the monastery, by advice of the lawyers, of whom there are plenty among the priests in Friesland, reported their ill life and conversation to the archbishop of Utrecht. None of them was chaste, all were proprietors [that is, possessed something which they called their own in money or goods], and they had nuns with them in the monastery who sometimes brought forth children. I knew the abbot there, a learned man, whose father had been called a convert, and his mother a nun. He afterwards resigned his abbacy and entered into a monastery of our chapter near Haarlem, and having there become a monk, he ended his days well.

The bishop, however, Frederic de Blankenheym, a wise and learned man, sent his ambassadors, men learned and skilful in the law, who, visiting the inmates of that monastery, found that almost all the converts had entered without rule or profession, and that they had remained up to that time, a period of many years, in that predicament. Being asked how they came to take upon them the habit of converts, they answered, "When first we came here, we saw many persons clothed with white tunics and scapulars, and at the same time wearing arms, so we bought ourselves white cloth, and had it made into white tunics, white hoods, and scapulars, and put them on ourselves." It was asked whether they had heard anything about a rule. They answered, "Never; but each one took to himself a nun, a female convert, or other woman, with whom he cohabited without being married." The bishop of Utrecht, therefore, hearing this, by the advice of men learned in the law, in which he too was learned himself, adjudged and decreed that all the persons of this description were not monks, but might lawfully go out and marry wives, and be secular persons; and that they should put off that habit, and resume their secular dress; and this they immediately did, and also made protestation that they had no right or claim to the monastery, or any property belonging to it. A few, however, two or three, obtained leave to remain there, because they were old; and for a time retained also the women who had belonged to them, that they might wait on them in their infirmity, until all the women being expelled, they were collected together and formed into a monastery of our order hard by. After this the agents of the bishop sent to Windesheim to request that they would bring the monastery into a proper state of reformation; and upon that the prior of Windesheim sent thither some monks of Windesheim and of Mount St. Agnes—viz., Jacobus Oem, afterwards prior of Tabor and rector of the nuns in Bronopia, Gerard Wesep, John Lap, priest of Berg, and Engelbert Tentinel, with one convert who was very expert in temporal matters; and these first began the reformation in that place, with John Gerard of Zwoll, professed in Berg, whom they appointed rector there. But as they had not monks enough for its reformation and refoundation, the prior of Windesheim sent Godfrey de Tyela, and one John Busch, to the aforesaid monastery, in order to make up the number for its complete reformation; and he said to me, "Brother John, you did not do much out beyond Cologne, at Bodingen; you may see whether you can convert the Frisians."

In the year 1429, therefore, on the festival

of the Conversion of St. Paul, I was sent to
Ludinkerka, where we carried forward the
reformation already begun, repairing the
choir, refectory, dormitory, and other buildings of the monastery, and taking in clerks
for its new reformation, and instructing them
according to rule and discipline; and in like
manner lay brethren and servants.

When, therefore, in obedience to the apostolic see (for the pope had laid the diocese
of Utrecht under his ban; and the Lord
Rudolph of Defolt, whom the towns of
Deventer, Zwoll, and Campen, with their
adherents set up, and the Lord Zweder of
Culenborch, to whom the pope had given it,
were striving for the bishopric), all the
monks of the Overyssel district were compelled to leave it, the prior of Mount St.
Agnes, of our order, by the advice of the
prior of Windesheim, with all his convent,
came to Ludinkerka with the lay brethren
and servants, and completely reformed the
monastery there, according to the rule of our
order, in every particular. And there are now
more than fifty persons, as well brethren as
laity, faithfully serving the Lord God in the
simplicity of their hearts day and night, and
maintaining themselves on the fields and
pastures, which are very rich, and well
suited for cattle; the name of abbot being
exchanged for that of prior, owing to its
incorporation into our chapter of Windesheim. Therefore, "my song shall be alway of
the loving-kindness of the Lord," who hath
made me a partaker of all the good that shall
be done there for evermore. For at first we
suffered a great deal for the want of furniture and other necessary things; and, there
being very few trees in that part of the
country, the wind, in the winter time, blew
round us on every side, and the cold became
intense, so that, after the service of the
canonical hours, I sat in bed to warm myself.
And the water, even in the canals and running streams, having a salt taste from being
so near the sea, which is apt to run into
them, disagreed with me very much. For in
all reformations or new foundations of monasteries it is necessary that the first set of
monks who go there should take a great
stock of patience with them, otherwise they
will never be able to live there without

words of disgust and murmuring; and thus,
murmuring and seeking their own, instead of
the things that are Jesus Christ's, they will
go away without credit and without fruit.

B. NICHOLAS OF CUSA (c. 1431/1434–1451) ON GENERAL COUNCILS, HERESY, AND CHURCH UNITY

37. *Mystical Body, Church and Sacraments; Priesthood, Hierarchy, Papal Headship*

De Concordantia Catholica, 1:6 (Ed. Schard,
"De jurisdictione," pp. 465ff.). Reprinted from
Medieval Political Ideas by Ewart Lewis, by
permission of Alfred A. Knopf, Inc. Published
in 1954 by Alfred A. Knopf, Inc. Vol. II, pp.
415–17.

. . . Even as man is constituted of
spirit, soul, and body, so in this one body of
the church the sacraments are the spirit,
and the priesthood the soul, and the faithful
the body: for even as the soul adheres partly
to the body and partly to the spirit and is
the means through which the spirit flows
into the body, so also the priesthood is related to the faithful; wherefore the whole
priesthood is as one soul in the one body of
the faithful. . . . Therefore a ruling, vivifying, and illuminating virtue befits the priesthood. . . . And there is a hierarchic order in
this soul, which is the priesthood, in regard
to its ruling, presidential charge: because,
although all members of the upper hierarchy, who are the bishops, are equal in
regard to order and pontifical judgment, yet
there are grades and distinctions among
them in regard to their ruling charge; and
in regard to the presidency, it is considered
hierarchic on the basis of a certain concordance which relates the one and the many.
For there is one episcopacy in which all
partake; but there is a differential order in
regard to the presidential charge. Certainly
all the other apostles shared equally in
honour and power with Peter, but Peter was
prelate of the others, that, as Cyprian said,
there might be unity in concordance. . . .
And Jerome said . . . , 'Among the equal
apostles Peter was chosen to preside, that
occasion of schism might be abolished
through the institution of a head.' Thus, even
as there is one episcopacy, so there is one

chair and one presidency, constituted in hierarchic gradation. . . . And since this presidency was instituted by Christ the Head for the avoidance of schism and the preservation of the peace and unity of the faithful, it has its gradation, to which temporal lordship figuratively corresponds. Whence, according to Jerome, one should notice that even as an army constitutes a captain for itself, and he then, bearing in himself the consent of all, becomes one presidential, public person: so also the bishop is constituted president (*Decretum*, c. 24, di. 93). Thus even as a republic is a common thing of the people, and a common thing is a thing of the state, and the state is a multitude of men brought to a kind of bond of concord, as Augustine writes . . . , so he who presides in the pastoral court corresponds to him to whom a republic is entrusted. Whence all who are under the court are understood to be united in him who presides as if he were one soul and they the body which the soul has to animate. Whence such a people, thus united with their pastor, constitute a church. . . . Whence even as the universal church is the mystic body of Christ, so particular churches are the mystic bodies of those who preside over them as delegates of Christ. . . . And this is one premise of our proposition: that the church is in the bishop through union, and thus the bishop symbolizes and represents them, since he is a public person with regard to that group; and this is a premise of all that will be said hereafter. Moreover, there are gradations within the bishopric, as Leo IX says in the letter he wrote to the two African bishops, saying: 'The order of bishops is one, however much some are set before others. . . . For even as all earthly powers differ from one another by gradations of dignity, . . . so also the ecclesiastical powers are found by the holy fathers to be related in a hierarchic order . . . ; in those cities in which the pagans had their chief priests and teachers of the law, primates or patriarchs were established . . . ; where the pagans had their archpriests, the archbishops of the Christians have been established . . . ; where lesser cities had only priests or counts, bishops have been estab-

lished; moreover, the tribunes of the people can be said to correspond to the priests, or to the rest of the lower order of the clergy; over them all the Roman pontiff is set by divine and human law.' From this it is clear that the presidential ecclesiastical power was superadded to the temporal even as the soul to the body, so that wherever there was a temporal unification in an earthly government there was superadded through the way of peace or concord a presidency to direct men to Christ, that all things might be brought to a suitable mean under one supremely powerful head.

38. The Primacy of Peter Was not Superiority over the Church but Within It

Ibid., 2:34, p. 420.

. . . Although all the apostles were rectors, pastors, and vicars of Christ, . . . yet the holy doctors affirm that in that pastorate, rectorate, and vicarage Peter had the primacy by more abundant grace, through this fact: that the keys were promised and given to him and, by the words 'Feed My sheep,' the pastorate was assigned to him as representing the whole church. . . . Moreover, that principate of Peter does not consist in superiority in the power of binding and loosing in the penitential court or in the confection of the sacraments; no one has any doubt concerning the latter, nor ought there to be doubt concerning the former . . . because the spiritual judicial power of all bishops is the same, as was that of the apostles, since this flows from Christ by way of the priesthood. . . . Nor was Peter through that primacy superior to the church, since he was named for the church and for its sake. . . . Therefore the superiority of Peter was not superiority over the church, but within it. Whence, although he was the mouth and head of the apostles of the church, and made proposals in its name, as in Acts 1:[15–22], and made answers in its name, as in Acts 2:[38–39], yet nevertheless he was under it as a member. . . .

39. On the Place of Popes and General Councils in Church and Empire

De Concord. Cath. 2:12–13. Items 39 and 40 reprinted from *Readings in Political Philosophy,* rev. ed. edited by F. W. Coker © 1938 The Macmillan Company, New York, and used with their permission. This item, pp. 259–61.

In short, one conclusion can be drawn from the laws, based in part on the endorsement of the signatories and partly on the reasoning in the councils: that the Roman pontiff does not have, in the making of general statutes, the authority which certain flatterers attribute to him—namely, that he alone has the power to legislate while the others merely serve as counsellors. I do not deny that the Pope has always had authority to respond to a consultation, to advise, and to address [the council] in writing; I am talking of statutes that have the force of canons and of decretals that are universally binding in the Church. Whether even today the Pope alone may decree, as universally binding, that which has been transmitted by long usage, I am not at present considering. I do say that even though he has such power it does not contradict our thesis, which holds merely that the authority of enacting canons depends, not on the Pope alone, but on common agreement.

No rule or custom can prevail against this conclusion any more than against the divine or natural law upon which the conclusion depends. The preëminent power of the Roman pontiff in respect to this matter in a general or universal council is no different from that of a metropolitan in a provincial council; or rather the pontiff's power, in respect to authoritative action, is less in a universal council of the whole catholic church than in a patriarchal council. In the latter, indeed, the Pope is rightly likened to the metropolitan in a provincial council, as we have shown. Accordingly, the Roman pontiff is frequently called "archbishop" by the ancients. Indeed a lesser preëminence is attributable to the Roman pontiff in a universal council of the whole church than to the same pontiff in a patriarchal council or to a metropolitan in a provincial council, as will be shown below.

Ch. XIII. This will perhaps appear strange to any who have read the writings of Roman pontiffs declaring that plenitude of authority is in the Roman pontiff and that all others may be called by virtue of his favor; as well as to those who have read Gelasius, Sylvester, Nicholas, Symmachus and other Roman pontiffs, maintaining that the Pope passes judgment on other ecclesiastical authorities but that none passes judgment on him: since the authority of the Pope is divine, transmitted to him by God with the words "Whatsoever ye shall bind," and accordingly, the Pope, as vicar of Christ, presides over the universal church; and since he himself holds this supreme authority and is known to have condemned and absolved subjects of any bishops whatsoever even when their own bishops were not negligent; and he may be appealed to without any intermediary. The power of making statutes depends on a power of jurisdiction; therefore [according to this argument] it is absurd to say that something more than his will is necessary to the validity of any statute, since what pleases the prince has the force of law. Furthermore: it can not be doubted that the head of a corporation has authority to exercise jurisdiction, although jurisdiction itself remains ostensibly in the corporation. And no one doubts that the Pope is the "rector" of the ship of St. Peter and of the universal church; wherefore the validity of fundamental laws depends upon him, just as it is impossible to legislate for a corporation without the head. . . .

However, in order to discover the truth of this statement that inferior prelates hold jurisdiction under positive law *papa derivative*—that is derived from the Pope himself, it would be necessary, if that were true, that in the beginning Peter should have received something special from Christ and that the Pope was his successor in this. Yet we know that Peter received from Christ no more authority than the other apostles; for nothing was said to Peter that was not also said to the others. Is it not true that just as it was said to Peter, "Whatsoever thou shalt bind upon the earth," it was also said to the others, "Whomsoever ye shall bind"? And although it was said to Peter, "Thou art Peter and upon this Rock"; nevertheless, by rock we understand Christ, whom Peter confessed. And if by *petra* ("rock"), Peter is to be understood as the foundation stone of the church, then, according to St. Jerome, all the other apostles were similarly foundation stones of the church (concerning which there is a discussion in next to the last chapter of the Apocalypse, wherein by the twelve foundation stones of the city of Jerusalem—that is, the holy church—no one doubts that the apostles are meant). If it was said to Peter, "Feed the sheep," it is nevertheless clear that this feeding is by word and example. So also, according to St. Augustine in his gloss upon the same passage, the same command was given for all. In the verse—"Go ye into all the world" (Matthew and Mark, at the end), it does not appear that anything was said to Peter that implied any supremacy. Therefore, we rightly say that all the apostles are equal in authority to Peter. It should also be remembered that at the beginning of the church there was only one general episcopate, diffused throughout the whole world, without division into dioceses. . . .

Therefore, since the power of binding and loosing, on which all ecclesiastical jurisdiction is founded, is immediately from Christ, and since from this power comes the power of divine jurisdiction, it is evident that all bishops, and perhaps even presbyters, are of equal authority in respect to jurisdiction, although not in respect to the execution, which is confined within certain positive limits. . . .

40. Consensus, not the Pope's Authority, Determinative in General Councils

Ibid., 3:4 and 12, pp. 264–65, 267.

So also in general councils, the pontiff's authority rightly concurs by consent, in the first degree, with all others attending the same council. The force of a decree depends, nevertheless, not on the chief pontiff, but on the common consent of himself and the others. The fact that in setting up a king or emperor the consent of priests as well as of laymen must be obtained, is not because the authority of kings is outweighed by the priesthood in matters of government, for we know that the priesthood of the sun and the imperium of the moon are equal, but because the temporal possessions of the church, without which the priesthood cannot survive in this perishable life, are subject to the imperium and its laws. . . .

In sum and substance then, this ought to be understood: the aim of a ruler should be to establish laws by agreement. It is, therefore, fitting that all general matters affecting the commonwealth should be decided and ordered in a council of the two estates of primates and bishops (*primatum et praesulum*). Indeed the king must be the executor of what is enacted by the council, since this very legislation is the rule according to which the subjects desire the authority of the king to be controlled. No one doubts that a universal council has the power to regulate, by agreement of the head and members, the chief governing (*praesidentialem*) authority, for the good of the commonwealth.

41. The Pope, though Supreme in Administration, Is Subordinate to the Judgment of a Universal Council

De auctoritate presidendi in concilio generali (1434), trans. by the editor from *Cusanus-Texte*, II, ed. G. Kallen (Heidelberg: Carl Winters, 1935), pp. 24–28.

The Roman pontiff, who is a member of the church and admittedly supreme in administration, is himself subject to the Universal Council and to its judgment. Indeed, whatever the Universal Council in its plenary capacity shall decide upon shall be preferred to the judgment of any one man, even the pope himself, in any situation whatsoever. . . .

. . . The church is able, in keeping with its own welfare and necessity to order the papacy as it deems best—because in cases bearing upon its well being, the church itself cannot err—and may depose the pope, not merely because of matters of the faith, but whenever he may prove unprofitable and negligent. . . . However this judgment as to carelessness and uselessness belongs more properly to the church, on whose account the papacy exists, than to a man who is only the subject material (or carrier) of this papacy. Wherefore, there can be no doubt that the pope is universally subject to every decision of the church when, for its own welfare, it ordains canons or laws, even

541

those concerning the pope, or deposes the pope himself because of his ineffectiveness. Granting that the collected priesthood, as in a synod, does not constitute the whole church; conceding, further, that the pope represents the whole church as a council represents the priesthood; even so, the representation through the council is more truly a representation than that through the pope; that of the pope being farthest removed, that of the council nearest at hand. Whence, the representation of the council, coming closer to the truth of the church and in a more definite way representing it is, likewise, to be preferred to the confused papal representation in authority and judgment. Furthermore, the truth is promised, not only to the universal church, but likewise to the priesthood itself and to the governing part of the church. To this truth the universal council comes closest. For the priesthood is there in its totality, either actually or potentially. . . .

42. To the Bohemians on Double Communion, the Dissipation of Unity, Variety in Rites, Schism

Ep. II, *ad Bohemos* (Bâle, pp. 830ff.), trans. by the editor via M. de Gandillac, *Oeuvres Choisies de Nicolas de Cues* (Paris: Aubier, 1942), pp. 356–58.

You mistakenly believe that there is more profit in drinking the chalice of division than in taking the paschal lamb alone in peace and unity. To accept with a separatist will the chalice of the Lord of unity and peace is to receive it in vain, for it is powerless to bestow life on a member sundered from this church which is the body of Christ. Do not say that it is the rest of the church that is separated from you and that it is you who comprise the true church, restricted to this little part of Bohemia. It is surely beyond doubt that in the unity of the church the variety of rites is without danger. But if one, out of presumption and temerity, prefers a particular rite to unity and peace, though he is good, holy and worthy of praise, personally, yet he merits condemnation, notwithstanding. You say that it is necessary first to obey the precepts of Christ, and the church only after that, and if it teaches other

requirements than Christ, it is not the church but Christ who is to be obeyed. But this is the very beginning of all presumption when particular persons judge their private opinion concerning the divine commands to be more in keeping with the divine Will than that of the universal church.

It is necessary then to follow the church undeviatingly when it judges what is appropriate to a given time, for it possesses the faith and guards the received trust, even if it should slip into some error of judgment. The situation is that of a judge who, misled by a false witness, excommunicates an innocent person without knowingly committing a reprehensible act. This judge does not transgress, but on the contrary follows, the rule which requires him to judge according to testimonies and evidences. And the guiltless person, in obeying the sentence, in thus cutting himself off from the body of the church, does not lose the grace or the life that would have been forthcoming from the sacrament. Rather, by obeying the church even if it has made a mistake, he obtains salvation, although deprived of the sacrament. But all presumption against the church is condemnable, as well as the refusal to obey which goes to the lengths of schismatic division, notwithstanding every specious pretext drawn from the practice of the Scriptures and adduced in support of the resistance or rebellion. A conclusion that ruins your plans with all their reasons, for the actual usage of the universal church and the precepts of the Roman church founded rationally on this usage permit of no dispensation. . . .

43. On the Sacrament of the Eucharist, Common Faith, and the Diversity of Rites

De pace fidei, 18:66, trans. by the editor from R. Klibansky–H. Bascom, *Opera Omnia* (Hamburg: F. Meiner, 1959), VII, pp. 60–61.

This sacrament, insofar as it depends upon sensible signs—according to the keeping of the faith—is not so indispensable that one may not be saved without it; for it suffices unto salvation if one believes and, in this way, eats the bread of life. And, there-

542

fore, concerning its distribution, whether and to whom and how often it should be given to the people, no binding law is laid down. Wherefore, if any one having faith judges himself unworthy to approach the table of the highest King, this very humility is the more praiseworthy. Likewise, concerning this use and its rites, whatever seems to the rulers of the church to be more suitable for meeting the circumstances of the time in every religious community—the faith always being safeguarded—may be legitimately ordained so long as the peace of the faith is preserved no less inviolate through the common law by reason of the diversity of rites.

SUGGESTED READINGS

Bett, H., *Nicholas of Cusa*. London: Methuen & Co., Ltd., 1932.

Carlyle, R. W. and A. J. Carlyle, *A History of Medieval Political Theory in the West*, Vol. V. London: William Blackwood & Sons, Ltd., 1928.

Connolly, J. L., *John Gerson: Reformer and Mystic*. Louvain: Librairie Universitaire, 1928.

Coulton, G. G., *Five Centuries of Religion*, Vol. IV. Cambridge: Cambridge University Press, 1950.

Figgis, J. N., *Studies of Political Thought from Gerson to Grotius*, 2nd ed. Cambridge: Cambridge University Press, 1916.

Gavin, F., *Seven Centuries of the Problem of Church and State*, 2 vols. Princeton, N. J.: Princeton University Press, 1938.

Gewirth, A., *Marsilius of Padua, the Defender of Peace*, 2 vols. New York: Columbia University Press, 1951–56.

Hertz, F., *The Development of the German Public Mind*. New York: The Macmillan Co., 1957.

Jacob, E. F., *Essays in the Conciliar Epoch*, 2nd ed. Manchester: Manchester University Press, 1953.

Jordan, G. J., *The Inner History of the Great Schism of the West*. London: Williams and Norgate, 1930.

McFarlane, K. B., *John Wycliffe and the Beginnings of English Non-Conformity*. London: English Universities Press, Ltd., 1952.

Spinka, M., *Advocates of Reform*, Library of Christian Classics, Vol. XIV. Philadelphia: Westminster Press, 1958.

———, *John Hus and the Czech Reform*. Chicago: University of Chicago Press, 1941.

Thompson, A. H., *The English Clergy and Their Organization in the Later Middle Ages*. New York: Oxford University Press, Inc., 1947.

Tierney, B., *Foundations of the Conciliar Theory*. Cambridge: Cambridge University Press, 1955.

Ullmann, W., *Origins of the Great Schism*. London: Burns, Oates and Washbourne, Ltd., 1948.

Workman, H. B., *John Wyclif*, 2 vols. New York: Oxford University Press, Inc., 1926.

CHRONOLOGY

c. 1180–c. 1235	Eike of Repgow—Saxon Mirror c. 1220 and Saxon World Chronicle
c. 1241/51–1306/16	John of Paris—Conciliar theorist
1265–1321	Dante—Author of Divine Comedy, and On Monarchy (1308–1313)
1274	Death of Bonaventura and Thomas Aquinas
1275–c. 1342	Marsilius of Padua—Defensor Pacis (1324)
1294–1303	Pope Boniface VIII
1296	Bull, Clericis Laicos
1300	Papal Jubilee
1302	Unam Sanctam; First French Estates General
1303	William Nogaret and Sciarra Colonna take Boniface VIII prisoner at Anagni

1415	Decree Sacrosancta at fifth session of Constance; John Hus burnt; Pope John XXIII deposed; Wyclif and his writings condemned
1416	Jerome of Prague burnt
1417	Decree "Frequens" of Constance at 39th Session; conciliar reforms declared for at 40th
1417–1431	Pope Martin V
1418	Death of Dietrich of Niem, church unionist
1419	Hussite War; Ziska at Prague
1423–1424	Councils of Pavia and Siena
1428	Wyclif's body exhumed and burnt by order of Constance
1429	Jeanne d'Arc frees Orleans; death of Jean Gerson, conciliarist, mystic, educator
1430	Jeanne d'Arc captured at Compiegne
1430	Jeanne d'Arc burned at Rouen
1431–1447	Pope Eugenius IV
1431–1449	Council of Basel—Lausanne (Basel 1431–1448; Lausanne 1448–1449)
1433/34	Pacification of Bohemia; Communion in both kinds for the Hussites; Council of Basel finally recognized by Pope Eugenius IV
1434/35	Gutenberg (?) and printing
1437	Conflict of Council of Basel and Pope
1438	Pope convokes Council at Ferrara; Pragmatic Sanction of Bourges
1438–1445	Council of Ferrara-Florence-Rome

1439	Pope Eugenius IV transfers Council of Ferrara to Florence; Basel elects antipope Felix V after declaring Eugenius IV suspended (1438) and deposed (1439)
1439	Temporary healing of Eastern-Western Schism
1440–1449	Felix V, Basel Pope
1443	Temporary closing of Council of Basel; Felix V remains (anti) pope
1444	Death of Bernardine of Siena
1447–1455	Pope Nicholas V (successor to Eugenius IV); humanist and founder of Vatican Library (1447/50)
1448	Concordat between Frederick III and Nicholas V
1449	Felix V abdicates pontificate; Fathers of Basel, reassembled at Lausanne, submit themselves to Nicholas V; End of Great Schism
1450	Unitas Fratrum formed
1453	Turks capture Constantinople
1457	Lorenzo Valla's exposure of Donation of Constantine
1459	Death of Poggio Bracciolini, humanist
1471	Death of Thomas à Kempis, compiler of Imitation of Christ
1476	Caxton's printing press at Westminster
1479/80	Death of Johann Busch, German reformer
1492	Columbus discovers San Salvador
1498	Savonarola burnt at Florence

1294–1303   *Boniface VIII*
1303–1304   *Benedict XI*
1305–1314   *Clement V*
1316–1334   *John XXII*
1334–1342   *Benedict XII*
1342–1352   *Clement VI*
1352–1362   *Innocent VI*
1362–1370   *Urban V*
1370–1378   *Gregory XI*

Roman Line

1378–1389   *Urban VI*
1389–1404   *Boniface IX*
1404–1406   *Innocent VII*
1406–1415   *Gregory XII*

Avignon Line (Antipopes)

1378–1394   *Clement VII*
1394–1424   *Benedict XIII*

Conciliar Line (Antipopes)

1409–1410   *Alexander V*
1410–1415   *John XXIII*

1417–1431   *Martin V*
(1424   *Benedict XIV, antipope*)
(1424–1429 *Clement VIII, antipope*)
1431–1447   *Eugenius IV*
(1439–1449 *Felix V, antipope*)
1447–1455   *Nicholas V*
1455–1458   *Calixtus III*
1458–1464   *Pius II (Aeneas Silvius Piccolomini)*

Index

Contemplation and action (*see also* Monasticism, Mysticism), 130; in Joachim of Flore, 470–77; in Pseudo-Dionysius, 170–73; St. Augustine and, 167–69; with St. Gregory, 169–70; (*illus.*, 169); in St. Hildegarde of Bingen, 466–71

Contrition (*see also* Absolution, Penance, Sacraments), 247, 328

Conversion, sacramental (*see also* Transubstantiation), 321–22, 446

Cornificians, 379, 398

Corpus Christianum, 498

Cosmology (*see also* Philosophy, Theology): and the Christian tradition, 81–85; heretical, 85–97, 342–44; of Origen, 99–100; in St. Basil, 104–05

Councils (*see also* Conciliarism): Ancyra, 67; Arles, 58–60, 67; Chalcedon, 67–69; Clermont, 242–43; Constance, 533–36; Constantinople, 68; Ephesus, 117; IV Lateran, 251–53, 322; Nicaea, 63–64, 267–68; Pisa, 525–28; Troyes, 244–45

Courts (*see also* Curia, Justice), 234–35

Covenensa, 345

Creation (*see also* Cosmology), 45, 82–83, 87, 97, 104–05, 112, 192, 350

Credo (Symbol), 4

Creed, the (*see also* Rule of Faith), 4, 97, 127, 131; of Chalcedon, 68; of Nicaea, 63

Cross of Christ (*see also* Crusades), 22, 41, 97, 166, 203, 331, 338–39, 343–44, 346–47, 369, 399, 437, 446, 456, 461–63, 472, 480, 484

Crown of Thorns, relic of, 387, 456–57 (*illus.*, 457)

Crusades (*see also* Commerce, Feudalism, Towns, Trade): and Christian society, 228–30, 242–65; first and Urban II, 242–44; fourth and Innocent III, 259–62; St. Francis and the mendicants, 253–54; second and St. Bernard, 245–48; seventh, eighth and St. Louis, 259–65; sixth and Frederick II, 254–59; and the Templars, 244–45

Cult (*see also* Church, Liturgy): Christian, 41–42; imperial, 36

Cura animarum, in early church, 3–4; monastic, 194, 389–92; and the Middle Ages, 329–41, 393–99, 442-88, 503

Curia, papal, 315, 334, 499–502, 530

Customs, and uses: feudal, 230–34; monastic, 149–165, 281–93

Cyprian, 51–53, 103–04, 106, 121

Cyril of Jerusalem, 130–33

D'Ailly, Pierre, 501–02, 526–27

Damasus, Pope, 188

Damian, St. Peter, 227

Damietta, 259–262

Dance, medieval, 420, 427, 431, 433–35, 485

Dante Alighieri, 479–80, 499, 508–10

Darkness, Divine, 171–172

Deacons and Deaconesses, early Christian, 8–11, 15, 27–29, 52, 55–56, 62

Deans, rural, 332, 336

De Catholicae Ecclesiae Unitate, 103–04

Decius, 37–38, 50–51

De Concordantia Catholica, 502, 538–41

Decretals (*see also* Canon Law), 515, 527, 530

Decretum (*see also* Canon Law), 388, 396–97 (*illus.*, 396), 515–16, 527, 530, 539

Defensor Pacis, 500, 510–15

Degrees: Bachelor's, 406; Master's, 400–01, 405–06, 408–09, 524; Doctor's, 365, 408, 523–24

Demiurge (*see also* Dualism, Heresies), 94–96

De Musica, 384, 417–19

De Unitate Ecclesiastica, 525–26

Deutsche Grammophon Gesellschaft, 385, 489

Dialectic, medieval (*see also* Scholasticism, Universities), 379–81, 397–99

Dialogues: Catherine of Siena, 306–07; Gregory the Great, 161–64 (*illus.*, 162)

Dictatus Papae, 236–37

Didache, 4–5, 13–15

Didascalia, 4, 128, 375

Didascalicon, 394–95

Dies Irae, 436–38

Dietrich of Niem, 501, 528–31

Diocletian, 38–39, 52–56, 477–79

Diognetus, Epistle to, 18–21

Dionysius the Pseudo-Areopagite, 128, 143–47, 170–73

Discs (*see* Recordings)

Disputations, scholastic (*see* Scholasticism, Universities)

Divine Names, 146

Divine Service (*see* Liturgy, *Opus Dei*)

Docetism (*see also* Dualism, Gnostics, Heresies), 82–83, 86, 89

Doctrines, Christian (*see also* Church, Creed, Eschatology), 45, 59, 64, 131

Dominic, St., 279

Dominicans (*see also* Friars, Franciscans, Mendicants): as inquisitors, 279, 343–47; in

learning, 407–08, 413–17; as mystics, 302–07; and preachers, 358–60 (*illus.*, 360)

Domitian, 42–43

Donatello, 485

Donation of Pepin, 206–07

Donatism and Donatists, 58–59, 67, 116–17

Dualism (*see also* Docetism, Heresies): Bogomil, 342–43; Catharist, 343–49; gnostic, 85–89; Manichaean, 91–94; monastic, 128–29, Neo-Manichaean, 342

Dunstan, St., 393

Durandus, William, 387, 464–65

Easter, 59, 98, 186, 295, 474–75

Eastern Church, 7, 128; Fathers of (*see* Fathers: Greek); liturgy in, 126–28, 131–47; monasticism in, 149–56

Ecclesia, 125, 498

Ecclesiastical Hierarchy, 143–46

Ecclesiology (*see* Church)

Eckhart, Meister, 302–04

Economic theory, medieval (*see also* Church, Interest, Loans, Money, Usury), 222–68

Ecstasies (*see* Contemplation, Mysticism)

Ecumenicity, 3

Education (*see also* Liberal Arts, Scholasticism, Schools, Universities): early Christian, 374–75; Greek and Roman, 375; medieval, 375–488

Eike of Repgow, 234–35, 477–79, 498, 503

Einhard, 207–08

Election, doctrine of (*see* Predestination)

Elections: monastic, 281, 290–92, 294; papal, 235–36, 496–500, 513, 516–18, 523–26, 533, 536

Elements, consecrated (*see* Communion, Eucharist, Mass), 22

Elevation of the Host (*see also* Communion, Eucharist), *illus.*, 340

Emanations (*see* Gnostics)

Emperors and Empire, 37–40, 42–75

Enchiridion, 4

Encyclopedias and encyclopedists, medieval, 382-83, 413–17

End of world (*see* Eschatology)

Episcopacy (*see* Bishops, Church; episcopacy)

Eremites (*see* Anchorites, Cenobitism, Monasticism): 129, 149–50

Eschatology (*see also* Apocalyptic, Kingdom of God), 388, 407–08, 415, 466–68, 470–77; and the Antichrist, 12, 249, 521,

eral Arts, Music, Mysticism, Scholasticism, Universities)

Melioramentum, 345, 348–49

Mendicants (*see also* Franciscans, Dominicans, Monasticism): and the crusading era, 230; 253–54, 276–80; and renunciatory ideal, 276–80, 293–98, 302–07; as inquisitors, 279, 343–47; missions of, 365–69, 415–17; popular ministry by, 278–80; preaching of, 332, 358–60, 362; and the towns, 254, 278–80; at the universities, 279, 381–82, 399, 407–09, 413–17, 431–32

Mercantilism (*see* Commerce, Crusades, Towns, Trade, Usury)

Merits, Treasury of, 340–41

Merode altarpiece, 450–51

Merovingians, 181, 200–206

Messiah (*see* Christ, Jesus)

Metalogicon, 397–99

Microcosm, 380

Middle Ages (*see* Christianity, Church, Medieval Civilization)

Military service, early Christian (*see also* Armies), 30, 101–02, 136–37

Miniatures (*see* Acknowledgments for Illustrations)

Ministry (*see* Clergy, Deacons, Episcopacy, Hierarchy, Priesthood)

Minuto populo, 278

Miracles (*see also* Church), 86, 97, 162–63, 169, 261, 343, 369, 426, 446–47, 456

Missals (*see also* Books of Hours, Breviaries, Liturgy, Mass), 442–47, 454–55

Missi dominici, 211–12

Missions: English, 165–67, 180; German, 180–81; mendicant, 365–69, 415–17; monastic, 165–67, 180–81; and Polo brothers, *illus.,* 366–67

Mobility, mendicant, 276–79

Mohammed, 203–04

Monasticism (*see also* Mendicants, Orders, Rules): and asceticism, dualism, 128–30; of Basil and Cassian, 129, 151–56; Benedictine, 129, 156–67, 280–93; of Cassiodorus, 160–61; cenobitic, 150–61, 164–65, 280–93; Cistercian, 274–75, 283–90; Cluniac, 274–75, 280–81; and Columban, 129, 164–65; eremitic, 129–30, 149–50; liturgical hours and offices of, 157–59; and manual labor, 158–59, 284, 295, 297; as (new) martyrdom, 129, 152–53; mendicants and, 276, 279–80, 365–69, 415–17; and mysticism, 128–30, 167–70; Pachomian, 150–51; of Pope Gregory I, 161–67; vows of, 159–60; and worship in,

128–30, 155–57, 165, 274, 281–82, 284–85, 289–90, 294–98, 389, 393, 422–25, 431–32, 462

Monepiscopate, 5, 9–11

Money (*see also* Interest, Loans, Towns, Trade, Usury): 58, 68, 70, 243, 247, 258, 265–66, 268, 295, 341, 361, 525, 532

Monks and Nuns (*see* Cenobitism, Eremites, Monasticism)

Montanism, 89–90

Mummers, masked, *illus.,* 443

Murals, 478, 480–81, 483

Music and Musicians (*see also* Architecture, Builders, Liberal Arts, Liturgy): angelic, *illus.,* 372; *Ars antiqua et ars nova,* 432–38; dance and theology, 431–36, 440–43; drama, liturgy, and liberal arts, 425–27, 432–42; leading theorists of, and *De Musica,* 417–22, 425–27, 429; in medieval architecture, 429; and medieval games, 441, 443; numbers and *numerositas* in, 417–20

Myrc, John, 338–39

Mystagogue, 126

Mysteries (*see also* Liturgy, Sacraments): in early Christianity, 9, 19, 131, 139, 142; Ps.-Dionysian, 146–47

Mystic Wine Press, Church as, *illus.,* 462

Mystical Body and Blood (*see* Eucharist; *also* Communion, Liturgy, Sacraments)

Mystical Mirror, 459–64

Mystical Theology, 171–73

Mysticism (*see also* Contemplation, Liturgy, Monasticism): *Abgeschiedenheit,* 302–04; affirmative and negative theology, 172–73; Bride and Bridegroom in, 300–01; cell of self-knowledge and, 306–07; common life in, 309–10; darkness of unknowing, 171–72; degrees and grades of, 302; deification in, 143; early Christian leaders of, 167–73; illumination, 170–71; Inward Word, 304–06; medieval representatives of, 298–310, 466–77; and mystical theology, 171–73; soul seeking God in, 298–302; *Sparkling Stone* and, 307–09; Spiritual Deafness and, 304–06; *theoria* in, 130, 146

Negative theology (*see* Mysticism)

Neo-Manichaeism, 317–18, 342

Neoplatonism, 167, 377, 380, 422–23

Nero, 37, 42, 530

Nestorius, 116–17, 366

Nicaea, 60–67

Nicholas of Clémanges, 524–25

Nicholas of Cusa (*see also* Conciliarism), 502–03, 538–43

Nicholas II, Pope, 235–36

Nominalism (*see* Realism)

Notre Dame, 377, 412

Numbers, and *De Musica* (*see* Music)

Numerositas (*see* Music)

Offices (*see* Books of Hours, Canonical Hours, Liturgy, Monasticism)

Opus Dei, 129–30, 375

Orchestra, medieval, 435

Ordeals, feudal, 233–34

Orders (*see also* Monasticism, Sacraments): and clerical ordination, 27–30, 67, 193, 324–25, 328–30, 335, 350; mendicant, 276–80, 293–98; military, 244–45; monastic, 128–30, 149–67 (*illus.,* 272), 280–93; of worship, 5, 13–15, 27–31, 127–28, 131–49

Origen of Alexandria (*see also* Fathers), 99–103

Ostrogoths, 196–200

Ownership, church (*see* Property)

Pachomius, 150–51

Painters and painting, 385–89

Palladius, 150–51

Papacy (*see also* Church, Conciliarism, Councils): Avignon and Babylonian Captivity, 510–17; Boniface VIII and, 504–10; in conciliar era, 510–43; in crusades, 242–53; feudalism and Gregory VII, 236–39; finances and reforms of, 500, 504–06, 524–25, 530–33, 536; Great Schism, 517–36; Innocent III and, 248–53, 313–21; rise of, 177–214; schools and universities, 391–92, 399, 405–07

Paraclete, 89–90

Paradiso (*see* Dante)

Paris, University of (*see also* Education, Scholasticism, Schools, Universities), 376–82, 399–410

Parish (*see also* Clergy, Diocese, Hierarchy, Pastors, Priesthood): organization of, 315–17, 332; pastoral care in, 329–42, 385–92, 414–17, 442–88; rural deans and, 332, 336; visitations of, by diocesans, 332, 335–38

Parousia, 5

Suggested Readings
General Works and Collections

Altaner, B., *Patrology*, trans. H. C. Graef. New York: Herder & Herder, Inc., 1960.

Baillie, J., J. T. McNeill, and H. P. van Dusen, general eds., *The Library of Christian Classics*, Vol. I–XIV. Philadelphia: Westminster Press and London: Student Christian Movement Press, Ltd., 1953–1958.

Cannon, W. R., *History of Christianity in the Middle Ages*. Nashville, Tennessee: Abingdon Press, 1961.

Coulton, G. G., *Five Centuries of Religion*. 4 vols. Cambridge: Cambridge University Press, 1923, 1927, 1936, 1950.

Deanesly, M., *A History of the Medieval Church 590–1500*, 2nd ed. London: Methuen & Co., Ltd., 1928.

La Monte, J. L., *The World of the Middle Ages*. New York: Appleton-Century-Crofts, Inc., 1949.

Latourette, K. S., *A History of Christianity*. New York: Harper & Brothers, 1953.

———, *A History of the Expansion of Christianity*. 7 vols. Harper & Brothers, 1937–1945.

McNeill, J. T., *Christian Hope for World Society*. Chicago: Willet, Clark & Co., 1937.

———, *A History of the Cure of Souls*. New York: Harper & Brothers, 1951.

Walker, W., *A History of the Christian Church*, rev. by C. C. Richardson *et al*. New York: Charles Scribner's Sons, 1959.

Abbreviations Frequently Encountered

References

ANF   *The Ante-Nicene Fathers. Translations of the Fathers down to A.D. 325*, 9 vols. Edited by A. Roberts and J. Donaldson. Buffalo, 1885–1897.

LF   *A Library of Fathers of the Holy Catholic Church*, 48 vols. Oxford and London, 1848–.

NPNF   *A Select Library of Nicene and Post-Nicene Fathers of the Christian Church*. Edited by P. Schaff and A. Wace in two series; 1st ser. 14 vols., New York, 1886–1890; 2nd ser., 14 vols., New York, 1890–1900.

PTR   *Translations and Reprints from the Original Sources of European History*. Philadelphia: University of Pennsylvania, 1894–1900.

ThM   O. J. Thatcher and E. H. McNeal, *A Source Book for Medieval History*, New York, 1905.

Illustrations

ALINARI, Photo Fratelli Alinari, Florence

ANDERSON, Photo Anderson, Rome

BM, Trustees of the British Museum

BN, Bibliothèque Nationale, Paris

BRB, La Librairie De Bourgogne Au Cabinet Des Manuscrits De La Bibliothèque Royale De Belgique

CCC, Corpus Christi College, Oxford

CHAMPION, Librairie Honoré Champion, Éditeur, for permitting reproductions from *Documents Parisiens . . .* par A. Lognon

CNMH—AP, Caisse Nationale Des Monuments Historiques, Archives Photographiques, Paris

A. COLIN, Librairie Armand Colin for permitting reproduction of Figures 213–218, pp. 382–87 from É. Mâle, *L'art religieux de la fin du moyen âge en France*, 1931

CUTTS, adaptation from E. L. Cutts, *Scenes and Characters of the Middle Ages*, London, 1872

FMC, miniatures reproduced by permission of the Syndics of the Fitzwilliam Museum, Cambridge

GAI, German Archeological Institute

HD, M. René Metz, Président de la Société pour la conservation des Monuments Historiques d'Alsace, for permitting reproduction of plates from Herrade de Landsberg, *Hortus Deliciarum*, ed. A. Straub and G. Keller, Strasbourg, 1901

LF, adaptations from J. Lenfant, *Histoire des Concile de Constance*, Amsterdam, 1914, Tome II

MMA, Metropolitan Museum of Art (—CCP, The Cloisters Collection, purchase —GPM, gift of Pierpont Morgan —DF, Dick Fund —RF, Rogers Fund)

NGAK, National Gallery of Art, Washington, D. C., Samuel H. Kress Collection

NYPL, The New York Public Library

PCAS, Pontifica Commissione de Archeologia Sacra

PML, The Pierpont Morgan Library

RA, Rijksmuseum, Amsterdam

Unabbreviated acknowledgments at appropriate points of reference.

Special acknowledgment to Mr. Ernest Nash and the Fototeca Di Architettura E Topografia Dell'-Italia Antica for securing photographs of Italian provenance.